The Impact of Blockchain in Token Economies

Guneet Kaur
University of Stirling, UK

Lorena Nessi
Fairleigh Dickinson University, UK

Pooja Lekhi
https://orcid.org/0009-0008-0053-106X
University Canada West, Canada

IGI Global
Scientific Publishing
Publishing Tomorrow's Research Today

Vice President of Editorial Melissa Wagner
Director of Acquisitions Mikaela Felty
Director of Book Development Jocelynn Hessler
Production Manager Mike Brehm
Cover Design Jose Rosado

Published in the United States of America by
IGI Global Scientific Publishing
701 East Chocolate Avenue
Hershey, PA, 17033, USA
Tel: 717-533-8845 | Fax: 717-533-7115
Website: https://www.igi-global.com E-mail: cust@igi-global.com

Library of Congress Cataloging-in-Publication Data

Names: Kaur, Guneet, 1994- editor | Nessi, Lorena, 1979- editor | Lekhi, Pooja, 1990- editor
Title: The impact of blockchain in token economies / edited by Guneet Kaur, Lorena Nessi, and Pooja Lekhi.
Description: Hershey, PA : IGI Global Scientific Publishing, [2026] | Includes bibliographical references and index. | Summary: "The book provides readers with a clear understanding of the theoretical foundations, technological infrastructure, and economic principles driving tokenized economies"-- Provided by publisher.
Identifiers: LCCN 2025027519 (print) | LCCN 2025027520 (ebook) | ISBN 9798337333717 hardcover | ISBN 9798337333724 paperback | ISBN 9798337333731 ebook
Subjects: LCSH: Blockchains (Databases) | Blockchains (Databases)--Economic aspects | Finance--Technological innovations | Tokens | NFTs (Tokens)
Classification: LCC HG1710 .I546 2026 (print) | LCC HG1710 (ebook)
LC record available at https://lccn.loc.gov/2025027519
LC ebook record available at https://lccn.loc.gov/2025027520

British Cataloguing in Publication Data
A Cataloguing in Publication record for this book is available from the British Library.

Table of Contents

Detailed Table of Contents

harbors risks of power concentration and surveillance. The chapter concludes that neither pure decentralization nor complete centralization is viable. Instead, hybrid models are emerging that combine the efficiency and innovative power of tokenized systems with the stability and democratic legitimacy of public institutions.

Decentralized Finance (DeFi) has emerged as a transformative force in the financial sector, leveraging blockchain technology to enable permissionless and automated financial services. A key component of DeFi's expansion is the rise of tokenized assets, which represent digital ownership of real-world and virtual assets. This chapter explores the various forms of tokenization, including cryptocurrencies, asset-backed tokens, and Central Bank Digital Currencies (CBDCs), and their integration into the DeFi ecosystem. It examines how tokenized assets enhance liquidity, facilitate financial inclusion, and create new investment opportunities. Additionally, the chapter discusses the interplay between decentralized and centralized financial models, regulatory challenges, and the risks associated with smart contracts, price volatility, and governance. By analyzing case studies and emerging trends, the chapter provides insights into the future of the tokenized economy and its potential to bridge traditional finance with decentralized innovations.

Tokenized lending is a major application of decentralized finance (DeFi) that has evolved as an innovative platform for credit intermediation through blockchain-based smart contracts. Early token lending platforms such as MakerDAO (now Sky), Compound, and Aave were permissionless, built for decentralized retail lending. More recently, however, there has been an increase in the interest of tokenized lending by institutional investors and regulated entities looking for compliant, risk-managed solutions. This chapter explores the institutionalization of tokenized lending, including an overview and conceptual analysis of the growth, technology, and potential role in the financial system. Additionally, the chapter highlights the fragmented landscape of regulation on tokenized lending and more nuanced

tokenization acts as a catalyst for legal evolution, forcing a revision of fundamental concepts such as jurisdiction and state coercion.

This chapter delves into the rise of tokenized science economies, where blockchain infrastructure redefines how we fund, govern, and share scientific knowledge. At the heart of this shift is Decentralized Science (DeSci), a movement that challenges legacy systems by embedding transparency, programmability, and economic alignment into the research lifecycle. Through real-world case studies, the chapter explores tools like intellectual property NFTs, tokenized research outputs, DAO-led funding models, and scientific prediction markets. Together, these mechanisms offer new ways to incentivize peer review, coordinate global collaboration, and democratize access to discovery. Framing tokenization as a structural innovation, the chapter makes the case for a research economy that is not only open and sustainable, but fundamentally interoperable across platforms, disciplines, and communities.

The chapter explores the transformative potential of blockchain and tokenomics in reshaping education through secure micro-credentialing, equitable access, and lifelong learning. Drawing on recent peer-reviewed literature, it examines how blockchain enables tamper-proof academic records, portable micro-credentials, and learner-owned digital wallets, while tokenomics introduces incentive-driven ecosystems such as "learn-to-earn" and peer-to-peer knowledge sharing. The chapter also investigates the role of decentralized autonomous organisations in collaborative curriculum governance and community-led accreditation. Emphasising global case studies and policy implications, it critically assesses challenges including data privacy, regulatory uncertainty, and digital divides. The analysis highlights how blockchain-based systems can democratise education by recognising informal and modular learning across borders. It concludes by advocating for inclusive, ethical, and scalable implementation strategies to ensure blockchain and tokenomics advance equity and continuous learning in education.

Token economies offer a transformative solution to the enduring challenges of funding and coordinating public goods. Through blockchain-enabled mechanisms such as smart contracts, decentralized governance, and incentive-aligned tokens, communities can address traditional market failures in the provision of non-rivalrous and non-excludable resources. This chapter explores the theoretical foundations of public goods economics, analyzes innovative funding models like quadratic funding, retroactive public goods funding, augmented bonding curves, and emerging regenerative finance systems, and examines how blockchain-based systems can support decentralized, transparent, and scalable public goods provisioning. Drawing on real-world case studies, the chapter evaluates the strengths and limitations of token economies in this domain, highlighting both the promises and the complexities of decentralized coordination.

Blockchain technology is revolutionizing the hospitality sector by providing creative post-crisis recovery options and guaranteeing strong data protection. This chapter examines how blockchain builds confidence among players in the hospitality industry, improves operational efficiency, and secures transactions. Blockchain reduces data breaches, stops fraud, and simplifies consumer interactions using decentralized ledgers, smart contracts, and cryptographic security. The chapter also looks at how blockchain might help secure digital identities, smooth payment processes, and transparent supply chain management—all essential for boosting industry resilience and regaining consumer trust. The conversation also focuses on the practical uses, difficulties, and potential future developments of blockchain integration in the hospitality industry. Ultimately, this chapter offers a thorough foundation for comprehending how blockchain might aid in the industry's recovery while upholding strict data protection regulations.

Preface

Blockchain has moved rapidly from a niche technical innovation to an enabling infrastructure for new forms of economic coordination. What began as a mechanism for peer to peer digital cash has developed into an ecosystem of programmable assets, decentralised governance arrangements, and market architectures that increasingly interact with mainstream institutions. Token economies sit at the heart of this transition. They combine distributed ledger technology with incentive design, digital property rights, and automated execution to create systems in which value can be issued, exchanged, governed, and audited in novel ways.

The Impact of Blockchain in Token Economies is conceived as an academic contribution to understanding these developments as more than a succession of technical upgrades or financial products. Tokenization has become a broad organizing concept that applies to assets, rights, data, and access. It is relevant not only to cryptocurrency markets but also to securities infrastructure, credit intermediation, intellectual property, education, scientific research, public goods provision, and data governance. Yet token economies also expose unresolved tensions: how decentralization is implemented in practice, how governance power concentrates, how legal categories adapt to on-chain transactions, and how risks are distributed across participants and communities.

The purpose of this edited volume is to examine token economies as socio technical systems. A token is simultaneously a technical artifact, a legal representation, an economic incentive, and a governance instrument. Its meaning and function depend on protocol design, institutional context, regulatory interpretation, and user behavior. For that reason, the volume gathers interdisciplinary perspectives spanning blockchain systems, finance, political economy, law, governance, and ethics. The contributors analyze both enabling mechanisms and frictions, and they do so through theory, case analysis, and critical evaluation of emerging practices.

A second motivation for the book is the need to distinguish between what tokenization promises and what it delivers in operational settings. Public discussion often swings between two extremes: token economies are either framed as inherently emancipatory or dismissed as speculative. Neither position offers an adequate basis for scholarship, policy, or responsible adoption. A careful account must address how token systems work, what they incentivize, where they fail, and how they interact with existing structures of authority, regulation, and trust.

The volume begins with conceptual foundations. The opening chapter presents a systematic review of blockchain technology as a catalyst for decentralized token economies. It identifies patterns in the literature on governance design, wealth distribution, and incentive alignment, and highlights a recurring empirical observation: blockchain can decentralize infrastructure while economic and governance power may remain concentrated. This analytical starting point is complemented by a chapter that adopts a forward looking lens, examining the maturation of blockchain technology and the ways in which advances in artificial intelligence may interact with decentralized architectures. These foundational chapters establish a shared vocabulary for the rest of the book and set out core questions that recur throughout the volume: what is being decentralized, for whom, and at what cost.

The middle chapters examine token economies in financial markets. Decentralized finance is addressed as a system of permissionless financial services executed through smart contracts, with tokenized assets serving as collateral, liquidity primitives, and governance instruments. This is followed by an extended discussion of tokenized lending and the institutionalization of DeFi, which considers how regulated entities, large investors, and policymakers respond to both the opportunities and the risks of on-chain credit markets. The analysis then expands to financial market integration and tokenized securities, highlighting how tokenized instruments interact with cross border market dynamics, regulatory coordination, and systemic risk. These chapters collectively show that token economies are neither separate from traditional finance nor fully absorbed by it. They are increasingly hybrid, and this hybridity creates both innovation pathways and governance challenges.

Beyond finance, the volume explores tokenization as a mechanism for reconfiguring ownership and rights. Real world asset tokenization is examined as an evolving practice with significant implications for liquidity, fractional ownership, and market access, while also confronting barriers such as regulatory uncertainty and uneven infrastructure readiness across jurisdictions. Intellectual property receives focused treatment in two distinct but complementary chapters. One introduces tokenized digital rights management as a set of tools for managing licensing, attribution, and protection of creative and innovative outputs. Another offers a critical legal analysis of intellectual property tokenization, emphasizing the normative conflicts that arise when global on chain transfers meet territorially grounded legal frameworks and formal requirements. Together, these contributions demonstrate that tokenization is not merely technical representation but a legal and institutional reordering that demands careful scrutiny.

Several chapters extend the scope to public value creation and knowledge infrastructures. Decentralized science is addressed as a movement that aims to rewire incentives for research funding, governance, and dissemination through tokenized mechanisms such as DAO led grants, tokenized research outputs, and prediction markets. A chapter on education considers how blockchain based credentials and token economics can support micro credentialing, portability of learning records, and new incentive models for lifelong learning, while also acknowledging practical concerns about digital divides, privacy, and regulatory uncertainty. The chapter on public goods provision examines token based approaches to collective action, including quadratic funding and regenerative finance, and evaluates the conditions under which these mechanisms improve transparency and participation. These chapters collectively argue that token economies can influence domains where the goal is not only market efficiency, but also public trust, inclusion, and sustainable coordination.

The volume includes applied perspectives that anchor conceptual claims in sector specific practice. The chapter focused on hospitality examines how blockchain technologies can support operational recovery, strengthen data privacy, and enhance transparency in supply chains and customer interactions. Such applied analyses are necessary for identifying implementation constraints and for clarifying where tokenization adds value compared to conventional database systems and contractual arrangements.

The concluding chapters address risks, ethics, and governance. Tokenized systems introduce technical vulnerabilities, market manipulation risks, regulatory gaps, and complex governance dynamics. They also raise ethical concerns such as exclusion, surveillance, environmental impacts, and accountability failures. One chapter analyzes these issues at a systemic level, drawing lessons from well known failures and proposing principles for responsible tokenization. The final chapter offers a supplementary Indigenous case study to explore ethical and structural risks in a context where sovereignty, knowledge systems, and community governance require particular care. This perspective underscores a central claim of the book: token economies are never neutral. Their design embeds values, and their outcomes depend on whose interests are represented in governance and whose costs are externalized.

Across all chapters, a key theme is that token economies are shaped by design choices. Incentive structures can promote resilience or extraction. Governance mechanisms can broaden participation or entrench insiders. Transparency can support accountability or enable new forms of surveillance. For researchers, this means token economies must be studied with methods that connect protocol mechanics to social outcomes. For policymakers, it means regulation should be informed by how systems behave in practice rather than by abstract categories alone. For practitioners, it means technical innovation must be accompanied by responsible governance, risk management, and ethical consideration.

The Impact of Blockchain in Token Economies is intended for a diverse academic and professional audience. Researchers and academics will find current analyses that can inform future scholarship across blockchain systems, finance, law, governance, and data science. Graduate and advanced undergraduate students can use the volume to understand both the foundational concepts and the live debates shaping tokenization. Practitioners, entrepreneurs, and builders working on decentralized applications will find structured discussion of the technical and conceptual frameworks, the institutional constraints they will encounter, and the design tensions that shape real world deployment. Regulators and policy professionals may also find value in the grounded discussion of risks, governance, and cross jurisdictional challenges.

The editors, **Guneet Kaur, Lorena Nessi, and Pooja Lekhi**, are grateful to the contributors for their scholarship, care, and interdisciplinary engagement. The speed of change in this field makes sustained academic work both difficult and necessary. Each chapter reflects an effort to document, analyze, and assess token economies with rigor and clarity, resisting both hype and cynicism.

We believe that *The Impact of Blockchain in Token Economies* will serve as a valuable resource for a diverse audience. Researchers, academics, and students in computer science, finance, law, and related fields can gain insight into how token economies function and where their key challenges lie, helping to guide future research. Developers, entrepreneurs, and organizations building applications within decentralized ecosystems will find a clear account of the technical and conceptual foundations, along with the governance, regulatory, and ethical issues that shape adoption and long term viability. We hope this book supports academic courses, research programs, and training initiatives, sparks curiosity, inspires responsible innovation, and fosters meaningful discussion about how blockchain and tokenization may contribute to more transparent, inclusive, and accountable digital economies.

ORGANIZATION OF THE BOOK

The book is organized into twelve chapters. A brief description of each chapter follows.

Chapter 1 examines blockchain's development from its early phase as a disruptive innovation to a more mature infrastructure that continues to evolve despite barriers such as scalability constraints, regulatory ambiguity, and limited public understanding. It explains how innovation persisted beyond initial hype cycles and focuses on how recent advances in artificial intelligence are being positioned as a way to address longstanding limitations. The chapter explores the convergence of AI and blockchain, emphasizing blockchain's role in decentralized trust, secure data governance, and auditability, alongside AI's role in intelligent automation and adaptive decision making. It concludes with a forward looking discussion of AI enabled blockchain ecosystems.

Chapter 2 analyzes the tensions between the tokenization of tangible assets and the idea of a People's Ledger, asking whether these are opposing models of future financial architecture or complementary approaches. Using an interdisciplinary lens that combines economic, legal, and political, and economic perspectives, it presents the functioning and potential of tokenization, together with risks such as fragmentation, smart contract vulnerabilities, and cyber threats. It then assesses the People's Ledger as a centralization oriented solution that promises stability, inclusion, and public control, but may also concentrate power and enable surveillance. The chapter concludes that neither pure decentralization nor complete centralization is viable, and that hybrid models are emerging.

Chapter 3 examines decentralized finance as a transformative development that uses blockchain to enable permissionless and automated financial services. It focuses on tokenized assets as a key driver of DeFi growth and surveys multiple forms of tokenization, including cryptocurrencies, asset backed tokens, and central bank digital currencies. The chapter explains how tokenized assets can enhance liquidity, support financial inclusion, and create new investment opportunities, while also addressing the relationship between decentralized and centralized models. It discusses regulatory challenges and risks associated with smart contracts, volatility, and governance, and draws on case based discussion and emerging trends to consider how tokenized economies may connect traditional finance with decentralized innovation.

Chapter 4 explores tokenized lending as a major DeFi application that enables credit intermediation through blockchain based smart contracts. It describes early permissionless platforms and the more recent shift toward institutional interest, as regulated entities seek compliant and risk managed solutions. The chapter provides a conceptual analysis of the institutionalization of tokenized lending, including its underlying technologies and potential role within the broader financial system. It highlights the fragmented regulatory landscape and compares approaches across the United States, Canada, the European Union, and Singapore. The chapter argues that regulatory diversity creates room for experimentation, but also introduces risks of fragmentation and regulatory arbitrage that can shape market development.

Chapter 5 presents an interdisciplinary study of real world asset tokenization as a significant blockchain application with implications for ownership structures, liquidity, and investment accessibility. It combines theoretical foundations with practical perspectives and identifies gaps in literature and practice, including regulatory uncertainty, limited integration with existing infrastructure, and the underrepresentation of developing economies. The chapter evaluates conceptual frameworks and reviews real world implementations through case studies, outlining both benefits and limitations of tokenized ecosystems. It frames the discussion as relevant to academic and policy audiences, aiming to support better alignment between innovation and regulation while encouraging more globally inclusive participation in digital asset markets.

Chapter 6 provides a critical legal analysis of intellectual property rights tokenization and argues that while blockchain based mechanisms may improve liquidity, valuation, and commercialization of intangible assets, they also generate normative conflicts that challenge legality and effectiveness under current legal orders. Using dogmatic and comparative law methods, the chapter focuses on three problem areas: the clash between blockchain's global character and the territoriality principle in IP law, the mismatch between traditional formal requirements such as written form and on chain transactions, and classification difficulties for IP tokens under capital market regimes. The chapter concludes that tokenization pressures legal systems to reconsider core concepts such as jurisdiction and state enforcement.

Chapter 7 examines tokenized science economies and explains how blockchain infrastructure can reshape how research is funded, governed, and shared. It situates the discussion within the Decentralized Science movement and emphasizes transparency, programmability, and economic alignment across the research lifecycle. Through case based discussion, the chapter examines mechanisms such as intellectual property NFTs, tokenized research outputs, DAO led funding structures, and scientific prediction markets. It argues that these tools can support new incentives for peer review, enable global collaboration, and expand access to discovery. The chapter frames tokenization as a structural innovation and presents a vision of a research economy designed to be open, sustainable, and interoperable across platforms and communities.

Chapter 8 explores how blockchain and tokenomics can reshape education through secure micro credentialing, equitable access, and lifelong learning. Drawing on peer reviewed literature, it discusses tamper resistant academic records, portable micro credentials, and learner controlled digital wallets. It explains how tokenomics can support incentive based learning environments, including learn to earn approaches and peer to peer knowledge exchange, and considers the role of decentralized autonomous organizations in curriculum governance and community led accreditation. The chapter emphasizes global case examples and policy implications while critically assessing challenges such as privacy, regulation, and digital divides. It concludes by advocating inclusive, ethical, and scalable strategies so that blockchain and tokenomics can support equity and continuous learning.

Chapter 9 examines token economies as a response to the long standing challenge of funding and coordinating public goods. It connects public goods economics to blockchain enabled mechanisms such as smart contracts, decentralized governance, and incentive aligned token design. The chapter analyzes innovative funding and coordination models, including quadratic funding, retroactive public goods funding, augmented bonding curves, and regenerative finance systems. Drawing on real world case discussion, it evaluates both strengths and limitations of token based approaches, highlighting promises of transparency and scalability alongside complexities of decentralized coordination. The chapter provides a structured assessment of how token economies may address market failures in public goods provision while acknowledging practical constraints and implementation trade offs.

Chapter 10 examines how blockchain technology can support hospitality sector recovery while strengthening data privacy and security. It explains how decentralized ledgers, smart contracts, and cryptographic mechanisms can improve trust among stakeholders, increase operational efficiency, and secure transactions. The chapter discusses how blockchain may reduce data breaches, prevent fraud, and streamline customer interactions, and it considers applications in secure digital identity, payment processes, and transparent supply chain management. It also addresses practical implementation issues and adoption challenges relevant to hospitality organizations. Overall, the chapter provides a focused foundation for understanding how blockchain can enhance industry resilience while supporting data protection and regulatory compliance in a sector where trust and privacy are operational priorities.

Chapter 11 analyzes tokenized economic systems as blockchain enabled arrangements that transform ownership, finance, and governance through digital tokens representing assets, rights, or value. It outlines key risks including technical vulnerabilities, market volatility, regulatory gaps, and governance failures, and it addresses ethical concerns such as exclusion, manipulation, environmental harm, and accountability deficits. Using examples of real world failures including TerraUSD, The DAO, and OpenSea, the chapter highlights both the promise and pitfalls of token economies. It proposes principles for responsible tokenization, emphasizing transparency, equity, sustainability, and hybrid governance supported by interdisciplinary collaboration. The chapter aims to guide stakeholders in developing resilient, ethical, and inclusive digital economies.

Chapter 12 critically examines risks, challenges, and ethical considerations associated with tokenized systems and presents an Indigenous focused case study as a supplementary illustration. It surveys risk categories including financial, liquidity, market, operational, fraud, and cybersecurity risks, as well as constraints related to blockchain networks, adoption, scalability, sustainability, and governance, including the integration of artificial intelligence. The chapter also discusses ethical issues such as algorithmic bias, data privacy, accountability, and sustainability. It proposes a conceptual framework and offers policy oriented insights to support ethical and responsible adoption of tokenized systems globally and within indigenized contexts. The discussion is illustrated through a case framed through the lens of two eyed seeing, presented in the annex.

Guneet Kaur
University of Stirling, UK

Lorena Nessi
Farleigh Dickinson University, UK

Pooja Lekhi
University Canada West, Canada

Chapter 1
The Slow but Unstoppable Journey of Blockchain:
A Forward-Looking Lens Into the Intelligent, Decentralized Systems Shaping Our Future

Yashodhan Karulkar
https://orcid.org/0000-0002-0991-3565
Mukesh Patel School of Technology Management and Engineering, NMIMS, India

Samyukta Gurudanti
https://orcid.org/0009-0000-5797-6555
Mukesh Patel School of Technology Management and Engineering, NMIMS, India

ABSTRACT

Blockchain emerged in 2009 as a disruptive innovation but struggled with scalability, regulatory ambiguity, and limited public understanding. Though early hype faded, steady innovation persisted. Today, advances in artificial intelligence (AI) are revitalizing blockchain by resolving these longstanding challenges. AI brings intelligent automation and adaptive decision-making, while blockchain ensures decentralized trust, secure data governance, and auditability. This chapter explores the powerful convergence of AI and blockchain, showcasing how their synergy is enabling intelligent, autonomous digital ecosystems. Through theoretical insights and real-world cases—such as JPMorgan's Onyx, IBM Food Trust, and Ocean Protocol—it illustrates practical impact and industry transformation. It also revisits initial adoption barriers

DOI: 10.4018/979-8-3373-3371-7.ch001

and shows how AI integration is unlocking scalable, secure solutions. The chapter concludes with a forward-looking vision of AI-enabled blockchain infrastructure shaping the next generation of decentralized digital environments.

INTRODUCTION

Blockchain technology first entered public consciousness through the publication of Satoshi Nakamoto's white paper in 2008, proposing a peer-to-peer electronic cash system that would become known as Bitcoin. Initially lauded as a technological breakthrough in establishing decentralized trust without central intermediaries, blockchain represented a novel fusion of cryptography, distributed systems, and economic incentives. Its ability to create tamper-proof, append-only ledgers through consensus protocols like Proof of Work introduced the idea of trust less systems, wherein multiple parties could transact securely without reliance on centralized authorities (Crosby et al., 2016).

The early 2010s witnessed an explosion of enthusiasm, with proponents envisioning blockchain as a panacea for inefficiencies plaguing traditional sectors—from reducing reconciliation times in finance to ensuring traceability in global supply chains, improving identity management, and even enabling fairer democratic voting systems. The promise of immutable, transparent, and decentralized infrastructure garnered attention from academia, industry, and government sectors alike.

However, as theoretical excitement gave way to real-world implementation attempts, a series of practical bottlenecks began to surface. The limitations of early blockchain systems such as Bitcoin and Ethereum included low transaction throughput, high latency, and significant energy consumption, particularly in proof-based consensus mechanisms (Casino, Dasaklis, & Patsakis, 2019). For instance, while Visa can process over 24,000 transactions per second, early blockchain networks struggled with single-digit throughput, hindering scalability. Moreover, the lack of interoperability among blockchain platforms and the difficulty in integrating with legacy enterprise infrastructures created friction for large-scale adoption.

Regulatory ambiguity compounded these challenges. As cryptocurrencies surged in popularity, many governments reacted with caution or outright bans, largely due to concerns around money laundering, fraud, and consumer protection. The absence of universally accepted standards and legal definitions for blockchain-based assets created uncertainty, making institutional adoption slower than expected (Atzori, 2017). Additionally, blockchain suffered a perception problem: despite its vast applicability, much of the public and media attention remained confined to its use in volatile cryptocurrency markets, which were often marred by speculative behavior, scams, and security breaches.

While blockchain was grappling with these headwinds, Artificial Intelligence (AI) was undergoing its own transformative renaissance. Building on decades of theoretical development, recent advancements in machine learning, natural language processing, and computer vision—largely driven by increases in computational power and data availability—enabled AI systems to outperform humans in various specialized tasks (Russell & Norvig, 2021). Enterprises began leveraging AI for intelligent automation, fraud detection, personalization, and dynamic pricing, while governments and healthcare systems experimented with AI for predictive diagnostics and public service optimization.

However, AI's meteoric rise was not without critique. The concentration of AI development in the hands of a few technology giants raised significant ethical and governance concerns, particularly surrounding data monopolies, algorithmic bias, opaque decision-making, and lack of auditability. AI systems, often described as "black boxes," made critical decisions with limited human understanding of their logic or fairness, making them difficult to regulate or trust. Furthermore, many AI applications relied on centralized datasets—collected without explicit user consent—raising red flags about data privacy and surveillance.

It is against this backdrop that the convergence of AI and blockchain emerges not merely as a technological trend, but as a strategic necessity. Individually, each technology has transformative potential—but also severe limitations. Together, they can address each other's shortcomings. AI can enhance blockchain by offering intelligent solutions to scalability, energy efficiency, and transaction validation. For instance, machine learning can dynamically adjust consensus parameters based on network load, and AI-powered oracles can enable more complex and reliable smart contracts. Additionally, AI can process and analyze data recorded on-chain to generate real-time predictions, detect anomalies, or personalize services—thereby augmenting the functionality of decentralized applications.

Conversely, blockchain offers AI a much-needed framework for transparency and accountability. A decentralized ledger can record the data sources, model iterations, and decision logs used by AI systems, making them auditable and reproducible. This addresses critical challenges in responsible AI development by enabling verifiable data provenance, secure model sharing, and tamper-resistant audit trails. Moreover, blockchain can enable distributed AI models, where collaborative training across multiple nodes ensures that no single party monopolizes the system—a concept being explored through technologies like federated learning and decentralized autonomous organizations (DAOs).

The fusion of AI and blockchain is not just theoretical—it is already materializing in emerging applications across multiple domains. From decentralized finance (DeFi) platforms that use AI for risk modeling, to smart supply chains with AI-driven predictive logistics, and governance systems that integrate automated compliance via blockchain-based smart contracts, the intersection is proving to be fertile ground for innovation.

Figure 1. Core features of AI and Blockchain

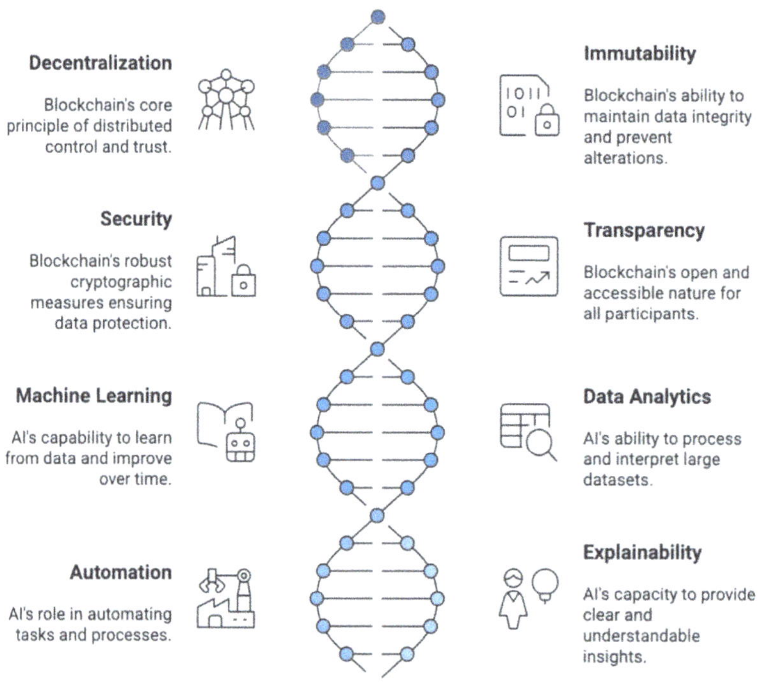

This chapter offers a comprehensive exploration of this evolving intersection. It begins by tracing the origins of both blockchain and AI, outlining their core principles and respective limitations. It then delves into the synergistic potential of their integration, highlighting how one can amplify the strengths and mitigate the weaknesses of the other. Through industry case studies and real-world implementations, we examine how this convergence is transforming sectors such as finance, supply chain, legal systems, and public governance. Particular attention is given to how AI is solving critical pain points in blockchain adoption, including scalability, regulatory compliance, and user trust.

The chapter also investigates cutting-edge projects at the forefront of this convergence, such as Ocean Protocol, Fetch.AI, and AI-governed DAOs—illustrating the diversity and depth of innovation in this space. Finally, it offers a forward-looking perspective on the opportunities, challenges, and ethical considerations that will shape the road ahead, urging stakeholders—technologists, policymakers, and investors—to collaboratively design intelligent systems that are not only efficient, but also transparent, secure, and aligned with democratic values.

As we move deeper into the 21st century, the integration of blockchain and AI is poised to usher in a new paradigm of intelligent decentralization. The quiet rise of these technologies—once seen as fringe or speculative—has become an unmistakable signal of change. Together, they are redefining not only how systems are built, but how trust, intelligence, and autonomy are engineered into the fabric of digital infrastructure.

BACKGROUND

Blockchain and artificial intelligence (AI) are two transformative technologies that are increasingly intersecting to redefine digital systems. Blockchain, introduced through Bitcoin in 2009, offers decentralized, tamper-proof data storage through cryptographic and consensus mechanisms. Its use cases have expanded beyond cryptocurrency into sectors like finance, healthcare, and logistics, though challenges like scalability, energy consumption, and regulatory ambiguity remain (Catalini & Gans, 2016; Agbo et al., 2019).

AI, encompassing machine learning and intelligent decision-making systems, has revolutionized fields such as healthcare diagnostics, financial forecasting, and autonomous systems. However, its opacity, susceptibility to bias, and lack of accountability raise ethical concerns (Binns, 2018; Floridi et al., 2018).

Recent research highlights the potential synergy between these technologies: blockchain can enhance AI transparency and trust, while AI can improve blockchain efficiency and adaptability. This convergence is laying the groundwork for decentralized, intelligent ecosystems that are secure, scalable, and ethically governed.

THEORETICAL FOUNDATIONS OF BLOCKCHAIN AND AI SYNERGY

The convergence of blockchain and artificial intelligence (AI) represents more than just the fusion of two technologies—it signals a foundational reimagining of digital infrastructure, trust, automation, and decision-making. To fully appreciate their synergy, it is crucial to dissect the core theoretical underpinnings of both systems and examine how their complementary attributes create a robust technological ecosystem with unprecedented potential.

At its essence, blockchain technology seeks to address a long-standing problem in computer science and economics: how to coordinate trust among untrusted parties without centralized control. This is achieved through a triad of foundational principles—decentralization, consensus, and cryptographic security—which collectively underpin blockchain's promise of secure, verifiable, and tamper-resistant digital transactions.

Decentralization is perhaps blockchain's most radical departure from conventional computing models. Traditional systems—whether financial ledgers, identity registries, or supply chain databases—operate under centralized authority, where data storage and control are consolidated. In contrast, blockchain distributes data across a peer-to-peer network of nodes, each maintaining a copy of the ledger and participating in its validation (Crosby et al., 2016). This disaggregation ensures fault tolerance, censorship resistance, and increased transparency, as no single entity can unilaterally manipulate or withhold information.

To coordinate this decentralized architecture, blockchain employs consensus algorithms that allow independent nodes to agree on the state of the ledger. Early systems like Bitcoin used Proof of Work (PoW)—a computationally expensive process designed to make tampering economically unviable. Later developments introduced alternatives such as Proof of Stake (PoS), Delegated PoS (DPoS), and Practical Byzantine Fault Tolerance (PBFT), which aim to enhance scalability and reduce energy consumption (Casino, Dasaklis, & Patsakis, 2019). These mechanisms form the operational backbone of blockchain, enabling collective agreement while maintaining system integrity in the presence of adversaries.

Blockchain's security model is grounded in cryptographic primitives. Hash functions ensure that each block is mathematically linked to its predecessor, making tampering with historical records computationally infeasible. Digital signatures authenticate transaction originators, while public-private key infrastructure governs access control and identity verification. The result is an immutable ledger, where every transaction is permanently recorded and can be independently verified, fostering high levels of transparency and auditability. These attributes are especially valuable in multi-stakeholder environments where trust is decentralized by design.

Artificial Intelligence, by contrast, is rooted in the goal of simulating intelligent behaviour in machines. It encompasses a wide array of subfields—from knowledge representation and search algorithms to statistical modeling and deep learning. The recent AI resurgence has been driven by three core capacities: intelligent automation, machine learning (ML), and adaptive decision-making.

At the heart of modern AI is machine learning, where algorithms learn from data rather than relying on explicitly coded instructions. Through supervised, unsupervised, and reinforcement learning, models can classify patterns, predict outcomes, or optimize strategies. Deep learning, a subset of ML, uses layered neural networks to extract hierarchical features, powering breakthroughs in image recognition, speech processing, and natural language understanding (Russell & Norvig, 2021).

AI also excels at automating complex workflows, mimicking human decision logic with greater speed, consistency, and scalability. Rule-based systems, decision trees, and expert systems enable machines to execute high-volume tasks with minimal human intervention. In financial services, for example, AI models detect fraud, automate underwriting, and provide real-time market insights. The ability to reason over dynamic data environments allows AI to adjust decisions based on feedback—an essential property for real-time, context-aware systems.

The integration of blockchain and AI is not just complementary—it is mutually enabling. While blockchain introduces data trustworthiness and decentralized governance, AI contributes intelligence, adaptability, and scalability. Their intersection addresses the weaknesses inherent in each technology and unlocks use cases previously unattainable in isolation.

One of blockchain's principal drawbacks lies in its scalability. Traditional consensus mechanisms like PoW are inherently slow and resource-intensive, limiting transaction throughput and energy efficiency. Here, AI can be leveraged to optimize consensus protocols. Through predictive modeling, AI systems can anticipate network traffic, dynamically adjust block sizes, or optimize node selection for consensus, reducing latency and improving throughput. Furthermore, AI can assist in automated anomaly detection in blockchain systems, identifying fraudulent transactions or protocol attacks before they cause systemic harm.

In the realm of smart contracts—self-executing digital agreements stored on-chain—AI enhances context awareness and decision flexibility. Traditional smart contracts are deterministic and limited to predefined conditions. By integrating AI models, contracts can incorporate real-time external data (via AI-powered oracles), learn from historical outcomes, and adapt to unforeseen scenarios. This leads to intelligent smart contracts capable of nuanced execution and self-adjustment in complex environments such as supply chains or decentralized insurance.

Conversely, AI's dependence on large, centralized datasets raises significant privacy, security, and ethical concerns. Centralized training environments are susceptible to data breaches, manipulation, and misuse. Blockchain mitigates these risks by offering decentralized, tamper-resistant data storage. By embedding data provenance and time-stamped audit logs into the ledger, blockchain provides a trust layer that enhances the integrity of AI model inputs.

Moreover, blockchain enables federated and collaborative AI, where models can be trained across distributed datasets without exposing raw data—a technique particularly relevant in privacy-sensitive domains like healthcare or finance. In such environments, blockchain can coordinate model updates, track contributions, and enforce access permissions, ensuring ethical and decentralized AI development.

The emergence of decentralized AI marketplaces—such as Ocean Protocol—exemplifies this model. These platforms allow data owners, model developers, and application users to transact securely and transparently, exchanging value without centralized intermediaries (Casino et al., 2019). Such models not only democratize access to AI but also incentivize fair data sharing, contributing to more equitable innovation ecosystems.

In sum, blockchain and AI, when viewed through a theoretical lens, are technological complements that together form the backbone of future intelligent systems. Blockchain provides the integrity, transparency, and trust infrastructure, while AI offers the intelligence, efficiency, and adaptive capability required to operate complex digital systems at scale.

This synergy sets the stage for a wide range of transformational applications—from algorithmically governed financial systems and autonomous supply networks to real-time legal arbitration and intelligent public governance. By weaving together these foundational technologies, it becomes possible to architect digital ecosystems that are not only smart but also secure, ethical, and resilient.

GOVERNMENT: ESTONIA'S E-GOVERNANCE AND DUBAI'S AI-AUGMENTED BLOCKCHAIN PUBLIC SERVICES

Estonia is frequently cited as a global leader in digital governance, owing to its integrated e-government system known as e-Estonia, built around the X-Road platform. Although some independent audits have questioned the actual deployment of blockchain in X-Road, the overall architecture exemplifies digital sovereignty. The system enables nearly all public services to be accessed online, including digital identity, healthcare, and electronic voting, at any hour of the year (Nordic Institute for Interoperability Solutions, 2021; Wiki Contributors, 2025). Although blockchain has not been uniformly adopted across every subsystem, Estonia's e-Governance infrastructure remains one of the most comprehensive globally. To augment service integrity, AI models have been deployed for fraud detection, policy simulation, and personalized citizen engagement. For example, fraud indicators are flagged by systems that cross-validate identity credentials and transaction histories, while AI assists in modeling alternative policy scenarios to forecast social and economic outcomes (Tiits & Kaska, 2018). This fusion of distributed system trust, automated oversight, and citizen-centric digital identity has enabled Estonia to scale public services while preserving transparency and legislative alignment.

In contrast, Dubai's Smart Dubai initiative represents a deliberate strategy to merge blockchain and AI across government services. Launched via the Dubai Blockchain Strategy in 2016—whose goal was for Dubai to become the first fully blockchain-powered government by 2020—this initiative envisions government efficiency, industry creation, and international leadership as its strategic pillars (Smart Dubai Office & Dubai Future Foundation, 2023; DMCC, 2025). In practice, blockchain underpins services such as property title registration, visa processing, digital identity (UAE Pass), and healthcare record exchange, eliminating paper-based inefficiencies and permitting auditable transactional transparency (Digital Dubai, 2024; Websima DMCC, 2025). AI enters this ecosystem via several channels: the AI Lab, in partnership with IBM, develops predictive analytics applications; Rashid, an AI assistant operating across eleven government entities, handles over 60,000 citizen queries per month; Salama, a visa renewal platform using AI to auto-recognize user inputs and expedite approvals; and city-wide intelligent hiring and procurement tools that leverage machine learning to assess vendor proposals or personalize training programs (Websima DMCC, 2025; Gulf News, 2025).

The inaugural Dubai State of AI Report (Digital Dubai & Dubai Future Foundation, 2025) underscores the institutional depth of this integration. It documents over 100 high-impact AI use cases already in operation or development across sectors including healthcare, procurement, compliance, licensing, and urban mobility. The accompanying AI Policy for Government Entities, introduced concurrently, institutionalizes principles such as explainability, interoperability, and human-centric deployment—which reflect Dubai's ambition to lead not only in technological implementation but also in ethical AI governance (Digital Dubai & Dubai Future Foundation, 2025).

Functionally, the integration of AI and blockchain in Dubai enables predictive government services, anticipatory resource allocation, and proactive responsiveness. For example, licensing—a formerly manual and siloed process—is now executed via AI decision support systems backed by blockchain logs, reducing turnaround time and strengthening. Similarly, procurement systems equipped with machine learning provide instant technical assessments of vendor proposals, while blockchain records supply transparency in contract awarding (Digital Dubai & Dubai Future Foundation, 2025; DMCC, 2025).

Dubai's leadership has also signaled ambition for legislative innovation. The UAE is piloting the use of AI as a co-legislator through a newly created Regulatory Intelligence Office, aiming to accelerate legislative drafting and propose legal amendments based on data-driven insights—an approach expected to increase efficiency by up to 70% (Financial Times, 2025). The wider governance architecture even anticipates an "AI Minister" integrated into cabinet decision-making by early 2026, reflecting a bold vision for AI-infused statecraft (The Sun, 2025).

Figure 2. Estonia V/S Dubai Digital Governance

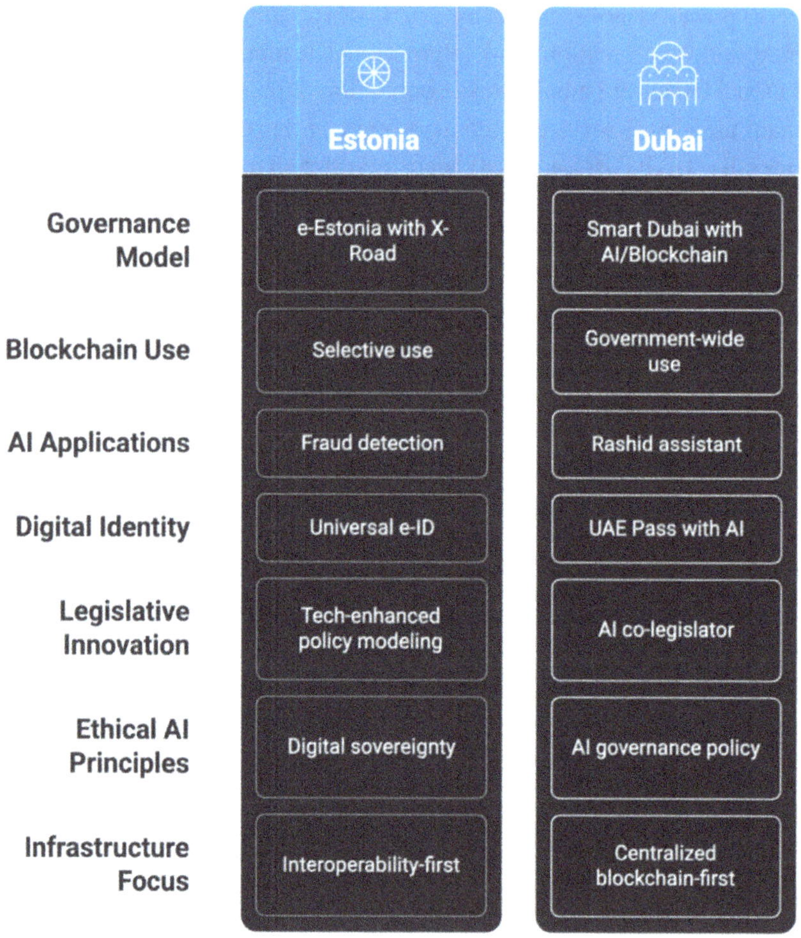

Together, the Estonian and Dubai case studies illustrate distinct but complementary models of AI-enabled blockchain governance. Estonia emphasizes digital identity, interoperability, and policy transparency; Dubai emphasizes service centralization through blockchain infrastructure and pervasive AI across public-facing applications. Both approaches foreground citizen-centric governance and digital trust. For researchers, policymakers, and technologists, these examples offer strategic models for designing modern governance systems that are efficient, resilient, and ethically governed—anchored by transparent ledgers and intelligent automation.

The fusion of AI and blockchain is reshaping multiple industries by establishing new standards of trust, efficiency, and adaptability. In finance, AI enhances the security and analysis of decentralized systems; supply chains gain predictive power that strengthens blockchain's transparency; the legal sector benefits from smart contracts that dynamically enforce compliance and resolve disputes; and governments leverage this synergy to deliver more transparent, responsive public services. Collectively, these innovations reveal how AI-enabled blockchain is creating smarter, more resilient infrastructures that will underpin the evolving digital economy.

OVERCOMING BLOCKCHAIN'S ROADBLOCKS WITH AI

While blockchain technology holds immense promise for revolutionizing numerous sectors, its path to widespread adoption has been obstructed by a series of persistent challenges. Chief among these are technical constraints such as scalability bottlenecks and energy inefficiencies, regulatory uncertainties that vary across jurisdictions, public mistrust fueled by misconceptions and associations with volatile cryptocurrencies, and the inherent complexity of integrating blockchain with entrenched legacy systems. Each of these factors has slowed blockchain's progress from experimental innovation to mainstream deployment. Yet, recent advancements in artificial intelligence (AI) are proving instrumental in overcoming these obstacles, paving the way for blockchain's evolution into a dependable, efficient, and user-trusted technology. This section explores the multifaceted role AI plays in addressing blockchain's limitations, enabling more scalable, compliant, and accessible blockchain ecosystems.

Technical limitations remain a significant barrier to blockchain's scalability and operational efficiency. Traditional consensus mechanisms like Proof of Work (PoW) demand extensive computational power, resulting in high latency and excessive energy consumption (Casino, Dasaklis, & Patsakis, 2019). AI's capacity for real-time data analysis and predictive modeling can optimize these consensus protocols by forecasting network traffic, dynamically allocating resources, and automating node participation to enhance throughput without compromising security. Machine learning algorithms also contribute to anomaly detection within blockchain networks, identifying irregular behaviors or security threats faster and with higher accuracy than conventional rule-based systems. By intelligently managing network conditions and safeguarding against malicious actors, AI fosters a more robust and efficient blockchain infrastructure.

Regulatory ambiguity represents another critical challenge. The decentralized and cross-border nature of blockchain complicates governance, leading to fragmented legal frameworks and compliance hurdles (Atzori, 2017). AI facilitates regulatory compliance by automating the monitoring and interpretation of evolving legal requirements across jurisdictions. Natural language processing (NLP) tools analyze regulatory texts, extracting relevant mandates that smart contracts can incorporate dynamically, ensuring real-time adherence to laws. Furthermore, AI-driven risk assessment models help organizations anticipate regulatory impacts, adapt operational strategies, and generate transparent audit trails that satisfy regulatory scrutiny. This proactive approach reduces the uncertainty and cost associated with compliance in complex legal environments.

Public skepticism toward blockchain, often rooted in misconceptions or negative associations with speculative cryptocurrency markets, limits broader acceptance. AI-enhanced user interfaces, such as conversational agents and personalized dashboards, simplify blockchain interactions and improve user understanding by translating complex technical concepts into accessible insights (Russell & Norvig, 2021). Additionally, AI-powered reputation systems aggregate and analyze network participant behaviors, offering transparent trust scores that help users distinguish reliable actors from fraudulent entities. These features build confidence by fostering transparency and accountability, thereby mitigating skepticism and promoting wider adoption.

SCALABILITY SOLUTIONS ACCELERATED BY AI OPTIMIZATION

Scalability has persistently been one of the most formidable technical challenges confronting blockchain technology, especially in networks reliant on energy-intensive consensus mechanisms such as Proof of Work (PoW). These limitations manifest as high transaction latency, constrained throughput, and substantial energy consumption, which collectively hinder blockchain's deployment in environments demanding real-time processing and handling of large transaction volumes (Croman et al., 2016). To surmount these challenges, artificial intelligence (AI) techniques—particularly machine learning and predictive analytics—are increasingly leveraged to optimize scalability across multiple dimensions of blockchain architecture.

One critical area where AI delivers significant impact is in the dynamic optimization of consensus protocols. Traditional consensus algorithms are generally static, lacking the ability to adjust operational parameters in response to fluctuating network conditions. AI algorithms, by contrast, utilize predictive models to forecast network congestion and other performance bottlenecks. This foresight allows for real-time adjustments to essential parameters such as block size, block interval, and validation timing, thereby maximizing throughput while preserving the core security guarantees of the blockchain. Reinforcement learning, a branch of machine learning where systems improve decision-making by learning from feedback, enables blockchain nodes to iteratively discover optimal configurations based on historical data, effectively fine-tuning resource allocation and accelerating transaction confirmation times over successive cycles.

Another promising scalability enhancement involves sharding, a technique that partitions the blockchain ledger into smaller, more manageable segments or "shards" to enable parallel transaction processing. However, the orchestration of sharding demands precise coordination to ensure workload is evenly distributed and data consistency is maintained across shards. AI-powered orchestration systems facilitate this by analyzing workload patterns and network states, thereby intelligently balancing shard assignments and minimizing cross-shard communication overheads. This adaptive management contributes significantly to scalability gains by preventing hotspots and bottlenecks within the blockchain network.

MITIGATING PUBLIC MISPERCEPTIONS THROUGH TRANSPARENT AI-DRIVEN AUDIT TRAILS

Public skepticism represents a formidable barrier to blockchain technology adoption despite its widely recognized potential to revolutionize industries through decentralization, enhanced security, and data immutability. Many laypersons and even institutional stakeholders often associate blockchain............n primarily with negative connotations such as its initial use in illicit marketplaces, extreme price volatility of cryptocurrencies, and the perceived complexity of its cryptographic underpinnings. This mistrust is further compounded by the lack of transparency around blockchain processes, which are often opaque to non-expert users, regulators, and decision-makers. The intricate, distributed nature of blockchain networks, combined with the complexity of consensus algorithms and smart contract execution, creates a steep cognitive barrier to understanding and trusting the technology's operation. Without clear visibility into these processes, fears regarding data misuse, transaction fraud, and technological failure persist, undermining confidence and slowing mainstream adoption.

To overcome these challenges, AI-driven transparent audit trails emerge as a critical solution that not only bolsters blockchain's inherent security and immutability but also addresses the cognitive and perceptual barriers that fuel public skepticism. Traditional audit trails merely record transaction logs, which can be voluminous and inscrutable. However, by leveraging advanced AI methodologies—particularly explainable AI (XAI), natural language processing (NLP), and anomaly detection—

these audit trails can be transformed into intelligent, user-friendly systems that elucidate blockchain operations in real time and provide verifiable assurances of integrity and compliance.

Explainable AI, in particular, addresses the "black box" problem commonly associated with complex machine learning models by providing human-interpretable explanations of decisions and actions taken by algorithms (Doshi-Velez & Kim, 2017). When applied to blockchain, XAI frameworks analyze the sequence of transactions, the conditions triggering smart contract executions, and the consensus mechanisms to generate clear, step-by-step narratives that explain the provenance and validation of each transaction. This capability is especially vital in regulated environments such as finance and healthcare, where auditability and traceability are legal requirements. For example, an AI-powered audit system can describe why a certain smart contract clause was executed or why a transaction was flagged for further scrutiny, enabling auditors and regulators to verify compliance without requiring deep technical expertise.

Transparency is further enhanced through AI-powered visualization tools and user interfaces that translate raw blockchain data into accessible formats. Interactive dashboards leverage AI to provide real-time metrics on network performance, transaction throughput, and security incidents, often coupled with predictive analytics that forecast potential risks or bottlenecks. These visualizations are customizable, catering to different stakeholder groups—from everyday users wanting to verify the status of their transactions to regulators conducting compliance audits. By democratizing access to blockchain insights, these tools reduce the "black box" effect, empowering users to make informed decisions and participate confidently in blockchain ecosystems.

Figure 3. AI-Blockchain Audit-ability Framework

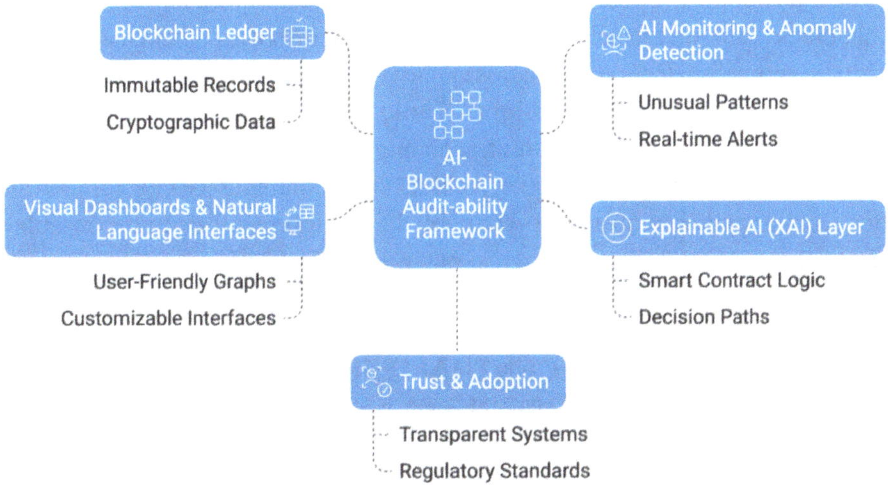

Moreover, AI's integration with blockchain audit trails facilitates regulatory compliance and public accountability. Regulatory bodies increasingly require transparent record-keeping and proof of compliance with anti-money laundering (AML), know-your-customer (KYC), and data privacy laws. AI automates the extraction and summarization of relevant data points from blockchain ledgers, producing audit-ready documentation that expedites reporting and regulatory review (Arner, Barberis, & Buckley, 2017). This automation not only lowers the cost and complexity of compliance but also reduces human errors and potential manipulation, thereby enhancing trustworthiness.

Importantly, transparent AI-driven audit trails enable continuous improvement of blockchain systems themselves. By analyzing patterns in transaction failures, bottlenecks, or security breaches, AI can provide actionable insights to developers and administrators for optimizing network protocols, smart contract design, and consensus algorithms. This iterative feedback loop is essential for scaling blockchain technologies to meet enterprise demands and ensuring long-term sustainability.

Real-world deployments underscore the effectiveness of AI-enhanced audit trails. For instance, the Hyperledger Foundation—a leading open-source blockchain consortium—has explored integrating AI tools for enhanced network analytics and automated compliance monitoring (Hyperledger, 2023). Similarly, companies like Chainalysis utilize AI to track and explain cryptocurrency flows, providing law enforcement and financial institutions with transparent, actionable intelligence about blockchain transactions, which helps counteract the illicit-use narrative and builds mainstream trust.

In conclusion, public misperceptions rooted in distrust and complexity can be significantly mitigated by harnessing AI-driven transparency mechanisms embedded within blockchain infrastructures. Explainable AI demystifies blockchain decision processes, anomaly detection safeguards against fraud, and AI-powered visualizations democratize access to network insights. These capabilities collectively transform opaque ledger systems into transparent, accountable platforms that foster trust across users, regulators, and developers alike. As blockchain continues its trajectory towards mainstream adoption, embedding AI-enabled audit trails will be indispensable in bridging the gap between technological potential and societal acceptance.

OCEAN PROTOCOL: DECENTRALIZED DATA MARKETPLACES LEVERAGING AI AND BLOCKCHAIN

Ocean Protocol represents a pioneering initiative in the emerging domain of decentralized data marketplaces, combining the immutable transparency and security of blockchain technology with the adaptive intelligence of artificial intelligence (AI) to create an ecosystem that fundamentally reshapes how data is shared, monetized, and consumed (Ocean Protocol Foundation, 2023). At the heart of Ocean Protocol's architecture is a decentralized network that empowers data providers—ranging from individuals to large enterprises—to retain sovereignty over their data assets. Unlike traditional centralized data platforms, where intermediaries often control access and dictate terms, Ocean Protocol leverages blockchain-based smart contracts to enforce immutable, automated agreements governing data access and usage rights (Brody et al., 2021). These smart contracts provide cryptographically secure, transparent records of every transaction and interaction within the marketplace, ensuring data provenance, accountability, and trustworthiness throughout the data lifecycle.

One of the key innovations within Ocean Protocol is the seamless integration of AI tools that enhance marketplace functionality far beyond simple data exchange. Machine learning models embedded in the platform perform sophisticated data quality assessments and enable intelligent data discovery mechanisms that allow potential data consumers to evaluate the utility and relevance of datasets before making acquisition decisions (Ocean Protocol Foundation, 2023). This is critical in addressing the pervasive issue of data trustworthiness, as buyers face significant risk when procuring datasets of uncertain provenance or quality. By leveraging AI-driven metadata analysis and pattern recognition, Ocean Protocol minimizes such risks and facilitates more informed, data-driven decision-making. For instance, advanced anomaly detection and data validation algorithms analyze incoming data streams, flagging inconsistencies or potential biases that might compromise downstream analytics.

Moreover, AI-powered recommendation engines within Ocean Protocol tailor the marketplace experience by dynamically matching data providers with consumers based on contextual relevance, user behavior, and historical transaction patterns (Brody et al., 2021). This personalization optimizes marketplace liquidity, ensuring that valuable data assets find the most appropriate and high-impact applications. Such AI-enhanced matchmaking not only drives efficiency but also fosters innovation by uncovering novel use cases and facilitating interdisciplinary data collaborations that traditional siloed systems rarely enable.

Figure 4. Building a secure data ecosystem

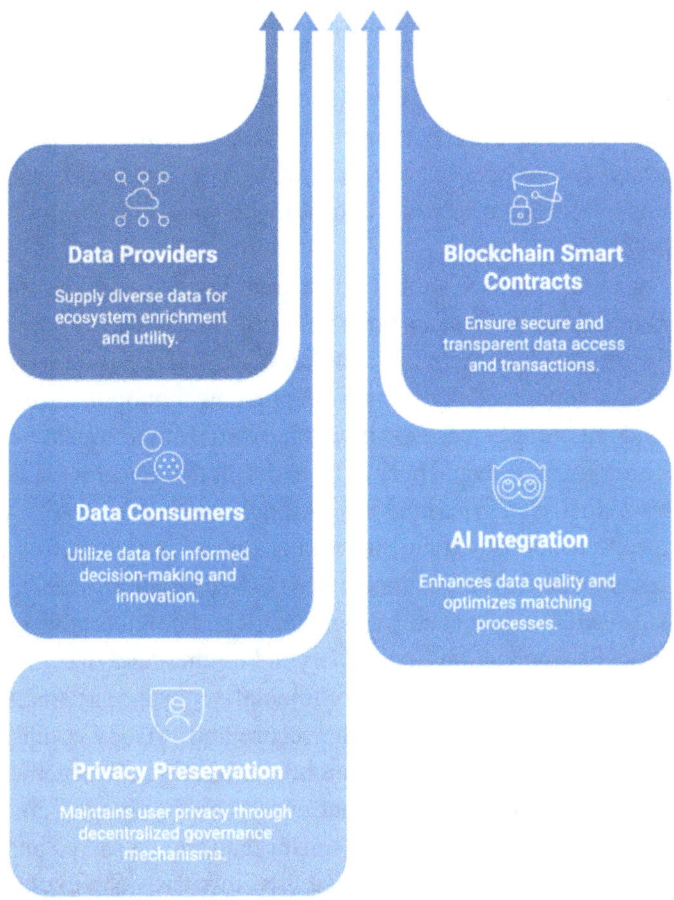

Ocean Protocol's hybrid architecture addresses several entrenched challenges inherent in the data economy. Privacy preservation, for example, is deeply embedded through blockchain's decentralized governance combined with privacy-enhancing AI techniques. Instead of transferring raw data outright, Ocean supports privacy-preserving computation frameworks such as federated learning and secure multi-party computation, allowing AI models to train on distributed data sources without exposing sensitive information. This mitigates regulatory and ethical concerns related to data sharing, such as compliance with the General Data Protection Regulation (GDPR) and other data protection laws, by ensuring that data ownership and control remain firmly in the hands of providers while still enabling valuable insights to be derived.

Another significant barrier Ocean Protocol tackles is data siloing, a pervasive problem where valuable datasets remain isolated within organizational boundaries, inaccessible for broader societal benefit or cross-industry innovation (Ocean Protocol Foundation, 2023). By establishing a decentralized marketplace governed by blockchain consensus, Ocean facilitates secure and permissioned data exchanges that transcend institutional boundaries without compromising security or control. This shift promotes a more fluid and democratized data economy, where data liquidity increases as assets can be licensed or rented with verifiable terms, generating new revenue streams for data owners while expanding the data availability for AI model development.

Vendor lock-in, a common limitation in traditional cloud and data platform ecosystems, is mitigated by Ocean's open protocol design, which supports interoperability with multiple blockchain networks and data storage systems (Brody et al., 2021). This open-source, modular framework prevents monopolistic control by any single entity and encourages a competitive, innovative environment where diverse stakeholders can contribute to and benefit from the platform's growth. Furthermore, Ocean incentivizes ecosystem participation through a native utility token (OCEAN), which facilitates transaction settlement, staking for data curation, and governance voting. This token economy aligns incentives between data providers, consumers, and curators, fostering sustained ecosystem health and collaborative governance.

Ocean Protocol's implications extend beyond commercial data exchanges into critical sectors such as healthcare, environmental science, and smart cities. For example, in healthcare, Ocean enables the secure and privacy-compliant sharing of sensitive medical datasets for AI research, accelerating advancements in diagnostics and personalized medicine without compromising patient confidentiality. In environmental monitoring, distributed sensor data can be shared and monetized transparently, supporting AI-driven sustainability initiatives. Smart cities can leverage Ocean's infrastructure to integrate disparate urban data sources, facilitating intelligent service delivery and real-time policy analytics.

The Ocean Protocol model exemplifies how the confluence of AI and blockchain can disrupt traditional data paradigms by introducing trust, transparency, and intelligence at scale. As data continues to be a critical economic and social asset, platforms like Ocean provide a blueprint for creating decentralized, privacy-respecting, and AI-augmented ecosystems that unlock the full potential of data while safeguarding ethical and regulatory principles. This transformative approach not only democratizes data access but also catalyzes innovation by lowering barriers to high-quality, diverse datasets necessary for training robust AI models.

HEALTHCARE: AI-ENHANCED BLOCKCHAIN FOR DATA SECURITY AND PATIENT PRIVACY

Healthcare remains one of the most critical sectors where the safeguarding of sensitive data, seamless interoperability among disparate systems, and stringent patient privacy protections are non-negotiable imperatives. The integration of blockchain technology with artificial intelligence (AI) presents a transformative paradigm that addresses these complex challenges, offering robust solutions to ensure data security, foster trust, and accelerate healthcare innovation.

At its core, blockchain's immutable, decentralized ledger provides a tamper-resistant record-keeping framework that can securely log patient data, medical histories, and transactional interactions across healthcare ecosystems. This ensures provenance, auditability, and transparency, reducing risks associated with data manipulation, unauthorized access, and fraud. However, blockchain alone cannot solve the challenges of data utility and actionable insights without intelligent processing — a gap that AI effectively fills by offering sophisticated data analytics, anomaly detection, and predictive modeling capabilities.

One pioneering example is the MediLedger Project, which utilizes blockchain to authenticate and track pharmaceutical supply chains with high precision (MediLedger, 2022). Counterfeit drugs pose a major global health risk, costing lives and undermining confidence in healthcare systems. MediLedger leverages blockchain's decentralized verification to record every transaction and shipment immutably, ensuring end-to-end traceability of medicines from manufacturers to pharmacies. Integrating AI models into this blockchain infrastructure elevates its capabilities by analyzing transaction patterns, identifying anomalies indicative of counterfeit or diversion attempts, and predicting supply chain disruptions before they escalate. AI-driven insights empower stakeholders to intervene proactively, safeguarding the integrity of pharmaceuticals and enhancing patient safety.

Beyond supply chain authentication, AI and blockchain converge powerfully in privacy-preserving collaborative medical research. Traditional approaches to data sharing are hindered by regulatory constraints such as HIPAA (Health Insurance Portability and Accountability Act) in the U.S. and GDPR (General Data Protection Regulation) in Europe, which impose strict controls on patient data usage. AI techniques such as federated learning enable multiple healthcare providers and research institutions to collaboratively train machine learning models on decentralized datasets without exchanging raw patient data. When combined with blockchain's secure ledger and access control mechanisms, federated learning frameworks ensure that models improve continuously while patient confidentiality remains intact.

For example, AI algorithms can be deployed directly on encrypted blockchain-stored medical data using advanced cryptographic methods like homomorphic encryption, which permits computations on encrypted data without decrypting it (Acar et al., 2018). This allows healthcare organizations to gain clinical insights and predictive diagnostics from aggregated data across hospitals or research centers, accelerating precision medicine initiatives and early disease detection while fully respecting patient privacy. Blockchain ensures immutable logging of AI model training and access events, fostering accountability and auditability in sensitive clinical environments.

Innovative platforms such as BurstIQ exemplify the potential of AI-enhanced blockchain in healthcare (BurstIQ, 2023). BurstIQ provides a comprehensive ecosystem where healthcare data is tokenized and exchanged within secure marketplaces, enabling patients, providers, and researchers to retain ownership and control of their data. AI-powered analytics integrated into BurstIQ's platform support advanced risk stratification, outcome prediction, and operational efficiency improvements. For instance, AI algorithms analyze vast longitudinal patient records to identify early indicators of chronic disease progression, enabling clinicians to personalize treatment plans more effectively. Meanwhile, blockchain's

Figure 5. AI and Blockchian integration spectrum

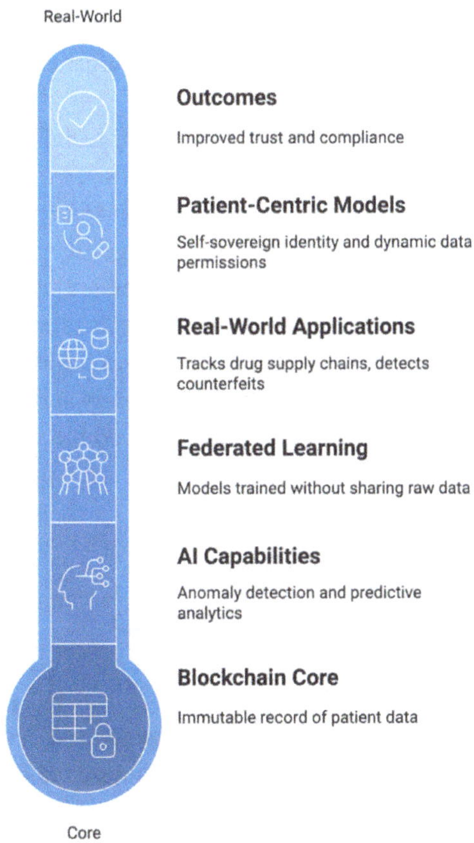

decentralized governance ensures data provenance and regulatory compliance, fostering trust among participants in the healthcare value chain.

Moreover, AI and blockchain facilitate patient-centric care models by empowering individuals with greater control over their health data. Through blockchain-based self-sovereign identity solutions, patients can securely grant and revoke data access permissions to providers, researchers, or insurers in real time. AI agents can monitor usage patterns to detect unusual access or potential privacy breaches, triggering alerts and reinforcing security. This model not only enhances patient autonomy but also streamlines administrative processes such as insurance claims, consent management, and clinical trial recruitment, reducing friction and administrative costs.

The integration also extends to clinical trial management, where AI-driven blockchain platforms improve transparency and trust in trial data integrity. By recording trial protocols, participant consent, and outcome data on an immutable blockchain ledger, these platforms prevent data tampering and selective reporting. AI analytics further optimize patient recruitment by identifying suitable candidates based on complex criteria extracted from decentralized datasets, speeding up trial timelines and reducing costs.

In summary, the confluence of AI and blockchain technologies in healthcare creates a powerful synergy that transcends the limitations of existing systems. Blockchain guarantees secure, decentralized data management and provenance, while AI provides the intelligence to extract actionable knowledge, detect fraud, and preserve privacy through cutting-edge cryptographic and federated approaches. Together, they enable interoperable, transparent, and patient-centric healthcare ecosystems that comply with rigorous regulations and empower stakeholders—from providers and researchers to patients themselves—to innovate safely and efficiently. As these technologies mature and adoption expands, AI-enhanced blockchain solutions will play an indispensable role in advancing healthcare security, privacy, and personalized medicine worldwide.

FUTURE DIRECTIONS: THE ROAD AHEAD FOR AI AND BLOCKCHAIN

As blockchain technology and artificial intelligence (AI) evolve and increasingly interconnect, their convergence promises to redefine the digital landscape by creating ecosystems that are simultaneously intelligent, secure, and decentralized. This fusion unlocks unprecedented opportunities to transform industries, enhance governance models, and address societal challenges through innovative applications that leverage the unique strengths of both technologies. However, achieving this ambitious vision demands careful consideration of technical, ethical, and regulatory complexities that arise from the interplay of AI and blockchain systems.

Looking forward, future development must prioritize building interoperable frameworks that enable seamless integration between heterogeneous blockchain networks and diverse AI models. Advances in cross-chain communication protocols, combined with federated learning and privacy-preserving AI techniques, will be essential to enable large-scale, collaborative intelligence without compromising data sovereignty or user privacy. Additionally, research into scalable AI-driven consensus mechanisms can address performance bottlenecks, enabling these hybrid systems to operate efficiently at the scale required by real-world applications.

Ethical considerations will play a critical role in shaping responsible AI-blockchain deployments. Embedding fairness, transparency, and accountability directly into system design through decentralized governance structures and explainable AI will be vital to prevent bias, misuse, and unintended consequences. The establishment of global standards and regulatory harmonization will further support trustworthy innovation while safeguarding individual rights and societal values.

Moreover, fostering multi-stakeholder collaboration between technologists, policymakers, industry leaders, and civil society will be crucial to align incentives and co-create inclusive ecosystems. Investment in education, research, and open-source initiatives can accelerate innovation while democratizing access to these powerful technologies.

In summary, the road ahead for AI and blockchain is marked by vast potential and equally significant challenges. By addressing technical scalability, ethical integrity, and regulatory clarity through collaborative efforts, the integration of AI and blockchain can become the backbone of next-generation digital infrastructures that empower individuals, organizations, and communities worldwide.

For technologists, the ongoing convergence of artificial intelligence (AI) and blockchain technology presents a complex yet promising frontier that necessitates a multidisciplinary and holistic approach to system design and development. To build robust, scalable, and resilient AI-blockchain systems, technologists must integrate cutting-edge advances across several technical domains, including consensus mechanisms, cryptographic protocols, data privacy techniques, and explainable AI frameworks. For instance, the evolution of consensus algorithms—from traditional proof-of-work models to more efficient proof-of-stake, delegated proof-of-stake, and novel AI-assisted consensus approaches—can significantly improve network scalability and energy efficiency while maintaining decentralization and security guarantees. Meanwhile, cryptographic innovations such as zero-knowledge proofs, homomorphic encryption, and secure multi-party computation enable privacy-preserving computations that allow AI models to operate on encrypted data, thus protecting user confidentiality and complying with increasingly stringent data protection regulations (Jin et al., 2023).

Figure 6. The future of AI-Blockchain Integration

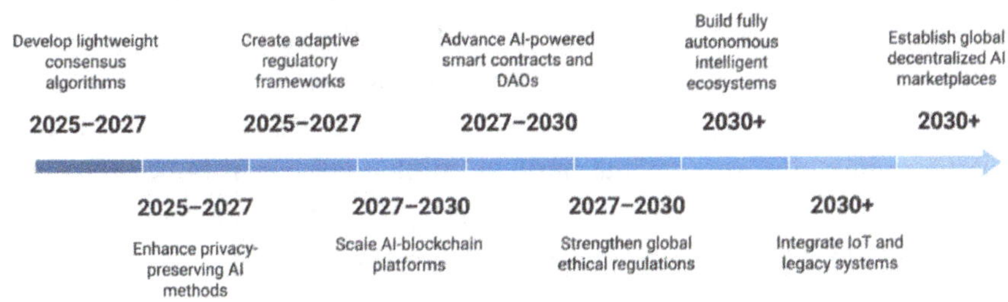

Central to unlocking new business models and application domains are decentralized autonomous organizations (DAOs), which utilize blockchain to automate governance and decision-making processes without centralized intermediaries. When combined with AI, DAOs can dynamically adapt rules and strategies based on real-time data and stakeholder inputs, creating intelligent governance ecosystems capable of self-optimization and resilience against manipulation or failure (López & Garay, 2021). Furthermore, AI-powered smart contracts elevate traditional automated contract execution by embedding machine learning algorithms that enable conditional reasoning, anomaly detection, and contextual decision-making, thereby expanding contract flexibility and responsiveness in complex environments. Prioritizing privacy-preserving AI techniques—including federated learning and differential privacy—ensures that sensitive data can be utilized for model training and inference while preventing data leakage, a critical concern as AI-blockchain applications increasingly operate in domains like healthcare, finance, and identity management.

Open-source collaboration and the development of interoperable standards are indispensable to reduce fragmentation within the AI-blockchain ecosystem. Efforts to harmonize protocols, APIs, and data models facilitate cross-platform compatibility, enabling diverse blockchain networks and AI services to interoperate seamlessly. Standardization bodies and industry consortia must spearhead these initiatives to foster an ecosystem that mitigates vendor lock-in, accelerates innovation cycles, and expands market accessibility (ISO/IEC, 2023). Additionally, embracing modular, composable architectures allows technologists to build flexible systems where AI and blockchain components can be independently upgraded or replaced, ensuring long-term adaptability in a rapidly evolving technological landscape.

Policymakers face the nuanced challenge of balancing the imperative to foster technological innovation with the responsibility to protect public interest, privacy, and security. To achieve this, they must craft adaptive, forward-looking regulatory frameworks that accommodate the decentralized nature of AI-blockchain systems, which often defy traditional jurisdictional and institutional boundaries. Regulations should address data sovereignty concerns, ensuring that individuals retain control over their personal data even as it is processed and shared across distributed networks. Moreover, frameworks must mandate algorithmic transparency and accountability, requiring developers to document AI decision-making processes and implement safeguards against bias, discrimination, and unintended harm. Policymakers can harness AI-driven regulatory technologies (RegTech) to monitor real-time compliance, automate reporting, and enhance oversight capabilities, thus enabling efficient governance without imposing onerous burdens that stifle experimentation and innovation (Arner, Barberis, & Buckley, 2017).

Given the global and cross-border nature of AI-blockchain applications, international cooperation and harmonization of standards and ethical guidelines are crucial. Collaborative efforts among governments, intergovernmental organizations, and standards bodies can establish universal principles for data protection, AI ethics, and decentralized governance. Such coordination helps prevent regulatory arbitrage, enhances trust among users and investors, and supports the development of interoperable infrastructures that transcend geopolitical boundaries (European Commission, 2020). Policymakers should also engage in public-private partnerships to promote responsible innovation, facilitate knowledge exchange, and support capacity-building initiatives that educate stakeholders about the risks and benefits of AI-blockchain convergence.

Investors stand at the forefront of an unprecedented technological evolution, presented with diverse opportunities across sectors ranging from finance and supply chain to healthcare and governance. Identifying ventures with strong technical foundations requires due diligence that extends beyond superficial metrics to include rigorous assessment of the underlying architecture's scalability, security, and privacy capabilities. Equally important is evaluating whether projects adhere to ethical design principles—such as fairness, transparency, and user empowerment—given the increasing scrutiny by regulators and consumers alike (Binns, 2018). Investments that prioritize these attributes are better positioned to generate sustainable, long-term value and mitigate reputational risks associated with ethical lapses or regulatory non-compliance.

Furthermore, supporting projects with demonstrable real-world use cases—where AI and blockchain symbiotically enhance each other's strengths—offers higher potential for market traction and impact. For example, ventures that combine blockchain's immutable ledger with AI-driven predictive analytics can deliver novel solutions for fraud detection, supply chain transparency, and personalized finance, thus creating competitive advantages and unlocking new revenue streams. Investors should also recognize the importance of fostering ecosystem development by backing open-source initiatives, cross-industry consortia, and platform-agnostic solutions that accelerate adoption and interoperability.

Finally, given the dynamic nature of this emerging field, investors must embrace a flexible, long-term perspective. Early-stage projects may require patience and iterative refinement before achieving commercial viability. Engaging closely with technical teams, contributing to governance structures, and supporting regulatory compliance efforts can enhance project resilience and maximize returns. By strategically channeling capital towards scalable, privacy-conscious, and ethically grounded AI-blockchain innovations, investors can catalyze the creation of intelligent decentralized infrastructures that define the future digital economy.

POTENTIAL CHALLENGES AND ETHICAL CONSIDERATIONS IN AI-BLOCKCHAIN CONVERGENCE

The convergence of artificial intelligence (AI) and blockchain technologies, while promising transformative impacts across industries and society, also brings forth a series of significant challenges and ethical dilemmas that must be addressed for sustainable and responsible adoption. These challenges encompass technical limitations, data governance complexities, and profound ethical considerations surrounding accountability, fairness, and human agency.

Technical Challenges: Scalability and Energy Consumption

One of the foremost technical obstacles in AI-blockchain integration is scalability. Blockchain networks, especially those based on traditional proof-of-work consensus mechanisms, face inherent throughput and latency limitations that constrain transaction processing speeds and network capacit. These constraints become especially critical when AI applications demand real-time data ingestion, processing, and feedback loops—scenarios common in decentralized finance, supply chain optimization, and autonomous agent coordination. Addressing scalability requires advancing lightweight consensus protocols such as proof-of-stake, delegated proof-of-stake, and emerging AI-assisted consensus algorithms that dynamically optimize network participation and resource allocation. Parallelization techniques, sharding, and layer-2 solutions also show promise but introduce additional complexity regarding cross-shard communication and security guarantees.

Energy consumption represents a related concern. The environmental footprint of blockchain networks that rely on energy-intensive consensus algorithms has attracted criticism, especially when combined with AI workloads that are also computationally demanding due to large model training and inference cycles. Innovations in green computing, energy-efficient AI models (such as pruning and quantization), and sustainable blockchain infrastructures are therefore critical areas of research. Balancing performance with environmental responsibility is a vital challenge that stakeholders must prioritize to ensure long-term viability and public acceptance.

Data Privacy and Security Concerns

Data privacy intensifies as a challenge in AI-blockchain convergence. AI's appetite for vast, diverse datasets for training and decision-making conflicts with the need to maintain strict data sovereignty and confidentiality in decentralized networks. While blockchain offers immutability and transparency, these characteristics complicate data privacy since transaction records and smart contract executions are typically publicly accessible or replicated across nodes (Casino et al., 2019). Privacy-preserving technologies such as homomorphic encryption, zero-knowledge proofs, and federated learning have emerged as promising solutions that allow AI models to train or infer on encrypted or distributed data without exposing raw information (Jin et al., 2023). Nonetheless, these techniques are computationally expensive and often limited in scope, necessitating ongoing research to enhance their efficiency, scalability, and practical deployment.

In addition, securing AI models themselves is critical. Models are vulnerable to adversarial attacks, data poisoning, and model theft, which could undermine trust and reliability in decentralized AI-blockchain applications. Integrating robust security protocols and continuous monitoring mechanisms within the AI-blockchain stack is essential to preserve integrity and prevent malicious exploitation.

Ethical Challenges: Accountability, Bias, and Transparency

Ethical considerations permeate the AI-blockchain landscape, driven by the interplay of AI's algorithmic opacity and blockchain's immutable record-keeping. The "black-box" nature of many AI models complicates the attribution of accountability when adverse outcomes occur, such as erroneous decisions, discriminatory impacts, or financial losses. Immutable blockchain records may exacerbate these issues by preserving decisions and transactions permanently, making redress or correction difficult once errors or biases have been recorded (Hagendorff, 2020).

Bias in AI algorithms poses a particularly pernicious risk. Without deliberate design and oversight, AI models trained on biased data can perpetuate or amplify systemic inequalities, which may be codified in blockchain-based smart contracts or autonomous agent behaviors. Decentralized governance models must embed fairness as a core principle, incorporating bias detection, auditing, and mitigation tools alongside transparent reporting mechanisms. Community participation and stakeholder inclusivity in governance decisions can provide critical checks against discrimination and ensure equitable outcomes (Binns, 2018).

AI-Driven Automation Across Industries

The synergy between AI's automation capabilities and blockchain's decentralized infrastructure will revolutionize complex workflows across multiple sectors. In finance, autonomous agents powered by AI will execute decentralized finance (DeFi) operations such as lending, trading, and insurance with real-time risk assessment and fraud detection, all anchored on transparent and immutable smart contracts. Supply chains will achieve unprecedented efficiency through AI-enhanced, blockchain-verified tracking of goods, enabling dynamic adjustments in logistics and inventory based on predictive analytics and environmental factors. Healthcare systems will benefit from AI models that analyze encrypted patient data on blockchain, delivering personalized diagnostics while preserving privacy (BurstIQ, 2023). Governance models will similarly incorporate AI decision-support tools within blockchain frameworks to facilitate participatory, transparent policymaking and resource allocation.

Democratization of AI Through Decentralized Marketplaces

The future envisions decentralized AI marketplaces that democratize access to sophisticated AI models and services. By leveraging blockchain's tokenization and smart contract capabilities, these marketplaces will incentivize collaboration, data sharing, and innovation across a broad spectrum of participants—including startups, researchers, and individual developers—rather than concentrating AI power within a few dominant technology firms. Such open ecosystems will foster diversity in AI development and use cases, catalyzing novel applications tailored to niche and underserved communities. AI models will be auditable and upgradeable via blockchain governance, ensuring continuous improvement and alignment with evolving societal needs.

Ethical AI and Transparent Automated Decision-Making

Ethical considerations will be deeply embedded in these intelligent ecosystems. Blockchain's inherent transparency and immutability will complement AI's explainability efforts, creating verifiable audit trails of automated decision-making processes that stakeholders can inspect to ensure fairness, accountability, and compliance with regulations (Hagendorff, 2020). Smart contracts enhanced with ethical AI protocols will enforce privacy-preserving principles, protect against bias, and balance automation with human oversight. Token-based incentive mechanisms may reward ethical behaviors such as transparency and user consent, cultivating a culture of trustworthiness.

CONCLUSION

The evolution of blockchain technology over the past decade tells a compelling story of resilience, adaptation, and continuous innovation. What began as a groundbreaking innovation promising to disrupt entrenched centralized systems encountered practical challenges that tempered early enthusiasm and slowed mass adoption. Yet, this phase of slower maturation was far from failure; rather, it served as an essential incubation period. During this time, blockchain's core principles—decentralization, transparency, and cryptographic security—were rigorously tested, refined, and fortified, setting a solid foundation for future growth.

The integration of artificial intelligence (AI) has acted as a powerful catalyst in accelerating blockchain's evolution. AI's strengths in intelligent automation, predictive analytics, and adaptive decision-making have effectively addressed critical limitations in blockchain's scalability, throughput, and user experience. Conversely, blockchain provides AI systems with immutable audit trails, decentralized governance frameworks, and trust guarantees that mitigate issues around transparency, bias, and accountability—concerns that are especially vital given AI's growing autonomy and impact. Throughout this chapter, the rich and multifaceted synergy emerging from the convergence of AI and blockchain has been explored. This fusion is reshaping a broad spectrum of industries and redefining what decentralized intelligent systems can accomplish. In finance, AI-augmented blockchain platforms have enabled the rise of more secure, transparent, and efficient decentralized finance ecosystems that provide real-time risk management, fraud detection, and automated compliance. In supply chain management, AI-driven predictive analytics layered on blockchain's tamper-proof ledgers have enhanced traceability, responsiveness, and resilience to disruptions, improving operational efficiencies and stakeholder trust. Legal and compliance domains have benefited from AI-enabled smart contracts automating complex regulatory workflows and dispute resolution processes with unprecedented accuracy and speed, reducing costs and enhancing enforceability. Governments worldwide are increasingly leveraging this technology fusion to build more citizen-centric, transparent, and resilient public services, improving trust and engagement while safeguarding data sovereignty.

Figure 7. Journey to AI-Blockchain Convergence

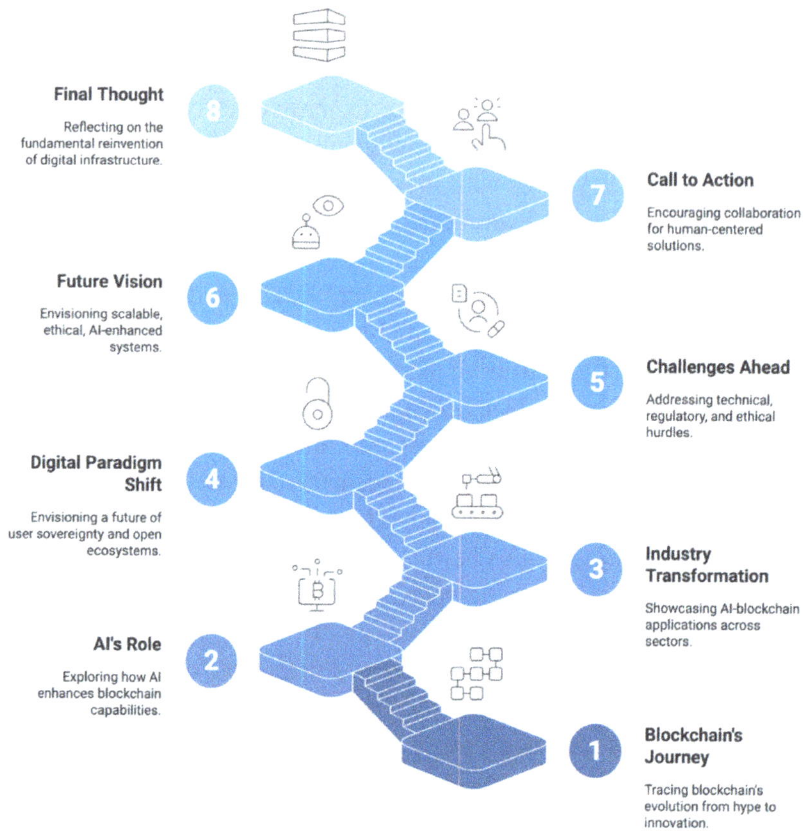

Beyond these specific applications, the AI-blockchain fusion represents a broader paradigm shift in digital infrastructure—one that moves away from centralized control and opaque processes toward open, distributed networks prioritizing user sovereignty, ethical governance, and collaborative innovation. Autonomous agents governed by AI-enhanced smart contracts are already demonstrating the potential to create self-regulating ecosystems that dynamically adapt to changing environmental conditions and stakeholder needs.

However, this transformative journey is not without significant challenges. Technical obstacles such as blockchain scalability and energy consumption demand ongoing innovation in consensus mechanisms and AI-driven optimization. Regulatory frameworks must evolve carefully to balance the drive for innovation with critical concerns for privacy, security, and ethical safeguards. Ethical challenges related to AI bias, accountability, and transparency of autonomous systems require robust, blockchain-embedded governance structures that enable fairness, auditability, and community participation.

Looking ahead, the convergence of AI and blockchain holds immense promise to underpin a new generation of intelligent, secure, and decentralized systems that are not only technologically advanced but also socially equitable and environmentally sustainable. These systems will empower individuals with greater control over their data and digital identities, enable more resilient economic and governance models, and foster innovation ecosystems transcending traditional silos and geographic boundaries.

For researchers, technologists, and investors alike, the mandate is clear: engage deeply with the interdisciplinary challenges and opportunities presented by AI-blockchain convergence, prioritizing solutions that are scalable, ethical, and aligned with human-centered values. The synergy between AI and blockchain is poised to fundamentally redefine the digital landscape, providing a pathway toward a future where intelligent automation and decentralized trust coalesce to create a more transparent, inclusive, and trustworthy digital society.

In sum, the ongoing revolution in decentralized intelligent systems is more than a technological evolution—it represents a profound transformation in how we conceive of and interact with digital infrastructure. The promise of AI-enhanced blockchain systems is immense; as these technologies mature in tandem, they hold the potential to unlock unprecedented innovation and societal benefit, ultimately shaping the very fabric of our digital future.

REFERENCES

Acar, A., Aksu, H., Uluagac, A. S., & Conti, M. (2018). A survey on homomorphic encryption schemes: Theory and implementation. *ACM Computing Surveys*, *51*(4), 79. Advance online publication. DOI: 10.1145/3214303

Agbo, C. C., Mahmoud, Q. H., & Eklund, J. M. (2019). Blockchain technology in healthcare: A systematic review. *Health Care*, *7*(2), 56. Advance online publication. DOI: 10.3390/healthcare7020056 PMID: 30987333

Arner, D. W., Barberis, J., & Buckley, R. P. (2017). FinTech, RegTech, and the reconceptualization of financial regulation. *Northwestern Journal of International Law & Business*, *37*(3), 371–413.

Atzori, M. (2017). Blockchain technology and decentralized governance: Is the state still necessary? *Journal of Governance and Regulation*, *6*(1), 45–62. DOI: 10.22495/jgr_v6_i1_p5

Binns, R. (2018). Fairness in machine learning: Lessons from political philosophy. In Friedler, S. A., & Wilson, C. (Eds.), *Proceedings of the 1st Conference on Fairness, Accountability and Transparency* (pp. 149–159). PMLR.

Brody, P., Halamka, J., & Singh, H. (2021). *Decentralized data marketplaces: The future of digital information sharing*. IEEE Computer Society Press.

Burst, I. Q. (2023). Blockchain and AI in healthcare: Securing precision medicine through intelligent automation. *HealthTech Journal*, *14*(1), 32–47.

Casino, F., Dasaklis, T. K., & Patsakis, C. (2019). A systematic literature review of blockchain-based applications: Current status, classification and open issues. *Telematics and Informatics*, *36*, 55–81. DOI: 10.1016/j.tele.2018.11.006

Catalini, C., & Gans, J. S. (2016). Some simple economics of the blockchain (Working Paper No. 22952). National Bureau of Economic Research.

Croman, K., Decker, C., Eyal, I., Gencer, A. E., Juels, A., Kosba, A., Miller, A., Saxena, P., Shi, E., Sirer, E. G., Song, D., & Wattenhofer, R. (2016). On scaling decentralized blockchains. In Clark, J., Meiklejohn, S., Ryan, P., Wallach, D., Brenner, M., & Rohloff, K. (Eds.), *Financial cryptography and data security: FC 2016 international workshops* (pp. 106–125). Springer., DOI: 10.1007/978-3-662-53357-4_8

Crosby, M., Nachiappan, Pattanayak, P., Verma, S., & Kalyanaraman, V. (2016). Blockchain technology: Beyond bitcoin. *Applied Innovation Review*, *2*, 6–19.

Digital Dubai. (2024). *AI integration in public services*. Digital Dubai Office.

Digital Dubai & Dubai Future Foundation. (2025). Dubai State of AI Report. Government of Dubai. https://www.digitaldubai.ae/knowledge-hub/publications/dubai-state-of-ai-report-2025

DMCC. (2025). *Blockchain and AI for government efficiency*. Dubai Multi Commodities Centre.

Doshi-Velez, F., & Kim, B. (2017). Towards a rigorous science of interpretable machine learning. arXiv. https://arxiv.org/abs/1702.08608

European Commission. (2020). White paper on artificial intelligence: A European approach to excellence and trust. Publications Office of the European Union.

Fetch.AI. (2023). *Technical whitepaper: Building autonomous economic systems with agents and smart contracts. Fetch*. AI Foundation.

Financial Times. (2025). UAE experiments with AI-driven legislative drafting. Financial Times Middle East Edition.

Floridi, L., Cowls, J., Beltrametti, M., Chatila, R., Chazerand, P., Dignum, V., Luetge, C., Madelin, R., Pagallo, U., Rossi, F., Schafer, B., Valcke, P., & Vayena, E. (2018). AI4People—An ethical framework for a good AI society: Opportunities, risks, principles, and recommendations. *Minds and Machines*, *28*(4), 689–707. DOI: 10.1007/s11023-018-9482-5 PMID: 30930541

Gulf News. (2025). *AI transforms public services in Dubai*. Gulf News Tech.

Hagendorff, T. (2020). The ethics of AI ethics: An evaluation of guidelines. *Minds and Machines*, *30*(1), 99–120. DOI: 10.1007/s11023-020-09517-8

Hyperledger Foundation. (2023). *AI-integrated compliance monitoring in distributed networks*. Hyperledger Technical Reports.

ISO/IEC. (2023). *ISO/IEC 38505-1: Information governance—Governance of data—Part 1: Application of ISO/IEC 38500 to the governance of data*. International Organization for Standardization.

Jin, C., Wang, J., & Li, Y. (2023). Blockchain and AI integration: Opportunities, challenges and future directions. *Journal of Network and Computer Applications*, *214*, 103513. Advance online publication. DOI: 10.1016/j.jnca.2023.103513

Nordic Institute for Interoperability Solutions. (2021). X-Road: Data exchange layer technology. https://niis.org/x-road

Russell, S. J., & Norvig, P. (2021). *Artificial intelligence: A modern approach* (4th ed.). Pearson.

Smart Dubai Office & Dubai Future Foundation. (2023). *Dubai Blockchain Strategy progress and implementation*. Government of Dubai.

Tiits, M., & Kaska, K. (2018). *Estonian digital government architecture and the role of emerging technologies*. Estonian Information System Authority.

Websima, D. M. C. C. (2025). *AI and blockchain in Dubai government services: Case studies and insights*. Websima DMCC.

Wiki Contributors. (2025). X-Road. In Wikipedia. Retrieved December 23, 2025, from https://en.wikipedia.org/wiki/X-Road

KEY TERMS AND DEFINITIONS

AI Ethics: A multidisciplinary framework that addresses the moral implications, risks, and governance of AI systems, focusing on fairness, accountability, transparency, and privacy.

AI-Enhanced Blockchain: A hybrid system where artificial intelligence is used to optimize and manage blockchain functions such as consensus, security, and scalability.

Artificial Intelligence (AI): A branch of computer science focused on creating systems capable of performing tasks that typically require human intelligence, such as learning, reasoning, and problem-solving.

Autonomous Agents: Software entities powered by AI that operate independently to perform tasks, make decisions, and interact with other agents or systems—often deployed on blockchain networks.

Blockchain: A decentralized, distributed ledger technology that records transactions in a secure, immutable, and transparent manner across a network of nodes.

Data Sovereignty: The concept that data is subject to the laws and governance structures within the nation or entity where it is collected, stored, or processed.

Decentralized AI Governance: The use of blockchain to distribute authority and oversight in the development, deployment, and monitoring of AI systems, promoting fairness and trust.

Decentralized Autonomous Organization (DAO): An organization governed by rules encoded as smart contracts on a blockchain, allowing collective decision-making without centralized leadership.

Decentralized Identity (DID): A digital identity system where users control their personal data without relying on a centralized authority, supported by blockchain technology.

Explainable AI (XAI): Techniques in artificial intelligence that make the decision-making processes of complex models understandable and interpretable to humans.

Immutable Audit Trail: A permanent, tamper-proof log of transactions or system activities recorded on a blockchain to ensure transparency and accountability.

Interoperability: The ability of different blockchain systems or AI frameworks to work together, exchange information, and use each other's services effectively.

Privacy-Preserving AI: AI techniques that ensure data privacy during training and inference, often using methods like federated learning, homomorphic encryption, or differential privacy.

Smart Contracts: Self-executing code stored on a blockchain that automatically enforces rules and agreements when predetermined conditions are met, without intermediaries.

Tokenization: The process of converting rights to an asset into a digital token recorded on a blockchain, enabling fractional ownership and secure transfers.

Chapter 2
Tokenization and the People's Ledger: Two Sides of the Same Coin?

Silvio Andrae
https://orcid.org/0000-0002-8586-7812
Independent Researcher, Germany

ABSTRACT

This chapter examines the tensions between the tokenization of tangible assets and the concept of the 'People's Ledger'. The aim is to determine whether both approaches can be viewed as opposing models of a future financial architecture or whether they can complement each other in hybrid forms. Methodologically, the analysis follows an interdisciplinary approach that integrates economic, legal, and political-economic perspectives. First, the functionality and potential of tokenization, along with its associated risks—namely, fragmentation, smart contract vulnerabilities, and cyber risks—are presented. Next, the People's Ledger is discussed as a radical centralization solution that promises stability, inclusion, and public control, but simultaneously harbors risks of power concentration and surveillance. The chapter concludes that neither pure decentralization nor complete centralization is viable. Instead, hybrid models are emerging that combine the efficiency and innovative power of tokenized systems with the stability and democratic legitimacy of public institutions.

INTRODUCTION

The digital transformation of financial markets has reached a critical point. Over the past decade, the emergence of distributed ledger technologies (DLT), tokenization, and decentralized finance (DeFi) has been hailed as a paradigm shift comparable

DOI: 10.4018/979-8-3373-3371-7.ch002

to the introduction of joint-stock companies or electronic trading platforms. Tokenization—the process of representing real-world assets, such as stocks, bonds, real estate, or commodities, as digital tokens on a blockchain—promises to fundamentally reshape the architecture of finance. By enabling fractional ownership, automated settlement via smart contracts, and 24/7 trading on global platforms, tokenization is expected not only to reduce transaction costs, increase market liquidity, and expand access to capital markets for previously underserved individuals and businesses, but also to foster financial inclusion and efficiency.

However, as with previous waves of financial innovation, the disruptive potential of tokenization is inextricably linked to significant risks. Market fragmentation due to competing technological standards and protocols, liquidity silos, and interoperability challenges could undermine the efficiency gains promised by tokenization. Furthermore, the shift toward decentralized infrastructures introduces new systemic vulnerabilities: errors in smart contracts, manipulation of oracles, cyberattacks, and governance failures can spread shocks at unprecedented speed. The rapid proliferation of tokenized assets and DeFi platforms has already raised regulatory concerns at the national and international levels, as evidenced by the debates surrounding the European Union's Markets in Crypto Assets Regulation (MiCAR), the controversial jurisdiction of the US Securities and Exchange Commission (SEC) over digital assets, and the repeated warnings from the Bank for International Settlements about the fragility of decentralized systems.

Against this backdrop, debates about the future of financial intermediation are intensifying. If tokenization undermines the traditional role of banks and market infrastructures, a fundamental rethinking of the institutional foundations of the economic system seems inevitable. One particularly radical proposal is the so-called People's Ledger, presented by Saule Omarova (2021). Her vision is to transfer commercial bank deposits to the central bank's balance sheet, thereby establishing a direct relationship between citizens and the monetary authority. In such a system, the central bank would become a universal public platform for money and payments, offering programmable accounts, direct lending mechanisms, and macroprudential instruments embedded in the architecture of money itself. The People's Ledger thus represents not only a monetary reform, but a comprehensive reorganization of the financial system under public control.

Proponents argue that this model could prevent bank runs, improve financial stability, and democratize access to credit by eliminating dependence on for-profit intermediaries. The People's Ledger, with its potential to democratize access to credit, offers a ray of hope for a more equitable financial system. Critics, however, warn of equally serious drawbacks: the concentration of economic power in the state, the potential misuse of sensitive transaction data, and the erosion of innovation in the private sector. The People's Ledger thus embodies the opposite of tokenization-driven decentralization: while tokenization distributes functions across a multitude of actors and protocols, the People's Ledger consolidates them into a single institutional actor—the central bank.

This contrast raises a central question that guides this chapter: Are tokenization and the People's Ledger inherently antagonistic, or could they develop into complementary pillars of a future financial architecture? In other words, does tokenization amplify systemic risks to such an extent that a public ledger is necessary as a regulatory counterweight, or can both concepts coexist in hybrid models that balance innovation and stability? This tension between decentralization and centralization is at the heart of current debates on the modernization of finance.

The analytical task is further complicated by the fact that both tokenization and the People's Ledger are not static concepts, but evolving ideas. Tokenization spans a broad spectrum, from private blockchain consortia and tokenized bank deposits to completely permissionless decentralized protocols. Similarly, the People's Ledger can be interpreted in a narrow technical sense—as a form of central bank digital currency (CBDC) for the retail segment—or in a broader sense as a fundamental redistribution of financial power. Both are viewed as controversial, politically charged terms shaped by technological, regulatory, and socioeconomic dynamics.

The discussion is embedded in a fundamental monetary theory orientation of our thinking. The mainstream views money as an apolitical tool for market operations. However, money is not just a set of functions; it is also a social construct. In this respect, the creation of money must once again be brought more into focus. The discussion initiated in this chapter on the tokenization of assets in the People's Ledger is well-suited to deepening our understanding of the role of money. The conventional view of money as apolitical sells a social infrastructure as a private tool. In this way, questions of money creation become a purely technical variable and are subsumed under the concerns of price stability. The result is the privatization of monetary sovereignty. Hockett and Omarova (2017) argue that private banks do not autonomously create money, but rather act as franchisees of the state. The state monetary system (central bank money, deposit insurance, liquidity provision) forms the foundation on which banks create private scriptural money. Money creation is thus a public privilege that has been outsourced to private hands but remains based on state guarantees.

This chapter adopts a conceptual and comparative analytical approach rather than a hypothesis-testing empirical design. Its objective is not to predict adoption outcomes or quantify welfare effects, but to clarify the structural trade-offs embedded in emerging monetary architectures. Drawing on monetary political economy and theories of financial instability, the chapter develops a typology of digital monetary infrastructures. It evaluates their implications for financial stability, democratic accountability, and distributive outcomes.

Methodologically, this chapter takes an interdisciplinary and comparative approach. It builds on insights from law, economics, and political economy to analyze the institutional implications of tokenization and the People's Ledger. The analysis is conducted in four steps. First, the conceptual foundations of tokenization and the People's Ledger are described and placed in the context of broader debates on financial intermediation and monetary sovereignty. Second, it examines the systemic risks associated with tokenization and considers whether these risks justify the use of centralized solutions. Third, it examines the People's Ledger as a possible regulatory response and draws parallels to current CBDC projects and public banking initiatives. Fourth, it assesses the potential for hybrid models that combine decentralized innovation with centralized stabilization.

In doing so, the chapter contributes to three strands of literature. The first concerns the growing body of research on tokenization and DeFi, which has primarily focused on technical feasibility, efficiency gains, and regulatory classification. By emphasizing systemic risk and institutional design, this chapter adds a macrofinancial perspective to this debate. The second strand is the emerging debate on public banking and digital central bank currencies. While most analyses treat CBDCs as evolutionary improvements to existing payment systems, this chapter explores the more radical implications of Omarova's People's Ledger. It situates it within the spectrum of centralization measures. The third strand is the political economy of financial architecture. Here, the chapter addresses broader questions about the distribution of power among states, banks, and technology providers in shaping the future of money and finance.

Ultimately, this chapter is not about declaring tokenization or the People's Ledger as superior alternatives, but rather about assessing the conditions under which they can serve as mutually reinforcing components of a sustainable financial system. The analytical proposition is that hybrid models—in which decentralized token infrastructures provide technological innovation and efficiency, while centralized public institutions ensure stability and accountability—offer a promising path forward. This perspective challenges the dichotomy between decentralization and centralization, opening the way for a financial system that is both resilient and inclusive.

CONCEPTUAL FOUNDATION

Tokenization of Real Assets

Tokenization has become one of the most significant financial innovations of the digital age. At its core, tokenization is the process of representing ownership rights to tangible assets—such as securities, commodities, real estate, or even works of art—through digital tokens recorded on a distributed ledger, thereby establishing a claim against the issuer (FSB, 2024). These tokens serve as cryptographically secure, transferable units that embody the economic value and legal claims of the underlying asset. By embedding ownership and transfer rules directly into the digital representation of an asset, tokenization aims to streamline financial transactions and radically reduce dependence on traditional intermediaries. The limited publicly available data on tokenization suggests that its adoption is still very low but appears to be growing. Tokens are currently used for trading, investment, and in some cases, payments, but may find other uses in the future.

Recent developments in tokenized real-world assets (RWAs) illustrate both the transformative potential and the systemic risks associated with decentralized finance and programmable tokens. Industry and central bank reports document rapid growth in tokenization activities—including sovereign and corporate debt, private credit, and other collateralized instruments—driven by institutional demand for efficiency, settlement speed, and collateral mobility. These trends suggest that tokenization increasingly replicates core functions of the traditional financial system, often in the absence of equivalent public safeguards (BIS, 2023a; Banerjee et al., 2024).

The technical basis of tokenization lies in distributed ledger technology (DLT). Unlike centralized databases, which a single institution manages, DLT records transactions across a decentralized network of nodes. Each node maintains a synchronized copy of the ledger, ensuring resistance to manipulation and enabling transparency of financial flows. Within such a framework, smart contracts—self-executing programs encoded in the ledger—enable the automated enforcement of contractual obligations (Schär, 2021). For example, dividend payments on tokenized shares can be automatically distributed once certain conditions are met, eliminating the need for custodians, transfer agents, or clearinghouses. This programmability distinguishes tokenization from earlier forms of digital representation, underscoring its transformative potential.

Projects to date, including some public-private partnerships, cover a range of use cases. These include issuing DLT-based tokens representing sovereign debt or holdings in debt funds, creating DLT-based tokens for payments, and tokenizing gold bullion.

Tokenization also overlaps with the rapidly evolving field of decentralized finance (DeFi). In DeFi ecosystems, tokenized assets can be traded, lent, or staked on decentralized platforms without the need for centralized intermediaries. For example, tokenized real estate shares could be pooled and used as collateral to borrow stablecoins, increasing the liquidity of traditionally illiquid assets. By connecting tokenized assets to programmable protocols, DeFi creates a modular, composable financial infrastructure often referred to as 'money Legos' (Harvey et al., 2021).

From an economic perspective, tokenization promises several benefits. First, it increases efficiency by reducing settlement times from days to near real-time, lowering operating costs, and minimizing counterparty risk. Traditional post-trade infrastructures—clearing, settlement, reconciliation—could be compressed into a single transaction validated by the ledger. Second, tokenization increases market accessibility and inclusion. Fractional ownership enables high-value assets, such as commercial real estate or works of art, to be divided into affordable units, thereby opening up investment opportunities for retail investors who were previously excluded from these markets. Third, tokenization enables global interoperability. Digital tokens are inherently borderless, potentially enabling cross-border capital flows with less friction than today's fragmented correspondent banking systems.

Despite the potential benefits, tokenization also presents significant challenges and risks. Market fragmentation, driven by competing technological standards, could diminish the network effects needed for robust, efficient markets. Legal uncertainty about the status of tokenized property rights across jurisdictions could hinder widespread adoption. These challenges underscore the need for caution and careful consideration when navigating the world of tokenization.

Another challenge is legal uncertainty. The legal status of tokenized property rights remains a matter of controversy across jurisdictions. While some countries, such as Switzerland, Liechtenstein, and Singapore, have introduced legal frameworks that recognize tokenized securities, many important jurisdictions—including the United States and parts of the European Union—still rely on case-by-case interpretations of the rules. This uncertainty hinders widespread adoption, particularly for institutional investors who require clear, enforceable property rights and investor protection.

Furthermore, tokenization is giving rise to new forms of financial intermediation rather than eliminating intermediaries. Private key custodians, oracle service providers (who feed off-chain data into smart contracts), governance token holders, and decentralized platform developers all play essential roles in the emerging ecosystem. These actors may lack the accountability and regulatory oversight that traditionally applies to banks and exchanges, creating new vulnerabilities. For example, oracle manipulation has already been exploited in DeFi markets, resulting in millions of dollars in losses. Similarly, governance tokens can concentrate decision-making power in a small group of technologically savvy or financially dominant actors, undermining the promise of decentralization.

In short, tokenization is not just a technical innovation, but a structural transformation of financial intermediation. It has the potential to democratize access and increase efficiency, but it also creates new risks that pose challenges for both regulators and market participants. These tensions form the basis for considering whether entirely new institutional concepts—such as the People's Ledger—are necessary to stabilize the financial system in the age of tokenization.

The People's Ledger

While tokenization represents a decentralized approach to financial activities, the People's Ledger offers a radical alternative: centralizing money and credit under public sector control. The People's Ledger, as presented by Saule Omarova (2021), is a conceptual framework that redefines the central bank's role as the core institution of the financial system. Its defining feature is the transfer of all deposits from commercial banks to the central bank's balance sheet. This shift could transform the central bank into society's primary financial intermediary, offering a new perspective on financial intermediation.

The People's Ledger would thus transform the central bank from a 'bank of banks' to the primary financial intermediary for society as a whole. Beyond accepting deposits, it envisions the central bank directly creating and lending money, possibly using programmable accounts to target lending toward socially desirable goals such as green investment, infrastructure, or financial inclusion. In this sense, the People's Ledger is not merely a proposal for a central bank digital currency (CBDC), but a radical restructuring of financial intermediation, shifting functions traditionally performed by private banks—such as deposit taking, lending, and payment processing—to the public sector.

The objectives of such a system are manifold. First, the People's Ledger aims to improve financial stability by eliminating the risk of bank runs. Since deposits would no longer be liabilities of commercial banks but of the central bank, depositors would have no incentive to flee in times of crisis, thereby eliminating an important source of systemic fragility. Second, the system aims to democratize money and credit. By subjecting decisions about fund allocation to public oversight, it promises to align the financial world more closely with societal priorities than with shareholder profits. Third, the People's Ledger could improve macroprudential control. Programmable money and direct accounts would enable the central bank to implement measures such as negative interest rates, targeted liquidity injections, or real-time monitoring of systemic risks more effectively than under the current intermediary system.

However, the People's Ledger is not free from significant criticism. The biggest concern is the concentration of power. By taking over the core banking functions, the central bank would exert unprecedented influence over lending and the flow of financial resources. Critics warn that such a concentration could undermine pluralism, stifle private innovation, and expose the economy to technocratic or political manipulation.

A second criticism concerns data protection and surveillance. By centralizing all deposits at the central bank, the authorities would have direct access to detailed transaction data on all citizens and businesses. While such access could improve oversight and the fight against money laundering, it also raises profound questions about civil liberties. The potential for abuse—whether by authoritarian regimes, political persecution, or cybersecurity breaches—poses serious risks.

Third, there is the issue of political influence. The independence of central banks, carefully built up over decades, could be jeopardized if they take on functions that directly affect lending to specific sectors or companies. In democratic systems, such decisions are inherently political and can expose monetary authorities to pressure from elected officials or powerful interest groups.

In summary, the People's Ledger represents a radical counterproposal to tokenization-driven decentralization. While tokenization fragments ownership and transactions across networks of private actors, the People's Ledger consolidates them into a single public institution. Its promise lies in stability, inclusivity, and democratic accountability; its danger lies in concentration, surveillance, and politicization.

Taken together, tokenization and the People's Ledger offer two opposed visions of the future financial system. One distributes power and relies on technological infrastructures to replace trust in intermediaries; the other centralizes power and relies on public authority to ensure stability and accountability. Both promise efficiency and resilience, but also introduce new risks. It is essential to comprehend their conceptual foundations before evaluating whether tokenization itself can create the conditions that necessitate a People's Ledger, or whether hybrid models can effectively integrate the strengths of both approaches.

Hybrid Monetary Architectures: Combining Tokenization and Public Ledgers

Rather than framing tokenization and the People's Ledger as mutually exclusive alternatives, this chapter conceptualizes a hybrid monetary architecture that deliberately separates monetary sovereignty from financial programmability. The core premise is that the functions of money as a public institution—namely the provision of a unit of account, settlement finality, and systemic stability—should remain anchored in a publicly governed infrastructure. At the same time, innovation in financial contracts and asset allocation can unfold in a complementary, privately driven layer.

In such a dual-layer system, a publicly governed ledger, potentially implemented as a central bank digital currency (CBDC), serves as the monetary backbone. This public layer provides a stable unit of account, ensures settlement finality, and enables macro-financial oversight and intervention where necessary. Crucially, it embeds monetary operations within democratic governance structures and public law, thereby safeguarding monetary sovereignty, legal certainty, and the capacity for countercyclical stabilization.

Built on top of this public backbone, privately issued tokens and smart-contract-based instruments operate as a programmable financial layer. This layer enables the tokenization of assets, automated contractual execution, and new forms of liquidity provision and risk-sharing. Importantly, these instruments do not replace public money but remain denominated in, settled through, or ultimately convertible into the public monetary unit. Their operation is thus constrained by clearly defined regulatory, prudential, and economic boundaries, preventing the emergence of parallel, uncontrolled monetary systems.

This architectural separation mirrors long-standing historical and theoretical distinctions between money as a public institution and finance as a competitive and innovation-driven allocation mechanism. In monetary theory, money has never been a neutral technological artifact but a socially and politically constituted institution, embedded in legal frameworks and collective trust. Finance, by contrast, has always been characterized by experimentation, leverage, and competition—processes that generate efficiency gains but also systemic fragilities if left unchecked.

By rearticulating this distinction in a digital context, the hybrid model allows societies to capture the efficiency and flexibility gains associated with tokenization without relinquishing the stabilizing, coordinating, and redistributive functions traditionally performed by public monetary authorities. Rather than suppressing financial innovation or fully privatizing monetary functions, the proposed architecture seeks to align technological dynamism with institutional responsibility.

Figure 1 illustrates the proposed hybrid monetary architecture. It visualizes the analytical distinction between a publicly governed monetary core and a programmable financial layer operating on top of it. While the public layer provides the unit of account, settlement finality, and macro-financial stability, the upper layer enables tokenization and smart-contract-based financial innovation within clearly defined monetary and regulatory boundaries. The figure emphasizes that programmability is subordinated to economic sovereignty, rather than replacing it.

Figure 1. A Hybrid Monetary Architecture: Public Monetary Core and Programmable Financial Layer

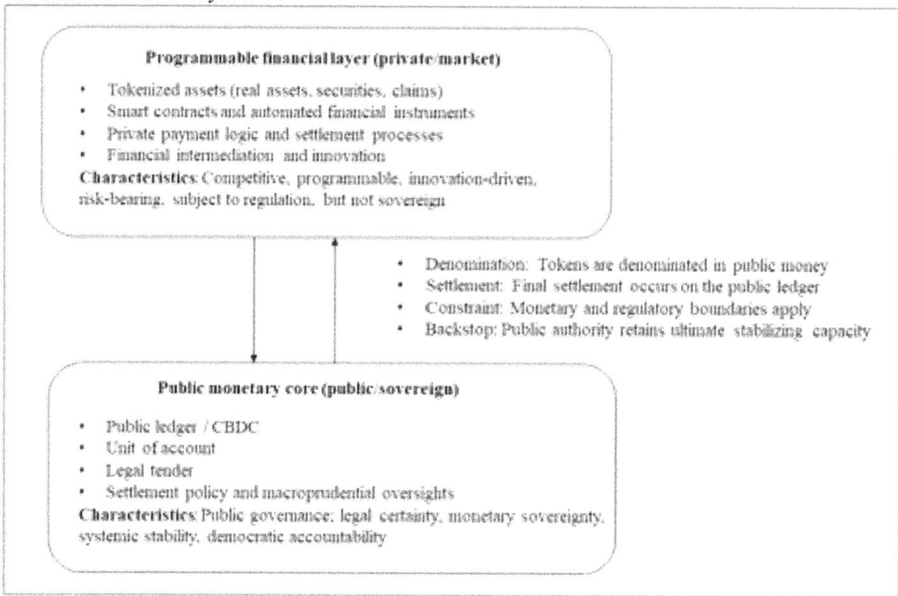

Source: own representation.

In this sense, the hybrid approach does not represent a compromise between opposing visions. Still, a functional integration: monetary stability and democratic accountability are treated as non-negotiable public goods. At the same time, programmability and experimentation are channelled into a financial layer that remains institutionally subordinate to the public monetary core.

DECENTRALIZATION VS. CENTRALIZATION IN FINANCE

Developments in Financial Intermediation

The tension between decentralization and centralization is not a recent phenomenon but a historical one that has significantly shaped financial systems for centuries. The early Renaissance financial markets were characterized by decentralized networks of merchants and moneylenders who relied on their reputations, family ties, and local notaries to enforce contracts (Graeber, 2014). The subsequent rise of modern banking in the 17th and 18th centuries marked a decisive step toward institutionalized intermediation, as banks began pooling deposits, lending money, and processing payments on behalf of their customers. This process centralized trust and reduced transaction frictions, but at the same time created concentrated vulnerabilities that manifested themselves in recurring banking crises (Laeven, 2011).

The 19th and 20th centuries saw the consolidation of large universal banks and the emergence of central banks as 'lenders of last resort.' Centralization at the monetary authority level provided protection against systemic crises but reinforced the hierarchical structure of financial systems. The post-Bretton Woods era reinforced this centralization through regulatory frameworks and the dominance of major currencies such as the US dollar.

The turn of the 21st century ushered in a new wave of digital finance. Online banking, electronic trading platforms, and the rise of fintech companies challenged established banks by offering more user-friendly, data-driven services. However, the real challenge to centralization only emerged with the advent of blockchain technology and decentralized finance (DeFi) after the 2008 financial crisis (Zhang et al., 2024. The original Bitcoin white paper explicitly framed decentralization as a response to perceived failures of centralized financial institutions and to the discretionary power of central banks.

DeFi platforms based on smart contracts represent a radical departure from the logic of bank-based intermediation. They attempt to replicate lending, trading, and settlement without trusted intermediaries, relying instead on algorithmic governance and distributed consensus. In these platforms, algorithmic governance refers to the use of predefined rules and conditions encoded in smart contracts to make decisions, while distributed consensus is a method for achieving agreement on a single data value among distributed processes or systems. The historical pendulum is thus swinging back toward decentralization, albeit through technological rather than social or reputational mechanisms.

Theoretical Perspectives

Various theoretical approaches can shed light on the central debate. Intermediation theory (Diamond, 1984; Allen & Santomero, 1998) explains banks as institutions that enhance efficiency by eliminating information asymmetries, pooling risks, and providing liquidity. From this perspective, decentralization through DeFi seems paradoxical: Why eliminate intermediaries that reduce transaction costs? Distributed ledgers and smart contracts can replace institutional trust with technological trust, potentially rendering intermediaries redundant. Critics counter that DeFi merely creates new intermediaries—developers, oracle providers, or governance token holders—without the accountability structures typically found in traditional banks.

Public banking theory emphasizes the state's role in providing a stable monetary infrastructure. Historically, public banking models—from 19th-century savings banks in Europe to development banks in emerging economies—have sought to align the financial world with public objectives (Marois, 2023). The People's Ledger, a concept rooted in this tradition, represents a public alternative to profit-oriented intermediation. It is a decentralized ledger system, collectively owned and managed by the public, that aims to provide financial services transparently and equitably. Here, decentralization is interpreted not as efficiency but as fragmentation, while centralization provides stability and democratic accountability.

Minsky's hypothesis of financial instability (1992) offers another perspective. Minsky argued that financial systems are inherently prone to cycles of stability and instability driven by speculative leverage and euphoria during boom phases. Centralized oversight by the state is therefore essential to dampen destabilizing dynamics (Nikolaidi & Stockhammer, 2017). From this perspective, tokenization and DeFi exacerbate fragility by enabling unregulated leverage, maturity mismatches, and algorithmic amplification of shocks. Conversely, centralization via a people's ledger or CBDCs could internalize stability functions, but at the expense of innovation.

Together, these theories underscore that the tension between centralization and decentralization is not binary but a continuum characterised by trade-offs among efficiency, innovation, and stability.

Efficiency and Innovation vs. Stability and Control

The promise of decentralization lies in efficiency and innovation. Tokenized systems enable instant settlement, fractional ownership, and 24/7 open markets. DeFi lending platforms, such as Aave or Compound, demonstrate how algorithmic protocols — sets of rules and conditions encoded in smart contracts — can lend globally without intermediaries and often at lower cost. In addition, decentralized architectures promote composability, allowing new products to be built modularly on top of existing protocols, thereby accelerating innovation cycles.

However, these advantages come at the expense of stability and control. Decentralized systems are inherently prone to coordination failures and technological risks. Smart contract exploits, flash loan attacks, and cascading liquidations illustrate how algorithmic rigidity can amplify volatility. The lack of central oversight complicates crisis management: unlike banks, DeFi protocols lack a lender of last resort.

Centralized systems, on the other hand, are characterized by stability and control. Central banks can act countercyclically, cushion shocks, and restore confidence. Deposit insurance, regulatory oversight, and macroprudential instruments provide additional safeguards. However, these mechanisms often slow down innovation, cement the position of established institutions, and can exclude disadvantaged populations. The trade-off is thus clear: decentralization accelerates innovation at the expense of fragility, while centralization offers resilience but carries the risk of rigidity and power concentration.

This tension is not easy to resolve. It reflects profound normative choices about the roles of markets and the state, technological autonomy and democratic accountability, and efficiency and fairness.

Comparison of Contemporary Initiatives

The current financial landscape illustrates these tensions through parallel experiments in decentralization and centralization.

Central bank digital currencies (CBDCs) represent the centralist path. Dozens of central banks, including the European Central Bank (digital euro) (ECB, 2023) and the People's Bank of China (e-CNY) (People's Bank of China, 2021), are exploring digital currencies that aim to combine the convenience of digital payments with the stability of central bank money. CBDCs can be designed for retail (accessible to households) or wholesale (restricted to financial institutions or businesses) use. They promise stability, interoperability, and monetary sovereignty, but raise concerns about privacy, political control, and potential disintermediation of banks.

Stablecoins are an example of a hybrid form of decentralization. They are issued by private companies (e.g., Tether, Circle's USDC) or embedded in DeFi protocols (e.g., DAI from MakerDAO) and aim to replicate the stability of fiat money while maintaining the programmability and borderlessness of tokens. Their rapid growth highlights the increasing demand for digital currencies in global markets. However, stablecoins are exposed to risks related to collateral, governance failures, and regulatory controls, as demonstrated by the collapse of TerraUSD in 2022. In addition, stablecoins may further exacerbate the conflict between state and private sovereignty in payment transactions.

DeFi lending platforms such as Aave, Compound, and MakerDAO embody pure decentralization. They automate lending using smart contracts, leveraging crypto assets or tokenized collateral. While efficient, they are susceptible to market volatility and have no shock absorbers. The market crashes of 2020 and 2022 demonstrated how cascading liquidations can destabilize protocols and spill over to the entire crypto ecosystem.

The coexistence of these initiatives underscores that the future of finance is likely to be neither exclusively decentralized nor centralized. Instead, a pluralistic architecture is emerging, where CBDCs coexist alongside stablecoins and DeFi platforms, and where regulated banks experiment alongside them. The crucial question is whether these systems will evolve toward integration—with interoperable standards, shared governance mechanisms, and regulatory harmonization—or remain fragmented, thereby amplifying systemic risks.

Historical and theoretical analysis shows a pendulum swinging between decentralization and centralization. Both have different strengths and weaknesses:

decentralization promotes innovation but carries the risk of instability, while centralization ensures stability but risks concentration and inertia. The current coexistence of CBDCs, stablecoins, and DeFi platforms suggests that future financial systems will likely operate in a hybrid equilibrium that balances efficiency and resilience.

Understanding these dynamics is essential to determining whether tokenization requires radical centralization via a People's Ledger or whether hybrid solutions can reconcile both logics. The following sections, therefore, examine the systemic risks of tokenization (Section 4) in more detail and evaluate the People's Ledger as a possible regulatory response (Section 5).

TOKENIZATION AND SYSTEMIC RISKS

Market Fragmentation and the Challenge of Standards

Market fragmentation, a significant systemic risk in tokenization, is a complex challenge. The representation of assets as digital tokens has not followed a uniform technological or legal path. Instead, a variety of standards and platforms have emerged, each vying for acceptance. Ethereum's ERC-20 and ERC-721 token standards dominate the open blockchain ecosystem, while other blockchains, such as Solana, Polkadot, and Avalanche, offer alternative frameworks. In parallel, private or permissioned blockchains operated by financial consortia (e.g., Hyperledger Fabric, Corda, Quorum) are striving to meet institutional requirements.

While this diversity reflects a healthy appetite for experimentation, it undermines liquidity consolidation. Without a common standard, the same asset—for example, a tokenized bond—can exist in multiple incompatible forms on different platforms. Liquidity that would otherwise be concentrated in a single market becomes scattered, reducing depth and increasing volatility. The result is a proliferation of 'walled gardens' rather than a unified global market, diminishing the efficiency gains promised by tokenization.

The lack of standardization also hinders institutional adoption. Institutional investors need legal certainty, interoperability, and reliable custody solutions. When tokenized assets are scattered across non-interoperable platforms, the costs of compliance, custody, and settlement increase significantly. It creates barriers to entry for smaller players and risks entrenching dominant players who can afford proprietary infrastructure, reinforcing concentration rather than democratization.

Interoperability and the Emergence of Liquidity Islands

Closely linked to fragmentation are issues related to interoperability. Even when token standards are technically compatible, cross-platform integration often remains constrained by governance rules, regulatory silos, or infrastructure bottlenecks. For example, tokenized securities issued on a private, permissioned blockchain may be legally recognized in a single jurisdiction but remain inaccessible to global investors due to conflicting regulatory regimes. Similarly, DeFi protocols operating on public blockchains often lack mechanisms to securely integrate tokenized real-world assets (RWAs), leading to isolated liquidity pools.

These obstacles lead to what scientists and regulators refer to as liquidity islands, which are difficult to connect. Fragmented liquidity means that there is no single 'pool' of assets that traders, investors, or decentralized finance (DeFi) applications can draw on. Instead, each blockchain or sidechain has its own fixed liquidity. This isolation creates numerous problems for users who want to buy tokens or access a particular lending platform. Capital and users are scattered across an ever-growing maze of blockchains. With so many chains and significant value spread across them, participants are confronted daily with the hassle of bridges, swaps, and wallet changes. Liquidity islands undermine the core promise of tokenisation: freeing up capital and increasing market efficiency. Instead, capital remains trapped in fragmented ecosystems, making pricing difficult and increasing volatility. Many users employ bridges to transfer funds between chains, but these bridges are often targets for attacks, fueling fear and mistrust. DeFi cannot achieve mass adoption if liquidity transfers are too cumbersome or risky.

Furthermore, the existence of parallel markets—regulated vs. unregulated, approved vs. unapproved—creates arbitrage opportunities that can destabilize the system. For example, liquidity-seeking returns could quickly migrate from regulated to unregulated markets, increasing systemic fragility. Solutions to this dilemma already exist. Bridges and wrapped assets enable basic interoperability, but the user experience remains cumbersome. Cross-chain aggregators can route tokens across multiple exchanges, but they typically do not aggregate underlying liquidity. They merely help users navigate.

The problem is fundamental: every chain believes it is different. Every new chain or subnetwork must be 'plugged' into the bottom layer to truly unify liquidity. Otherwise, another universe of liquidity emerges that users must discover and bridge. This challenge is exacerbated by the fact that blockchains, bridges, and aggregators view each other as competitors, leading to deliberate isolation and further fragmenting the ecosystem. Integration at the base layer addresses liquidity fragmentation by embedding bridge and routing functions directly into the chain's core infrastructure.

This approach is found in some Layer 1 protocols and specialized frameworks where interoperability is a fundamental element.

Efforts continue to address interoperability challenges. Initiatives such as the InterWork Alliance or the Token Taxonomy Framework aim to create common industry standards, while central banks are experimenting with cross-border CBDC platforms (e.g., the BIS's mBridge project). However, progress remains uneven, and there is still a risk that tokenization will cement new forms of segmentation rather than global integration. Yet, as these initiatives gain traction, there is promising potential for international integration in the future. Some observers fear that fragmentation could lead to a return to a few dominant blockchains or centralized exchanges, thereby undermining the decentralization that has driven the rise of blockchain.

Stability Implications of DLT-based Tokenization

Beyond fragmentation and interoperability, tokenization introduces new systemic vulnerabilities that are qualitatively different from those of traditional financial markets. The vulnerabilities of DLT-based tokenization can be traced to three factors that operate both individually and in combination:

1. The underlying reference value that is tokenized.
2. The market participants involved in tokenization projects.
3. The technologies used and their interaction with existing systems.

These factors can exacerbate many of the traditional financial system's known vulnerabilities. However, their specific manifestations depend heavily on design decisions, market penetration, and the scope of the initiatives. For example, the choice of settlement asset (especially tokenized private money) can exacerbate liquidity risks. The companies involved often include new market participants that are not subject to the applicable regulations in all jurisdictions. Additionally, DLT is a relatively young, still untested technology that entails operational risks.

Despite these weaknesses, tokenization does not currently pose a significant risk to financial stability. The main reasons for this are its still limited scope, the focus on permissioned rather than permissionless platforms, the restricted use of programmability features to date, and the limited interoperability both between DLT platforms and between DLT and existing financial infrastructures.

Smart contracts form the backbone of tokenized systems by embedding contractual rules directly into the code. While this reduces dependence on intermediaries, it also introduces new risks: coding errors, logical errors, or overlooked contingencies can block or misallocate billions in assets. Unlike traditional contracts, smart contracts are executed automatically and are immutable once deployed. High-profile incidents—such as the 2016 DAO hack or repeated DeFi exploits—demonstrate how vulnerabilities can drain liquidity from protocols in mere minutes. These events spread systemic stress because smart contracts are highly combinable: a malfunction can affect multiple interconnected platforms.

Tokenization represents a change in how we define and transfer assets. This change in medium opens up new opportunities for financial innovation, but the exact nature of tokenized rights should remain clear. The robustness of the chain of rights linking a natural or legal person to the asset is a critical factor in the benefits of tokenization. In fact, tokenization enables the combinability of financial functions. Assets and financial services can be combined and recombined to offer new services in a trust-minimized manner, amplifying opportunities and risks. Therefore, each additional link in the chain of rights requires a strong legal foundation to maintain the integrity of the system (Lavayssière, 2025).

Tokenized systems often rely on external data feeds, also known as 'oracles,' to execute smart contracts. For example, a tokenized derivative may require a price feed to trigger settlement. If the oracle is manipulated or fails, the contract may be executed incorrectly, resulting in losses. Since many DeFi protocols rely on the same oracles, a single point of failure can have system-wide implications. Governance presents a parallel challenge. Decentralized protocols are governed by voting mechanisms that distribute power among users. In practice, however, voting rights are often concentrated among a few large shareholders, such as venture capital funds or early adopters. It creates vulnerabilities to capture, collusion, or apathy, undermining the claim to decentralization. Governance failures can lead to inconsistent policies, delayed responses to crises, or opportunistic decisions that privilege insiders over the broader ecosystem.

Tokenized infrastructure is an attractive target for cyberattacks due to the high concentration of value in digital form. Attack vectors include denial-of-service attacks on blockchain nodes, theft of keys from custodians, or exploitation of protocol vulnerabilities. Unlike traditional financial institutions, which can rely on deposit insurance or regulatory safeguards, tokenized systems often lack recourse mechanisms. A single cyberattack can therefore undermine trust and trigger systemic contagion.

Under certain circumstances, tokenization could become systemically important—for example, if its share of the financial system grows significantly, if the complexity and opacity of projects trigger unpredictable dynamics in times of crisis, or if vulnerabilities are not addressed through supervision, regulation, and enforcement.

Regulatory Perspectives

In light of these systemic risks, regulators worldwide are seeking effective responses. Several international and national frameworks illustrate the diversity of approaches.

International Organization of Securities Commissions (IOSCO). IOSCO (2022) has emphasised that the principle of 'same activity, same risk, same regulation' must apply to tokenized markets. It has published reports calling on regulators to address risks to investor protection, custody arrangements, and market integrity posed by crypto assets and DeFi. IOSCO warns that the illusion of decentralization often masks concentrated risks in governance and infrastructure.

Bank for International Settlements (BIS). The BIS has repeatedly highlighted the systemic vulnerabilities of tokenized finance. In its 2023 report, 'A blueprint for the future monetary system,' it highlights the dangers of liquidity fragmentation and advocates for public infrastructures—possibly CBDCs—that provide an anchor of trust. The BIS views tokenization as a technological innovation that must be embedded in sound institutional frameworks rather than developed in parallel with them.

European Union—MiCA Regulation. The EU's MiCA (Markets in Crypto-Assets) Regulation, adopted in 2023, represents one of the most comprehensive frameworks for addressing risks associated with tokenization. MiCAR sets licensing requirements for crypto-asset issuers, imposes capital and governance obligations on stablecoin providers, and establishes consumer protection rules. While MiCAR does not yet comprehensively cover DeFi or tokenized securities, it demonstrates the EU's ambition to integrate tokenised assets into existing regulatory frameworks. Decentralized stablecoins are not yet explicitly covered by EU regulation, even though they could, in principle, be classified as crypto-assets or e-money tokens under MiCAR. However, MiCAR only applies if no other regulation—such as MiFID II—is relevant. Under current law, decentralized stablecoins are not classified as financial instruments within the meaning of MiFID II, as they do not confer ownership rights on a legal entity nor are they associated with repayment obligations. In addition, MiFID only covers financial products for which a central counterparty—typically a limited liability company or public limited company—is legally established. Critics generally argue that excessive compliance requirements could hinder innovation and shift activities abroad.

United States—SEC vs. CFTC. The U.S. regulatory landscape is more fragmented. The Securities and Exchange Commission (SEC) claims jurisdiction over tokenized assets that meet the Howey test and treats them as securities. It has led to enforcement actions against numerous token issuers and platforms. The Commodity Futures Trading Commission (CFTC), on the other hand, claims jurisdiction over digital commodities, including Bitcoin and certain derivatives. The resulting overlap of jurisdictions creates uncertainty for market participants. Legislation such as the Digital Commodities Consumer Protection Act attempts to clarify the boundaries, but progress has been slow. Of particular note is the recently enacted U.S. law, the Guiding and Establishing National Innovation for U.S. Stablecoins Act (GENIUS Act), which aims to regulate stablecoins under private law.

Overall, these regulatory perspectives reflect the tension between innovation and stability. While regulators aim to mitigate systemic risks, they must also strike a balance between competitiveness, technology neutrality, and consumer protection. Although various regulatory initiatives, such as MiCAR and the GENIUS Act, represent significant regulatory progress, they pursue distinctly different approaches (Odinet & Tosato, 2025). The diversity of approaches in other jurisdictions carries the risk of increased fragmentation, as companies engage in regulatory arbitrage by migrating to more liberal regulatory environments.

Tokenization offers transformative potential for financial markets, but also poses systemic risks. Fragmentation and interoperability issues can lead to liquidity silos. Vulnerabilities in smart contracts, oracle manipulation, and governance failures threaten market integrity. Cyber risks and technological path dependencies exacerbate fragility. Regulatory responses remain inconsistent and fragmented, further complicating the situation.

The key question is whether the systemic risks of tokenization can be managed within the existing institutional framework or require more radical solutions, such as the People's Ledger. This question is addressed in the next section, which evaluates the People's Ledger as a regulatory response to the vulnerabilities of the tokenized financial world.

THE PEOPLE'S LEDGER AS A REGULATORY RESPONSE

From Tokenization to the Demand for Central Stability

The preceding analysis has shown that tokenization presents both opportunities and vulnerabilities. By distributing financial activities across networks of smart contracts, private platforms, and decentralized protocols, tokenization undermines the stability functions traditionally performed by banks and centralized infrastructures. The result is an ecosystem characterized by fragmented liquidity, rapid contagion channels, and limited crisis management mechanisms. This dynamic raises the question of whether tokenization itself creates a structural need for centralized stabilization—a mechanism that can hedge the financial system against volatility.

The People's Ledger, conceived by Omarova (2021), can be understood as precisely such a response. By shifting deposits to the central bank and consolidating payment, clearing, and settlement functions into a single public infrastructure, the People's Ledger counterbalances the centrifugal forces of tokenization. While tokenization distributes trust across code and distributed consensus, the People's Ledger refocuses trust on a sovereign institution whose job is to ensure monetary and financial stability.

The logic is straightforward: as more financial activity migrates to tokenized environments prone to instability, the case for a central stabilizing anchor that prevents systemic collapse becomes stronger. From this perspective, the People's Ledger is not merely an ideological project, but a pragmatic response to the destabilizing effects of decentralization.

In The Citizens' Ledger, Hockett (2022) draws a visionary analogy, viewing modern economies as giant 'social balance sheets' in which individual and institutional assets are recorded, stored, and balanced daily. From this perspective, Hockett argues that it is possible and justified to create a universal digital system that gives all citizens access to secure, inexpensive, and inclusive payment and savings facilities—directly through the central bank or the treasury, without the detour via private intermediaries. Hockett argues that modern technology enables a kind of public digital wallet that replaces all previous payment systems: free, inclusive, barrier-free, and shielded from private rent-seeking. It corresponds to the central claim of the People's Ledger: programmable money, direct payment channels, and the central bank as the institutional guardian of the monetary architecture. He emphasizes that payment and savings infrastructures should be public goods. The private sector is often inefficient, exclusionary, and profit-maximizing—an argument that supports the normative logic of the People's Ledger.

Institutional Design: A 'Single Ledger' for Retail and Wholesale

A central component of the People's Ledger proposal is the creation of a 'single ledger' operated by the central bank. This ledger would serve as a universal infrastructure for recording monetary claims and transactions, and would be accessible to both retail customers and wholesale customers.

For retail customers, the central bank would offer direct accounts—often referred to as 'FedAccounts' in the US debate or 'digital euro wallets' in the European context. These accounts would serve as secure storage locations for digital money and eliminate credit risk by posting deposits directly on the central bank's balance sheet. Payments would be executed instantly and at low cost, without going through commercial banks and private payment providers.

For large customers, the unified ledger could integrate the settlement of tokenized securities, cross-border transactions, and interbank transfers. It would streamline the post-trade process and reduce the need for fragmented clearing houses. By embedding wholesale and retail customer levels into a unified infrastructure, the People's Ledger envisions a converged financial architecture in which all monetary transactions are ultimately recorded and settled within the central bank system.

The technological feasibility of such a design has been demonstrated in pilot projects. The Bank of England's 'Omnibus Account,' the BIS's 'Project Helvetia,' and the People's Bank of China's experiments with the digital yuan all point to models in which central banks take on a greater infrastructural role. The People's Ledger takes this logic a step further by eliminating the distinction between central bank money and bank deposits.

Programmable Money and Macroprudential Control

Beyond providing a secure payment infrastructure, the People's Ledger opens up the possibility of programmable money. By embedding rules directly into digital accounts, the central bank could implement targeted monetary and macroprudential measures.

For example, programmable accounts could enable the following:

- Conditional transfers, such as economic stimulus payments, are restricted to certain goods or services.
- Negative interest rates are applied directly to balances to stimulate spending.
- Automatic tax collection is integrated into transaction flows.
- Lending policies that direct funds to environmentally friendly investments or underserved communities.

From a macroprudential perspective, programmable money could enhance the central bank's ability to monitor and manage systemic risks in real-time. Instead of relying on lagging indicators and incomplete reports from commercial banks, the central bank would have direct insight into transaction flows across the economy. This transparency could enable dynamic regulation, with liquidity or leverage limits adjusted immediately to dampen emerging bubbles.

In theory, the combination of programmable money and central oversight transforms the central bank not only into a guardian of stability, but also into an active lender. It represents a profound shift from the traditional model of central banks as neutral guarantors of monetary stability to a vision of them as engines of targeted economic development.

Advantages

The potential advantages of a People's Ledger can be divided into three dimensions.

Stability. By eliminating bank runs and consolidating the payment infrastructure, the People's Ledger addresses the key vulnerabilities of both tokenized and traditional banking systems. Deposits at the central bank are risk-free, and settlement within a single ledger reduces counterparty risk. This makes the financial system less vulnerable to liquidity crises and contagion effects.

Transparency. A unified ledger enables unprecedented transparency of financial flows. Regulators can monitor risks in real time, allowing them to intervene more effectively before crises escalate. Transparency also promotes accountability: public scrutiny of the central bank's operations could strengthen confidence in the financial system.

Democratic control. Advocates argue that the People's Ledger could democratize the financial world by aligning money creation and lending with public goals rather than private profits. Central bank accounts could be universally accessible, ensuring financial inclusion. Additionally, targeted credit policies could support the transition to green energy, infrastructure renewal, or social justice initiatives. In this sense, the People's Ledger represents not only a technical reform but a normative realignment of the financial world toward public goals.

Risks

The advantages of a people's ledger must be weighed against equally significant risks.

Surveillance. Centralizing all financial transactions at the central bank enables comprehensive surveillance of individual and corporate behavior. Even if data protection is formally guaranteed, the mere existence of such detailed information raises concerns about government abuse or unauthorized access by hackers. In societies with weak control mechanisms, there is a particularly high risk that financial surveillance will be used against political opponents or vulnerable groups.

Concentration of power. The People's Ledger would effectively nationalize the core banking functions and concentrate financial power in a single institution. While this could increase stability, it carries the risk of stifling innovation in the private sector and reducing the diversity of financial intermediation. Monopolization of infrastructure could slow technological progress and make societies dependent on bureaucratic processes rather than market competition.

Politicization. The most controversial risk is the politicization of lending. If the central bank takes responsibility for managing lending, it could lose its independence and be subject to pressure from elected officials or interest groups. History shows that public banks often struggle to strike a balance between efficiency and political objectives. A people's ledger risks blurring the line between monetary and fiscal policy, thereby undermining the central bank's credibility.

Comparison with CBDC debates

The proposal for a People's Ledger is often confused with debates about central bank digital currencies (CBDCs), but there are significant differences.

Digital euro. The ECB's digital euro project aims to complement, not replace, deposits at commercial banks. It envisages a two-tier model in which commercial banks continue to manage customer relationships, while the ECB provides the digital infrastructure. This cautious approach contrasts with the People's Ledger, which would bypass banks entirely.

Digital yuan (e-CNY). China's digital yuan represents a more expansive vision. Although technically processed through commercial banks, the e-CNY grants the People's Bank of China comprehensive oversight of transaction data. It illustrates how CBDCs can serve both monetary and political objectives, including surveillance and geopolitical influence. However, even the e-CNY does not go as far as completely disintermediating banks from financial intermediation, unlike the People's Ledger.

FedNow and FedAccounts. In the United States, the Federal Reserve has introduced FedNow, a real-time payment system that enhances efficiency while maintaining the existing bank-centric model. However, parallel proposals for 'FedAccounts' are more in line with the People's Ledger, as they provide for direct retail accounts with the Fed. The debate reflects the deep tensions in US political circles between maintaining the role of private banks and expanding public access to central bank money.

In summary, while CBDC initiatives experiment with digital forms of central bank money, they essentially operate within an evolutionary framework that preserves the role of commercial banks. The People's Ledger, on the other hand, represents a revolutionary leap: a comprehensive redesign of financial intermediation under public control.

The People's Ledger addresses the systemic risks arising from tokenization by providing a centralized stabilizing infrastructure. Its potential to ensure stability, transparency, and inclusivity is undeniable, but so are its dangers of surveillance, concentration, and politicization. Compared to incremental CBDC models, the People's Ledger represents a more radical departure from current practices that could fundamentally alter the balance of power in the financial system.

Whether such a radical change is feasible or desirable depends as much on political decisions as on technological feasibility. The following section examines whether hybrid models can reconcile the strengths of decentralization and centralization, offering a more balanced approach to shaping the future financial system.

HYBRID MODELS: COMPLEMENTARITY AND COEXISTENCE

Beyond the Dichotomy: Rethinking Centralization and Decentralization

The analysis so far has contrasted tokenization and the People's Ledger as opposing poles: one distributes financial activities across decentralized networks, the other concentrates them within a central public institution. In practice, however, it is unlikely that the future of finance will unfold as an either/or scenario. Instead, hybrid models that integrate elements of decentralization and centralization appear increasingly plausible. These models would combine the efficiency and innovation of tokenized infrastructures with the stability and accountability of public institutions, thereby overcoming the limitations of both extremes.

The hybrid approach, as demonstrated by the history of financial development, is a testament to the financial system's adaptability. Innovations that initially appeared disruptive were often integrated into existing institutional frameworks rather than being completely replaced. This adaptability is a key feature of the financial system, ensuring its resilience amid technological advancements. Electronic trading platforms did not abolish stock exchanges; instead, they were integrated into regulated markets. Similarly, securitization did not displace banks, but changed their role in credit intermediation. Analogously, tokenization may not destroy central banking, but instead form the technological basis for new public infrastructures such as the People's Ledger.

Tokenization as the Technological Basis for the People's Ledger

One possible hybrid model envisions tokenization as the technological basis for a People's Ledger. In this scenario, the central bank does not build its ledger from scratch; instead, it uses tokenization standards and distributed ledger technologies that are already in use in private markets.

The programmability of tokenization could be integrated into central bank accounts, enabling the automated issuance of policy instruments and the seamless settlement of a wide range of assets. For example, tokenized government bonds could be issued and traded directly on a central bank ledger, while households and businesses interact via retail accounts that accept programmable payments. Such an architecture would combine the transparency and efficiency of tokenization with the trust and legal certainty of public backing.

Importantly, this model does not imply the complete displacement of private actors. Commercial banks and fintech companies could continue to offer front-end services—such as wallets and interfaces—while the central bank manages the back-end infrastructure. The result is a multi-layered ecosystem in which tokenization and centralization reinforce each other rather than compete with each other.

When machines make investment decisions, human understanding becomes a prerequisite for the legitimacy of regulatory decisions. Grobys et al. (2022) demonstrate that hedge funds with a high degree of automation outperform their less automated counterparts. However, this does not mean that humans become redundant; on the contrary, they remain responsible for model architecture, data selection, and governance mechanisms.

Public Ledgers and Private Token Ecosystems

Another hybrid scenario involves a pluralistic ledger architecture, where a public ledger coexists alongside private token ecosystems. Here, the central bank provides a 'settlement backbone' that builds trust, while private markets experiment with tokenizing various asset classes.

In such a design, interoperability is ensured through the use of common standards and gateways between public and private ledgers. For example, a tokenized corporate bond issued on a private blockchain could be settled by transferring central bank tokens on the public ledger. Similarly, DeFi protocols could integrate central bank-issued tokens as collateral, increasing stability while preserving innovation.

This approach is similar to the current two-tier banking system, in which central bank reserves form the basis for private lending. The difference is that the settlement assets themselves would be tokenized and programmable, enabling deeper integration between public and private systems.

Practical Examples of Hybridization

Several ongoing initiatives illustrate the feasibility of hybrid models.

Project mBridge (BIS). Led by the BIS Innovation Hub in collaboration with the central banks of China, Thailand, the United Arab Emirates, and Hong Kong, Project mBridge is developing a multi-CBDC platform for cross-border payments (BIS, 2023b). Using distributed ledger technology, participating central banks issue digital currencies that can be exchanged directly on a shared infrastructure. While maintaining public oversight, the project also involves private-sector participants, such as banks and payment providers. mBridge demonstrates how public infrastructure can utilize tokenization to enhance the efficiency of wholesale transactions, thereby reducing costs and settlement delays in international trade. If mBridge is successfully established, China, for example, would be less dependent on the dollar.

DeFi/CeFi collaborations (Aave Arc, MakerDAO, Sovereign Debt). The line between decentralized and centralized finance is already blurring due to collaborations. Aave Arc, for example, is a permissioned version of the Aave lending protocol that integrates regulatory compliance. Institutional investors can participate in decentralized lending while fulfilling their KYC and AML obligations. Similarly, MakerDAO has begun experimenting with purchasing tokenized U.S. Treasury bonds, effectively linking the issuance of decentralized stablecoins to the government bond market. These initiatives illustrate how DeFi protocols can collaborate with traditional assets and institutions, creating hybrid spaces that combine innovation with oversight.

Tokenized deposits in the banking system. An emerging concept in the banking industry is the issuance of tokenized deposits—bank liabilities recorded in distributed ledgers. Unlike stablecoins, tokenized deposits remain fully backed by traditional deposit insurance and regulatory frameworks while benefiting from the technological advantages of tokenization, including programmability and real-time settlement. Several major banks, including JPMorgan, are currently testing tokenized deposits for cross-border settlements and wholesale transactions via their Onyx platform. Tokenized deposits thus represent a point of convergence between the existing banking model and tokenized infrastructures, bridging the gap between private intermediation and public stability.

the gap between private intermedi

Potential of Hybrid Models

Hybrid models demonstrate promise in balancing efficiency and stability.

Efficiency gains. By leveraging tokenization, hybrid systems can enable real-time settlements, fractional ownership, and interoperability across different asset classes. Programmable features enable cost reductions and product design innovation.

Anchors of stability. By embedding tokenized assets in a public ledger or linking them to central bank-issued tokens, hybrid models reduce systemic risks. Liquidity islands can be bridged, vulnerabilities in smart contracts mitigated through regulatory frameworks, and oracles anchored in trusted institutions.

Inclusivity and competition. Hybrid models, by preserving the role of private actors in providing innovative services while ensuring universal access via public infrastructure, can promote inclusivity and healthy competition in the financial industry. This pluralistic architecture prevents monopolization by private technology giants or central banks, promoting a balanced ecosystem and a more competitive market.

Global integration. Projects such as mBridge show that hybrid models can eliminate long-standing inefficiencies in cross-border payments. By linking multiple CBDCs and tokenized assets on shared infrastructures, they improve monetary cooperation and reduce dependence on dominant reserve currencies.

Challenges and Unanswered Questions

Despite their potential, hybrid models face several unresolved challenges.

- Governance complexity. Integrating public and private systems raises governance questions: Who sets standards, resolves disputes, and ensures fairness among participants?
- Regulatory alignment. Differing national approaches to tokenization and CBDCs can hinder cross-border interoperability. Without coordination, hybrid models risk perpetuating fragmentation on a larger scale.
- Technological risks. Hybrid systems remain vulnerable to cyberattacks, software bugs, and technological obsolescence. The challenge is to design architectures that are resilient yet flexible enough to evolve.
- Political economy. Hybrid models do not resolve the underlying conflict over financial power. The balance between public oversight and private innovation will remain contentious, particularly in countries with differing attitudes toward government intervention.

Hybrid models show that the relationship between tokenization and the People's Ledger need not be antagonistic. Instead, they can form complementary components of a new financial architecture that harnesses the innovative potential of tokenization while embedding it in public institutions that ensure stability and accountability. The coexistence of public ledgers and private token ecosystems could thus form the backbone of a resilient, efficient, and inclusive financial system.

The following section will explore the normative and political-economic implications of such hybrid architectures, analyzing how they redistribute power between states, banks, and technology providers, and what this means for the future of money and finance.

NORMATIVE AND POLITICAL-ECONOMIC PERSPECTIVES

Political Economy of Money: Distribution of Power

Money is not a neutral medium of exchange, but an institution that reflects and reproduces power relations in society (Andrae, 2026a). The debate between tokenization and the People's Ledger illustrates this dimension particularly clearly.

Tokenization distributes financial functions across decentralized infrastructures, often operated by private technology developers and global platforms. In contrast, the People's Ledger centralizes these functions within the state, particularly the central bank.

The result is a shift in the distribution of financial power between three key players: the state, the banking sector, and technology platforms. For much of the 20th century, commercial banks acted as dominant intermediaries, controlling access to credit and payments under the supervision of central banks. Since the 2000s, however, technology platforms such as PayPal, Alipay, and Stripe have begun to undermine the banks' monopoly on payment services by leveraging data-driven business models and global user networks (Andrae, 2022). Tokenization reinforces this trend by enabling new market entrants—such as crypto exchanges, decentralized autonomous organizations (DAOs), and DeFi protocols—to offer financial services without relying on banks at all. The People's Ledger would reverse this trend by restoring the state's primacy in financial intermediation. However, this carries the risk of disempowering both banks and private innovators, raising concerns about efficiency, diversity, and political influence. The political economy of money thus becomes a contest over who controls the financial infrastructure: private code, bank balance sheets, or public authorities.

In *The Code of Capital*, Katharina Pistor (2019) demonstrates that the material substance or economic productivity of capital does not define it; instead, it is determined by the legal coding of assets. This 'code of capital' refers to the set of laws and regulations that govern the transformation of assets into capital. Property, contractual clauses, trust and corporate structures, and liability limitations are key mechanisms through which assets are transformed into capital. Capital thus does not arise 'naturally,' but through a specific legal framework that gives it permanence, convertibility, and global enforceability. This 'code' is not neutral, but rather an expression of social power and distribution structures.

Pistor's analysis is directly relevant to the debate on tokenization and the People's Ledger. Tokenization can be understood as a new phase of capital coding, in which property and usage rights are no longer regulated solely by legal contracts but increasingly by digital tokens and smart contracts, and are anchored in technology. Tokenization thus promises to facilitate access to capital, make markets more efficient, and broaden investment opportunities, offering a hopeful perspective on its potential benefits. Lavayssière (2025) shows that the effectiveness of these new infrastructures depends on the robustness of their legal foundations. Once tokenization is complete, tokens embody legal assets.

At the same time, however, it carries the risk of further privatization of the capital code. It is because the technical and legal standards for tokenization are predominantly set by private actors—platforms, protocols, consortia—that are neither democratically legitimized nor systematically supervised. Tokenization thus reinforces the trends described by Pistor: capital is 'privatized' in legally and technically secure forms and increasingly subject to the logic of returns and competition.

The People's Ledger, on the other hand, can be interpreted as an attempt to return the power to code money and capital to the public sphere. If deposits are held directly at the central bank and payment and credit flows are processed via a central, state-controlled infrastructure, this means a re-politicization of capital coding. The 'code of capital' would no longer be written solely by private lawyers, banks, and technology providers, but by a public institution democratically legitimized and mandated to maintain stability and the common good.

Pistor's perspective thus opens up a normative axis for the current debate:

- Tokenization refers to the privatization of code—capital is generated through new legal and technical constructs in privatized infrastructures.
- The People's Ledger stands for the socialization of code—the fundamental architecture of money and capital is once again placed under public authority.

From this perspective, the core issue is less about technology than about institutional power: Who has the right to transform assets into capital and thus control social resources? Private platforms and banks, as in the case of tokenization? Or public institutions, as the People's Ledger strives for?

The integration of Pistors' approach makes it clear that the future of money and capital will not be determined solely by market forces or technological innovations, but by the legal and institutional framework in which these innovations are embedded. The debate about tokenization and the People's Ledger is, therefore, ultimately a debate about the design of the capital code in the digital age.

Democratization vs. Technocratization of the Financial World

One of the most essential normative questions is whether new financial architectures democratize or technocratize the financial world. Tokenization is often praised for its potential to democratize: fractional ownership and borderless networks enable broader participation in markets that were previously reserved for wealthy or institutional investors. Communities can issue their own tokens to finance projects. Individuals in emerging markets can access capital globally without going through local banking oligopolies.

At the same time, tokenization carries the risk of replacing old hierarchies with new ones. The governance of DeFi protocols is often concentrated among early adopters, venture capital firms, or technologically savvy players. 'Decentralization' usually masks new forms of exclusion, in which participation is restricted by technical knowledge, access to digital infrastructure, and the ability to manage cryptographic keys. Far from democratizing finance, tokenization can thus lead to technocratization, strengthening a small elite of programmers, miners, and large token holders.

The People's Ledger presents similar ambiguities. On the one hand, universal central bank accounts could expand access to secure money and payments for all citizens, representing an essential step toward financial democratization. On the other hand, embedding financial decisions in programmable accounts risks turning finance into a highly technocratic domain governed by algorithms and central bank officials. Without robust mechanisms of democratic control, such technocratization could undermine public trust and limit pluralism in financial intermediation.

Social Impacts of Tokenization and Centralization

Financial inclusion. Tokenization is touted as a tool for inclusion, particularly through fractional ownership and mobile access to global capital markets. For people in regions with limited banking infrastructure, tokenized assets and stablecoins can provide access to savings and investment opportunities. The People's Ledger could further improve inclusion by ensuring universal access to central bank accounts, effectively creating a public option for financial services. However, both systems face obstacles: tokenization requires digital literacy and internet access, while the People's Ledger raises questions about whether marginalized groups would trust government infrastructure.

Data protection and data security. The normative challenges associated with data differ greatly between tokenization and the People's Ledger. In decentralized systems, privacy can be improved through pseudonymity, though the transparency of the blockchain often makes transaction patterns traceable. In centralized systems, the People's Ledger would concentrate large amounts of sensitive financial data in the hands of public authorities. The balance between enforcing anti-money laundering measures and civil liberties becomes particularly delicate. Normatively, this raises the question of whether financial privacy in the digital age should be considered a fundamental right or a conditional privilege subject to government oversight.

Inequality and access to capital. Both tokenization and centralization have distributional effects. Tokenization could democratize capital markets, but it could also exacerbate inequality by enabling speculative bubbles that disproportionately benefit early movers and wealthy investors. Similarly, a people's ledger could level the playing field in terms of access to secure deposits, but it could also concentrate lending in the hands of central banks. Decisions about which sectors or communities receive targeted loans can either reinforce or challenge existing inequalities, depending on the governance structures in place. The political economy of design decisions thus determines whether these innovations reduce or reinforce inequalities.

Global North vs. Global South

The global impact of tokenization and the People's Ledger further underscores their political dimensions.

For the Global South, tokenization presents a potential solution to underdeveloped local financial systems. Stablecoins denominated in US dollars, for example, are already widely used in countries with high inflation or weak currencies, offering households a hedge against local instability. Tokenized microfinance, or the use of tokens for remittances from the diaspora, could expand access to capital where traditional banks are absent. However, such developments could also increase dependence on infrastructures controlled by actors in the Global North, particularly US-based stablecoin issuers or global crypto exchanges (Andrae, 2026b).

The People's Ledger offers a range of other opportunities and risks. For developing countries, the introduction of a public ledger model could improve financial inclusion, reduce dependence on fragile banking sectors, and provide tools for targeted development lending. A central bank with direct citizen accounts could channel resources into infrastructure, healthcare, or education. At the same time, however, the technological and institutional capacities required to operate such systems could be prohibitively expensive. In weaker states, centralization could exacerbate corruption or political misuse of financial data.

At the global level, the introduction of infrastructures modeled on the People's Ledger in major economies could also reshape the international monetary order. If advanced economies centralize their financial infrastructures under their central banks, the Global South could face increasing dependence on dominant currencies and governance models. Conversely, regional cooperation—such as the African Continental Free Trade Area, which is experimenting with regional tokenized settlement systems—

Monetary Sovereignty between Privatization and Re-politicization

The concept of 'apolitical money' is one of the most influential ideologies in modern financial systems. Money has increasingly been understood as a technical, seemingly neutral instrument that supposedly obeys the laws of supply and demand, with political negotiation processes being deemed irrelevant. However, this depoliticization had tangible political consequences: it led to the privatization of monetary sovereignty.

Over the course of the 20th century, the central function of money creation shifted almost entirely to the banking sector. Bank money, i.e., the book money created by banks through lending, now dominates the money supply. The result was a decoupling of money production and real economic growth. While banks were able to create large amounts of credit for speculative purposes, the financing of productive investments took a back seat. This imbalance not only contributed to the instability of financial systems—for example, through credit-driven bubbles, as Minsky described—but also exacerbated social inequality. Lending and wealth accumulation became increasingly concentrated among economically privileged actors, while risks were socialized to them.

Against this backdrop, it becomes clear that money is not neutral, but deeply political. It determines which social activities are financed and which are not, who has access to capital, and who is excluded. The idea that money creation is a 'technical' task of private banks has obscured the political nature of money, while the consequences—instability, inequality, cyclical crises—are very real.

The discussion about the People's Ledger aims to regain the monetary sovereignty that central banks have lost. By keeping deposits directly with the central bank and, at least in part, transferring credit allocations back to public responsibility, the political controllability of money is strengthened. The People's Ledger thus represents not only an instrument of stability, but also a claim to the re-politicization of money—away from privately dominated money production and toward a public mandate.

In contrast, tokenization can be interpreted as another wave of privatization of money creation. Tokenized assets, stablecoins, or DeFi protocols create new forms of 'private money' that often arise outside of direct regulatory control. Even if these innovations promise efficiency and inclusion, they risk deepening dependence on privately controlled infrastructure and further exacerbating the decoupling of money production from social prosperity.

At its normative core, therefore, a fundamental question arises: Should the future of money production continue to be organized in a private, fragmented, and profit-oriented manner—as tokenization tends to suggest? Or should it be placed back under greater public control to regain monetary sovereignty in the interests of social stability and equality—as the concept of the People's Ledger promises?

DISCUSSION

Tokenization as Disruptive Innovation, the People's Ledger as Radical Order

The analysis in the previous sections has highlighted the stark contrast between tokenization and the People's Ledger. Tokenization, a disruptive innovation, harnesses the transformative power of DLT, smart contracts, and DeFi architectures to fragment financial intermediation and reconfigure trust relationships based on code rather than institutions. Its disruptive power —not just in efficiency gains (such as faster settlements, fractional ownership, and new liquidity channels), but also in its ability to challenge established banks and other traditional financial intermediaries —is a source of intrigue and excitement.

In contrast, the People's Ledger embodies a radical project to build a new order. It does not aim to decentralize finance, but to reconsolidate it under public oversight. Instead of dispersing intermediation, it integrates deposits, payments, and lending into a centralized public infrastructure. While tokenization reimagines finance as a network of distributed protocols, the People's Ledger reimagines finance as a single sovereign ledger. Both visions are transformative, pointing in opposite directions: one toward diversity, the other toward unity. Both hold significant potential.

This juxtaposition makes the debate particularly consequential. If tokenization undermines systemic stability, the People's Ledger may appear as a necessary corrective. Conversely, tokenization offers a counterweight to the potential threats to pluralism and innovation posed by the People's Ledger. The discussion, therefore, revolves not around choosing one model or the other but around the crucial task of assessing their relative risks, opportunities, and complementarities.

Risks and Opportunities

The most important opportunities of tokenization include efficiency, accessibility, and innovation. Tokenized assets can mitigate settlement issues, broaden access to capital markets, and foster innovation in financial engineering. However, these advantages are mitigated by systemic risks, including fragmentation, interoperability problems between DLT platforms and between these platforms and traditional financial infrastructure, the unavailability of money settlement assets, vulnerabilities in smart contracts and governance capture, and differences in legal and regulatory frameworks due to the cross-border nature of many projects. In practice, tokenization often creates new intermediaries (oracles, custodians, protocol developers) that may be less accountable than traditional banks. Therefore, the normative claim that tokenization inherently democratizes finance must be qualified.

The People's Ledger, on the other hand, promises financial stability, inclusivity, and alignment of credit with public priorities. By eliminating bank runs and embedding macroprudential controls in programmable money, it offers tools for mitigating systemic risks that are not available in decentralized markets. However, its risks are equally serious: concentration of power, potential surveillance, and the politicization of credit. A People's Ledger may offer stability, but at the expense of pluralism and individual autonomy.

A comparative assessment suggests that both models entail asymmetric trade-offs. Tokenization maximizes innovation but minimizes systemic safeguards; the

People's Ledger maximizes stability but minimizes diversity of intermediation. Neither model can be considered a complete solution.

Prerequisites for Viable Hybrid Solutions

A key finding from the analysis is that sustainable financial architectures are unlikely to emerge from pure decentralization or pure centralization, but rather from hybrid models that balance their strengths. Several conditions appear to be crucial for the feasibility of such hybridization:

1. Interoperable standards. Tokenized assets must be issued under harmonized conditions that ensure compatibility between platforms and with central bank infrastructures. Without interoperability, there is a risk that hybrid models will reproduce fragmentation.
2. Multi-layered architecture. Hybrid systems should have a multi-layered design, with the central bank providing the settlement infrastructure, while private actors offer front-end services and innovative technologies. This structure mirrors the two-tier banking system, but adapts it to the age of tokenization.
3. Balanced governance. Hybrid models must avoid both the capture of governance by private platforms and excessive concentration in the state. Mechanisms for public-private co-governance, transparent rule-making, and democratic accountability are essential.
4. Resilience mechanisms. The vulnerabilities of tokenization—such as smart contract exploits and oracle risks—should be addressed by integrating safety nets, insurance mechanisms, and backstops alongside public institutions.
5. Global coordination. Because tokenization and digital ledgers operate across borders, hybrid models require international standards to prevent regulatory arbitrage and ensure financial stability in the global system.

When these conditions are met, hybrid systems can combine the efficiency frontier of tokenization with the stability anchor of the people's ledger, creating a financial architecture that is both dynamic and resilient.

Comparing Existing Reform Proposals

Hybrid models are not merely theoretical; they are consistent with existing reform proposals in CBDCs, DeFi regulation, and public banking.

CBDC models. Most CBDC designs—whether the ECB's digital euro or the Federal Reserve's exploratory frameworks—reflect an incremental rather than a radical approach. They aim to provide digital central bank money while preserving the role of commercial banks in distribution and intermediation. This two-tier model is consistent with hybrid logic: central banks provide trust and refinance financial institutions, while private banks and fintechs drive innovation at the user interface. However, without programmability and interoperability with tokenized assets, CBDCs could remain limited in scope. In this respect, it is understandable that the first central banks, such as the Bank of England and the Bank of Korea, are now distancing themselves from further development of CBDCs. Even Sweden, a pioneer of digital money in Europe with its e-krona, has put the brakes on. The Swedish central bank identifies data protection issues and concerns about the integrity of payment transactions in the event of unforeseen events, such as power outages or cyberattacks.

DeFi regulation. International standard-setting bodies, such as IOSCO and the Financial Stability Board (2022), advocate for the principle of 'same activity, same risk, same regulation.' Under this approach, DeFi platforms are treated as functionally equivalent to traditional intermediaries if they perform similar tasks. By embedding tokenized systems into existing regulatory frameworks, this reform path aims to mitigate risks without stifling innovation. Hybridization refers to the process of transferring decentralized innovations into regulated environments, thereby bridging the gap between DeFi and CeFi.

Approaches to public banking. The People's Ledger is consistent with long-standing proposals for public or postal banking, which aim to expand financial inclusion through government-backed institutions. These models demonstrate that centralization does not necessarily displace private banking, but can coexist alongside it. A hybrid model could therefore combine universal central bank accounts with tokenized private services, ensuring that citizens have a secure public option while maintaining diversity in the financial ecosystem.

Towards a Sustainable Financial Architecture

The convergence of debates on tokenization and centralization suggests the possibility of designing a sustainable financial architecture for the digital age. Such an architecture would not eliminate risks, but would redistribute and manage them more effectively:

- Tokenization contributes to innovation, efficiency, and the creation of new channels for accessing capital.
- The People's Ledger contributes to stability, inclusion, and democratic accountability.
- Hybrid models integrate by embedding tokenized infrastructures into public safety nets.

The challenge for policymakers is to create frameworks that leverage these complementarities while mitigating the risks of capture, surveillance, and fragmentation. The future of finance will likely not be determined solely by technological feasibility, but will depend on normative choices about power, inclusion, and accountability.

The concluding section summarizes these findings and outlines the broader policy implications, and outlines the contours of a financial system well-suited to the challenges of the digital age.

CONCLUSION

This chapter has explored the interplay between tokenization, as a disruptive innovation, and the People's Ledger, as a radical proposal for building a new order. At first glance, they appear to be pursuing opposite paths: tokenization distributes financial activities across decentralized infrastructures, whereas the People's Ledger consolidates them into a single public authority. However, the analysis reveals that both approaches address similar systemic challenges—the fragility of traditional banking, the inefficiencies of outdated infrastructures, and the pursuit of greater inclusivity in finance.

Our research has revealed that neither tokenization nor the People's Ledger offers a comprehensive solution on its own. While tokenization enhances access, fosters innovation, and reduces friction losses, it also introduces systemic vulnerabilities such as fragmentation, interoperability issues, governance capture, and technological fragility. On the one hand, the People's Ledger promises stability, transparency, and public accountability; on the other hand, it also carries the risks of power concentration, surveillance, and the politicization of lending.

The primary contribution of this chapter is to underscore the potential of hybrid models that merge the efficiency of tokenization with the stability of the People's Ledger. These hybrid solutions, ranging from tokenized deposits to multi-CBDC platforms to regulated DeFi protocols, demonstrate that complementarities can be achieved. Under the right conditions, such architectures could effectively mitigate systemic risks while fostering innovation.

The debate about the future of finance often oscillates between two extremes: libertarian visions of decentralized protocols on the one hand and statist visions of sovereign digital currencies on the other. By juxtaposing tokenization and the People's Ledger, this chapter has reframed the discussion. The real question is not whether decentralization will triumph over centralization, but how their logics can be combined to design sustainable financial architectures.

This article covers three aspects. First, it integrates insights from technology, law, and political economy to show how institutional design interacts with technological possibilities. Second, it situates both tokenization and the People's Ledger within the historical development of intermediation, demonstrating that financial systems evolve through hybridization rather than binary replacement. Third, it identifies normative trade-offs—between efficiency and stability, between democratization and technocratization, and between privacy and oversight—that must guide policymaking in the digital age.

Based on this analysis, several policy recommendations emerge for regulators, central banks, and market participants:

1. Promote interoperable standards. Regulators and standards bodies should prioritize frameworks that ensure compatibility between tokenization platforms and central bank infrastructures. Interoperability reduces fragmentation and supports liquidity consolidation.
2. Introduction of multi-layered governance. Central banks should provide stability and settlement, while private actors should offer innovative front-end services. This multi-layered design strikes a balance between public trust and private dynamism.
3. Embed risk management in the code. Smart contracts, oracles, and tokenized assets must undergo rigorous audits, stress tests, and security measures to ensure their integrity. Embedding safety nets into programmable infrastructures reduces the risk of chain failures.
4. Protect privacy and civil liberties. Any centralization of financial data under a people's ledger or CBDC must be accompanied by robust privacy measures and independent oversight to prevent abuse.
5. Promote inclusive access. Whether through universal central bank accounts or fractional tokenized assets, policymakers should ensure that marginalized groups have access to secure and
6. Promoting global coordination. As tokenized finance and digital currencies cross borders, international institutions such as the BIS, IMF, and IOSCO must take a leading role in harmonizing regulations, preventing arbitrage, and combating cross-border spillover effects.

Looking ahead, the future of financial systems will be shaped by the interplay of technological innovation and institutional reform. Several development paths are conceivable:

- Global scaling of tokenized ecosystems. Once interoperability challenges are resolved, tokenization could underpin global capital markets, reduce friction losses, and expand access.

- Expansion of central bank infrastructures. CBDCs and possibly People's Ledger-style systems could extend public control over money and payments, embedding stability functions directly into the monetary base.
- Hybrid convergence. The future will bring multi-layered hybrid systems: tokenized assets integrated into central bank settlement infrastructures, regulated DeFi protocols operating alongside public options, and tokenized deposits bridging the gap between traditional banks and digital ledgers.

It is about more than just efficiency; it is about the political economy of money in the digital age. Decisions about how to integrate tokenization and centralization will determine who controls credit, how risk is distributed, and whether the financial world serves primarily private wealth accumulation or the public interest.

The digital age promises to enable the creation of pluralistic financial architectures that harness the innovative energy of decentralization while embedding it in a framework of stability, inclusivity, and accountability. Realizing this promise requires not only technical innovation but also political will, normative clarity, and institutional imagination.

The metaphor of ‘two sides of the same coin’ captures the relationship between tokenization and the People's Ledger. They appear to be opposites—one distributed, the other concentrated—but both reflect a common realization: that the status quo of financial intermediation is inadequate for the challenges of the 21st century. Whether through disruption, centralization, or hybridization, the task ahead is to design a financial system that can withstand systemic shocks, empower citizens, and align the financial world with collective goals. The path to the future is not predetermined, but the decisions made today will shape money, intermediation, and public control for decades to come.

REFERENCES

Allen, F., & Santomero, A. (1998). The theory of financial intermediation. *Journal of Banking & Finance*, *21*(11–12), 1461–1485. DOI: 10.1016/S0378-4266(97)00032-0

Andrae, S. (2022). The role of BigTech in emerging markets. In Nguyen, D. K. (Ed.), *Handbook of Banking and Finance in Emerging Markets* (pp. 433–463). Edward Elgar., DOI: 10.4337/9781800880900.00032

Andrae, S. (2026a). Money as a cultural artifact: An economic anthropology analysis of its social and environmental impacts. In Christiansen, B., & Branch, J. D. (Eds.), *Examining modern economic anthropology* (pp. 31–72). IGI Global Publishing., DOI: 10.4018/979-8-3373-1260-6.ch002

Andrae, S. (2026b). U.S. strategy to dominate the Dollar with stablecoins: Geopolitical and economic implications. In Akhtar, S., Khan, M., Almaqtari, F. A G., Selvam, V., & Bahl, S. (Eds.), *Policy implications on international financial economics and banking* (pp. 195–236). IGI Global Publishing., DOI: 10.4018/979-8-3373-3725-8.ch007

Banerjee, A., Sevillano, J., Higginson, M., Rigo, D., & Spanz, G. (2024). From ripples to waves: The transformational power of tokenizing assets. McKinsey Company. https://www.mckinsey.com/industries/financial-services/our-insights/from-ripples-to-waves-the-transformational-power-of-tokenizing-assets

Bank for International Settlements (BIS). (2023a). A blueprint for the future monetary system: Improving the old, enabling the new. BIS Annual Economic Report, Chapter III. https://www.bis.org/publ/arpdf/ar2023e3.pdf

Bank for International Settlements (BIS). (2023b). Project mBridge: Connecting economies through CBDC. BIS Innovation Hub. https://www.bis.org/about/bisih/topics/cbdc/mcbdc_bridge.htm

Commodity Futures Trading Commission (CFTC). Digital assets primer (2020). https://www.cftc.gov/LabCFTC/primers

Diamond, D. W. (1984). Financial intermediation and delegated monitoring. *The Review of Economic Studies*, *51*(3), 393–414. DOI: 10.2307/2297430

European Central Bank (ECB). (2023). Progress on the investigation phase of a Digital Euro. ECB Reports. https://www.ecb.europa.eu/paym/digital_euro/investigation/progress/html/index.en.html

European Union (2023). Regulation (EU) 2023/1114 on markets in crypto-assets (MiCA). Official Journal of the EU. https://eur-lex.europa.eu/eli/reg/2023/1114/oj

Financial Stability Board (FSB). (2022). Assessment of risks to financial stability from crypto-assets. https://www.fsb.org/2022/02/assessment-of-risks-to-financial-stability-from-crypto-assets

Financial Stability Board (FSB). (2024). The financial stability implications of tokenisation. October 22, 2024. https://www.fsb.org/uploads/P221024-2.pdf

Graeber, D. (2014). *Debt: The First 5,000 Years*. Melville House.

Grobys, K., Kolari, J. W., & Niang, J. (2022). Man versus machine: On artificial intelligence and hedge funds performance. *Applied Economics*, *54*(40), 4632–4646. DOI: 10.1080/00036846.2022.2032585

Harvey, C., Ramachandran, A., & Santoro, J. (2021). *DeFi and the future of finance*. Wiley.

Hockett, R. C. (2022). *The citizens' ledger digitizing our money, democratizing our finance*. Springer., DOI: 10.1007/978-3-030-99566-9

Hockett, R. C., & Omarova, S. (2017). The finance franchise. *Cornell Law Review*, *102*, 1143–1218. https://scholarship.law.cornell.edu/clr/vol102/iss5/2

IOSCO. (2022). Decentralized Finance Report. International Organization of Securities Commissions. https://www.iosco.org/library/pubdocs/pdf/IOSCOPD699.pdf

Laeven, L. (2011). Banking crises: A review. *Annual Review of Financial Economics*, *3*(1), 17–40. DOI: 10.1146/annurev-financial-102710-144816

Lavayssière, X. (2025). Legal structures of tokenised assets. *European Journal of Risk Regulation*, •••, 1–13. DOI: 10.1017/err.2024.88

Marois, T. (2023). *Public Banks: Decarbonisation, Definancialisation and Democratisation*. Cambridge University Press. DOI: 10.4324/9781003344292

Minsky, H. (1992). The financial instability hypothesis. The Jerome Levy Economics Institute Working Paper No. 74. https://www.levyinstitute.org/pubs/wp74.pdf

Nikolaidi, M., & Stockhammer, E. (2017). Minsky models: A structured survey. *Journal of Economic Surveys*, *31*(5), 1304–1331. DOI: 10.1111/joes.12222

Odinet, C. K., & Tosato, A. (2025). Regulating stablecoins: Comparing MiCAR and the GENIUS Act. DOI: 10.2139/ssrn.5383158

Omarova, S. (2021). The People's Ledger: How to democratize money and finance the economy. *Vanderbilt Law Review*, *74*(5), 1231–1314. https://scholarship.law.vanderbilt.edu/vlr/vol74/iss5/3

People's Bank of China. (2021). Progress of Research & Development of e-CNY in China. PBoC Report. https://www.pbc.gov.cn/en/3688110/3688172/4157443/4293696/2021071614584691871.pdf

Pistor, K. (2019). *The Code of Capital: How the Law Creates Wealth and Inequality*. Princeton University Press.

Schär, F. (2021). Decentralized finance: On Blockchain- and Smart Contract-based financial markets. *Review - Federal Reserve Bank of St. Louis*, *103*(2), 153–174. DOI: 10.20955/r.103.153-74

U.S. Securities and Exchange Commission (SEC). Ongoing enforcement releases on crypto assets. https://www.sec.gov/about/divisions-offices/division-enforcement/cyber-crypto-assets-emerging-technology/enforcement-actions#crypto

Zhang, Y., Gong, B., & Zhou, P. (2024). Centralized use of decentralized technology: Tokenization of currencies and assets. *Structural Change and Economic Dynamics*, *71*, 15–25. DOI: 10.1016/j.strueco.2024.06.006

Chapter 3
Decentralized Finance and the Role of Tokenized Assets

Pooja Lekhi
https://orcid.org/0009-0008-0053-106X
University Canada West, Canada

Kamal Nain Sharma
https://orcid.org/0000-0002-0732-0299
Lovely Professional University, India

ABSTRACT

Decentralized Finance (DeFi) has emerged as a transformative force in the financial sector, leveraging blockchain technology to enable permissionless and automated financial services. A key component of DeFi's expansion is the rise of tokenized assets, which represent digital ownership of real-world and virtual assets. This chapter explores the various forms of tokenization, including cryptocurrencies, asset-backed tokens, and Central Bank Digital Currencies (CBDCs), and their integration into the DeFi ecosystem. It examines how tokenized assets enhance liquidity, facilitate financial inclusion, and create new investment opportunities. Additionally, the chapter discusses the interplay between decentralized and centralized financial models, regulatory challenges, and the risks associated with smart contracts, price volatility, and governance. By analyzing case studies and emerging trends, the chapter provides insights into the future of the tokenized economy and its potential to bridge traditional finance with decentralized innovations.

DOI: 10.4018/979-8-3373-3371-7.ch003

INTRODUCTION

The past few years have seen an influx of blockchain financial innovations. As the Bitcoin technology was introduced in 2008, thousands of so-called crypto projects have been created. Ethereium was released in 2015, to support smart contracts based on a blockchain. Since it has been applied to fund start-up projects (e.g., initial coin offerings, or ICOs), support institutional governance (e.g., decentralized autonomous organization, or DAO), provide financial services (e.g., decentralized finance, or DeFi), and address asset ownership (e.g., non-fungible tokens, or NFTs). This new ecosystem, however, requires a safe payment device in order to release all the promises. Well-known cryptocurrencies as Bitcoin and Ether are highly price volatile and not as attractive as a store of value or unit of account. Consequently, numerous people believe that they are too unstable to serve as a valuable mode of exchange in the crypto world. In order to close the gap that is created by the traditional payment methods, which cannot easily be expressed in the crypto space through regulatory and technological challenges, the private efforts have introduced different recipes to a stable crypto money (a.k.a. stablecoins). The rise of decentralized finance (DeFi) and tokenized assets could be considered as the most radical technological change in the financial services industry since the invention of internet. Since 2008 when the proof-of-concept of Bitcoin was first developed, all the way up to the prosperous ecosystems of decentralized exchanges, lending protocols and tokenized real-world assets (RWAs) the world financial system is radically being restructured. This has been marked in particular by the institutionalization of blockchain infrastructure since 2020, the emergence of Layer-2 scaling infrastructure, like Polygon and Arbitrum, and increased regulatory attention around markets in digital assets (BIS, 2023; McKinsey and Company, 2024). Decentralized finance is supposed to eliminate the need to rely on traditional intermediaries such as banks, clearing houses, and brokers and instead have direct, programmable financial relationships between participants based on blockchain-based smart contracts. The structural building blocks of this system are tokenized assets, which are partial or whole ownership of real or digital assets in a transparent and programmable and secure way (OECD, 2021). The convergence of DeFi and tokenization therefore reinvents the 21 st century way of forming, trading, and governing capital.

EVOLUTION OF TOKENIZATION IN FINANCIAL MARKETS

From Digitization to Tokenization

Financial markets have long pursued efficiency through digitization. The late 20th century saw dematerialization of securities, moving from physical share certificates to electronic records. Tokenization represents the next evolutionary step, in which ownership rights are recorded as blockchain-based tokens that can be transferred in real time across global networks (Carapella et al., 2023). While digitization merely replaced paper with bytes, tokenization embeds ownership and transaction logic directly into the asset through code.

Early Use Cases

The first commercial applications appeared around 2015–2017, when firms such as tZERO and Overstock experimented with issuing blockchain-based securities under U.S. regulations (Heines et al., 2021). Switzerland's SIX Digital Exchange (SDX) and Germany's Deutsche Börse D7 later launched pilot programs for tokenized bond issuances, paving the way for institutional acceptance.

By 2025, consulting estimates suggested that global tokenized assets could exceed $10 trillion in value by 2030, driven by tokenization of funds, private credit, and real estate (Boston Consulting Group [BCG], 2023).

Tokenization vs. Securitization

Tokenization is often compared to securitization because both transform illiquid assets into tradable units. However, securitization relies on centralized intermediaries and legal structures, whereas tokenization employs decentralized ledgers and programmable governance (Hentov & Gorshkov, 2024). In tokenization, the settlement, custody, and ownership transfer occur natively on-chain, reducing counterparty and operational risks.

Concept of Tokenization

The concept of tokenization is the creation of a digital form of a physical or real-life object. It also may be used as a way to save some secret information or simplify the processing of big data. The concept of tokenization is the conversion of ownership of the real or digital asset into digital form, and such a token may be stored and transmitted on a distributed system of ledger or blockchain basis. The Organisation for Economic Co-operation and Development (OECD, 2021) describes tokenization as the process of creating assets or claims of assets on a digital token registry, with the focus on the fact that it is possible to represent in digital form and transfer rights or claims to a physical or financial asset. On the same note, the Bank for International Settlement (BIS, 2023) defines token arrangements as programmable structures that facilitate financial market operations by using digital tokens to facilitate the process of issuing, owning, and trading assets with the help of smart contracts and the possibility of issuing assets in fractions. It is possible to split high-value assets, like real estate or art, into smaller digital units so that an investor may enter previously inaccessible markets with high entry barriers (Heines et al., 2021). Besides, the trading of asset tokens becomes more efficient and transparent through blockchain networks that decrease the number of intermediaries and the settlement period (Carapella et al., 2023).However, the concept also brings regulatory, operational, and legal challenges. Since tokenized assets blur the lines between securities, commodities, and digital currencies, determining their legal status is often complex (OECD, 2021). Additionally, issues such as valuation, custody, and cybersecurity remain barriers to mainstream adoption (Hentov & Gorshkov, 2024).

Overall, tokenization represents a significant innovation in the financial ecosystem—bridging traditional asset markets and digital infrastructures—by combining the benefits of blockchain transparency and programmability with real-world asset value (BIS, 2023; Carapella et al., 2023).

How does tokenization function?

According to McKinsey & Company (2024), tokenization refers to the creation of a digital, unique, and typically anonymous representation of a real-world item. In Web3 applications, tokens are often deployed on private blockchains and are used within specific protocols. These tokens can symbolize a variety of assets—physical (e.g., real estate or art), financial (e.g., stocks or bonds), intangible (e.g., intellectual property), or even personal data and identity. This allows for increased control by creators and more efficient monetization (World Economic Forum, 2020).

Types of Tokens

1. Utility Tokens — It provide access to a network or product but do not represent ownership (e.g., Filecoin).
2. Security Tokens —It is represent ownership in a financial asset, subject to securities regulation (e.g., tokenized bonds).
3. Stablecoins — Pegged to fiat currencies to maintain stable value (Arner et al., 2020).

4. Non-Fungible Tokens (NFTs) — It represent unique assets such as art, collectibles, or intellectual property rights.
5. Governance Tokens — Grant voting power within decentralized protocols (Schär, 2021).

Tokenization relies on standardized frameworks such as ERC-20 for fungible tokens and ERC-721/1155 for non-fungible assets. The development of ISO 20022 messaging standards and token identification numbers by the International Organization for Standardization enhances interoperability between traditional and decentralized systems (OECD, 2021).

Several types of tokens can be developed through Web3 tokenization. For example, stablecoins are cryptocurrencies tied to traditional currencies and are designed to be interchangeable. In contrast, nonfungible tokens (NFTs) are unique and non-replicable, serving as verifiable digital proofs of ownership.

The concept of tokenization also exists in artificial intelligence but differs significantly. In AI, especially in large language models (LLMs), tokenization breaks down text into smaller units (tokens), such as words, enabling the model to interpret relationships between them—for instance, the word "cat" and its context.

Web3 tokenization offers notable benefits to financial institutions, including programmability (embedding smart contract logic), composability (interacting with other digital assets), and enhanced operational efficiency through automation and streamlined processes (McKinsey & Company, 2024)

Web3 tokenization offers several advantages to financial institutions, including:

Programmability: Tokens can carry embedded code that interacts with smart contracts, allowing for advanced automation. (Lekhi, P., & Kaur, G, 2023)
Composability: Tokens can seamlessly interact with other digital assets and decentralized applications within the same ecosystem.
Operational efficiency: Tokenization can simplify workflows, enable automatic transactions, and enhance overall operational productivity. (McKinsey& Company, 2024).

Impacts on Market Infrastructure

Tokenization enhances efficiency by replacing multiple intermediaries with automated smart-contract processes. Settlement cycles shorten from T+2 days to near-instantaneous exchange of assets and payment (Delivery vs Payment on-chain). The process also allows fractional ownership, enabling smaller investors to participate in previously inaccessible markets, thereby enhancing inclusivity (World Economic Forum, 2022).

Challenges of Institutional Integration

Despite progress, integration with legacy systems remains complex. Custody solutions must meet institutional security standards; valuation methods must adapt to continuous 24/7 markets; and compliance teams must reconcile blockchain transparency with confidentiality requirements (McKinsey & Company, 2024).

Governance and Functioning of DeFi Ecosystems

1 Architecture of Smart-Contracts. The work of DeFi is based on smart contracts. Exchange, lending, and collateral management platforms like Uniswap, Aave, and Compound are automated and do not include intermediaries (Zetzsche et al., 2020). Governance credentials such as UNI and AAVE enable users to suggest protocol upgrades and vote on parameters and receive fee revenue.
2 Interoperability Across Chains. The current state of DeFi is not based on disconnected chains anymore. Polkadot, Cosmos IBC, and LayerZero are all frameworks that use cross-chain communication to allow tokens to move across ecosystems with ease. This interoperability plays a crucial role in scaling the tokenized finance (Makarov and Schar, 2022).

3. Hybrid CeFi-DeFi Models The convergence of centralized and decentralized models is evident in initiatives such as Aave Arc (institutional DeFi compliant with KYC) and Circle's USDC bridges connecting bank deposits to DeFi protocols. Such hybrids offer regulatory comfort while preserving decentralized efficiencies (Aramonte et al., 2022).

Understanding the Functioning of Blockchain and Crypto-Assets

Blockchain technology reduces the need for centralized institutions by validating transactions using cryptographic protocols and economic incentives (Bank for International Settlements [BIS], 2021). At its core, a blockchain is an append-only digital ledger comprising chronologically ordered blocks. These records are upheld by selected network actors such as miners or validators. The system works without a central authority, and every device in the network keeps an exact copy of the record book (BIS, 2021). To illustrate, consider the difference between traditional banking and blockchain transactions. In conventional systems, if Alice transfers $1,000 to Bob, her bank verifies her balance, communicates with Bob's bank, credits his account, and debits hers. This process relies entirely on trusted intermediaries. In contrast, blockchain transactions are submitted to a public queue and shared across the network. The transaction is expressed in cryptocurrency—a native digital asset backed by blockchain technology. Network participants engage in a consensus process, often involving solving complex cryptographic puzzles, to verify the transaction and group it into a new block (BIS, 2021). The successful participant broadcasts the validated block to the network, where other nodes verify its correctness and update their ledgers. Each block contains a cryptographic hash of the previous one, making it nearly impossible to alter past records without redoing all subsequent ones, a task that requires majority agreement across the network. Participants are motivated to carry out these resource-intensive processes through rewards in the form of newly minted cryptocurrency or user-paid transaction fees (BIS, 2021).

Decentralised Finance: Smart Contracts, DeFi Protocols, and DApps

The creation of Bitcoin brought blockchain technology to the world, which led to many new projects within the cryptocurrency space. A key early development was the emergence of cryptocurrency exchanges, which enabled users to convert bitcoin into traditional fiat currencies. These exchanges helped attract large waves of new participants, often triggering price surges followed by dramatic declines. (Lekhi, P, 2024)

Meanwhile, blockchain's potential captured the attention of computer scientists, leading to the creation of alternative blockchain platforms. Among these, Ethereum—launched in 2015—was particularly groundbreaking. Unlike Bitcoin, Ethereum allowed developers to create and deploy applications using programmable transactions known as *smart contracts*. These contracts enable conditional transactions that execute automatically once predefined conditions are met, thereby expanding blockchain use beyond simple peer-to-peer transfers (Aramonte et al., 2022; Zetzsche et al., 2020).

The emergence of smart contracts laid the foundation for a decentralized ecosystem of financial services, now known as Decentralized Finance (DeFi). DeFi systems eliminate traditional intermediaries by using self-executing code and blockchain networks. According to Schär (2021), the DeFi ecosystem can be structured into five main layers: blockchains, digital assets, protocols, applications, and aggregators. However, a simpler model suggests looking at four key parts—blockchains, smart contracts, protocols, and decentralized applications (DApps)—to make things clearer and easier to understand (Makarov & Schär, 2022).

Key Functions of Decentralized Finance (DeFi) and Their Traditional Finance Equivalents

Decentralized Finance (DeFi) replicates several core functions of traditional financial intermediaries by using smart contracts on blockchain platforms. The table below summarizes the major DeFi use cases and maps them to traditional finance functions they aim to replicate.

Table 1. DeFi Function

DeFi Function	Description	Traditional Finance Function Mimicked
1. Lending & Borrowing	Users lend and borrow cryptoassets. Due to user anonymity, loans are typically over-collateralized.	Credit intermediation, Risk transformation
2. Staking	Users lock cryptoassets into the blockchain to help validate transactions and secure the network, earning rewards.	Credit intermediation
3. Asset Management	Smart contracts pool funds and automatically allocate them into portfolios based on predefined strategies.	Portfolio management, Credit intermediation
4. Yield Farming	A strategy where users move assets across platforms to maximize returns via lending, borrowing, and staking.	Portfolio management, Credit intermediation
5. Tokenization	Users hold crypto tokens that represent ownership or participation in a protocol's value or success.	Portfolio management
6. Derivatives & Synthetic Assets	Smart contracts create instruments that simulate traditional derivatives, linking different cryptoassets.	Risk transfer via derivatives
7. Decentralized Insurance	Offers protection against DeFi-specific risks (e.g., hacks) or automates payouts based on pre-defined events.	Risk transfer via insurance

Source: Bank for International Settlements. (2021).

Limitations: Even though DeFi copies many features of traditional finance, it still has a small impact on the real world economy. It does not yet support core financing needs like mortgages, SME financing, or real-world hedging.

STABLECOINS AND NEW FORMS OF CENTRAL BANK MONEY

Stablecoins

Stablecoins are a type of crypto tokens that are supposed to have a constant value, most commonly linked to the US dollar. This aspect allows them to provide one to one convertibility and it also seems less volatile as compared to traditional cryptocurrencies. The proponents tend to market stablecoins as the currency of choice in the crypto sphere (Arner et al., 2020). There are 3 categories of stablecoins depending on the way they preserve the price stability. The former group consists of fiat-backed stablecoins, i.e. Tether (USDT) and USD Coin (USDC), and they take a majority of the market. The traditional financial assets such as the US Treasuries, commercial paper, repurchase agreements, and bank deposits support these stablecoins. They are very similar to money market funds (MMFs) in structure (Aldasoro et al., 2024). The second type is those crypto-backed stablecoins such as Dai, where other cryptocurrencies are used as assets instead of fiat. A particular group of these include decentralized stablecoins which are fully based on smart contracts and crypto collateral to stabilize around a target value. The third one is algorithmic stablecoins, which stabilize supply by automatic minting and burning protocols. One example is the widely-known TerraUSD that collapsed in May of 2022 and lost its dollar peg. Although the idea of stablecoins is promoted as a means of effective cross-border payments that allow avoiding excessive charges that are characterized by the conventional services, at the moment, they are predominantly used as platforms to enter the wider DeFi space. Although the stablecoins are believed to be a safe haven in a volatile market, the studies show that the fiat-backed stablecoins which constitute more than 90 percent of the market can be affected by both crypto-specific shocks and changes in the monetary policy of the US. Such stressors usually lead to considerable capital leakage, which complicates the story according to which stablecoins can be used as safe assets (Aldasoro et al., 2024).

New Forms of Central Bank Money

Central bank digital currencies (CBDCs) are a new kind of digital money that can perform some tasks similar to stablecoins. CBDCs are digital tools that are valued in a country's own currency and act as a direct obligation of the central bank that issues them (Bank for International Settlements [BIS], 2020, 2021; Group of Central Banks, 2020). In simple terms, they are like digital versions of either physical cash or the money that banks keep at the central bank. Essentially, they are digital equivalents of either physical cash or commercial bank reserves.

CBDCs are of two main types: wholesale and retail. Wholesale CBDCs are used for transactions between banks and usually rely on distributed ledger technology, which lets them work like digital reserves that only approved financial institutions can access.

. In contrast, *retail CBDCs* are intended for the general public—including households and businesses—and can be viewed as digital cash. Unlike conventional e-money, which is a liability of private institutions, retail CBDCs are direct claims on the central bank, similar to physical currency.

CBDC development varies widely by country. As of now, three countries—The Bahamas, Nigeria, and Jamaica—have fully launched retail CBDCs. Over 25 other jurisdictions are at the pilot stage, and many have also conducted trials of wholesale CBDCs. According to Auer et al. (2023), the level of CBDC advancement is positively correlated with a country's technological capacity, especially mobile phone penetration and innovation. Retail CBDC initiatives are more common in economies with larger informal sectors, while wholesale projects align with broader financial infrastructure goals.

Figure 1. DeFi TVL of multiple blockchains combined as of February 25, 2025

Total value locked in DeFi blockchains across different networks from April 2018 up to February 25, 2025, measured in billions of U.S. dollars.

Figure 1 illustrates the fluctuating growth of DeFi TVL, highlighting its vulnerability to systemic events like stablecoin collapses and overall crypto market performance.

By April 2023, the decentralized finance (DeFi) market had dropped to less than 50 billion U.S. dollars, showing a big drop from its highest point in 2021. This fall happened after several bad events, especially the collapse of Terra (LUNA) and its stablecoin TerraUSD (UST) in May 2022. The problems didn't stop there—other stablecoins like USDD also lost their value compared to the dollar in June 2022. Also, the general drop in the crypto market helped push DeFi down. Since Ethereum is the main blockchain used for DeFi activities, changes in its price have a big effect on how well the DeFi sector is doing.

Tokenization of Real-World Assets through Decentralized Finance Platforms

Case Study 1: RealT — Tokenized Real Estate on Blockchain

The emergence of blockchain technology has disrupted numerous industries, with real estate being a notable beneficiary. RealT, a U.S.-based company, exemplifies how blockchain can be leveraged to fractionalize ownership and increase accessibility to property investment. By tokenizing residential real estate assets on the Ethereum blockchain, RealT allows investors to purchase fractional interests in properties using security tokens. Each token represents a legally enforceable ownership share in a specific property and entitles the holder to a proportionate share of rental income and capital appreciation (Kaal, 2020).

RealT introduces a major change by removing the need for usual middlemen like real estate agents, escrow companies, and property managers. Instead, smart contracts automate rent distribution and ownership verification, providing enhanced transparency and efficiency. Investors receive daily or weekly rental income in stablecoins like USDC or cryptocurrency such as Ethereum (ETH), depending on the platform's settings and user preference (Zhao, 2021).

RealT targets properties in stable rental markets, such as Detroit and Chicago, where acquisition costs are lower, making fractional investment feasible. For instance, a property priced at USD 120,000 might be divided into 1,000 tokens at USD 120 each. These tokens are available on decentralized exchanges, such as Uniswap or secondary platforms like RealtySwap, allowing for greater liquidity in a traditionally illiquid market (Ammous, 2021). This enables investors from countries like Canada, Germany, or Singapore to seamlessly participate in the U.S. real estate market without physical presence or traditional cross-border legal complexities.

The economic impact of such democratized access to property markets is significant. A 2022 study by the World Economic Forum estimates that blockchain could save the real estate industry up to $160 billion annually in transaction and processing costs by 2030 through automation and disintermediation (World Economic Forum, 2022). Moreover, tokenization can increase trust and reduce fraud, especially in jurisdictions with weak land registry systems.

However, the model is not without challenges. RealT must navigate U.S. securities laws and KYC/AML compliance. It restricts offerings to accredited investors in some jurisdictions due to SEC regulations under Reg D or Reg A+. Furthermore, the relatively nascent state of regulation around digital assets means that legal uncertainties remain, particularly around secondary trading of these tokens (Kaal, 2020).

Despite these limitations, RealT showcases how blockchain-based tokenization can reshape asset ownership by increasing transparency, reducing entry barriers, and improving liquidity. It exemplifies how fintech and decentralized finance (DeFi) can merge with traditional sectors to drive innovation and inclusion in global real estate investment.

Case Study 2: Centrifuge — Bridging Real-World Assets with DeFi

Centrifuge represents a cutting-edge effort in the decentralized finance (DeFi) space to tokenize and bring real-world assets (RWAs) such as invoices, purchase orders, and trade receivables onto blockchain networks. Unlike other DeFi platforms that mainly use crypto assets like ETH or USDC, Centrifuge allows businesses, especially small and medium-sized ones, to get financing by using their real-world financial documents as collateral via its Tinlake protocol. This approach aims to address the $1.7 trillion global trade finance gap—especially affecting SMEs in emerging economies—by improving access to liquidity (World Bank, 2020).

At the core of Centrifuge's system is asset tokenization, where real-world financial claims are converted into non-fungible tokens (NFTs), uniquely representing underlying off-chain documents. These NFTs are then pooled into smart contracts that issue two types of ERC-20 tokens: DROP (senior, lower-risk, lower-yield) and TIN (junior, higher-risk, higher-yield), creating a decentralized form of securitization. Investors can purchase these tokens and earn returns from the interest paid by borrowers, while the smart contracts enforce the lending and repayment terms transparently and automatically (Schär, 2021).

Centrifuge integrates with DeFi lending platforms like MakerDAO, where DROP tokens serve as collateral for DAI issuance—effectively connecting traditional asset-backed financing to decentralized stablecoin systems. As of mid-2022, Tinlake had facilitated over $100 million in financing and supported asset originators from sectors like freight forwarding, music royalties, and e-commerce (Messari, 2022). For example, New Silver, a U.S.-based real estate lender, successfully tokenized fix-and-flip loans on Centrifuge and borrowed DAI against them, shortening funding cycles for real estate projects.

The use of smart contracts enhances operational efficiency by reducing the need for human intermediaries such as credit analysts, underwriters, and clearinghouses. In traditional finance, invoice factoring or receivables financing often takes weeks due to compliance and manual processing. Centrifuge shortens this to a matter of hours or days, drastically improving cash flow management for businesses (Schär,

2021). Additionally, blockchain ensures tamper-proof data and verifiable transaction history, enhancing trust among global investors.

Yet, there are notable challenges. Legal enforceability of tokenized assets in case of borrower default remains complex, as smart contracts cannot enforce claims in traditional courts. Regulatory uncertainty—particularly around security classification of tokens—adds compliance risks. Furthermore, because Centrifuge bridges traditional finance and DeFi, it must carefully vet asset originators to avoid default risks that could affect both investors and partner protocols like MakerDAO (DeFi Pulse, 2021).

Despite everything, Centrifuge shows that using decentralized platforms can help unlock capital from real-world assets that aren't connected to the blockchain. It allows small and medium-sized businesses to get financing across borders at lower costs, without needing traditional financial institutions. This is a big move towards making the global financial system more inclusive and easier to program.

Case Study 3: The European Investment Bank (EIB) — Tokenized Bonds on Blockchain

The European Investment Bank (EIB) pioneered sovereign-grade tokenized securities through its €100 million digital bond issuance in April 2021. In partnership with Goldman Sachs, Société Générale, and Banco Santander, the EIB issued digital notes on the Ethereum blockchain, marking the first large-scale bond offering on a public distributed ledger (EIB, 2021).

This transaction represented more than a technological experiment—it tested the feasibility of replacing traditional intermediaries such as central securities depositories (CSDs) and clearing systems with blockchain settlement. Investors could purchase and hold the tokenized bonds directly through on-chain wallets, while settlement and interest payments were executed via smart contracts.

Following the success of this pilot, EIB launched another €100 million tokenized bond in 2023, this time using HSBC Orion, a permissioned blockchain network that complies with European settlement standards (HSBC, 2023). The issuance demonstrated how distributed ledgers can provide real-time delivery versus payment (DvP) and transparent investor ownership records.

The EIB's experiment is now widely seen as a model for sovereign and supranational bond digitization, potentially saving millions annually in post-trade reconciliation costs. The success also paved the way for private-sector replication by other institutions such as UBS and Société Générale Forge (Carapella et al., 2023).

Case Study 4: Franklin Templeton's Tokenized Money Market Fund

In April 2021, Franklin Templeton Investments became one of the first global asset managers to tokenize a U.S. registered mutual fund on the Stellar blockchain, later integrating Polygon for scalability (Franklin Templeton, 2022). The Franklin OnChain U.S. Government Money Fund (FOBXX) allows investors to own blockchain-based shares that mirror traditional fund units, with all transactions recorded on-chain.

Unlike earlier tokenization projects, this fund is regulated under the Investment Company Act of 1940, providing full investor protection. Shareholders access the fund via the Benji Investments App, which uses blockchain to verify ownership and process subscriptions or redemptions without intermediaries. The blockchain ledger operates in parallel with the transfer agent's traditional system, ensuring regulatory compliance and transparency.

By March 2024, the fund had exceeded $360 million in assets under management, demonstrating institutional and retail appetite for blockchain-based funds (Franklin Templeton, 2024). The project showcases how tokenization can coexist with existing regulatory structures rather than replace them, illustrating a viable path for asset managers seeking operational efficiency and investor engagement.

Case Study 5: JPMorgan's Onyx and Tokenized Deposits

J.P. Morgan has emerged as a key institutional player in blockchain finance through its Onyx Digital Assets and JPM Coin platforms. The Onyx network, launched in 2020, enables tokenized representations of deposits—known as "deposit tokens"—that settle instantaneously between clients on permissioned blockchains (Chiu & Monnet, 2024).

The network uses the Liink and Onyx Digital Assets platforms to tokenize financial instruments like U.S. Treasuries and commercial paper, facilitating intraday repo transactions. For instance, in 2022, JPMorgan executed the first blockchain-based intraday repo between itself and Goldman Sachs, reducing settlement from 48 hours to minutes (BIS, 2023).

Furthermore, JPMorgan tested programmable payments using its JPM Coin in Singapore's Project Guardian with MAS, demonstrating cross-border tokenized asset transfers under real regulatory conditions (MAS, 2023). The system's programmability allows conditional settlement, such as automatic release of payment upon asset delivery.

This case highlights how tokenized deposits and assets can operate within a bank-regulated environment, bridging the gap between DeFi principles and compliance standards—offering a prototype for the "regulated DeFi" model envisioned by central banks.

Case Study 6: BlackRock and the BUIDL Fund — Institutional Tokenization at Scale

In March 2024, BlackRock launched its BUIDL Fund—the world's first tokenized asset fund by a top-tier asset manager—on the Ethereum blockchain. The fund, managed via Securitize, represents tokenized shares of a U.S. Treasury money-market fund, allowing 24/7 issuance and redemption through blockchain wallets (BlackRock, 2024).

The BUIDL Fund issues ERC-20 tokens backed by short-term U.S. Treasuries, repurchase agreements, and cash. Investors include corporate treasuries and institutional players, with Coinbase Custody providing custody and transfer services. The blockchain-based model drastically reduces administrative overhead and increases transparency in asset flows.

Larry Fink, BlackRock's CEO, described tokenization as the "next generation for markets," predicting that "every financial asset will eventually exist on-chain." The success of BUIDL accelerated other asset managers' exploration of tokenized fund models, including Fidelity and WisdomTree (Hentov & Gorshkov, 2024).

BlackRock's initiative confirms that tokenization has reached institutional legitimacy, moving from concept to multi-billion-dollar commercial deployment.

Case Study 7: Goldfinch — Decentralized Credit for Emerging Economies

Goldfinch Finance illustrates how DeFi and tokenization can serve real-world lending in developing markets. Operating on Ethereum, Goldfinch provides unsecured loans to off-chain businesses—such as microfinance institutions, agricultural co-ops, and fintechs—through tokenized credit pools.

Investors supply stablecoins (USDC or DAI) into senior and junior tranches, with yield varying by risk exposure, similar to Centrifuge's model (Schär, 2021). Borrowers, vetted by community governance and off-chain audits, receive capital through local intermediaries, repaying in crypto or fiat equivalents.

By 2023, Goldfinch had distributed over $150 million in loans to businesses in Africa, Asia, and Latin America, including fintech lenders in Nigeria and Kenya (Messari, 2023). The model proves how tokenization can channel global liquidity into emerging markets while maintaining transparency and risk control via smart contracts.

However, challenges persist—currency volatility, borrower creditworthiness, and limited legal recourse in defaults. Still, Goldfinch demonstrates how DeFi can extend financial inclusion and impact investing through tokenized credit models.

Case Study 8: Toucan Protocol and the Tokenization of Carbon Credits

The Toucan Protocol, launched in 2021, tokenizes carbon offset credits, transforming them into fungible blockchain tokens to facilitate transparent and efficient carbon trading (World Economic Forum, 2020). Toucan bridges the Verified Carbon Standard (VCS) registry with blockchain networks, issuing Base Carbon Tonnes (BCTs) representing verified CO_2 offsets.

Once carbon credits are brought on-chain, they can be traded or "retired" automatically using smart contracts, ensuring double-spending prevention. By 2023, over 22 million carbon credits had been tokenized through Toucan, enabling decentralized climate financing via DeFi integrations like KlimaDAO, which incentivizes carbon sequestration through market-based mechanisms.

This initiative transforms carbon accounting by ensuring traceable, tamper-proof, and programmable ESG assets. It aligns with the broader tokenized sustainability finance trend, where environmental assets are digitized to improve liquidity and accountability (Hentov & Gorshkov, 2024).

Case Study 9: Singapore's Project Guardian — Regulated DeFi in Practice

Project Guardian, led by the Monetary Authority of Singapore (MAS) in collaboration with J.P. Morgan, DBS Bank, and SBI Digital, serves as one of the world's most significant regulatory pilots for tokenized finance (MAS, 2023). The initiative explores decentralized finance for institutional use, focusing on tokenized bonds, deposits, and foreign exchange.

In 2023, Project Guardian executed live transactions of tokenized Singapore Government Securities (SGS) and Japanese Government Bonds (JGBs) between DBS and SBI, settled instantly using tokenized deposits. These transactions occurred on a public blockchain but under strict compliance supervision, marking the first successful cross-border tokenized government bond swap (MAS, 2023).

The experiment validated that regulation and decentralization can coexist, offering a framework for "compliant DeFi." It also demonstrated that smart contracts could enforce financial integrity and transparency without manual intervention.

Singapore's model is now influencing similar projects globally—such as the UK's Project Rosalind and the EU's Digital Euro Pilot—indicating a future convergence of central bank policy, blockchain infrastructure, and tokenized financial markets.

Case Study 10: Sygnum Bank — Tokenized Equity and Dividend Distribution

Sygnum Bank, a Swiss digital-asset bank licensed by FINMA, provides one of the earliest operational examples of tokenized equity issuance. In 2020, Sygnum tokenized its own company shares on the Sygnum DLT platform, enabling fully on-chain shareholder management and dividend distribution via smart contracts (Sygnum, 2022).

Shareholders received digital tokens representing their equity positions, which could be traded or held in regulated digital wallets. Dividends were automatically distributed in CHF stablecoins through smart contracts, ensuring efficiency and transparency.

The project highlighted the potential of DLT-based corporate governance, where shareholder voting, cap table management, and profit distribution occur seamlessly on-chain.

Since then, Sygnum has extended the platform to other issuers, facilitating tokenized equity and debt products for Swiss SMEs under the DLT Act of 2021. The model illustrates how tokenization can modernize corporate finance and democratize access to private equity investments.

Case Study 11: Siemens — Tokenized Corporate Bonds in Germany

In 2023, Siemens AG issued a €60 million tokenized bond on the Polygon blockchain, marking the first corporate bond issuance under Germany's Electronic Securities Act (eWpG) (Siemens, 2023). The three-month bond was issued directly to investors without central securities depositories or paper documentation.

The issuance process was automated via smart contracts, with payments conducted using traditional banking channels. By bypassing intermediaries, Siemens demonstrated a potential reduction in issuance time from weeks to days, cutting operational costs by up to 30 percent (BCG, 2023).

This case emphasizes how large corporates are adopting tokenization not merely for experimentation but for efficiency and cost optimization, setting a precedent for other multinational issuers.

Synthesis of Case Studies

Across these diverse examples—ranging from DeFi-native protocols like Centrifuge and Goldfinch to institutional pilots like EIB, BlackRock, and Siemens—a clear trend emerges:

1. Tokenization has matured beyond proof-of-concept to regulated, large-scale implementations.
2. It enables real-world utility, including faster settlement, fractionalization, and programmable compliance.
3. Collaboration between traditional financial institutions and blockchain innovators is key to mainstream adoption.
4. Jurisdictions like Singapore, Switzerland, and the EU are leading in establishing legal frameworks that balance innovation with investor protection.

These cases collectively demonstrate that tokenization is not merely a crypto experiment but a foundational evolution in capital markets, capable of reshaping liquidity, inclusion, and transparency across global finance.

Regulatory Landscape and Compliance Challenges

1 Global Regulatory Frameworks

Regulators worldwide are developing frameworks to balance innovation with consumer protection:

- European Union – MiCA (2024): classifies crypto-assets and establishes licensing requirements.
- United Kingdom – FCA Consultation (2023): extends securities rules to stablecoins and DeFi protocols.
- United States – SEC vs. CFTC: jurisdictional disputes create uncertainty, particularly for security tokens.
- Asia – Monetary Authority of Singapore (MAS) and Hong Kong SFC promote sandboxes and digital-asset guidelines.

2.AML/KYC and Custody Issues

Decentralization poses compliance challenges for Anti-Money-Laundering (AML) and Know-Your-Customer (KYC) regulations. DeFi protocols lack traditional account identification, raising concerns under the Financial Action Task Force (FATF) "travel rule." Emerging solutions include decentralized identity (DID) frameworks and zero-knowledge proofs to ensure privacy-preserving compliance (OECD, 2021).

Custody is another focal area. Legal ownership of on-chain tokens depends on wallet control; courts are still determining whether private-key possession equates to beneficial ownership (BIS, 2023). Institutional custodians such as Anchorage Digital and Fidelity Digital Assets have emerged to bridge this gap.

3.Taxation and Accounting

Tokenized assets blur distinctions between securities, commodities, and currencies, complicating taxation and accounting. International bodies including the IMF and OECD advocate unified reporting frameworks to prevent regulatory arbitrage (OECD, 2021).

Socioeconomic Implications and Financial Inclusion

1 Democratization of Investment

Tokenization lowers entry barriers by enabling fractional ownership. Small investors can now hold slices of real estate, fine art, or private equity funds through blockchain-based tokens . Such democratization promotes broader wealth distribution and inclusion (World Economic Forum, 2022).

2 Empowering Emerging Markets

In developing economies, tokenization facilitates new financing models. For example, agricultural cooperatives in Africa are exploring tokenized crop receipts to secure loans, while Southeast-Asian startups use tokenized micro-bonds to fund renewable-energy projects (World Bank, 2020). These initiatives bypass traditional credit bottlenecks, giving SMEs and rural producers access to capital.

3 Gender and Wealth Inclusion

Research suggests blockchain-based ownership models can empower women entrepreneurs by offering transparent, traceable ownership records without reliance on patriarchal property systems (WEF, 2022). Tokenization also allows diaspora investors to support projects in home countries through small, digital contributions.

4 Risks of Digital Divide

Despite potential, risks remain. Access to digital wallets and internet connectivity is uneven, leading to a new "tokenization divide." Moreover, speculative behavior in crypto markets may divert attention from productive investment (Aldasoro et al., 2024). Financial literacy programs and responsible innovation are essential to ensure inclusive benefits.

The Future of the Tokenized Economy

The tokenized economy is on the brink of becoming a foundational layer in global finance. With the rapid evolution of blockchain technologies, tokenized real-world assets (RWAs)—such as real estate, invoices, and sovereign bonds—are expected to fuel financial innovation across sectors (World Economic Forum, 2020). These digital representations of physical or intangible assets, when combined with smart contracts, enable programmable ownership and real-time value exchange, thereby reducing reliance on intermediaries and enhancing transparency (Schär, 2021).

Institutional involvement is growing, driven by potential efficiency gains and new investment opportunities. Governments and regulators are also increasingly interested in issuing Central Bank Digital Currencies (CBDCs), which can coexist with private stablecoins and contribute to a more efficient and inclusive financial infrastructure (Auer et al., 2023). Furthermore, advances in composability and decentralized identity (DID) are expected to accelerate integration between traditional finance and decentralized systems.

Yet, this future depends on addressing several key challenges—particularly legal enforceability of tokenized claims, security of smart contract protocols, and regulatory standardization across jurisdictions (Aramonte et al., 2022). Despite these obstacles, tokenization is likely to play a transformative role in shaping a more open and interoperable financial future.

The Future Outlook: Convergence of Tokenization, AI, and Web3

1 Integration with Artificial Intelligence

AI and tokenization are converging to enable *autonomous finance*. Machine-learning algorithms can analyze on-chain data to price tokenized assets dynamically, forecast market risks, and automate portfolio adjustments. For example, AI-driven DeFi oracles can provide real-time credit scoring for tokenized loan platforms (Lekhi, 2024).

2 Machine-to-Machine and IoT Economies

Tokenization also extends to the Internet of Things (IoT). Connected devices may use crypto tokens to conduct micro-transactions automatically—such as electric vehicles paying for charging or drones purchasing airspace routes. This machine-to-machine (M2M) economy could be underpinned by stablecoins and CBDCs (Auer et al., 2023).

3 ESG and Sustainability Tokens

Environmental, Social, and Governance (ESG) tokenization is emerging as a vital trend. Carbon-credit tokens, renewable-energy certificates, and social-impact tokens enhance transparency and accountability in sustainability initiatives. Platforms such as Toucan Protocol and Climate Trade use blockchain to track and retire carbon credits (World Economic Forum, 2020).

4 Predictions Toward 2030

By 2030, analysts expect most major asset classes—bonds, equities, real estate, and alternative investments—to have tokenized versions. WEF (2024) projects that tokenized assets could represent 10 percent of global GDP, while BIS (2023) envisions integrated "unified ledgers" linking central-bank money and tokenized deposits. The line between traditional and decentralized finance will blur, giving rise to a programmable, interoperable financial internet.

CONCLUSION

This chapter highlighted how decentralized finance (DeFi) and tokenized assets are converging to reshape traditional financial systems. Through the examples of RealT and Centrifuge, we observed how tokenization empowers fractional ownership and democratizes access to investments traditionally limited by geography, cost, or institutional gatekeeping (World Bank, 2020). These innovations reduce friction in asset issuance, management, and settlement while enhancing efficiency, trust, and global participation.

Although DeFi adoption faces headwinds such as regulatory ambiguity and technological risks, its alignment with tokenized assets positions it as a powerful tool for addressing longstanding gaps in access to finance—especially for small and medium enterprises and underserved markets. As blockchain platforms mature and legal frameworks evolve, tokenization will likely become a standard mechanism for managing and transferring ownership in the digital economy (McKinsey & Company, 2024). Ultimately, this convergence has the potential to create a more accessible, transparent, and programmable financial system.

The evolution of DeFi and tokenized assets represents not just a technological advancement but a structural reimagining of global finance. Tokenization provides a framework for digitizing value in a programmable and interoperable way, while DeFi ensures that value can move seamlessly without central intermediaries. Together, they offer a blueprint for an open, inclusive, and transparent financial ecosystem.

However, realizing this potential demands collaboration among regulators, technologists, and institutions. Legal clarity, cybersecurity resilience, and standardization across jurisdictions will determine the pace of adoption. Education and digital-literacy initiatives will be crucial to ensure that tokenized finance benefits society broadly rather than deepening inequalities.

In sum, DeFi and tokenized assets together herald a new monetary era—one defined by programmable trust, fractional ownership, and borderless participation. The coming decade will likely see convergence of blockchain, artificial intelligence, and digital identity systems, forming the backbone of a tokenized global economy.

REFERENCES

Aldasoro, I., Aramonte, S., Huang, W., & Zoss, M. (2024). Stablecoins: A safe haven or a source of instability? Bank for International Settlements. https://www.bis.org

Ammous, S. (2021). *The fiat standard: The debt slavery alternative to human civilization.* Saifedean.com Publishing.

Aramonte, S., Huang, W., & Schrimpf, A. (2022). DeFi risks and the decentralisation illusion. Bank for International Settlements. https://www.bis.org/publ/qtrpdf/r_qt2112b.htm

Arner, D. W., Auer, R., & Frost, J. (2020). Stablecoins: Risks, potential and regulation. Bank for International Settlements. https://www.bis.org/publ/bisbull21.pdf

Auer, R., Cornelli, G., & Frost, J. (2023). CBDC development and cross-country experiences. Bank for International Settlements. https://www.bis.org/publ/bppdf/bispap136.pdf

Bank for International Settlements. (2021). CBDCs: An opportunity for the monetary system. https://www.bis.org/publ/othp42.pdf

Bank for International Settlements (BIS). (2021). CBDCs: Financial stability implications. https://www.bis.org/publ/bppdf/bispap114.pdf

Bank for International Settlements (BIS). (2023). *Blueprint for the future monetary system: Improving the old, enabling the new.* BIS Annual Economic Report 2023. https://www.bis.org

BlackRock. (2024). *Introducing the BlackRock BUIDL Fund: The next evolution of digital assets.* https://www.blackrock.com

Boston Consulting Group (BCG). (2023). *Revolution in asset markets: The trillion-dollar potential of tokenization.*

Carapella, F., Chuan, G., Gerszten, J., Hunter, C., & Swem, N. (2023). *Tokenization: Overview and financial stability implications* (Finance and Economics Discussion Series No. 2023-060). Board of Governors of the Federal Reserve System. DOI: 10.17016/feds.2023.060

Chiu, J., & Monnet, C. (2024). Public and private money creation for distributed ledgers: Stablecoins, tokenized deposits, or central bank digital currencies? Bank of Canada. https://www.bankofcanada.ca/wp-content/uploads/2024/10/swp2024-35.pdf

DeFi Pulse. (2021). Centrifuge and Tinlake overview: Real-world assets on DeFi. https://defipulse.com/blog/centrifuge-real-world-assets/

Franklin Templeton. (2022). *Franklin OnChain U.S. Government Money Fund launched on Stellar.* https://www.franklintempleton.com

Group of Central Banks. (2020). Central bank digital currencies: Foundational principles and core features. https://www.bis.org/publ/othp33.pdf

Heines, R., Dick, C., Pohle, C., & Jung, R. (2021). *The tokenization of everything: Towards a framework for understanding the potentials of tokenized assets*. Proceedings of the Pacific Asia Conference on Information Systems (PACIS). https://aisel.aisnet.org/pacis2021/86

Hentov, E., & Gorshkov, V. (2024). *Asset tokenization in capital markets: A primer*. State Street Global Advisors (SSGA) White Paper. https://www.ssga.com

HSBC. (2023). *HSBC Orion platform completes EIB digital bond issuance.* https://www.hsbc.com

Kaal, W. A. (2020). Blockchain innovation in wealth and asset management: The RealT case. *Journal of Financial Transformation*, *52*(2), 34–45.

Lekhi, P. (2024). Central Bank Digital Currencies: Concept, Benefit, Impact, and Challenges. In *Exploring Central Bank Digital Currencies: Concepts, Frameworks, Models, and Challenges* (pp. 13-20). IGI Global Scientific Publishing.

Lekhi, P. (2024). Megatrends and Innovations Shaping the Future of Finance. *Innovation, Sustainability, and Technological Megatrends in the Face of Uncertainties: Core Developments and Solutions*, 41.

Lekhi, P., & Kaur, G. (Eds.). (2023). *Concepts, Technologies, Challenges, and the Future of Web 3*. IGI Global. DOI: 10.4018/978-1-6684-9919-1

Makarov, I., & Schär, F. (2022). *Permissionless blockchains and the future of financial intermediation*. National Bureau of Economic Research., DOI: 10.3386/w30006

MAS (Monetary Authority of Singapore). (2023). *Project Guardian expands cross-border tokenized asset pilots.* https://www.mas.gov.sg

McKinsey & Company. (2024, July). What is tokenization? https://www.mckinsey.com/featured-insights/mckinsey-explainers/what-is-tokenization

Messari. (2022). State of Centrifuge Q2 2022. https://messari.io/report/state-of-centrifuge-q2-2022

Messari. (2023). *Goldfinch Q3 Report: Decentralized credit growth.* https://messari.io

Organisation for Economic Co-operation and Development (OECD). (2021). *Understanding the tokenisation of assets in financial markets.* OECD Blockchain Policy Series. https://www.oecd.org

Schär, F. (2021). Decentralized finance: On blockchain- and smart contract-based financial markets. *Review - Federal Reserve Bank of St. Louis, 103*(2), 153–174. DOI: 10.20955/r.103.153-74

Siemens, A. G. (2023). *Siemens issues first digital bond on blockchain under eWpG.* https://press.siemens.com

Statista. Retrieved June 13, 2025, from https://www.statista.com/statistics/1272181/defi-tvl-in-multiple-blockchains/

Sygnum Bank. (2022). *Sygnum tokenizes own shares and distributes first tokenized dividend.* https://www.sygnum.com

World Bank. (2020). Trade finance gaps, growth, and jobs survey. https://www.worldbank.org/en/topic/trade/publication/trade-finance-gaps-growth-and-jobs-survey

World Economic Forum. (2020). The tokenization of products and services. https://www.weforum.org/reports/the-tokenization-of-products-and-services

World Economic Forum. (2022). Tokenization of real estate and the future of property investment. https://www.weforum.org/reports/tokenization-in-real-estate-2022/

Zetzsche, D. A., Buckley, R. P., & Arner, D. W. (2020). Decentralized finance (DeFi). *Journal of Financial Regulation, 6*(2), 172–203. DOI: 10.1093/jfr/fjaa010

Zhao, L. (2021). How blockchain is changing real estate: A case study of RealT. Forbes Technology Council. https://www.forbes.com/sites/forbestechcouncil/2021/06/21/how-blockchain-is-changing-real-estate

Chapter 4
Tokenized Lending and Defi Institutionalization:
Global Trends and Regulatory Tensions

Bismark Addai
https://orcid.org/0000-0003-0550-5983
University Canada West, Canada

Adjei Gyamfi Gyimah
https://orcid.org/0000-0003-3158-6051
The Eastern and Southern African Trade and Development Bank, Nairobi, Kenya

Peilin Li
University Canada West, Canada

Shahinaz Hanem R. Abdellatif
https://orcid.org/0009-0005-1528-1567
University Canada West, Canada

ABSTRACT

Tokenized lending is a major application of decentralized finance (DeFi) that has evolved as an innovative platform for credit intermediation through blockchain-based smart contracts. Early token lending platforms such as MakerDAO (now Sky), Compound, and Aave were permissionless, built for decentralized retail lending. More recently, however, there has been an increase in the interest of tokenized lending by institutional investors and regulated entities looking for compliant, risk-managed solutions. This chapter explores the institutionalization of tokenized lending, including an overview and conceptual analysis of the growth, technology, and potential role in the financial system. Additionally, the chapter highlights the fragmented land-

DOI: 10.4018/979-8-3373-3371-7.ch004

scape of regulation on tokenized lending and more nuanced strategies taken by the United States, Canada, the European Union, and Singapore. Although this mixed picture provides the avenue for innovation, it also evinces risks of fragmentation and regulatory arbitrage. The chapter contextualizes the development, potential, and risks of the institutionalization of tokenized lending relative to the global and selected credit markets.

1. INTRODUCTION

Decentralized finance (DeFi) is an innovative configuration of financial services on the blockchain technology. By displacing intermediaries with programmable smart contracts, DeFi has the prospect to offer stronger accessibility, lower transaction costs, and greater transparency (Gogel et al., 2021). Among the numerous use cases of the Applications (Apps) in the DeFi ecosystem, tokenized lending, the act of taking or extending credit secured by blockchain tokens, has controversially emerged as one of the most momentous. Although previous literature has thoroughly covered retail-focused DeFi platforms like MakerDAO, Compound, and Aave (see e.g., Schär, 2021; Cornelli et al., 2024; Qin et al., 2021), there is still a gap in understanding how tokenized lending is developing with the increasing institutional acceptance and regulatory scrutiny. Research on Institutional adoption of DeFi lending in developed regions like Canada, the U.S., and the EU remains limited, especially as different compliance and regulatory frameworks are being evaluated. Therefore, this chapter conceptually explores the institutionalization of tokenized lending across global case studies.

The leading DeFi lending platforms as of 2025 are Compound, Aave, Uniswap, Balancer, Yearn Finance, SushiSwap, MakerDAO (now Sky Protocol), Curve Finance, Synthetix, and Lido. Aave continues to dominate with its flash loan option, enabling uncollateralized borrowing within a single transaction, whereas Yearn Finance has grown in popularity for automated yield optimization, which suits those who prefer little to no human intervention. Conversely, Lido has emerged as a key participant in the liquid staking space, enabling its users to earn staking rewards without compromising the liquidity of their assets (Solulab, 2025).

In its early stages, DeFi lending was heavily retail-focused and largely dominated by crypto-native and individual investors looking for permissionless access to credit and yield opportunities. DeFi platforms generally allow retail users to deposit assets, take out loans, and yield farm with relatively little oversight. The current literature tends to stop at a retail level, either ignoring or glossing over the institutional aspect of tokenized lending. For example, questions remain unanswered about how banks, institutional investors, and asset managers are adopting tokenized lending for governance, compliance, profit, and systemic risk management. This chapter aims to address that gap by exploring the nature of institutional participation in tokenized lending, the current regulatory design, and how these regulations enable or constrain that participation, and financial stability considerations, and how that may vary participation in the retail and institutional context.

With the passage of time, the DeFi lending ecosystem has shown substantial signs of institutionalization. Traditional financial institutions, asset managers, and corporates are starting to invest in tokenized lending models, finding a way to access the efficiency benefits of DeFi protocols in a way that also conforms with some level of regulation and risk controls. This is due to multiple factors, including a general need for yield enhancement, a potential reduction in the costs of capital, and regulatory clarity in some jurisdictions (Wyman et al., nd). Specifically, permissioned platforms illustrate this new trend Aave Arc, for example, places participation and liquidity pool access restrictions for KYC/AML-compliant institutions only (Evans, 2024). Maple Finance, on the other hand, offers undercollateralized institutional loans with onboarding and credit underwriting standards that more closely mirror existing banking relationships (Chiu et al., 2023). Finally, JPMorgan's Onyx used in Singapore's Project Guardian shows how financial institutions (banks) tokenize assets and perform activities on-chain on a permissioned blockchain in a regulatory sandbox setting (OECD, 2022).

Nevertheless, the institutional activities in the DeFi lending space do not occur under a common regulatory environment, but rather different jurisdictional regulations. Canadian securities regulators have taken an approach in which most crypto trading and lending platforms have been ordered to register and provide investor protection features (CSA, 2023). The EU has proposed Markets in Crypto-Assets Regulation (MiCA), a legislative initiative to bring digital asset regulation more in line across the entire bloc (ESMA, 2024). By contrast, the U.S. remains in an enforcement-first phase of its approach to digital assets, at least under the current administration, by applying existing securities laws (Gensler, 2023). Singapore has primarily focused on engaging institutions via a regulatory sandbox, though it has issued some compliance expectations as well (MAS, 2023). The above-mentioned examples are not fully comprehensive, but they highlight both a potential for regulatory arbitrage, as well as for possible differences in consumer protections and market fragmentation.

Institutional participation in the DeFi lending space should generally lead to better outcomes with respect to compliance, governance, and operational risk management, yet there is still intrinsic risk in tokenized lending. Smart contract flaws, oracle manipulation, and protocol interconnectivity risk remain very real considerations in the space (Capponi et al., 2023). In many ways, composability, which is both a competitive advantage and a disruptive force of DeFi, creates its own pathways for potential cascading failures and susceptibility to exogenous shocks. Furthermore, governance models, ranging from DAOs to more centralized arrangements, have revealed their own sets of trade-offs between decentralization, accountability, and financial stability (Darlin et al., 2022).

This chapter is therefore novel and contributes to the body of knowledge in three ways. First, to the best of our knowledge, this chapter is among the first to provide a detailed exploration of the institutionalization of tokenized lending. This approach thus adds to a prior literature that is focused mostly on retail-centric platforms and DeFi applications (Gogel et al., 2021; Chiu et al., 2023). Second, this chapter seeks to build upon prior literature in regulatory and comparative studies by looking at how various institutional tokenized lending activities sit within the differing regulatory frameworks of Canada, the U.S., the EU, and Singapore. In doing so, the chapter elucidates the role of regulatory design in the continued adoption of DeFi lending by institutional actors. Finally, this chapter attempts to enrich the nascent literature on financial stability and DeFi governance by comparing the risks present between permissionless retail platforms and permissioned models targeted at institutions. In sum, this chapter forms a body of work that contributes to the emerging intersection of DeFi innovation, institutional adoption, regulatory policy, and systemic financial risk. Thus, this chapter has important ramifications from both academic and practical, applied perspectives.

The remaining parts of the chapter proceed as follows: Section 2 is dedicated to the theoretical foundation; Section 3 explores the overview of tokenized lending; Section 4 explores Institutional Entry and Adoption, including a tokenized fund from BlackRock on Ethereum, the JPMorgan Onyx platform and MAS pilot, and custodians, that encourage the adoption. Section 5 is dedicated to regulatory developments and challenges, including the OSC and CSA's position on crypto trading and lending platforms, US SEC enforcement actions, legal uncertainty, Europe's Markets in Crypto-Assets Regulation (MiCA) and its implications, identity verification (KYC), and compliance tools. Section 6 highlights risk and the ethics of tokenized lending institutionalization, including smart contract risk, liquidity risks, oracle manipulation. This section will also discuss the debate on decentralization and whether institutional models are still DeFi. Section 7 presents possible disruptions in credit intermediation and risk pricing, including regulatory arbitrage, systemic risk concerns, and the need for global coordination and regulatory clarity. Section 8 focuses on future directions for Institutional DeFi governance frameworks, Central Banks Digital Currencies (CBDCs) and the role of tokenized government securities, and long-term integration scenarios for tokenized lending and Section 9 concludes the chapter.

2. THEORETICAL FOUNDATIONS

Existing theories of finance and organizational behavior must be explored to make sense of the explosive growth of tokenized lending in decentralized finance (DeFi). On one hand, tokenized lending questions traditional concepts of intermediation because it substitutes banks with smart contracts. On the other hand, it re-inscribes the key functions of intermediaries, such as monitoring, risk allocation, and liquidity provision, but in algorithmic form. The institutionalization of tokenized lending can also be understood as a process by which organizations respond to both regulation and legitimacy in their absorption of decentralized innovation by the financial mainstream. For these reasons, this chapter utilizes the theory of financial intermediation and the institutional theory as the main underpinnings. Financial intermediation theory sheds light on how and to what extent DeFi platforms replace or distribute traditional banking functions of managing information asymmetries and reducing transaction costs. At the same time, institutional theory is useful in explaining how regulation and isomorphic pressures nudge tokenized lending towards more compliance-oriented models. The two combined show that tokenized lending is as much a process of institutional transformation as a wholesale technological disruption of existing forms of finance.

2.1 Institutional Theory

Institutional theory has been applied across a range of disciplines to demonstrate how organizational and social structures, as well as processes, become relevant and persist beyond their original technical mandate (Ozili, 2023; Suddaby, 2010). This theory provides a framework for understanding how both informal and formal structures, such as norms, rules, schemes, and routines, become recognized as authoritative guides for social interaction (Ozili, 2023; Peters, 2022; Munir, 2015; Willmott, 2015). The theory addresses the lifecycle of these structures: how they come into being, spread, are embraced or modified, and ultimately, how they may decline and fade away over time (Scott, 2005). Institutionalism, contextually for tokenized lending, considers the advent and changes undergone by tokenization and its crisis of acceptance in the financial landscape, partially orchestrated by the presently “laissez-faire” nature of tokenized assets and lending by extension. . Regulation, conscious bolstering of the underlying infrastructure which underpins tokenized lending, and other adoption considerations of the digital lending community are the bedrock of institutionalized tokenization.

Institutional isomorphism answers the question of why DeFi protocols like Aave Arc implement processes such as KYC/AML checks. They are required to achieve the legitimacy of regulators and to demonstrate this legitimacy to institutional investors by mimicking structures from the traditional world. Coercive pressures from regulators, normative isomorphic pressures from other global financial institutions and market participants, as well as mimetic isomorphism due to the uncertainties in the DeFi ecosystem, all play a role in the institutionalization process of DeFi.

Thus, the movement towards institutional-grade protocols from the retail-led protocols does not only involve technical convergence but institutional isomorphism as well. That is, DeFi platforms find themselves under coercive pressures from regulators, central banks, and policy groups that mandate them to follow existing financial rules. For instance, in Canada, the CSA has made it clear that crypto trading and lending platforms must register under securities regulation, thereby coercing all DeFi-linked entities to register or lose Canadian investors. In the EU, the MiCA proposal brings a uniform licensing regime for issuers and service providers in an effort to develop a top-down legal code for scaling tokenized lending, whereas the SEC in the US applies coercive enforcement actions against platforms that offer unregistered securities, issuing regulatory guidance that deters or conditions the development of tokenized lending instead of providing forward-looking regulatory support. In Singapore, Project Guardian by MAS (Monetary Authority of Singapore) has opened the space for experimentation, but within regulated sandboxes, thereby conditioning market entry and expansion on expectations of meeting prudential safeguards and AML/KYC requirements.

Institutional investors impose additional sets of expectations for capital adequacy requirements, custodial safeguards and risk governance, which bring additional normative pressures for platforms to adopt familiar financial practices. The outcome is that institutional convergence takes place, whereby tokenized lending platforms begin to look, act, and feel like traditional financial intermediaries, but within decentralized protocols.. In that way, coercive isomorphism, in which peer organizations are compelled by regulators and laws to become more similar, shapes the development of DeFi into institutional-grade finance.

2.2 Financial Intermediation Theory

Hirshleifer (1971), in a treatise on private information in commercial settings, indicated the prospect of commercial actors who are armed with private information and the possibility of selling this information for financial gain. Yet, in the same treatise, Hirshleifer (1971) dismissed the practicality of such an undertaking for financial gain. Leland and Pyle (1977) advanced the thought with the argument that intermediation could solve the challenge of what to do with this private information. However, Allen (1990) and Allen and Santomero (1998) formalized this thought with a postulate of financial intermediation, arguing that holding transaction cost constant, the supposed custodian of private information which could lead to financial returns from investing in a given asset could better harness this value if the engagement with the buyer of this information is brokered by an intermediary who understands the unique needs, fears, and risks faced by the two commercial actors. This is the foundation of modern borrowing and lending, brokered by financial intermediaries. Against this backdrop, tokenized lending is fraught with apprehensions of both ultimate lenders and ultimate borrowers, especially ultimate lenders. Thus, financial intermediaries are required to calm these apprehensions while managing and sharing the risks inherent in these transactions.

Yet, institutional involvement brings back many of the traditional intermediation issues, for instance, the problem of information asymmetry. In many cases, institutional borrowers may still have an incentive to ask for undercollateralized credit. For example, Maple has provided loans to trading companies and market makers who could not function effectively on a fully collateralized model (Gogel et al., 2021). The Maple example shows that even in DeFi, as soon as credit is extended without full collateralization, the market needs intermediaries to enforce discipline and mitigate information asymmetry. This buttresses our argument that tokenized lending does not represent the full disintermediation of finance but a reshuffling of intermediation functions, with smart contracts taking over collateral management and settlement functions and institutional pool delegates taking over screening and monitoring functions. Again, Institutions require risk-adjusted returns, custodial assurances, and compliance standards, demonstrating that there still is a need for monitoring and governance functions in a decentralized ecosystem. From this angle, tokenized lending is more a form of reintermediation, with functions being reallocated between algorithms, institutional gatekeepers, and regulators.

3. TOKENIZED LENDING: AN OVERVIEW

To tokenize embodies the process of conversion of financial instruments, such as bonds and loans or real world assets (RWA) such as intellectual property (IP), real estate, and commodities, into digital tokens on the blockchain. This involves using smart contracts to transform the credit assets into their digital forms (Braithwaite, 2025). Smart contracts are applications which transform traditional financial operations into different formats. Thus, a token will represent a unique digital identifier of one's investment which mirrors the traditional bond certificate, title deed, IP certificate, loan document or share certificate. WEF (2025) details that to be eligible for tokenization, an asset should have a tangible form, carry complex ownership or administrative structures, be reusable or adaptable for repurposing, have low infrastructure maturity to benefit from tokenization, possibly belong to unstructured over-the-counter markets, have limited fractionalization or divisibility, or be already well-regulated to make tokenization easier.

For lending, tokens, created by blockchain technology for clear ownership and kept in digital wallets for safety, represent portions of the debt. These features enhance the trading efficiency of debt securities; thus, tokenized debt assets are tradable instruments. While the specific mechanisms of tokenization may vary, the basic process involves completing the deal terms before creating digital representations of the underlying debt asset on the blockchain. Polled forecasts from Citibank, Mckinsey & Company, and Bernstein puts the asset tokenization market value at a peg of $1-$5 trillion by 2030 (Kaur, 2024). Private credit, which describes non-bank loans, is persistently emerging as a principal component of the global debt market with a compound annual growth rate (CAGR) of 17% (S&P, 2024). Presently, the global private credit market is valued at assets under management of $1.5 trillion (Braithwaite, 2025), of which $13.9 billion (0.9%) is tokenized relative to the U.S. tokenized treasuries of $7.38 billion (Redman, 2025).

Private lending is particularly saddled with issues of liquidity, high manager fees, risk-return mismatch, high default risk, and less transparency and regulation. Tokenization potentially addresses these issues by offering efficiency from smart contracts to reduce back-office costs, liquidity from efficient trading, and transparency through a shared ledger of record (S&P, 2024). The value proposition of tokenized lending, relative to conventional lending, also includes the potential of shared unified records in tokenized lending to enhance information symmetry and reduce ambiguity in asset ownership, custodial models which enhance end-user control over assets, asset fractionalization which allows micro-units (fragmented) of asset ownership and composability or enhanced multi-asset mobility and reuse of collateral across lending activities (WEF, 2025; FSB, 2024).

While tokenization could be payment, data, cryptographic, transaction or asset tokenization (George & Soofi, 2024), the models are either backed (hybrid) or native tokens as categorised in Table 1. Native tokens represent assets issued on-chain without reference to any off-chain counterparts, underlying or reference assets; while backed tokens digitally represent legal ownership of an off-chain immobilized RWA (e.g. real estate, gold), represented as an on-chain token. Contemporary tokens are predominantly modelled as backed tokens due to physical limitations, regulatory uncertainty, and issuer restrictions.

Table 1. Tokenization models

MODEL	CONVENTIONAL	BACKED TOKEN		NATIVE TOKEN
Purpose	To allow investors to trade, hold and settle off-chain	To allow investors to trade, hold and settle on-chain, with the ability to redeem the underlying reference asset		To allow investors to trade, hold and settle on-chain
Component(s)	Conventional asset	Reference asset	Token	Token
Issuance	Asset is issued off-chain	Asset is issued off-chain	Token is issued on-chain	Token is issued on-chain
Proof of value	Driven by issuer credibility	Driven by issuer credibility		Driven by issuer credibility
Proof of ownership	Evidenced by off-chain records	Evidenced by on-chain records		Evidenced by on-chain records
Proof of transaction	Recorded off-chain	Recorded on-chain		Recorded on-chain
Custody	Qualified custodian	Qualified custodian	Flexible custodial arrangements	Flexible custodial arrangements
Redemption	No token	Token may be redeemable for the reference asset or its par value		No reference asset
Example	Public equities	Physical gold (commodity)		Sovereign digital bonds

Off-chain On-chain

Source: WEF (2025)

DeFi is a contestable, competitive, non-custodial, and composable financial infrastructure built on the blockchain, a technology with no safety net and which does not need a centralized institution to operate. Its financial protocols are applied as smart contracts, operated through linked computers to automatically handle financial transactions (Auer et al., 2023). Decentralized Finance (DeFi) essentially shifts the paradigm of lending to disintermediation, as the use of distributed ledger technologies (DLTs) to offer lending services omits the reliance on a traditional financial intermediary. Thus, the borrower and the original provider of funds could transact directly. Auer et al. (2023) assert that DeFi is greater than singular cryptocurrencies like Ethereum. On the contrary, the entire ecosystem for DeFi gives the image of a fragmented yet compositiecomposite union of singular subsystems, with each constructed on top of a single DLT having definite technical structures that delimit and delineate the design options of the financial protocols which are executable on it. While this is evolving and systematically changing as numerous projects presently try to actualize communication channels across DLTs, Ethereum arguably represents a typical relevant DeFi sub-ecosystem, for the locked value and the significance of the built-in financial protocols (Auer et al., 2023). The DeFi layered approach to disintermediation through DLT is conceptualised in Figure 1 as the DeFi Stack Reference (DSR) Model, adopted from Auer et al. (2023).

Figure 1. DeFi stack reference (DSR) model

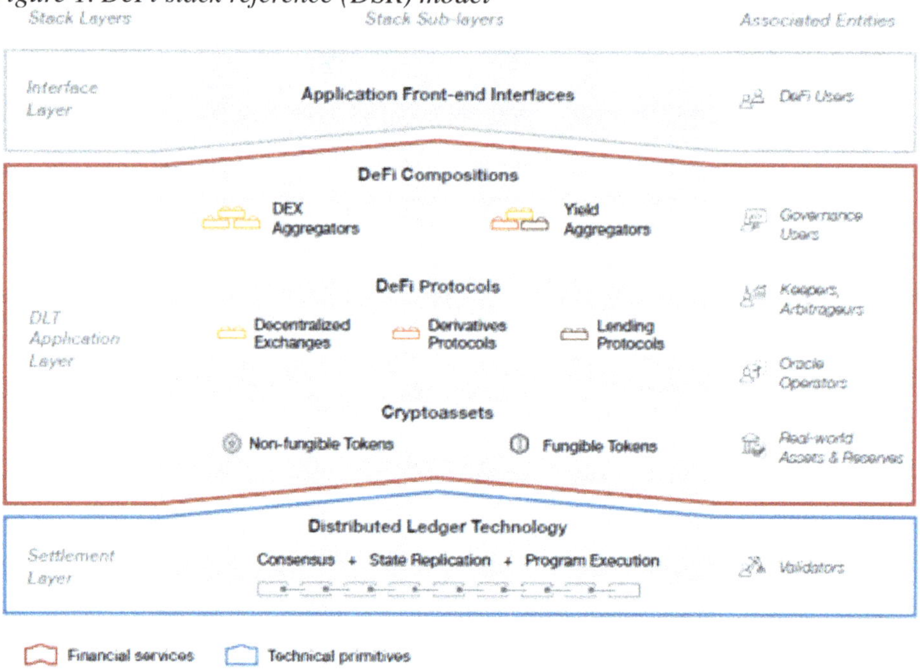

Source: Auer et al. (2023)

At the settlement layer of the DSR Model in Figure 1, DLTs permit the reaching of an agreement on the system, duplicate it throughout the network, and implement programs which facilitate the exchange of native token transactions. The mid-stream DLT application layer is made up of DeFi protocols, arbitrary crypto assets, and DeFi compositions, providing peculiar financial services, that are executed in smart contracts. Different protocols can execute similar financial functionalities. The final layer offers a front-end pictorial interface to users of DeFi. Every layer is related to off-chain entities: arbitrageurs and keepers enforce incentive mechanisms, validators ensure that consensus is reached, on-chain real-world asset information are loaded by oracles, and fiat currencies are the reserves for many crypto assets. DeFi protocols are employed by final users to interact, while decision-making DeFi users make up protocol governance.

The adopted Auer et al. (2023) model is extended in Figure 2 to specifically introduce the DeFi lending protocol or Protocols for loanable funds (PLFs) which automate the lending and borrowing of crypto assets. Figure 2 illustrates the interaction between financial services and economic agents offered by lending platforms like Compound, with token borrowing and lending as core services. Lenders load funds and receive token assets in return which permits redemption of these dpeosits in future, plus interest or a premium. To illustrate, the PLF generates wrapped tokens (cTokens) whose growth over time is pegged to the exchange rate linked to the underlying asset. Thus, the value of funds would have risen at the point of redemption. The flip side involves borrowers paying interest before closing their positions. Collateralizing debt positions is a fundamental function, the foundation on which PLF contracts stand. Usually, collateral provision precedes borrowing as a cushion against default risk. However, there are emerging models which attempt to use other safeguards beside collateral provision.

Figure 2. DeFi lending protocol

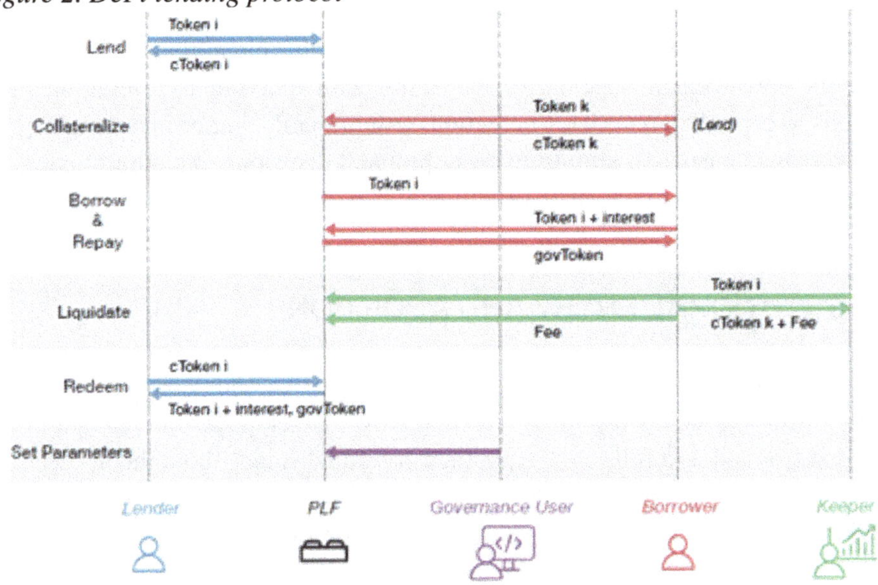

Source: Auer et al. (2023)

Thus, borrowers source loans from lenders' provided funds, and borrowers over-collateralize their positions to hedge against default. Keepers take a fee to fill gaps of inadequately collateralized tickets. Fees earned by governance members come from the use of the protocol.

Retail investors are observed to be primarily motivated by yield pursuit, particularly during low interest periods (Cornelli et al., 2024). Aave's on-chain data indicates that 65% of depositors possess crypto assets under $5,000, with mean annual percentage yields (APYs) ranging from 7% to 12% for stablecoins in 2024, relative to 0.5% to 1% for conventional savings accounts. Decentralized finance (DeFi) platforms provide considerably greater returns than traditional savings accounts, attracting yield-seeking depositors. For instance, Aave's variable interest rates on stablecoins surpass 10% annually, while bank savings yield less than 1% (DeFi Rate, 2024).

At the other end of the spectrum, speculation and governance incentivise lending activity. According to compound data, 70% of lending activities (approximately 112,000 loans from 2019 to 2021) were directed towards leveraged yield farming, with significant investors borrowing an average of $50,000 to acquire governance tokens such as COMP (Saengchote, 2023). Both retail and large investors engage in borrowing to enhance their positions and speculate on price appreciation. Furthermore, large investors also borrow to obtain governance tokens, thereby increasing their power over protocol decisions. Ultimately, speculation is predominant, and DeFi intermediation tends to direct funds towards speculators rather than productive enterprises. The main incentive for lending in DeFi lending pools is the pursuit of higher yields, especially where traditional interest rates remain low. The primary driver for borrowing is speculative in nature, with individuals leveraging their positions to capitalize on price fluctuations. Additionally, larger investors borrow for governance purposes, aiming to sway protocol decisions, including voting on project development initiatives (Cornelli et al., 2024).

4. INSTITUTIONAL ENTRY AND ADOPTION

The institutionalization and adoption of tokenized lending is gaining momentum in a slow and steady fashion, given that most market players are caught in the transition from pilot to full scale. Apprehension and disquiet about the uncertainty of structure, ecosystem acceptability, and regulation could partly explain why the transition from pilot to full scale has dragged among most major market players. Firms in financial services had adopted at least 72 distributed or programmable ledgers as of May 2025 (Accenture et al., 2025).

Global tokenization adoption demands standards harmonization. Inadequate collaboration among industry players and fragmented innovation has also been cited as principal in impeding tokenization adoption (La Salla, 2024). This need is credited by the fact that About 74% of DLT projects had fewer than six participants in 2023 (ISSA, 2023). Swift (n.d.) identifies five critical variables which need alignment to guarantee enhanced adoption; the cash leg and settlement, roles and responsibilities, cross-chain interoperability, token standards, and reference data.

Token use case patterns in financial markets could be broadly segregated into the asset classes of securities financing, asset issuance and asset management. Tokenized lending under the asset issuance category includes sovereign corporate and municipal bonds and private debt. Use cases for the securities financing class include collateral and repurchase agreements; while the asset management class comprises tokenized treasury funds and money market funds. The World bank, in October 2023, issued its first digital securities on Euroclear's DLT, a new Digital Financial

Market Infrastructure (D-FMI). The Digital Native Notes raised €100 million for sustainable development projects. Euroclear's DLT-powered D-FMI showcases tokenized lending for the issuance and settlement of digitized international securities.

Product innovation, which addresses market failures such as over-collateralization as a requirement for tokenized lending, is highly necessary to spur patronage and adoption. Through the Bank of Canada's exploration, it emerged that flash loans native to blockchain ecosystems demonstrate how uncollateralized lending, which wields zero default risk, transforms access to liquidity for sophisticated market participants (Mandin, 2025).

The European Investment Bank has six issued tokenized bonds totalling about €550 million, with its first in 2021on Ethereum. The last was issued on the Orion platform of HSBC and settled on DL3S of Banque de France (Ledgerinsights, 2024). Eight (8) tokenized agency, sovereign, and supranational bonds and 18 commercial tokenized bonds with International Securities Identification Numbers have been issued globally since 2019 (Aldasoro et al., 2025). About €1.3 billion worth of DLT-based bonds had been issued globally as of 2024 with a distribution of 38%, 31%, 21%, 10% and 0.3% hailing from APAC, Switzerland, EU, U.S., and the rest of the world respectively (AFME, 2024). The U.S. Commodity Futures Trading Commission has accepted tokenized treasuries and classified them as non-cash collateral (CFTC, 2024). While the Hong Kong government has normalized tokenized bond issues, the Hong Kong Monetary Authority is on the cusp of a third tokenized bond tranche issue while musing the prospect of tokenizing existing bonds (HKSAR, 2025).

Flash loans, which are essentially uncollateralized near-zero default risk loans, were initially conceived as guaranteed lending by Marble; but Aave (protocol) was the pioneer in writing the smart contract embedding the functionality of flash loan to Ethereum blockchain for a Dai arbitrage deal (worth $33.10). Flash loans have catalyzed lending activity of $2 trillion involving 10 million different flash loan events, with established and potential use cases in arbitrage, liquidations, and liquidity management (Mandin, 2025). Kinexys was launched as a JP Morgan program at the forefront of the tokenization campaign. The bank earlier, in 2017, launched their Liink platform, to facilitate money transfers on blockchain among banks. Subsequently, Kinexys extended the effort to incorporate a collateral system for settlement based on blockchain, with transactions settled in JPM Coin, their tokenized deposit. Its Tokenized Collateral Network (TCN) also permitted BlackRock to load tokenized shares of money market fund as an OTC-trade collateral with Barclays. JP Morgan also recently pursued efforts to demonstrate how tokenizing alternative assets might enable alts to be included at scale in client portfolios which are discretionary. Citibank launched Citi Token Services in 2025, a trade finance and cash management solution on blockchain for institutional clients (Ava Labs & Mastercard, 2024).

Broadridge's Distributed Ledger Repo (DLR) platform enables financial institutions (FIs) to digitally represent US treasury securities outright purchase and sale and repos in real time. The platform has an average monthly transaction value of $1.5 trillion to a clientele which includes 19 U.S. primary treasury dealers. The immutable, programmable, and time-stamped ledger architecture, through smart contracts, decreases discrepancies, counterparty risks, settlement and operating costs. The on-chain DLR Intraday Repo offering improves liquidity, decreases capital buffer requirements, and averagely reduces transaction costs by 50-60% (WEF, 2025).

It is noteworthy that in spite of the numerous use cases and institutions which have either piloted or explored tokenization in general, and tokenized lending specifically, a 2025 survey of 15 sovereign and public pension funds, and 75 central banks found that no central bank in the sample holds any digital asset. It is revealing that 82% of these public FIs do not intend to invest in digital assets over the next 5 to 10 years, 10% have aspirations of building an allocation in digital assets while a paltry 3% intend to build bitcoin allocation in their reserves (OMFIF, 2025).

Tanveer et al. (2025) ascertained how block chain-enabled asset tokenization impacts value creation, transaction efficiency, and risk distribution for use cases in carbon credits, real estate, gaming assets, and gold. Tokenization is decidedly found to create novel value propositions and improve transaction efficiency, but also engenders risk distribution complexities and governance haziness, which could threaten stability in markets. Thus, institutional players may be pre-disposed to pursue and anchor the advantages of asset tokenization; however, balance is required by preserving sustainability and trust in markets.

Zeiß et al. (2024) establishes that, in the matter of acceptance and adoption, awareness directly impacts the perceived behavioural control, ease of use, and usefulness of investing in crypto assets; but inversely influences the perceived risk of investing in crypto assets. Beyond awareness, perceived trust positively influences attitude; while perceived behavioural control positively influences behavioural intention of investing in crypto assets. Perceived ease of use positively influences both perceived usefulness and attitude of investing in crypto assets. Consequently, awareness, trust, and objective sensitization could impact the bottom line of institutional adoption.

Goshie (2024) draws on the viewpoint of political economy to establish another principal motivation for traditional banks to adopt blockchain technology in their operations. Power dynamics dictate that the most influential entities wield the greatest agency in the grand scheme of markets and ecosystems. Against this thinking and through a technological lens, it is not far-fetched that banks move to attain principal positions within the evolving blockchain infrastructure, dynamically influencing the interplay between technology and financial institutions. Tokenization thus transcends mere technology, evolving into a phenomenon that demonstrates how banks actively interact with blockchain, effortlessly incorporating it into their frameworks to influence the narratives surrounding infrastructure. By providing insights into the consequences of blockchain integration by conventional banks, Goshie (2024) exudes the comprehension of power dynamics within financial infrastructure and their capacity for transformation, highlighting the effort, motivation and rationale to achieve a central role within an infrastructure.

Kowsar and Mintoo (2025) comparatively established, across the regions of Asia-Pacific, North America, Africa, and Europe, that regulatory compliance is enhanced by blockchain using live audit trails and automated AML/KYC reporting, though low interoperability, non-standardized data protocols, and lack of legal clarity limit adoption. Crucial enablers for adoption include leadership commitment for institutional readiness, regulatory flexibility and IT infrastructure. Finally, public-private partnerships and national policies impact the scope and pace of adoption.

5. REGULATORY DEVELOPMENTS AND CHALLENGES

Elements in the previous sections point to the conclusion that inadequate regulation, and no regulation in some cases, is a major sticking point for low patronage and slow adoption of tokenization and tokenized lending. FSB (2024) asserts that the case for regulation in DLT, DeFi, and tokenization hovers around issues of adoption, settlement asset choice and availability, speed, and level of automation in the context of programming, fragmentation and interoperability among platforms, transaction complexity, and the level of programming employed in tokenized transactions.

The DeFi market has been challenging from a regulatory oversight perspective, partially due to fintech complexities. leading to market misconduct and cybersecurity attacks, while exacerbating market harm and investor mistrust (IOSCO, 2023).

Market manipulations in decentralized finance dominantly feature wash trading, which involves the concurrent buying and selling of financial instruments without any intrinsic change in the manipulator's position. Tokenized transactions such as flash loans have involved wash trades through the swapping of a token between a lender and borrower, respectively, in a borrow-and-repay cycle, is creat a synthetic increase in trading volumes between the token pair in question. While traditional markets have effectively stemmed the menace of wash trades, the lack of form, structure, clear rules, and design in most DeFi markets has limited the ability to address wash trading. Regulation is needed to address wash trading in DeFi and tokenized lending markets (Mandin, 2025; Wang et al., 2021).

Furthermore, IOSCO (2023) criticizes vulnerabilities related to services and products which depend on DLT activities and arrangements. These services and products include smart protocols and contracts, blockchain networks, governance mechanisms, cross-chain bridges, oracles, and access control points. These cybersecurity attacks often lead to colossal loss for DeFi players and investors. Given the susceptibility of DeFi infrastructure to hacks and attacks as well documented by ImmuneBytes (2024) and DeFiLlama (n.d.), regulation is required to instill sanity in the market and reduce or avoid loss, theft, and value depletion. These vulnerabilities have been detected in smart contract infrastructure and oracle protocols, which link the real world with the on-chain DeFi system.

Furthermore, Europe grapples with the prospect of innovating without increasing systemic risk in financial markets. A case in point, in reference to MiCA regulation, is the unease and differing opinions which have arisen among policy makers and regulators from the approval granted by Malta's regulator to a crypto asset service provider. Countries such as France have registered their unease about this approval granted in Malta. The recent action is part of broader initiatives by national regulators aimed at preventing fragmentation and fostering much-needed integration of capital markets; however, it poses a direct threat to the originally intended mechanisms of MiCA. The European Securities and Markets Authority (ESMA) may emerge as the Pan-European supervisor of MiCA, backed by pressure from larger member states within the Council of the European Union, while facing opposition from smaller states. ESMA had offered a rapid educational verdict to the Maltese regulators, who predictably declined the proposal for direct oversight (Orchard & Voloder, 2025).

The latest tripartite stance from three European regulators - Austria's Financial Market Authority (FMA), France's Autorité des marchés financiers (AMF), and Italy's Commissione Nazionale per le Società e la Borsa (CONSOB) - illustrates the delicate balancing act that has emerged. Their joint paper in September 2025 cautions that national discrepancies could create opportunities for regulatory arbitrage and harm to investors. They advocate for stricter oversight of third-country platforms, more transparent authorisation processes, and a unified filing point for token offerings (AMF et al., 2025).

MiCA was explicitly crafted to standardise regulations while allowing member states to oversee their own markets. The team responsible for guiding the legislation through the Commission intentionally left space for a range of regulatory approaches within established and agreed-upon rules. The arrangement, which substitutes for a single official supervisor, necessitates that member states protect each other against serious violations by forwarding complaints to the Commission. They are discouraged from pursuing trivial or protectionist complaints due to the potential for reciprocal actions against them. However, there remains an opportunity for local preferences, which could foster innovation. Some historians might even argue that this unique European characteristic contributed to its success (Orchard & Voloder, 2025).

Proponents of blockchain innovation fear that the unfolding regulatory and supervisory annexation and usurpation may stifle innovation in financial markets much to the detriment of what could potentially be for future financial markets. Worried stakeholders liken the potential foreboding abyss to the experience of Europe in the Markets in Financial Instruments Directive and MiFID II, which were intended to support the Capital Markets Union, which devolved into a chaotic mix of overly stringent national regulations, inconsistent conduct standards, and ongoing obstacles. There is a danger that MiCA, which aims to establish a cohesive framework for digital assets, may ultimately result in a fragmented system.

MiCA may require re-ratification at a moment when the United States is rapidly advancing the authorization of systemic stablecoins through the Genius Act, which openly endorses the extraterritorial use of the dollar and is typically perceived by European policymakers as a threat to European financial sovereignty. In summary, a decision that may initially appear to be a favorable European initiative could, in fact, be counterproductive.

Historically, Europe has previously witnessed the unfortunate scenario of a Single Market initiative in finance self-sabotaging in this manner. The Markets in Financial Instruments Directive and MiFID II, which were intended to support the Capital Markets Union, devolved into a chaotic mix of overly stringent national regulations, inconsistent conduct standards, and ongoing obstacles. There is a danger that MiCA, which aims to establish a cohesive framework for digital assets, may ultimately result in a fragmented system.

The oversight of Crypto-Asset Service Providers (CASPs), akin to that of banks, serves as a pertinent example. While it is secure, it poses the risk of driving tokenized finance to other regions, potentially leaving Europe lagging in a financial revolution and ultimately becoming a subordinate in the face of an emerging US 'oligopoly', as referred to by the EU Council. A regulatory victory has been achieved, yet the war for economic sovereignty has been forfeited.

ESMA, in June 2025 guided on shared order book restrictions, instructing that a unified order book that encompasses both EU and non-EU platforms is deemed non-compliant unless every operator holds MiCA authorization. Furthermore, the AMF-FMA-CONSOB position paper (AMF et al., 2025) intensifies this concern by advocating that intermediaries should only execute trades on platforms that are either subject to MiCA or adhere to rules that are demonstrably equivalent. This situation engenders a troubling tension between the quality of execution and the enforcement of formal regulatory boundaries. The practical implication is that brokers may be compelled to prioritize compliance with established norms over considerations of fill probability and price, even when clients would benefit from broader access to trading venues.

Conclusively, regulation must quickly overtake market events to establish structures while tokenization remains nascent in its development and before its scaling within financial systems. Regulatory action could also spur increased adoption. IOSCO (2023) and FRA (2024) advocate that more supervision is needed and regulatory emphasis must be placed on governance, risk management standards, interoperability between traditional financial infrastructure and DLT systems, and among two or more DLT systems in the ecosystem, as well as multi-asset transactional execution. Markets that are already mature in regulatory and institutional arrangements could also rethink tokenization to focus on scalability and broadening use cases. Stress-test frameworks could also be instituted to stem unnoticed and hidden risk augmentation, which characterizes tokenized transactions and hence, tokenized lending. Composability and programmability of DLT also imply complex relations among financial market elements and players. Such interrelations should be checked by regulatory checks and balances to avoid contagion and systemic shocks. DeFi and tokenized lending markets, like conventional financial markets, also warrant mitigants for liquidity and credit risks related to the given settlement asset deployed, misalignment in maturity and liquidity between reference assets and tokens, hypothecation and associated issues, among other fragilities.

Global Cross-Jurisdictional Comparison.

As mentioned earlier, international regulatory bodies diverge and vary across the various countries and jurisdictions as follows:

- International Organization for Securities Commissions (IOSCO) International Organization for Securities Commissions (IOSCO), as a global regulator-setter, adopts an results-oriented, principles-based method to identifying, assessing, and reducing risk. IOSCO aligns its present regulatory structure with major risks recognized in DeFi, by mapping its Standards to DeFi activities, products, arrangements, and services (IOSCO, 2023). FSB (2024) is advocating more governance to DeFi and introducing new regulations that will put more restrictions on tokenized lending firms; in terms of the type of collateral and leverage ration
- Canada In jurisdictions like Canada, for example, the Ontario Securities Commission (OSC) and the Canadian Securities Administrators (CSA) used a Securities-law supervision of CTPs and VRCAs via CSA Staff Notice 21-333 and refrains from using a digital sandbox. The Canadian regulator is introducing new regulations, relating to the supervision of cross—borders tokenized assets - with no clearly defined intermediaries (CSA, 2023).
- USA The U.S. Securities and Exchange Commission (U.S. SEC) is adopting a different enforcement-focused and agency driven approach compared to other jurisdictions (Gensler, 2023; U.S. Securities and Exchange Commission, 2024).
- Europe In contrast, the European Union (European Commission, 2020) adopts a MICA code-driven approach to the markets in crypto-assets regula-

tion to provide a more general oversight of digital asset activities by ESMA (2024).

- Asia Asian countries, such as Singapore, South Korea, and China, have recently worked together to introduce new blockchain and digital asset policies. The Monetary Authority of Singapore (MAS) took steps to lead the region and updated the Payment Services Act for digital assets in 2024.

Figure 2 sums up the regulatory discussion with a timeline of how regulatory and policy developments have unfolded in different jurisdictions from 2019 to 2024.

Figure 3. Regulatory and policy developments on digital assets

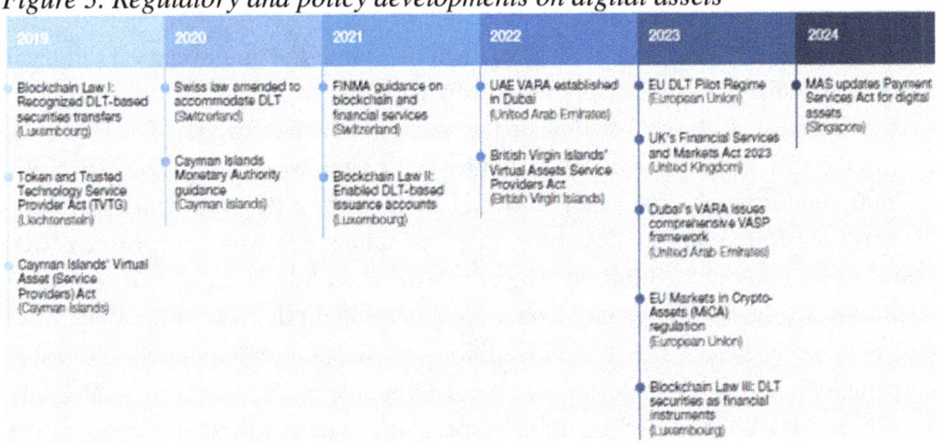

Source: WEF (2024)

6. RISK AND ETHICAL CONSIDERATIONS

Conventional financial products and markets harbour risks and ethical hazards, and so does the market for blockchain-based DeFi and tokenized lending. The difference persistently lies in the robust frameworks which exist in conventional markets for risk identification, trigger points and indicators and risk management. While liquidity and credit risks are usual suspects for financial markets, cybersecurity leads the pack of risk considerations in tokenization. The 2025 Bybit crypto exchange hack involving a $1.5 billion loss in ETH (cryptocurrency) is arguably the grandest theft in time related to crypto assets (Berkowitz, 2025).

Borrower profiling is another key consideration in tokenized lending; given that information asymmetry, adverse selection, and ultimately, credit default could stem from wrong, inadequate or poor borrower profiling. Kowsar and Mintoo

(2025) established from 29 studies that blockchain infrastructure could install decentralized and robust credit history infrastructure which delivers greater value than conventional credit bureaus. The greater value is found in enhanced accuracy, informal data inclusion, and reduced data breaches. However, most of the use cases in the reviewed studies featured pilot and not full-scale projects. This underscores the need for more work to be done on improving the perception of market players about the transparency and robustness of blockchain platforms. Poor perception is a grave risk hampering the growth of DeFi, tokenization generally, and tokenized lending specifically. Without an enhanced perception about tokenized assets and blockchain-based DeFi, the touted value proposition may not drive patronage and allay perceived risk. Instituting regulation could do much to improve market perception of DeFi and tokenization.

The uncertainty and want of clarity which surrounds the classification and legal status of tokenized assets, as opposed to conventional financial instruments, is also a risk which casts a gloomy shadow on the future of tokenized assets. The landmark case of the U.S. SEC versus Ripple captures this picture accurately. The U.S. SEC, in 2000, sued Ripples, a private firm which created the XRP cryptocurrency. Ripple was sued by the SEC in December 2020, in connection with unregistered XRP sales valued at about $1.3 billion. The courts ruled, in July 2023, classifying these institutional sales as unregistered securities, but upheld that exchange sales were registered securities. A fine of $125 million was slapped on Ripple who was also perpetually barred from undertaking unregistered institutional sales. The SEC and Ripple, in May 2025, withdrew their respective appeals of certain aspects of the court's decision, thereby bringing finality to the suit (Helms, 2025).

Contagion and concentration risks could be mitigated by creating access for micro players and emerging entrants to spur competition and redistribute liquidity and market power. Furthermore, composability should be applied in a fashion that limits wrapped asset creation in alignment with the risk profile of assets and the involved parties. Smart contract risks could also be curbed by employing thorough test mechanisms. Moreover, robust governance frameworks to safeguard the interest of all stakeholders is necessary, especially through an independent mediator in the event of disputes (WEF, 2025; FSB, 2024).

Ethical considerations include scrupulous data usage, privacy, the immutability of data, and the risk of exclusion which stems from the use of algorithms for decision making (Kowsar & Mintoo, 2025; Wamba & Queiroz, 2020). European economies such as Estonia, the Netherlands, and Switzerland have ridden on the back of General Data Protection Regulation (GDPR) and other policy aids to foster ethical and safe blockchain banking operations (Bhuiyan et al., 2024). The European Blockchain Services Infrastructure (EBSI) from the European commission has also spurred a regional wave of blockchain protocol harmonization ((Dasgupta & Islam, 2024).

South Korea, China, and Singapore have also led the way in blockchain and digital asset policy development in Asia (MAS, 2023).

7. DISRUPTIVE TENDENCIES

Disruptive tendencies that accrue from DeFi and tokenization cannot be overlooked. The order of financial systems, industries, and markets have been ruffled by the advent of tokenized transactions and DeFi. For example, independent third parties, usually, are missing in cases where financial intermediaries depend on permissionless blockchains for settlement, trading, and issuance of tokenised instruments. This implies that the burden of operational risk management associated with the infrastructure, in the absence of a third-party auditor, reverts to the financial intermediary. In the event of any major incident, the intermediary is faced with the option of either moving to an off-chain platform or another blockchain, which may be disruptive or just not viable (FSB, 2024).

DeFi and tokenized lending is set to disrupt the financial system from payment systems, banking, asset management, and insurance (Henriquez et al., 2019).

The gradual movement towards DeFi and tokenized lending borders on the disruption it creates through variables such transaction costs, process automation, information symmetry, collateralization, fractionalization, auditability, reconciliation costs and operational efficiency (Ciccio, 2024; Kassen, 2022). Disruption could reduce costs and increase efficiency, but this could also be offset by uncertainty, crashes in traditional financial markets, especially if regulation for mainstreaming the disruption is delayed or ignored.

Studies have pointed out the advent of blockchain message queues, adapters, and gateways which serve as facilitators to synchronize system interactions without the need for a complete architectural reinvention. API-driven models, for example, make interfacing scalable and modular-friendly, thereby permitting disruption-free interaction between enterprises and blockchain networks (Li et al., 2024; Alam et al., 2023; Mori, 2016). Oracle's Blockchain Cloud Service and IBM's Blockchain Platform have been cited as middleware tools supporting Hyperledger compatibility and REST APIs (Zachariadis et al., 2019). APIs support audit trails for transactions, real-time compliance enforcement, and data transformation. It is crucial to also acknowledge the potential latency and dependency risks, as well as performance bottlenecks which could loom from middleware layers, especially in financial ecosystems characterized by high frequency (Bin et al., 2023; Ivanov, 2022; Bünz et al., 2018).

8. FUTURE DIRECTIONS

Considering the enumerated constraints and potential disruptions for DeFi and tokenized lending, future platform configurations should consider robust hybrid models where traditional infrastructure and blockchain technology can co-exist. Greater collaboration among ecosystem players such as software manufacturers, platform builders, regulators and FIs should be promoted for compliance, fair play, transparency, and enhanced interoperability (Chang et al., 2019).

Closing information and data gaps in tokenized lending adoption is critical to provide the cushion and comfort market players desire. Reporting to a regulated entity is a key consideration for the future of accountability in tokenization markets. The issue of data also borders on privacy and security. Markets are usually considered safe, especially by institutional clients and high net-worth individuals, if safety, privacy and informational security are assured. Rapid developments in tokenization demands experience sharing and best-practice exchanges among national, global, and regional regulatory bodies with the view to developing pathways that work and help to address the operational and adoption challenges of tokenization and DeFi established in this chapter. Thus, information sharing on a cross-border basis among principal financial system players is a non-negotiable imperative. Regulatory sandboxes could be a vital starting point to undertake this daunting task (FSB, 2024).

The future outlook for financial institutions could witness a flurry of blockchain technologies being instituted for back-end activities, purposely to boost existing conventional infrastructure and improve overall user experience and robustness in a latent manner, thus not making the blockchain infrastructure visible to the final consumer (Ava Labs & Mastercard, 2024).

Decentralized insurance powered by blockchain has emerged on DeFi platforms such as Etherisc and Nexus Mutual. Smart contracts for risk pooling could be apt for managing (transferring) the risk associated with tokenized lending. Furthermore, parametric insurance has also been introduced on platforms such as Etherisc. The proximate cause associated with parametric insurance include climatic conditions or climate-induced losses (Singhal et al., 2024; Feng et al., 2024).

9. CONCLUSION

The main argument in this chapter is that the institutionalization of tokenized lending is a testament to the innovation, potential disruption of DeFi, and the resilience and continued importance of traditional financial institutions, theories, and regulations. The motivation for this dual perspective is driven by the observation that tokenized lending has evolved from being predominantly a retail-focused to one that is increasingly influenced by institutional investors, banks, and regulators. The financial intermediation theory is used to highlight how DeFi protocols and their native tokens replicate and redistribute the classic functions of financial intermediation, such as monitoring, liquidity creation, and risk sharing, as observed in traditional banking. Institutional theory is then used to show how regulatory, normative, and coercive pressures from the external environment are driving DeFi platforms towards permissioned and compliant models. Overall, the chapter contributes to three strands of literature. First, this is one of the first, if not the first, conceptual narratives of tokenized lending institutionalization across advanced economies. Second, it contributes to the regulatory divergence debate in highlighting what consequences such divergence might have on global market integration. Third, it enriches the systemic risk and trade-off discussions of which tokenized lending as an intersection of DeFi and traditional finance.

Tokenized lending is evolving from a decentralized credit experiment to a sector that is drawing increasing attention from regulated financial institutions, asset managers, and global banks, and more scrutiny by regulators across the world. This shift is being facilitated by permissioned protocols such as Aave Arc and Maple Finance, which are integrating various controls such as KYC, AML, and credit underwriting into DeFi protocols. This integration of controls into DeFi is a prime example of how DeFi infrastructure is evolving towards an interoperable system that is becoming more accessible to financial institutions.

Given the fragmented environment, tokenized lending is being shaped by divergent regulatory frameworks across the globe. In Canada, crypto-asset trading platforms have to register. The EU is working towards MiCA as a harmonized regulatory framework for the EU. The United States is taking an enforcement-led approach based on existing securities laws and regulations, and Singapore continues to innovate with Project Guardian. However, regulatory fragmentation could lead to regulatory arbitrage, and there is a need for coordination, not just between regulators and regulators but across regulators to develop a set of common baseline standards to ensure investor protection and system-wide consistency.

The growing involvement of regulated institutions is positive for the maturing tokenized lending sector, but several risks remain in tokenized lending markets. From an operational perspective, smart contract bugs and oracle manipulation, and in some cases, cross-protocol exposures, could result in systemic contagion risks. From a governance perspective, centralized governance with non-transparent practices and decentralized governance with very little checks and balances are two extremes in this maturing sector, which raises questions around accountability, long-term legitimacy, and financial stability. This complex dynamic between technology and governance underscores that technological design alone is not enough to provide resilience to the system, which means that regulation, market discipline, and governance are also crucial in the system.

The dynamics and evolution of the tokenized lending market provide both policymakers and institutions with the opportunity to learn from innovation and better understand how best to design policy and risk management frameworks that help to manage systemic risks while still allowing room for innovation. For regulators, the question is how to regulate, and for institutions, it is about how to better understand DeFi tools, including tokenized lending and other DeFi instruments, and use them while continuing to maintain transparency and efficiency as well as prudential oversight. Tokenized lending is an example of a highly innovative DeFi subsector that is an increasingly important part of the global financial system. The chapter aims to provide a better understanding of the evolution of tokenized lending and the interactions between DeFi and the traditional financial system, and what this means for the future of credit markets, regulation, and global financial stability.

REFERENCES

Accenture, Chainlink, & RWA.xyz. (2025, forthcoming). *Liquidity without borders: Why cross-chain interoperability matters.*

Alam, M. A., Sohel, A., Hossain, A., Eshra, S. A., & Mahmud, S. (2023). Medical imaging for early cancer diagnosis and epidemiology using artificial intelligence: Strengthening national healthcare frameworks in the USA. *American Journal of Scholarly Research and Innovation, 2*(1), 24–49. DOI: 10.63125/matthh09

Aldasoro, I., Cornelli, G., Frost, J., Koo W. P., & Shreeti, V. (2025). *Tokenisation of government bonds*, mimeo

Allen, F. (1990). The market for information and the origin of financial intermediation. *Journal of Financial Intermediation, 1*(1), 3–30. DOI: 10.1016/1042-9573(90)90006-2

Allen, F., & Santomero, A. M. (1998). The theory of financial intermediation. *Journal of Banking & Finance, 21*(11-12), 1461–1485. DOI: 10.1016/S0378-4266(97)00032-0

AMF. FMA, & CONSOB (2025). European crypto-asset markets' framework: proposals from the French, the Austrian, and the Italian financial markets authorities. Available at https://www.amf-france.org/sites/institutionnel/files/private/2025-09/final_amf-fma_conso b_mica-2-position-paper_clean-consob_logo.pdf

Association for Financial Markets in Europe (AFME) (2024). *Use of DLT and tokenisation in financial markets.*

Auer, R., Haslhofer, B., Kitzler, S., Saggese, P., & Friedhelm, V. (2023). *The technology of decentralized finance (DeFi).* Bank for International Settlements (BIS), Monetary and Economic Department, Working Papers, No. 1066

Ava Labs & Mastercard (2024). Asset tokenization: A comprehensive report and why you should start caring about the technology

Berkowitz, J. (2025, March 14). *The Bybit hack of 2025 - potential implications.* Paul Hastings. https://www.paulhastings.com/insights/crypto-policy-tracker/the-bybit-hack-of-2025-potential-implications

Bhuiyan, S. M. Y., Mostafa, T., Schoen, M. P., & Mahamud, R. (2024). Assessment of machine learning approaches for the predictive modeling of plasma-assisted ignition kernel growth. *ASME 2024 International Mechanical Engineering Congress and Exposition.* DOI: 10.1115/IMECE2024-145906

Bin, A. F., Kumar, R. P., & Majharul, I. M. (2023). AI-Powered predictive failure analysis in pressure vessels using real-time sensor fusion: Enhancing industrial safety and infrastructure reliability. *American Journal of Scholarly Research and Innovation*, *2*(2), 102–134. DOI: 10.63125/wk278c34

Braithwithe, C. (2025, June 25). What is private credit tokenization and how does it work? *Onchain*. Retrieved from https://onchain.org/magazine/what-is-private-credit-tokenization-and-how-does-it-work/

Bünz, B., Bootle, J., Boneh, D., Poelstra, A., Wuille, P., & Maxwell, G. (2018). Bulletproofs: Short proofs for confidential transactions and more. *2018 IEEE Symposium on Security and Privacy (SP)*, 315-334. DOI: 10.1109/SP.2018.00020

Canadian Securities Administrators. (2023). CSA Staff Notice 21-332: Crypto Asset Trading Platforms: Term and Conditions of Trading. Retrieved from https://www.securities-administrators.ca/news/csa-publishes-updated-approach-to-crypto-asset-trading-platforms/

Capponi, A., Iyengar, G., & Sethuraman, J. (2023). Decentralized finance: Protocols, risks, and governance. Foundations and Trends® in Privacy and Security, 5(3), 144-188. DOI: 10.1561/3300000036

Carstens, A. (2020). Shaping the Future of Payments. BIS Quarterly Review, March 2020, Available at *SSRN*: https://ssrn.com/abstract=3561177

Chang, Y., Iakovou, E., & Shi, W. (2019). Blockchain in global supply chains and cross border trade: A critical synthesis of the state-of-the-art, challenges and opportunities. *International Journal of Production Research*, *58*(7), 2082–2099. DOI: 10.1080/00207543.2019.1651946

Chiu, J., Koeppl, T., Yu, H., & Zhang, S. (2023). Understanding DEFI through the lens of a Production-Network model. Bank of Canada. DOI: 10.34989/swp-2023-42

Ciccio, C. D. (2024). *Blockchain and Distributed Ledger Technologies*. Cambridge University Press., DOI: 10.1017/9781009411783.003

Commodity Futures Trading Commission (CFTC). (2024, November 21). *CFTC's Global Markets Advisory Committee advances recommendation on tokenized non-cash collateral* [Press release]. https://www.cftc.gov/PressRoom/PressReleases/9009-24

Cornelli, G., Gambacorta, L., Garratt, R., & Reghezza, A. (2024). Decoding DeFi lending: Motivations, risks, and investor behaviours. CEPR. https://cepr.org/voxeu/columns/decoding-defi-lending-motivations-risks-and-investor-behaviours

Darlin, M., Palaiokrassas, G., & Tassiulas, L. (2022, September). Debt-financed collateral and stability risks in the defi ecosystem. In 2022 4th Conference on Blockchain Research & Applications for Innovative Networks and Services (BRAINS) (pp. 5-12). IEEE. DOI: 10.1109/BRAINS55737.2022.9909090

Dasgupta, A., Islam, M., Nahid, M., Omar, F., Rahmatullah, R. (2024). Engineering management perspectives on safety culture in chemical and petrochemical plants: A systematic review. *Academic Journal On Science, Technology, Engineering & Mathematics Education, 1*(1), 10.69593.

DeFi Rate. (2024). *Compare crypto lending rates.* Available at https://defirate.com/lend/

DeFiLlama. (n.d.) Total value locked (DeFi) all chains. *DeFiLlama.* Retrieved from https://defill ama.com/ chains

European Commission. (2020). *Proposal for a Regulation of the European Parliament and of the Council on Markets in Crypto-assets and amending Directive (EU) 2019/1937.* Retrieved from https://eur-lex.europa.eu/legal-content/EN/TXT/?uri=CELEX%3A52020PC0593

European Securities and Markets Authority. (n.d.). Markets in Crypto-Assets Regulation (MiCA). https://www.esma.europa.eu/esmas-activities/digital-finance-and-innovation/markets-crypto-assets-regulation-mica

Evans, D. (2024). Permissioned DeFi goes live with Aave Arc + Fireblocks. Fireblocks. https://www.fireblocks.com/blog/permissioned-defi-goes-live-with-aave-arc-fireblocks/#:~:text=We're%20excited%20to%20announce,active%20whitelister%20for%20the%20protocol

Finance, U. K. (2024, November). *Digital gilt roadmap 2024.* https://www.ukfinance.org.uk/system/files/2024-11/UK%20Finance%20Digital%20Gilt%20roadmap%202024.pdf

Financial Stability Board (FSB). (2024). *The financial stability implications of tokenization.* Financial Stability Board.

Gensler, G. (2023). You may have seen this before - Remarks before the Piper Sandler Global Exchange and FinTech Conference. U.S. Securities and Exchange Commission. https://www.sec.gov/newsroom/speeches-statements/gensler-remarks-piper-sandler-060823

Gogel, D., Baker-Taylor, T., Cloots, A. S., Forster, B., Gustave, J. L., Schär, F., & Sokolin, L. (2021). DeFi Beyond the Hype: The Emerging World of Decentralized Finance. Wharton Blockchain and Digital Asset Project, in collaboration with the World Economic Forum. https://wifpr.wharton.upenn.edu/wp-content/uploads/2021/05/DeFi-Beyond-the-Hype.pdf

Government of the Hong Kong Special Administrative Region (HKSAR). (2025, February 26). *The 2025–26 budget: Speech by the financial secretary*, the Hon Paul MP Chan. https://www.budget.gov.hk/2025/eng/pdf/e_budget_speech_2025-26.pdf

Helms, K. (2025, June 27). XRP legal saga concludes as Ripple withdraws appeal, SEC expected to follow. *Bitcoin*. Retrieved from https://news.bitcoin.com/xrp-legal-saga-concludes-as-ripple-withdraws-appeal-sec-expected-to-follow/

Henriquez, R., Cohen, I., Bittan, N., & Tulbassiyev, K. (2019). Blockchain and business model innovation: Designing a P2P mortgage lending system. SSRN *Electronic Journal*. DOI: 10.2139/ssrn.3371850

Hirshleifer, J. (1971). The private and social value of information and the reward to inventive activity. *The American Economic Review*, *61*(4), 561–574.

ImmuneBytes. (2024). Crypto hacks directory. *ImmuneBytes*. Retrieved from https://immunebyte s.com/blog/category/web3-security/crypto-hacks-directory/

International Organization of Securities Commissions (IOSCO). (2023, December). Final report with policy recommendations for decentralized finance (DeFi) (FR/14/2023). https://www.iosco.org/library/pubdocs/pdf/IOSCOPD753.pdf

International Securities Services Association (ISSA). (2023, July). *DLT in the real world survey 2023 – key findings*. https://issanet.org/content/uploads/2023/07/DLT-in-the-Real-World-2023_Survey-Key-Findings.pdf

Ivanov, D. (2022). The industry 5.0 framework: Viability-based integration of the resilience, sustainability, and human-centricity perspectives. *International Journal of Production Research*, *61*(5), 1683–1695. DOI: 10.1080/00207543.2022.2118892

Kassen, M. (2022). Blockchain and e-government innovation: Automation of public information processes. *Information Systems*, 103, 101862. https://doi.org/. 101862DOI: 10.1016/j.is.2021

Kaur, G. (2024, December 11). What are tokenized debt instruments? A beginner's guide. *Cointelegraph*. Retrieved from https://cointelegraph.com/learn/articles/what-are-tokenized -debt-instruments

Kowsar, M. M., & Mintoo, A. A. (2025). Blockchain in banking: A review of distributed ledger applications in loan processing, credit history, and compliance. *American Journal of Scholarly Research and Innovation*, *4*(1), 101–138. DOI: 10.63125/gp61va54

La Salla, F. (2024, January 16). *Why standards and controls are essential to the future offinancial assets.* World Economic Forum. https://www.weforum.org/stories/2024/01/digital-financia l-markets-developing-standards-controlsdavos24/

Ledger Insights. (2024, November 26). EIB issues second €100m digital bond in a week using wCBDC. *Ledgerinsights.* https://www.ledgerinsights.com/eib-issues-second-e100m-digital -bond-in-a-week-using-wcbdc/

Leland, H. E., & Pyle, D. H. (1977). Informational asymmetries, financial structure and financial intermediation. *The Journal of Finance*, *32*(2), 371–387. DOI: 10.2307/2326770

Li, M.-Y., Jiang, Z.-H., & Wang, L. (2024). Grain storage security in context of government digital governance: A tripartite evolutionary game analysis of speculative behavior. *Kybernetes.* Advance online publication. DOI: 10.1108/K-12-2023-2670

Mandin, J. (2025, March 21). *Risk free uncollateralized lending in decentred markets.* https://www.bankofcanada.ca/wp-content/uploads/2025/03/sdp2025-6.pdf

Monetary Authority of Singapore. (2023). MAS partners financial industry to expand asset tokenisation initiatives. https://www.mas.gov.sg/news/media-releases/2023/mas-partners-financial-industry-to-expand-asset-tokenisation-initiatives

Mori, T. (2016). Financial technology: Blockchain and securities settlement. *Journal of Securities Operations & Custody*, *8*(3), 208. DOI: 10.69554/YEJN7450

Munir, K. A. (2015). A loss of power in institutional theory. *Journal of Management Inquiry*, *24*(1), 90–92. DOI: 10.1177/1056492614545302

OECD. (2022). Institutionalisation of crypto-assets and DeFi–TradFi interconnectedness. OECD. https://www.oecd.org/en/publications/institutionalisation-of-crypto-assets-and-defi-tradfi-interconnectedness_5d9dddbe-en.html

Official Monetary and Financial Institutions Forum (OMFIF). (2025). *Global public investor 2025.* London.

Orchard, J., & Voloder, E. (2025, October 6). European regulators jostle for control of MiCA. *OMFIF.* Retrieved from https://www.omfif.org/2025/10/european-regulators-jostle-for-contro l-of-mica/?mc_cid=d482b2a27d&mc_eid=1fd274c085

Ozili, P. K. (2023). Institutional theory of financial inclusion. (Munich Personal RePEc Archive Paper No. 115770). Retrieved from https://mpra.ub.uni-muenchen.de/115770/

Peters, B. G. (2022). Institutional theory. In *Handbook on Theories of Governance*. Edward Elgar Publishing. DOI: 10.4337/9781800371972.00039

Qin, K., Zhou, L., Gamito, P., Jovanovic, P., & Gervais, A. (2021, November). An empirical study of defi liquidations: Incentives, risks, and instabilities. In *Proceedings of the 21st ACM internet measurement conference* (pp. 336-350). DOI: 10.1145/3487552.3487811

Redman, J. (2025, June 19). Blockchain lending boom: Tokenized private credit nears $14 billion. *Bitcoin.* Retrieved from https://news.bitcoin.com/blockchain-lending-boom-tokenized-priv ate-credit-nears-14-billion/

Saengchote, K. (2023). Decentralized lending and its users: Insights from Compound. *Journal of Banking & Finance*, *151*, 106839. DOI: 10.1016/j.jbankfin.2023.106839

Schär, F. (2021). Decentralized finance: On blockchain- and smart contract-based financial markets. *Review - Federal Reserve Bank of St. Louis*, *103*(2), 153–174. DOI: 10.20955/r.103.153-74

Scott, W. R. (2005). Institutional theory: Contributing to a theoretical research program. *Great Minds in Management: The Process of Theory Development*, *37*(2), 460–484. DOI: 10.1093/oso/9780199276813.003.0022

Solulab (2025). *Top DeFi Lending Platforms in 2025.* Available at https://www.solulab.com/top-defi-lending-platforms/

S&P Global. (2024). *Tokenized Private Credit: A New Digital Frontier for Real World Assets*. Retrieved from https://www.spglobal.com/en/research-insights/special-reports/tokenized-private-credit

Suddaby, R. (2010). Challenges for institutional theory. *Journal of Management Inquiry*, *19*(1), 14–20. DOI: 10.1177/1056492609347564

Swift. (n.d.). Unlocking the potential of digital asset securities. Retrieved April 14, 2025, from https://www.swift.com/campaign/unlocking-potential-digital-asset-securities

Tanveer, U., Ishaq, S., & Hoang, T. G. (2025). Tokenized assets in a decentralized economy: Balancing efficiency, value, and risks. *International Journal of Production Economics*, *282*, 109554. DOI: 10.1016/j.ijpe.2025.109554

U.S. Securities and Exchange Commission. (2024, January 10). *Order approving the application for the ProShares Bitcoin Strategy ETF.* Retrieved from https://www.sec.gov/news/press-release/2024-6

Wamba, S. F., & Queiroz, M. M. (2020). Blockchain in the operations and supply chain management: Benefits, challenges and future research opportunities. *International Journal of Information Management*, 52, 102064. https://doi.org/. ijinfomgt.2019.102064DOI: 10.1016/j

Wang, D., Wu, S., Lin, Z., Wu, L., Yuan, X., Zhou, Y., Wang, H., & Ren, K. (2021). Towards a first step to understand flash loan and its applications in DeFi ecosystem, *Proceedings from Ninth International Workshop on Security in Blockchain and Cloud Computing* (pp. 22-28). DOI: 10.1145/3457977.3460301

Willmott, H. (2015). Why institutional theory cannot be critical. *Journal of Management Inquiry*, *24*(1), 105–111. DOI: 10.1177/1056492614545306

World Economic Forum (WEF). (2025). *Asset tokenization in financial markets: The next generation of value exchange.* Cologny, Switzerland

Wyman, O., De Lima, L., Ekberg, J., Ho, M., & Hung, T. (n.d.). It's Time to Explore Institutional DeFi. Oliver Wyman Forum. https://www.oliverwymanforum.com/future-of-money/2022/Nov/institutional-defi.html

Zachariadis, M., Hileman, G., & Scott, S. V. (2019). Governance and control in distributed ledgers: Understanding the challenges facing blockchain technology in financial services. *Information and Organization*, *29*(2), 105–117. DOI: 10.1016/j.infoandorg.2019.03.001

Zeiß, C., Schaschek, M., Straub, L., Tomitza, C., & Winkelmann, A. (2024). Re-intermediation of the crypto asset ecosystem by banks: An empirical study on acceptance drivers among the populace. *Electronic Markets*, *34*(1), 37. DOI: 10.1007/s12525-024-00720-4

Chapter 5
Tokenization of Real-World Assets:
Theoretical and Practical Perspectives

Honnur Md Thazuddin
https://orcid.org/0009-0006-2491-4730
Dayananda Sagar College of Engineering, India

Vinod Krishna Makkimane
https://orcid.org/0009-0009-5150-3701
Dayananda Sagar College of Engineering, India

ABSTRACT

The tokenization of real-world assets (RWAs) is increasingly recognized as a significant application of blockchain technology, with transformative implications for ownership structures, liquidity, and investment accessibility. This chapter presents a descriptive and interdisciplinary study that examines both the theoretical foundations and practical applications of asset tokenization. It identifies key gaps in existing literature and practice, including regulatory uncertainty, limited infrastructure integration, and underrepresentation of developing economies. Guided by these gaps, the research aims to evaluate conceptual frameworks, analyse real-world implementations through case studies, and provide insights into the benefits, challenges, and future directions of tokenized ecosystems. By offering a comprehensive academic and policy-oriented perspective, the chapter seeks to support efforts to align innovation with regulation and promote global inclusivity in digital asset markets.

DOI: 10.4018/979-8-3373-3371-7.ch005

1. INTRODUCTION

Tokenization refers to the digital representation of real-world assets (RWAs) on a blockchain or distributed ledger. It enables the division of ownership of an asset into tradable digital units, commonly known as tokens. Whether applied to real estate, commodities, debt instruments, or intellectual property, tokenization allows assets to become more accessible, divisible, and liquid. These characteristics position tokenization as a disruptive force in traditional finance and a foundational element in the evolution of decentralized finance (DeFi).

The global interest in tokenization has accelerated over the past five years, driven by advancements in distributed ledger technologies (DLT), increased institutional experimentation, and the potential to streamline asset issuance and transfer. Policymakers and regulators are gradually acknowledging this shift. For instance, the European Union's DLT Pilot Regime, Switzerland's legal recognition of tokenized securities, and India's IFSCA guidelines for FinTech entities reflect regional efforts to craft enabling legal and infrastructural environments for tokenized assets (World Economic Forum, 2020; IFSCA, 2023; Zetzsche et al., 2020).

Despite this momentum, critical uncertainties remain. Regulatory fragmentation, lack of legal enforceability, technological interoperability, and limited inclusion of emerging economies are persistent issues. Furthermore, existing research often treats tokenization from either a purely technical or financial angle, without integrating socio-legal, institutional, and governance considerations.

This chapter seeks to address these gaps by offering a comprehensive academic investigation of tokenization from theoretical, empirical, and policy standpoints. The research is guided by the following objectives:

- To examine the conceptual foundations and classification of tokenized assets;
- To evaluate the technical infrastructure enabling tokenization and its limitations;
- To analyze real-world case studies across sectors and jurisdictions;
- To identify the benefits and challenges of tokenization as a financial innovation;
- To propose policy recommendations and outline future research directions.

Methodologically, the chapter adopts a qualitative, exploratory approach rooted in embedded case study analysis. Eight global use cases are examined across real estate, trade finance, public infrastructure, and commodities. By integrating academic theory, technological design, and practical experience, the chapter aims to support a broader understanding of how tokenization may evolve from a speculative innovation into a mainstream mechanism for global capital formation.

Guided by these gaps, the research aims to evaluate conceptual frameworks, analyze real-world implementations through case studies, and provide insights into the benefits, challenges, and future directions of tokenized ecosystems. By offering a comprehensive academic and policy-oriented perspective, the chapter seeks to support efforts to align innovation with regulation and promote global inclusivity in digital asset markets.

2.1 DEFINITION AND SCOPE

Tokenization, in the context of blockchain and distributed ledger technologies (DLT), refers to the process of digitally representing ownership or rights over a real-world asset (RWA) as a unique cryptographic token.

These tokens can be transferred, stored or exchanged on the blockchain network, which enables rapid and more transparent asset management at boundaries (International Monetary Fund [IMF], 2021; World Economic Forum, 2020). Unlike traditional digitization, where assets are represented in centralized databases or scanned documents, the token takes advantage of the irreversibility, program and decentralization of the blockchain system. Each token acts as a partial or full asset as a cryptographic and legally structured stand-in, and can embed rights such as ownership, income distribution, governance, governance, or utility access (bank [BIS], 2022) for international settlements. The scope of the token is the expander and it continues. Property for tokens usually comes in two broad categories: • Tangible property: These include physical property such as real estate, infrastructure, goods (eg, gold, oil) and fine arts. For example, a commercial building can be divided into 100,000 tokens, each property represents a proportional share in income or value.

Intangible Assets:

These encompass financial instruments (e.g., bonds, equities, receivables), intellectual property, carbon credits, or structured finance products. These are frequently tokenized to boost capital market accessibility, boost liquidity, and streamline compliance procedures.

Depending on the technical framework and the jurisdiction, tokenized assets may have different structures. Nonetheless, the tokenization procedure is typically defined by three crucial components:

1. Legal Structuring: Outlining the token's rights and guaranteeing their enforceability under the law. To manage off-chain claims, this involves establishing custodial contracts, trusts, or Special Purpose Vehicles (SPVs).

2. Smart contracts: These lessen the need for manual administration by encoding the logic of ownership, transfer restrictions, payment flows, and governance (Catalini & Gans, 2016).
3. Custodianship and Oracles: Systems for safely connecting off-chain assets with on-chain tokens. These could be real-world data feeds (oracles) or regulated custodians.

The most significant effects of tokenization occur when it allows:
Fractional ownership lowers the required minimum investment.

- 24/7 Market Access: Via decentralized exchanges or regulated digital marketplaces.
- Cross-border Interoperability: Reducing settlement delays and fees.

However, as the IMF (2021) and FATF (2022) note, tokenized assets must be distinguished from cryptocurrencies. Cryptocurrencies (e.g., Bitcoin) are native digital assets with no underlying claim, while tokenized RWAs represent legal rights to off-chain value. This distinction has implications for regulatory classification, taxation, and investor protection.

Thus, tokenization must be viewed not merely as a technological innovation, but as a multidimensional reconfiguration of ownership rights, market access, and legal accountability. It is not the digitization of finance—it is the financialization of digital space.

2.2 Technical Infrastructure

The technical infrastructure supporting the tokenization of real-world assets (RWAs) is composed of several interlocking components across blockchain protocol layers, token design standards, custody arrangements, identity solutions, and application interfaces. These components work together as the foundation for asset exchange, compliance automation, and decentralized ownership.

Fundamentally, tokenization relies on distributed ledger technology (DLT), which guarantees participant synchronization, transparency, and immutability. The three most popular DLT networks—Ethereum, Polygon, and Hyperledger Fabric—offer different degrees of transaction throughput, scalability, and decentralization (Pinna & Ruttenberg, 2016).

Crucial Elements of the Tokenization Stack

1. The Protocol Layer Blockchain platforms that verify and log transactions make up this foundational layer. While permissioned chains (like R3 Corda, Hyperledger) offer customizable access control and are preferred by financial institutions, public chains (like Ethereum) offer transparency and openness.
2. Standard Tokens Protocol-specific templates are used to standardize the functionality of tokens:

   ERC-20 refers to fungible tokens, such as tokenized equity, that have the same value units.

   - ERC-721 and ERC-1155: Non-fungible token (NFT) standards used for unique, indivisible assets (e.g., real estate deeds, artwork).
   - ERC-1400: A security token standard that embeds regulatory compliance, transfer restrictions, and identity requirements into the token contract (Tokeny, 2022). By ensuring interoperability, these standards allow tokens to function across custodial platforms, wallets, and exchanges.
3. Contracts with smart features The logic controlling asset ownership, transfer terms, dividend payments, and compliance procedures are carried out by smart contracts. These contracts improve auditability while reducing operational risk and human intervention (Catalini & Gans, 2016). However, as demonstrated by previous exploits (such as the DAO hack in 2016), smart contracts are susceptible to bugs and logical errors. Applications involving high-value tokens require formal audit and verification frameworks (Finck, 2018).
4. Linking Custody and Off-chain Custody continues to be a hybrid function for tokenized RWAs. The underlying asset (such as a gold reserve or real estate title) needs to be secured off-chain by a custodian even though tokens are on-chain. The following are examples of custody models:
   - Direct Custody: Regulated entities issue and hold the asset
   - Smart Custody: Multi-signature wallets and escrow arrangements managed by smart contracts.
   - Oracles: Trusted data feeds that confirm off-chain events (e.g., payment received, court judgment) for on-chain execution. Linking tokens to real-world legal claims is technically and legally complex. Without secure and trustworthy custodianship, the integrity of the tokenized asset system may be compromised.
5. Compliance and Identity Infrastructure Tokenization platforms integrate Know-Your-Customer (KYC), Anti-Money Laundering (AML), and sanctions screening into their issuance and transfer systems. Identity frameworks such as Decentralized Identifiers (DIDs) and Verifiable Credentials (VCs) are increas-

ingly used to facilitate compliant, privacy-preserving identity checks (World Bank, 2020).

Protocols like Chainalysis, Tether's TRM Labs, and Fireblocks provide institutional-grade monitoring of transactions and on-chain behaviour to mitigate financial crime risk.

6. Cybersecurity and Operational Resilience As tokenization platforms become more closely integrated with mainstream financial activity, cybersecurity and operational resilience emerge as core design requirements rather than peripheral add-ons. In addition to traditional credit, market, and legal risks, tokenized systems introduce exposure to smart contract flaws, key-management failures, oracle manipulation, and vulnerabilities in the underlying ledger protocols. Incidents in adjacent digital asset markets demonstrate that exploited contract logic, compromised private keys, or inaccurate data feeds can quickly translate into financial losses, service disruptions, and reputational damage.

Smart contracts, which automate issuance, compliance checks, cash-flow distribution, and governance processes, are particularly sensitive points of failure. Their deterministic execution and persistence on-chain make it difficult to correct errors once contracts are deployed, especially when assets are widely held. For high-value or regulated tokenized instruments, this reality strengthens the case for formal code review, independent security audits, and, in some contexts, carefully designed upgrade or circuit-breaker mechanisms that permit controlled intervention during emergencies. The challenge lies in enhancing safety without undermining legal certainty or contradicting expectations around transparent, rules-based execution.

Operational resilience extends beyond code security to encompass custody operations, infrastructure management, and business continuity planning. Platforms must define how underlying assets and digital keys are safeguarded, what happens when service providers fail, and how systems recover from outages or cyberattacks. Questions around insurance coverage, segregation of duties, and regulatory notification in incident scenarios link tokenization to broader debates on critical financial market infrastructures. Over time, key tokenization platforms may be expected to meet resilience standards similar to those applied to exchanges, central securities depositories, or payment systems

Challenges in Technical Implementation

Despite advancements, tokenization infrastructure faces several roadblocks:

- Interoperability: Cross-chain token mobility remains limited, often locking liquidity in isolated ecosystems (Pinna & Ruttenberg, 2016).
- Scalability: Many public blockchains suffer from congestion and high fees during periods of peak activity.
- Security Risks: Smart contract vulnerabilities and key management failures remain persistent.
- Legacy Integration: Interfacing token platforms with traditional finance systems (e.g., SWIFT, clearinghouses) is incomplete.

Emerging solutions include:

- Cross-chain bridges (e.g., Polkadot, Cosmos) for interoperability,
- Zero-Knowledge Proofs (ZKPs) for privacy-preserving compliance,
- Regulatory nodes for supervisory oversight in real-time

2.3 Classification of Tokens

Token classification is essential for understanding the legal, technical, and functional characteristics of digital assets. Proper classification informs regulatory treatment, investor rights, technological standards, and the design of secondary markets. However, the absence of a globally unified taxonomy continues to create ambiguity, especially where tokens straddle multiple functions (Zetzsche et al., 2020; FATF, 2021).

This section categorizes tokens based on their purpose, structure, and regulatory implications, using frameworks from the Financial Action Task Force (FATF), International Monetary Fund (IMF), and European Securities and Markets Authority (ESMA).

1. Security Tokens

Security tokens represent traditional financial instruments issued in tokenized form—such as equity shares, debt instruments, or revenue-sharing claims. These tokens often fall under the definition of "securities" in most jurisdictions and are subject to applicable laws such as the U.S. Securities Act or the EU's Markets in Financial Instruments Directive (MiFID II) (SEC, 2020; ESMA, 2022).

Key features:

- Backed by off-chain legal claims or contractual rights.
- Require regulatory compliance (e.g., KYC/AML, prospectus).
- Often issued via Security Token Offerings (STOs).

Examples include tokenized equity of a startup, tokenized bonds, and income-linked tokens.

2. Utility Tokens

Utility tokens provide access to a platform, product, or service. They do not generally confer ownership or profit rights and are often used for network participation (e.g., governance, staking) or access to digital content.

Key features:

- Non-investment in nature (but may still be speculative).
- Common in blockchain projects and ICOs.
- May fall under consumer protection laws, not securities regulation.

However, many utility tokens have economic features similar to securities, leading regulators (e.g., SEC and FCA) to apply the "Howey Test" or similar standards to determine their true nature (SEC, 2020).

3. Payment Tokens

Also referred to as cryptocurrencies, payment tokens function as a medium of exchange, unit of account, or store of value. Examples include Bitcoin (BTC), Litecoin (LTC), and stablecoins like USDC or USDT.

Key features:

- No underlying asset or issuer (in most cases).
- Used primarily for value transfer and settlement.
- Subject to AML/CFT laws but not usually securities laws.

Stablecoins—especially those backed by fiat reserves—have come under increasing scrutiny for systemic risk potential, with ongoing regulatory proposals worldwide (BIS, 2022).

4. Asset-Backed Tokens

These tokens are collateralized by off-chain assets—such as gold, real estate, or agricultural commodities. Each token represents a claim to a specific quantity or share of the asset held in reserve.

Key features:

- Require robust custody and audit mechanisms.
- Must have clear legal enforceability to prevent misrepresentation.
- Used for fractional ownership, diversification, or inflation hedging.

Examples: Paxos Gold (PAXG), tokenized REITs, and commodity-backed instruments.

5. Non-Fungible Tokens (NFTs)

NFTs are unique, indivisible tokens that represent ownership of specific assets—digital or physical. While widely used in art and gaming, NFTs are increasingly being explored for title deeds, patents, and property registries.

Key features:

- Immutable ownership proof.
- Metadata includes details of the underlying asset.
- Governance challenges around royalties, metadata storage, and permanence.

NFTs may fall under different legal classifications depending on their structure and use case (Finck, 2021).

Hybrid Tokens and Classification Challenges

Many tokens blur the boundaries between categories. For instance:

- A token may provide governance rights (utility), yield (security), and access (utility) simultaneously.
- Cross-jurisdictional offerings create multiple regulatory burdens.
- Some tokens evolve in function post-issuance ("function creep").

To mitigate confusion, regulators and scholars recommend applying a function-based or activity-based analysis, where the use case, economic intent, and issuer role define the regulatory status (FATF, 2021; Zetzsche et al., 2019).

2.4 Theoretical Frameworks

Tokenization of real-world assets intersects multiple academic disciplines, including financial economics, institutional theory, legal studies, and technology adoption.

To understand the drivers, constraints, and transformative potential of tokenization, it is essential to ground the analysis in established theoretical frameworks.

The study is framed by four conceptual lenses, which are presented in this section:

Financial Market Infrastructure Theory, Institutional Theory, Technology Adoption Models, and Property Rights Theory.

The Theory of Property Rights

According to property rights theory, when ownership rights are well-defined, transferable, and enforceable, economic efficiency is maximized (Coase, 1960; Demsetz, 1967). Tokenization essentially reorganizes the recording, trading, and enforcement of rights to tangible and intangible assets.

Traditional systems use centralized organizations (like stock exchanges and land registries) to manage rights; tokenization suggests a distributed model in which ownership is encoded in code and verified by consensus procedures. This change enables fractionalization without compromising enforceability, lowers transaction costs and dependency on middlemen, and adds programmability to rights (e.g., conditional access, auto-payment) (BIS, 2022).

However, in order to without legal infrastructure and dispute resolution mechanisms, tokenized ownership risks becoming economically and socially fragile (De Filippi & Wright, 2018).

2. Institutional Theory

Institutional theory explores how social structures, norms, and formal rules shape organizational behavior and adoption of innovation (Scott, 2001). The rise of tokenized systems challenges institutional norms in financial regulation, governance, and infrastructure.

Key insights include:

- Institutional Isomorphism: Traditional financial actors (banks, funds, custodians) may mimic early adopters of tokenization to maintain legitimacy, even without full understanding or capacity (DiMaggio & Powell, 1983).
- Path Dependency: Regulatory and infrastructural inertia may delay tokenization despite evident efficiencies.
- Legitimacy Gaps: Blockchain-native institutions may struggle to earn trust from investors or regulators due to non-traditional governance models.

  Adoption of tokenized systems will depend not just on technical capability but on alignment with institutional expectations, risk perceptions, and existing power structures (North, 1990).

3. Technology Adoption Models

Technology adoption theories such as the Technology Acceptance Model (TAM) and Diffusion of Innovation (DOI) provide behavioral insights into why and how individuals and institutions adopt new technologies (Davis, 1989; Rogers, 2003).

Key variables include:

- Perceived Usefulness: Tokenization must offer tangible benefits over traditional systems—such as liquidity, transparency, or access.
- Perceived Ease of Use: Complexity of custody, key management, or compliance may hinder adoption.
- Relative Advantage: Institutional actors compare new systems to legacy ones across cost, speed, and risk.

The rate of adoption is also influenced by external factors like regulatory support, network effects, and availability of infrastructure. Early adopters often operate in regulatory sandboxes or under specific legal exemptions (Arner et al., 2017).

4. Financial Market Infrastructure (FMI) Theory

FMI theory focuses on the systems that enable securities clearing, settlement, and custody. Tokenization represents a new layer of infrastructure-as-code, where smart contracts replace post-trade operations and regulatory compliance is embedded on-chain (Pinna & Ruttenberg, 2016).

Tokenized ecosystems challenge existing FMI models in three ways:

- Decentralization: Removes central counterparties and introduces peer-to-peer settlement.
- Real-Time Operations: Eliminates traditional settlement delays (T+2/T+3).
- Programmable Compliance: Automates issuer and investor obligations through smart contracts (e.g., dividend payments, cap table management).

The integration of tokenized systems into existing FMIs (e.g., SWIFT, Euroclear) remains under development. Hybrid models may evolve where traditional systems validate, host, or integrate blockchain-based instruments under regulatory oversight.

2.4.5 Game Theory and Network Effects

Game theory provides a lens for analyzing strategic interactions in tokenized ecosystems (Von Neumann & Morgenstern, 1944). Issuers, investors, and validators engage in cooperative or competitive behaviors, where trust in smart contracts or oracles determines outcomes. For example, Centrifuge's Tinlake pools align incentives by assigning higher risks to junior tranche (TIN) holders to attract conservative senior (DROP) investors, resembling a Stackelberg model. Misaligned incentives, such as oracle manipulation, could destabilize trust, as seen in early DeFi exploits (Finck, 2018).

Network effects theory suggests that tokenized platforms gain value as user participation grows (Katz & Shapiro, 1985). Increased adoption, as observed in Ondo Finance's DeFi integrations, enhances liquidity and reduces transaction costs. However, interoperability challenges, such as Ethereum's high gas fees, can limit scalability (Pinna & Ruttenberg, 2016). Research is needed to design governance models that balance cooperation and competition while ensuring cross-platform compatibility. This framework highlights tokenization's potential to reshape market dynamics, provided incentives and network structures are robustly aligned.

2.5 Identified Research Gaps

Despite increasing scholarly and industry attention, the literature on tokenization remains fragmented and nascent. While technological frameworks, pilot implementations, and high-level regulatory commentaries are available, systematic research addressing the legal, institutional, and developmental dimensions of tokenization is limited. This section identifies five key areas where further inquiry is urgently needed.

1. Legal Enforceability and Recognition

Tokenized rights often lack clear legal status in most jurisdictions. While some regions, such as Switzerland and Liechtenstein, have provided legal recognition for tokenized securities, most countries still treat tokenized assets as experimental or undefined under current legal codes (Zetzsche et al., 2020; De Filippi & Wright, 2018).

Research Gap: How can legal systems be updated to ensure that tokenized claims are enforceable in courts, particularly in cross-border contexts?

2. Regulatory Coordination and Standardization

Current regulation of tokenized assets varies widely across jurisdictions. Disparate classifications (security vs. commodity vs. utility), conflicting disclosure requirements, and overlapping jurisdictions create uncertainty for issuers and investors

(FATF, 2021; SEC, 2020). The lack of unified regulatory taxonomies and standards also hinders international adoption.

Research Gap: What role can global institutions (e.g., IOSCO, BIS, IMF) play in developing harmonized regulatory standards for tokenized markets?

3. Technological Interoperability and Infrastructure Gaps

Blockchain platforms used for tokenization are often siloed, with limited cross-chain interoperability. Legacy financial infrastructure (e.g., SWIFT, DTCC) is not yet fully integrated with tokenization platforms. As a result, liquidity is fragmented, settlement is delayed, and institutional trust remains limited (Pinna & Ruttenberg, 2016).

Research Gap: What technological and governance models can bridge the gap between blockchain-based token ecosystems and existing financial infrastructure?

4. Underrepresentation of Emerging Markets

Most tokenization initiatives and studies are concentrated in developed economies, despite the potential benefits for financial inclusion and infrastructure funding in emerging markets (World Bank, 2020). There is little empirical research on the conditions needed for tokenization to succeed in low-income settings.

Research Gap: How can tokenization be adapted for use in emerging and developing economies with limited legal, technical, and institutional capacity?

5. Longitudinal Performance and Risk Assessment

There is limited empirical evidence on the long-term financial performance, volatility, default risk, and investor behavior related to tokenized assets. Most existing analyses are based on pilot projects, anecdotal data, or simulation models (Catalini & Gans, 2016). Without rigorous data, regulators and institutional investors face uncertainty about adoption.

Research Gap: What are the long-term risk-return profiles, liquidity dynamics, and market behaviors associated with tokenized asset classes?

2.6 Recent Empirical Developments (2023–2025)

Since the initial wave of conceptual and pilot-oriented studies, tokenization has begun to generate a richer empirical record across jurisdictions and asset classes. New reports by international institutions and industry bodies document gradual but steady growth in tokenized markets, especially in short-term government securities, money-market instruments, real estate, and gold. These studies show that many projects now operate within formal sandboxes or tailored regulatory frameworks, rather than purely experimental environments, marking a shift from proof-of-concept pilots toward more institutionalized deployments.

The emerging data also highlight several cross-cutting trends. Institutional investors and regulated intermediaries feature prominently in larger pilots and early production systems, often in partnership with specialized technology providers and public authorities. Interoperability between tokenized assets and existing financial market infrastructures is becoming a central concern, reflected in experiments that link DLT platforms to central securities depositories, payment rails, and central bank digital currency (CBDC) testbeds. Comparative evidence suggests that jurisdictions offering clear legal recognition of tokenized securities together with structured sandbox regimes are seeing more persistent experimentation than those relying on informal guidance alone.

These developments reinforce the research gaps identified above. Longitudinal data remain limited, particularly on risk–return profiles, default behaviour, and secondary-market liquidity for tokenized instruments. However, the newer empirical work provides an important bridge between theory and practice by grounding discussions of legal design, infrastructure choices, and governance models in observed patterns of usage and adoption

3. METHODOLOGICAL APPROACH

This chapter adopts a qualitative, exploratory multiple case study design to investigate the implementation and impact of tokenization of real-world assets (RWAs) across different asset classes and regulatory environments. The method is selected to provide a rich, contextual understanding of tokenization as a socio-technical and legal phenomenon, in contrast to purely quantitative performance metrics. The framework emphasizes thematic depth, case diversity, and variable-pattern identification.

3.1 Research Design

The research employs an embedded multiple case study approach (Yin, 2018), analyzing eight distinct tokenization projects across sectors such as real estate, infrastructure, SME finance, commodities, and sovereign public goods. This design enables within-case and cross-case analysis while accounting for sectoral and jurisdictional variation. The guiding research question is:

What are the key regulatory, institutional, and technical variables shaping the outcomes of tokenized real-world asset implementations across different geographies and asset classes?

Theoretical grounding is drawn from:

- Property Rights Theory (Coase, 1960; Demsetz, 1967)
- Institutional Theory (Scott, 2001)
- Technology Adoption Models (Davis, 1989; Rogers, 2003)
- Financial Infrastructure Theory (Pinna & Ruttenberg, 2016)

These frameworks inform both variable selection and the interpretation of observed outcomes.

3.2 Case Selection Criteria

Cases were selected using purposive sampling with the goal of maximizing diversity in geography, asset type, governance model, and regulatory structure. Inclusion criteria:

- Must involve a real-world, asset-backed tokenization (not native crypto assets),
- The project must have a clearly defined legal or operational structure (e.g., whitepapers, SPV documents),
- It must have some form of regulatory engagement (sandbox, approval, or exemption),
- Public documentation should exist to support triangulation.

Selected cases include: Aspen Coin (USA), SCCF–Taurus (Switzerland), ReitBZ (Brazil), Ondo Finance (USA), Centrifuge (Global), Digibrixx (Europe), Belt and Road Hydropower (China), and HSBC Digital Gold (UK).

3.3 Data Collection and Ryzer Integration

The study relies on secondary qualitative data from:

- Whitepapers, technical documentation, and platform websites,
- Regulatory filings and legal summaries,
- Academic papers and policy briefs,
- Media articles and institutional interviews,
- Project dashboards and audited performance reports.

Each case was validated through triangulation to ensure reliability of evidence. Additionally, Ryzer, a real-time financial intelligence and analytics platform, was used to gather structured insights from public announcements, developer updates, and regulatory communications. This tool played a supporting role in identifying sentiment trends, institutional responses, and compliance shifts for tokenization projects—particularly Ondo Finance, Centrifuge, and Digibrixx.

3.4 Analytical Framework: Variables and Relationships

To structure the analysis, the study defines a set of independent and dependent variables derived from theory and case context. While no statistical testing is performed, the relationships are explored qualitatively through pattern matching and cross-case synthesis (Miles & Huberman, 1994).

Independent Variables (IVs):

- Regulatory Environment (supportive, neutral, restrictive)
- Legal Infrastructure (presence of SPV, trust law, token enforceability)
- Token Design (ERC standard, programmable compliance, asset backing)
- Custody Model (centralized, decentralized, hybrid)
- Asset Type (real estate, debt, commodity, public utility)

Dependent Variables (DVs):

- Capital Raised
- Market Accessibility (retail/institutional reach)
- Liquidity and Tradability
- Investor Participation
- Regulatory Compliance Success

Examples of Observed Relationships:

- Strong legal frameworks and programmable compliance (IVs) correlate with higher capital raised and institutional interest (DVs), as seen in Aspen Coin and SCCF.
- Token projects with regulatory sandbox participation (IV) were more likely to achieve post-launch liquidity and cross-border scaling (DV), e.g., HSBC and Digibrixx.

Thematic coding was applied to map these variables across each case. The analysis focused on both confirming expected patterns and identifying anomalies.

3.5 Reliability and Validity

To ensure methodological robustness:

- Triangulation was applied across multiple data sources.
- A structured variable coding template was used to enable cross-case comparability.
- Replicability is supported through transparent documentation of case selection and coding.
- Transferability is strengthened by selecting globally diverse cases.

Limitations:

- No primary interviews were conducted, which restricts insider insights.
- Reliance on secondary data introduces potential reporting bias.
- Causal relationships are inferred, not proven, due to qualitative method constraints.

Despite these limitations, the approach enables a nuanced, theory-informed analysis of real-world tokenization implementations and their contextual success factors.

4. CASE STUDIES IN TOKENIZATION

4.1 Aspen Coin – Tokenized Real Estate Equity (USA)

Context and Motivation

In 2018, Aspen Digital, a real estate investment platform, launched the Aspen Coin, the first Security Token Offering (STO) backed by a U.S.-based luxury hotel — the St. Regis Aspen Resort in Colorado. The goal was to raise capital while providing fractional investment opportunities in high-end commercial real estate (Zetzsche et al., 2020).

Implementation and Technology

Aspen Coin was issued under Regulation D of the U.S. Securities and Exchange Commission (SEC), targeting accredited investors. The token was deployed on the Ethereum blockchain using the ERC-20 standard with added compliance features. Securitize, a registered transfer agent and tokenization platform, managed issuance, KYC/AML onboarding, and investor registry.

Regulatory and Legal Considerations

The offering was legally structured as a digital equity share in a Special Purpose Vehicle (SPV) holding the hotel asset. It was registered with the SEC as a security, ensuring legal enforceability and investor rights. The use of a regulated platform allowed for secondary trading on Alternative Trading Systems (ATS), such as tZERO.

Outcomes and Impact

- The project successfully raised over $18 million from global investors.
- It provided proof of concept for asset-backed security tokens in U.S. real estate.
- Secondary trading was made possible under SEC exemptions, improving liquidity.

Aspen Coin became a reference model for regulated, institution-friendly real estate tokenization in the U.S.

Challenges and Lessons Learned

- Regulatory compliance significantly limited investor access to accredited participants only.
- Custodial and secondary market infrastructure was still evolving, delaying liquidity realization.
- Education and investor trust-building were major hurdles in marketing the offering.

4.2 SCCF-Taurus – Tokenized Trade Finance Debt (Switzerland)

Context and Motivation

In 2021, Swiss-based SCCF (Structured Commodity & Corporate Finance) partnered with Taurus Group, a digital asset infrastructure provider, to tokenize a short-term debt instrument that financed a biofuel trade transaction. The objective was to accelerate funding for small-to-medium commodity traders, who often face liquidity bottlenecks in traditional financing environments (Taurus, 2021).

Implementation and Technology

The tokenized debt note was issued on the Ethereum blockchain using Taurus' proprietary platform. The instrument was structured as a fixed-income product backed by trade receivables. Investors could purchase digital tokens representing fractional ownership of the debt instrument. Compliance was ensured via Taurus' TDX platform, which includes integrated identity checks, transfer restrictions, and programmable governance.

Regulatory and Legal Considerations

The issuance was fully compliant with Swiss financial law, particularly under the DLT Framework for Securities, which allows for tokenized financial instruments to be traded on licensed digital asset exchanges. No prospectus was required due to the private offering structure and investor qualification criteria. Swiss legislation recognises book-entry securities in tokenized form, giving the tokens full legal enforceability.

Outcomes and Impact

- The instrument enabled rapid capital deployment in a complex, low-liquidity trade finance deal.
- Reduced intermediation resulted in cost savings and greater transparency.
- The deal attracted attention from institutional and accredited investors interested in real-world yield opportunities.

This case illustrates how tokenization can extend beyond real estate and equities into short-term, real-economy debt markets, particularly for SME and cross-border trade financing.

Challenges and Lessons Learned

- Regulatory clarity in Switzerland was an enabler, but such frameworks are not yet globally harmonized.
- Investor onboarding required stringent identity checks, limiting speed and scale.
- Market liquidity remains thin due to lack of integration with broader institutional investor pools.

4.3 ReitBZ by BTG Pactual – Tokenized Real Estate Investment (Brazil)

Context and Motivation

In 2019, BTG Pactual, one of Brazil's largest investment banks, launched ReitBZ, a tokenized real estate investment product aimed at global investors. The project sought to democratize access to Brazilian real estate assets by leveraging blockchain technology to facilitate borderless, low-cost, and fractional ownership of distressed properties under bank management (BTG Pactual, 2019).

Implementation and Technology

ReitBZ was launched as an Ethereum-based ERC-20 token, supported by a custom-built smart contract system designed to handle compliance and distribution logic. The token represented equity participation in a real estate portfolio held by a dedicated SPV. BTG Pactual used Mynt, its in-house digital asset platform, for onboarding, wallet services, and investor interface. Investors could participate using fiat or cryptocurrencies, including Bitcoin and Ethereum.

Regulatory and Legal Considerations

ReitBZ was structured to comply with Brazilian securities law, but because it targeted global investors, the offering was made via Regulation S, exempting it from U.S. registration requirements. The tokens were backed by underlying real estate assets and income flows, and dividends were distributed in crypto. Legal enforceability was ensured through contractual arrangements governed by Brazilian law.

However, the lack of a dedicated digital securities framework in Brazil at the time created complexity, especially for institutional investors needing regulatory clarity.

Outcomes and Impact

- ReitBZ successfully raised $3.3 million in its initial offering.
- It served as a pioneering use case for real estate tokenization in Latin America.
- Enabled global crypto investors to access Brazilian property markets without traditional barriers such as currency conversion or real estate licensing.

ReitBZ demonstrated how emerging market institutions can leverage blockchain to attract foreign capital and develop digital capital market infrastructure.

Challenges and Lessons Learned

- While the issuance was compliant, secondary trading was limited due to jurisdictional friction and lack of digital exchanges accepting ReitBZ.
- Crypto-dividend mechanisms introduced volatility in yield for non-crypto-native investors.
- The project revealed a need for better regulatory harmonization between traditional financial systems and tokenized investment vehicles.

4.4 Ondo Finance – Tokenized U.S. Treasury Products (USA)

Context and Motivation

In response to increased demand for low-risk, yield-generating digital assets, Ondo Finance, a U.S.-based DeFi infrastructure firm, launched tokenized representations of U.S. Treasury products in 2023. The primary motivation was to offer blockchain-native investors and protocols access to real-world yield, while maintaining the composability and programmability of decentralized finance (Ondo Finance, 2023).

Implementation and Technology

Ondo introduced two primary instruments:

- OUSG: A tokenized share in short-term U.S. Treasury ETFs.
- USDY: A tokenized interest-bearing stablecoin backed by short-duration notes.

The tokens were issued on Ethereum and compatible with multiple DeFi platforms. Flux Finance, a lending protocol developed by Ondo, allowed users to borrow against these tokens in decentralized markets. Smart contracts governed issuance, yield accrual, and transfer restrictions. The tokens interfaced with qualified custodians and broker-dealers, such as BlackRock and Coinbase Custody, to manage off-chain settlement.

Regulatory and Legal Considerations

Ondo structured the products as regulated securities, available to qualified purchasers under Rule 144A of the U.S. Securities Act. Legal enforceability was ensured via custodial agreements and third-party attestations. Transfer restrictions were embedded in smart contracts to comply with U.S. securities regulations.

USDY, the stablecoin variant, was issued via a Bahamas-based structure to target non-U.S. investors while staying outside certain domestic compliance burdens. However, Ondo maintained KYC/AML infrastructure across all platforms to remain institution-ready.

Outcomes and Impact

- Ondo attracted both institutional DeFi protocols and DAOs (e.g., MakerDAO) as early adopters.
- The project demonstrated that tokenized Treasuries can function as decentralized "risk-free" assets, enabling a new class of collateral in DeFi lending.
- Enhanced trust among crypto-native treasurers and traditional finance firms exploring on-chain solutions.

This case showed that tokenization of government securities is not only technically feasible but increasingly desirable in a post-stablecoin regulatory environment.

Challenges and Lessons Learned

- The fragmented U.S. regulatory landscape limited the scalability of token offerings to retail investors.
- Cross-border issuance structures added legal and operational complexity.
- Secondary market development remained in its infancy, with limited integration into mainstream broker networks.

Ondo's case exemplifies the intersection of institutional finance and decentralized protocols, demonstrating how on-chain yield generation can coexist with traditional regulatory requirements.

4.5 Centrifuge – SME Financing through DeFi (Global)

Context and Motivation

Centrifuge is a decentralized asset financing protocol that enables small and medium-sized enterprises (SMEs) to tokenize real-world assets such as invoices, purchase orders, and accounts receivable. Launched in 2021, the initiative was motivated by the need to provide alternative financing to SMEs that are often excluded from traditional capital markets due to lack of collateral or credit history (Centrifuge, 2022).

The project aimed to bridge DeFi liquidity with real-world use cases, allowing institutional and retail DeFi investors to earn yield by financing tokenized debt from real-world businesses.

Implementation and Technology

Centrifuge operates on its own blockchain (Centrifuge Chain) with interoperability to Ethereum through bridges. The protocol enables asset originators (typically fintech lenders or SMEs) to create non-fungible tokens (NFTs) representing financial documents (e.g., invoices), which are then pooled into Tinlake pools—smart contract-based asset pools.

Investors can purchase junior (TIN) or senior (DROP) tokens, representing tranches of the asset pool. DROP token holders receive fixed yields, while TIN token holders bear default risk but earn higher returns. The pools are governed by smart contracts and transparently manage interest payments, defaults, and collateralization.

Centrifuge has integrated with MakerDAO, enabling its senior tokens to be used as collateral to mint DAI, a decentralized stablecoin.

Regulatory and Legal Considerations

The project operates in a decentralized architecture but collaborates with regulated asset originators for off-chain enforceability. Asset originators are responsible for KYC/AML procedures and for validating the legitimacy of tokenized documents. Each pool is managed under a legal framework, often with SPVs or trusts that facilitate claims enforcement in case of default.

Centrifuge's global reach allows it to operate across jurisdictions, but this also introduces regulatory uncertainty in terms of investor protection and classification of tokenized debt instruments.

Outcomes and Impact

- Over $350 million in assets have been financed via Tinlake pools.
- Dozens of SMEs across sectors (e.g., logistics, e-commerce, renewable energy) have gained access to fast, affordable capital.
- The protocol demonstrates the potential for DeFi-native infrastructure to finance traditionally underserved markets.

Centrifuge stands out for offering a decentralized yet legally grounded solution to a long-standing financial inclusion problem.

Challenges and Lessons Learned

- Legal enforcement of claims remains off-chain, introducing counterparty and documentation risks.
- Liquidity in secondary markets is thin; DROP and TIN tokens are not yet widely tradable.
- Bridging between Ethereum and Centrifuge Chain adds technical complexity and user friction.

Despite these limitations, Centrifuge proves that DeFi can finance real-world economic activity in a scalable, transparent, and semi-regulated manner—pushing the boundaries of what tokenization can achieve.

4.6 Digibrixx – Tokenized Infrastructure Investment (Europe)

Context and Motivation

Digibrixx is a European fintech initiative launched to tokenize public infrastructure projects, such as roads, bridges, housing, and energy facilities. Motivated by the increasing financing gaps in municipal infrastructure and the limitations of public-private partnerships (PPPs), Digibrixx aims to enable fractional citizen investment in long-term infrastructure via blockchain-based tokens (Digibrixx, 2021).

The project aligns with the European Commission's push toward digital capital markets and inclusive financial systems, especially in underfunded or rural regions.

Implementation and Technology

Digibrixx operates using a hybrid blockchain architecture, combining permissioned ledgers for compliance and public chains for transparency. Infrastructure project rights (e.g., concession income, usage fees) are tokenized as revenue-participation tokens backed by legally binding contracts.

Tokens are issued through regulated platforms in compliance with the EU's MiFID II and Prospectus Regulation frameworks. Smart contracts manage the distribution of revenue (e.g., tolls, rents) to token holders and enforce time-based or milestone-triggered payouts.

The issuance process includes:

- Token Prospectus submitted to national authorities,
- Digital ID onboarding (eIDAS-compliant),
- Asset token registration via Eurozone-compliant custodians.

Digibrixx's investor interface integrates e-wallets, Euro-pegged stablecoins, and traditional bank transfers to increase accessibility.

Regulatory and Legal Considerations

The platform works closely with European regulators to align with:

- MiFID II (Markets in Financial Instruments Directive),
- DLT Pilot Regime,
- EU AML directives,
- National-level sandbox programs (e.g., Germany's BaFin and France's AMF).

The tokens qualify as regulated financial instruments, and issuers are required to provide full risk disclosures, audited cash flow models, and governance rights to token holders. SPVs hold asset rights and act as fiduciaries on behalf of investors.

Outcomes and Impact

- Enabled community-based funding of infrastructure assets in multiple EU regions.
- Attracted both retail and institutional investors, with ticket sizes as low as €100.
- Introduced a transparent and traceable model for infrastructure financing in compliance-heavy jurisdictions.

The platform's model has been praised for increasing citizen engagement, lowering capital entry thresholds, and creating alternative infrastructure finance pipelines outside traditional PPPs and state bonds.

Challenges and Lessons Learned

- Lengthy regulatory approvals delayed initial rollouts.
- Liquidity of infrastructure tokens remains low due to their long maturity cycles.
- Public perception of risk in infrastructure tokens requires active investor education.

Digibrixx demonstrates how tokenization can unlock infrastructure as an investable asset class, while complying with stringent regulatory frameworks in developed capital markets.

4.7 Belt and Road Hydropower – Sovereign Infrastructure Tokenization (China)

Context and Motivation

As part of China's Belt and Road Initiative (BRI), a group of regional development banks and energy consortiums proposed the tokenization of hydropower infrastructure projects in 2022. The goal was to pilot sovereign-backed digital asset issuance to fund community-scale renewable energy in Central Asia and Southeast Asia, while offering global investors exposure to infrastructure-linked yield (BRI Investment Forum, 2022).

The project marked one of the first serious attempts to explore how nation-states and state-owned enterprises (SOEs) could use blockchain for project financing and citizen bond-like products.

Implementation and Technology

The hydropower token initiative used a permissioned blockchain network, co-developed by Chinese blockchain firms and supported by regional SOEs. Each token represented a share of project cash flows (from electricity tariffs), issued in the form of a sovereign-backed infrastructure token (SBIT).

Tokens were:

- Denominated in a digitally collateralized currency (e.g., e-CNY equivalents).

- Issued and governed via smart contracts that automated distribution of revenues.
- Integrated with a national ID-based KYC system tied to digital wallets.

Infrastructure projects were vetted by sovereign lenders, and tokens were linked to physical progress indicators (e.g., completion of turbine installation, environmental compliance).

Regulatory and Legal Considerations

The initiative operated under a special regulatory sandbox hosted within China's BRI FinTech Innovation Zone. While the tokens were not classified as securities, they required:

- Government guarantees,
- Project audits,
- Risk disclosures.

Cross-border token purchases were restricted to jurisdictions with memoranda of understanding (MOUs) with the People's Bank of China (PBoC), limiting legal conflict. Chinese state ownership of the infrastructure assets provided sovereign backstop for investor protection.

Outcomes and Impact

- Over $100 million equivalent was raised for small-scale hydropower in Kyrgyzstan and Laos.
- Enabled real-time monitoring and financing of sustainability-linked infrastructure.
- Introduced a programmable state-backed bond instrument with potential for replication across green finance sectors.

The project highlighted how blockchain and tokenization can be aligned with state-led development goals, rather than just private capital markets.

Challenges and Lessons Learned

- Cross-border capital controls and data localization laws limited investor scope.

- Trust-building with international investors was difficult due to lack of third-party governance.
- Public-private integration of systems (e.g., state banks, utilities, blockchain nodes) created coordination delays.

This case illustrates the emerging role of sovereign actors in blockchain ecosystems, potentially reshaping how infrastructure is financed and governed in the developing world.

4.8 HSBC Digital Gold – Tokenized Commodities Pilot (United Kingdom)

Context and Motivation

In 2023, HSBC, one of the world's largest custodial and bullion banks, initiated a tokenized gold pilot to enable fractional ownership and instant settlement of physical gold stored in institutional vaults in London. The goal was to modernize the trading and settlement of precious metals, reduce operational costs, and provide investors with real-time exposure to gold using blockchain technology (HSBC, 2023).

This initiative was particularly timely as global demand for gold surged amid macroeconomic uncertainty, and institutional clients sought digital-first instruments for hedging and collateral purposes.

Implementation and Technology

The pilot used a private, permissioned blockchain, built on HSBC's Orion digital asset platform. Each token represented a gram of London Good Delivery (LGD) gold held in HSBC vaults, with real-time audit and asset provenance enabled through blockchain records and integrated RFID tags on the gold bars.

Tokens were:

- Issued and redeemed through smart contracts, linked to client accounts.
- Transferable within HSBC's institutional network and compatible with whitelisted OTC partners.
- Settled using tokenized fiat in sandbox environments simulating Delivery-versus-Payment (DvP) models.

The platform was integrated with HSBC's existing global custodial system and could generate both trade confirmations and regulatory audit trails automatically.

Regulatory and Legal Considerations

Though the pilot was internal, HSBC ensured alignment with the UK's Financial Conduct Authority (FCA) regulations and Basel III requirements for collateral and liquidity treatment. The tokens did not constitute securities or e-money under UK law but were treated as digital warehouse receipts governed by contractual enforceability.

The platform was also compatible with the UK Regulatory Sandbox, allowing for feedback from the FCA and market participants throughout the testing phase.

Outcomes and Impact

- Demonstrated significant improvements in settlement speed (from T+2 to near-instant).
- Reduced transaction reconciliation costs by over 30%, according to internal reports.
- Created a foundation for a future institutional tokenized commodities marketplace, with expansion possibilities into silver, platinum, and palladium.

HSBC's pilot proved that digital gold tokens can retain regulatory and operational integrity when managed within traditional banking infrastructure.

Challenges and Lessons Learned

- Interoperability with external exchanges and custodians remained limited, creating siloed liquidity.
- Legal classification of digital gold tokens remained undefined in some jurisdictions.
- Token distribution was restricted to institutional clients, limiting broader market validation.

This case reinforces that tokenization of commodities can succeed within regulated financial institutions, particularly when designed with legal enforceability, full asset backing, and institutional workflow integration.

4.9 Verra's Tokenized Carbon Credits – Sustainability-Linked Assets (Global)

Context and Motivation

In 2022, Verra collaborated with Toucan Protocol to tokenize verified carbon credits from reforestation projects, aiming to enhance transparency and accessibility in voluntary carbon markets (World Economic Forum, 2022). The initiative addressed double-counting concerns and sought to enable fractional trading for diverse investors.

Implementation and Technology

Credits were tokenized as ERC-1155 NFTs on Polygon, with metadata linked to Verra's registry via oracles. Smart contracts facilitated retirement upon offset claims, integrating with DeFi platforms like KlimaDAO (Toucan Protocol, 2022). Hybrid custody ensured Verra's off-chain verification complemented on-chain tradability, leveraging Polygon's low-cost transactions.

Regulatory and Legal Considerations

Tokens aligned with EU ETS and UN Article 6 guidelines, classified as utility assets requiring AML compliance. Legal enforceability was supported by SPVs in Singapore, with audited registries ensuring transparency (World Bank, 2020).

Outcomes and Impact

The pilot tokenized credits worth millions, attracting institutional and retail investors. It reduced verification times significantly, boosting market efficiency. The case demonstrated tokenization's potential for ESG-focused assets in emerging economies.

Challenges and Lessons Learned

Carbon price volatility and oracle reliability posed risks. Limited investor education hindered retail adoption. Nonetheless, the project set a precedent for scalable, transparent carbon markets.

5. BENEFITS AND CHALLENGES OF TOKENIZATION

Tokenization of real-world assets presents a paradigm shift in how ownership, access, and value are distributed across markets. While the preceding chapters have illustrated the technical and legal underpinnings of tokenization, this chapter critically analyzes the key advantages and systemic risks based on real-world evidence and theoretical frameworks.

5.1 Benefits of Tokenization

1. Enhanced Liquidity and Fractional Ownership

One of the most frequently cited benefits is liquidity transformation. Assets that are traditionally illiquid—such as real estate, infrastructure, or invoices—can be fractionalized and traded in smaller units, improving accessibility and marketability (BIS, 2022). Platforms like Aspen Coin and ReitBZ enabled investment in high-value real estate projects with minimal capital thresholds, demonstrating how tokenization can democratize access to exclusive asset classes.

2. Increased Market Efficiency

Smart contracts and decentralized ledgers automate previously manual and fragmented processes such as clearing, settlement, dividend distribution, and investor onboarding. This can reduce settlement times from days to minutes (e.g., HSBC Digital Gold), lower operational costs, and minimize counterparty risks.

3. Transparency and Auditability

Blockchain's immutable ledger enables real-time audit trails for asset provenance, ownership changes, and transaction histories. This is particularly important in sectors where fraud, double-pledging, or opaque practices are common, such as trade finance or SME lending (Centrifuge, 2022).

4. Customization and Programmable Resources

Rules for investor rights, compliance, or revenue sharing may be integrated into tokenized assets. For instance, real-time yield mechanisms are embedded in Ondo Finance's tokens. Dynamic financial instruments that automatically enforce legal or governance terms are made possible by this programmability.

5. Disintermediation and Cost Cutting

Tokenization lessens the need for numerous middlemen, including clearinghouses, registrars, and custodians. Tokenized trade finance instruments can be issued, verified, and settled with significantly fewer middlemen, negating issuance costs and delays, as demonstrated by case studies such as SCCF-Taurus.

6. Broader Involvement and Financial Inclusion

Especially when combined with mobile wallets and decentralized identity, tokenization can open up investment opportunities to retail, unbanked, and underbanked populations. Centrifuge and Digibrixx presented models in which SMEs and citizens, respectively, were able to access working capital and infrastructure funding.

7. Automation of Regulations and Real-Time Compliance

In order to automate regulatory requirements, issuers can incorporate compliance logic (such as whitelisting, transfer restrictions, and real-time KYC) into tokens and smart contracts. Both Taurus and HSBC employed programmable compliance modules to allow innovations that are friendly to regulators without compromising operational agility.

8. Diversification of Portfolios and Innovative Investment Products

New avenues for portfolio diversification are made possible by tokenization, which gives investors access to specialized asset classes such as hydropower revenue streams (BRI projects), tokenized treasuries (Ondo), and SME invoices (Centrifuge). It makes hybrid portfolios possible by obfuscating the distinction between digital and conventional assets.

5.2 Challenges of Tokenization

While the case studies illustrate the diverse benefits of tokenization, they also reveal a set of persistent challenges that cut across projects and jurisdictions. For clarity, these challenges can be organized into three broad categories: regulatory and institutional, technological and operational, and ethical and environmental. This structure helps to show how legal frameworks, infrastructure choices, and socio-economic factors interact to shape outcomes in tokenized markets.

Against this backdrop, the sub-sections that follow re-examine the previously discussed obstacles through these three lenses, drawing on the case studies to highlight where risks have materialized in practice and how different actors have attempted to mitigate them.

1. Regulatory Uncertainty and Fragmentation

Include fragmented classification regimes, uncertain legal enforceability of tokenized claims, and uneven access to sandbox arrangements or tailored guidance.

Technological and operational challenges encompass interoperability constraints, cybersecurity and custody risks, scalability limits, and the difficulty of integrating DLT platforms with legacy payment, settlement, and messaging systems. Ethical and environmental challenges involve questions of financial inclusion, governance, privacy, and sustainability, particularly where participation requires specialized technical knowledge or relies on energy-intensive consensus mechanisms.

To avoid American scrutiny, ReitBZ was forced to issue tokens under Regulation S, and SCCF-Taurus profited from Switzerland's progressive position. However, these cases also demonstrated how regulatory dissonance continues to limit cross-border operations.

2. Digital Rights' Legal Enforcement

Legal rights are not automatically conferred by token ownership unless specifically supported by legally binding agreements or local laws. According to De Filippi and Wright (2018), many jurisdictions do not yet accept smart contract-mediated claims in court or blockchain-based ownership.

Whereas Belt and Road hydropower tokens needed sovereign guarantees to be legally credible, Aspen Coin relied on an SPV structure to protect investor rights under US law. Tokenized claims are still brittle and dangerous in the absence of solid legal foundations.

3. Infrastructure, Security, and Custody Risks

Tokenized asset custody arrangements are still being developed. Significant operational risks include issues with integration between off-chain assets and on-chain tokens, protocol-level vulnerabilities, and private key loss.

HSBC's digital gold pilot addressed this through institutional custody and programmable audit layers, but most retail-focused platforms lack this robustness. Meanwhile, token-custodian relationships are often poorly defined in law, complicating recovery in cases of fraud or bankruptcy.

4. Limited Secondary Market Liquidity

Although tokenization promises liquidity, in reality, secondary markets remain illiquid for most tokenized RWAs. ReitBZ and SCCF tokens had limited tradability outside private channels or ATSs. Absence of standardized exchange infrastructure and low institutional adoption stifles price discovery and investor confidence.

5. Fragmented Technical Standards and Interoperability

The proliferation of blockchain protocols (Ethereum, Solana, Hyperledger, etc.) has led to a lack of interoperability, fragmenting liquidity and forcing platforms to build custom bridges or siloed ecosystems (Pinna & Ruttenberg, 2016). This reduces composability and produces technical debt, two essential characteristics of scalable token markets.

User reach was restricted by Ondo and Centrifuge's difficulties integrating across DeFi protocols, custodians, and fiat onramps.

6. Dispute Resolution and Investor Protection

Token platforms frequently lack explicit investor protection measures, in contrast to traditional markets. Rights like redemption, voting, and disclosures that are normally available in the stock or bond markets might not be included in tokenized investment contracts. In many DeFi or global token contexts, it is also unclear how disputes are resolved.

For Centrifuge and Digibrixx, this problem is especially pressing because SME borrowers and infrastructure developers function under disparate legal frameworks, which results in unequal or opaque investor recourse.

7. Legacy Integration Obstacles and Institutional Reluctance

Due to compliance risk, reputational issues, and the ambiguity of the law surrounding tokenized products, traditional financial institutions frequently show caution. HSBC's pilot, although successful, was limited to internal clients. In order to support token models, Belt and Road projects needed sovereign infrastructure, demonstrating the continued importance of institutional and political guarantees.

Furthermore, integration is being delayed by the incomplete interoperability of blockchain-based platforms with legacy systems like Euroclear, DTCC, and SWIFT.

8. Intricacy of User Experience and Product Design

Environmental concerns also challenge tokenization's scalability and inclusiveness. While early blockchain networks attracted criticism for energy-intensive validation, many newer platforms and tokenization projects rely on more efficient setups and, in some cases, explicitly support green finance initiatives (World Economic Forum, 2023). The key challenge is to ensure that the environmental benefits of directing capital to sustainable projects are not undermined by the ecological footprint of the digital infrastructure itself.

9. Ethical, Social, and Environmental Considerations

Tokenization carries significant promise for democratizing access to capital markets and expanding financial inclusion, yet the case studies reveal that these outcomes depend critically on design choices and implementation contexts. Three dimensions—social inclusion, environmental sustainability, and governance—merit particular attention as the tokenization landscape matures.

Social Inclusion and User Experience

While fractional ownership and 24/7 market access can lower barriers to entry, tokenization can simultaneously reinforce existing inequalities if not carefully designed. Onboarding processes that rely heavily on cryptocurrencies, complex wallet management, or unfamiliar user interfaces may deter non-technical users and exclude those lacking reliable digital infrastructure, stable internet connectivity, or access to specific exchanges. ReitBZ's experience demonstrates this risk: the requirement for investors to manage crypto wallets and accept crypto-denominated dividends limited participation to crypto-native participants and sophisticated investors, thereby undermining the stated goal of democratizing access to Brazilian real estate for a broad investor base.

Ethical design therefore requires attention to user education, accessible interface design, and inclusive identity solutions. Platforms designed for institutional and retail audiences alike must balance security and compliance with simplicity. Projects operating in emerging markets have an additional responsibility to consider whether tokenization genuinely lowers costs and improves access relative to existing alternatives, or merely shifts barriers from one form to another.

Environmental and Sustainability Concerns

The environmental footprint of tokenized systems depends on infrastructure choices, particularly the consensus mechanism underlying the blockchain platform. Early deployments on energy-intensive proof-of-work systems attracted criticism for contradicting commitments to green finance and climate goals. However, many recent tokenization projects—including those examined in this chapter—have adopted more efficient proof-of-stake architectures, Layer 2 solutions, or application-specific chains with lower per-transaction energy costs.

Crucially, the net environmental impact depends not only on technology efficiency but also on the ultimate use of capital. A tokenized project that channels investment into renewable energy infrastructure or climate mitigation may deliver a positive environmental outcome even on a moderately energy-intensive platform, whereas a speculative asset may provide negligible social benefit regardless of platform efficiency. Regulators and industry participants can reinforce these priorities by incorporating sustainability criteria into guidelines for tokenized offerings, setting energy benchmarks for platforms, and ensuring transparent disclosure of environmental footprints alongside financial performance metrics.

Governance and Democratic Participation

Tokenization also raises governance questions about who controls smart contracts, how disputes are resolved, and whether token holders have meaningful voice in platform or asset decisions. Decentralized governance models—exemplified by Centrifuge's Tinlake structure and MakerDAO's governance token voting—attempt to distribute decision-making power, yet often result in voting concentration among large holders and face challenges around voter participation and information asymmetry. Conversely, centralized governance by issuers or platforms ensures rapid decision-making but may not reflect diverse stakeholder interests and increases counterparty risk.

Hybrid approaches, wherein key platform decisions are subject to multi-stakeholder review (e.g., custodians, regulators, and community representatives), show promise but require developing new institutional frameworks and coordination mechanisms. As tokenization matures and encompasses larger asset pools and more diverse stakeholders, governance models will need to balance efficiency, transparency, and legitimate representation.

Looking forward, regulators and standard-setters can strengthen the tokenization landscape by explicitly incorporating ethical and environmental criteria into guidance and oversight frameworks. This includes transparency requirements on governance structures, energy use disclosures, inclusion metrics (e.g., percentage of retail vs. institutional participation, geographic distribution of investors), and dispute-resolution mechanisms. Public-private collaboration on these standards—drawing on expertise from financial regulators, sustainability certifiers, and technology providers—will be essential to ensure that tokenization contributes to a more efficient, inclusive, and sustainable financial system rather than reproducing or amplifying existing inequalities.

Table 1. The following matrix synthesizes key challenges, observed trends, and their short-, medium-, and long-term implications for tokenized markets:

Issue	Current trend	Short-term impact	Long-term systemic impact
Regulatory fragmentation	Growth of national regimes and sandboxes with only partial harmonization	Legal uncertainty and higher compliance costs for cross-border deals	Stratification between "token-friendly" and lagging jurisdictions
Interoperability limitations	Proliferation of siloed platforms and bespoke integration solutions	Liquidity trapped in closed ecosystems; operational complexity	Risk of parallel infrastructures and weaker network effects
Cybersecurity and operational risk	Increasing awareness but uneven adoption of best-practice frameworks	Periodic incidents that erode investor confidence and delay adoption	Pressure to apply FMI-grade standards to critical token infrastructures
Governance and inclusion	Experiments with decentralized, hybrid, and state-led governance models	Mixed levels of access for SMEs and retail investors; learning effects	Potential for broader participation—or deeper inequalities—depending on design
Environmental and ethical concerns	Shift toward more efficient consensus and impact-oriented token projects	Scrutiny of energy use and distributional effects of tokenization	Integration of sustainability and inclusion criteria into digital asset regulation

6. PROSPECTIVE PATHS AND POLICY CONSEQUENCES

The evidence assembled in this chapter suggests that tokenization of real-world assets is evolving into a foundational layer of financial market infrastructure rather than remaining a niche or speculative phenomenon. When embedded in appropriate legal structures and supported by robust technical and governance standards, tokenization can streamline issuance and settlement, broaden access to capital, and enable programmable forms of ownership and control. Yet the trajectory from isolated pilots to systemic relevance is contingent on how regulators, market participants, and technology providers collectively address the unresolved challenges identified in previous sections.

The evidence assembled in this chapter suggests that tokenization of real-world assets is evolving into a foundational layer of financial market infrastructure rather than remaining a niche or speculative phenomenon. When embedded in appropriate legal structures and supported by robust technical and governance standards, tokenization can streamline issuance and settlement, broaden access to capital, and enable programmable forms of ownership and control. Yet the trajectory from isolated pilots to systemic relevance is contingent on how regulators, market participants, and technology providers collectively address the unresolved challenges identified in previous sections.

Against this backdrop, the subsections that follow elaborate five strategic levers—legal harmonization, public–private collaboration, interoperable infrastructure, inclusion-oriented token design, and a strengthened research agenda—that will shape whether tokenization contributes to a more efficient and inclusive financial system or remains confined to fragmented, privileged niches

6.1 Legal Infrastructure and Harmonization of Regulations

One of the biggest obstacles to large-scale tokenization is the absence of a single, worldwide regulatory framework. Despite regional advancements like the Swiss DLT Act, the EU's DLT Pilot Regime, and India's IFSCA sandbox guidelines, cross-border legal recognition of tokenized claims is still dispersed (Zetzsche et al., 2020).

Suggestion for Policy:

International organizations like the IMF, BIS, and IOSCO ought to take the lead in creating legal models and standards that are compatible with tokenized assets. Standardized token classification frameworks, cross-border digital rights enforceability, and international AML/CFT coordination for token-based platforms are among the priority areas.

6.2 Public-Private Collaborations and Institutional Integration

Tokenization must be embraced by regulated organizations and integrate with traditional finance (TradFi) infrastructures in order to attain systemic relevance. Institutional entry necessitates regulatory clarity, custodial controls, and investor protections, as case studies like HSBC, BTG Pactual, and Ondo Finance show.

Future Direction:

- Increase the number of public-private sandbox programs to enable joint experimentation.
- Create hybrid market models that allow traditional and tokenized assets to coexist in a single regulatory framework.
- Promote the involvement of sovereign funds and central banks in green finance and tokenized infrastructure.

6.3 Open Standards and Interoperability in Infrastructure

Proprietary systems and siloed blockchains restrict composability and liquidity. To enable price discovery, cross-platform use cases, and token portability, an interoperable architecture is required. This covers not only technical standards but also identity frameworks, data models, and compliance procedures.

Technological focus areas include: Decentralized Identity (DID) systems for regulatory onboarding; Zero-Knowledge Proofs (ZKPs) for privacy-preserving compliance; and cross-chain bridges and interoperability protocols (such as Cosmos and Polkadot).

An open-source tokenization middleware that connects the TradFi custody and on-chain asset layers is a promising option for infrastructure unification.

6.4 Financial Inclusion and Token Design for Emerging Markets

Tokenization has the potential to address financing gaps in emerging and developing economies (EMDEs), where SME access to credit and infrastructure funding remains limited. However, adoption in these contexts requires simplified interfaces, localized legal models, and low-cost custody options.

Policy Direction:

- Build tokenization pilots in low-income countries with support from development banks (e.g., World Bank, ADB).
- Use tokenization for community infrastructure, remittance-backed assets, or mobile-money–linked collateral systems.
- Encourage localization of regulatory sandboxes with focus on rural economies and informal sectors.
- Ethical design is critical to ensure tokenization does not exacerbate digital divides, as seen in ReitBZ's crypto-heavy onboarding, which limited access for non-technical users (World Bank, 2020).

Projects like Digibrixx and Centrifuge offer early proof points for socially impactful token economies.

6.5 Research, Innovation, and Future Inquiry

As tokenization evolves, so too must the academic and regulatory understanding of its mechanics. Key areas for future research include:

- Governance models for decentralized asset ownership,
- Cross-chain dispute resolution,
- AI-integrated compliance monitoring,
- Macroeconomic effects of asset tokenization on monetary policy and capital flow controls.

Call to Action

Universities, think tanks, and regulatory labs should collaborate to track, simulate, and evaluate the performance of tokenized economies across various scenarios.

Academic research must also expand to measure longitudinal outcomes, such as liquidity shifts, investor behaviour, and socio-economic effects.

Looking ahead, several research priorities emerge from the intersection of theory and practice in tokenized markets. First, longitudinal studies are needed to assess the stability, liquidity, and default behaviour of tokenized asset classes across macroeconomic cycles. Second, governance models for tokenized systems—spanning on-chain voting mechanisms, delegated authority structures, and supervisory overlays—require further conceptual and empirical refinement. Third, cross-chain dispute resolution and the legal recognition of events occurring in multi-network environments represent underexplored frontiers for both legal scholarship and protocol design. Finally, the integration of artificial intelligence into compliance monitoring, surveillance, and contract management invites new questions about algorithmic bias, accountability, and privacy in tokenized ecosystems

6.6 AI and Machine Learning in Tokenized Systems

Artificial intelligence (AI) enhances tokenization by improving compliance and efficiency. Machine learning models, such as those used by Chainalysis, analyse on-chain transactions to detect AML/CFT risks, supporting platforms like Centrifuge (Chainalysis, 2022). Natural language processing can automate regulatory compliance by parsing legal texts, reducing manual overhead for issuers. However, challenges include algorithmic bias and privacy concerns under frameworks like GDPR (Zetzsche et al., 2020). For instance, decentralized platforms struggle to balance transparency with data protection. Future research should explore AI-driven smart contracts for real-time risk assessment and governance, building on MakerDAO's experiments with automated collateral management (MakerDAO, 2022–2023). Collaboration between academia and industry is needed to develop ethical AI frameworks that ensure equitable access, particularly in emerging markets with varying technical literacy.

7. CONCLUSION

The tokenization of real-world assets (RWAs) is not merely a technological advancement—it represents a fundamental transformation in how economic value is created, accessed, and governed. This chapter has sought to provide a comprehensive, research-based understanding of tokenized ecosystems by integrating conceptual theory, empirical case studies, and policy-oriented insights.

Beginning with a detailed examination of the definition, scope, and infrastructure of tokenization, the chapter outlined how blockchain and distributed ledger technologies (DLT) enable the representation of real-world claims—such as real estate, commodities, debt, and infrastructure—as programmable, transferable digital tokens. These innovations challenge existing financial market structures and regulatory norms, particularly around custody, asset transfer, compliance, and investor protection.

A core contribution of this research lies in the theoretical grounding of tokenization. Drawing on Property Rights Theory, Institutional Theory, and Technology Adoption Models, the study explains how tokenized systems reshape ownership structures, influence institutional adoption, and reconfigure market incentives. These theories provided the scaffolding for interpreting eight diverse, real-world cases—from Aspen Coin and ReitBZ to Centrifuge and HSBC's digital gold pilot.

The case studies underscored tokenization's potential to democratize access, lower issuance costs, enhance transparency, and expand capital formation. They also revealed key implementation models—ranging from fully decentralized platforms to institutionally managed pilots—and highlighted how regional contexts, regulatory environments, and asset types influence outcomes. Importantly, they illustrated that success requires not only robust technical design but also legal enforceability, institutional trust, and investor education.

At the same time, the analysis revealed persistent challenges: regulatory fragmentation, lack of interoperability, legal ambiguity, and thin secondary markets. These risks are not merely operational—they raise questions about governance, systemic resilience, and equitable access. Tokenization, if not thoughtfully implemented, could replicate or even exacerbate existing inequities in global capital markets.

Looking forward, this chapter outlined five strategic directions: harmonizing regulatory frameworks, fostering institutional integration, investing in infrastructure interoperability, designing inclusive token economies, and expanding academic inquiry. These imperatives are necessary to transition from fragmented pilots to mature tokenized markets capable of reshaping how economies mobilize capital and manage assets.

In conclusion, tokenization holds immense promise—but it is not a panacea. Its impact will depend on how well stakeholders balance innovation with regulation, efficiency with inclusion, and technical design with social purpose. As the digital asset economy evolves, interdisciplinary collaboration among technologists, regulators, financiers, and researchers will be critical to ensuring that tokenization contributes to a more open, transparent, and equitable global financial system.

REFERENCES

Arner, D. W., Barberis, J., & Buckley, R. P. (2017). FinTech, RegTech, and the reconceptualization of financial regulation. *Northwestern Journal of International Law & Business*, *37*(3), 371–413.

Bank for International Settlements. (2022). *The future monetary system: A BIS perspective*. https://www.bis.org/publ/arpdf/ar2022e3.htm

Catalini, C., & Gans, J. S. (2016). *Some simple economics of the blockchain* (MIT Sloan Research Paper No. 5191-16). DOI: 10.3386/w22952

Centrifuge. (2022). *Protocol overview and Tinlake documentation*. https://docs.centrifuge.io

Coase, R. H. (1960). The problem of social cost. *The Journal of Law & Economics*, *3*, 1–44. DOI: 10.1086/466560

Davis, F. D. (1989). Perceived usefulness, perceived ease of use, and user acceptance of information technology. *Management Information Systems Quarterly*, *13*(3), 319–340. DOI: 10.2307/249008

De Filippi, P., & Wright, A. (2018). *Blockchain and the law: The rule of code*. Harvard University Press.

Digibrixx. (2021). *Infrastructure tokenization platform documentation*. https://www.digibrixx.eu/docs

European Securities and Markets Authority. (2022). *ESMA report on trends, risks and vulnerabilities*. https://www.esma.europa.eu/sites/default/files/library/esma50-165-2238_trv_1_2022.pdf

Financial Action Task Force. (2021). *Updated guidance for a risk-based approach to virtual assets and virtual asset service providers*. https://www.fatf-gafi.org/content/dam/fatf-gafi/guidance/Updated-Guidance-VA-VASP.pdf

Finck, M. (2018). *Smart contracts as a form of private ordering: An empirical study* (Max Planck Institute for Innovation and Competition Research Paper No. 18-10). https://doi.org/DOI: 10.2139/ssrn.3266668

HSBC. (2023). *HSBC Orion platform pilot on digital gold*. https://www.hsbc.com/news-and-insight/2023/hsbc-launches-digital-gold-token

International Monetary Fund. (2021). *The rise of digital money*. https://www.imf.org/en/Publications/fintech-notes/Issues/2019/07/12/The-Rise-of-Digital-Money-47097

MakerDAO Governance Forum. (2022–2024). *Real-world asset proposals and research.* https://forum.makerdao.com/c/rwa/16

Miles, M. B., & Huberman, A. M. (1994). *Qualitative data analysis: An expanded sourcebook* (2nd ed.). Sage Publications.

Ondo Finance. (2023). *OUSG and USDY product documentation.* https://ondo.finance/whitepaper

Pactual, B. T. G. (2019). *ReitBZ whitepaper.* https://www.reitbz.io/whitepaper.pdf

Pinna, A., & Ruttenberg, W. (2016). *Distributed ledger technologies in securities post-trading* (ECB Occasional Paper No. 172). European Central Bank. https://www.ecb.europa.eu/pub/pdf/scpops/ecbop172.en.pdf

Rogers, E. M. (2003). *Diffusion of innovations* (5th ed.). Free Press.

Scott, W. R. (2001). *Institutions and organizations* (2nd ed.). Sage Publications.

Securities and Exchange Commission. (2020). *Framework for "investment contract" analysis of digital assets.* https://www.sec.gov/corpfin/framework-investment-contract-analysis-digital-assets

Taurus Group. (2021). *SCCF-Taurus trade finance tokenization report.* https://www.taurusgroup.ch/reports/sccf

Tokeny. (2022). *ERC-3643 and ERC-1400 token standards overview.* https://www.tokeny.com/erc-3643-overview

World Bank. (2020). *Digital financial services for development.* https://www.worldbank.org/en/topic/financialinclusion/publication/digital-financial-services

World Economic Forum. (2020). *Tokenization of assets and the future of finance.* https://www.weforum.org/reports/tokenization-of-assets-and-potential-implications-for-financial-markets

Yin, R. K. (2018). *Case study research and applications: Design and methods* (6th ed.). Sage Publications.

Zetzsche, D. A., Buckley, R. P., Arner, D. W., & Barberis, J. N. (2020). The future of data-driven finance and RegTech. *European Business Organization Law Review, 21*(3), 353–394.

ADDITIONAL READING

Catalini, C., & Gans, J. S. (2016). *Some Simple Economics of the Blockchain. MIT Sloan Research Paper No. 5191-16.*

De Filippi, P., & Wright, A. (2018). *Blockchain and the Law: The Rule of Code.* Harvard University Press.

FATF (2021). *Updated Guidance for a Risk-Based Approach to Virtual Assets and Virtual Asset Service Providers.*

IMF (2022). *The Impact of Fintech on Financial Intermediation.*

BIS Innovation Hub. (2023). *Project Helvetia and Project Jura Reports.*

MakerDAO Governance Forum & Research Publications.

Pinna, A., & Ruttenberg, W. (2016). *Distributed Ledger Technologies in Securities Post-Trading. European Central Bank Occasional Paper Series.*

Tapscott, D., & Tapscott, A. (2016). *Blockchain Revolution: How the Technology Behind Bitcoin Is Changing Money, Business, and the World.* Penguin.

World Economic Forum. (2020). Tokenization of Assets and Potential Implications for Financial Markets.

Zetzsche, D. A., Buckley, R. P., Arner, D. W., & Barberis, J. N. (2020). The Future of Data-Driven Finance and RegTech. *European Business Organization Law Review*, *21*(3), 353–394.

KEY TERMS AND DEFINITIONS

Asset-Backed Token: A digital token collateralized by off-chain assets (e.g., gold, real estate), providing investors with claims on those underlying holdings.

Decentralized Finance (DeFi): An open financial system built on blockchain networks that uses smart contracts to replicate and innovate upon traditional financial services without centralized intermediaries.

DLT (Distributed Ledger Technology): A decentralized database architecture in which data is shared, replicated, and synchronized across multiple nodes without a central administrator.

Fractional Ownership: The division of asset ownership into smaller units that can be purchased and traded individually, lowering barriers to entry for investors.

Interoperability: The ability of different blockchain networks, protocols, or platforms to communicate and exchange data or assets seamlessly.

Programmable Compliance: The embedding of legal and regulatory requirements into token logic or smart contracts to automate compliance processes such as KYC, AML, and transfer restrictions.

Real-World Assets (RWAs): Physical or intangible assets with economic value in traditional markets—such as real estate, commodities, invoices, or securities—that can be tokenized.

Security Token: A tokenized financial instrument that represents ownership, debt, or profit-sharing rights and is subject to securities regulations.

Smart Contracts: Self-executing agreements coded into blockchain platforms that automatically enforce the terms and logic of transactions without human intervention.

Tokenization: The process of converting rights to a real-world asset into a digital token recorded on a blockchain or distributed ledger, enabling transfer, trading, and fractional ownership.

Chapter 6
Tokenization of Intellectual Property in Research and Innovation Processes:
Between Technological Utopia and Dogmatic Paralysis

Aneta Napieralska
https://orcid.org/0009-0004-0463-3646
University Humanitas, Italy

Przemysław Kępczyński
https://orcid.org/0009-0006-8427-3162
Legalteq Law Office, Poland

ABSTRACT

This article provides a critical legal analysis of the phenomenon of intellectual property (IP) rights tokenization. The paper posits the thesis that the implementation of mechanisms based on blockchain technology, while offering revolutionary solutions to the problems of liquidity, valuation, and commercialization of intangible assets, is fraught with fundamental normative conflicts that undermine its legality and effectiveness within current legal orders. The analysis, conducted using dogmatic and comparative law methods, focuses on three key problem areas: (1) the collision of the global nature of blockchain with the principle of territoriality of IP rights; (2) the inadequacy of traditional formal requirements, particularly the written form, for the specifics of on-chain transactions; and (3) the crisis of regulatory classification

DOI: 10.4018/979-8-3373-3371-7.ch006

of IP tokens under capital market law regimes. In conclusion, the authors assert that tokenization acts as a catalyst for legal evolution, forcing a revision of fundamental concepts such as jurisdiction and state coercion.

INTRODUCTION

A New Paradigm in Intellectual Property Management: Blockchain Technology as a Catalyst for the Transformation of the Intellectual Property System

Blockchain technology, originally developed as a decentralized infrastructure for cryptocurrencies (Nakamoto, 2008), has evolved into a universal platform enabling the tokenization of a broad spectrum of assets (De Filippi & Wright, 2018). In the context of intellectual property (IP), this technology creates the possibility of representing abstract exclusive rights in the form of digital tokens that function within distributed ledgers. The process of tokenization itself involves creating a digital equivalent of an intellectual property right, which, depending on its technical and legal construction, can be subject to transfer, division into smaller, transferable units (fractionalization), or be subject to automated management through smart contract protocols (Savelyev, 2017).

The fundamental innovation that blockchain technology brings is the cryptographic solution to the double-spending problem in a digital environment, which eliminates the need for a trusted central institution (Catalini & Gans, 2020). For the intellectual property system, this implies the ability to create digital representations of rights characterized by uniqueness, the impossibility of arbitrary duplication, and the finality of transfers made on them. In this way, the technology addresses one of the longest-standing challenges related to the digitization of intellectual property rights—ensuring the attribute of scarcity and excludability in an environment where copying is inherently trivial (Fairfield, 2021).

It should be emphasized, however, that the potential of intellectual property tokenization extends beyond simple digitization. It introduces the possibility of programming rights through smart contracts, which opens the way to automating complex licensing processes, as well as creating liquid secondary markets for assets traditionally considered illiquid (Werbach, 2018). Smart contracts can be programmed to automatically distribute royalties due to creators, enforce territorial or temporal restrictions arising from licensing agreements, and implement complex remuneration structures without the need for constant human intervention (Szabo, 1997).

Structural Limitations of the Current Intellectual Property Management System

The current system of managing and commercializing intellectual property, especially in the research and development (R&D) sector, is characterized by many structural limitations that hinder the effective allocation of resources and slow the pace of innovation (OECD, 2023). The valuation of intangible assets remains a highly subjective, costly, and time-consuming process. The lack of standard, universally accepted valuation methodologies leads to significant discrepancies in the estimated values of the same assets by different experts (Lev, 2001). The due diligence process in intellectual property transactions often takes months and generates costs reaching hundreds of thousands of dollars, making smaller transactions economically unviable (Hagiu & Yoffie, 2013).

The low liquidity of intellectual property rights stems from the lack of organized secondary markets and high transaction costs. Unlike stocks or bonds, there are no liquid, transparent exchanges for patent rights or advanced licenses (Kamiyama et al., 2006). Transactions are mainly conducted bilaterally, often through specialized brokers, which limits price transparency and deepens information asymmetry between parties. This lack of liquidity naturally increases investment risk and raises the required rate of return, ultimately limiting the availability of capital for early-stage research projects (Hall & Lerner, 2010).

Furthermore, the transfer of rights encounters significant jurisdictional barriers arising from the territorial nature of intellectual property protection (Dinwoodie, 2009). A patent granted in one jurisdiction does not provide protection in others, which requires the coordination of transfer processes across multiple legal systems. Differences in formal requirements—from simple notification to the patent office to the necessity of a notarial deed—further complicate international transactions. Moreover, differing interpretations of the scope of protection in various jurisdictions introduce uncertainty regarding the actual value and effectiveness of the transferred rights (Trimble, 2012).

Finally, innovation financing remains concentrated in a limited number of institutional sources, such as venture capital funds, corporate R&D departments, and government grants (Kerr & Nanda, 2015). This concentration of capital excludes smaller, individual investors from participating in the value generated by breakthrough scientific discoveries. Crowdfunding, while theoretically possible, faces regulatory barriers related to public securities offerings and practical problems with managing the rights of a large number of small investors (Belleflamme et al., 2014).

Research Problem, Thesis, and Structure of Argumentation

In light of the structural challenges presented, the phenomenon of intellectual property tokenization emerges as a potential remedy, offering mechanisms to increase liquidity, democratize access to investment in innovation, and radically automate rights management. The authors of this article, however, posit the thesis that the implementation of these mechanisms within current legal orders is fraught with fundamental normative conflicts that undermine their legality and effectiveness. Tokenization is not merely a technological optimization but generates profound challenges for legal dogmatics, which is based on the principles of territoriality, the formalism of legal acts, and the central enforcement of rights (De Filippi & Hassan, 2016).

The main research objective of this article is, therefore, a critical analysis of these conflicts and the identification of key legal problems that must be resolved for intellectual property tokenization to become a safe and effective instrument of commerce. Specifically, the authors aim to answer the following research questions:

1. In what way does the global and decentralized nature of blockchain technology collide with the principle of territoriality of intellectual property rights, and what are the practical consequences thereof?
2. Can the transfer of a token representing an intellectual property right satisfy the formal requirements of civil law, particularly the requirement of written form for the transfer of economic copyrights?
3. How should IP tokens be classified under capital market law regimes, and what regulatory consequences arise from adopting a specific classification in key jurisdictions, such as the USA and the European Union?

To achieve this research objective, the argumentation in the article is structured progressively. First, the authors will analyze the legal ontology of the token, examining its nature as a digital representation of a right. Next, the fundamental conflicts between tokenization mechanisms and the dogmatics of the international intellectual property protection system will be explored. The subsequent chapter will be devoted to a comparative legal analysis of the regulatory classification of tokens, identifying both barriers and emerging practices in leading legal systems. The final part of the work will discuss the practical challenges related to jurisdiction and the enforcement of rights in a decentralized ecosystem. This structure will allow for the construction of a comprehensive picture of the issue, and consequently, the formulation of conclusions regarding both the current legal state and the desired directions of its evolution.

THE LEGAL ONTOLOGY OF AN INTELLECTUAL PROPERTY TOKEN

The Token as a Digital Representation of a Right – Fundamental Distinctions

Understanding the legal nature of a token first requires making a fundamental distinction between the intellectual property right itself and its digital representation. This is a distinction of an ontological nature that determines the entire subsequent legal analysis (Guadamuz, 2019). An intellectual property right—be it a patent, a registered design right, a copyright, or a trademark—remains an abstract juridical construct, existing within a specific legal system and subject to its rules. A token, on the other hand, is merely a digital record in a distributed database, whose authenticity and integrity are cryptographically secured (Antonopoulos & Wood, 2018).

This distinction is of paramount practical importance. A token in itself is not an intellectual property right, just as a share certificate is not a share in a company but merely a document confirming its existence (Low & Teo, 2017). One can imagine a situation in which a token exists on the blockchain, while the right it represents has expired, been invalidated, or transferred outside the blockchain system. Such a discrepancy between the legal state and the state on the blockchain ledger raises fundamental questions about the value and effectiveness of the token (Michels, 2018).

In legal doctrine, three basic models for conceptualizing the relationship between a token and an intellectual property right are emerging. The incorporation model assumes that the token contains the right within itself, becoming its carrier in a manner analogous to a bearer security (Rodrigues, 2019). In this view, possession of the token is tantamount to possession of the right, and its transfer automatically results in the transfer of the represented right. This model, though conceptually elegant, faces serious obstacles arising from the territorial nature of intellectual property rights and the diverse formal requirements of various jurisdictions (Reyes, 2019).

The representation model treats the token as a digital certificate attesting to the existence of certain rights within the traditional legal system (Schrepel, 2021). The transfer of the token does not automatically cause the transfer of the intellectual property right—it merely constitutes an obligation to perform the assignment in accordance with the requirements of the applicable law. This model maintains full compliance with existing legal frameworks but, at the same time, significantly limits the benefits of automation and eliminates the possibility of an immediate, definitive transfer of rights.

The hybrid model, which appears to be gaining the most acceptance in practice, treats the token as a bundle of contractual rights related to intellectual property (Cong & He, 2019). The token may incorporate the right to receive a certain portion of royalties, the right to vote on matters concerning the management of the IP portfolio, an option to acquire full intellectual property rights upon the fulfillment of certain conditions, or the right to use the work or invention to a specified extent. The smart contract managing the token implements the logic for the automatic execution of these rights, *de facto* creating a new category of property rights of an obligatory nature, the subject of which is intellectual property (Durovic & Janssen, 2019).

A Typology of Intellectual Property Tokens and Their Legal Construction

An empirical analysis of intellectual property tokenization projects allows for the identification of several basic types of tokens, which differ in both their technical construction and their legal regime (OECD, 2023). This typology is functional in nature—the classification is based not on the technical characteristics of the token, but on the economic and legal function it performs within the intellectual property ecosystem.

Utility tokens, in the context of intellectual property, provide the holder with specific rights of access or use. An example is the token of the Ocean Protocol platform, which enables access to copyrighted datasets used in artificial intelligence research (Ocean Protocol, 2023). The legal construction is based on an automatic, limited license—the acquisition of the token results in the granting of a non-exclusive license to use specific IP resources to the extent and under the conditions specified in the smart contract (Finck, 2019).

The challenge lies in precisely encoding the scope of the license. Consider the real-world case of Audius ($AUDIO) tokens, which manage access to a music streaming platform (Audius, 2023). The smart contract must take into account the complexity of rights in the music industry—composition rights (often managed by music publishers), recording rights (master rights belonging to record labels), and performance rights (managed by collective management organizations). Each of these rights may be subject to different territorial and temporal restrictions (Torbey, 2020).

Security tokens represent an economic interest in the revenue streams generated by intellectual property. A flagship example is the Royal.io platform, founded by the musician 3LAU, which sells NFTs representing a percentage share in the royalties from specific musical works (Royal, 2023). The purchasers of a token representing 0.5% of the rights to the song "Worst Case" receive a proportional share of the revenue from streaming, sales, and licensing of the work.

An analysis of Royal.io's legal structure reveals the complexity of such constructions (O'Dair & Owen, 2019). For each work, a special purpose vehicle (LLC) is created in Delaware, which acquires a certain percentage of the royalty rights from the artist. The NFT tokens represent membership interests in this company. The smart contract automates the distribution of revenue—when royalties are received from streaming platforms or collective management organizations, they are automatically distributed in proportion to the tokens held. This structure was designed to comply with U.S. securities law—sales are restricted to accredited investors, and the offering is subject to an exemption under Regulation D (Securities Act of 1933, 17 C.F.R. § 230.506).

Non-fungible tokens (NFTs) in the intellectual property ecosystem serve as unique certificates associated with specific assets. The Molecule Protocol uses the IP-NFT standard to tokenize the early stages of pharmaceutical research (Molecule Protocol, 2023). Each IP-NFT represents a package of intellectual property related to a specific research project—this may include preliminary research results, patent applications, know-how, and clinical data.

The Molecule case provides a fascinating implementation study. VitaDAO, a decentralized autonomous organization that finances research on longevity, used an IP-NFT to fund research on autophagy inhibitors conducted at Newcastle University (VitaDAO, 2023). The token contains a hash of legal documents stored on IPFS, metadata identifying specific patent applications, and smart contract logic defining voting rights in commercialization decisions. Importantly, the structure provides for a "waterfall" payment mechanism—first, patenting costs are reimbursed, then the initial investment with a specified return, and only then are profits divided among the university, the researchers, and the token holders (Koepsell, 2022).

The Technical-Legal Architecture of Smart Contracts for IP

The effective tokenization of intellectual property requires the creation of smart contracts that can reflect the complexity of the legal relationships characteristic of this field (Cannarsa, 2019). An analysis of leading implementations allows for the identification of the key components of such an architecture.

The identification and verification layer forms the foundation of the system. The smart contract must unambiguously identify the represented intellectual property right and verify the issuer's authority to tokenize it. IPwe, a patent tokenization platform collaborating with IBM, uses AI for this purpose to analyze and standardize patent descriptions, creating unique "fingerprints" for each patent (IPwe, 2023). The system integrates with the USPTO, EPO, and WIPO databases, verifying the legal status and ownership of the patent before issuing the token (Clark, 2018).

The rights management layer implements the business logic specific to a given type of intellectual property. An example of an advanced implementation is the smart contract of the Artory platform for copyrighted works of art (Artory, 2023). The contract tracks not only ownership but also the history of exhibitions, publications, and licensing of the work. It also implements *droit de suite*—the artist's automatic right to receive a percentage of each resale of the work, in accordance with Directive 2001/84/EC.

The economic distribution layer is responsible for the division and transfer of economic value. Async Art, a platform for tokenizing programmable digital art, has created a particularly innovative model (Async Art, 2023). The work of art is divided into layers, each tokenized separately. The owners of the layer tokens can modify their elements, changing the final work. The smart contract automatically divides the revenue from sales or licensing between the owner of the main work (Master) and the owners of the layers according to predetermined proportions (Franceschet et al., 2021).

The compliance and reporting layer ensures adherence to regulatory requirements. Securitize, a platform for tokenizing assets subject to securities regulations, implements KYC/AML mechanisms, transfer restrictions (e.g., only to verified accredited investors), and automatic tax report generation in its smart contracts (Securitize, 2023). For IP tokens, this means the ability to implement restrictions arising from export sanctions (e.g., for dual-use technology) or reporting requirements for transactions above certain thresholds (Maas, 2019).

The Problem of On-Chain and Off-Chain State Synchronization

One of the most fundamental challenges of intellectual property tokenization is ensuring synchronization between the state recorded on the blockchain (on-chain) and the actual legal state in the external world (off-chain). This dichotomy, referred to in the literature as the "oracle problem," takes on a particularly complex form in the context of intellectual property rights (Adler et al., 2018).

Consider a real-world case. In 2022, a project to tokenize a portfolio of battery technology patents encountered a problem when one of the key patents was invalidated by the USPTO following an *inter partes* review proceeding (35 U.S.C. § 311). The token representing the portfolio continued to function on the blockchain at its full value, while the actual value of the portfolio had significantly depreciated. The lack of an automatic mechanism to update the legal status in the smart contract led to a situation where some token holders conducted transactions based on outdated information (Casey & Niblett, 2019).

Tokenization projects have developed various strategies to address this problem. The legal oracle model uses trusted third parties to verify and report on the legal status. For example, the Vaultie platform for trademark tokenization collaborates with international law firms that act as oracles, regularly verifying the registration status and validity of trademarks in various jurisdictions (Vaultie, 2023). The smart contract can automatically suspend trading of the token or adjust its parameters based on the oracle's reports (Breidenbach et al., 2021).

The conditional escrow model assumes that the transfer of a token is not definitive until the legal effectiveness of the off-chain transaction is confirmed. A group tokenizing a portfolio of copyrights for a stock photo library implemented a system where the funds from a transaction are held in a smart contract for 30 days (Getty Images, 2023). During this time, the parties must complete the formal transfer of rights in accordance with the requirements of the relevant jurisdictions. Only after providing proof of the assignment's registration (e.g., with the Copyright Office) are the funds released, and the token transfer becomes irreversible (Mik, 2017).

The insurance model introduces an additional layer of protection by tokenizing not the rights themselves, but insurance claims related to those rights. The InsurAce Protocol project is experimenting with tokens that represent insurance policies for intellectual property (InsurAce Protocol, 2023). In the event of a loss of IP value (e.g., through patent invalidation or infringement), the smart contract automatically pays compensation to the token holders, minimizing the risk of a discrepancy between the on-chain and off-chain value (Gatteschi et al., 2018).

TOKENIZATION IN CONFRONTATION WITH THE DOGMATICS OF INTELLECTUAL PROPERTY LAW

The implementation of tokenization mechanisms encounters a series of fundamental barriers arising from the basic principles upon which the international system of intellectual property protection is founded (WIPO, 2022). In the authors' assessment, these conflicts are systemic in nature and cannot be resolved merely through interpretation or technological adaptation; they require deep dogmatic reflection and, potentially, legislative intervention. The most significant of these conflicts manifest themselves in the clash between the global nature of blockchain technology and the principle of territoriality of rights, in the collision with the formal requirements of legal acts, and in the tension between the automation of rights enforcement and the statutory rights of users.

The first and most fundamental conflict is that between the principle of territoriality and the inherently global nature of blockchain technology (Trimble, 2019). Intellectual property law, whether it concerns patents, trademarks, or even to some extent copyright, is a strictly territorial construct. An exclusive right is effective only within the territory of the state that granted it or in which it is recognized under international agreements (Paris Convention, 1883; Berne Convention, 1886). Meanwhile, blockchain operates as a global, supranational, and distributed system in which transactions are verifiable by all network participants, regardless of their geographical location (Swan, 2015). This fundamental asymmetry creates almost insurmountable practical challenges, especially in the context of tokenizing a portfolio of rights protected in multiple jurisdictions. A smart contract managing such a token would have to implement an extremely complex logic, taking into account different scopes of protection, terms of duration, exceptions and limitations, and legal status in each country (Banda & Schwienbacher, 2023). The attempt to create a single, universal token representing a "global right" is doomed to failure from a dogmatic point of view, as such a legal entity simply does not exist (Peukert, 2021).

The second, equally significant conflict concerns the formal requirements for the effectiveness of legal acts, especially in the context of transferring copyrights. Many legal systems, including the Polish one (Article 53 of the Act on Copyright and Related Rights), require a written form on pain of nullity for an agreement to transfer economic copyrights (Act of February 4, 1994, on Copyright and Related Rights, Dz.U. 1994 No. 24 item 83). A blockchain transaction, which consists of creating a digitally signed, cryptographic entry in a distributed ledger, *prima facie* does not meet this requirement (Allen, 2018). This raises the fundamental question of whether such a record can be considered a functional equivalent of a document in written form. The answer to this question is highly ambiguous and depends on the specific jurisdiction and its approach to electronic forms of declarations of will (UNCITRAL Model Law on Electronic Commerce, 1996). In systems that strictly interpret written form as requiring a handwritten signature on a tangible medium, the transfer of copyright by means of a token will be absolutely void (Savelyev, 2018). Even in jurisdictions that recognize documentary or electronic forms, doubts may arise as to whether a pseudonymous transaction on the blockchain network allows for sufficient identification of the parties to the legal act (Bacon et al., 2021).

The third area of conflict is the tension between the automation of rights enforcement and the flexibility of the legal system, particularly in the context of statutory limitations on exclusive rights (Mezei, 2020). Smart contracts, by their nature operating in a binary ("if-then") manner, enable the creation of technological protection measures (DRM) that can absolutely prevent access to content without the possession of the appropriate token (Efroni & Geiger, 2018). Such rigid, automated control contradicts doctrines such as fair use (in common law systems) or private and public permitted use (in continental systems) (Directive 2001/29/EC, art. 5). These doctrines are an essential element of systemic balance, allowing the use of protected works without the rightholder's consent for specific, socially justified purposes (e.g., educational, scientific, as part of the right to quote) (Geiger et al., 2018). Encoding in a smart contract the complex, contextual, and assessment-requiring criteria that determine the possibility of invoking permitted use is practically impossible (Quintais, 2017). As a result, token-based systems can lead to the *de facto* elimination of these statutory user rights, disrupting the fundamental balance of interests on which all copyright law is based (Senftleben, 2019). Similar problems concern the doctrine of exhaustion of rights, which, in relation to digital copies, is still a subject of controversy and differing rulings in various legal systems (UsedSoft GmbH v. Oracle International Corp., C-128/11; Capitol Records v. ReDigi, 934 F.Supp.2d 640), further complicating the possibility of creating an interoperable, global tokenization system.

THE REGULATORY MOSAIC: A COMPARATIVE ANALYSIS OF INTELLECTUAL PROPERTY TOKEN CLASSIFICATION

The United States: A Labyrinth of Precedents and Regulatory Uncertainty

The American approach to the regulation of intellectual property tokens is characterized by a lack of dedicated legislative frameworks, coupled with the active enforcement of existing regulations by the Securities and Exchange Commission (SEC). This "regulation by enforcement" strategy creates an environment of high legal uncertainty, in which tokenization projects must navigate a complex labyrinth of precedents and regulatory guidelines (Rohr & Wright, 2019).

The foundation of American analysis remains the *Howey* test, formulated in the 1946 Supreme Court ruling in *SEC v. W.J. Howey Co.*, 328 U.S. 293 (1946). The application of this test to IP tokens reveals particular interpretive challenges. Consider the real-world case of the tokenization of rights to future royalties from a portfolio of biotechnology patents by a Silicon Valley fund. The SEC challenged the structure, arguing that the tokens met all four prongs of the *Howey* test: (1) the purchasers invested money in the form of cryptocurrencies, (2) in a common enterprise of managing the IP portfolio, (3) with an expectation of profits from growing licensing royalties, (4) which were to be derived primarily from the efforts of the management team in commercializing the patents (see, e.g., *SEC v. Kik Interactive Inc.*, No. 19-cv-5244 (S.D.N.Y. 2020)).

The ruling in *SEC v. Ripple Labs* from July 2023 is of breakthrough significance (*SEC v. Ripple Labs, Inc.*, No. 20-cv-10832 (S.D.N.Y. July 13, 2023)). Judge Analisa Torres made a precedential distinction between the institutional sale of tokens (which constituted an offering of securities) and programmatic sales on cryptocurrency exchanges (which were not deemed to be an offering of securities). This distinction, based on the theory that exchange purchasers cannot reasonably expect profits from the issuer's efforts because they do not know from whom they are buying, introduced a new dimension to the analysis (Goforth, 2021). For IP tokens, this implies a potential avenue for avoiding classification as securities when sold on decentralized exchanges, although uncertainty remains regarding the broader applicability of this precedent (Henderson & Raskin, 2019).

An analysis of no-action letters issued by the SEC reveals criteria that may help IP tokens avoid classification as securities. In the case of *TurnKey Jet* (SEC No-Action Letter, April 3, 2019), the SEC did not take action against tokens that were: fully functional at the time of sale, sold at a fixed price corresponding to their utility value, not promoted as an investment, and contained built-in mechanisms to prevent speculation. IP tokenization projects are attempting to adapt these guidelines, for example, by creating tokens that provide immediate access to a patent database at a fixed subscription price (Robinson, 2020).

The practical consequences of the American regime are severe. A full registration of an offering with the SEC entails costs of $1-5 million and a process lasting 6-12 months (Cohney et al., 2019). Alternatives in the form of exemptions also have significant limitations: Regulation D (17 C.F.R. § 230.501-508) restricts the offering to accredited investors and imposes restrictions on secondary trading; Regulation S (17 C.F.R. § 230.901-905) excludes U.S. persons; and Regulation A+ (17 C.F.R. § 230.251-263), while allowing for a public offering of up to $75 million, requires SEC approval and ongoing reporting. As a result, many IP tokenization projects completely exclude Americans from their offerings, which paradoxically limits the access of American innovators to this new source of financing (Dell'Erba, 2020).

The European Union: Comprehensive Harmonization through MiCA

The European Union has adopted a diametrically different approach, creating a comprehensive regulatory framework in the form of the Regulation on Markets in Crypto-Assets (Regulation (EU) 2023/1114 - MiCA), which came into full effect in December 2024. MiCA represents the most ambitious attempt to create a coherent regulatory regime for tokens in the world, offering both legal clarity and significant compliance burdens (Zetzsche et al., 2021).

A key element in the analysis of IP tokens in the context of MiCA is determining whether a given token constitutes a financial instrument within the meaning of MiFID II (Directive 2014/65/EU). This classification is binary and decisive—financial instruments are excluded from the scope of MiCA and are subject to traditional, often more restrictive, capital market regulations. The European Securities and Markets Authority (ESMA) indicates in its guidelines that tokens offering rights similar to shares or bonds, including the right to participate in profits, should be classified as transferable securities (ESMA, 2019).

The case of the French AMF (Autorité des marchés financiers) illustrates the practical application of this analysis. In 2023, the AMF assessed a project to tokenize the copyrights of a catalog of musical works (AMF, 2023). The tokens offered holders a proportional share in royalties and voting rights in licensing decisions.

The AMF concluded that such a structure met the criteria of a transferable security, requiring a full prospectus in accordance with the Prospectus Regulation (Regulation (EU) 2017/1129). The project had to be restructured, limiting the rights of the tokens to simple access to the works, in order to qualify as a utility token under MiCA (Gurrea-Martínez & Remolina, 2020).

For IP tokens that qualify for the MiCA regime, the requirements depend on the specific category. Utility tokens only require the notification of a white paper to the competent supervisory authority at least 20 days before the offering (MiCA, Art. 7). The white paper must contain detailed information about the issuer, the project, the rights granted by the token, the technology, and the risks. For a project tokenizing a patent database, the white paper would need to precisely describe the scope of access, territorial restrictions, database update mechanisms, and the risks associated with the possible invalidation of patents (Ferrari, 2020).

Asset-referenced tokens (ARTs) are subject to much more stringent requirements. If the value of an IP token is linked to a basket of intellectual property rights and is intended to maintain a stable value, it may be classified as an ART (MiCA, Art. 16). This requires obtaining authorization from the competent authority, maintaining own funds of the greater of €350,000 or 2% of the value of the reference assets, and detailed plans for reserve management and recovery (MiCA, Art. 34-35). In practice, these requirements make the ART structure unviable for most IP tokenization projects (Annunziata, 2020).

MiCA also introduces extensive requirements for crypto-asset service providers (CASPs), including platforms for trading IP tokens (MiCA, Title V). The requirements include initial capital of €50,000 to €150,000 (depending on the type of services), segregation of client assets, risk management systems, and detailed anti-money laundering procedures. For specialized IP token trading platforms, this means significant barriers to entry and operational costs (Möslein, 2019).

A positive aspect of MiCA is the passporting mechanism—authorization in one member state allows for the provision of services throughout the EU (MiCA, Art. 60). For global IP tokenization projects, a single authorization opens up access to a market of 450 million consumers. Nevertheless, MiCA does not harmonize the underlying IP law—a token representing French *droits d'auteur* is still subject to different rules than German *Urheberrecht*, which complicates the creation of truly pan-European IP tokens (Jacobs, 2021).

Innovative Regulatory Models: Switzerland, Singapore, and Regulatory Sandboxes

Small but highly developed jurisdictions have crafted innovative regulatory approaches that often serve as laboratories for solutions later adopted by larger economies. Switzerland, Singapore, and Liechtenstein stand out for their particularly progressive frameworks for tokenization (Blandin et al., 2019).

Switzerland, through the legal amendment known as the "DLT Act" (Federal Act on the Adaptation of Federal Law to Developments in Distributed Ledger Technology, effective from February 2021), has created what is perhaps the most complete legal framework for tokenization in the world. The key innovation is the introduction of "DLT securities"—a new category of securities that can exist exclusively in the form of tokens on a blockchain (Swiss Code of Obligations, Art. 973d). For IP tokenization, this means the ability to issue legally recognized tokens representing shares in intellectual property revenues without the need to create traditional securities (Kramer, 2021).

The case of the Swiss company Tokengate illustrates the practical application of this framework. The company issued DLT securities representing shares in a portfolio of software rights (Tokengate, 2023). The tokens are traded on the SIX Digital Exchange—the world's first fully regulated token exchange integrated with a traditional stock exchange. The structure allows for immediate settlement (T+0) and 24/7 trading, radically increasing liquidity compared to traditional instruments (Schär, 2021).

FINMA (Swiss Financial Market Supervisory Authority) applies a functional approach to token classification, publishing detailed guidelines with specific examples (FINMA, 2018). A token representing the right to receive royalties from a patent is classified as an asset token (subject to securities regulations), while a token providing access to a patent database may be a payment token (subject only to AML regulations). This regulatory clarity, combined with a competitive tax system, has made Switzerland a hub for IP tokenization projects—the Crypto Valley in Zug hosts over 1,000 blockchain companies (Crypto Valley Association, 2023).

Singapore, through the Monetary Authority of Singapore (MAS), has adopted an equally innovative, though more flexible, approach. The Payment Services Act of 2019 regulates "digital payment token services," while the Securities and Futures Act covers tokens of a securities nature (Payment Services Act 2019, No. 2 of 2019). A key innovation is the FinTech Regulatory Sandbox, which allows projects to test tokenization models with limited regulatory requirements (MAS, 2016).

The example of ADDX (formerly iSTOX) shows the potential of this approach (ADDX, 2023). The platform, licensed by MAS, enables the tokenization and trading of intellectual property rights, including rights to future revenues from patents and copyrights. Using the sandbox, ADDX tested a model for fractionalizing IP rights, allowing investors to acquire shares starting from just $10,000 USD—radically lowering the barriers to entry compared to traditional IP transactions. After the testing period, the platform received a full license as a Recognised Market Operator (Arner et al., 2017).

Liechtenstein has gone the furthest, creating an entirely new legal framework through the Token and Trusted Technology Service Provider Act (TVTG), also known as the "Blockchain Act" (TVTG, LGBl. 2019 No. 301). The act introduces a revolutionary "Token Container Model"—a token is treated as a digital container that can hold any right (TVTG, Art. 2). The transfer of the token automatically means the transfer of the contained right, eliminating uncertainty about the legal effects of blockchain transactions (Konashevych, 2020).

For IP tokenization, the TVTG offers unprecedented legal certainty. The company IP Bridge Liechtenstein has used this framework to tokenize a portfolio of luxury brand trademarks (IP Bridge Liechtenstein, 2023). The tokens, registered as "IP Right Tokens" with the Financial Market Authority, represent direct ownership rights to the trademarks. The smart contract automatically manages licensing, and revenues are distributed proportionally to the tokens held. Importantly, in the event of a dispute, the courts of Liechtenstein recognize the blockchain record as proof of ownership, radically simplifying legal proceedings (Nägele & Xander, 2020).

Conclusions from the Comparative Analysis: Towards Convergence or Fragmentation?

The comparative analysis reveals fundamental differences in regulatory philosophy among jurisdictions. The USA represents an *ex post* approach, based on the enforcement of broad, flexible standards. The EU opts for comprehensive *ex ante* harmonization, creating detailed frameworks for every aspect of tokenization. Small, innovative jurisdictions are experimenting with new legal constructs, often leading larger economies by a decade (Auer, 2019).

These differences create both opportunities and challenges for IP tokenization projects. On one hand, regulatory arbitrage allows for choosing the most favorable environment—be it Swiss legal certainty, Singapore's sandbox, or Liechtenstein's Token Container Model (Cong et al., 2021). On the other hand, regulatory fragmentation complicates projects with a global reach, forcing costly navigation through a mosaic of requirements (Mangano, 2018).

However, we are observing signs of a slow convergence. IOSCO (International Organization of Securities Commissions) is working on global standards for crypto-assets (IOSCO, 2023). The FATF has introduced the Travel Rule, *de facto* harmonizing AML requirements globally (FATF, 2021). Bilateral regulatory cooperation agreements, such as the one between the UK's FCA and Singapore's MAS, are creating bridges between regimes. For IP tokenization, this evolving convergence offers hope for a future in which innovative financing models will be globally accessible without artificial regulatory barriers (Yeoh, 2017).

The Crisis of State Coercion: Jurisdiction and Enforcement in a Decentralized Reality

The analysis of substantive law problems, while fundamental, does not capture the full shock that blockchain technology sends through the legal system. It is on the procedural level, in the collision with issues of jurisdiction and the effectiveness of enforcement, that traditional legal paradigms, based on the Westphalian model of state sovereignty, undergo a complete deconstruction (Lehmann, 2019). These problems are not merely technical inconveniences; they strike at the very essence of the state as an organization possessing, according to Max Weber's classic definition, a monopoly on the legitimate use of physical force (Weber, 1919). An analysis of these issues leads to the conclusion that the decentralized nature of blockchain technology undermines this monopoly, forcing a search for radically new models of legal order (Wright & De Filippi, 2015).

Determining the appropriate jurisdiction for disputes concerning IP tokens is a problem that can be described as "squaring the circle" in private international law. Traditional jurisdictional connecting factors, such as the place of contract conclusion (*lex loci contractus*), the place of performance of an obligation (*lex loci solutionis*), or the defendant's domicile (*forum rei*), lose all clarity and rationality in the context of transactions executed by autonomous smart contracts (Ortolani, 2019). Each of these connecting factors is based on the assumption of a geographically tangible anchor point. Meanwhile, in a blockchain network, a transaction has no single location—it is a globally distributed event, existing simultaneously in thousands of places (Möslein, 2018). Attempts to apply existing conflict-of-law rules, such as the Brussels I bis Regulation in the EU (Regulation (EU) No 1215/2012) or the "minimum contacts" test in the USA (*International Shoe Co. v. Washington*, 326 U.S. 310 (1945)), lead to contradictory and often absurd results. One could argue that the court of every state where even one network node is located has jurisdiction, which would lead to an unacceptable multiplicity of jurisdictions (*forum shopping* on a global scale) and would violate the principle of predictability (Guillaume, 2019). One could also, with equal justification, claim that no court has jurisdiction, as no state has a sufficiently strong, "targeted" connection with the transaction. Both of these conclusions are unacceptable from the perspective of legal certainty and lead to procedural paralysis (Dickinson, 2019).

Even if, through legal acrobatics, it were possible to establish the proper court, an even greater challenge emerges: the illusory nature of judgment enforcement. The effectiveness of any legal system ultimately rests on the existence of a coercive apparatus capable of physically enforcing a judgment against the debtor's will (Kelsen, 1967). This is the transition from the sphere of *sollen* (ought) to the sphere of *sein* (being). Traditional enforcement mechanisms—bank account seizure, bailiff seizure of movables, forced mortgage entry—rely on the existence of central, regulated intermediaries (banks, state organs, land registry systems) who serve as the "arm" of the justice system (Mann, 2019). In a decentralized ecosystem, such trusted intermediaries, by definition, do not exist. There is no central entity that a court could order to freeze tokens in an anonymous user's self-custody wallet (Kiviat, 2015). The irreversibility of blockchain transactions means that an unlawful disposal of tokens cannot simply be "reversed" by a court order. This is a situation where a court judgment becomes merely a non-binding declaration, devoid of real executive power—a kind of *nudum ius* (a naked right, devoid of protection) (Van Hoecke, 2002). Although courts in some jurisdictions, e.g., in the United Kingdom, have issued innovative asset freezing orders (*freezing injunctions*) directed against "persons unknown" operating at specified wallet addresses (*AA v Persons Unknown* EWHC 3556 (Comm)), the practical enforceability of such orders is minimal without the voluntary cooperation of the defendant or centralized exchanges, which are, however, increasingly being bypassed by advanced users (Fox et al., 2021).

In the authors' assessment, these challenges indicate the inevitable need to seek radically new solutions, which can be described as the privatization of justice or the development of code-based legal orders (*lex cryptographica*) (De Filippi & Wright, 2019). This is not an entirely new concept—legal history knows examples of non-state orders, such as medieval merchant law (*lex mercatoria*) (Calliess & Zumbansen, 2010). Today, however, thanks to technology, this phenomenon can take on a global scale. One direction may be the development of hybrid dispute resolution systems that combine the legitimacy and authority of traditional arbitration with the efficiency of blockchain technology (Ortolani, 2016). Parties could agree in advance, in the smart contract code, to submit disputes to the jurisdiction of a specialized arbitration tribunal, whose decision, after being transmitted to the network through a trusted "oracle," would then be automatically enforced by the smart contract itself (e.g., by unlocking funds deposited in escrow or through a forced token transfer) (Schmitz & Rule, 2019). In such a model, state coercion is replaced by technological coercion, built into the system's architecture (Werbach, 2018).

Another, more futuristic direction is the development of fully decentralized justice systems (such as Kleros or Aragon Court), where disputes are resolved by randomly selected, economically motivated "judges" from around the world, and their decisions are enforced directly by code (Ast & Dimov, 2021). Although these systems are still in an early stage of development and raise serious doubts about their compliance with fair trial guarantees (such as the right to be heard, judicial independence, or the right to appeal) (European Convention on Human Rights, Art. 6), they point to a potential future in which law is enforced not through state coercion but through cryptographically secured mechanisms built into the system's architecture (Barnett & Treleaven, 2018). The development of these alternative legal orders may be the most important and lasting consequence of the blockchain revolution, leading to the emergence of a global, polycentric legal system in which the state is only one of many providers of jurisdictional services (Cutts, 2019).

CONCLUSIONS: TOWARDS A NEW LEGAL ORDER FOR INNOVATION

The multi-faceted analysis conducted in this article leads to an unequivocal conclusion: the phenomenon of intellectual property rights tokenization constitutes a fundamental challenge to existing legal paradigms, the scale and depth of which are still underestimated in mainstream legal discourse (Finck, 2019). This is not merely another technological innovation that can be easily fitted into existing frameworks through careful interpretation. Rather, it is a catalyst that exposes the limitations, anachronisms, and dogmatic assumptions of many fundamental institutions of civil, commercial, and financial law (Yeung, 2019). Attempts to mechanically apply twentieth-century legal tools, created for a centralized, territorial, and analog world, to describe and regulate decentralized, global, and programmable digital assets are doomed to failure and lead to a regulatory paralysis that stifles innovation (Zetzsche et al., 2020).

In the course of the argumentation, the authors have posited the thesis that the implementation of tokenization mechanisms is fraught with fundamental normative conflicts. This thesis has, in our assessment, been fully confirmed through the analysis of problems on three key levels. First, at the level of intellectual property law, where the global nature of blockchain enters into an irresolvable, ontological conflict with the principle of territoriality of rights, and where rigid formal requirements for the transfer of rights, designed to protect parties in traditional commerce, become an irrational barrier to fluid digital trade (Savelyev, 2017). Second, at the level of regulatory law, where binary, rigid categories created for the simple, analog world of finance prove to be completely inadequate for describing complex, hybrid, and multifunctional IP tokens, leading to absurd classification dilemmas (Hacker et al., 2019). Third, at the level of procedural law, where traditional mechanisms for establishing jurisdiction and enforcing judgments, based on the state's monopoly on the use of coercion, become helpless in a decentralized, borderless reality (De Filippi, 2016).

De Lege Ferenda Recommendations

Emerging from this intellectual and regulatory impasse requires courage and openness from both legislators and legal dogmatists. It is necessary to abandon attempts to forcibly fit new phenomena into old frameworks and to begin work on creating a new, flexible, and functional legal order for digital innovations (Brownsword et al., 2017). Based on the analysis conducted, we formulate the following *de lege ferenda* postulates:

At the international level, an initiative within the World Intellectual Property Organization (WIPO) is necessary, aimed at developing a convention on the recognition of token-based transfers of intellectual property. The convention should establish minimum technical and legal standards for tokenization, principles for determining jurisdiction in disputes concerning IP tokens, and mechanisms for international cooperation in enforcement (WIPO, 2022). The model for such a convention could draw from the experience of the New York Convention on the Recognition and Enforcement of Foreign Arbitral Awards (New York Convention, 1958), adapting its solutions to the specificity of blockchain (Benedetti & Kostovetsky, 2021).

At the European Union level, we postulate the introduction of a dedicated regime for intellectual property tokens within the review of the MiCA regulation. The current categories of utility tokens and asset-referenced tokens do not account for the specificity of intellectual property rights (European Commission, 2020). We propose creating a new category of "IP tokens" with tailored requirements that consider the long-term nature of IP rights, the need for flexibility in structuring economic rights, and the necessity of integration with national intellectual property registration systems (Busch et al., 2021).

At the national level, it is crucial to introduce provisions recognizing blockchain records as a documentary form for the purpose of transferring intellectual property rights. Following the example of Estonia (Digital Signatures Act, RT I 2000, 26, 150) or Switzerland (Swiss Code of Obligations, Art. 973d), legislators should explicitly recognize that a transaction that is cryptographically signed and recorded on a blockchain meets the requirements of written form, provided that the parties can be identified and the integrity of the record is ensured (Konashevych, 2019). Additionally, it is necessary to create frameworks for "blockchain-ready" intellectual property registers, enabling the automatic verification of the legal status of tokenized assets (Lim et al., 2019).

Towards a New Philosophy of Law for the Digital Era

For a legal order for intellectual property tokenization to be effective, it must be based on several fundamental principles that go beyond traditional legal paradigms (Murray, 2019):

The principle of technological neutrality requires that the law regulate economic functions and risks, not specific technological implementations. It does not matter whether the transfer of rights occurs through blockchain, another distributed ledger technology, or future innovations—what is essential are the legal and economic effects of the transaction (Reed, 2018).

The principle of regulatory proportionality postulates that the burden of compliance requirements should be adequate to the scale of risk and the nature of the activity. The tokenization of rights to an amateur musical work should not be subject to the same requirements as the tokenization of a pharmaceutical patent portfolio worth billions of dollars (Baldwin et al., 2012).

The principle of technological autonomy recognizes the right of parties to choose not only the applicable law and forum but also the technological mechanism for dispute resolution. If parties consciously choose to submit a dispute to the "jurisdiction" of a decentralized arbitration protocol, the law should respect this, provided that minimal procedural guarantees are maintained (Nakamoto, 2008).

The principle of legal interoperability requires that legal systems be designed with cooperation in the digital environment in mind. This means the standardization of data formats, APIs for public registers, and mechanisms for the automatic recognition of decisions made in other jurisdictions (Lessig, 2006).

Epilogue: Blockchain as a Catalyst for Legal Evolution

The tokenization of intellectual property is not an end in itself. It is a tool that can unlock the enormous, dormant economic potential inherent in intangible assets, democratize access to innovation financing, and accelerate the pace of technological development (Chen & Bellavitis, 2020). History shows that great technological innovations—from the printing press through the railroad to the Internet—have always forced fundamental changes in the legal system (Brownsword, 2019). Blockchain is no exception.

The task for lawyers and legislators is to create legal frameworks that allow this potential to be realized in a safe, predictable, and fair manner. This will require not only amendments to laws but, above all, a change in the way we think about law in the digital era (De Filippi et al., 2021). We must be ready for a world in which state law is only one of many competing normative orders, and the effectiveness of law depends not only on the force of coercion but also on the intelligence of its architecture (Reidenberg, 1998).

Perhaps blockchain's greatest contribution to the evolution of law will be forcing us to reconsider the fundamental assumptions on which our legal system is based. Is territoriality an indispensable attribute of law? Is the state's monopoly on coercion the only guarantee of order? Does written form really protect parties better than a cryptographic signature? The answers to these questions will determine the shape of law in the 21st century (Wright, 2021).

The tokenization of intellectual property is thus more than a technical innovation—it is a mirror reflecting all the tensions between the traditional, territorial, hierarchical legal order and the emerging, global, decentralized digital reality. How we resolve these tensions will determine not only the future of innovation but also the fundamental question of the role of law and the state in the society of the future (Katzenbach & Ulbricht, 2019).

REFERENCES

ADDX. (2023). Digital securities exchange platform. https://addx.co/

Adler, J., Berryhill, R., Veneris, A., Poulos, Z., Veira, N., & Kastania, A. (2018). Astraea: A decentralized blockchain oracle. *2018 IEEE International Conference on Internet of Things*.

Allen, J. G. (2018). Wrapped and stacked: "Smart contracts" and the interaction of natural and formal language. *European Review of Contract Law*, *14*(4), 307–343. DOI: 10.1515/ercl-2018-1023

AMF. (2023). Position-recommendation DOC-2023-04: Guide to the regulatory framework applicable to initial coin offerings (ICOs). Autorité des marchés financiers.

Annunziata, F. (2020). Speak, if you can: What are you? An alternative approach to the qualification of tokens and initial coin offerings. *European Company and Financial Law Review*, *17*(2), 129–154. DOI: 10.1515/ecfr-2020-0007

Antonopoulos, A. M., & Wood, G. (2018). *Mastering Ethereum: Building smart contracts and DApps*. O'Reilly Media.

Arner, D. W., Barberis, J., & Buckley, R. P. (2017). *FinTech and RegTech in a nutshell, and the future in a sandbox*. CFA Institute Research Foundation. DOI: 10.2139/ssrn.3088303

Art, A. (2023). Programmable art platform. https://async.art/

Artory. (2023). Blockchain registry for art and collectibles. https://artory.com/

Ast, F., & Dimov, D. (2021). The crowdjury, a crowdsourced justice system for the collaboration era. In *Legal Tech and the New Sharing Economy* (pp. 45–67). Springer.

Audius. (2023). Decentralized music streaming protocol. https://audius.co/

Auer, R. (2019). Embedded supervision: How to build regulation into blockchain finance. BIS Working Papers No. 811.

Bacon, J., Bazinas, G., Goldenfein, J., Grigera-Naón, J. J., & Rauchs, M. (2021). *Blockchain and digital assets: International legal and regulatory challenges*. Sweet & Maxwell.

Baldwin, R., Cave, M., & Lodge, M. (2012). *Understanding regulation: Theory, strategy, and practice*. Oxford University Press.

Banda, P., & Schwienbacher, A. (2023). Blockchain-based corporate governance. *Journal of Corporate Finance*, *78*, 102338.

Barnett, J., & Treleaven, P. (2018). Algorithmic dispute resolution—The automation of professional dispute resolution using AI and blockchain technologies. *The Computer Journal*, *61*(3), 399–409. DOI: 10.1093/comjnl/bxx103

Belleflamme, P., Lambert, T., & Schwienbacher, A. (2014). Crowdfunding: Tapping the right crowd. *Journal of Business Venturing*, *29*(5), 585–609. DOI: 10.1016/j.jbusvent.2013.07.003

Benedetti, H., & Kostovetsky, L. (2021). Digital tulips? Returns to investors in initial coin offerings. *Journal of Corporate Finance*, *66*, 101786. DOI: 10.1016/j.jcorpfin.2020.101786

Berne Convention for the Protection of Literary and Artistic Works. Sept. 9, 1886, as revised at Paris on July 24, 1971, and amended on September 28, 1979, S. Treaty Doc. No. 99-27 (1986).

Blandin, A., Cloots, A. S., Hussain, H., Rauchs, M., Saleuddin, R., Allen, J. G., & Cloud, K. (2019). *Global cryptoasset regulatory landscape study*. Cambridge Centre for Alternative Finance. DOI: 10.2139/ssrn.3379219

Breidenbach, S., Glatz, F., Schrey, J., & Schmid, A. (2021). *Rechtshandbuch Smart Contracts*. C.H. Beck.

Bridge Liechtenstein, I. P. (2023). Intellectual property tokenization platform. https://ipbridge.li/

Brownsword, R. (2019). *Law, technology and society: Reimagining the regulatory environment*. Routledge. DOI: 10.4324/9781351128186

Brownsword, R., Scotford, E., & Yeung, K. (Eds.). (2017). *The Oxford handbook of law, regulation and technology*. Oxford University Press.

Busch, C., Mak, V., Twigg-Flesner, C., & Schulze, R. (2021). The EU digital services act and the EU digital markets act: A primer. *EuCML*, *10*(6), 256–261.

Calliess, G. P., & Zumbansen, P. (2010). *Rough consensus and running code: A theory of transnational private law*. Hart Publishing.

Cannarsa, M. (2019). Interpretation of contracts and smart contracts: Smart interpretation or interpretation of smart contracts? *European Review of Private Law*, *27*(4), 773–785.

Casey, A. J., & Niblett, A. (2019). Framework for the new personalization of law. *The University of Chicago Law Review. University of Chicago. Law School*, *86*(2), 333–358.

Catalini, C., & Gans, J. S. (2020). Some simple economics of the blockchain. *Communications of the ACM*, *63*(7), 80–90. DOI: 10.1145/3359552

Chen, Y., & Bellavitis, C. (2020). Blockchain disruption and decentralized finance: The rise of decentralized business models. *Journal of Business Venturing Insights*, *13*, e00151. DOI: 10.1016/j.jbvi.2019.e00151

Clark, B. (2018). Blockchain and IP law: A match made in crypto heaven? WIPO Magazine, February 2018.

Cohney, S., Hoffman, D., Sklaroff, J., & Wishnick, D. (2019). Coin-operated capitalism. *Columbia Law Review*, *119*(3), 591–676.

Cong, L. W., & He, Z. (2019). Blockchain disruption and smart contracts. *Review of Financial Studies*, *32*(5), 1754–1797. DOI: 10.1093/rfs/hhz007

Cong, L. W., Li, Y., & Wang, N. (2021). Tokenomics: Dynamic adoption and valuation. *Review of Financial Studies*, *34*(3), 1105–1155. DOI: 10.1093/rfs/hhaa089

Crypto Valley Association. (2023). CV VC Top 50 Report. https://cryptovalley.swiss

Cutts, T. (2019). Smart contracts and consumers. *West Virginia Law Review*, *122*(2), 389–447.

De Filippi, P. (2016). The interplay between decentralization and privacy: The case of blockchain technologies. Journal of Peer Production, 7.

De Filippi, P., & Hassan, S. (2016). Blockchain technology as a regulatory technology: From code is law to law is code. *First Monday*, *21*(12). Advance online publication. DOI: 10.5210/fm.v21i12.7113

De Filippi, P., Mannan, M., & Reijers, W. (2021). The alegality of blockchain technology. *Policy and Society*, *41*(3), 358–372. DOI: 10.1093/polsoc/puac006

De Filippi, P., & Wright, A. (2018). *Blockchain and the law: The rule of code.* Harvard University Press.

De Filippi, P., & Wright, A. (2019). Decentralized blockchain technology and the rise of lex cryptographia. SSRN Electronic Journal.

Dell'Erba, M. (2020). Initial coin offerings: The response of regulatory authorities. *NYU Journal of Law & Business*, *16*(3), 543–608.

Dickinson, A. (2019). Cryptocurrencies and the conflict of laws. In Fox, D., & Green, S. (Eds.), *Cryptocurrencies in public and private law* (pp. 253–289). Oxford University Press. DOI: 10.1093/law/9780198826385.003.0005

Digital Signatures Act, RT I 2000, 26, 150 (Estonia).

Dinwoodie, G. B. (2009). Developing a private international intellectual property law: The demise of territoriality. *William and Mary Law Review, 51*(2), 711–800.

Directive 2001/29/EC of the European Parliament and of the Council of 22 May 2001 on the harmonisation of certain aspects of copyright and related rights in the information society, OJ L 167, 22.6.2001.

Directive 2001/84/EC of the European Parliament and of the Council of 27 September 2001 on the resale right for the benefit of the author of an original work of art, OJ L 272, 13.10.2001.

Directive 2014/65/EU of the European Parliament and of the Council of 15 May 2014 on markets in financial instruments, OJ L 173, 12.6.2014.

Durovic, M., & Janssen, A. (2019). The formation of blockchain-based smart contracts in the light of contract law. *European Review of Private Law, 27*(4), 753–771.

Efroni, Z., & Geiger, C. (2018). Limitations in the digital single market: Has the court of justice developed a crystal clear vision? IIC - International Review of Intellectual Property and Competition Law, 49(8), 881-885.

ESMA. (2019). Advice on Initial Coin Offerings and Crypto-Assets. ESMA50-157-1391.

European Commission. (2020). Proposal for a Regulation on Markets in Crypto-assets. COM(2020) 593 final.

European Convention on Human Rights, November 4, 1950, E.T.S. 5, 213 U.N.T.S. 221.

Fairfield, J. (2021). Tokenized: The law of non-fungible tokens and unique digital property. *Industrial Law Journal, 97*(4), 1261–1331.

FATF. (2021). *Updated guidance for a risk-based approach to virtual assets and virtual asset service providers*. Financial Action Task Force.

Federal Act on the Adaptation of Federal Law to Developments in Distributed Ledger Technology (DLT Act), AS 2021 33 (Switzerland).

Ferrari, V. (2020). The regulation of crypto-assets in the EU – Investment and payment tokens under the radar. *Maastricht Journal of European and Comparative Law*, *27*(3), 325–342. DOI: 10.1177/1023263X20911538

Finck, M. (2019). *Blockchain and the General Data Protection Regulation: Can distributed ledgers be squared with European data protection law?* European Parliamentary Research Service.

FINMA. (2018). *Guidelines for enquiries regarding the regulatory framework for initial coin offerings (ICOs).* Swiss Financial Market Supervisory Authority.

Fox, D., Green, S., & Hsiao, K. (2021). Cryptocurrencies in the common law of property. In Fox, D., & Green, S. (Eds.), *Cryptocurrencies in public and private law* (pp. 143–177). Oxford University Press.

Franceschet, M., Colavizza, G., Smith, T., Finucane, B., Ostachowski, M. L., Scalet, S., Perkins, J., Morgan, J., & Hernández, S. (2021). Crypto art: A decentralized view. *Leonardo*, *54*(4), 402–405. DOI: 10.1162/leon_a_02003

Gatteschi, V., Lamberti, F., Demartini, C., Pranteda, C., & Santamaría, V. (2018). Blockchain and smart contracts for insurance: Is the technology mature enough? *Future Internet*, *10*(2), 20. DOI: 10.3390/fi10020020

Geiger, C., Frosio, G., & Bulayenko, O. (2018). The exception for text and data mining (TDM) in the proposed directive on copyright in the digital single market. Centre for International Intellectual Property Studies Research Paper No. 2018-02.

Goforth, C. R. (2021). Regulation of crypto: Who is the securities and exchange commission protecting? *American Business Law Journal*, *58*(3), 643–705. DOI: 10.1111/ablj.12192

Guadamuz, A. (2019). Blockchains and legal institutions. In Brownsword, R., Scotford, E., & Yeung, K. (Eds.), *The Oxford handbook of law, regulation and technology* (pp. 311–330). Oxford University Press.

Guillaume, F. (2019). Blockchain: La réponse de la CNUDCI et d'UNIDROIT. *Revue de Droit Commercial Belge*, *6*, 513–532.

Gurrea-Martínez, A., & Remolina, N. (2020). Global challenges and regulatory strategies to fintech. *SSRN*, *35*(3), 421–465. DOI: 10.2139/ssrn.3576506

Hacker, P., Lianos, I., Dimitropoulos, G., & Eich, S. (Eds.). (2019). *Regulating blockchain: Techno-social and legal challenges.* Oxford University Press. DOI: 10.1093/oso/9780198842187.001.0001

Hagiu, A., & Yoffie, D. B. (2013). The new patent intermediaries: Platforms, defensive aggregators, and super-aggregators. *The Journal of Economic Perspectives, 27*(1), 45–66. DOI: 10.1257/jep.27.1.45

Hall, B. H., & Lerner, J. (2010). The financing of R&D and innovation. In Hall, B. H., & Rosenberg, N. (Eds.), *Handbook of the economics of innovation* (Vol. 1, pp. 609–639). North-Holland. DOI: 10.1016/S0169-7218(10)01014-2

Henderson, M. T., & Raskin, M. (2019). A regulatory classification of digital assets: Toward an operational Howey test for cryptocurrencies, ICOs, and other digital assets. *Columbia Business Law Review, 2019*(2), 443–493.

Images, G. (2023). Stock photo licensing platform. https://www.gettyimages.com/

InsurAce Protocol. (2023). Decentralized insurance protocol. https://www.insurace.io/

International Shoe Co. v. Washington, 326 U.S. 310 (1945).

IOSCO. (2023). *Policy recommendations for crypto and digital asset markets.* International Organization of Securities Commissions.

IPwe. (2023). Global patent marketplace. https://ipwe.com/

Jacobs, L. (2021). Financial regulation of crypto-assets under MiFID II/MiFIR and MiCA. *European Company and Financial Law Review, 18*(6), 844–878.

Kamiyama, S., Sheehan, J., & Martinez, C. (2006). Valuation and exploitation of intellectual property. OECD Science, Technology and Industry Working Papers 2006/05.

Katzenbach, C., & Ulbricht, L. (2019). Algorithmic governance. *Internet Policy Review, 8*(4). Advance online publication. DOI: 10.14763/2019.4.1424

Kelsen, H. (1967). *Pure theory of law.* University of California Press. DOI: 10.1525/9780520312296

Kerr, W. R., & Nanda, R. (2015). Financing innovation. *Annual Review of Financial Economics, 7*(1), 445–462. DOI: 10.1146/annurev-financial-111914-041825

Kiviat, T. I. (2015). Beyond Bitcoin: Issues in regulating blockchain transactions. *Duke Law Journal, 65*(3), 569–608.

Koepsell, D. (2022). NFTs, IP rights, and policy. *Frontiers in Blockchain, 5*, 1077343.

Konashevych, O. (2019). Constraints and benefits of the blockchain use for real estate and property rights. Journal of Property. *Planning and Environmental Law, 12*(2), 109–127.

Konashevych, O. (2020). General concept of real estate tokenization on blockchain. *European Property Law Journal*, *9*(1), 21–66. DOI: 10.1515/eplj-2020-0003

Kramer, X. (2021). Swiss DLT Act enters into force. *Computer Law Review International*, *22*(2), 51–53.

Lehmann, M. (2019). Who owns Bitcoin? Private law facing the blockchain. *SSRN*, *21*(1), 93–136. DOI: 10.2139/ssrn.3402678

Lessig, L. (2006). *Code: Version 2.0.* Basic Books.

Lev, B. (2001). *Intangibles: Management, measurement, and reporting*. Brookings Institution Press.

Lim, C., Saw, T. J., & Sargeant, C. (2019). Smart contracts: Bridging the gap between expectation and reality. Oxford Law Faculty Research Paper.

Low, K. F. K., & Teo, E. (2017). Bitcoins and other cryptocurrencies as property? *Law, Innovation and Technology*, *9*(2), 235–268. DOI: 10.1080/17579961.2017.1377915

Maas, T. (2019). Initial coin offerings: When are tokens securities in the EU and US? SSRN Electronic Journal. DOI: 10.2139/ssrn.3337514

Mangano, R. (2018). Blockchain securities, insolvency law and the sandbox approach. *European Business Organization Law Review*, *19*(4), 715–735. DOI: 10.1007/s40804-018-0123-5

Mann, M. (2019). Technological architecture as law: Affordances and the dynamics of digital regulation. *Regulation & Governance*, *14*(3), 466–481.

MAS. (2016). *FinTech regulatory sandbox guidelines*. Monetary Authority of Singapore.

Mezei, P. (2020). Revisiting the concept of exhaustion in the online environment. *GRUR International*, *69*(11), 1107–1120.

Michels, J. D. (2018). Blockchain in securities markets: Toward a new ecosystem. *Journal of Securities Operations & Custody*, *10*(4), 310–321.

Mik, E. (2017). Smart contracts: Terminology, technical limitations and real world complexity. *Law, Innovation and Technology*, *9*(2), 269–300. DOI: 10.1080/17579961.2017.1378468

Möslein, F. (2018). Legal boundaries of blockchain technologies: Smart contracts as self-help? In Braegelmann, R., & Kaulartz, M. (Eds.), *Rechtshandbuch Smart Contracts* (pp. 313–326). C.H. Beck.

Möslein, F. (2019). Conflicts of laws and codes: Defining the boundaries of digital jurisdictions. In Hacker, P., Lianos, I., Dimitropoulos, G., & Eich, S. (Eds.), *Regulating blockchain* (pp. 264–282). Oxford University Press. DOI: 10.1093/oso/9780198842187.003.0016

Murray, A. (2019). *The regulation of cyberspace: Control in the online environment.* Routledge.

Nägele, T., & Xander, P. (2020). Liechtenstein's innovative Blockchain Act. *Trusts & Trustees, 26*(10), 876–888.

Nakamoto, S. (2008). Bitcoin: A peer-to-peer electronic cash system. https://bitcoin.org/bitcoin.pdf

New York Convention on the Recognition and Enforcement of Foreign Arbitral Awards, June 10, 1958, 21 U.S.T. 2517, 330 U.N.T.S. 38.

O'Dair, M., & Owen, R. (2019). Monetizing music in the blockchain age. *Journal of Revenue and Pricing Management, 18*(4), 330–337.

OECD. (2023). *The tokenisation of assets and potential implications for financial markets.* OECD Publishing.

Ortolani, P. (2016). Self-enforcing online dispute resolution: Lessons from Bitcoin. *Oxford Journal of Legal Studies, 36*(3), 595–629. DOI: 10.1093/ojls/gqv036

Ortolani, P. (2019). The impact of blockchain technologies and smart contracts on dispute resolution: Arbitration and court litigation at the crossroads. *Uniform Law Review, 24*(2), 430–448. DOI: 10.1093/ulr/unz017

Paris Convention for the Protection of Industrial Property, March 20, 1883, as revised at Stockholm on July 14, 1967, 21 U.S.T. 1583, 828 U.N.T.S. 305.

Payment Services Act. 2019, No. 2 of 2019 (Singapore).

Peukert, A. (2021). Fictitious commodities: A theory of intellectual property inspired by Karl Polanyi's "Great Transformation". Fordham Intellectual Property. *Media & Entertainment Law Journal, 29*(4), 1151–1210.

Protocol, M. (2023). Intellectual property NFTs for biotech. https://molecule.to/

Protocol, O. (2023). Data tokenization protocol. https://oceanprotocol.com/

Quintais, J. P. (2017). *Copyright in the age of online access: Alternative compensation systems in EU law.* Kluwer Law International.

Capitol Records, LLC v. ReDigi Inc., 934 F.Supp.2d 640 (S.D.N.Y. 2013).

Reed, C. (2018). How should we regulate algorithms? *Philosophical Transactions of the Royal Society A*, *376*(2128), 20170360. DOI: 10.1098/rsta.2017.0360

Regulation (EU) 2017/1129 of the European Parliament and of the Council of 14 June 2017 on the prospectus to be published when securities are offered to the public or admitted to trading on a regulated market, OJ L 168, 30.6.2017.

Regulation (EU) 2023/1114 of the European Parliament and of the Council of 31 May 2023 on markets in crypto-assets (MiCA), OJ L 150, 9.6.2023.

Regulation (EU) No 1215/2012 of the European Parliament and of the Council of 12 December 2012 on jurisdiction and the recognition and enforcement of judgments in civil and commercial matters (recast), OJ L 351, 20.12.2012.

Reidenberg, J. R. (1998). Lex informatica: The formulation of information policy rules through technology. *Texas Law Review*, *76*(3), 553–593.

Reyes, C. L. (2019). If Rockefeller were a coder. *The George Washington Law Review*, *87*(2), 373–429.

Robinson, R. (2020). The new digital wild west: Regulating the explosion of initial coin offerings. *Tennessee Law Review*, *85*(4), 897–960.

Rodrigues, U. R. (2019). Law and the blockchain. *Iowa Law Review*, *104*(2), 679–729.

Rohr, J., & Wright, A. (2019). Blockchain-based token sales, initial coin offerings, and the democratization of public capital markets. *The Hastings Law Journal*, *70*(2), 463–524.

Royal. (2023). Music NFT marketplace. https://royal.io/

Savelyev, A. (2017). Contract law 2.0: 'Smart' contracts as the beginning of the end of classic contract law. *Information & Communications Technology Law*, *26*(2), 116–134. DOI: 10.1080/13600834.2017.1301036

Savelyev, A. (2018). Copyright in the blockchain era: Promises and challenges. *Computer Law & Security Review*, *34*(3), 550–561. DOI: 10.1016/j.clsr.2017.11.008

Schär, F. (2021). Decentralized finance: On blockchain- and smart contract-based financial markets. *Review - Federal Reserve Bank of St. Louis*, *103*(2), 153–174.

Schmitz, A. J., & Rule, C. (2019). Online dispute resolution for smart contracts. *Journal of Dispute Resolution*, *2019*(1), 103–126.

Schrepel, T. (2021). Smart contracts and the digital single market through the lens of a "Law + Technology" approach. European Commission. SEC v. Kik Interactive Inc., No. 19-cv-5244 (S.D.N.Y. 2020). SEC v. Ripple Labs, Inc., No. 20-cv-10832 (S.D.N.Y. July 13, 2023). SEC v. W.J. Howey Co., 328 U.S. 293 (1946).

Securities Act of 1933, 15 U.S.C. §§ 77a–77aa.

Securitize. (2023). Digital asset securities platform. https://securitize.io/

Senftleben, M. (2019). User-generated content: Towards a new use privilege in EU copyright law. In Aplin, T. (Ed.), *Research handbook on intellectual property and digital technologies* (pp. 136–162). Edward Elgar Publishing.

Swan, M. (2015). *Blockchain: Blueprint for a new economy*. O'Reilly Media.

Swiss Code of Obligations, SR 220 (as amended by the DLT Act).

Szabo, N. (1997). Formalizing and securing relationships on public networks. *First Monday*, *2*(9). Advance online publication. DOI: 10.5210/fm.v2i9.548

Token and Trusted Technology Service Provider Act (TVTG). LGBl. 2019 No. 301 (Liechtenstein).

Tokengate. (2023). DLT securities platform. https://tokengate.io/

Torbey, C. (2020). Reconciling music streaming and blockchain: Transparency and smart contracts. *Hastings Communications and Entertainment Law Journal*, *42*(2), 145–178.

Trimble, M. (2012). The future of cybertravel: Legal implications of the evasion of geolocation. Fordham Intellectual Property. *Media & Entertainment Law Journal*, *22*(3), 567–657.

Trimble, M. (2019). Blockchain and intellectual property. In Brownsword, R., Scotford, E., & Yeung, K. (Eds.), *The Oxford handbook of law, regulation and technology* (pp. 817–836). Oxford University Press.

UNCITRAL Model Law on Electronic Commerce. G.A. Res. 51/162, U.N. Doc. A/RES/51/162 (Dec. 16, 1996).

UsedSoft GmbH v. Oracle International Corp., Case C-128/11, ECLI:EU:C:2012:407.

Ustawa z dnia 4 lutego 1994 r. o prawie autorskim i prawach pokrewnych, Dz.U. 1994 nr 24 poz. 83 (Poland).

Van Hoecke, M. (2002). *Law as communication*. Hart Publishing.

Vaultie. (2023). Trademark tokenization platform. https://vaultie.io/

VitaDAO. (2023). Decentralized biotech research collective. https://vitadao.com/

Weber, M. (1919). *Politik als Beruf.* Duncker & Humblot.

Werbach, K. (2018). *The blockchain and the new architecture of trust.* MIT Press. DOI: 10.7551/mitpress/11449.001.0001

WIPO. (2022). WIPO Blockchain Whitepaper: Blockchain technologies and IP ecosystems: A WIPO white paper. World Intellectual Property Organization.

Wright, A. (2021). The rise of decentralized autonomous organizations: Opportunities and challenges. *Stanford Journal of Blockchain Law & Policy*, *4*(2), 152–203.

Wright, A., & De Filippi, P. (2015). Decentralized blockchain technology and the rise of lex cryptographia. SSRN Electronic Journal. DOI: 10.2139/ssrn.2580664

Wyoming Digital Assets Act, W.S. § 34-29-101 (2019).

Yeoh, P. (2017). Regulatory issues in blockchain technology. *Journal of Financial Regulation and Compliance*, *25*(2), 196–208. DOI: 10.1108/JFRC-08-2016-0068

Yeung, K. (2019). Regulation by blockchain: The emerging battle for supremacy between the code of law and code as law. *The Modern Law Review*, *82*(2), 207–239. DOI: 10.1111/1468-2230.12399

Zetzsche, D. A., Arner, D. W., & Buckley, R. P. (2020). Decentralized finance. *Journal of Financial Regulation*, *6*(2), 172–203. DOI: 10.1093/jfr/fjaa010

Zetzsche, D. A., Buckley, R. P., Arner, D. W., & Föhr, L. (2021). The ICO gold rush: It's a scam, it's a bubble, it's a super challenge for regulators. *Harvard International Law Journal*, *60*(2), 267–315.

Chapter 7
DeSci and Tokenized Science Economies: Rewiring Research Incentives With Blockchain

Sasha Shilina
https://orcid.org/0000-0003-4696-0739
Paradigm Research, Georgia

ABSTRACT

This chapter delves into the rise of tokenized science economies, where blockchain infrastructure redefines how we fund, govern, and share scientific knowledge. At the heart of this shift is Decentralized Science (DeSci), a movement that challenges legacy systems by embedding transparency, programmability, and economic alignment into the research lifecycle. Through real-world case studies, the chapter explores tools like intellectual property NFTs, tokenized research outputs, DAO-led funding models, and scientific prediction markets. Together, these mechanisms offer new ways to incentivize peer review, coordinate global collaboration, and democratize access to discovery. Framing tokenization as a structural innovation, the chapter makes the case for a research economy that is not only open and sustainable, but fundamentally interoperable across platforms, disciplines, and communities.

1. INTRODUCTION

1.1 From Centralized Science to DeSci

Modern science emerged as a public, collaborative enterprise governed by communal norms: communalism, universalism, disinterestedness, and organized

DOI: 10.4018/979-8-3373-3371-7.ch007

skepticism (Merton, 1973). Over the past half-century, however, the research system has been progressively financialized and bureaucratized: funding concentrated in gatekeeping agencies, evaluation outsourced to opaque peer-review cartels, and intellectual property (IP) enclosed within university–industry technology transfer offices (Mirowski & Sent, 2007; Mirowski, 2011; Sarewitz, 2016). The result is a growing misalignment between what advances knowledge and what advances careers: publishable novelty trumps cumulative verification, proprietary licensing trumps open reuse, and incremental grant-friendly projects crowd out high-risk exploration (Nosek et al., 2015).

Against this backdrop, Decentralized Science (DeSci) has emerged as a heterogeneous movement that applies cryptonative primitives: blockchain networks, token economies, smart contracts, decentralized autonomous organizations (DAOs), to rebuild scientific infrastructure around transparency, programmability, and incentive alignment (Asgaonkar & Krishnamachari, 2018; Bamakan et al., 2022; Bischof et al., 2022; Buterin et al., 2019; DeFrancesco & Klevecz, 2022; Fantaccini et al., 2024; Shilina, 2023; Weidener and Spreckelsen, 2024; Weidener & Boltz, 2025; Weiss, 2022). Rather than treating papers, data, and peer review as static artifacts governed by slow institutions, DeSci treats them as on-chain objects whose provenance, access rules, and financial flows can be natively coordinated across networks (Nielsen, 2012; Buterin, Hitzig, & Weyl, 2018; De Filippi & Wright, 2018). Tokenization is not an add-on; it is the economic substrate that allows communities to fund, govern, and verify research in ways that are legible and enforceable without centralized trust (Heines et al., 2021).

1.2 Why Tokenization Matters for Research

Tokenization refers to the process of converting the core elements of scientific labor (ideas, datasets, experimental protocols, peer review contributions, and researcher reputation) into automatable, exchangeable units that can be tracked, governed, and incentivized across distributed systems. Unlike static, PDF-bound outputs or siloed databases, tokenized representations of scientific work are composable: they can interface with smart contracts, governance modules, and financial protocols. When carefully designed, token systems align incentives with epistemic value by rewarding activities such as replication, data curation, methodological rigor, and constructive critique, behaviors often undervalued in conventional academic metrics that prioritize novelty and citation accumulation.

Tokenized mechanisms also unlock new financial architectures. Communities can pool capital through DAOs, issue IP-backed tokens that fractionalize ownership of emerging knowledge assets, and stream micro-payments directly to contributors based on real-time milestones or post hoc impact. Governance becomes embedded within the research assets themselves: an intellectual property non-fungible token (IP-NFT) might automatically route future royalties to a DAO treasury, while review tokens can grant voting power over methodological standards or funding decisions. Additionally, tokenized infrastructure strengthens provenance and reproducibility through decentralized storage networks, enabling cryptographically verifiable links between data, claims, and review events.

Beyond funding and validation, tokenization enables scientific coordination at scale. Market-based mechanisms such as prediction markets or quadratic funding (QF) translate belief and preference into prices, allowing communities to collectively surface high-leverage research directions and allocate resources dynamically. These tools are not merely economic, they function as epistemic feedback loops, continuously updating community belief states based on evolving data and incentives.

In short, tokenization provides a protocol-defined coordination grammar for science, answering foundational questions such as: who contributed what, who governs what, who benefits, and under what conditions? These rules are formalized, enforceable, and transparent by design. While the open science movement has increased access to publications and data, it has not fundamentally restructured the incentive systems that govern research behavior (Sunyaev et al., 2021). To make this concrete, the chapter will map specific token primitives to stages of the research lifecycle (see Figure 1) and analyze real-world case studies to demonstrate how design choices in token architecture reshape scientific behavior, power dynamics, and knowledge outcomes.

Figure 1. Token Primitives Across the Research Lifecycle

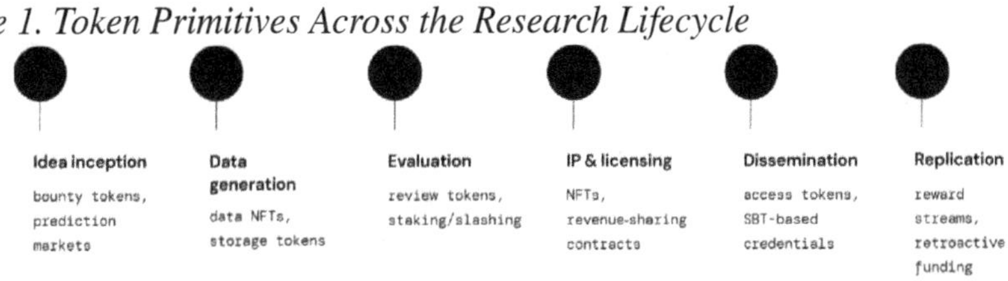

1.3 Chapter Objectives and Structure

This chapter pursues three primary objectives. First, it seeks to conceptualize tokenized science as a socioeconomic system, drawing from classical frameworks in the sociology and economics of science, as well as contemporary innovations in cryptoeconomics and digital governance. Second, it aims to analyze how specific token mechanisms, across funding, IP, and validation, restructure the incentive architecture of research, shifting who participates, who benefits, and how knowledge-related authority is distributed. Third, it offers a critical assessment of the risks and limitations inherent in tokenizing scientific Inquiry.

The chapter is structured as follows:

- Section 2 grounds tokenized science in established theories of knowledge production and institutional coordination. It examines the incentive misalignments of traditional academic structures and introduces blockchain as a potential veridiction and coordination layer. A typology of token primitives relevant to the scientific lifecycle is also developed.
- Section 3 analyzes governance and collaboration within scientific DAOs. It discusses mechanisms such as token voting, Sybil resistance systems (e.g., Gitcoin Passport, Proof-of-Humanity, Humanode), and the role of artificial intelligence (AI) agents in verification and proposal triage.
- Section 4 explores new architectures made possible by token economies, including DAO-based research funding (e.g., VitaDAO, Bio Protocol), quadratic and retroactive public goods funding (RPGF) (e.g., Gitcoin, Optimism RPGF).
- Section 5 focuses on the tokenization of IP. It examines the lifecycle of IP-NFTs, smart licensing contracts, and royalty-sharing mechanisms, drawing on cases such as Molecule and VitaDAO.
- Section 6 deepens the analysis of decentralized peer review, with ResearchHub as a case study for token-incentivized evaluation, curation, and reputation systems.
- Section 7 turns to issues of reproducibility and data infrastructure. It assesses decentralized storage solutions (e.g., Arweave, IPFS), provenance protocols, interoperability standards.
- Section 8 examines the cultural and participatory dimensions of tokenized science. Topics include meme tokens, gamification, citizen science bounties, scientific prediction markets (e.g., Episteme, Stadium Science), the emergence of autonomous agents as epistemic actors.
- Section 9 surfaces critical risks and limitations, including equity and access concerns, token-based governance fragility, speculative distortion, and philosophical critiques of incentivized knowledge systems.
- Section 10 concludes with a forward-looking synthesis. It outlines key trajectories for tokenized science economies, presents unresolved questions and research priorities, and proposes a normative framework for designing inclusive, reflexive, and sustainable epistemic infrastructures.

Together, these sections aim to provide a comprehensive map of the tokenized science landscape, its promises, its architectures, and its dilemmas, while equipping researchers, technologists, and policymakers with the tools to engage critically and constructively with this emerging paradigm.

2. THEORETICAL FOUNDATIONS OF TOKENIZED SCIENCE

2.1 Science as a Socioeconomic System

Science is not only a cognitive enterprise; it is a political economy of knowledge structured by incentives, institutions, and material flows (Latour & Woolgar, 1986; Partha & David, 1994). Merton's CUDOS norms[1] articulated an idealized moral order (Merton, 1973), yet empirical studies show how priority races, prestige economies, and IP regimes shape what gets researched and published (Mirowski, 2011; Azoulay, Zivin, & Manso, 2011). Benkler (2006) reframed knowledge production as "commons-based peer production," emphasizing distributed collaboration beyond firm and market logics. DeSci extends this lineage by positing that cryptoeconomic primitives can instantiate commons governance rules directly in code, making contribution, coordination, and compensation natively programmable.

2.2 Incentive Misalignments in Traditional Research

Classic public-goods problems (free riding, under-provision of replication, tragedy of the anti-commons in IP) persist in academic science (Ostrom, 1990; Heller & Eisenberg, 1998). "Publish or perish" rewards speed and novelty over robustness (Ioannidis, 2005; Sarewitz, 2016); peer review concentrates gatekeeping power in small elites; and tech-transfer offices monetize outputs through exclusionary licensing that often stalls diffusion (Mirowski, 2011). Funding pipelines are slow, centralized, and risk-averse (Stokes, 1997). In short, epistemic value (truth, reproducibility, usefulness) is weakly coupled to economic reward and career advancement.

Tokenization offers new levers: stake-based review markets can pay for rigorous critique; RPGF can reward replication after impact is demonstrated; IP-NFTs can route royalties back to communities instead of siloed institutions; and prediction markets can expose belief states and penalize inaccuracy.

2.3 Blockchain as a Coordination and Veridiction Layer

Blockchains provide three properties crucial to scientific coordination: (1) credible neutrality, rules apply equally to all addresses; (2) composability, financial and governance primitives interlock like Lego bricks; and (3) verifiable provenance, hash-linked histories of data, decisions, and transfers (Buterin et al., 2018; De Filippi

& Wright, 2018). Following Foucault's notion of 'veridiction', the set of procedures through which truth claims are validated, blockchains can serve as protocolal veridiction layers: they do not determine scientific truth, but they fix the conditions under which claims are recorded, challenged, rewarded, or penalized.

Smart contracts allow conditional payouts (e.g., release funds only if pre-registered endpoints are met); DAOs instantiate polycentric governance (Ostrom, 2010) at internet scale; zero-knowledge proofs (ZKP) and cryptographic tools preserve privacy while verifying computations; and identity primitives like Proof-of-personhood (PoP) systems, soulbound tokens, SBTs (Ohlhaver, Weyl& Buterin, 2022) mitigate Sybil attacks. Combined with AI agents that can score evidence or check reproducibility, these tools can create recursive feedback loops where epistemic labor is continuously priced, audited, and refined.

2.4 Literature Review

To ground tokenized science in established scholarship, we draw on four intertwined literatures: (1) the economics of science and innovation, (2) commons governance and knowledge commons, (3) sociology and anthropology of scientific fields, and (4) information and coordination theory. They illuminate why incentives drift, how communities self-govern resources, and which design levers matter when rebuilding infrastructures with cryptoeconomic tools.

2.4.1 Economics of Science and Incentive Structures

Classical economic theory treats scientific knowledge as a non-rival, only partially excludable public good (Arrow 1962; Nelson 1959). Because private markets systematically under-incentivize its production, the state subsidizes basic research, yet public-allocation mechanisms introduce their own distortions, often favoring low-variance, committee-palatable projects over high-risk discovery (Stokes 1997; David 2004). Partha and David (1994) crystallized this tension by distinguishing two interacting regimes: an Open-Science order, which rewards rapid disclosure and communal validation, and a Proprietary/IP order, which privileges secrecy and downstream monetization. Subsequent scholarship maps the consequences of this duality. Stephan (1996, 2012) shows that academic labor markets compensate researchers largely with prizes (priority, prestige, and citations) rather than wages, producing winner-take-most dynamics and strategic behavior around visibility. Building on the "Mode 1 / Mode 2" distinction introduced by Gibbons et al. (1994), Ziman (2000) argues that contemporary science has shifted toward a transdisciplinary, market-responsive model that erodes the self-correcting norms idealized by Merton. Finally, Mirowski & Sent (2008) and Mirowski (2011) trace the neoliberal turn in detail: universities adopt corporate logics, patents proliferate, and knowledge becomes increasingly financialized.

Token economies intervene precisely at these fault lines. By encoding reward functions and ownership modalities directly in smart contracts, cryptoeconomic systems can, at least in principle, tie compensation to verifiable intellectual outputs; automate revenue-sharing for communal IP; and open funding flows to broader publics. Whether they genuinely escape the old distortions or merely recode them on-chain depends on how closely their design aligns with the commons and governance principles outlined in Section 2.5.

2.4.2 Commons Theory and Knowledge Commons

Ostrom's design principles (1990) challenged Hardin's tragedy narrative by showing communities can sustainably govern common-pool resources. Later work extended this to knowledge commons (Hess & Ostrom, 2007; Madison, Frischmann, & Strandburg, 2010; Frischmann, Madison, & Strandburg, 2014): information is non-rival but requires rules for contribution, curation, and access. Boyle (2003) and Lessig (2001) warned of the "second enclosure movement", IP overreach that fences the informational commons. In tokenized systems, smart contracts become institutional rulesets that can embody Ostromian principles (clear boundaries, graduated sanctions, collective-choice arrangements) if carefully designed. Conversely, without pluralistic governance, tokens may simply instantiate new enclosures (anticommons, Heller & Eisenberg, 1998).

2.4.3 Sociology of Scientific Fields and Capital

Bourdieu (1975, 2004) analyzed science as a field where actors accumulate scientific capital (recognition, citations) convertible into economic or social capital. Polanyi (1962) emphasized tacit knowledge and the "republic of science" as a self-coordinating order. Latour & Woolgar (1986) showed how facts are socially constructed through inscriptions and negotiations. Tokenization must therefore reckon with symbolic capital and tacit labor: if only quantifiable outputs get tokens, we risk ignoring invisible work (mentoring, negative results). Reputation tokens should capture diverse forms of efforts, not just publication metrics.

2.4.4 Information, Coordination and Mechanism Design

Coordination failures in science mirror those in public-goods provision generally (Samuelson, 1954), but mechanism design offers tools: quadratic funding and voting (Buterin et al., 2019; Weyl, 2012), futarchy (Hanson, 2000), bonding curves, and staking as incentive-alignment devices (Posner & Weyl, 2018). Benkler (2006) theorized networked peer production as an alternative to firm/market dichotomies; token economies instantiate programmable peer production, where knowledge production is recorded and rewarded automatically. Cryptoeconomic security analyses (Budish, 2018; Roughgarden, 2020), protocol and game-theoretic work on adversarial behavior in blockchains (Douceur, 2002; Kroll, Davey, & Felten, 2013; Eyal & Sirer, 2014) extend incentive design to hostile environments—crucial for Sybil resistance, validator incentives, and oracle robustness.

DeSci's novelty is not that it discovered incentives or commons, it is that it can encode institutional rules, incentive flows, and audit trails directly into assets. The challenge is choosing which rules to encode and how to keep them adaptable. Commons theory teaches us to embed participatory governance and graduated sanctions; economics of science warns us where misaligned metrics corrupt behavior; sociology of science reminds us to value tacit and symbolic labor; mechanism design provides the primitives to wire it all together.

2.5 Design Principles for Tokenized Science

To guide the development of tokenized infrastructures in scientific research, it is essential to ground system design in clear principles that reflect the normative goals of science itself. Drawing from the theoretical foundations outlined above, we propose a set of commitments aimed at ensuring that token systems enhance, rather than compromise, the integrity and advancement of knowledge.

First, token architectures must prioritize *epistemic alignment*: that is, they should reward verifiable contributions to scientific knowledge rather than surface-level activity metrics. Token incentives ought to promote behaviors such as replication, data curation, methodological transparency, and rigorous critique—core practices that uphold the integrity and reliability of research but which are often undervalued in traditional academic metrics.

Equally critical is *pluralistic governance*. Decision-making power within scientific token economies should not be reducible to financial capital or technical credentialing alone. Instead, governance frameworks should integrate multiple vectors of legitimacy, including token-weighted voting, reputation-based influence, and PoP mechanisms that assert the dignity and equality of participants. Such pluralism ensures that no single stakeholder group, be it investors, senior academics, or early adopters, can dominate the direction of scientific funding and validation.

In systems handling sensitive data, especially in fields like biomedicine, the principle of *progressive disclosure and privacy preservation* must be embedded from the outset. Technologies such as ZKP, differential privacy, and revocable access controls can help preserve confidentiality while still enabling verifiability. Rather than forcing transparency as an absolute, progressive disclosure empowers contributors and data subjects to control what is revealed, to whom, and under which conditions.

Tokenized science must also be *interoperable by design*. This means adopting open standards, decentralized identifiers (DIDs), verifiable credentials (VCs), and content-addressable storage that allow knowledge assets, attestations, and reputations to circulate freely across protocols and platforms. Without interoperability, DeSci risks replicating the siloed inefficiencies of traditional academia, undermining the composability and scalability that make blockchain-native infrastructure powerful.

Finally, sustainable systems should support *retroactive and recursive funding*. Rather than relying solely on speculative forward-looking grants, token economies can retroactively reward contributions based on demonstrated impact. Through mechanisms such as RPGF, scientific communities can recognize and support high-value work after the fact, thereby encouraging exploration and long-term commitment even when short-term incentives are lacking. Recursive feedback loops, where governance, funding, and evaluation influence one another dynamically, can foster a more adaptive and resilient epistemic ecosystem.

These principles serve not only as normative aspirations but as actionable design heuristics for the systems examined in the following sections. They will inform the evaluation of decentralized governance (Section 3), token-based funding (Section 4), IP tokenization (Section 5), and verification mechanisms (Section 6), while providing a framework for understanding the limitations and risks addressed in Section 9. In essence, they are a call to treat infrastructure design as a form of epistemic ethics: not merely as engineering, but as the careful construction of environments in which truth, inclusion, and responsibility can co-evolve.

2.6 Typology of Tokens in Science Economies

To understand the role of tokenization in DeSci, it is essential to categorize the various types of tokens not merely by their technical specifications but by their knowledge-oriented function. Tokens in science economies can be analyzed along two primary axes: what is being tokenized, whether a resource, action, or identity, and what role the token plays, whether as a mechanism for access, governance, signaling, or economic yield.

Table 1 offers a functional typology of token classes observed across leading DeSci platforms and protocols. Each category addresses distinct layers of scientific coordination: from decision-making and labor compensation to knowledge ownership and belief formation.

- *Governance tokens* encapsulate decision rights within DAOs. Typically implemented via ERC-20 standards and deployed in off-chain voting platforms such as Snapshot or conviction voting systems, these tokens grant holders proposal power and treasury influence.

- *Contribution tokens* represent verifiable units of scientific labor: peer review, data curation, replication, or annotation. They serve as payment instruments and, in some cases, as staking devices in reputation-weighted systems.
- *Reputation tokens*, particularly non-transferable ones, encode track records, credentials, and domain expertise. Their value lies in enabling weighted governance or access permissions based on demonstrable contribution histories.
- *IP and asset tokens*, including IP-NFTs and other real-world asset (RWA) representations, fractionalize ownership over scientific outputs such as patents, cell lines, or protocols. These tokens enable licensing flows and royalty distribution via smart contracts.
- *Prediction market tokens* make beliefs about scientific hypotheses tradable. By encoding collective probabilities and conditional outcomes, they provide price-discovered signals around research validity, replication likelihood, or expected impact.
- *Funding and matching tokens* facilitate the distribution of capital through mechanisms such as QF or RPGF. These tokens act as receipts or multipliers that align incentives between funders and communities.
- *Data and storage tokens* secure rights to access or preserve datasets. Decentralized storage systems ensure data persistence and availability, bolster provenance and reproducibility.
- *Liquidity Provider (LP) tokens* represent pooled assets in scientific token markets, whether prediction instruments, IP positions, or funding primitives. They incentivize market depth and trading activity.

This typology sets the stage for subsequent empirical analyses. The mechanisms discussed here function as a foundation for epistemic infrastructure, formalizing how knowledge is produced, validated, distributed, and rewarded in the emerging scientific economies of the blockchain age.

Table 1. Token Types and Functions in DeSci

Token Class	What's Tokenized	Primary Function	Examples	Risks
Governance	Decision rights in a DAO	Voting, proposal power, treasury control	Conviction voting, futarchy	Plutocracy, voter apathy, token capture
Contribution	Labor units (review, curation, replication)	Payment, reputation accrual, staking/ slashing	Review bounties, curation markets, stake-to-signal	Sybil attacks, low-quality spam, metric gaming
Reputation	Non-transferable credentials, track records	Sybil resistance, weighted voting, access control	SBTs, Gitcoin Passport stamps	Privacy leakage, bias ossification, forgiveness problem
IP/Asset	Patents, data sets, cell lines, protocols	Fractional ownership, licensing, royalty streams	Molecule IP-NFTs, royalty routing contracts	Commodification, legal ambiguity, anti-commons
Prediction Market	Belief states about hypotheses	Price discovery, resolution payouts	Episteme hypothesis tokens, Pump.Science claims	Speculative bubbles, manipulation, oracle risk
Funding/ Matching	Capital allocation receipts, matching multipliers	QF, retroactive rewards	Gitcoin Grants, Optimism RPGF	Collusion, Sybil amplification, short-termism
Data/Storage	Storage rights, retrieval guarantees	Provenance, persistence, pay-per-access	Filecoin, Arweave profit-sharing tokens	Data hoarding, sustainability of incentives
Liquidity	Claims on pooled liquidity	Market depth, fee accrual	LP tokens for IP pairs	Impermanent loss, capital inefficiency

3. GOVERNANCE AND COLLABORATION IN DESCI

At the heart of DeSci lies a core challenge: how can tokenized systems facilitate collective decision-making about science in a way that is epistemically sound, socially inclusive, and resilient to manipulation? Governance in scientific DAOs is not merely a matter of technical procedure, it directly shapes what gets funded, who gets to evaluate truth claims, and how research trajectories unfold. This section explores the emerging design space of token-based governance mechanisms and the trade-offs they introduce.

3.1 Tokenized Governance: From Snapshot Polls to Futarchy

Contemporary DAO governance mechanisms span a spectrum from simple off-chain signaling to sophisticated market-based epistemics. The most widely adopted approach is token-weighted voting, typically implemented through platforms like Snapshot (Snapshot Labs, 2021). This model allows gasless off-chain voting, with results executed via multisig signers or on-chain automation. While this ensures usability and speed, it often inherits plutocratic dynamics: influence scales linearly with token holdings.

To mitigate capital dominance, alternative models such as quadratic voting have gained traction. Here, the cost of each additional vote increases quadratically, amplifying the influence of many small holders over a few whales (Weyl, 2012; Buterin, Hitzig, & Weyl, 2019). Similarly, conviction voting, accumulates voting weight over time, rewarding sustained support and reducing the impact of short-term swings or opportunistic participation.

More experimental yet philosophically aligned with scientific inquiry is futarchy, a governance mechanism proposed by Robin Hanson (2000) under the maxim: "Vote on values, bet on beliefs." In futarchy, prediction markets are used to determine which policy or research proposal is most likely to maximize a predefined metric, such as replication rate, citation index, or long-term epistemic value. While implementations remain limited, emerging DeSci platforms aim to pioneer domain-specific futarchy, embedding forecasting and resolution mechanisms directly into the scientific process.

Another key innovation involves multicameral governance. Rather than relying on a single voting mechanism, these systems partition authority across distinct chambers (token holders, reputation-bearing contributors, and verified unique humans). This design introduces structural checks and balances, distributing power across epistemic, economic, and civic dimensions.

3.2 Coordination Tools for Cross-Disciplinary Research

Scientific inquiry is inherently pluralistic. It traverses disciplines, methodologies, cultures, and temporal rhythms, from long-horizon benchwork to rapid computational iterations. For decentralized scientific collectives, this heterogeneity poses a profound coordination challenge: how can distributed communities of researchers, funders, and evaluators, often without prior affiliation, align on shared standards, synchronize their efforts, and make decisions across complex knowledge domains?

To meet this challenge, emerging scientific DAOs are assembling coordination stacks: modular toolchains that formalize key interactions, from proposal intake to dispute resolution. One foundational layer involves proposal schemas, standardized, machine-readable formats that structure hypotheses, methodologies, budget requests, and licensing preferences. These formats not only streamline review workflows across domains but also enable AI agents to assist in parsing, summarizing, or simulating proposals.

Second, curation markets and decentralized juries, such as those powered by Kleros, introduce incentivized review and adjudication layers. These systems allow community members or experts to stake tokens on the relevance or quality of a submission, with slashing mechanisms or reputation loss deterring fraud and misrepresentation. When disputes arise, whether over authorship, IP validity, or research misconduct, these systems offer lightweight, credibly neutral adjudication processes.

Third, DAOs are integrating on-chain project management tools, platforms like Dework, which link task bounties, milestone deliverables, and contributor attestations to verifiable reputational records. This embeds scientific labor into a transparent ledger of accountability, enabling both coordination and credit attribution across globally distributed teams.

Fourth, inter-DAO agreements are emerging as protocols for collaboration across scientific domains. These range from cross-treasury token swaps to federated review bodies and co-authored funding frameworks. In biotech, for instance, alliances between VitaDAO, AthenaDAO, ValleyDAO, and other domain-specialized collectives point to the rise of decentralized consortia with research standards.

Finally, AI co-pilots are becoming integral to coordination. Systems such as Bio Protocol's agentic stack and elizaOS reviewers assist with proposal triage, highlight missing experimental controls, simulate budget forecasts, and even suggest prior art. These agents reduce the cognitive burden of distributed review and amplify the ability of small teams to participate meaningfully in large, interdisciplinary networks.

Together, these tools point to an infrastructural shift: from informal, ad hoc collaborations to composable, auditable, and intelligence-augmented coordination protocols, tailored for the epistemic and organizational complexities of modern science (Table 2).

Table 2. Governance Mechanisms and Anti-Capture Tools

Layer	Mechanism	What It Solves	Example	Residual Risks
Decision	Token voting, QV, conviction, futarchy	Aggregating preferences	Snapshot, 1Hive, Episteme markets	Plutocracy, complexity
Identity	PoP, VC, DID, SBT	Sybil, credentialing	Gitcoin Passport, POH, Humanode	Privacy, exclusion
Dispute	Juried arbitration, stake-slash courts	Fraud, low-quality proposals	Kleros, Aragon	Collusion, juror apathy

continued on following page

Table 2. Continued

Layer	Mechanism	What It Solves	Example	Residual Risks
Execution	Multisigs, timelocks, optimistic exec	Secure enactment	Gnosis Safe, UMA	Bottlenecks, signer capture
Privacy	ZK voting	Coercion, vote buying	Semaphore	UX friction, parameter trust

4. FUNDING SCIENTIFIC DISCOVERY IN DESCI

Who funds science, when funds are released, and under what terms are questions fundamentally reshaped in tokenized economies. This section examines how tokenization mechanisms reconfigure incentive flows, distribute epistemic risk, and shift control over research agendas.

4.1 DAO-Based Funding Models

Scientific DAOs constitute automatic grant-makers: they pool capital, native governance tokens, stablecoins, or partner involvement, and disburse it through on-chain proposals that specify hypotheses, milestones, budgets, and licensing terms.

Across DeSci, several design patterns recur (Table 3). Domain-specific working groups integrate expert review into token-weighted governance, balancing technical rigor with broad participation. Milestone-based vesting releases tranches only when verifiable deliverables (datasets, preprints, patent filings) are confirmed on-chain. Treasuries diversify across governance tokens, stable assets, and IP-backed instruments to hedge volatility and sustain runway.

Empirically, VitaDAO has deployed more than $4 million into longevity research via token raises and IP-NFT acquisitions, experimenting with licensing structures that recycle revenues to token holders (Friday, 2023). Similarly, BIO Protocol acts as a launchpad, facilitating global collaboration to fund and govern research initiatives from universities, researchers, and companies. Its ecosystem includes specialized DAOs such as HairDAO (targeting hair loss), CerebrumDAO (boosting brain health), CryoDAO (cryogenics), and others. By integrating liquidity and incentive mechanisms, BIO Protocol accelerates the commercialization of science while fostering decentralized governance. Moreover, Bio Protocol operates an “agentic” grant stack, where LLM-based BioAgents triage proposals before community voting allocates rapid micro-grants (Brennan, 2025). ValleyDAO applies the template to climate biotechnology, while AthenaDAO focuses on women’s health, both adapting IP-tokenization and community governance to distinct scientific domains.

The incentive landscape shifts accordingly: scientists, reviewers, and token holders become equity-like stakeholders in downstream outcomes, aligning epistemic risk-taking with potential upside through royalties, token appreciation, and continued governance influence.

4.2 Quadratic and Retroactive Funding, and DeFi Integration

Quadratic funding (QF), formalized by Buterin, Hitzig, and Weyl (2019), introduces a mechanism for capital allocation that privileges pluralistic support over concentrated wealth. By matching donations in proportion to the square of the sum of square roots of individual contributions, QF amplifies collective signal rather than whale influence. In a scientific context, this mechanism is particularly well-suited to support underfunded but widely valued efforts (replication studies, dataset maintenance, and open tooling) that often fall outside the scope of conventional grant systems.

Core to QF are three design pillars: (1) signal aggregation, where broad but modest donor support carries more weight than a few large events; (2) matching pools, typically funded by philanthropic organizations, protocol treasuries, or DAOs, with smart contracts ensuring transparent distribution; and (3) Sybil resistance, implemented through systems such as Gitcoin Passport or proof-of-personhood (PoP) networks like Idena, BrightID, World, or proof-of biometric uniqueness (PoBU) Humanode protocol, which help ensure the integrity of the matching logic (Kavazi et al., 2021).

RPGF extends this model by allocating funds *after* projects demonstrate measurable impact, reversing the conventional logic of forward-facing grants. Initiatives such as Optimism's RPGF rounds (Optimism, 2021) have pioneered this approach. For scientific ecosystems, it is especially promising for surfacing latent value: from failed experiments that clarify boundaries to infrastructure that supports reproducibility.

DeFi-native infrastructure further augments these funding models. Protocol treasuries can deploy idle assets in yield-bearing strategies to replenish or expand matching pools. Streaming protocols like Superfluid and Sablier enable continuous micro-payments to researchers, dynamically tied to KPIs or milestone oracles. More experimental approaches, such as bonding curves and continuous organizations (COs), offer mechanisms for creating perpetual liquidity and incentive alignment around research tokens, embedding sustainability into the funding substrate itself.

Table 3. Comparison of Funding Mechanisms in Tokenized Science

Mechanism	Capital Source	Signal Type	Payout Logic	Strengths	Key Risks
DAO Grants	Treasury (token sales, donations)	Token + expert vote	Milestone tranches	Aligned community governance	Plutocracy, review bottlenecks
Quadratic Funding	Community + matching pool	Broad small donations	Algorithmic match	Democratic signal aggregation	Sybil collusion, metric gaming
Retroactive Funding	Protocol/DAO surplus	Impact metrics post hoc	Lump-sum rewards	Rewards real impact, reduces upfront bias	Impact measurement subjectivity

5. INTELLECTUAL PROPERTY AND RESEARCH TOKENIZATION

A key question in tokenized science is how IP changes when brought on-chain. Traditionally managed by institutions like tech transfer offices or licensing firms (Hellmann, 2007; Ouellette, 2012), IP is now becoming composable and programmable: patents can be made liquid, datasets collectively governed, and revenue flows automated via smart contracts.

5.1 IP-NFTs and the New Lifecycle of Knowledge Assets

The IP-NFT is an emerging cryptolegal construct designed to represent a bundle of rights associated with a scientific asset, whether a patent filing, dataset, cell line, research protocol, or material transfer agreement (MTA). While the NFT itself cannot instantiate legal ownership, it cryptographically links to off-chain legal documents (e.g., license agreements, LLC membership units) whose terms are mirrored on-chain. This dual-layer architecture enables automation of revenue routing, access control, and governance logic, while remaining anchored in enforceable law.

This model introduces a new lifecycle for knowledge assets:

- Creation and disclosure: The process begins when a research output, such as an invention disclosure, dataset, or biological material, is formalized with metadata describing its provenance, authorship, and timestamp. This metadata is hashed and stored on-chain, anchoring the claim in a tamper-resistant record.
- Tokenization: The scientific asset is bound to a legal wrapper, such as an LLC or licensing agreement, which is then represented by an ERC-721 or ERC-

1155 token. In many cases, this IP-NFT can be fractionalized into ERC-20 tokens or hybridized, enabling more accessible participation and liquidity.

- Financing and governance: DAOs, investors, or community members can purchase fractional governance or economic rights in the asset. Token holders may collectively decide on licensing strategies, fund follow-up studies, or spin out startups that develop the IP. This participatory model reconfigures IP ownership from a bilateral negotiation to a multilateral governance process.
- Monetization: Smart contracts route royalties, milestone payments, or equity event proceeds to relevant parties. For example, revenue might be split programmatically (e.g., 30% to the inventors, 50% to the DAO treasury, and 20% to a public goods pool) removing friction and opacity from the distribution process.
- Expiration: As patents expire or data becomes obsolete, the IP-NFT can execute pre-programmed conditions to relicense assets under open-access terms. The NFT may then continue to serve as a provenance token, anchoring the historical record of contribution.

Why does this matter? IP-NFTs introduce a radically more transparent and participatory mechanism for managing research translation. They expand the universe of potential backers beyond venture capital and pharma incumbents to include distributed communities, early-stage DAOs, and mission-aligned patrons. At the same time, they offer a portfolio logic: DAOs can spread capital across a range of IP-NFTs, hedging scientific risk while inviting collective curation of future research directions.

However, these benefits must be weighed against potential pitfalls: the risk of speculative bubbles, the legal enforceability of on-chain representations, and the political question of who governs licensing in decentralized regimes. As such, IP-NFTs represent not just a new financial instrument, but a reimagining of how society coordinates, allocates, and governs the fruits of scientific labor.

5.2 Case Studies

Molecule helped architect the contemporary IP-NFT model, in which inventors place patent rights (or comparable assets) into a special-purpose vehicle (e.g., an LLC/SPV). That entity signs a licensing agreement with the buyer, often a DAO, and the corresponding NFT cryptographically references this contract while embedding payment and governance logic.

As for VitaDAO, a widely cited early example is the University of Copenhagen senolytic project acquired by the project in 2021–2022. Since then, VitaDAO has completed over a dozen IP-NFT transactions (as of mid-2025), spanning early-stage acquisitions and at least one biotech spin-out. Decisions to out-license, continue funding, or divest are put to token-holder governance, illustrating how translational strategy can be community-directed.

AthenaDAO applies a similar framework to women's health research, foregrounding patient-centered benefit sharing. Draft revenue-share arrangements channel a fixed portion of future income to advocacy or patient groups, operationalizing ethical commitments in code.

ValleyDAO and LabDAO extend tokenization beyond patents to include scientific processes and infrastructure, experimenting with tokenized protocols, "lab credits," or reagent access, thereby creating markets for modular research capacity rather than only end-stage IP.

5.3 Smart Contracts for Licensing, Royalties, and Revenue Sharing

The tokenization of IP introduces the possibility of programmable, modular licensing frameworks that adapt dynamically to usage, context, and performance. Instead of static bilateral agreements, licensing can be encoded in smart contracts that respond to on-chain signals, automate compliance, and align stakeholder incentives over time.

For instance, dynamic royalty structures can be implemented wherein token holders receive revenue share until their principal and a predefined return are recovered, after which the royalty rate decreases or transitions to a perpetual fee directed toward public goods funding. This enables early investors to be repaid while ensuring long-term benefit-sharing.

Field-of-use licenses may be encoded via separate token classes (e.g., ERC-1155 variants) representing different application domains for the same underlying technology, such as oncology, neurology, or infectious disease. This permits differentiated commercialization strategies without fragmenting ownership entirely.

To address the problem of underutilized or "dead" IP, auto-open licensing clauses can be incorporated, such that if an asset remains unlicensed beyond a set duration (e.g., 12 months post-tokenization), the terms automatically convert to a non-exclusive open license. This ensures knowledge circulation even in the absence of commercial uptake.

Milestone-based escrows enable conditional disbursement: research funds are streamed to recipients in tranches, with each tranche contingent on the completion of verifiable outcomes. These outcomes (clinical endpoints, data deposition, preprint publication) can be validated via decentralized oracles or AI-assisted review agents.

Finally, ZK usage accounting allows for the metering of sensitive dataset access while preserving privacy. ZK proofs confirm that a user meets access conditions and has not exceeded usage quotas, with aggregate payments calculated and settled on-chain, ensuring transparency without compromising confidentiality.

These mechanisms collectively represent a shift from static, paper-based contracts to living, executable agreements.

Table 4 outlines emerging licensing patterns for tokenized intellectual property, detailing smart-contract logic, real-world analogies, and the trade-offs between automation, precision, and legal or technical complexity.

Table 4. Licensing Patterns in Tokenized IP

Pattern	What It Does	Smart-Contract Logic	Example/Analogy	Pros	Cons
Revenue-Share Split	Distributes % of income to stakeholders	Split contract, milestone-based sliders	NFT rev splits	Transparent, automatic	Securities treatment, oracle accuracy
Dynamic Royalty Decay	Lowers royalties after payback	State machine w/ thresholds	VC clawback waterfalls	Aligns early risk/reward	Complexity, gaming metrics
Auto-Open Fallback	Defaults to open license after inactivity	Timelock + condition check	Copyleft time bombs	Prevents IP hoarding	May deter cautious licensees
Field-of-Use Tokens	Separate rights per domain	Multi-class ERC-1155 mapping	Patent field-of-use carve-outs	Precision licensing	Fragmentation, coordination cost
Milestone Escrow	Conditional release of funds/IP	Oracle-verified unlocks	Milestone grants in biotech	Accountability	Oracle disputes, false negatives
ZK Metered Access	Private usage tracking + payment	ZK proofs of access counts	Privacy-preserving data co-ops	Balance privacy and monetization	Tech overhead, verifier trust

6. DECENTRALIZED VALIDATION AND PEER REVIEW

How can scientific evaluation become transparent, incentive-aligned, and continuously self-correcting? Usually, peer review obscures process and under-rewards rigor. In contrast, decentralized validation architectures offer visible, traceable, and economically incentivized alternatives, shifting epistemic assessment from static gatekeeping to dynamic, participatory verification.

6.1 The Limits of Traditional Peer Review

Traditional peer review, long upheld as a cornerstone of scientific quality control, increasingly shows signs of systemic failure. Its structural weaknesses are well-documented: opaque decision-making, significant inter-reviewer disagreement, limited detection of methodological flaws or fraud, and pervasive biases linked to institutional prestige, geography, and gender (Lee et al., 2013; Smith, 2006; Garcia-Costa et al., 2022). Rather than functioning as a rigorous epistemic filter, peer review often operates as a gatekeeping mechanism that reinforces status hierarchies while under-rewarding substantive critique and replication.

The replication crisis across psychology, medicine, and other disciplines has sharpened these concerns, revealing that many widely cited findings cannot be reproduced under scrutiny (Nosek et al., 2015; Baker, 2016). Journals and funders continue to prioritize novelty and publication metrics over robustness and reuse, skewing incentives away from verification, incremental knowledge building, or negative results. Efforts to reform the system, such as open peer review, post-publication commentary, or reviewer recognition programs, have had modest success but fail to address deeper incentive misalignments (Tennant et al., 2017).

At its core, peer review is under-incentivized intellectual labor. Reviewers are typically unpaid, and their contributions remain invisible within formal scholarly credit systems. As a result, essential functions like replication, critique, and methodological refinement are frequently sidelined. Decentralized validation architectures, driven by tokenized incentives, transparent protocols, and modular reputation, offer a promising alternative to reimagine how scientific claims are evaluated, challenged, and refined.

6.2 Token-Incentivized Feedback Platforms

Emerging decentralized platforms introduce financial and reputational incentives into the peer review process, addressing long-standing critiques of opacity, slowness, and uncompensated labor in traditional systems. By embedding stake-based mechanisms and transparent attribution, these systems align epistemic rigor with economic reward. For instance, ResearchHub compensates reviewers with cryptocurrency for high-quality feedback, with reports of average payouts reaching $150 per review (Else, 2024). This marks a significant departure from conventional academic models, where peer review is largely uncompensated despite its central role in knowledge validation.

6.3 AI-Augmented Evaluation and Protocolal Verification

AI is increasingly integrated into scientific validation workflows (Stokel-Walker, 2023). In tokenized science systems, AI agents function not just as assistants but as protocolal components embedded in evaluation logic.

Automated checks, power analysis, p-hacking detection, and code execution, can flag issues early. LLMs acting as evidence oracles cross-reference claims with public databases, producing confidence scores that inform staking or challenge processes. These AI evaluations are further secured through smart contracts encoding conditional validation (e.g., milestone-triggered disbursements) and ZKPs that confirm computations were performed on specific data without revealing sensitive inputs (Ben-Sasson et al., 2014; Thaler, 2013). This emerging stack enables hybrid peer review: AI provides scalable, auditable first-pass scrutiny, while human reviewers refine judgment and accountability.

Projects such as NobleBlocks and YesNoError exemplify emerging paradigms in blockchain-native scholarly communication. NobleBlocks secures peer-reviewed manuscripts on-chain, ensuring tamper-evident provenance and verifiable authorship. YesNoError integrates LLMs to autonomously detect methodological and factual inconsistencies, marking a shift toward AI-augmented post-publication review.

In parallel, the DeScAI model (Decentralized Science and Artificial Intelligence) envisions a multi-stratum architecture where AI agents operate across the research lifecycle, from hypothesis triage to post hoc evaluation, within a decentralized, incentive-aligned ecosystem (Shilina, 2025). This approach formalizes recursive, autonomous verification as a native function of scientific infrastructure, blending distributed governance, machine intelligence, and epistemic accountability.

Table 5 compares verification mechanisms in tokenized science, highlighting who performs validation, what incentives are used, what gets verified, and common failure modes across approaches from peer review bounties to cryptographic proofs.

Table 5. Verification Mechanisms in Tokenized Science

Mechanism	Who Verifies?	Incentive Primitive	What's Verified?	Example	Failure Modes
Bounty Review	Independent reviewers	Fixed bounty + rating bonus	Methods, stats, ethics	ResearchHub bounties	Low-effort spam, echo chambers
Stake-to-Validate	Reviewers/replicators staking tokens	Slashing on failure, rewards on success	Replication outcomes, code/ data fidelity	Episteme verification circuit	Collusion, oracle gaming
Prediction Markets	Traders/experts	Profit from accuracy	Future success/ replication of claims	Science markets	Thin liquidity, info asymmetry
AI Pre-Checks	LLM/agents	None (tooling), or agent rewards	Statistical soundness, duplication	DeSci bots and agents	Model bias, false flags
ZK Proofs	Cryptographic verifiers	Gas fees, grants	Correctness of computation	ZKML	Complexity, trusted setup

7. REPRODUCIBILITY AND DECENTRALIZED DATA INFRASTRUCTURE

How can we guarantee that scientific data, code, and methodologies remain accessible, auditable, and ethically stewarded across time? As research lifecycles extend beyond institutional memory, decentralized storage, cryptographic provenance, and persistent identifiers are emerging as foundational tools for long-term reproducibility and trust.

7.1 Decentralized storage and Blockchain-Based Provenance

Ensuring the time-resilient accessibility and integrity of scientific artifacts (data, code, protocols) requires infrastructure that is both resilient and verifiable. Decentralized storage networks such as IPFS (Benet, 2014), Filecoin, and Arweave (Williams et al., 2020) offer tamper-evident systems by distributing data across peer-to-peer nodes and anchoring content via cryptographic content identifiers (CIDs) or transaction hashes. When combined with blockchain anchoring, these systems enable researchers to timestamp and verify the exact state of a file, be it a preprint, dataset, or analysis script, at a given moment in time.

Unlike centralized repositories, such systems allow provenance tracking without relying on a single institutional custodian. Storage incentives differ by design: Filecoin utilizes a collateralized retrieval model, while Arweave promises "permaweb" availability via upfront payments encoded into its protocol-level economics. Smart contracts can automate such payments, facilitating long-term persistence without manual renewal.

A reproducibility-oriented workflow thus involves storing large assets off-chain (IPFS CID or Arweave TXID), anchoring their hashes on-chain, and including semantic metadata using machine-readable formats. Timestamps can be cryptographically verified using protocols like OpenTimestamps, and author attestations can be linked to persistent researcher identifiers (e.g., ORCID). This stack not only enables technical reproducibility but also embeds trust into the infrastructure of science itself.

7.2 Interoperability and Open Access in DeSci

The scalability of tokenized science depends on whether data, assets, and reputations can circulate meaningfully across platforms. Interoperability is thus not merely a technical convenience but a necessity. Core components of this infrastructure include content-addressable systems (e.g., IPFS CIDs) that ensure the cryptographic integrity of referenced datasets across DAOs, and evolving token standards such as ERC-6551, which enable NFTs to function as accounts embedding lab records, or ERC-5218, which explores revocable and condition-bound NFT rights. Semantic interoperability follows the FAIR principles—Findable, Accessible, Interoperable, Reusable (Wilkinson et al., 2016), but now extends into on-chain systems through DIDs, VCs, and cross-protocol schemas.

These frameworks allow scientific reputation to become portable, composable, and context-aware, enabling a researcher's identity and efforts to accrue trust across DeSci networks without redundant verification.

7.3 Long-Term Archival Strategies and Considerations

Ensuring the longevity and ethical governance of scientific data in decentralized systems requires both technical foresight and normative sensitivity. Scientific records must persist beyond grant cycles, which decentralized storage models like Arweave's endowment or multisig DAO custodianship help address. Yet permanence introduces its own challenges: protocol upgrades and file format changes demand periodic migration strategies embedded into governance.

Biomedical and sensitive data raise further complications. Immutable ledgers can conflict with privacy rights and evolving consent, especially the "right to be forgotten" (Eichhorn, 2019). Mitigation approaches include off-chain encryption with on-chain key management, ZK queries that reveal aggregate insights without exposing raw inputs, and time-locked cryptographic commitments that allow for future deletion or disclosure.

Finally, decentralized archiving entails ecological considerations. Permanent storage and L1 transactions consume energy (Mora et al., 2018); sustainable design requires using energy-efficient networks, adopting L2 solutions, and embedding carbon accountability into treasury policy.

Table 6 outlines key data infrastructure choices in DeSci, comparing storage, anchoring, access, and identity layers along technical guarantees, incentive models, and design trade-offs.

Table 6. Data Infrastructure Choices and Trade-offs

Layer	Option	Guarantees	Incentive Model	Pros	Cons
Storage	IPFS/Filecoin	Content-addressed, incentive storage	Miner rewards, deals	Flexible, open	Pinning overhead, retrieval latency
Storage	Arweave	Permaweb, endowment	Upfront fee, perpetual storage	Strong permanence	Token economics risk, write costs
Anchor	L1 chain	High security, permanence	Gas fees	Credible neutrality	Costly, low throughput
Anchor	L2 / rollups	Lower fees, batch commits	Sequencer fees	Cheap, scalable	Relies on L1 escape hatches
Access	ZK-gated APIs	Privacy, verifiability	Compute markets	Protects sensitive data	Complexity, UX friction
Identity	DID/VC + ORCID	Portable credentials	None/protocol grants	Interop, self-sovereign	Standard fragmentation

8. COMMUNITY, CULTURE, INCENTIVE INNOVATION

Tokenized science is not only a financial shift, it reconfigures the cultural fabric of research. Tokens act as semiotic tools, shaping identity, participation, and legitimacy. Memes, quests, and gamified rituals move from the margins to the center, becoming instruments that mobilize attention and coordinate distributed labor.

In this scheme, culture is infrastructure: playful incentives align with serious inquiry, and community becomes a method of knowledge production. This section examines how tokens reshape who participates in science, how meaning is signaled, and how new forms of coordination emerge through shared symbolic and economic frameworks.

8.1 Meme Tokens, Gamification, Citizen Science

Drawing from Web3's memetic grammar, where narratives spread virally and capital flows through cultural signal, DeSci experiments with playful mechanics that democratize research participation while embedding epistemic function into social interaction. Models include:

- On-chain quests and experience points (XP) systems: Participants earn VCs (e.g., POAPs, attestations) for discrete contributions, reviewing datasets, contributing protocols, or attending research seminars. These accrue into XP, which can be converted into tokens, governance power, or symbolic status, creating a cumulative incentive structure for sustained engagement.
- NFTs as cultural-scientific artifacts: Art-infused tokens tied to research events, such as dataset releases or experimental breakthroughs, anchor provenance, celebrate contribution, and foster symbolic alignment. These artifacts create a shared aesthetic and mnemonic layer within scientific communities.
- Tokenized citizen science: Inspired by platforms like Metaculus and Foldit, DeSci DAOs deploy micro-bounties for distributed tasks (e.g., environmental sampling, gene annotation, hypothesis formulation) payable in native tokens. This expands the sensemaking surface of science by allowing non-academics to contribute to research in meaningful, rewarded ways.
- Design cautions remain critical: Gamification, if overused, risks incentivizing visibility over rigor, or reducing epistemic labor to attention games. To counterbalance this, platforms must structure layered reward systems, combining playful surface-level engagement with retroactive grants, expert stipends, and long-horizon impact metrics, to ensure that depth is rewarded alongside breadth.

Accounts such as Isaac, Causality Network, Big Pharmai, DeSci World, HealthSci.AI, and Bill the DeSci Guy operate as contemporary intellectual salons and memetic catalysts within the ecosystem. Through reproducibility memes, protocol explainers, and epistemic satire, these platforms play a pivotal role in shaping discourse, cultivating shared norms, and fostering public literacy around emerging scientific infrastructure. While lacking formal on-chain primitives, their cultural influence extends into norm formation, onboarding, and scaffolding across DeSci communities.

8.2 Tradable Hypotheses and Prediction Markets

Prediction markets reconceive scientific hypotheses as tradeable claims, letting prices aggregate and update collective beliefs as evidence accumulates. In doing so, they supply continuous, incentive-compatible signals about which questions are promising, which results are fragile, and how communities should prioritize scarce resources.

Markets can (i) triage hypotheses, channeling funding toward propositions with the highest expected impact-to-probability ratio; (ii) run replication markets, where traders stake on whether published findings will reproduce, thereby disciplining hype and rewarding methodological caution; and (iii) inform research roadmaps, allowing DAOs to compare competing directions by market-implied expected value rather than rhetoric or hierarchy.

There are several platforms pioneering this approach. Pump.Science hosts small, fast-turnaround prediction markets on narrow biotech hypotheses, typically with modest liquidity, aimed at surfacing early signals and gauging expert sentiment in underexplored areas. Stadium Science runs open prediction markets around scientific goals, framing research as competitive "seasons" and inviting broad participation; prices update as evidence streams in, and outcomes are resolved under transparent, pre-registered criteria. Emerging Episteme platform is developing AI-assisted resolution of formally specified scientific claims, aiming to reduce ambiguity in outcomes.

Thin liquidity in more esoteric domains can yield noisy prices; ambiguous endpoints invite oracle disputes; and financial stakes risk perverse incentives to influence experiments. Mitigations include strict pre-registration of resolution criteria, hybrid AI–human oracle panels, caps or circuit breakers for sensitive questions, and separating "signal" markets from direct funding decisions when moral hazard is high. In short, tradable hypotheses convert belief into a measurable, auditable coordination primitive, but only when market design is as rigorous as the science it seeks to guide.

8.3 The Role of AI Agents

The integration of autonomous and semi-autonomous AI agents into scientific process marks a significant evolution in both knowledge system and institutional design. AI agent frameworks such as domain-specific agents are increasingly being deployed across DeSci ecosystems to support and, in some cases, enact core functions, ranging from proposal drafting and milestone tracking to grant evaluation and constrained governance participation.

Emergent agentic patterns include:

- Guardian agents: Automated watchdogs that monitor treasury flows, detect anomalous transactions, and flag potential governance attacks or collusion patterns.
- Research copilots: Agents that support under-resourced research groups by synthesizing relevant literature, scaffolding experimental protocols, or simulating outcomes under defined constraints.
- Mediators of scale: Systems that process and summarize large volumes of community input, such as open calls or citizen science data, into actionable signals for token-weighted or multistakeholder governance processes.

While the epistemic and operational gains of agentic augmentation are substantial, concerns persist around model opacity, embedded bias, prompt injection vulnerabilities, and the difficulty of auditing agent behavior post-hoc. Mitigation strategies include the cryptographic hashing of prompt or model states to ensure reproducibility, publicly accessible agent activity logs, and the incorporation of human-in-the-loop override councils for high-impact decisions.

Table 7 summarizes key coordination mechanisms in tokenized science, detailing their goals, token types, examples, and tradeoffs between participation benefits and systemic risks.

Table 7. Cultural and Participation Mechanisms in Tokenized Science

Mechanism	Primary Goal	Token Primitive	Example	Benefits	Risks
Meme/Gov Tokens	Identity and mobilization	Meme tokens, POAPs	DeSci meme coins	Fast attention, community glue	Hype cycles, shallow engagement
Quest/XP Systems	Micro-task rewards	Attestations, claimable tokens	Quests	Granular incentives, onboarding	Task spamming, metric gaming
Prediction Markets	Belief discovery	Conditional tokens	Episteme, Stadium Science	Price signals, accountability	Oracle risk, low liquidity
Citizen Bounties	Data/annotation crowdsourcing	Bounties, SBT badges	Bio Protocol microgrants	Rapid scaling, inclusivity	Quality control, consent issues
AI Agents	Scale review and ops	Agent reward tokens, KPIs	HealthSci.AI, Bill the DeSci Guy	Efficiency, coverage	Bias/ opacity, over-automation

9. RISKS, LIMITS, AND CRITICAL REFLECTIONS

9.1 Commodification of Knowledge and Epistemic Inequity

The integration of tokenized mechanisms into the scientific process risks re-inscribing existing hierarchies under the guise of decentralization. In the absence of robust public-access guarantees, token-gated models may inaugurate a new regime of enclosure, paywalled science 2.0, where access to knowledge production and validation is contingent upon asset ownership. The financialization of epistemic labor, tethered to the volatility and speculative dynamics of crypto markets, may warp research priorities, incentivizing market-friendly or ideologically fashionable domains at the expense of foundational inquiry, critical disciplines, or epistemologies emerging from the Global South.

Structural exclusions are further exacerbated by infrastructural asymmetries: prohibitive gas fees, monolingual interfaces, and jurisdictional KYC requirements disproportionately burden under-resourced, non-Western, and independent researchers. Left unaddressed, these design choices risk converting epistemic decentralization into a geographically and economically narrow technocracy.

Proposed mitigations include reserving treasury allocations for open-access infrastructure; retroactively funding replication studies, negative results, and null findings; and subsidizing participation through gasless interfaces, multilingual tooling, and targeted grants for underrepresented communities.

9.2 Governance Capture and the Fragility of Decentralized Institutions

While decentralized governance promises pluralism and resistance to central capture, empirical trends reveal persistent tendencies toward oligopoly and protocol stagnation. Token concentration by early adopters, venture funds, or founding teams often translates into enduring agenda-setting power, exacerbated by delegation markets that professionalize governance and disincentivize grassroots deliberation. Ostensibly decentralized systems may conceal de facto centralization behind multisig wallets, foundation boards, or opaque legal entities.

Furthermore, the epistemic legitimacy of scientific prediction markets and DAO-led funding mechanisms is vulnerable to the same tensions that haunt political constitutions: the dilemma between rigidity and plasticity. Excessively rigid governance ossifies error; overly malleable systems undermine trust in procedural fairness.

Institutional countermeasures include the adoption of polycentric governance models that integrate token-weighted, reputation-based, and biometric (e.g., Proof-of-Personhood) voting schemes; rotating validator or curator councils to prevent entrenchment; constitutional modules that require supermajority consensus for core protocol changes; and explicit "exit-to-fork" rights as a formal safeguard of minority dissent.

9.3 Ethical, Philosophical, Regulatory Ambiguities

The transposition of scientific labor into a tokenized incentive economy raises foundational questions about the ethics of motivation and the ontology of research itself. By externalizing intellectual value into market price and staking rewards, such systems risk displacing intrinsic drivers, curiosity, collaboration, the pursuit of truth, with extrinsic metrics of profitability or speculative gain. In doing so, they may erode the communal and intergenerational character of science.

Data permanence introduces a further layer of concern. The immutable storage of biomedical, behavioral, or ecological datasets, particularly when coupled with AI-based prediction and inference, collides with emerging regulatory frameworks such as the GDPR, HIPAA, and future iterations of AI law. While cryptographic techniques such as differential privacy, revocable encryption, and ZKPs offer partial solutions, their implementation requires delicate trade-offs between transparency, accountability, and confidentiality.

On the legal front, tokenized IP instruments, DAO governance mechanisms, and revenue-sharing protocols increasingly intersect with securities and bioethics regulation. Scientific activities under these new models may fall within the purview of agencies such as the FDA, EMA, or biosafety boards, particularly in dual-use domains like synthetic biology or neurotechnology.

Ultimately, tokenization must not be fetishized as a metric of progress. Its legitimacy should be judged not by Total Value Locked (TVL) or Gross Market Value (GMV), but by its contributions to truth-oriented robustness, equitable participation, and the long-term flourishing of planetary life. A science worth decentralizing is one that resists commodification not only in name but in practice, one that holds truth, not trade volume, as its telos.

Table 8 outlines major risk domains, associated failure modes, and proposed countermeasures, highlighting the need for thoughtful design across equity, compliance, privacy, and incentive alignment.

Table 8. Major Risk Domains and Countermeasures

Risk Domain	Failure Mode	Example Scenario	Countermeasure Stack
Equity and Access	Token gates exclude publics	IP-NFT dataset only for token whales	Public-goods share, open license fallback
Governance Capture	Whale cartel blocks replication grants	Early investor bloc vetoes	Multicameral votes, veto chambers, PoP quorum
Regulatory	SEC classifies governance token as security	Enforcement action halts DAO ops	Legal wrappers, airdrop exclusions, compliance modules
Privacy/Bioethics	Immutable leak of patient data	Hash reveals re-identifiable info	Off-chain encryption, ZK queries, consent revocation
Speculative Bubbles	Hype token pumps distort research	Meme cycle funds nonsense experiments	Impact-weighted retrofunding, cap speculation arenas

10. CONCLUSION

10.1 The Future of DeSci in Token Economies

DeSci is transitioning from niche experimentation to infrastructural consolidation. What began as isolated primitives (tokenized grants, DAO-based peer review, IP-NFTs) now signals a deeper reconfiguration of the research economy. Over the next decade, several trajectories are likely to define this shift:

- Composable research stacks: Modular token systems for funding, IP, peer review, and data will interoperate across blockchains and disciplines. These stacks will form the substrate of a programmable scientific internet, enabling dynamic, cross-domain reconfiguration of research processes.
- Agentic epistemic loops: Autonomous AI agents will take on increasingly active epistemic roles, evaluating data, allocating funding, flagging reproducibility issues, and even proposing governance updates. Crucially, these systems must remain accountable to pluralistic human oversight, not self-perpetuating algorithms.
- Institutional integration: Public research agencies, universities, and national labs will begin to experiment with quadratic and retroactive funding models. Tokenized IP and DAO-based governance may form the basis of new public–private–academic hybrids.
- Cross-domain spillover: Mechanisms prototyped within DeSci, such as outcome-based retrofunding or staking open data for credibility, will migrate

to other knowledge domains, including climate science, open hardware, decentralized education, and citizen sensing networks.

10.2 Open Questions and Research Opportunities

As tokenized science matures, a new set of challenges and research questions emerges:

- Measuring epistemic value: What alternative metrics, beyond citations or token price, can meaningfully quantify scientific contribution, methodological rigor, or social relevance?
- Reputation without reification: How can we build reputation systems that reward diligence and domain expertise without reproducing entrenched hierarchies or excluding newcomers?
- Privacy-preserving verification: In sensitive domains, can cryptographic tools enable validation without compromising safety or confidentiality?
- Global inclusion: What design choices in funding, governance, and UX truly reduce structural barriers for underrepresented researchers, beyond mere token distribution?
- Regulatory adaptation: As scientific assets become tokenized and governed on-chain, how should laws around securities, IP, and data protection evolve, or be reimagined entirely?

10.3 Designing for Reflexivity and Justice

Tokenization, if designed reflexively, is more than a financing tool, it is a primitive for rethinking how knowledge is produced, validated, and shared. Yet its emancipatory potential depends entirely on institutional design. Without careful safeguards, the financialization of epistemic labor risks commodifying science, deepening inequities, and undermining credibility.

To realize its promise, tokenized science economies must be:

- Transparent, yet privacy-preserving;
- Efficient, yet procedurally just;
- Open to innovation, yet protected against exploitation.

This calls for pluralistic governance frameworks, ethical constraints on incentive design, and a deep commitment to epistemic justice. Science is not merely a market, it is a public, planetary process. The legitimacy of any new infrastructure must be measured not by capital inflows or token price, but by its contribution to truth, reproducibility, and the collective flourishing of knowledge.

In this light, tokenization should be understood as a structural opportunity, not a technological inevitability. Its true test lies in whether it can help us build a science system that is not only faster and more open, but also more inclusive, more resilient, and more just.

REFERENCES

Arrow, K. J. (1962). Economic welfare and the allocation of resources for invention. In *The rate and direction of inventive activity* (pp. 609–626). Princeton University Press. DOI: 10.1515/9781400879762-024

Asgaonkar, A., & Krishnamachari, B. (2018). Token curated registries: A game theoretic approach. arXiv. https://arxiv.org/abs/1809.01756

Azoulay, P., Zivin, J. S. G., & Manso, G. (2011). Incentives and creativity: Evidence from the academic life sciences. *The RAND Journal of Economics*, *42*(3), 527–554. DOI: 10.1111/j.1756-2171.2011.00140.x

Baker, M. (2016). 1,500 scientists lift the lid on reproducibility. *Nature*, *533*(7604), 452–454. DOI: 10.1038/533452a PMID: 27225100

Bamakan, S. M., Nezhadsistani, N., Bodaghi, O., & Qu, Q. (2022). Patents and intellectual property assets as non-fungible tokens: Key technologies and challenges. *Scientific Reports*, *12*(1), 1–13. DOI: 10.1038/s41598-022-05920-6 PMID: 35140251

Ben-Sasson, E.. (2014). *Zerocash: Decentralized anonymous payments from Bitcoin*. IEEE S&P.

Benet, J. (2014). IPFS - Content Addressed, Versioned, P2P File System. ArXiv. https://arxiv.org/abs/1407.3561

Benkler, Y. (2006). *The wealth of networks: How social production transforms markets and freedom*. Yale University Press.

Bischof, E., Botezatu, A., Jakimov, S., Suharenko, I., Ostrovski, A., Verbitsky, A., Yanovich, Y., Zhavoronkov, A., & Zmudze, G. (2022). Longevity foundation: Perspective on decentralized autonomous organizations for special-purpose financing. *IEEE Access : Practical Innovations, Open Solutions*, *10*, 33048–33058. DOI: 10.1109/ACCESS.2022.3161392

Bourdieu, P. (1975). The specificity of the scientific field and the social conditions of the progress of reason. *Social Sciences Information. Information Sur les Sciences Sociales*, *14*(6), 19–47. DOI: 10.1177/053901847501400602

Bourdieu, P. (2004). *Science of science and reflexivity*. University of Chicago Press.

Boyle, J. (2003). The second enclosure movement and the construction of the public domain. *Law and Contemporary Problems*, *66*(1/2), 33–74.

Brennan, S. (2025, February 28). BioAgents: Accelerating decentralized science with AI agents. Bio Protocol. https://www.bio.xyz/blog-posts/bioagents-pioneering-decentralized-science-with-ai-agents

Budish, E. B. (2018). The economic limits of Bitcoin and the blockchain (Chicago Booth Research Paper No. 18-07). SSRN. DOI: 10.2139/ssrn.3197300

Buterin, V., Hitzig, Z., & Weyl, E. G. (2018). Liberal radicalism: A flexible design for philanthropic matching funds [Working paper]. *SSRN*. DOI: 10.2139/ssrn.3243656

Buterin, V., Hitzig, Z., & Weyl, E. G. (2019). A flexible design for funding public goods. *Management Science*, *65*(11), 5171–5187. DOI: 10.1287/mnsc.2019.3337

David, P. A. (2004). Understanding the emergence of 'open science' institutions: Functionalist economics in historical context. *Industrial and Corporate Change*, *13*(4), 571–589. DOI: 10.1093/icc/dth023

De Filippi, P., & Wright, A. (2018). *Blockchain and the law: The rule of code*. Harvard University Press.

DeFrancesco, L., & Klevecz, A. (2022). Decentralized investor communities gain traction in biotech. *Nature Biotechnology*, *40*(9), 1310–1315. DOI: 10.1038/s41587-022-01459-z PMID: 36042297

Douceur, J. R. (2002). The Sybil attack. In Druschel, P., Kaashoek, F., & Rowstron, A. (Eds.), *Peer-to-Peer Systems (IPTPS 2002)* (pp. 251–260). Springer., DOI: 10.1007/3-540-45748-8_24

Eichhorn, K. (2019). *The end of forgetting: Growing up with social media*. Harvard University Press. DOI: 10.4159/9780674239333

Else, H. (2024). 'Getting paid to review is justice': Journal pays peer reviewers in cryptocurrency. *Nature*. Advance online publication. DOI: 10.1038/d41586-024-04027-4 PMID: 39663443

Eyal, I., & Sirer, E. G. (2014). Majority is not enough: Bitcoin mining is vulnerable. *Communications of the ACM*, *61*(7), 95–102. DOI: 10.1145/3212998

Fantaccini, S., Grassi, L., & Rampoldi, A. (2024). The potential of DAOs for funding and collaborative development in the life sciences. *Nature Biotechnology*, *42*(4), 555–562. DOI: 10.1038/s41587-024-02189-0 PMID: 38565972

Foucault, M. (2014). On the government of the living (A. Davidson, Ed.). Palgrave.

Friday, S. (2023, June 18). VitaDAO letter: Zuzalu & shaping the future of autophagy research. VitaDAO.

Frischmann, B. M., Madison, M. J., & Strandburg, K. J. (2014). *Governing knowledge commons*. Oxford University Press. DOI: 10.1093/acprof:oso/9780199972036.001.0001

Garcia-Costa, D., Squazzoni, F., Mehmani, B., & Grimaldo, F. (2022). Measuring the developmental function of peer review: A multi-dimensional, cross-disciplinary analysis of peer review reports from 740 academic journals. *PeerJ*, *10*, e13539. DOI: 10.7717/peerj.13539 PMID: 35694383

Hanson, R. (2000). Shall we vote on values, but bet on beliefs? Department of Economics, George Mason University. https://mason.gmu.edu/~rhanson/futarchy2000.pdf

Heines, R., Dick, C., Pohle, C., & Jung, R. (2021). The tokenization of everything: Towards a framework for understanding the potentials of tokenized assets. In PACIS 2021 Proceedings (Paper 40). Pacific Asia Conference on Information Systems. https://aisel.aisnet.org/pacis2021/40

Heller, M. A., & Eisenberg, R. S. (1998). Can patents deter innovation? The anticommons in biomedical research. *Science*, *280*(5364), 698–701. DOI: 10.1126/science.280.5364.698 PMID: 9563938

Hellmann, T. (2007). The role of patents for bridging the science to market gap. In Academic science and entrepreneurship: Dual engines of growth (pp. [insert page range if known]). National Bureau of Economic Research. DOI: 10.1016/j.jebo.2006.05.013

Hess, C., & Ostrom, E. (Eds.). (2007). *Understanding knowledge as a commons*. MIT Press.

Ioannidis, J. P. A. (2005). Why most published research findings are false. *PLoS Medicine*, *2*(8), e124. DOI: 10.1371/journal.pmed.0020124 PMID: 16060722

Kavazi, D., Smirnov, V., Shilina, S., Li, M., Contreras, R., Gajera, H., & Lavrenov, D. (2021). You are [not] a bot. arXiv preprint arXiv:2111.13189. https://arxiv.org/abs/2111.13189

Kroll, J. A., Davey, I. C., & Felten, E. W. (2013). The economics of Bitcoin mining, or Bitcoin in the presence of adversaries. In Proceedings of WEIS 2013. https://w.econinfosec.org/archive/weis2013/papers/KrollDaveyFeltenWEIS2013.pdf

Latour, B., & Woolgar, S. (1986). *Laboratory life: The construction of scientific facts* (2nd ed.). Princeton University Press.

Lee, C. J., Sugimoto, C. R., Zhang, G., & Cronin, B. (2013). Bias in peer review. *Journal of the American Society for Information Science and Technology*, *64*(1), 2–17. DOI: 10.1002/asi.22784

Lessig, L. (2001). *The future of ideas: The fate of the commons in a connected world*. Random House.

Madison, M. J., Frischmann, B. M., & Strandburg, K. J. (2010). Constructing commons in the cultural environment. *Cornell Law Review*, *95*(4), 657–709.

Merton, R. K. (1973). *The sociology of science: Theoretical and empirical investigations*. University of Chicago Press.

Mirowski, P. (2011). *Science-mart: Privatizing American science*. Harvard University Press. DOI: 10.4159/harvard.9780674061132

Mirowski, P., & Sent, E.-M. (2007). The Commercialization of Science, and the Response of STS. In *Edward Hackett, Olga Amsterdamska, Michael Lynch & Judy Wajcman, The Handbook of Science and Technology Studies* (pp. 635–689). MIT Press.

Mora, C., Rollins, R. L., Taladay, K., Kantar, M. B., Chock, M. K., Shimada, M., & Franklin, E. C. (2018). Bitcoin emissions alone could push global warming above 2°C. *Nature Climate Change*, *8*(11), 931–933. DOI: 10.1038/s41558-018-0321-8

Nelson, R. R. (1959). The simple economics of basic scientific research. *Journal of Political Economy*, *67*(3), 297–306. DOI: 10.1086/258177

Nielsen, M. (2012). *Reinventing discovery: The new era of networked science*. Princeton University Press.

Nosek, B. A.. (2015). Estimating the reproducibility of psychological science. *Science*, *349*(6251), aac4716. Advance online publication. DOI: 10.1126/science.aac4716 PMID: 26315443

Ohlhaver, P., Weyl, E. G., & Buterin, V. (2022). Decentralized society: Finding Web3's soul. *SSRN*. DOI: 10.2139/ssrn.4105763

Optimism. (2021, July 20). Retroactive public goods funding. Optimism PBC Blog. https://medium.com/ethereum-optimism/retroactive-public-goods-funding-33c9b7d00f0c

Ostrom, E. (1990). *Governing the commons: The evolution of institutions for collective action*. Cambridge University Press. DOI: 10.1017/CBO9780511807763

Ostrom, E. (2010). Polycentric systems for coping with collective action and global environmental change. *Global Environmental Change*, *20*(4), 550–557. DOI: 10.1016/j.gloenvcha.2010.07.004

Ouellette, L. L. (2012). How many patents does it take to make a drug? *Nature Biotechnology*, *30*(6), 556–560.

Partha, D., & David, P. A. (1994). Toward a new economics of science. *Research Policy*, *23*(5), 487–521. DOI: 10.1016/0048-7333(94)01002-1

Polanyi, M. (1962). The republic of science: Its political and economic theory. *Minerva*, *1*(1), 54–73. DOI: 10.1007/BF01101453

Posner, E. A., & Weyl, E. G. (2018). *Radical markets: Uprooting capitalism and democracy for a just society*. Princeton University Press.

Roughgarden, T. (2020). Transaction fee mechanism design. *ACM SIGecom Exchanges*, *19*(1), 52–55. DOI: 10.1145/3476436.3476445

Samuelson, P. A. (1954). The pure theory of public expenditure. *The Review of Economics and Statistics*, *36*(4), 387–389. DOI: 10.2307/1925895

Sarewitz, D. (2016). The pressure to publish pushes down quality. *Nature*, *533*(7602), 147. DOI: 10.1038/533147a PMID: 27172010

Shilina, S. (2023). Decentralized science (DeSci): Web3-mediated future of science. URL: https://medium. com/paradigm-research/decentralized-science-desci-web3-mediated-future-of-science-2547f9a88c40

Shilina, S. (2025). Worlds that verify themselves: DeScAI as a recursive epistemic ecology. *SSRN*. DOI: 10.2139/ssrn.5272669

Smith, R. (2006). Peer review: A flawed process at the heart of science and journals. *Journal of the Royal Society of Medicine*, *99*(4), 178–182. DOI: 10.1177/014107680609900414 PMID: 16574968

Stephan, P. (1996). The economics of science. *Journal of Economic Literature*, *34*(3), 1199–1235.

Stephan, P. (2012). *How economics shapes science*. Harvard University Press. DOI: 10.4159/harvard.9780674062757

Stokel-Walker, C. (2023, January 18). ChatGPT listed as author on research papers: Many scientists disapprove. Nature. https://www.nature.com/articles/d41586-023-00107-z

Stokes, D. E. (1997). *Pasteur's quadrant: Basic science and technological innovation*. Brookings Institution Press.

Sunyaev, A., Kannengießer, N., Beck, R., Treiblmaier, H., Lacity, M., Kranz, J., Fridgen, G., Spankowski, U., & Luckow, A. (2021). Token Economy. *Business & Information Systems Engineering*, *63*(4), 457–478. DOI: 10.1007/s12599-021-00684-1

Tennant, J. P.. (2017). A multi-disciplinary perspective on emergent and future innovations in peer review. *F1000 Research*, *6*, 1151. DOI: 10.12688/f1000research.12037.3 PMID: 29188015

Thaler, J. (2013). Time-optimal interactive proofs for circuit evaluation. CRYPTO 2013.

Weidener, L., & Boltz, L. (2025). Challenges of DAOs in decentralized science: A qualitative analysis of expert interviews. *SSRN*. DOI: 10.3389/fbloc.2025.1641294

Weidener, L., & Spreckelsen, C. (2024). Decentralized science (DeSci): Definition, shared values, and guiding principles. *Frontiers in Blockchain*, *7*, 1375763. DOI: 10.3389/fbloc.2024.1375763

Weiss, K. (2022). Gitcoin grants – Quadratic funding for the world. Gitcoin. https://gitcoin.co

Wilkinson, M. D., Dumontier, M., Aalbersberg, I. J. J., Appleton, G., Axton, M., Baak, A., Blomberg, N., Boiten, J.-W., da Silva Santos, L. B., Bourne, P. E., Bouwman, J., Brookes, A. J., Clark, T., Crosas, M., Dillo, I., Dumon, O., Edmunds, S., Evelo, C. T., Finkers, R., & Mons, B. (2016). The FAIR guiding principles for scientific data management and stewardship. *Scientific Data*, *3*(1), 160018. DOI: 10.1038/sdata.2016.18 PMID: 26978244

Williams, S., Diordiiev, V., Berman, L., Raybould, I., & Uemlianin, I. (n.d.). Arweave: A protocol for economically sustainable information permanence (DRAFT-1). Arweave. Retrieved from https://www.arweave.org/yellow-paper.pdf

Wolfers, J., & Zitzewitz, E. (2004). Prediction markets. *The Journal of Economic Perspectives*, *18*(2), 107–126. DOI: 10.1257/0895330041371321

Ziman, J. (2000). *Real science: What it is, and what it means*. Cambridge University Press. DOI: 10.1017/CBO9780511541391

KEY TERMS AND DEFINITIONS

Agentic Epistemic Loop: A feedback mechanism in which autonomous AI agents evaluate research proposals, validate claims, or trigger funding flows, creating continuous cycles of machine-assisted knowledge refinement within decentralized ecosystems.

Decentralized Autonomous Organization (DAO): A collective, blockchain-based governance structure in which rules and decision-making processes are encoded in smart contracts, enabling communities to manage resources, fund research, and coordinate labor without central intermediaries.

Decentralized Science (DeSci): An emerging movement that applies blockchain, smart contracts, token economies, and decentralized governance to reimagine how scientific knowledge is funded, validated, owned, and shared, aiming to replace institutional gatekeeping with transparent, incentive-aligned coordination.

Intellectual Property Non-Fungible Token (IP-NFT): A digital representation of ownership rights or licensing claims over a scientific asset, such as a patent or dataset, that links on-chain smart contracts with off-chain legal agreements to automate revenue sharing, governance, and provenance tracking.

Prediction Market: A market mechanism that allows participants to trade shares in the outcome of future events, such as whether a scientific hypothesis will replicate, producing price signals that reflect collective belief about epistemic validity or expected impact.

Protocolal Veridiction: A concept introduced in this chapter, referring to the use of blockchain protocols as layers for recording, challenging, and rewarding scientific truth claims through formalized and transparent rules.

Quadratic Funding (QF): A matching funding model that allocates funds in proportion to the square of the sum of individual contributions, amplifying the voice of many small donors over a few large ones, and promoting democratic prioritization of scientific work.

Reputation Token: A non-transferable digital credential that represents a researcher's verified contributions or expertise within a decentralized system, used to weight governance votes, grant access, or build trust without relying on institutional affiliations.

Retroactive Public Goods Funding (RPGF): A funding mechanism that allocates rewards to projects after they have demonstrated measurable impact, reversing the forward-facing logic of traditional grants and allowing communities to retroactively finance valuable contributions.

Tokenization: The process of converting research-related assets, such as datasets, hypotheses, peer reviews, or IP, into programmable digital tokens that can be exchanged, governed, or incentivized across decentralized systems.

ENDNOTES

1 Merton's CUDOS norms are a foundational set of principles describing the ideal values guiding scientific research, first articulated by sociologist Robert K. Merton in 1942. The acronym CUDOS stands for: Communalism, Universalism, Disinterestedness, Organized Skepticism.

Chapter 8

Blockchain and Tokenomics for Education:

Unlocking Micro-Credentials, Equity, and Lifelong Learning — An Overview

Mussa Saidi Abubakari
https://orcid.org/0000-0003-3782-281X
Dig Connectivity Research Laboratory (DCRLab), Uganda & Universiti Brunei Darussalam, Brunei

Lawal Abdulwahab Olamilekan
https://orcid.org/0000-0003-4955-244X
Accord University, Mogadishu, Somalia

ABSTRACT

The chapter explores the transformative potential of blockchain and tokenomics in reshaping education through secure micro-credentialing, equitable access, and lifelong learning. Drawing on recent peer-reviewed literature, it examines how blockchain enables tamper-proof academic records, portable micro-credentials, and learner-owned digital wallets, while tokenomics introduces incentive-driven ecosystems such as "learn-to-earn" and peer-to-peer knowledge sharing. The chapter also investigates the role of decentralized autonomous organisations in collaborative curriculum governance and community-led accreditation. Emphasising global case studies and policy implications, it critically assesses challenges including data privacy, regulatory uncertainty, and digital divides. The analysis highlights how blockchain-based systems can democratise education by recognising informal and

DOI: 10.4018/979-8-3373-3371-7.ch008

modular learning across borders. It concludes by advocating for inclusive, ethical, and scalable implementation strategies to ensure blockchain and tokenomics advance equity and continuous learning in education.

1. INTRODUCTION

Background: Contextualising the Digital Transformation in Education

Education systems worldwide are undergoing rapid digital transformation. Emerging technologies like artificial intelligence, big data, and blockchain are reshaping how learning is delivered, tracked, and recognised. In particular, blockchain technology- originally devised for cryptocurrency – has expanded into non-financial domains, offering new ways to manage data and credentials. Its unique features of decentralisation, transparency, and immutability have attracted interest in education as a means to address persistent challenges in record-keeping, credential verification, and trust (Silaghi & Popescu, 2025). Across all sectors of education (K-12, higher education, vocational training, and informal learning), stakeholders are exploring blockchain-based solutions to improve efficiency and equity in credentialing and student data management.

The Rise of Blockchain and Tokenomics in Global Sectors: Beyond finance, blockchain has been piloted in supply chains, healthcare, government, and now education as a tool for secure information exchange. In parallel, "Tokenomics" – the design of economic systems using digital tokens – has gained prominence in the context of Web3 (the decentralised web). Tokenomics leverages blockchain tokens (fungible or non-fungible) to create incentive structures within ecosystems (Freni et al., 2022). Education is beginning to tap into Tokenomics by issuing tokens as rewards for learning achievements or as governance tools in academic communities. This convergence of blockchain and token economies in education has given rise to experiments like learn-to-earn programs that reward students with cryptocurrency for completing learning tasks (Weiss & Salman, 2022), and pilot projects using blockchain tokens to fund students in rural schools. Globally, initiatives span from Europe's exploration of cross-border blockchain credentialing to developing countries testing blockchain for combating credential fraud and improving access (Alnafrah & Mouselli, 2021; de Alwis et al., 2025; Silaghi & Popescu, 2025). These efforts signal a burgeoning interest in harnessing blockchain and tokens to foster more trustworthy, learner-centred education systems.

The transformational potential of Tokenomics and blockchain in digital education is vast but fragmented, holding promise for more equitable access to and recognition of learning throughout life. Nonetheless, while a clear movement towards openness and accessibility for digitalised education is gathering momentum in the education landscape, it is not clear that this will necessarily redirect towards more equitable opportunities at a global level. Potentially, it could consolidate inequities based on the same structural forces that have contributed to them historically, with regard to education more generally, and with the same unintended consequences of new forms of social stratification (Park, 2021).

At present, both blockchain and Tokenomics in education are in a more nascent stage than in other domains, with only a small number of educational institutions making serious efforts to investigate, launch pilot initiatives, or deploy solutions using blockchain technologies (Fernandes & Werner, 2023). However, this time lag affords an opportunity to engage with the prospect of blockchain in education proactively and reflectively. Analysis of the ideal architecture for openness and accessibility for blockchain and education, and the research on pedagogical frameworks, practices, processes, and systems for Tokenomics in education, must also be carried out. Tokenomics strategies have the potential to disrupt traditional learning designs for transparency, equity, and accessibility while supporting more rewarding experiences in education. The combination of said strategies has the potential to scale this disruption to a level able to challenge the educational status quo. The educational status quo has the potential to co-opt blockchain and/or Tokenomics in ways that empower their transformational potential for creating more educational equity, accessibility, and lifelong curricula.

Lifelong learning evolved as a concept at the end of the 20th century upon the realisation that education must be a continuous process throughout life rather than a single event. Today, lifelong learning is critical to the personal and collective adaptation to rapid changes in knowledge, work, and life (Abubakari, 2025b; Mendoza-Chan & Pee, 2024). It is a training that never ends and takes place in an ever-expanding space of possibilities. It results in a diverse collection of micro-credentials, certificates, badges, and degrees from various providers. Through these myriad credentials, how can individuals prove their skills or understanding to other individuals or organisations? How can education assets be interoperable, verifiable, transparent, and accessible? Blockchain has been proposed as a solution to maximise the potential of lifelong learning by managing micro-credentials (Do et al., 2022; Mikroyannidis et al., 2025). It is an online distributed ledger technology that stores information in an encrypted way, that is maintained across distributed nodes, and that is immutable, meaning information cannot be altered (Capetillo et al., 2022). There is growing interest from industry, academia, policy-makers, and non-governmental organisations to capitalise on this technology to rethink, redesign, repurpose, and even redevelop education and to better align it with the rapid acceleration by which knowledge, skills, and competencies are created and shared. However, the nascent blockchain education solutions landscape is mixed. It is thus intriguing to evaluate where digital-based education will land in this competitive and dynamic landscape of these emerging technologies.

Therefore, this chapter intends to explore the transformative potential of emerging decentralised technologies in reshaping contemporary education systems. While organised in nine logically progressive sections, the chapter builds a comprehensive narrative that situates blockchain and Tokenomics within the broader discourse of digital educational innovation, access, and learner empowerment. The focus is on how these technologies can support inclusive, learner-centred, and skills-based learning ecosystems, particularly through the lens of micro-credentials, equitable access, and the promotion of lifelong learning.

Chapter Objectives, Structure, and Methods

This chapter aims to provide an analytical, evidence-based examination of how blockchain technology and Tokenomics are being applied in education, and how they might unlock new opportunities for micro-credentials, educational equity, and lifelong learning. We synthesise peer-reviewed research published recently to evaluate the potential benefits, practical implementations, and challenges of these innovations across different educational contexts. Key objectives are: (1) to explain the foundational concepts of blockchain and Tokenomics in an educational setting; (2) to explore current applications of blockchain in managing academic records and micro-credentials; (3) to discuss how Tokenomics can incentivise learning and enable new forms of peer-to-peer educational engagement; (4) to assess the implications of these technologies for widening access and equity – including opportunities for marginalised learners and the Global South; (5) to consider the role of blockchain in supporting lifelong learning through portable, stackable credentials; and (6) to critically analyze the challenges, limitations, and ethical issues that must be addressed for these technologies to be implemented responsibly and at scale.

The chapter is organised as follows. Section 2 introduces the conceptual foundations: a primer on blockchain technology (definitions, characteristics, and types) and Tokenomics (types of tokens and economic principles), along with a discussion of how education is evolving in the Web3 era toward decentralised, learner-centred models. Section 3 examines current blockchain applications in education, including secure academic recordkeeping, blockchain-enabled micro-credentialing, and the use of smart contracts to automate educational transactions. Section 4 explores Tokenomics in education through emerging tokenised learning ecosystems, token-driven peer-to-peer knowledge sharing platforms, and the concept of Decentralised Autonomous Organisations (DAOs) for educational governance. In Section 5, we focus on micro-credentials and issues of equity and access: how blockchain-based credentials can democratise access to recognition, what equity challenges exist (such as the digital divide), and illustrative case studies from both developed and developing contexts. Section 6 discusses lifelong learning in the blockchain era, describing frameworks for recognising continuous learning, the idea of personal learning wallets owned by learners, and token incentive mechanisms to motivate ongoing skill development. Section 7 addresses the challenges, limitations, and ethical concerns associated with implementing blockchain and Tokenomics in education, including data privacy, sustainability, regulatory hurdles, and risks of token misuse. Finally, Section 8 outlines future directions and policy implications, offering recommendations for designing inclusive and scalable blockchain-education ecosystems and highlighting steps needed for international standards and collaboration. The Conclusion (Section 9) summarises the key insights and calls for cooperative innovation to harness blockchain and Tokenomics in advancing equity, recognition, and lifelong learning in education.

As for the chapter's method of researching, this chapter employed a qualitative, integrative review methodology, synthesising empirical, peer-reviewed literature published recently (but mostly between 2020 and 2025) from Scopus- and Web of Science-indexed journals, and other databases, including but not limited to Google Scholar. Keyword combinations used for the literature search included "blockchain in education," "educational tokenomics," "micro-credentials and blockchain," "lifelong learning and digital credentials," "decentralised learning systems," "token-based learning incentives," and "blockchain credentialing and equity." The search prioritised studies, systematic reviews, and case-based research across formal, non-formal, and informal education sectors globally. The chapter outline guided thematic analysis to extract insights on conceptual foundations, practical applications, and policy implications within blockchain- and tokenomics-enhanced education systems.

2. CONCEPTUAL FOUNDATIONS OF BLOCKCHAIN AND TOKENOMICS

Understanding Blockchain Technology and Its Types

Blockchain can be defined as a distributed ledger technology that records transactions or data across a peer-to-peer network in a verifiable and permanent way. Each record (or "block") is time-stamped, cryptographically secured, and linked to the previous block, forming a tamper-resistant chain (McGreal, 2023; Sun et al., 2018). Key characteristics of blockchain include: decentralisation – no single authority controls the data, instead it is maintained by a network of nodes; transparency – transaction records are visible to permitted participants, enabling auditability; and immutability – once data is recorded and validated on the blockchain, it cannot be altered retroactively, which is ideal for preserving the integrity of records (Steiu, 2020; Sun et al., 2018). These properties make blockchain a promising solution for securing sensitive educational records. For example, storing academic credentials on an immutable ledger ensures they cannot be forged or modified, thereby providing a tamper-proof way to store and verify academic credentials (Zeroual et al., 2024). Blockchain's trustworthiness comes from consensus algorithms that require network agreement to validate entries, making unauthorized changes exceedingly difficult. In sum, a blockchain is essentially a secure, shared database that, by design, builds trust among participants who may not trust each other solely through its protocol and cryptography.

There are several types of blockchain networks, generally distinguished by who is allowed to participate and read/write data. Public blockchains (permissionless) are open networks like Bitcoin or Ethereum, where anyone can join and contribute to the ledger. They prioritise decentralisation and transparency, but transactions are visible to all, and consensus mechanisms (like Proof of Work) can be resource-intensive. In contrast, private blockchains (permissioned) are closed networks controlled by a single organisation or a defined group; only authorised nodes can participate. These offer greater privacy and efficiency but are more centralised. A middle ground is the consortium blockchain, which is a permissioned network governed by a consortium of independent organisations rather than a single entity (Dinh et al., 2018; Jha, 2025). Consortium blockchains (also called federated blockchains) aim to balance decentralisation with privacy and speed – they allow multiple institutions to jointly maintain a ledger without making it public to everyone. In education, one can imagine a consortium blockchain operated by a group of universities or examination boards to verify credentials collectively. Indeed, the European Union's European Blockchain Services Infrastructure (EBSI) is an example of a consortium approach, where trusted nodes (e.g., government agencies or universities in each member state) validate transactions related to cross-border credentials (Silaghi & Popescu, 2025). Each type of blockchain has its use cases: public blockchains might be used for massive open credential platforms that anyone can verify, whereas private/consortium blockchains might be chosen by institutions that require compliance with data protection regulations and permission controls over who can access student data. Educational applications often favour permissioned models for privacy reasons – e.g., one study noted that, unlike public cryptocurrencies, educational blockchain systems usually require permission from the data owner for others to view credentials (McGreal, 2023). Overall, understanding these variations in blockchain architecture is important for designing systems that fit the governance and privacy needs of educational contexts.

Understanding Tokenomics and Its Types

Tokenomics, short for token economics, refers to the design and implementation of economic systems based on digital tokens. In a blockchain context, a token is a digital asset or unit of value that is recorded on the blockchain and can represent various things, from currency to utility or access rights to ownership of an asset. Tokenomics involves defining the role of tokens within an ecosystem, including their creation (token issuance), distribution, incentive mechanisms, and governance. It blends economic theory, game theory, and technology to ensure that the token's design motivates desired behaviours among participants (Longchamp et al., 2021). In simple terms, Tokenomics is about what makes a token valuable and useful within a system (Freni et al., 2022). For instance, tokens might be used to reward users for contributions, to grant voting power in decentralised governance, or to access services. A 2022 study by Freni et al. highlights the central role played by tokens within blockchain-based ecosystems, noting a shift from traditional economics to token-centric models in many decentralised applications. In education, Tokenomics principles are being applied in emerging platforms where students, teachers, or content creators earn tokens for their participation or achievements, aligning incentives to encourage learning and sharing of knowledge.

In terms of their types, Tokens can be categorised by their function. Utility tokens confer some use or service within a platform – for example, a token that students earn, which can be redeemed for access to advanced courses or tutoring. They are not primarily designed as investments, but rather as internal currency or points that drive the platform's economy. Governance tokens give holders a say in the management of a platform or organisation. In decentralised education platforms or academic DAOs (discussed later), governance tokens might allow educators and learners to vote on curriculum changes or how funds are allocated, thereby democratising decision-making. Both utility and governance tokens are typically fungible (interchangeable units of equal value, like one token is the same as another). By contrast, non-fungible tokens (NFTs) are unique tokens that represent distinct assets. NFTs have gained fame in art and collectables, but in education, they can represent one-of-a-kind credentials or achievements – for example, a diploma or a micro-certificate can be issued as an NFT that is cryptographically unique to the individual. An NFT-based credential system ensures that each certificate is non-transferable (if designed as such) and verifiably tied to its owner, preventing tampering or duplication (Delgado-von-Eitzen et al., 2024; Silaghi & Popescu, 2025). A recent conference paper demonstrated this by using non-transferable NFTs on the Algorand blockchain for issuing and verifying educational certificates, thereby combining the permanence of blockchain with the uniqueness of individual credentials (Tahlil et al., 2022).

In a well-designed educational token system, tokens might be awarded for positive behaviours such as completing courses, teaching others, contributing resources, or validating someone else's skills. The goal is to create a self-sustaining economy that encourages engagement – for example, a "learn-to-earn" model pays learners tokens for progressing through lessons (Weiss & Salman, 2022), leveraging the principles of operant conditioning (rewarding desired behaviour) in a modern, blockchain-mediated way. Game theory is often used to prevent exploitation of the system – for instance, making it costly to cheat or spam for tokens, and ensuring tokens have utility (so that they are not dumped immediately). Token value dynamics are a concern as well: if tokens can be traded on open markets, speculation could introduce volatility, potentially distracting from their educational purpose. In essence, Tokenomics in education needs to craft an economy where the token incentives reinforce learning outcomes. If done correctly, tokenised education platforms can motivate learners and contributors in ways that traditional systems (which often rely solely on intrinsic motivation or external accreditation) might not. However, token economies must be carefully balanced to avoid perverse incentives – a point we will revisit when discussing challenges in Section 7.

3. BLOCKCHAIN APPLICATIONS IN EDUCATION

Secure and Transparent Academic Records

One of the earliest and most prevalent applications of blockchain in education is to issue and verify academic credentials (diplomas, certificates, transcripts) in a secure digital format. By anchoring credentials on a blockchain, institutions can create digital certificates that are tamper-proof and instantly verifiable by third parties. This addresses long-standing issues of credential fraud and cumbersome verification processes. A blockchain-based credential typically involves publishing a cryptographic hash (a digital fingerprint) of the certificate data onto the blockchain. Anyone needing to verify the credential can compare the hash of the presented certificate with the hash on the blockchain to confirm authenticity and that it has not been altered (Silaghi & Popescu, 2025). Because the blockchain record is immutable and time-stamped, it provides a permanent audit trail for each credential. This significantly reduces the risk of fake diplomas and transcripts. As one source explains, by recording educational qualifications on a decentralised ledger, "blockchain ensures that diplomas cannot be tampered with or forged," allowing employers and institutions to authenticate applicants' qualifications confidently (Silaghi & Popescu, 2025).

Furthermore, the impact of secure digital credentials is perhaps most significant in contexts where credential fraud is rampant. Fake degrees and forged transcripts are a global problem that undermines trust in qualifications (Nguyen et al., 2018; Silaghi & Popescu, 2025). Traditional paper certificates and even PDFs can be forged, and verification often requires direct contact with issuing institutions, which is slow and prone to human error. Blockchain solutions directly tackle multiple forms of credential fraud. For example, "degree mills" (illegitimate entities that sell fake diplomas) would be thwarted if employers insist on verifiable blockchain credentials, since a fake institution would not be part of the trusted network to issue a valid hash (Nzaro et al., 2022). Likewise, if a legitimate diploma is maliciously altered (e.g., changing a GPA or graduation date), the hash would no longer match the blockchain record, immediately revealing the discrepancy. A study in Kenya by Nzaro et al. (2022) highlights how a blockchain-based model can curb institutional certificate fraud by validating each step of the certification process. In their model, smart contracts are deployed during admissions (to verify entry qualifications), examinations, and final certificate issuance, ensuring that each stage's integrity is independently verifiable and that no fake certificates can be produced without triggering a mismatch on-chain. This kind of end-to-end approach, using blockchain to audit every milestone of a student's journey, can significantly increase trust in the resulting credentials. Even in less extreme cases, the perceived trustworthiness of credentials can be enhanced: one cross-border pilot between Belgium and Italy used the European Blockchain Services Infrastructure to verify education credentials, demonstrating that two universities in different countries could instantly trust each other's issued credentials without lengthy manual checks (Tan et al., 2023). This is crucial for student mobility and international admissions/employment, where verifying foreign qualifications can be difficult. Blockchain credentialing also benefits learners by adding transparency – students can see and prove their accomplishments without needing to request official documents repeatedly.

Blockchain-Enabled Micro-Credentials

Micro-credentials are mini-certifications that attest to a specific skill or competency, often earned from short courses or training modules. They have gained popularity as a way to recognise lifelong learning and specific job-relevant skills that may not be reflected in traditional degrees. Blockchain provides an ideal infrastructure for micro-credentials because it can handle high volumes of credentials, issued by many different providers, in a secure and interoperable way. Unlike a diploma, which is issued by one authority, a learner might accumulate dozens of micro-credentials from various sources (e.g., a coding bootcamp, an online language course, a workplace safety training, etc.). A blockchain ledger can serve as a unified, tamper-proof ledger of all these achievements. Researchers note that blockchain is "particularly appropriate for micro-certifications" because of its ability to attest to students' accomplishments at a granular level, confidently (McGreal, 2023). Each micro-certificate can be logged as a transaction on the blockchain, creating a permanent record that the learner completed a specific learning unit or demonstrated a particular skill. This modular approach dovetails with the trend towards shorter, just-in-time learning – one study highlights that the 21st-century job market's shift from "just in case" (long degrees for possible future use) to "just in time" learning is driving growth in micro-credentials, which can be earned in a few months or less (de Alwis et al., 2025; Turkanovic et al., 2018). By using blockchain, these credentials can be independently verified and stacked together.

One of the promises of blockchain-enabled micro-credentials is to enable the portability of learning achievements across institutional and national boundaries. In traditional settings, transferring credits or getting recognition for learning done elsewhere is often complicated. But if multiple institutions issue micro-credentials on a common blockchain or interoperable networks, a learner can carry their credits from one institution to another seamlessly. A practical example of this is the EduCTX platform, proposed by researchers as a global credit transfer system using blockchain (Tariq et al., 2023; Turkanovic et al., 2018). EduCTX essentially creates a decentralised repository of academic credits (modelled on the European Credit Transfer System, ECTS) where universities act as nodes in a blockchain network and award students tokens that represent credits earned. Because all participating institutions share the ledger, a student earning credits at University A could have those recognised by University B without lengthy transcript exchanges – the blockchain tokens themselves are the proof of credit. EduCTX's prototype demonstrated the feasibility of uniting various higher education institutions on a blockchain to manage and regulate academic credit tokens, thereby addressing administrative and linguistic barriers in credit transfer (de Alwis et al., 2025). More broadly, the European Union has been actively exploring blockchain for credential portability: the EBSI pilot mentioned earlier not only verified degrees but also envisioned a network of trusted issuers across Europe (Tan & Du Seuil, 2025). In that pilot, a graduate of an Italian university used a blockchain credential to apply for work in Belgium, and the Belgian authority verified it via EBSI instantly (Tan et al., 2023). The success of that use case illustrates the potential for cross-border recognition of micro-credentials (and larger credentials) in a way that aligns with regional qualification frameworks.

4. TOKENOMICS IN EDUCATION

Tokenised Learning Ecosystems

Incentivising Learning through Token Rewards: One of the most intriguing developments at the intersection of tokenomics and education is the advent of incentive-aligned learning platforms – often sloganized as "learn-to-earn." In these tokenised learning ecosystems, students earn digital tokens (which may have real-world value or platform-specific utility) as a reward for engaging in learning activities. This model borrows inspiration from the success of "play-to-earn" in gaming (where players earn crypto tokens by playing games) (Weiss & Salman, 2022). The rationale is to boost learner motivation, persistence, and completion rates by providing extrinsic rewards that are transparently tied to learning outcomes. For example, a language learning app might reward users with tokens for each day they meet their practice goal, or an online academy could give tokens for completing courses and passing assessments. These tokens could then be used to unlock advanced courses, purchase learning materials, or even be traded on exchanges (depending on the design). Early experiments have shown promising results. Weiss and Salman describe a suite of blockchain projects aiming to incentivise learners to engage with educational content and, crucially, to stick with it over time. They cite examples where learners watch tutorials or take quizzes and, upon demonstrating mastery of the material, have crypto rewards deposited into their digital wallets automatically. This immediate positive feedback loop (answer questions → earn tokens) leverages basic behavioural psychology (reward reinforcement) through the medium of cryptocurrency. Such systems can be especially impactful for hard-to-reach student populations. A token reward system can encourage students to remain in school and improve performance. When students earn digital tokens (recorded on blockchain) for consistent homework completion and class attendance, these tokens could be exchanged for mobile data or other useful goods, providing a tangible incentive to continue schooling (Weiss & Salman, 2022)[REMOVED HYPERLINK FIELD]. Thus, blockchain combined with a Tokenisation mechanism can be the key to an educational program's success by ensuring that the incentive distribution is transparent and tamper-proof (preventing any local administrators from skimming funds) and that the conditions for rewards (e.g., a student's attendance record) are verifiable on an open ledger[REMOVED HYPERLINK FIELD].

Several platforms exemplify the learn-to-earn or tokenised learning approach in different contexts. Recently, researchers implemented a custom LMS for engineering students, where accomplishing certain learning tasks and self-assessments awarded the students blockchain-based learning tokens (Heizelman et al., 2024). These tokens were used as part of a self-audit and feedback mechanism aligned with

ABET student outcomes, effectively gamifying the attainment of competencies. The study found that the combination of an established outcomes framework and token rewards served as a powerful tool to enhance student engagement and give students greater autonomy in their learning process. Students could track their progress via tokens earned in various outcome categories, and the token ledger provided a transparent way for both students and instructors to monitor learning gains. This is a form of academic gamification using tokens as "points" that have real value in the educational context (and potentially beyond if the tokens are exchangeable or represent credentials).

Platforms like Mygrants (an application for refugees and migrants) provide another view of token-driven gamified education. Mygrants breaks training content into small missions or quizzes and rewards learners with points and ultimately digital payouts for reaching their learning goals. These kinds of platforms often combine multiple incentive techniques: badges and points for gamified feedback, NFT certificates for achievements, and fungible tokens as rewards (Weiss & Salman, 2022). The tokens also introduce economic concepts to learners – some programs allow learners to stake tokens on what topics they want to learn next, or earn interest, thereby boosting financial literacy as a side benefit. The overarching idea is that tokenisation can make learning more engaging and personalised. However, it is important to balance extrinsic and intrinsic motivation; token incentives must be designed so that they support and not undermine the love of learning. When well-implemented, token rewards can help learners overcome initial inertia and develop study habits. Evidence from the pilots suggests improved retention: for instance, anecdotally, the learn-to-earn projects reported that many learners who might have dropped out of an online course stayed longer when there was a small monetary reward at milestones.

Gamified token systems also have the advantage of providing instantaneous feedback and a sense of progression, which is often lacking in traditional education (Weiss & Salman, 2022). In summary, tokenised learning ecosystems are emerging as a novel way to align the goals of learners and educators by injecting a carefully crafted economic layer into the learning process. By rewarding effort and achievement with digital tokens, these models strive to increase engagement, democratize access (some learners effectively get paid to learn, which can support those with financial needs), and build communities (often tokens can be shared or pooled, creating a social learning economy). As these models are very new, ongoing research should be examining their efficacy. One must consider that over-reliance on tokens could potentially distract from learning or create "gaming the system" behaviours. But with thoughtful design and integration with pedagogical objectives, token rewards and gamification can have significant potential to make learning more fun and rewarding – literally and figuratively.

Token-Driven Peer-to-Peer Knowledge Sharing

Encouraging Tutoring, Mentoring, and Peer Assessment: Education is not only a one-way transfer from teacher to student; peer learning and knowledge sharing among students (and among educators) are critical components of a rich learning environment. Blockchain tokenomics can facilitate peer-to-peer (P2P) educational interactions by providing a system of incentives and trust for those interactions. Imagine a decentralised tutoring marketplace, where students who need help in a subject can connect with peer tutors or mentors, and payments or rewards are handled via tokens on a blockchain. In such a system, a student could pay a small amount of tokens to get 30 minutes of help from a peer who is proficient in, say, calculus. The transaction could be governed by a smart contract that holds the token payment in escrow and releases it to the tutor only if the session is completed and both parties confirm it was helpful (introducing a feedback mechanism). By eliminating a centralised tutoring company and letting students transact directly, the cost could be lower and the reach could be global. One example is peer mentoring: experienced students or alums could earn tokens by mentoring junior students, answering questions on a decentralised Q&A forum, or contributing study resources. A token economy can recognise and reward such contributions, which are often invisible in traditional systems. For example, one could design a university's blockchain-based intranet where every time a student answers a question for a peer or contributes a helpful study note, they get a token "thank you" that might later be exchanged for bookstore credits or additional academic resources. This not only motivates knowledge sharing but also creates a ledger of contributions, which could be useful for recognising student leadership and soft skills.

Importantly, blockchain's role is to provide trust and security in these peer transactions. Because all token exchanges and records of who provided which service are on-chain, users have recourse and transparency. If a peer tutor did not show up for a session, the smart contract would return the student's tokens. If someone tries to spam the system for tokens, their on-chain history would reveal that pattern, and they could be filtered out. Blockchain could also handle reputation in a decentralised way – e.g., an NFT badge could be automatically awarded to a student who has delivered one hundred successful peer tutoring sessions, which they could showcase as a credential in its right (demonstrating communication and leadership skills). While large-scale implementations of token-driven peer learning networks are still in early stages, the concept aligns well with the decentralised ethos: empower individuals to directly support each other's learning, and use tokens to measure and reward that support. Early research suggests that such models could especially help in resource-constrained environments (Chuing & Kutty, 2025; Heizelman et al., 2024). For example, a student in a country with a shortage of teachers might still learn effectively by connecting with retired educators or skilled volunteers elsewhere in the world via a blockchain platform that compensates those volunteers in tokens (which might be convertible to local currency). It is a way to crowdsource education and make it sustainable through a built-in reward system. Over time, if these networks grow, the tokens themselves could gain broader utility – potentially being recognised by educational institutions or employers as evidence of community contribution or even being exchangeable for certified credits (blurring lines between informal and formal learning recognition). Of course, careful design is needed to avoid issues like profiteering or ensuring quality (tokens should reward quality contributions, not just quantity). Mechanisms like peer review, staking tokens as a bond for quality (losing them if your contribution is downvoted for poor quality), and democratic governance of the platform (possibly through a DAO) can address these concerns. Ultimately, token-driven P2P knowledge sharing networks seek to decentralise not just content, but the act of teaching and support, creating a more collaborative and inclusive learning ecosystem where everyone's contributions are valued and visible.

Decentralised Autonomous Organisations for Education

A Decentralised Autonomous Organisation (DAO) is an organisation represented by rules encoded as smart contracts on a blockchain, and controlled by its members through a consensus mechanism (often token-based voting). Applying the DAO concept to education opens up novel ways of collaboratively designing and governing educational processes (Santana & Albareda, 2022). In a traditional educational institution, curricula, policies, and credentialing standards are set by central authorities (faculty boards, accreditation bodies, government education ministries). A DAO for education envisions shifting some of these decisions to the community of stakeholders – including educators, learners, alumni, and industry partners – who participate in governance via blockchain tokens. For instance, consider a "Curriculum DAO" for a rapidly evolving field like blockchain technology itself. Industry experts, professors, and even students could be part of the DAO, each holding governance tokens. When it is time to update the curriculum, proposals could be submitted, and token-holders vote on them. The accepted proposals are then adopted into the curriculum smart contract. This process would be transparent (everyone can see the proposals and votes on-chain) and inclusive, potentially resulting in curricula that are more responsive to real-world changes and stakeholder needs. A 2023 conceptual paper by Pulmano et al. touched on participatory governance in a blockchain credential system, indicating that a decentralised digital credential platform could allow multiple stakeholders to have a say in how it operates (Pulmano et al., 2023). While their focus was on a technical implementation using Hyperledger Fabric, they suggest the groundwork for adding participatory governance features whereby a consortium of universities could vote on the rules of issuing or revoking credentials or even the learners themselves (for example, deciding what metadata is included in a credential or how long it remains valid) (Pulmano et al., 2023).

One specific area where DAO-like structures could be transformative is in accreditation – the process of assuring the quality of educational programs and institutions. Traditional accreditation is done by centralised agencies or government bodies, usually through infrequent reviews. A decentralised approach could involve the community of experts continuously validating each other's courses or schools via blockchain records. Educational organisations could stake tokens to propose their credential for inclusion (basically applying for accreditation), and other members could challenge or vote on them. If approved, the credential stays on the list as accredited, giving it credibility. If the institution fails to maintain quality (detected perhaps by poor learner outcomes or complaints), a new vote could remove it. Such dynamic, crowd-based accreditation would be a big shift from current five- or ten-year accreditation cycles. It might allow new types of learning providers (like MOOCs, bootcamps, community-driven courses) to gain recognition through community validation even if they do not fit legacy frameworks. Indeed, some observers suggest blockchain could enable a soft accreditation by networks of trust rather than single authorities (de Alwis et al., 2025). They also pointed out that blockchain's consensus and transparency can provide comparability and trust across stakeholders (students, education bodies, employers) and could help build a globally trusted education system (de Alwis et al., 2025) – hinting that a decentralised consensus (not just technical, but social consensus) on what credentials are valuable is possible.

5. MICRO-CREDENTIALS, EQUITY, AND ACCESS TO EDUCATION

Democratising Access to Skills and Knowledge

Micro-credentials powered by blockchain can play a significant role in democratizing education by providing more accessible pathways to formal recognition of skills. Traditional degrees often require years of study, significant financial investment, and access to universities or colleges that may be out of reach for many (due to geography or admissions). In contrast, micro-credentials are typically short-term, focused on specific skills, and can be earned through flexible learning modes (online, part-time, etc.) (Jirgensons & Kapenieks, 2018). When these micro-credentials are issued on a blockchain, they gain a level of portability and trust that makes them function almost like 'mini-degrees' in the eyes of employers or other institutions (de

Alwis et al., 2025). This opens opportunities for learners who might not have the resources for a full degree to still obtain verifiable proof of their skills. For example, a person in a low-income community could take a series of free online courses offered by nonprofits or companies, earn blockchain certificates for each skill (say, IT support, digital marketing, basic accounting), and present these to employers as evidence of job readiness. Without blockchain, the burden would be on the learner to convince each employer of the legitimacy of those course certificates. With blockchain, the employer can easily verify that the certificates are authentic and see what competencies they represent (and even who endorsed them) (McGreal, 2023). This cuts out the 'middleman' in credential verification and can reduce scepticism over non-traditional qualifications, thereby lowering barriers for non-traditional learners. One of the primary benefits experts highlight is that blockchain credentials allow students to "attest to their knowledge" directly and own their data, rather than needing institutional gatekeepers to vouch for them (McGreal, 2023; Steiu, 2020).

Furthermore, many underserved communities face not just educational barriers, but also documentation and mobility barriers. For example, refugees and displaced persons often lose access to their academic records or have credentials that are not recognised in their host country. Blockchain credentials can empower these individuals by giving them a self-sovereign, portable record of their skills that is not dependent on any single government or institution. Recently, the United Nations began exploring blockchain for refugee education; one concept is a "learning passport" (developed by UNICEF and Microsoft), which could incorporate blockchain verification so that a refugee child's educational progress is recorded and continues across borders (So et al., 2024). In a similar vein, projects in war-torn or crisis regions (e.g., Syria, Somalia) have trialled blockchain to store academic records and training certificates for youth, to ensure continuity of learning evidence (de Alwis et al., 2025). By doing so, even if local schools are destroyed or records are lost, the students have a durable proof of what they learned, which can help them access opportunities elsewhere.

In marginalised communities, trust in institutions may be low or institutions themselves may be weak. Blockchain's trust-through-technology approach provides a neutral ground. Learners do not have to rely on potentially biased gatekeepers to certify their skills – they can present a blockchain credential that speaks for itself. Moreover, blockchain credentials can include rich metadata (like examples of work, evidence, endorsements) that give a fuller picture of one's ability than a traditional certificate (McGreal, 2023). This could help counter prejudice. For example, someone from an underrepresented group might face scepticism about their resume, but if they can produce a portfolio of verifiable micro-credentials, each with links to actual projects or assessments they completed, it could persuade evaluators to give them a chance. A study – though a bit earlier – envisioned blockchain in education as a means to widen participation by recognising diverse learning experiences and making credentials "open and interoperable" so learners can use them anywhere (Grech et al., 2017). Thus, blockchain-based micro-credentials and digital credentials help democratize education by decoupling learning proof from the traditional gatekeepers. They provide pathways for continuous, asynchronous learning achievements that can be tailored to individual life circumstances. This empowers marginalised learners – whether due to poverty, displacement, racial/gender biases, or simply being outside the conventional system – to take ownership of their educational narrative. They can progressively build a body of evidence for their skills that is widely trusted, thereby accessing jobs or further education that would otherwise require jumping through infeasible hoops.

Equity Implications of Blockchain Credentialing

Addressing Digital Divides and Access to Infrastructure: While blockchain and token-based systems can broaden access in principle, they also come with new requirements that could exacerbate inequity if not addressed: namely, reliable internet access, digital devices, and a basic level of digital literacy. The digital divide – the gap between those with access to technology and those without – is a critical consideration. If blockchain-based credentials become a norm, those without internet or smartphones could be left further behind, unable to obtain or use these new credentials. For example, if a rural student completes a training but does not have a smartphone to receive a blockchain certificate, they might not benefit from the innovation. It is encouraging that mobile penetration is increasing globally, and blockchain platforms are trying to be mobile-friendly, but connectivity gaps remain. Policymakers and practitioners must ensure that introducing blockchain in education goes hand-in-hand with investments in infrastructure and training. That is because regions with limited electricity or internet bandwidth may struggle with current blockchain networks – especially public ones that require constant synchronisation. Some scholars noted that technological infrastructure needs and high energy consumption are challenges for blockchain adoption in education (Garcia-Font, 2020; Steiu, 2020). Specifically, energy-intensive blockchains like Bitcoin's proof-of-work are infeasible in many developing areas. The good news is that newer blockchain technologies (proof-of-stake, consortium chains, etc.) are arguably far more energy-efficient, and these should be prioritised for educational use to be sustainable and accessible.

Another aspect is usability and digital literacy. The concepts of digital wallets, private keys, and tokens can be daunting for individuals who are not tech-savvy. If handling one's credentials requires managing cryptographic keys, there is a risk of losing credentials (if keys are lost) or being susceptible to scams. Educational programs will need to include digital literacy components to ensure learners can safely use blockchain tools (Abubakari et al., 2025; Abubakari & Kalinaki, 2024; Adel, 2024). Initiative projects can consider custodial wallets (managed by a trusted institution on behalf of learners) as an interim solution, though that reintroduces some centralisation. The design of user interfaces for blockchain credential apps targeting low-literacy populations is a major equity consideration: they must be simple, multilingual, and provide support (like recovery mechanisms, helpdesks, etc.) (Abubakari, 2025a; Musa et al., 2025). Otherwise, the very populations we aim to empower could be alienated by technology that seems too complex or risky.

Inclusion of Learners from the Global South and Non-Traditional Pathways: For blockchain in education to truly enhance equity, it has to be embraced and integrated in contexts outside the affluent, high-tech environments. Encouragingly, in 2025, we have seen multiple blockchain-education pilots in the Global South. For instance, countries like Kenya, Rwanda, and Bangladesh have been part of studies or trials for blockchain credentials (de Alwis et al., 2025). A 2021 study on the potential of blockchain in developing world education argued that blockchain could help leapfrog some systemic issues, but it also cautioned that local adoption would depend on government support and education of the populace on the tech (Alnafrah & Mouselli, 2021). The inclusion of non-traditional learners – such as adult learners reskilling, informal sector workers, or homemakers – is a major promise of micro-credentials. Blockchain adds value by giving these credentials legitimacy. For example, a cooperative of craftsmen without formal degrees could collectively issue an artisan skills certificate on blockchain for their members, which might then help those artisans find work or sell products by proving the authenticity of their skill. Global organisations (like the Commonwealth of Learning and UNESCO) have been exploring these community-driven credentialing ideas, noting that they could recognise skills learned on the job or through community mentorship that would otherwise never be formally certified (Grech et al., 2022; World Bank Group, 2020).

Case Studies and Lessons Learned

To ground the discussion, we examine a few notable case studies that illustrate the use of blockchain-based credentialing platforms and pilot projects targeting educational equity.

MIT Digital Certificates (Blockcerts)

MIT's Media Lab, in collaboration with learning machine companies, developed Blockcerts, an open standard for blockchain credentials, and in 2017 issued blockchain-based digital diplomas to a cohort of graduates (Blockcerts, 2018). Each student received a verifiable digital diploma in their smartphone wallet, which they could share with employers or other institutions. This case is significant as a pioneering demonstration of the technology. The impact was that graduates now had ownership of their credentials – even if MIT's systems were offline, the diploma could be verified against the blockchain. It proved the concept that a top university would entrust its credentials to a blockchain, giving confidence to others to follow. A key lesson from MIT's case was the importance of user experience: MIT provided an app that made it easy for students to retrieve and share their diplomas, abstracting away the technical details of the blockchain. This case also showed interoperability: Blockcerts was blockchain-agnostic (initially using Bitcoin's blockchain, later others), emphasising that open standards help adoption (Lam & Dongol, 2022; Silaghi & Popescu, 2025).

Pilot Projects in Developing Countries and International Agencies

A number of pilots led by international organisations illustrate blockchain's potential in improving access and record-keeping in developing regions. One example is the European Union's Blockchain in Education report (2017 and follow-ups) spurred the European Blockchain Partnership to test education use-cases on EBSI, culminating in the cross-border diploma verification pilot between Belgium and Italy discussed before (Tan et al., 2023). That pilot's success in 2023 led the EU to plan a service for recognising credentials across Europe on blockchain by default in the coming years. It shows a governmental approach: building a consortium chain (EBSI) specifically for public services, including education credentials, which can significantly streamline mobility within a region (Tan & Du Seuil, 2025).

For learners in the Global South or those who follow non-linear education paths, this portability is equally crucial. Someone in a remote area could collect micro-credentials from online courses offered by institutions worldwide; with blockchain, these carry weight even if the issuing institution is not locally known, because the verification does not rely on reputation alone but on cryptographic proof. A 2020 reference model by Cardoso et al. also showed how blockchain could support academic record portability for student mobility scenarios, indicating that a unified approach can significantly ease credit transfers and recognition across universities (Cardoso et al., 2020b, 2020a). In summary, blockchain-enabled micro-credentials act like digital LEGO bricks of education – learners can earn them from various sources and then assemble them as needed, with blockchain ensuring each piece is authentic and fits into the larger picture of the learner's qualifications. This enhances not only portability but also learner agency, as individuals are not locked into one institution's track but can curate their lifelong learning journey from a variety of providers. Thus, each of these case studies, in different ways, highlights both the potential and the practical challenges of blockchain in education. The case studies also emphasise that multi-stakeholder collaboration (tech providers, educational institutions, governments, NGOs) is often necessary to implement these solutions effectively and ensure they serve the goal of widening access and increasing trust globally.

6. LIFELONG LEARNING IN THE BLOCKCHAIN ERA

Recognition of Informal, Non-Formal, and Continuous Learning

In today's rapidly changing world, learning is a lifelong endeavour. People continually acquire new skills outside formal degree programs – through online courses, workshops, on-the-job experience, and personal projects. However, recognising and compiling this continuous learning into a coherent "education profile" is challenging with conventional methods. Blockchain offers a framework to capture all learning achievements, formal or informal, in a secure and unified manner. This is often discussed in terms of a "lifelong learning passport" or learning ledger (So et al., 2024; Terzi et al., 2022). The idea is that from early childhood through retirement, a person could have an evolving set of blockchain-verified credentials representing everything from school grades and diplomas to micro-credentials, workplace training certificates, and even community service or volunteering badges. By integrating these on a blockchain, the individual and any verifier can trust the authenticity of each record and see the progression over time. A key concept in such frameworks is stackable credentials: smaller credentials can be built into larger qualifications. For example, several professional development badges could stack up to a diploma, or a series of community college certificates could culminate in an associate's degree. Blockchain helps in stacking because it provides the chronological, tamper-proof record needed to show that prerequisite modules were completed. Projects like BlockAdemiC in the EU have worked on a blockchain-powered lifelong learning passport to facilitate exactly this: issuing verifiable credentials for every learning event and enabling them to be aggregated for higher qualifications (Tepelidis et al., 2024; Terzi et al., 2022).

Another scenario is recognising informal learning. For instance, if someone self-studies programming and creates a software project, they might not have a formal certificate, but could earn a community-issued blockchain badge (perhaps from an open-source community) attesting to their skill. If employers accept that, it essentially brings informal learning into the formal economy via blockchain validation. There is also interest in using blockchain to track and certify skills gained through apprenticeships or vocational experience, which are traditionally documented in cumbersome ways. A 2022 system developed in Vietnam, B4E (Blockchain for Education), aimed to create a complete record of lifelong education for each user, storing not only certificates but also detailed training data and transcripts (Do et al., 2022). Their goal was to facilitate verification and guard against any fake credentials by having a holistic view of an individual's learning history. This demonstrates the practical assembly of a lifelong record on a private blockchain network, indicating that technology is catching up to the vision of comprehensive lifelong learning accounts.

In summary, integrating blockchain into lifelong learning frameworks helps create a continuous, trustworthy narrative of an individual's learning journey. It blurs the lines between formal and informal education by providing a common trust layer for all credentials. A lifelong learning system underpinned by blockchain could mean that learning never goes unrecognised: any skill you gain, you can get a certificate or badge for it that will be respected, and you can keep building on it throughout your life. This is a dramatic shift from the current situation, where much learning is invisible or uncredited. With blockchain, the phrase "lifelong learning" becomes tangible, because we finally have a tool to track and validate it lifelong.

Motivating Continuous Education with Token Incentives

In many industries, the shelf-life of skills is shrinking; workers must reskill or upskill regularly to stay relevant. However, adult learners often face motivational and financial barriers to continuous education. Token incentives, as discussed previously, can be particularly valuable in spurring ongoing learning engagement beyond formal schooling. Imagine a scenario where a professional receives tokens for completing a new course or obtaining an in-demand skill certification. These tokens might be provided by an employer, an industry consortium, or even a government keen on upskilling the workforce. For instance, a tech company could allocate a budget in the form of tokens to employees, which are awarded whenever an employee finishes a certified training or earns a micro-credential. Those tokens could then be exchanged for bonuses, extra vacation days, or other benefits as per company policy. This creates a direct line of sight between learning and tangible reward, reinforcing the habit of continuous learning.

Furthermore, in gig economies or freelance careers, individuals could earn tokens from a community or platform by demonstrating new competencies that increase their value to clients. Some blockchain-based freelance marketplaces consider giving freelancers tokens for passing skill tests (to encourage them to improve their skill profile, which in turn makes the marketplace more robust). Those tokens might translate into lower platform fees or higher visibility on the platform. This is essentially a loyalty program, but for skill development.

Continuous education is also crucial for unemployed or transitioning workers. Governments and NGOs could deploy token incentives as part of workforce development programs. For example, an unemployment benefits system might be gamified: claimants could earn token rewards (which might translate into additional cash grants or other support) by completing certain upskilling activities that improve their employability. The World Economic Forum has even speculated about something akin to frequent flyer points, but for learning – accumulate enough learning points (tokens) and you get perks or recognition, perhaps even portable "learning equity" that you can spend on formal education later. Blockchain tokens make tracking and exchanging such "learning points" feasible on a large scale, and smart contracts ensure they are awarded fairly when conditions are met.

7. CHALLENGES, LIMITATIONS, AND ETHICAL CONCERNS

Implementing blockchain and tokenomics in education is not without significant challenges. While the potential benefits are clear, stakeholders must navigate technical, ethical, and organisational hurdles. Key concerns include data privacy, energy sustainability, regulatory compliance, institutional inertia, and the pitfalls of introducing market dynamics into learning.

Data Privacy and Surveillance Risks

Education records are sensitive personal data. Storing or linking these records on a blockchain raises concerns about privacy, especially if using public blockchains. Even if the actual content of credentials is not on-chain (with only hashes or identifiers recorded), the metadata of transactions might reveal information (like the fact that a person received a certain type of certificate at a certain time). In the EU, GDPR mandates the right to be forgotten, which conflicts with blockchain's immutability (Belen-Saglam et al., 2023; Silaghi & Popescu, 2025). How do you "forget" a credential on an immutable ledger? Solutions exist (like revocation or off-chain storage with on-chain proofs), but they add complexity. There is also the risk of surveillance if, for instance, a government decided to track all learning activities of citizens via blockchain. If not properly permissioned, a robust educational blockchain could inadvertently become a panopticon of citizens' skills and movements through learning institutions. Safeguards like permissioned access (only those granted see the data) and encryption are crucial. Techniques like zero-knowledge proofs can allow verification of a credential without revealing unnecessary data about the person, helping maintain privacy. Still, the ethical use of the data needs governance: Who owns the credential data on blockchain? Ideally, the learner (as argued), but institutions or platforms might try to co-own. Policies must ensure that learners' rights over their data are protected. We must also consider minors – recording K-12 credentials on blockchain could conflict with child data protection laws; parental consent and the ability to remove records upon reaching adulthood might need to be built in.

Sustainability and Energy Concerns of Blockchain

Early blockchains like Bitcoin and Ethereum (pre-2022) used energy-intensive consensus (Proof of Work). Bitcoin's annual energy consumption was famously compared to that of a small country (like Switzerland) (Steiu, 2020). Understandably, using such a blockchain at scale for education (which would involve millions or billions of transactions for credentials and tokens) is not eco-friendly or feasible for many education systems (Park, 2021). This concern has been a barrier, with some educators baulking at the carbon footprint of blockchain. Fortunately, the landscape has changed: many new blockchains use Proof of Stake or other low-energy algorithms. Consortium chains can use practically negligible energy since they rely on a few nodes with established trust (Aggarwal & Kumar, 2021; Chen et al., 2024). Nonetheless, sustainability is an ethical concern—especially in education, where we aim to instil responsibility. It would be counterproductive if an education solution contributed to climate change. Therefore, any large-scale blockchain credential system tends to use energy-efficient methods. For instance, the European EBSI uses a permissioned network with limited validators, and blockchains like Tezos or Algorand, which are PoS, have been considered by some educational pilot projects for their green profile (Tahlil et al., 2022; Tan et al., 2023). Another angle is e-waste: frequent upgrading of digital devices or the short lifecycle of tech could pose waste issues if blockchain tech requires newer devices. However, this is more of a general tech issue than a blockchain-specific one. Blockchain networks can also offset some carbon or use renewables (some networks are now marketing themselves as carbon-neutral). The bottom line is that tech choices must align with sustainability goals. If an existing high-energy blockchain is to be used for education, carbon offsetting, or transitioning to layer-2 solutions should be done.

Regulatory and Institutional Resistance

Education is a highly regulated sector. Introducing blockchain and tokenomics faces regulatory uncertainty. For instance, in some countries, issuing degrees is legally tightly controlled; would a blockchain credential be recognised under current laws? There might need to be new regulations to accept a digital diploma as legally equivalent to a paper one. Some accreditation bodies might resist or take time to adapt standards to accommodate micro-credentials and blockchain proofs. On the token side, tokenomics in education may flirt with financial regulations. If students are earning tokens that have monetary value, are those considered income? If a school creates a token to reward learning, does it inadvertently become an "issuer of a digital currency" needing oversight? These questions are largely untested in legal systems. In addition, institutions themselves can be resistant to change. Universities might be wary that blockchain could disrupt their control over credentialing – perhaps fearing a loss of gatekeeping power or revenue. There is also the human factor: administrators might not understand the tech and therefore distrust it. This can manifest as internal pushback or slow adoption. Education systems can be quite conservative and bureaucratic, often for good reason – they deal with important stakes like one's future. Thus, convincing stakeholders of blockchain's security and reliability is an ongoing challenge. A recent literature survey indicated that a lack of understanding and skills in blockchain among university staff is a major barrier to adoption (Wang et al., 2025).

To mitigate this, pilot programs and clear policy frameworks are needed. Governments could update rules to explicitly allow digital blockchain credentials as valid evidence for jobs and further study. International bodies can develop guidelines for quality assurance in blockchain credentialing. On institutional change management: starting with supplementary credentials (like issuing blockchain certificates alongside traditional ones) can help ease the transition. Once familiarity and trust are built, institutions may fully switch. There is precedent in other industries (finance, slowly moving to blockchain behind the scenes, etc.), but education might require special care, given its public service nature. Additionally, cross-institution collaboration (like consortia forming a shared credential blockchain) can help, so no single institution feels it is stepping into the unknown alone.

Risks of Token Speculation and Value Volatility

While token-based incentives offer benefits, they also introduce risks akin to any cryptocurrency or token economy. If an education token given to students is freely tradable, its value might fluctuate due to market speculation unrelated to educational purposes. This could distract from its intended use or even create perverse incentives (for instance, students might focus on gaming token gains, or external speculators could interfere in an education token system to make a profit). In the worst case, if a token crashes in value, learners might feel cheated or demotivated. Conversely, if tokens rise too much, the program might become financially unsustainable or attract misuse. One mitigation is to use stable-value tokens (pegged to a fiat currency or inherently stable asset) for educational rewards, to avoid volatility. Another approach is to restrict transferability: e.g., tokens can only be used within an ecosystem (to buy learning materials or pay tuition) and not cashed out, thus reducing speculative interest. However, that limits the flexibility for learners – a balance must be struck. Finally, we must consider the ethical use of data from token systems. These systems will generate a lot of data on who learns what and how actively, and so on. There is a risk that educational institutions or employers misuse this data for surveillance or high-pressure tactics (imagine an employer monitoring an employee's learning token activity to judge them). Clear agreements on data usage and respect for learner privacy and autonomy are needed.

8. FUTURE DIRECTIONS AND POLICY IMPLICATIONS

Looking ahead, the confluence of blockchain, tokenomics, and education will require intentional design and collaboration among stakeholders. Several future directions and policy considerations emerge from our analysis.

Designing Inclusive, Scalable, and Ethical Blockchain Ecosystems in Education

For blockchain credentials to realise their potential, they must be built on inclusive design principles. This means developing systems that accommodate users with varying levels of digital access and literacy. Future R&D should focus on offline functionality (e.g., credentials that can be verified with low connectivity via SMS-based queries or periodic sync) to include learners in remote or under-resourced areas. Scalability is also crucial; educational blockchains should be able to handle potentially billions of transactions (every quiz result or assignment could technically be a micro-credential). This may drive innovation in layer-2 solutions or education-specific blockchain networks optimised for high volume and low cost. From an ethical standpoint, design should incorporate privacy by design and security by design – for instance, using decentralised identifiers and giving users fine-grained control over which data they share, and employing the latest cryptographic techniques to protect personal information (Do et al., 2022). Usability testing with diverse learner groups (including those with disabilities) should guide interface development for personal learning wallets and credential platforms to ensure no one is left behind due to design negligence. Additionally, future systems might integrate AI to personalise learning while using blockchain to secure the credentials; policies will need to ensure such AI usage is fair and does not perpetuate bias (blockchain might store model decisions for transparency in such cases).

Recommendations for Policymakers, Educators, and Tech Developers

Policymakers should begin updating legal and educational frameworks to recognise and encourage blockchain credentials. For example, national qualification frameworks can be amended to include micro-credentials and blockchain verifiable credentials as legitimate evidence of skills. Governments might consider establishing national (or regional) blockchain networks for education – similar to the EU's EBSI – to provide a trusted public infrastructure that schools and companies can plug into (Silaghi & Popescu, 2025). This can reduce duplication and ensure standardisation. Investment in digital infrastructure (broadband, devices) remains a priority to enable these technologies broadly (aligning with SDG goals for equitable quality education). Policymakers should also facilitate pilot projects in collaboration with tech companies and educational institutions, perhaps via sandboxes where regulatory flexibility is allowed to experiment safely. On the international stage, bodies like UNESCO, the OECD, and the World Bank can create guidelines or principles for blockchain in education, covering ethics, quality, and inclusion (Weiss & Salman, 2022; World Bank Group, 2020). They can also help the Global South leapfrog by transferring knowledge from pilots in advanced economies and providing funding support for localised implementations.

Educators and academic leaders have a role in advocating for and shaping these innovations to serve pedagogical goals, not just administrative efficiency. Faculty should be involved in developing micro-credential curricula to ensure they represent meaningful learning outcomes. Teacher professional development needs to include digital credential literacy so that educators can guide students in using and benefiting from these tools. Educational institutions might consider forming consortia to share best practices in issuing blockchain credentials or to develop common token incentive systems so that students see consistency. Also, educators should keep the focus on learning: token incentives or blockchain tech are means to an end (learning), so pedagogical research should continue to evaluate how these tools impact student motivation, engagement, and learning depth. Adjustments should be made based on evidence (e.g., if token rewards for quizzes are leading to shallow learning, maybe restructure to reward project completion or mastery demonstration instead).

Tech developers should work closely with educational experts to ensure the solutions address real needs and constraints. They should adhere to open standards to avoid vendor lock-in of credentials (nothing would undermine the vision more than having credentials that only a particular software can verify). Collaboration on interoperability—like ensuring a credential from one system can be imported into another's wallet—is a key technical priority. Developers should also prioritise user-friendly experiences, perhaps abstracting blockchain jargon away from the end-user. For instance, a student app might say "Verified Certificate" rather than "Hash" or "Transaction ID." Tech companies also need to consider data security deeply; education data breaches can be very damaging, so rigorous security audits and perhaps decentralised storage solutions (like using IPFS for documents while storing hashes on blockchain) should be in the development roadmap (Do et al., 2022).

Potential for International Standardisation of Blockchain Credentials

Just as there are international standards for transcripts (like Europass) and qualification frameworks, there is a need for global standards in blockchain-based credentials. The W3C Verifiable Credentials (VC) standard is a strong foundation; broad adoption of it will allow credentials to be understood globally. Building on VC, an international standard for educational credential schemas (what fields to include for a diploma vs. a skill badge, etc.) would greatly aid interoperability. UNESCO's ongoing efforts in the Digital Credentials Consortium and other groups aim to define common taxonomies and metadata for micro-credentials (OECD, 2021); these should be extended to the blockchain context. Another layer is standardising the process and governance: e.g., an International Blockchain Academic Credential Council could certify issuers or provide a trust mark so verifiers know which blockchain credentials adhere to quality practices (somewhat analogous to accreditation agencies but for the credential process rather than content). Standards are also needed for the token side: guidelines on how to design token incentives ethically in education could be developed by organisations like IEEE or ACM, combining insights from educational psychology and blockchain economics.

At the policy level, mutual recognition treaties for education might incorporate blockchain. For example, UNESCO could update the global Convention on the Recognition of Qualifications to mention that verifiable digital (blockchain) credentials should be treated equivalently to traditional ones. This would push universities and employers to accept such credentials from abroad without prejudice (de Alwis et al., 2025). Cross-border initiatives, like those between developing countries and developed, could pilot allowing migrant workers to carry learning credentials from one country to another via blockchain, informing future frameworks for skills mobility.

Ultimately, achieving the envisioned transformation will require collaborative innovation in educational ecosystems. Technologists, educators, and policymakers must engage in constant dialogue – perhaps via working groups or innovation hubs dedicated to blockchain in education. Pilot programs should include all these stakeholders from the get-go to ensure a holistic understanding of impacts. For instance, a city that wants to become a "smart education hub" could bring local universities, school boards, employers, and tech startups together to create an integrated credential & learning incentive network for the city, with government oversight to align it with public interest goals. Successful models can then be replicated elsewhere with localisation as needed. In conclusion, the future of blockchain and tokenomics in education looks promising, but it will unfold correctly only with initiative-taking efforts to shape it. By focusing on inclusivity, standardisation, and evidence-driven policies, we can harness these technologies to build more equitable, efficient, and learner-centred education systems worldwide. Embracing innovation while safeguarding core educational values will be the balancing act for all involved.

9. CONCLUSION

The exploration of blockchain and tokenomics in education reveals a transformative potential to reconfigure how we recognise, reward, and share learning. In summary, blockchain-based micro-credentialing and personal learning wallets empower learners with ownership of their achievements and enable seamless portability of skills across institutions and borders, addressing long-standing issues of credential verification and mobility. Smart contracts and token incentives introduce new mechanisms to automate trust and motivation in educational transactions, whether by securing academic records against fraud or by incentivising lifelong learning through tangible rewards. These innovations carry the promise of making education systems more learner-centric, equitable, and responsive to the demands of a global knowledge economy.

Crucially, blockchain and tokenomics offer tools to advance equity and access. They lower barriers by validating skills learned in non-traditional settings, giving marginalised learners alternative pathways to gain recognition and improve their socioeconomic prospects. A securely verifiable skill passport means a refugee or a rural student can present credentials that hold weight internationally, potentially democratizing opportunities that were once reserved for those following conventional routes. Tokenised learning models, when thoughtfully implemented, can allocate resources and attention to learners who need it most (for example, by rewarding persistence in underserved communities or funding learning in emerging fields). These technologies also facilitate lifelong learning, which is increasingly critical as careers evolve; individuals can continually update and showcase their skill sets in real time, staying relevant and employable. However, the journey towards this vision demands careful navigation of challenges. Throughout this chapter, we noted the importance of guarding privacy, ensuring inclusivity, preventing misuse of token systems, and aligning technological innovation with educational values and policies. Blockchain in education should not be a solution looking for a problem, but a deliberate answer to clear needs – whether it is the need for trust in credentials or the need for new motivational frameworks in learning. The case studies we reviewed provide empirical evidence and lessons that can guide scaling up these ideas. They show that the technology works, but also that human and institutional factors are pivotal in adoption.

In concluding, we underscore a call for collaborative innovation: realising the benefits of blockchain and tokenomics for education will require educators, technologists, administrators, and policymakers to work in concert. Educators must articulate the pedagogical goals and safeguard academic integrity in these new modes. Technologists should continue to refine user-friendly, secure, and interoperable systems, ideally open-source and with open standards, so that the educational community as a whole can benefit rather than a few siloed platforms. Institutions and accreditation bodies need to be forward-thinking, updating norms and standards to integrate micro-credentials and digital verification as mainstream. Policymakers should craft enabling policies and invest in the necessary infrastructure and training to ensure no regions or populations are left behind in this digital transformation.

If done right, the integration of blockchain and tokenomics in education can be truly transformative. It could lead to an ecosystem where a learner's skills and knowledge are transparently and reliably acknowledged, wherever or however they were acquired, and where continuous learning is actively nurtured through aligned incentives. Such an ecosystem would better promote not just efficiency and trust, but also the ideals of equity and lifelong personal growth. In a world where learning is the new currency, blockchain provides the mint and tokenomics the market – together, they can help ensure that every individual has the means to earn, spend, and invest in their learning over a lifetime. The next decade will likely witness whether these technologies fulfil their promise. The evidence and analysis presented in this chapter suggest that, with mindful implementation, blockchain and tokenomics can indeed unlock a future of micro-credentials, equity, and lifelong learning that is more accessible and empowering than ever before.

REFERENCES

Abubakari, M. S. (2025a). Digital Competence for Enhancing Financial Inclusion in FinTech Adoption: Addressing the Digital Divide. In Masri, M., Sait, M. A., & Anshari, M. (Eds.), *Promoting Inclusivity and Accessibility With FinTech* (pp. 65–102). IGI Global Scientific Publishing., DOI: 10.4018/979-8-3373-1112-8.ch003

Abubakari, M. S. (2025b). Digital Technologies Adoption in Islamic Education for Fostering Lifelong Learning Culture: Pilot Survey Preliminary Insights. In Anshari, M., Almunawar, M. N., & Ordóñez de Pablos, P. (Eds.), *Multi-Industry Digitalization and Technological Governance in the AI Era* (pp. 103–126). IGI Global., DOI: 10.4018/979-8-3373-1681-9.ch005

Abubakari, M. S., & Kalinaki, K. (2024). Digital Competence in Islamic Education for Lifelong Learning: Preliminary Analysis Using DigComp 2.1 Framework. In Hawamdeh, M. M. K., & Abdelhafid, F. (Eds.), *Embracing Technological Advancements for Lifelong Learning* (pp. 1–31). IGI Global., DOI: 10.4018/979-8-3693-1410-4.ch001

Abubakari, M. S., Zakaria, G. A. N., & Musa, J. (2025). Validating the DigComp framework among university students across different educational systems. *Discover Education*, *4*(1), 200. DOI: 10.1007/s44217-025-00652-x

Adel, N. (2024). The impact of digital literacy and technology adoption on financial inclusion in Africa, Asia, and Latin America. *Heliyon*, *10*(24), e40951. DOI: 10.1016/j.heliyon.2024.e40951 PMID: 39720071

Aggarwal, S., & Kumar, N. (2021). A Consortium Blockchain-Based Energy Trading for Demand Response Management in Vehicle-to-Grid. *IEEE Transactions on Vehicular Technology*, *70*(9), 9480–9494. DOI: 10.1109/TVT.2021.3100681

Alnafrah, I., & Mouselli, S. (2021). Revitalizing blockchain technology potentials for smooth academic records management and verification in low-income countries. *International Journal of Educational Development*, *85*, 102460. DOI: 10.1016/j.ijedudev.2021.102460

Belen-Saglam, R., Altuncu, E., Lu, Y., & Li, S. (2023). A systematic literature review of the tension between the GDPR and public blockchain systems. *Blockchain: Research and Applications*, *4*(2), 100129. DOI: 10.1016/j.bcra.2023.100129

Blockcerts. (2018). *FAQ - Blockcerts: The Open Standard for Blockchain Credentials*. Blockcerts.Org. https://www.blockcerts.org/guide/faq.html

Capetillo, A., Camacho, D., & Alanis, M. (2022). Blockchained education: Challenging the long-standing model of academic institutions. [IJIDeM]. *International Journal on Interactive Design and Manufacturing*, *16*(2), 791–802. DOI: 10.1007/s12008-022-00886-1 PMID: 40477579

Cardoso, S., Mamede, H., & Santos, V. (2020b). Reference Model for Academic Results Certification in Student Mobility Scenarios. *Journal of Information Systems Engineering & Management*, *5*(4), em0125. Advance online publication. DOI: 10.29333/jisem/8491

Cardoso, S., Mamede, H. S., & Santos, V. (2020a). Reference model for academic results certification in student mobility scenarios : Position paper. *2020 15th Iberian Conference on Information Systems and Technologies (CISTI)*, 1–4. DOI: 10.23919/CISTI49556.2020.9141134

Chen, X., He, S., Sun, L., Zheng, Y., & Wu, C. Q. (2024). A Survey of Consortium Blockchain and Its Applications. *Cryptography*, *8*(2), 12. DOI: 10.3390/cryptography8020012

Chuing, S. S., & Kutty, F. M. (2025). The Effectiveness of Implementing a Token Economy System in Reducing Disruptive Behavior among Preschool Students. *International Journal of Academic Research in Progressive Education and Development*, *14*(1), 1812–1828. DOI: 10.6007/IJARPED/v14-i1/24769

de Alwis, A., Shrestha, A., & Sarker, T. (2025). Exploring Governance for accreditation in the education sector using blockchain technology: A systematic literature review. *Discover Education*, *4*(1), 57. DOI: 10.1007/s44217-025-00449-y

Delgado-von-Eitzen, C., Anido-Rifón, L., & Fernández-Iglesias, M. J. (2024). NFTs for the Issuance and Validation of Academic Information That Complies with the GDPR. *Applied Sciences (Basel, Switzerland)*, *14*(2), 706. DOI: 10.3390/app14020706

Dinh, T. T. A., Liu, R., Zhang, M., Chen, G., Ooi, B. C., & Wang, J. (2018). Untangling Blockchain: A Data Processing View of Blockchain Systems. *IEEE Transactions on Knowledge and Data Engineering*, *30*(7), 1366–1385. DOI: 10.1109/TKDE.2017.2781227

Do, B.-L., Nguyen, V.-T., Dinh, H.-N., Dao, T.-C., & Nguyen, B. (2022). Blockchain for Education: Verification and Management of Lifelong Learning Data. *Computer Systems Science and Engineering*, *43*(2), 591–604. DOI: 10.32604/csse.2022.023508

Fernandes, F., & Werner, C. (2023). Towards a Blockchain-based Software Engineering Education. *Proceedings of the 1st Colloquium on Blockchain and Decentralized Web*, 25–30. DOI: 10.5753/cblockchain.2023.230488

Freni, P., Ferro, E., & Moncada, R. (2022). Tokenomics and blockchain tokens: A design-oriented morphological framework. *Blockchain: Research and Applications, 3*(1), 100069. DOI: 10.1016/j.bcra.2022.100069

Garcia-Font, V. (2020). Blockchain: Opportunities and Challenges in the Educational Context. In Baneres, D., Rodríguez, M., & Guerrero-Roldán, A. (Eds.), *Engineering Data-Driven Adaptive Trust-based e-Assessment Systems* (Vol. 34, pp. 133–157). Springer., DOI: 10.1007/978-3-030-29326-0_7

Grech, A., Balaji, V., & Miao, F. (2022). *Education and Blockchain*. Commonwealth of Learning (COL). DOI: 10.56059/11599/4131

Grech, A., Camilleri, A. F., & Inamorato dos Santos, A. (2017). *Blockchain in Education*. Publications Office of the European Union., DOI: 10.2760/60649

Heizelman, I., Bittner, N., Alvarez Vazquez, E., Ewert, D., & Striker, R. (2024). Empowering Engineering Students: Blockchain Learning Tokens for Assessing ABET Student Outcomes and Enhancing Quality Control in Innovation-Based Education. *2024 ASEE Annual Conference & Exposition Proceedings*. DOI: 10.18260/1-2--47245

Jha, S. (2025). The Complete Guide for Types of Blockchain. In *Simplilearn*. Simplilearn. https://www.simplilearn.com/tutorials/blockchain-tutorial/types-of-blockchain

Jirgensons, M., & Kapenieks, J. (2018). Blockchain and the Future of Digital Learning Credential Assessment and Management. *Journal of Teacher Education for Sustainability, 20*(1), 145–156. DOI: 10.2478/jtes-2018-0009

Lam, T. Y., & Dongol, B. (2022). A blockchain-enabled e-learning platform. *Interactive Learning Environments, 30*(7), 1229–1251. DOI: 10.1080/10494820.2020.1716022

Longchamp, Y., Gupta, A., & Goel, K. (2021). *Tokenomics*. SEBA Bank AG.

McGreal, R. (2023). Blockchain and Micro-Credentials in Education. *International Journal of E-Learning & Distance Education, 38*(1), 1–17. DOI: 10.55667/ijede.2022.v38.i1.1250

Mendoza-Chan, J., & Pee, L. G. (2024). Digital skilling of working adults: A systematic review. *Computers & Education, 218*(March 2023), 105076. DOI: 10.1016/j.compedu.2024.105076

Mikroyannidis, A., Third, A., & Domingue, J. (2025). Blockchain-based decentralised micro-accreditation for lifelong learning. *Interactive Learning Environments*, *33*(3), 2201–2215. DOI: 10.1080/10494820.2024.2401485

Musa, S., Abubakari, M. S., & Abdulwahab, L. O. (2025). Evaluating the Potential of Adapting Artificial Intelligence (AI) in Small and Medium Enterprises for Competitive Advantage. In Anshari, M., Almunawar, M. N., & Ordóñez de Pablos, P. (Eds.), *Multi-Industry Digitalization and Technological Governance in the AI Era* (pp. 233–266). IGI Global., DOI: 10.4018/979-8-3373-1681-9.ch012

Nguyen, D.-H., Nguyen-Duc, D.-N., Huynh-Tuong, N., & Pham, H.-A. (2018). CVSS: A Blockchainized Certificate Verifying Support System. *Proceedings of the Ninth International Symposium on Information and Communication Technology - SoICT 2018*, 436–442. DOI: 10.1145/3287921.3287968

Nzaro, E. K., Ondimu, K., & Mwakondo, F. (2022). A Blockchain-Based Conceptual Model for Curbing Institutional Academic Certificate Fraud. *International Journal of Computer Applications Technology and Research*, *11*(07), 255–263. DOI: 10.7753/IJCATR1107.1002

OECD. (2021). *Micro-credential innovations in higher education : Who, What and Why* (Vol. 39). OECD Publishing., DOI: 10.1787/f14ef041-

Park, J. (2021). Promises and challenges of Blockchain in education. *Smart Learning Environments*, *8*(1), 33. DOI: 10.1186/s40561-021-00179-2 PMID: 40477765

Pulmano, C. E., Estuar, M. R. J. E., De Leon, M. M., Tan, H. C. L., Co, N. A. S., & Tamayo, L. P. V. (2023). Towards the Development of a Blockchain-based Decentralized Digital Credential System using Hyperledger Fabric for Participatory Governance. *Procedia Computer Science*, *219*, 99–106. DOI: 10.1016/j.procs.2023.01.269

Santana, C., & Albareda, L. (2022). Blockchain and the emergence of Decentralized Autonomous Organizations (DAOs): An integrative model and research agenda. *Technological Forecasting and Social Change*, *182*, 121806. DOI: 10.1016/j.techfore.2022.121806

Silaghi, D. L., & Popescu, D. E. (2025). A Systematic Review of Blockchain-Based Initiatives in Comparison to Best Practices Used in Higher Education Institutions. *Computers*, *14*(4), 141. DOI: 10.3390/computers14040141

So, H.-J., Lee, C., Lee, G.-Y., & Kim, M. J. (2024). *Artificial intelligence, blockchain and extended reality in lifelong learning*. UNESCO Institute for Lifelong Learning.

Steiu, M.-F. (2020). Blockchain in education: Opportunities, applications, and challenges. *First Monday*, *25*(9). Advance online publication. DOI: 10.5210/fm.v25i9.10654

Sun, H., Wang, X., & Wang, X. (2018). Application of Blockchain Technology in Online Education. [IJET]. *International Journal of Emerging Technologies in Learning*, *13*(10), 252–259. DOI: 10.3991/ijet.v13i10.9455

Tahlil, T., Gomasta, S. S., & Ali, A. B. M. S. (2022). AlgoCert: Adopt Non-transferable NFT for the Issuance and Verification of Educational Certificates using Algorand Blockchain. *2022 IEEE Asia-Pacific Conference on Computer Science and Data Engineering (CSDE)*, 1–8. DOI: 10.1109/CSDE56538.2022.10089274

Tan, E., & Du Seuil, D. (2025). European Digital Infrastructure Consortium (EDIC): A New Governance Framework for the European Blockchain Services Infrastructure (EBSI). In *Public Governance and Emerging Technologies* (pp. 83–101). Springer Nature Switzerland. DOI: 10.1007/978-3-031-84748-6_5

Tan, E., Lerouge, E., Du Caju, J., & Du Seuil, D. (2023). Verification of Education Credentials on European Blockchain Services Infrastructure (EBSI): Action Research in a Cross-Border Use Case between Belgium and Italy. *Big Data and Cognitive Computing*, *7*(2), 79. DOI: 10.3390/bdcc7020079

Tariq, A., Binte Haq, H., & Ali, S. T. (2023). Cerberus: A Blockchain-Based Accreditation and Degree Verification System. *IEEE Transactions on Computational Social Systems*, *10*(4), 1503–1514. DOI: 10.1109/TCSS.2022.3188453

Tepelidis, A., Mitsopoulou, E. E., Patenidis, A. T., Votis, K., & Tzovaras, D. (2024). A Multi-blockchain System for Verifiable Academic Credentials. In *Open Science in Engineering (REV 2023)* (Vol. 763, pp. 917–926). Springer., DOI: 10.1007/978-3-031-42467-0_86

Terzi, S., Ioannis, S., Votis, K., & Tsiatsos, T. (2022). A Life-Long Learning Education Passport Powered by Blockchain Technology and Verifiable Digital Credentials: The BlockAdemiC Project. In *Software Engineering and Formal Methods. SEFM 2021 Collocated Workshops* (pp. 249–263). Springer Publishing Company. DOI: 10.1007/978-3-031-12429-7_18

Turkanovic, M., Holbl, M., Kosic, K., Hericko, M., & Kamisalic, A. (2018). EduCTX: A Blockchain-Based Higher Education Credit Platform. *IEEE Access : Practical Innovations, Open Solutions*, *6*, 5112–5127. DOI: 10.1109/ACCESS.2018.2789929

Wang, X., Younas, M., Jiang, Y., Imran, M., & Almusharraf, N. (2025). Transforming Education Through Blockchain: A Systematic Review of Applications, Projects, and Challenges. *IEEE Access : Practical Innovations, Open Solutions*, *13*, 13264–13284. DOI: 10.1109/ACCESS.2024.3519350

Weiss, J., & Salman, Z. (2022). How Blockchain Can Encourage Learning. In *Stanford GSE Office of Innovation and Technology*. Stanford GSE Office of Innovation and Technology. https://medium.com/@stanfordgseit/blockchain-enthusiasts-eye-challenges-in-education-3064058fdfb2

World Bank Group. (2020). *Blockchain Technology for Youth Empowerment and Value Exchange: Final Project and Evaluation Report* (Vol. 1). World Bank Group. https://documents.worldbank.org/curated/en/948241602654046284

Zeroual, N., Lamia, M., & Hafidi, M. (2024). Blockchain-Based Payment System for Registration Fees in higher education: A Case Study of Algeria. *CEUR Workshop Proceedings: 7th International Conference on Informatics and Applied Mathematics, 3922*, 124–138.

Chapter 9
Leveraging Token Economies for Public Goods

Maria Shilina
https://orcid.org/0000-0002-1611-805X
Paradigm Research Institute, Russia

ABSTRACT

Token economies offer a transformative solution to the enduring challenges of funding and coordinating public goods. Through blockchain-enabled mechanisms such as smart contracts, decentralized governance, and incentive-aligned tokens, communities can address traditional market failures in the provision of non-rivalrous and non-excludable resources. This chapter explores the theoretical foundations of public goods economics, analyzes innovative funding models like quadratic funding, retroactive public goods funding, augmented bonding curves, and emerging regenerative finance systems, and examines how blockchain-based systems can support decentralized, transparent, and scalable public goods provisioning. Drawing on real-world case studies, the chapter evaluates the strengths and limitations of token economies in this domain, highlighting both the promises and the complexities of decentralized coordination.

1. INTRODUCTION

Public goods are the resources or services that are non-excludable and non-rivalrous. They are fundamental to societal well-being, yet have long suffered from chronic underinvestment due to market failures. Traditional funding for public goods relies on government taxation or philanthropy, but these mechanisms often

DOI: 10.4018/979-8-3373-3371-7.ch009

fall short, leaving critical needs underprovisioned. In recent years, the emergence of token economies has opened novel pathways for incentivizing and financing public goods. Tokenization allows the creation of digital assets and economic systems that can align individual incentives with collective benefit, offering a transformative approach to funding open-source software, climate stability, scientific knowledge, and other public goods.

This chapter provides an in-depth exploration of how token economies can address the public goods funding problem. It begins by outlining the characteristics of public goods and the problem of underprovision, followed by an overview of token economies as a novel framework for aligning individual incentives with collective outcomes. The chapter then examines key token-based funding models, including quadratic funding, retroactive public goods funding, augmented bonding curves, and regenerative finance (ReFi), detailing their mechanisms and real-world implementations. In addition, it addresses critical challenges, including governance vulnerabilities, regulatory ambiguity, and the influence of speculative market dynamics. The chapter concludes with a forward-looking discussion on the potential of token economies to scale global public goods funding, presenting both the opportunities and limitations of this emerging field at the intersection of blockchain economics and the public interest.

2. PUBLIC GOODS AND THE PROBLEM OF UNDERPROVISION

In economic terms, public goods are goods that are non-excludable (no one can be prevented from using them) and non-rivalrous (one person's use does not reduce availability to others) (Samuelson, 1954; Olson, 1965). Classic examples include clean air, national defense, basic scientific research, open-source software, and public knowledge. In the digital era, this category has expanded to include open-source software, open data, and internet infrastructure, resources that are essential yet remain systematically underfunded.

The core challenge lies in the free-rider problem. Because people can benefit from public goods without paying, markets left to themselves tend to undersupply these goods. Rational individuals have an incentive to "free ride," expecting others to contribute, leading to outcomes where everyone benefits but too few are willing to fund provision (Marwell & Ames, 1979; Andreoni, 1988; Benkler, 2002). As a result, public goods often suffer from chronic underinvestment or complete market failure in private markets (Hardin, 1968).

Historically, governments and philanthropic institutions have attempted to fill this gap. Governments use taxation and hierarchical budgeting processes or establish property rights where possible (turning a public good into a private good), while philanthropic actors allocate funding through grants and donations (Ostrom, 1990; Cornes & Sandler, 1996). However, these traditional mechanisms face limitations: government budgets are finite and subject to political cycles, while charity and grants can be inconsistent or insufficient to meet global needs (Kaul, et al., 1999; Stiglitz, 1999). Moreover, they struggle to keep pace with the funding needs of a rapidly evolving digital and ecological commons. This context has driven technologists and economists to seek innovative funding models that can solve the free-rider problem and sustainably finance public goods.

A key insight from the blockchain community is that cryptographic tokens can be designed to encode incentive structures and governance rules in a decentralized but reliable way. Instead of relying solely on altruism or coercion, these models attempt to contribute to public goods in one's self-interest. For example, a token-based system might reward contributors with tokens that confer future value or influence, thereby giving individuals a stake in the success of the public good. The broader field of cryptoeconomics explores how tokens and smart contracts can facilitate self-organizing systems for collective action. Within the Ethereum ecosystem (often considered a public good itself) early experiments such as the Ethereum Community Fund and grant-based programs have attempted to address funding challenges in decentralized environments. As Buterin et al. (2018) and others have noted, much of what is valuable in digital ecosystems (open standards, software infrastructure, educational content) takes the form of public goods. This recognition has catalyzed a wave of innovation in mechanism design: new funding models explicitly tailored to public goods, implemented via blockchain tokens and smart contracts.

3. TOKEN ECONOMIES AND NOVEL MECHANISMS FOR PUBLIC GOODS FUNDING

A token economy refers to an economic system built around digital tokens that represent some form of value or stake, and the rules and incentives that govern their distribution and use. On blockchain platforms, tokens can be fungible (interchangeable units like cryptocurrencies or utility tokens) or non-fungible (unique tokens like NFTs), and they can encode rights (e.g. governance voting power, access to services) or claims on future value. Token economies are enabled by smart contracts which allow complex rules for token issuance, transfer, and destruction to be enforced transparently (Liu & Szmigiera, 2021; Cong, et al., 2021). In essence, token economies let designers "program" incentive structures: for example, a protocol can automatically reward certain behaviors with newly minted tokens or fees. This programmability and automation is a novel feature compared to traditional funding systems. It means that communities can create their own micro-economies, raising funds and allocating resources according to rules they set, without needing centralized intermediaries.

Tokens offer the potential to overcome the misalignment in funding public goods by giving contributors a stake in the outcome. If a public good is associated with a token that appreciates in value as the good is more widely used or appreciated, early contributors can capture some of the positive externalities they create (Easley, et al., 2019; Rozas, et al., 2021; de Filippi & Loveluck, 2016). This transforms public goods provision into an investment or participatory act with upside. For instance, a group could launch a token to fund development of an open-source software project, and people who donate or build the software might receive tokens. If the software becomes critical infrastructure used widely, demand for the token (perhaps required for governance or integrated into the software's ecosystem) could increase, rewarding those early supporters. This dynamic (sometimes described as "capitalizing the commons") tries to replicate the feedback loop of private goods (where investment leads to profit) but for goods that are non-excludable. Additionally, tokens can confer governance rights, letting contributors directly influence how funds are spent or how a project evolves. This can engender a stronger sense of community ownership and responsibility for a public resource, in contrast to traditional top-down provision. The crypto space has seen the rise of Decentralized Autonomous Organizations (DAOs) which use tokens for governance of shared projects, many of which aim to produce public goods like open-source code or informational resources. The underlying principle is that those who value the public good most should have proportional say and stake, which can encourage more people to contribute and discourage free riding.

Tokenization allows implementation of funding mechanisms that have been theorized in economics but were impractical to execute at scale without blockchain technology. Importantly, token economies can leverage global networks of participants: anyone with an Internet connection can donate to a public goods project and potentially receive tokens or other rewards in return. This opens public goods funding to a broader base of contributors. While this introduces risks like speculation and governance attacks, it also creates programmable, transparent, and self-sustaining ecosystems. For example, some token models impose small fees on usage which are funneled back into a treasury to fund the public good continuously, creating a circular economy for public goods.

The novelty of token-based approaches lies in combining elements of markets and communities. Traditional public goods funding often relies on either government coercion or voluntary donations. Token models blur this line by creating quasi-markets for public goods, where people trade and speculate, but for a purpose that benefits all. This can unlock new sources of capital and enable experimentation: communities can try different governance rules (encoded in smart contracts) and quickly iterate if something fails. In effect, blockchain tokens allow mechanism design to be implemented among large groups of people with real assets at stake.

4. TOKEN-BASED FUNDING MODELS FOR PUBLIC GOODS

Token economies have given rise to several innovative funding models designed explicitly to tackle the public goods funding gap. This section examines five major models: quadratic funding, retroactive public goods funding, augmented bonding curves, and regenerative finance credit systems. Each of these approaches leverages tokens and smart contracts in a distinct way to incentivize contributions or allocate funds to public goods. Table 1 outlines key token-based models for funding public goods.

Table 1. Token-Based Funding Models for Public Goods

Model	Core Logic	Deployment
Quadratic Funding (QF)	Small donations are quadratically matched from a pool, privileging diverse support	Gitcoin Grants
Retroactive Funding (RetroPGF)	Ex-post token rewards for measurable impact	Optimism Collective
Augmented Bonding Curve (ABC)	Continuous token issuance funds a treasury while providing liquidity	Token Engineering Commons
Regenerative Finance (ReFi)	Tokenized ecological outcomes monetize externalities	Regen Network, Drex

4.1 Quadratic Funding

Quadratic funding (QF), also termed plural funding, is a mechanism that uses matching funds to amplify broad-based support for public goods projects. QF was first proposed in 2018 (Buterin, et al. 2018). The core idea is to optimize the distribution of a matching pool among projects based on the number of distinct contributors and the amounts they contribute, with a formula that increases matching for widely-supported projects. In simple terms, individual donations are matched not linearly, but proportional to the square of the sum of square roots of contributions (Pasquini, 2020, 2022). This formula means that ten people giving $1 each to a project generates a higher match than one person giving $10 to the same project, thus privileging broad small-donor support over single large donors. The result is that the matching amount grows quadratically with the number of contributors, encouraging widespread participation.

QF is the optimal way to fund public goods under certain assumptions. It aligns with the idea that if many people value a project enough to contribute something, even a small amount, then society should subsidize that project because it has broad positive externalities. The quadratic mechanism solves a coordination problem: individuals on their own might donate only a little to a public good, undervaluing their true preference if they think others won't contribute (Lalley & Weyl, 2017). But with QF, each small donation unlocks matching funds that reflect the latent support of the community. In effect, QF can achieve a near "first-best" public goods provision as if everyone had contributed according to their true valuation. Another key rationale behind QF is that it accounts for the diversity of contributors. A project supported by 100 individual donors is assumed to generate broader social value than one funded by just 10 donors contributing the same total amount, and thus is allocated more matching funds. This encourages project creators to seek many supporters, even small ones, rather than a few whales, democratizing funding. Imagine a matching pool of $M is available. Projects A and B receive community contributions. If Alice gives $16 to Project A, and Bob and Charlie each give $4 to Project B (total also $8, but from two people), the quadratic calculation would allocate more matches to Project B.

Table 2 summarizes the core features of QF.

Table 2. Quadratic Funding (QF)

Parameter	Description
Mechanism Type	Matching fund mechanism based on mathematical aggregation of contributions
Primary Goal	Democratic funding of public goods, reflecting community support
Timing of Funding	Ex-ante (before or during project execution)
Incentive Structure	Small, broad-based contributions receive greater matching than large, concentrated ones
Funding Source	Matching pool (donations, treasury, or protocol-set funds)
Key Advantages	Pluralistic, transparent, and scalable public goods mechanism
Limitations	Susceptible to sybil attacks and collusion without identity verification
Use Cases	Open-source software, community tech, public education

4.1.1. Case Study: Gitcoin Grants

The most famous implementation of QF is Gitcoin Grants, a platform for funding open-source software and other public goods in the Ethereum ecosystem. Since 2019, Gitcoin has run quarterly QF rounds where a pool matches community contributions to hundreds of projects. Over the past few years, Gitcoin Grants has distributed over $60 million in funding to more than 4000 projects using QF, with over 3 million individual donations contributing. This has helped support critical infrastructure, education initiatives, and public-good services in Web3. Gitcoin's results validate that QF directs funds toward what the community collectively values: many projects that were bootstrap-funded via Gitcoin QF (like the Uniswap exchange, WalletConnect protocol) later grew into essential ecosystem pieces. Moreover, QF has proven versatile: Gitcoin expanded it beyond Web3 to social causes (e.g., a round for COVID-19 relief). Cities have even piloted QF for local issues: for instance, town Boulder, Colorado ran a "Downtown Stimulus" QF program to support small businesses during the pandemic (Johnson, 2020). This demonstrates that QF is understandable and appealing to a broad public; people see their small donations get magnified, which encourages them to participate in funding causes they care about.

4.1.2. Benefits and Challenges

The democratic nature of QF is its greatest strength. However, it is not without challenges. It is vulnerable to Sybil attacks, where one donor creates many fake identities to pretend to be many people, thereby gaming the system. Gitcoin has invested heavily in Sybil-resistance measures (identity verification, contributions analysis) to combat this. There is also the issue of collusion: groups of contributors who know each other could coordinate donations to each other's projects or form circles to inflate matches. Some improvements like pairwise bonding (reducing match weight for closely affiliated contributors) have been proposed. Additionally, QF can turn into a popularity contest, favoring projects that market well or appeal to the masses. This is a subtler problem: projects that mobilize a lot of mild support may outweigh a niche but critical project that only a few experts recognize as important (Freitas & Maldonado, 2024). To address this, there have been experiments in incorporating expert input into QF. For example, the Token Engineering Commons (TEC) tested a Quadratic Funding + Subject Matter Expert boost where contributions from wallets holding certain knowledge certificates were given extra weight. This QF+SME approach aimed to combine the wisdom of the crowd with expert judgment to avoid purely popularity-driven outcomes. It showed promising initial results in directing slightly more funds to technically meritorious projects without entirely overriding community voice. Finally, running QF at scale requires education and trust: participants need to understand that the matching mechanism is fair and how their donations translate into impact. Despite these challenges,QF has proven to be a landmark innovation that provides a concrete tool for policymakers and communities to implement more democratic public funding.

4.2 Retroactive Public Goods Funding

While QF focuses on raising and allocating funds before or during a project's development (i.e. prospective funding), Retroactive public goods funding (Retro PGF) takes the opposite approach: rewarding projects after they have proven their impact. In a retroactive model, a pool of funds is set aside and periodically distributed to public goods projects that have demonstrated real value to a community or ecosystem (Wang, et al., 2025; Yu, et al., 2025). This concept was initially implemented by the Ethereum scalability project Optimism around 2021 (Buterin, 2021). The core principle is that it's easier to agree on what was useful than what will be useful. By waiting until outcomes are known, funders can direct rewards to the most impactful public goods, thus encouraging future actors to pursue similarly valuable work in hopes of later reward.

In practice, Retro PGF involves a "results oracle" or a community-driven evaluation process that periodically assesses public goods outcomes. For example, Optimism created a governance mechanism where a committee of respected community members would review nominations of projects that have benefited the ecosystem and then allocate a fixed pool of OP tokens to those projects in proportion to their perceived impact. Importantly, projects did not need to apply in advance or have any formal agreement; they could simply do good work (like developing open-source software, tooling, or educational resources), and if the community later deemed their work valuable, they could receive a reward. Retro PGF can complement upfront grants: initially, many public goods might be grant-funded or volunteer-driven, but the retroactive rewards create a profit motive for success. A team can take the risk of building a public good on their own dime, with the knowledge that if it truly becomes important, they might get a substantial payout later. This can mobilize private capital into public goods via impact investors: an investor could fund a team to build an open-source project, speculating that retroactive rewards will later compensate them if the project is successful.

Table 3 provides an overview of the Retro PGF model.

Table 3. Retroactive Public Goods Funding (RetroPGF)

Parameter	Description
Mechanism Type	Ex-post reward mechanism based on demonstrated public benefit
Primary Goal	Fund contributors after impact has occurred, incentivizing open innovation
Timing of Funding	Ex-post (after impact is measurable)
Incentive Structure	Contributors build without pre-approval, hoping for retroactive reward
Funding Source	Protocol treasury or allocated reward pool
Key Advantages	Rewards actual value creation; open to all contributors
Limitations	Difficult to assess impact fairly; potential for gaming or subjectivity
Use Cases	Ecosystem development, infrastructure maintenance, educational content

4.2.1. Case Study: Optimism's Retro PGF

The Optimism network pioneered Retro PGF by launching RetroPGF rounds. In its first round in late 2021, Optimism allocated a portion of its token supply and distributed millions of dollars to dozens of Ethereum community projects that had delivered exceptional value (e.g. infrastructure providers, educational programs, open-source development teams). By 2023, Optimism had conducted multiple rounds and even committed to fund public goods with all profits from its sequencer (the sequencer is the entity ordering Optimism's blockchain transactions, which has revenue from user fees). This means that the very operation of the network directly funds its commons, a novel model for sustainable funding. In a notable round in 2022, Optimism's RetroPGF Round 2 awarded $25 million (10 million OP tokens) to 90+ public goods projects in the Ethereum ecosystem, ranging from technical infrastructure to community resources. This was a demonstration of retro funding at scale. It essentially turned the typical grant model on its head. Vitalik Buterin praised this approach and even participated as a badgeholder (evaluator) in one of the rounds, emphasizing that such ex-post funding can create strong incentives for long-term, less immediately remunerative work that nonetheless benefits everyone. The expectation is that if a few high-profile successes get big retro rewards, it will inspire a generation of builders to aim for useful projects in hope of similar future rewards.

After Optimism's lead, other ecosystems have begun exploring retroactive funding. Gitcoin has announced initiatives to incorporate retro rewards on top of its grants rounds: projects that perform well or have lasting impact might get additional grants down the line. Protocols like Filecoin are also experimenting in this space, given Filecoin's mission to fund open science and their experience with incentive design (Daniels, 2025).

4.2.2. Benefits and Challenges

Retroactive funding addresses several issues of traditional funding. First, it reduces waste and speculation: money is only spent on things that have proven value, avoiding the problem of grants that funded projects which failed or never delivered. This makes resource allocation more efficient in hindsight. Second, it counters the bias towards good storytellers over good builders: in proactive grants, those who write proposals well or have existing reputation often secure funding, whereas retroactive rewards flow purely from output. Third, it can reveal underrecognized public goods. There are cases where a small project quietly produces huge value (for example, a tiny developer team maintaining a critical library). Retro PGF can "surface" these by asking the community what was impactful, rather than only funding visible projects upfront. Notably, Optimism's Retro PGF discovered and rewarded some unsung heroes of Ethereum development who had received little or no funding before. Another major advantage is creating a market for public goods: investors and entrepreneurs can treat public goods efforts as something that might generate returns (through retro payouts or impact certificates that can be sold), which could massively increase capital inflows to public goods.

Retroactive funding also has challenges. One is coordination and trust: people must believe that the retro funding will indeed be there and will be fairly distributed. This requires credible commitment by funding organizations or communities. Optimism addressed this by hard-coding some funding (treasury and token allocation) for retro rounds and involving credible community figures in the process. Another challenge is evaluation: deciding what was most impactful can be contentious. There is an inherent subjectivity and comparison when dozens of very different public goods all claim value. Optimism has tried both appointed expert committees and community input to get a balanced evaluation. They found that clear criteria and diverse evaluators are key, and that the combination of quantitative metrics (like usage stats) with qualitative judgment for things like research or community-building efforts is needed. There is also a risk of short-termism: evaluators might over-reward things with immediate visible impact versus foundational work that pays off later. A mitigation is to run retro funding rounds regularly, so that projects can be rewarded when their impact does manifest even if it's a few years after initial work. Another issue is gaming and fairness: since retro funding looks at actual usage or adoption, it's harder to fake than prospective promises, but some gaming is still possible. Careful design of metrics and having human judgment in the loop can help prevent gaming. Lastly, from a motivational perspective, some worry that if people start expecting retro rewards, will they still create public goods without an upfront guarantee. This flips the usual concern: instead of no one doing the work, everyone might chase retro bounties, potentially skewing efforts. However, because retro funding coexists with other funding, it likely will augment rather than replace upfront funding. In fact, a hybrid model is emerging: funding some things proactively, then using retro funding to double down on what works.

Thus, Retro PGF is a powerful complement to traditional grants: it flips the incentive model by offering ex-post rewards, which can galvanize individuals and teams to contribute to public goods in hopes of later recognition and payment. Early evidence from Optimism suggests it can direct significant funds to those who genuinely add value, while encouraging a culture of impact-driven development. As the model matures, it could become a pillar of public goods funding in Web3 and even a tool for governments or large institutions seeking efficient use of funds. The next challenge is scaling it, standardizing fair evaluation processes, and ensuring a steady influx of funds into the retro pools.

4.3 Augmented Bonding Curves

A different approach to funding public goods with tokens centers on the concept of bonding curves, specifically the Augmented Bonding Curve (ABC) developed by the Commons Stack and related communities. A bonding curve is a continuous token issuance model where the price of a token is mathematically determined by a formula based on the current supply (Zargham, et al., 2020). It effectively serves as an automated market maker that anyone can interact with to buy or sell tokens at transparent prices. The ABC modifies the basic model to direct a portion of every transaction into a funding pool (treasury) for public goods, while also incorporating mechanisms like vesting and exit fees to stabilize the system. This creates a circular micro-economy where a community token both represents membership/ownership in the commons and continuously generates funding for that commons' goals.

In a standard bonding curve, a smart contract issues a token that can be purchased by sending collateral (e.g., DAI stablecoin) to the contract. The contract sells tokens at a price that increases as more tokens are in circulation, often following a polynomial or exponential curve. Conversely, token holders can sell their tokens back to the contract for collateral at the current price. This means liquidity is always available from the contract; the token price automatically adjusts to supply and demand. Bonding curves allow communities to launch a token without listing on an exchange, the curve itself provides price discovery and liquidity. However, plain bonding curves have drawbacks: they can be highly volatile and are prone to speculative pump-and-dump behavior, since early buyers who get in at low prices might later cash out at higher prices once more people buy, which can crash the price.

The ABC addresses these issues by introducing several enhancements. First is the split reserve and funding pool: when someone buys tokens on an ABC, their payment is split, a portion goes into the reserve pool (to back the token's value as usual), and a portion is diverted into a funding pool/treasury that is not used for backing tokens but earmarked for funding public goods projects of the community. For example, if 70% of incoming funds go to reserve and 30% to funding pool (this split is a parameter often called θ, the "initial allocation" to funding), then every purchase of the token helps fill a community chest. This is a built-in fundraising mechanism: as members invest in the token, they simultaneously fund the cause.

Second is the closed hatch: the ABC typically starts with a "hatch" phase, a limited initial sale to founding contributors. During the hatch, people contribute funds which partially seed the reserve (minting initial tokens for them) and partially seed the funding pool as an initial endowment for project funding. Hatch participants receive tokens at a fixed initial price, but those tokens are vested (locked) for a period to prevent them from immediately selling when the open phase begins. The hatch ensures that the initial token holders are value-aligned and that the commons starts with some capital to deploy.

Third is the open trading phase: after the hatch, the curve is opened to the public; anyone can buy tokens along the curve, and the price starts at whatever was determined by the initial supply/reserve. As more people buy in, the price on the bonding curve goes up; if people sell, the price goes down. The reserve pool ensures liquidity, there is always collateral to redeem based on the formula. But to discourage immediate speculation, the ABC often imposes an exit tribute (tax) on sales: when you sell tokens back, a percentage of the collateral you would receive is diverted to the funding pool instead of back to you. It disincentivizes quick flips and ensures that even speculative activity feeds the public good.

Fourth is the vesting and governance integration. The tokens minted via the ABC aren't just financial, they usually carry governance rights over the funding pool. Using a governance mechanism (such as conviction voting or quadratic voting), token holders can vote on proposals to spend money from the funding pool on public goods projects that align with the community's mission. Importantly, the ABC can tie token vesting to governance participation and funding outcomes. In the Commons Stack model, tokens from the hatch unlock gradually only as funds from the pool are actually allocated to projects. This is a clever incentive: early supporters (hatchers) cannot liquidate their tokens unless the community is actively using the funds to achieve impact, aligning everyone's incentives to deploy capital for good rather than just sit on it. It prevents a scenario where token holders hoard value but never invest in the mission. Essentially, for the early investors to profit, the public good must be funded.

Table 4 describes the ABC model parameters.

Table 4. Augmented Bonding Curve (ABC)

Parameter	Description
Mechanism Type	Token issuance and reserve-backed bonding system with public goods extensions
Primary Goal	Sustainable funding for commons by embedding mechanisms in token design
Timing of Funding	Continuous; funds accrue through token buys/sells
Incentive Structure	Entry/exit tributes, bonding curve pricing, and governance participation
Funding Source	Reserve pool and tribute to commons pool from token interactions
Key Advantages	Continuous funding, internal sustainability, aligned tokenomics
Limitations	Requires careful economic design; sensitive to market behavior
Use Cases	DAO funding, open science, local economies, Web3 regenerative networks

4.3.1. Case Study: Token Engineering Commons (TEC)

The Token Engineering Commons is a real-world implementation of the ABC model. Launched in 2021, TEC is a community that funds token engineering research and open-source projects. During its hatch, the community raised an initial pool of over $1 million (in xDAI) from contributors who then received TEC tokens. After launch, anyone could buy TEC tokens via the bonding curve, and the price of TEC token floated accordingly. Importantly, TEC's bonding curve was calibrated for low volatility: since launch, $TEC's price has tracked roughly alongside ETH and did not experience the kind of boom-bust that many small tokens did. Commons Stack reports that TEC's token had much lower volatility compared to typical small-cap tokens because the ABC mechanism and governance discouraged rapid speculative swings. In 2023, the TEC had funded over $460,000 in grants to token engineering public goods using the accumulated common pool (TEC, 2023). The funding came from the tributes and initial raise made possible by the ABC. Additionally, the TEC has innovated on top of this model by later incorporating QF for their grants distribution, showing that these mechanisms can be combined: they used QF to allocate a portion of their pool to specific projects, thereby layering a democratic allocation on top of their continuous funding structure. The success of TEC's token maintaining value and continuing to fund projects suggests that an ABC can create a sustainable regenerative economy: people hold the token because they believe in the long-term mission and governance power, not merely short-term profit, and as the community demonstrates impact, it attracts more participants, which can drive token demand in a virtuous cycle.

4.3.2. Benefits and Challenges

A notable feature of ABC is how they align financial value with social value in a quantified way. The ABC allows public goods to "quantify their own qualitative value" (Commons Stack, 2021). Normally, public goods' value is not captured in a price, but by creating a token that people buy to support the cause, and whose price reflects supply/demand, you get a market signal for the value of that commons. Early supporters who took on risk by buying tokens are rewarded for the project's success via token appreciation. This inverts the usual frame where altruistic contributions are sunk costs; here, they become an investment that can grow if the public good succeeds and attracts more supporters. This philosophically shifts altruism into a sustainable loop: contributors don't necessarily lose their money; they park it in the token, which they can resell later, potentially even at a profit if the community thrives.

Despite its elegant design, an ABC system is complex and must be carefully tuned. One challenge is parametric design: choosing what fraction of funds goes to the reserve vs funding pool (e.g., θ), what the shape of the curve is (which determines how fast price rises with supply), the length of vesting, and the exit tax rate. Simulation tools are often employed to model different scenarios. Another challenge is governance of the funds: the community needs effective processes to decide what to fund from the treasury, otherwise money can be wasted or conflicts arise. The Commons Stack has paired ABCs with conviction voting, a continuous voting system where token holders signal preference for proposals over time, which gets around some issues of voter apathy and plutocracy by requiring continuous support rather than one-time votes. Nonetheless, governance vulnerabilities exist (e.g., a majority of token holders could in theory vote to misuse funds), so often a strong social layer and cultural build-up is necessary before launching the token. ABCs also face market risks: if the broader crypto market crashes, the collateral might fluctuate or community sentiment might falter, leading to many sales. The built-in exit tribute means even a mass exit would leave some funds for rebuilding. Finally, there are legal/regulatory aspects: an ABC token walks a fine line between being a charitable membership token and an investment instrument. Regulators might view some implementations as securities, given people have expectations of profit. Projects often frame them as social membership tokens with utility (governance rights) rather than profit intent, but this area is a gray zone legally.

Overall, ABC represents a sophisticated fusion of automated finance and community governance to create self-funding public goods ecosystems. The success of the TEC pilot with substantial capital raised for its commons pool from the ABC's tributes alone is a proof of concept that this model can maintain an ongoing funding stream. Other communities are following suit: for example, the Commons Stack plans to replicate the model for environmental commons, local communities, and more. The potential is that any group that wants to fund a public good can launch a token via an ABC and create a sustainable economy around it. This is a markedly different approach from one-off fundraising or continuous donation drives; it creates aligned incentives where contributing funds = gaining influence and stake = enabling impact, closing the loop between individual and collective benefit.

4.4 Regenerative Finance (ReFi) and Ecological Credit Systems

One of the compelling applications of token economies for public goods is in the domain of environmental and ecological assets, essentially funding and incentivizing positive environmental outcomes (a global public good) via tokenization. This movement is often referred to as Regenerative finance (ReFi). ReFi projects create token systems for things like carbon credits, biodiversity credits, or sustainable development goals, seeking to channel capital into ecological regeneration by making these contributions investable or economically rewarding (Bennett, 2025; Kenyon, et al., 2022). In traditional markets, carbon offsets and green bonds exist, but they face issues like opacity, fragmentation, and trust. Blockchain tokens can bring transparency, efficiency, and global accessibility to these markets (Saraji & Borowczak, 2021). This section explores two categories: 1) tokenized ecological credits (like carbon credits) exemplified by Regen Network, and 2) tokenized green bonds and government initiatives exemplified by pilots like Brazil's Drex CBDC sandbox and Hong Kong's tokenized green bonds. These illustrate how tokens can fund public environmental goods.

Table 5 outlines the features of ReFi models.

Table 5. Regenerative Finance (ReFi)

Parameter	Description
Mechanism Type	Broad category of financial systems aligned with ecological and social regeneration
Primary Goal	Restore natural systems, support communities, and fund long-term planetary health
Timing of Funding	Varies: includes ex-ante, ex-post, or continuous models
Incentive Structure	Impact-based rewards, tokenized credits, aligned economic participation
Funding Source	Carbon markets, DAOs, philanthropic capital, public goods treasuries
Key Advantages	Values long-term sustainability, incentivizes positive externalities
Limitations	Measurement difficulty, token volatility, greenwashing concerns
Use Cases	Tokenized carbon credits, biodiversity restoration, climate finance

4.4.1. Tokenized Carbon Credits: Regen Network

Regen Network is a pioneering blockchain project aimed at creating a marketplace for high-integrity carbon credits and other ecological assets. It operates its own proof-of-stake blockchain, specifically designed to register, verify, and trade carbon sequestration or ecological impact credits. The motivation is that current voluntary carbon markets are plagued by double-counting and unverifiable claims. Regen uses a public ledger to ensure that each credit (representing, for example, one ton of CO2 sequestered by a certain project) is unique and retired transparently when used. Importantly, Regen Network goes beyond just trading existing credits, it provides an end-to-end platform where ecological projects can scientifically monitor and verify their ecological outcomes, then mint those as tokens once verified by methodologies and possibly oracles. These tokens can then be sold to buyers (companies or individuals offsetting emissions) or used in decentralized finance (DeFi) applications. By integrating local monitoring (sometimes via satellite data or on-ground reports) with blockchain issuance, Regen aims to reward ecological regeneration directly through smart contracts. In Regen's model, the value flows as follows: investors buy Regen tokens or specific eco-credits, money flows to land stewards who implement regenerative practices, and those practices are certified and yield tokenized credits that can be consumed or traded, completing the loop.

A practical example is Regen Network's work with land restoration projects. Suppose a farmer transitions to agroforestry, increasing soil carbon. A Regen-approved methodology quantifies the carbon sequestered. The farmer (or a sponsor) can then issue Regen Carbon Standard credits on-chain. Buyers anywhere in the world can buy these tokens to offset their carbon footprint, confident in the provenance because every credit and its source are traceable on the ledger. Once a credit is used to offset, it's retired (burned) on-chain to prevent reuse. The blockchain ensures the credit isn't double-counted or double-spent. Additionally, governance via native $REGEN token is community-driven: credit methodologies and project approval can be governed by token holders including scientists, verifiers, and stakeholders. This is an attempt to democratize and decentralize what is otherwise a top-down market dominated by a few registries.

Regen Network has made concrete progress, such as partnering with existing carbon standard bodies. It collaborated with Toucan Protocol to bridge carbon credits onto the blockchain. Regen's approach focuses more on new credits rather than tokenizing legacy ones, to ensure quality. By 2023, the Regen marketplace was live with actual credit issuances being bought and sold by companies looking to offset, thereby channeling funds to regenerative agriculture projects. This is a direct funding of a public good (carbon drawdown and soil health) through token incentives. Regen Network's vision extends beyond carbon, to biodiversity credits, water quality credits, etc., all handled as digital assets. The broader significance is that such systems could allow international climate finance to scale up and be verifiable: imagine climate aid or green funds distributing to thousands of micro-projects, each issuing tokens for each ton of CO2 removed or each hectare reforested, with near real-time transparency.

4.4.2. ReFi and Governance

The mention of DAO models in these contexts is vital. Many ReFi projects use DAOs to govern funds and standards (Gutiérrez, et al., 2023). For instance, KlimaDAO used a token (KLIMA) to aggregate carbon credits: it created a treasury of tokenized credits and issued KLIMA tokens against them, effectively pushing carbon credits out of circulation to drive up price (a sort of carbon central bank approach). KlimaDAO's mechanism was highly financialized, and while it succeeded in taking a large volume of credits off-market and raising awareness, it faced sustainability issues when incentives became unsustainable and the token price collapsed. Nonetheless, KlimaDAO's experiment showed that there is huge interest and liquidity available for climate-oriented tokens: at its peak, it had accumulated over 17 million tons of carbon (valued at hundreds of millions of dollars) in its treasury. The lesson learned is that pure speculation without robust value anchoring can be risky.

4.4.3. Tokenized Assets for Public Good: Brazil's Drex CBDC Sandbox

Governments are also exploring tokenization for public goods through Central Bank Digital Currency (CBDC) projects. Brazil's forthcoming CBDC, officially named Drex (Digital Real Electronic Transaction), has a pilot that explicitly includes tokenized public assets and sustainability instruments. In 2024, the Central Bank of Brazil selected 13 use case themes for its Drex pilot, among them "credit transactions and decarbonization (CBIO)". CBIO refers to Brazilian carbon credit units (Crédito de Descarbonização) under the RenovaBio program which incentivizes biofuel producers for emissions reduction. The Drex sandbox is testing how these carbon credits can be issued, traded, or used as collateral on a blockchain-based platform integrated with the CBDC infrastructure. By tokenizing CBIO credits on a regulated platform, Brazil aims to increase transparency and liquidity in its carbon market, making it easier for companies to acquire credits and for environmental projects to sell them. This signals an understanding that climate-related public goods need market mechanisms and that tokenization can help modernize those markets. The initial phase of the Drex pilot even tested tokenization of a government bond between banks, showing the platform's capability for handling regulated assets. In phase two, beyond carbon credits, other themes include tokenized agribusiness assets and public securities, some of which can indirectly fund rural development (a public good in terms of food security and community livelihoods). The combination of a CBDC and tokenization suggests a future where everyday financial infrastructure can also support public goods funding. For instance, a government could issue green bonds as tokens to directly raise funds for sustainability projects from retail users on their digital currency wallets.

4.4.4. Tokenized Green Bonds

Another case study is the issuance of tokenized green bonds by governments. A green bond is a bond instrument where proceeds are dedicated to environmental or climate-friendly projects. Hong Kong, for example, made headlines by issuing the world's first tokenized government green bond in 2023. The Hong Kong Monetary Authority (HKMA) issued a HK$800 million (~US$100M) tokenized green bond, where the bond ownership and transactions were recorded on a distributed ledger (HKMA, 2023). They even followed up with a larger multi-currency digital green bond totaling US$750 million. This bond was fully subscribed by institutional investors and showed that even conservative debt instruments can benefit from blockchain. From a public goods perspective, the importance is that it lowers the friction to raise capital for sustainability: by streamlining issuance and potentially broadening investor base (such bonds could be sold in smaller slices to the public via digital wallets), more funds can flow into green infrastructure. The HKMA is actively promoting this by offering grants to future digital bond issuances. Similarly, German development bank KfW and others have conducted blockchain bond trials. While a bond is still a debt, making it tokenized could reduce costs and engage new stakeholders.

4.4.5. Challenges in ReFi

ReFi faces a set of unique challenges. One is verification: ensuring that what is tokenized corresponds to real impact. Projects like Regen rely on oracles, independent auditors, and science-based methodologies. This is still a human process being ported to code gradually; the risk of bad credits (e.g., a project over-claims its carbon impact) can undermine trust. Another challenge is fragmentation of standards: currently there are multiple token standards for carbon credits (Regen's, Toucan's, etc.) and some tension with traditional registries. This is being resolved through dialogues and perhaps a common registry bridging solution. Liquidity and price volatility is also an issue: when KlimaDAO suddenly bought lots of credits, it spiked prices; then as demand waned, prices crashed, which can hurt project funding expectations. A stable, gradually growing demand is healthier, some propose a protocol-owned approach or automated market makers to stabilize carbon price.

However, there is strong momentum. Traditional players (e.g., the World Bank or regional development banks) are also experimenting with blockchain for climate finance. For instance, the BIS (Bank for International Settlements) has run projects on tokenized green bonds for smaller economies. The reason is clear: climate change is the ultimate public goods problem, and token economies offer tools to mobilize private capital and grassroots participation in ways that bureaucratic mechanisms haven't.

Thus, ReFi uses tokenization to turn positive externalities, like carbon sequestration, biodiversity gains, into internalized, tradable assets, thereby aligning profit with the planet. Projects like Regen Network demonstrate how a decentralized approach can bring new credibility and inclusion to environmental markets. Government-linked projects like Drex and Hong Kong's green bond show that the public sector is also embracing tokenization to boost sustainable finance. Together, these indicate a future where funding environmental public goods is embedded in financial systems, where everyday transactions, investments, or even currency systems have hooks that feed into regenerating the commons.

5. CHALLENGES AND RISKS IN TOKENIZING PUBLIC GOODS

While token economies present innovative paths for funding public goods, they also introduce critical risks. This section addresses three primary challenges: governance vulnerabilities, regulatory uncertainty, and speculative dynamics.

5.1. Governance Vulnerabilities and Attacks

Decentralized governance mechanisms can empower community participation, yet they often create structural weaknesses that undermine democratic ideals. Token-weighted voting tends to result in plutocracy, where wealth equates to influence. This risks replicating existing inequalities and can result in capture by powerful actors. Moreover, participation in governance tends to be low, with small token holders often abstaining from votes, leading to decisions being made by a concentrated minority.

Systems that rely on unique identities for voting, such as one-person-one-vote or quadratic voting, face threats from Sybil attacks and collusion, where malicious actors use fake or coordinated identities to sway outcomes. Gitcoin's development of Passport highlights the importance and difficulty of building Sybil-resistant systems. Bribery and vote buying are additional concerns; financial incentives may corrupt governance processes, especially as decentralized systems scale and become more heterogeneous. A further vulnerability lies in flash loan attacks, where temporary acquisition of large token volumes can be used to pass malicious proposals and extract funds before the community can respond. Finally, governance decisions may reflect short-term self-interest rather than long-term public good outcomes, especially when token holders are incentivized by market performance rather than civic responsibility.

To mitigate these risks, projects can implement mechanisms such as quadratic or plural voting structures, voting delays, multi-layer governance with checks and balances, and targeted participation incentives. Transparent and well-audited processes are also essential for ensuring accountability and resilience.

5.2. Regulatory Uncertainty and Compliance

Token economies operate in a rapidly evolving and often ambiguous legal landscape. One of the most pressing concerns is the classification of tokens as securities, which can impose burdensome compliance requirements. Many tokens associated with public goods funding, particularly those sold with an expectation of profit, may fall under securities regulations, subjecting projects to potential enforcement actions. The lack of clear legal guidance, and instances of retroactive enforcement, has created a chilling effect on innovation and led some developers to halt projects or relocate operations to more favorable jurisdictions.

Legal ambiguity presents a formidable obstacle for tokenized public goods. A core issue is whether a token is classified as a security. If so, it becomes subject to regulatory regimes like the U.S. Howey Test, requiring registration, disclosures, and possibly restricting access to accredited investors. Many public goods tokens risk falling into this category, especially if they are distributed with expectations of profit. Recent SEC actions suggest increasing scrutiny and a willingness to apply enforcement retroactively, chilling innovation even among well-intentioned projects.

In addition to securities law, projects must comply with rules related to commodities, taxes, environmental credits, and charitable fundraising. For instance, tokenized carbon credits may be regulated as environmental commodities or financial instruments. Jurisdictions like the EU (through MiCA) and Switzerland offer clearer categorization frameworks, but multi-jurisdictional compliance remains resource-intensive.

To manage these risks, projects are adopting phased decentralization, starting under compliant legal entities before transitioning to community governance, while engaging proactively with regulators and using jurisdictions with established crypto laws. Transparent token utility, clear messaging to avoid speculative framing, and careful structuring of launches are increasingly standard. Jurisdictional arbitrage, while helpful in the short term, does not resolve the broader need for globally harmonized regulatory standards. Demonstration of good-faith governance practices may help projects build trust and operate within evolving legal boundaries.

5.3. Speculation, Volatility, and Misaligned Incentives

The integration of token economies into public goods funding introduces exposure to market volatility and speculative behavior. Tokens used for funding and governance are subject to price swings that complicate budgeting and resource planning. A token grant denominated in volatile assets may vary significantly in value by the time it is utilized, leading to funding uncertainty and operational instability. The speculative nature of crypto markets can also distort participation, attracting actors interested primarily in price appreciation rather than supporting long-term impact.

Speculation can skew community behavior, with sudden price increases encouraging cash-outs or short-term decisions that undermine sustainability. Public goods initiatives risk being conflated with hype-driven crypto projects if speculation overshadows their mission. Misaligned incentives in token design may lead to gaming of metrics or exploitation of funding mechanisms, such as Sybil attacks on quadratic funding rounds or manipulative behavior in retroactive grants. Poorly designed tokenomics can create adverse incentives. Bonding curve tokens may appear Ponzi-like if early entrants extract significant value at the expense of later participants. Liquidity mining and high-yield incentive programs can attract mercenary users who quickly exit, depleting treasuries and harming community cohesion. These effects not only damage trust but also risk conflating public goods efforts with speculative schemes.

To manage these dynamics, public goods projects are encouraged to diversify treasuries into stable assets, apply vesting and lockup mechanisms, and establish cultural norms that prioritize mission over token price. Designing tokens with intrinsic utility and clear governance roles, maintaining transparency, and focusing community attention on measurable public outcomes rather than market valuation are critical. Circuit breakers, communication strategies, and impact-oriented metrics can help anchor projects in their core purpose while benefiting from the liquidity and reach of token-based systems.

Thus, tokenized public goods systems must continuously balance the benefits of open, incentive-driven coordination with the risks of capture, regulatory backlash, and financial volatility. These are not merely technical issues but core institutional design challenges that will shape the future of decentralized cooperation.

6. PROSPECTS OF TOKEN ECONOMIES FOR PUBLIC GOODS

Token economies for public goods remain an emerging experiment, yet they have already demonstrated sufficient potential to justify substantial scaling in the coming years. Looking ahead to the 2025–2035 period, several major trajectories and developments appear likely.

6.1. Mainstream Adoption by Institutions

Traditional institutions (governments, NGOs, and multilateral organizations) are increasingly engaging with token-based mechanisms for funding public goods. Initiatives such as Brazil's Drex CBDC sandbox and Hong Kong's issuance of digital bonds suggest growing institutional interest in tokenization for social finance. In the near future, it is plausible that several countries will employ blockchain platforms to administer grants, subsidies, or participatory budgeting programs. Likewise, large-scale NGOs may adopt Gitcoin-style quadratic funding models to allocate resources globally. For instance, organizations like the United Nations or the World Bank could coordinate decentralized funding rounds, allowing citizens to signal their preferences over climate technology projects. In this way, blockchain-based tools tested within crypto-native communities may be repurposed by legacy institutions to improve the transparency and responsiveness of public spending.

6.2 Fusion of Web3 Infrastructure and "Real World" Impact Metrics

Token-based systems are expected to integrate more tightly with real-world data and metrics. This will likely involve the use of oracles and IoT devices to feed verified data into smart contracts that enable outcome-based funding. A retroactive public goods DAO focused on health, for example, might automatically issue rewards based on verifiable improvements in vaccination rates or disease reduction, using data from clinics or satellite systems. ReFi projects like Regen Network are already working to trigger token issuance automatically when a measurable environmental benefit, such as carbon sequestration, is confirmed. These innovations may lead to the emergence of widely recognized "impact tokens" that represent verified public goods outcomes, such as a quality-adjusted life year saved or a ton of plastic removed from oceans. Such tokens would allow global markets to price and allocate capital based on real, measurable public benefit.

6.3 Improved Synergies Between Funding Mechanisms

Currently, mechanisms such as quadratic funding, retroactive funding, and bonding curves tend to operate in isolation. In the next phase of development, these models are expected to hybridize. Gitcoin, for instance, is already integrating retroactive bonuses into its funding rounds. Retroactive funding DAOs may begin using QF signals to inform reward distributions. Communities leveraging bonding curves might allocate portions of their treasury to ongoing QF rounds. This convergence will be facilitated by "funding operating systems" such as Gitcoin's Allo protocol or Hypercerts, which enable modular integration of funding primitives. Hypercerts (NFT-like certificates representing public goods contributions) could bridge the gap between upfront and retroactive funding: funders might buy shares in a hypercert that will be redeemed if a certain impact is achieved, allowing for early capital infusion and later performance-based rewards. Such mechanisms promise to increase the liquidity and scalability of public goods financing.

6.4 Emergence of Global Public Goods Communities and Network States

Token economies are poised to underpin the rise of transnational communities organized around shared values. These entities, sometimes referred to as "network states," may develop their own token-based infrastructure to fund and govern public goods. A global coalition of educators, for example, might establish a bonding curve to support open educational resources, effectively functioning as a distributed education ministry. Similarly, a climate-focused network state could use ReFi tools to build resilient infrastructure. These digitally-native collectives could negotiate with traditional governments or provide parallel services, using tokens to coordinate and sustain efforts globally. As early examples, projects like the Internet Archive and Open Source collectives are already exploring crypto-native funding models. By 2035, some network states may operate micro-economies that fund public goods on a global scale, potentially with formal recognition from existing nation-states.

6.5 Cultural Normalization and Civic Engagement

The use of tokens for public goods may become culturally normalized, particularly among younger and more technologically literate populations. Just as crowdfunding became widespread in the 2010s, token-based public goods funding may become a mainstream civic activity by the late 2020s. Individuals might regularly contribute a portion of their income through QF platforms as a form of participatory democracy. This shift could reframe public narratives around cryptocurrency, from a vehicle for speculation to a tool for collective action. Educational curricula in civics and economics may begin to incorporate decentralized funding models, further embedding these practices into societal norms.

6.6 Interoperability and Infrastructure Integration

In the coming years, different token-based public goods platforms are likely to become more interoperable. Users may be able to move donations or investments seamlessly across multiple ecosystems. Aggregator platforms could emerge, allowing individuals to view and manage their entire portfolio of public goods contributions, including DAOs, impact bonds, and credits. This integration will lower barriers to participation and increase user engagement by offering unified interfaces and simplified user experiences.

Thus, the trajectory for token economies in public goods funding points toward increased institutional adoption, integration with real-world metrics, convergence of funding models, the rise of global digital communities, and cultural normalization. By 2035, tokenized funding could transition from a fringe Web3 experiment to a central pillar of how societies coordinate around collective challenges. If realized, this vision represents the emergence of a "crypto-driven public sector", a novel governance layer built on programmable, transparent, and incentive-aligned infrastructure. The next few years will be pivotal in determining whether this vision can be actualized at scale. As the Optimism Collective's very name suggests, optimism itself may become a core design principle, one powered not just by sentiment, but by the credible mechanisms that token economies now make possible.

7. CONCLUSION

Token economies represent a breakthrough in funding and governing public goods. By leveraging blockchain and cryptographic tokens, communities are addressing the age-old underprovision problem: aligning incentives so beneficiaries can directly support what they value. Mechanisms like quadratic funding, retroactive public goods funding, bonding curves, and regenerative finance offer practical ways to overcome the free-rider problem. These aren't just theories: Gitcoin has mobilized millions for open-source software through QF, Optimism uses retroactive rewards to grow its ecosystem, and the TEC funds niche research via bonding curves. ReFi efforts like Regen Network tokenized ecological services, while Brazil and Hong Kong explored digital bonds and CBDCs for public finance.

These successes show that token models can scale impact, from software to climate. Governments and institutions are beginning to take notice, signaling the potential for hybrid public-private funding models. However, challenges remain. Governance risks (e.g., plutocracy, Sybil attacks), regulatory uncertainty, and speculative distortions must be addressed. Best practices like identity systems, anti-collusion tools, diversified treasuries, and inclusive governance will be critical for credibility and sustainability.

Looking ahead, token economies may increasingly integrate with traditional systems. Governments could co-fund public goods with DAOs, or CBDCs might support social programs via smart contracts. Legal frameworks and technical standards will mature, boosting legitimacy and adoption. The potential is vast: these models can unlock global participation, fund what people truly value, and respond swiftly to crises, from pandemic relief to climate resilience. They empower communities to self-organize and manage shared resources effectively. The early evidence is promising. As theory becomes practice, and innovators refine these tools, token-based funding may evolve into a foundational pillar of a more participatory and coordinated global society.

REFERENCES

Andreoni, J. (1988). Why free ride? Strategies and learning in public goods experiments. *Journal of Public Economics, 37*(3), 291–304. DOI: 10.1016/0047-2727(88)90043-6

Benkler, Y. (2002). Coase's Penguin, or, Linux and the nature of the firm. *The Yale Law Journal, 112*(3), 369–446. DOI: 10.2307/1562247

Bennett, K. (2025). The ReFi movement in Web3: Implications for the global commons. *Frontiers in Blockchain, 8*, Article 1564073. https://www.frontiersin.org/articles/10.3389/fbloc.2025.1564073/full

Buterin, V. (2021, August 16). *Moving beyond coin voting governance* [Blog post]. https://vitalik.eth.limo/general/2021/08/16/voting3.html

Buterin, V. (2021). *Retroactive public goods funding*. Medium. https://medium.com/ethereum-optimism/retroactive-public-goods-funding-33c9b7d00f0c

Buterin, V., Hitzig, Z., & Weyl, E. G. (2018). Liberal radicalism: A flexible design for philanthropic matching funds [Working paper]. *SSRN*. https://ssrn.com/abstract=3243656

Commons Stack. (2019). *Deep dive: Augmented bonding curves* [Medium article by A. Titcomb]. https://medium.com/commonsstack/deep-dive-augmented-bonding-curves-b5ca4fad4436

Commons Stack. (2021a). *The augmented bonding curve, part 1: A Web3 way to fund public goods*. https://medium.com/commonsstack/the-augmented-bonding-curve-part-1-a-web3-way-to-fund-public-goods-7c9d1a871ae2

Commons Stack. (2021b). *Augmented Bonding Curve whitepaper*. https://www.commonsstack.org/augmented-bonding-curve

Cong, L. W., Li, Y., & Wang, N. (2021). Tokenomics: Dynamic adoption and valuation. *Review of Financial Studies, 34*(3), 1105–1155. DOI: 10.1093/rfs/hhaa089

Cornes, R., & Sandler, T. (1996). *The theory of externalities, public goods, and club goods* (2nd ed.). Cambridge University Press. DOI: 10.1017/CBO9781139174312

Daniels, J. (2025). *Introducing FIL ProPGF: A new era in community-led public goods funding for the Filecoin ecosystem*. Filecoin. https://filecoin.io/blog/posts/introducing-fil-propgf-a-new-era-in-community-led-public-goods-funding-for-the-filecoin-ecosystem

De Filippi, P., & Loveluck, B. (2016). The invisible politics of Bitcoin: Governance crisis of a decentralized infrastructure. *Internet Policy Review*, *5*(4). Advance online publication. https://ssrn.com/abstract=2852691. DOI: 10.14763/2016.3.427

Easley, D., O'Hara, M., & Basu, S. (2019). From mining to markets: The evolution of bitcoin transaction fees. *Journal of Financial Economics*, *134*(1), 91–109. DOI: 10.1016/j.jfineco.2019.03.004

Freitas, L., & Maldonado, W. (2024). Quadratic funding with incomplete information. *Social Choice and Welfare*, *64*(1), 43–67.

Gitcoin. (2023, April 18). *WTF is retro funding* [Blog post by S. Smith].

Gitcoin. (2023). *Gitcoin impact report – Funding stats 2019–2023.*

Gitcoin. (2025a). *GG23 results & recap.* Gitcoin Blog.

Giveth. (2021, May 10). *Deep dive: Augmented bonding curves.* Giveth Blog. https://blog.giveth.io/deep-dive-augmented-bonding-curves-3f1f7c1fa751/

Gutiérrez, A., Tran, T. T., & Wainwright, S. (2023). Governance of the ReFi ecosystem and the integrity of voluntary carbon markets as a common resource. *The International Journal of the Commons*, *17*(1), 1–24. DOI: 10.5334/ijc.1410

Hardin, G. (1968). The tragedy of the commons. *Science*, *162*(3859), 1243–1248. DOI: 10.1126/science.162.3859.1243

Hong Kong Monetary Authority. (2023, February 16). *HKSAR Government announces successful offering of the world's first tokenised government green bond.* https://www.hkma.gov.hk/eng/news-and-media/press-releases/2023/02/20230216-3/

Information Services Department. HKSAR Government. (2023, February 16). *World's first tokenised government green bond issued.* https://www.info.gov.hk/gia/general/202302/16/P2023021600466.htm

Internet Archive. (2025, August 1). *Do you accept cryptocurrency?* Internet Archive Help Center. https://help.archive.org/help/do-you-accept-cryptocurrency/

Johnson, K. (2020). *Downtown Stimulus Program Review.* Medium.https://medium.com/@katiebrenjohnson/downtown-stimulus-program-review-e89f67e29f4f

Kaul, I., Grunberg, I., & Stern, M. A. (Eds.). (1999). *Global public goods: International cooperation in the 21st century.* Oxford University Press., DOI: 10.1093/0195130529.001.0001

Kenyon, C., Berrahoui, M., & Macrina, A. (2022). Transparency principle for carbon emissions drives sustainable finance. *arXiv Preprint.* https://arxiv.org/abs/2202.07689

Klima, D. A. O. (2024). *The Klima Protocol Dashboard (Part 1)*. https://www.klimadao.finance/resources/the-klima-protocol-dashboard-pt1

Lalley, S., & Weyl, E. G. (2017). Quadratic voting: How mechanism design can radicalize democracy. *American Economic Association Papers and Proceedings, 1*(1). https://ssrn.com/abstract=2003531

Ledger Insights. (2024, October 28). *Hong Kong partners with Brazil and Thailand for tokenization, to offer digital bond grants*. https://www.ledgerinsights.com/hong-kong-partners-central-banks-of-brazil-thailand-for-tokenization-to-offer-digital-bond-grants

Marwell, G., & Ames, R. E. (1979). Experiments on the provision of public goods. I. Resources, interest, group size, and the free-rider problem. *American Journal of Sociology, 84*(6), 1335–1360. DOI: 10.1086/226937

Messari. (2024). *State of OP Mainnet Q3 2024*.

Olson, M. (1965). *The logic of collective action: Public goods and the theory of groups*. Harvard University Press. DOI: 10.4159/9780674041660

Optimism Collective. (2023). *Optimism case study – Retroactive public goods funding results*.

Optimism Collective. (2024). *Retro funding 5: OP Stack – Round details*. Governance Forum.

Optimism Collective. (n.d.). *How retro funding works*. Optimism Docs. https://community.optimism.io/citizens-house/how-retro-funding-works

Ostrom, E. (1990). *Governing the commons: The evolution of institutions for collective action*. Cambridge University Press. DOI: 10.1017/CBO9780511807763

Pasquini, R. A. (2020). *Quadratic funding and matching funds requirements*. SSRN Working Paper (Revised August 2022).

Pasquini, R. A. (2022). *Optimal allocation of limited funds in quadratic funding. arXiv Preprint*.

Regen Network. (2021). *Regen Network whitepaper v1.3*. https://regen.network

Regen Network. (2023, May). *Digital carbon market case study. Frontiers in Blockchain*. https://frontiersin.org

Regen Network Registry. (2024). *Indigenous-led biocultural jaguar corridor credits*. https://registry.regen.network

Roam Network. (2025). *Building a credential-based wireless network.* Messari. https://messari.io

Rozas, D., Tenorio-Fornés, A., Díaz-Molina, S., & Hassan, S. (2021). When Ostrom meets blockchain: Exploring the potentials of blockchain for commons governance. *Environmental Innovation and Societal Transitions, 69,* 100678.

Samuelson, P. A. (1954). The pure theory of public expenditure. *The Review of Economics and Statistics, 36*(4), 387–389. DOI: 10.2307/1925895

Saraji, S., & Borowczak, M. (2021). A blockchain-based carbon credit ecosystem. *arXiv Preprint.* https://arxiv.org/abs/2107.00185

Stiglitz, J. E. (1999). Knowledge as a global public good. In Kaul, I., Grunberg, I., & Stern, M. (Eds.), *Global public goods: International cooperation in the 21st century* (pp. 308–325). Oxford University Press., DOI: 10.1093/0195130529.003.0015

The Bank for International Settlements. (2025). *The next-generation monetary and financial system* (Annual Report, Chapter III). https://www.bis.org/publ/arpdf/ar2025e3

Token Engineering Academy. (2025). *TE Fundamentals course overview.* https://te-academy.netlify.app

Token Engineering Commons. (2022). [Medium article by S. Voshmgir]. https://sherminvoshmgir.medium.com/token-engineering-commons-69398048209a

Token Engineering Commons. (2023). *Tunable quadratic funding: Incorporating expertise into QF* [Medium article by G. Rosenblatt]. https://medium.com/token-engineering-commons/expertise-and-quadratic-funding-bd4f0c5c3e23

Wang, L., Yu, J., Bennett, A., Gao, B., & Joseph, R. (2025). Evaluating voting design vulnerabilities for retroactive funding. *arXiv Preprint, arXiv:2505.16068.* https://arxiv.org/abs/2505.16068

Zargham, M., Shorish, J., & Paruch, K. (2020). *From curved bonding to configuration spaces.* BlockScience. https://blog.block.science/from-curved-bonding-to-configuration-spaces/

KEY TERMS AND DEFINITIONS

Augmented Bonding Curve (ABC): An augmented bonding curve is an advanced token issuance mechanism that integrates features such as reserve pools, governance locks, and contribution tributes. It enables continuous funding for public goods while managing token supply dynamics and reinforcing community alignment through embedded incentive structures.

Free-Rider Problem: A situation in which individuals benefit from a public good without contributing to its provision. This leads to systematic underinvestment, and in extreme cases, the failure to produce or maintain the good, due to misaligned incentives in voluntary contribution models.

Public Good: A non-rivalrous and non-excludable resource, meaning its use by one individual does not diminish its availability to others, nor can access be easily restricted. Classic examples include clean air, national defense, and lighthouses, which benefit everyone regardless of individual contribution. In the digital era, public goods also include open-source software, scientific knowledge, and open data, which can be freely accessed and used without being depleted.

Quadratic Funding (QF): A mechanism for allocating resources to public goods, wherein the total funding a project receives is proportional to the square of the sum of the square roots of individual contributions. This design amplifies small, distributed donations, prioritizing projects with broad community support over those with few large backers.

Regenerative Finance (ReFi): Regenerative finance (ReFi) encompasses financial systems and instruments designed to repair and sustain ecological, social, and economic systems. ReFi mechanisms often utilize blockchain-based tools to direct capital flows toward activities that generate long-term positive externalities, such as biodiversity conservation or community resilience.

Retroactive Public Goods Funding (Retro PGF): A model that compensates contributors only after their work has demonstrated measurable positive externalities. By rewarding proven impact rather than speculative outcomes, RetroPGF seeks to align individual incentives with long-term collective benefit.

Token Economy: A digitally native economic system that utilizes cryptographic tokens to coordinate incentives, allocate value, and facilitate governance within decentralized networks. Token economies are employed in applications ranging from decentralized finance (DeFi) to community-based public goods funding.

Tokenized Ecological Credits: Blockchain-based representations of environmental assets (carbon offsets or biodiversity units) that enable transparent issuance, traceability, and programmability. These credits facilitate decentralized, market-based mechanisms for incentivizing ecological restoration and environmental accountability.

Tokenized Green Bond: A debt instrument issued and managed on a blockchain, where ownership, settlement, and lifecycle processes are transparently recorded on a distributed ledger. These instruments enhance operational efficiency and traceability while directing capital toward environmentally sustainable projects.

Chapter 10
Blockchain Technology: Enhancing Hospitality Recovery and Safeguarding Data Privacy

Mohammad Badruddoza Talukder
https://orcid.org/0009-0008-1662-9221
International University of Business Agriculture and Technology, Bangladesh

Sanjeev Kumar
https://orcid.org/0000-0002-7375-7341
Lovely Professional University, India

Musfiqur Rahoman Khan
https://orcid.org/0009-0005-7416-2533
Daffodil Institute of IT, Bangladesh

Firoj Kabir
https://orcid.org/0009-0001-3014-3163
Daffodil International University, Bangladesh

ABSTRACT

Blockchain technology is revolutionizing the hospitality sector by providing creative post-crisis recovery options and guaranteeing strong data protection. This chapter examines how blockchain builds confidence among players in the hospitality industry, improves operational efficiency, and secures transactions. Blockchain reduces data breaches, stops fraud, and simplifies consumer interactions using decentralized ledgers, smart contracts, and cryptographic security. The chapter also looks at how blockchain might help secure digital identities, smooth payment processes, and transparent supply chain management—all essential for boosting industry resilience and regaining consumer trust. The conversation also focuses on the practical uses, difficulties, and potential future developments of blockchain

DOI: 10.4018/979-8-3373-3371-7.ch010

integration in the hospitality industry. Ultimately, this chapter offers a thorough foundation for comprehending how blockchain might aid in the industry's recovery while upholding strict data protection regulations.

INTRODUCTION

Since it generates employment opportunities and significantly contributes to GDP, the hotel industry has been a cornerstone of economic growth worldwide for a long time. The risks previously present in traditional operational models have been brought to light due to current issues such as the COVID-19 pandemic, cyber threats, and data breaches (Mohammad, 2025a). Blockchain technology has emerged as a potentially transformative instrument when the industry looks for novel ways to restore confidence, improve efficiency, and guarantee data safety (Rafique et al., 2020).

Blockchain technology, a decentralized and tamper-proof digital ledger, can potentially change several elements of the hospitality industry (Talukder & Kumar, 2024). These aspects include the security of client data, the protection of safe transactions, and the transparency of supply chains and loyalty programs. In contrast to traditional centralized systems, blockchain technology guarantees immutability, transparency, and security. As a result, it is an excellent solution for resolving the growing concerns over data privacy and fraud prevention in the business. Bringing back customers' faith is one of the most critical obstacles in the hospitality industry's revival (Yvonne et al., 2024). The increase in cyber threats that target hotels, airlines, and online booking platforms has increased guests' anxiety over managing their personal information. The capacity of blockchain technology to encrypt and safely store client information helps mitigate these risks, ensuring that sensitive data will remain private and protected. In addition, smart contracts, which are agreements that automatically carry out their terms and conditions (Kamath et al., 2024), can stream operations, reduce the number of middlemen, and increase the level of trust between service providers and their clients.

This chapter aims to investigate the different applications of blockchain technology in the hospitality industry, specifically focusing on how it might help with post-crisis recovery, data protection, and operational efficiency. It examines case studies of practical blockchain implementations, draws attention to potential problems, and assesses the prospects for blockchain adoption in the industry. By gaining a grasp of the strategic role that blockchain plays, professionals in the hospitality industry can make use of this technology to develop experiences that are more secure, transparent, and customer-centric in an environment that is becoming increasingly digital (Legris et al., 2003).

The Importance of Blockchain Technology in the Hospitality Industry. The worldwide hospitality industry stopped due to the pandemic, which compelled businesses to implement digital solutions to guarantee safety, preserve operational efficiency, and regain customers' trust (Mohammad & Sanjeev, 2025). Check-ins that do not require physical contact, digital payments, and virtual concierge services have become the standard. Nevertheless, elevated worries over data security and privacy have emerged in tandem with the growing prevalence of digitalization. Identity theft, financial fraud, and a loss of client confidence have all resulted from cyberattacks on big hospitality businesses, exposing the risks of centralized data storage (Mohammad, 2020a). The fact that blockchain is decentralized eliminates the possibility of a single point of failure, which makes it an effective instrument for protecting visitor information, financial transactions, and operational records (S. C. Hassan & Kumar, 2024).

Additionally, the sector has had difficulties in supply chain operations, fraudulent bookings, and ineffective loyalty programs. All of these issues can be resolved by utilizing the capabilities of blockchain technology, which are transparent, tamper-proof, and entirely automated (Kumar et al., 2024). Hotels, airlines, and travel firms may streamline their operations, reduce the amount of fraud that occurs, establish ecosystems founded on trust, and allow stakeholders to engage smoothly by integrating blockchain technology.

Within the Hospitality Industry, Blockchain and Data Privacy, Particularly in light of the proliferation of severe data protection legislation such as the General Data Protection Regulation (GDPR) and the California Consumer Privacy Act (CCPA), the hotel industry has become increasingly concerned about the privacy of its customers' personal information (Grima et al., 2024). Because of the large amounts of personal information they acquire, such as information about passports, credit card numbers, and individual preferences, hotels, travel agencies, and online booking platforms are popular targets for cybercriminals. Blockchain's cryptographic security protocols ensure that only authorized parties can access sensitive data, protecting against breaches and illegal access. Blockchain is a distributed ledger technology.

Another important application of blockchain technology is the maintenance of identities. In traditional verification systems, several intermediaries are involved, which increases the likelihood of data leaks (Mohammad, 2020b). Guests can store their validated credentials on a safe, decentralized network and selectively distribute them without disclosing any unneeded information thanks to blockchain technology, which enables self-sovereign identity (SSI) solutions.

This ensures that identification verification at check-ins, border crossings, and loyalty program registrations is simple and focused on protecting individuals' privacy (Mohammad, 2021). Utilizing Blockchain Technology to Revolutionize Hospitality Operations

The capabilities of blockchain extend beyond security and anonymity and incorporate the enhancement of overall operational efficiency. Contracts that are self-executing and maintained on a blockchain are known as smart contracts (Waheed & Kumar, 2024). These contracts automate transactions, hence minimizing the need for manual intervention in booking confirmations, supplier payments, refund processes, and dispute resolutions. Furthermore, supply chain management systems driven by blockchain technology allow hotels and restaurants to check the authenticity and ethical sourcing of food and beverage goods, ensuring that they comply with sustainability criteria. Additionally, blockchain technology redefines loyalty and rewards programs by removing inefficiencies in point redemption, avoiding fraud, and enabling interoperability across many brands by eliminating inefficiencies (Chauhan et al., 2025). Travelers have access to loyalty points that are decentralized, transferable, and fraud-proof, which makes it simpler for them to accrue and redeem rewards across a variety of service providers, including airlines, hotels, and restaurants.

This chapter examines real-world cases of blockchain technology and the problems involved in its adoption. It focuses on blockchain's essential role in hospitality recovery and data protection (Talukder et al., 2024). While addressing potential obstacles such as high implementation costs, regulatory concerns, and the requirement for industry-wide collaboration, it explains how blockchain technology can improve trust, security, and efficiency by resolving these hurdles (Singh et al., 2025). By gaining an awareness of these elements, professionals working in the hotel industry will be able to make educated judgments regarding the utilization of blockchain technology to establish a hospitality ecosystem that is safer, more resilient, and more focused on the client (Huda et al., 2024).

OBJECTIVES

This chapter aims to explore the role of blockchain technology in the recovery of the hospitality industry and its impact on data privacy. The specific objectives include:

1. To provide a comprehensive overview of blockchain, its key components (decentralization, immutability, transparency, and security), and its relevance to the hospitality industry.
2. To explore how blockchain enhances data security, protects guest information, and ensures compliance with data privacy regulations.

3. To discuss the future potential of blockchain in hospitality, exploring emerging trends, innovative applications, and possible collaborations between blockchain developers and hospitality businesses.

LITERATURE REVIEW

The integration of blockchain technology in the hospitality industry has gained significant attention in recent years, particularly in post-crisis recovery, data privacy, supply chain management, and operational efficiency. This literature review explores existing research on blockchain applications in hospitality, highlighting key contributions, challenges, and potential future directions.

BLOCKCHAIN IN HOSPITALITY RECOVERY

Especially in the wake of the COVID-19 outbreak, several studies have investigated how blockchain technology might help the hospitality industry recover and become more resilient. Mohammad (2025c) asserts that the pandemic brought to light inefficiencies in conventional business models for the hospitality industry, which prompted a transition toward digital and decentralized business solutions (Dewangan & Kumar, 2025. It has been determined that blockchain is a mechanism that may be used to build trust by improving operational efficiency, financial transparency, and safe transactions. These are all necessary components for regaining the confidence of consumers. Talukder et al.(2024) a study address the possibilities of blockchain technology in rehabilitating the hotel industry after a pandemic. The study highlights the capabilities of blockchain technology to eliminate fraud in online bookings, streamline guest verification processes, and give immutable records of health certifications for safe travel. According to the research findings, digital health passports based on blockchain technology can facilitate health verification that is streamlined, secure, and tamper-proof, ensuring compliance with international travel rules (Talukder et al., 2024).

BLOCKCHAIN AND DATA PRIVACY IN HOSPITALITY

Those working in the hotel business manage massive volumes of sensitive consumer data, including personal identities, payment information, and travel records. Concerns over the privacy of personal details have consequently gained more attention, particularly in light of the implementation of rigorous rules such as the General Data Protection Regulation (GDPR) and the California Consumer Privacy Act (CCPA).

According to Khanna et al. (2020), blockchain technology's cryptographic security and decentralized nature offer a solid solution for securing visitor information, minimizing identity theft risk, and increasing the likelihood of data breaches. According to the findings of the study, self-sovereign identification (SSI) systems based on blockchain technology enable guests to exercise control over their data, allowing access only when required. This provides an increased level of privacy and regulatory compliance.

The findings of a study conducted by Rodríguez et al.(2025) lend credence to this contention by demonstrating how blockchain's distributed ledger technology (DLT) guarantees the safety of personal data and prevents it from being altered without consent. In addition, the research highlights that the encryption methods of blockchain technology prohibit unauthorized access, significantly decreasing the cybersecurity risks associated with hospitality operations (Karim et al., 2023).

SMART CONTRACTS AND AUTOMATION IN HOSPITALITY

Smart contracts driven by blockchain technology have been widely acknowledged as a game-changer for hospitality operations (Hamledari & Fischer, 2021). Regarding payments, reservations, refunds, and supplier transactions, these self-executing contracts eliminate the need for intermediaries, automating the process (Onder & Acikgoz, 2023). These contracts, which reduce the risk of fraudulent reservations and ensure transparent and automated reward distribution, are a significant benefit. According to the study's findings, automated smart contracts reduce the number of arbitrations, speed up the processing of transactions, and reduce operating expenses.

Similarly, Ktari et al. (2024) investigate the possible role that blockchain-based smart contracts could play in easing the hospitality industry's administrative constraints associated with supply chain management. According to their findings, computerized procurement and payment verification streamline inventory management, providing openness and efficiency in food supply chains for hotels and restaurants (Hole et al., 2023).

BLOCKCHAIN FOR SECURE PAYMENTS AND FRAUD PREVENTION

Regarding the hospitality industry, one of the most frequently mentioned applications of blockchain technology is its capacity to improve payment security and prevent fraudulent transactions. Hacking, chargebacks, and unlawful transactions are all potential threats to traditional payment systems because they depend on centralized financial institutions.

Following the findings of Balagolla et al. (2021), blockchain-based cryptocurrency payments and decentralized financial (DeFi) solutions offer a secure alternative to traditional means of payment. According to the study, blockchain transactions minimize the possibility of chargeback fraud while assuring that international passengers can make payments across borders quickly and at a reasonable cost. In addition, research conducted by Motahhir & Maleh (2022) highlights that the immutable ledger of blockchain technology eliminates fake reviews, prevents double bookings, and ensures secure direct transactions between customers and hospitality providers. This reduces the need for third-party intermediaries such as online travel agencies (Halima et al., 2024).

CHALLENGES AND LIMITATIONS OF BLOCKCHAIN ADOPTION IN HOSPITALITY

Despite its potential, blockchain adoption in hospitality faces several challenges. Studies by Acikgoz et al. (2024) highlight key barriers, including:

- High Implementation Costs – Integrating blockchain into existing hospitality systems requires significant investment in infrastructure, training, and development.
- Scalability Issues – Blockchain networks may struggle with high transaction volumes, leading to delays in processing reservations and payments.
- Regulatory and Legal Concerns – The lack of uniform global regulations for blockchain-based financial transactions and data storage creates legal uncertainties.
- Industry-Wide Adoption Hurdles – Blockchain solutions require collaborative adoption across multiple stakeholders (hotels, airlines, travel agencies, payment processors), which remains challenging.

A recent study by Filimonau & Naumova (2020) proposes hybrid blockchain models (combining public and private blockchains) to overcome some limitations, offering scalability, cost-effectiveness, and regulatory compliance while maintaining data security and transparency.

FUTURE PROSPECTS OF BLOCKCHAIN IN HOSPITALITY

With new research concentrating on combining artificial intelligence, the Internet of Things, and blockchain to create a hospitality ecosystem that is more intelligent and autonomous, the future of blockchain in the hospitality industry appears to be bright (Önder & Gunter, 2022). Research done by Rashideh (2020) addresses the possibilities of blockchain-powered artificial intelligence chatbots, Internet of Things (IoT)-enabled smart contracts, and decentralized AI-driven customer service. These technologies can revolutionize individualized visitor experiences and enhance hotel administration.

Moreover, (Jain et al., 2023) propose that blockchain technology will play a significant part in implementing sustainable hospitality efforts. This technology will make it possible to monitor carbon footprints transparently, ethically source goods, and provide green certificates to encourage environmentally responsible tourism practices.

BLOCKCHAIN FOR TRANSPARENT AND FRAUD-FREE BOOKINGS

Several issues have been brought about by the proliferation of online travel agencies (OTAs) and third-party booking platforms. These challenges include fraud, hidden costs, and a lack of transparency. The technology known as blockchain provides a decentralized approach that removes the need for intermediaries and results in increased confidence. Research conducted by Yadav et al. (2023) demonstrates that the distributed ledger of blockchain technology eliminates the possibility of fraudulent bookings and duplicate reservations. As a result of the immutability of blockchain records, confirmed bookings cannot be changed or manipulated, effectively reducing the number of fraudulent cancellations and chargebacks. Similarly, Vijayvergiya et al. (2024) contend that blockchain technology can potentially suppress misleading pricing strategies and fraudulent reviews, promoting authenticity in the booking process.

There is also the possibility of blockchain technology enabling the development of decentralized direct booking systems, eliminating the requirement for third-party aggregators like Expedia or Booking.com. Vanini et al. (2023) conducted research that points to the fact that blockchain-based platforms make it possible for hotels to engage directly with clients, drastically reducing commission costs. Travala and Winding Tree are two examples of start-ups that have already established peer-to-peer (P2P) travel marketplaces driven by blockchain technology. These marketplaces provide guests with booking alternatives that are more safe, transparent and cost-effective (Avi et al., 2021).

BLOCKCHAIN FOR SECURE DIGITAL IDENTITY AND CONTACTLESS TRAVEL

Checking in at hotels, ensuring passengers' safety at airports, and participating in reward programs require identity verification in the hospitality business (Bandara et al., 2021). The conventional method of verifying an individual's identity depends on centralized databases, which are susceptible to data breaches. Travelers can safely keep their digital identities, such as passports, visas, and immunization records, in a private blockchain wallet thanks to self-sovereign identification (SSI) systems based on blockchain technology. This solves the problem. In their study, Bissessar et al. (2016) believe that blockchain-powered SSI might facilitate secure verification with a single click at airports, hotels, and rental vehicle services. This would improve efficiency while also assuring compliance with privacy standards. The combination of blockchain technology and biometric authentication provides an additional layer of protection for identity management activities. Pande et al. (2025) researched how blockchain technology and biometrics, such as fingerprint and facial recognition, can simplify verifying an individual's identity at airports and hotels. Digital passports based on blockchain technology, such as those being tested by organizations like ID2020 and IATA's One ID, provide for more frictionless travel experiences while lowering the danger of document forgery (Srinivasan et al., 2024).

BLOCKCHAIN FOR SECURE PAYMENTS AND FINANCIAL TRANSPARENCY

Through the facilitation of safe and instantaneous transactions, blockchain technology has the potential to bring about a revolution in the payment systems utilized in the hotel industry. According to Rane et al. (2023), cryptocurrencies like Bitcoin, Ethereum, and stablecoins provide an alternative to conventional ways of payment, hence lowering the transaction fees that hotels and travel firms must pay. As a reflection of the growing trend toward decentralized finance, several hospitality firms, such as Soneva Resorts and Pavilions Hotels & Resorts, have already implemented cryptocurrency payments. One additional benefit of using blockchain technology for financial transactions is that it can prevent fraudulent activity and chargebacks. Their study by Mohammad (2025b) highlights that the immutable transaction records of blockchain technology prevent improper chargebacks, which is a typical problem in online tour bookings. Furthermore, smart contracts, which are agreements that automatically execute themselves and are kept on blockchain networks, automate the processing of payments after a service, thereby reducing conflicts between customers and service providers (Talukder et al., 2025).

BLOCKCHAIN FOR SUSTAINABLE SUPPLY CHAIN MANAGEMENT

Sustainability is becoming an increasingly important business component in the hospitality industry, notably in ethical sourcing, waste reduction, and tracking carbon footprint patterns. Through the provision of an immutable digital ledger that records each stage of the procurement and distribution processes, blockchain technology offers an improvement in supply chain transparency. According to Sahoo et al. (2024), blockchain technology has the potential to validate the procurement of food in luxury hotels and eco-resorts, thereby assuring that these establishments comply with sustainability criteria. Similarly, projects such as IBM Food Trust have proved the efficacy of blockchain technology in tracking organic, fair-trade, and farm-to-table food, providing a model for the hospitality industry (Queiroz et al., 2019). The management of waste and the monitoring of carbon footprints are two other crucial areas in which blockchain technology has the potential to deliver significant benefits. Gurtu & Johny (2019) propose that waste tracking systems based on blockchain technology can assist hotels in monitoring and reducing the amount of food waste, plastic usage, and energy consumption. Additionally, carbon credit trading platforms that are enabled by blockchain technology would allow hotels to offset their carbon emissions, which encourages environmentally responsible business practices (Saberi et al., 2019).

BLOCKCHAIN FOR LOYALTY PROGRAMS AND CUSTOMER RETENTION

As a result of factors such as fragmentation, fraud, and limited redemption possibilities, hotel loyalty programs frequently face issues. Blockchain technology provides a solution by making it possible to conduct loyalty point transactions in a safe, real-time, and interoperable manner. L. Wang et al. (2019) suggest loyalty programs that are built on blockchain technology. These programs allow customers to earn tokenized points that can be redeemed for various options, including hotel chains, airlines, and restaurants. This increases customer engagement with the brand. Similarly, Santos et al. (2023) discuss how smart contracts prevent point expiration and fraudulent transactions, ensuring customers receive their incentives fairly and securely.

Another application of blockchain technology that is only beginning to emerge in the hospitality industry is decentralized customer relationship management (CRM). The traditional customer relationship management systems maintain the preferences of guests and the history of transactions in centralized databases, which raises privacy concerns. Contrarily, customer relationship management (CRM) solutions based on blockchain technology enable hotels to keep customer data decentralized, thereby giving guests increased control over their personal information. Lim et al. (2019) state that decentralized customer relationship management (CRM) solutions improve data security while enhancing consumer trust and engagement.

CHALLENGES AND FUTURE DIRECTIONS OF BLOCKCHAIN IN HOSPITALITY

Implementing blockchain technology in the hospitality industry confronts several hurdles despite its tremendous benefits. According to Ratna et al. (2024), one of the most significant obstacles is the high initial expenses. Establishing blockchain infrastructure requires substantial investment in technology and workers' training. There is also a concern regarding the scalability of blockchain technology, as many networks face poor transaction speeds, making it difficult to make real-time reservations for hotels and airlines. Another problem is regulatory ambiguity, which arises from the absence of globally standardized standards, creating legal and compliance issues (Elkhwesky & Elkhwesky, 2022). Future research should concentrate on developing hybrid blockchain models to enhance scalability and regulatory compliance. These models would mix public and private blockchains (Sharma et al., 2021). Combining artificial intelligence with blockchain technology is another intriguing option, enabling AI-driven predictive analytics to improve fraud detection and client personalization. Several hospitality businesses also experiment with NFT-based hotel bookings, allowing users to trade or resell their reservations on blockchain marketplaces (Nam et al., 2021).

BLOCKCHAIN AND RECOVERY IN HOSPITALITY POST-PANDEMIC

For enterprises in the hotel industry, the COVID-19 epidemic has fundamentally altered the environment, causing them to face many obstacles. These challenges include a decline in bookings, a change in customer expectations, and an increased emphasis on contactless services. It is believed that blockchain technology has the potential to be a key driver of recovery since it can provide a framework that is safer, more efficient, and robust for hospitality operations (Meng & Bhutia, 2025).

One of the most important areas in which blockchain technology has shown value is implementing operational streamlining. During this period of recovery in the hotel industry, firms are looking for ways to improve service efficiency while simultaneously regaining the trust of their customers. By utilizing digital wallets and self-sovereign identities, blockchain technology has the potential to contribute by guaranteeing transparent and secure bookings as well as frictionless transactions. As an illustration, Agarwal et al. (2024) highlight that decentralized platforms powered by blockchain make it possible for hotels to engage with consumers directly, thereby avoiding the involvement of third-party individuals. In addition to lowering commission costs, this helps smaller hotel businesses recover more quickly and allows them to repair relationships with consumers who have been loyal to them from the beginning. In addition, blockchain technology offers a trustworthy method of monitoring compliance with health and safety regulations, an essential worry in the aftermath of a pandemic (Mittal & Sinha, 2022). Blockchain technology can record and verify guests' vaccination status or test results in a ledger that cannot be altered. This allows hotels to securely comply with health protocols and assure the safety of their guests. Morrone et al. (2024) Illustrate how blockchain platforms utilized by resorts in health-centric tourism provide a high quality of sanitation and transparency throughout the process. This creates a sense of trust and reassurance for passengers who have returned from a pandemic.

BLOCKCHAIN IN CONTACTLESS PAYMENTS AND SAFE TRANSACTIONS

The capacity of blockchain technology to guarantee the safety and transparency of financial transactions is fueling the acceleration of the transition toward digital payments and contactless interactions in the hospitality industry. When the hospitality industry is recovering from the epidemic, cryptocurrency payments and financial systems based on blockchain technology have become a potentially useful alternative to conventional payment methods.

According to Y. Patel et al. (2024), blockchain technology makes it possible to seamlessly process payments using cryptocurrencies and stablecoins, providing immediate and secure transactions. Hotels can accept payments in digital currencies, which decreases the transaction fees associated with payments made with credit cards and eliminates the possibility of chargebacks (Yeh, 2018). Additionally, smart contracts based on blockchain technology can automate payment processes. This allows payments to be triggered only after accomplishing particular service milestones, reducing the likelihood of disputes. This is especially helpful for online travel agencies (OTAs) and booking platforms, frequently facing customer disagreements over customer service, cancellations, or bookings. Guests are only required to pay for the services they have received, and incorporating blockchain technology into these platforms guarantees that all transactions are open and transparent (Rongali et al., 2023).

BLOCKCHAIN FOR DATA PRIVACY AND CUSTOMER TRUST

The hospitality industry is becoming increasingly dependent on digital technologies, which has increased the worry surrounding data privacy. During the process of making reservations or interacting with hospitality services, customers are required to supply sensitive personal information. This information may include payment card details, identification documents, and health information (Saxena et al., 2024). By allowing customers to own their data and determine how and when to share it, blockchain technology can offer a decentralized solution to those concerned about their data's privacy. According to research conducted by Rouhani & Deters (2021), blockchain-based solutions are proposed to improve privacy protection by enabling guests to save their personal information on encrypted digital ledgers. Compared to typical centralized databases, which are more susceptible to cyberattacks and data breaches, this solution starkly contrasts conventional databases (Hussain et al., 2024). The adoption of blockchain technology enables hotels and other suppliers of hospitality services to instill confidence in their clients by assuring them that their data is being maintained securely and that they will continue to retain control of it.

According to H. Wang et al. (2020), the implementation of Self-Sovereign Identity (SSI) makes it possible for customers to build and manage their digital identities across a variety of hospitality platforms without the need for multiple logins or passwords. SSI systems built on blockchain technology ensure that customers have control over how their personal information is shared. These systems allow customers to allow or cancel access to their data anytime. By addressing privacy concerns, this decentralized control helps to increase customer trust (Mukherjee et al., 2021). Moreover, smart contracts built inside blockchain networks allow users to regulate who can access their sensitive data, guaranteeing that it is only shared with people they can trust.

BLOCKCHAIN IN ENHANCING CUSTOMER EXPERIENCE AND PERSONALIZATION

It is essential to provide a personalized experience for customers to maintain their loyalty in the hotel industry, which is characterized by intense competition. By enabling hotels to generate comprehensive and secure visitor profiles based on immutable data records, blockchain technology supports the development of a new level of tailored services.

According to K. Patel (2024), blockchain technology has the potential to monitor a guest's preferences, previous bookings, and feedback across multiple hotels that are part of a hotel chain. Through the utilization of blockchain's transparent ledger, this information is not only readily available but also unchangeable, enabling customized experiences for returning guests. Using blockchain technology, for instance, a hotel may determine a guest's favorite room type, specific dietary preferences, or special requests, and then utilize that information to ensure that those preferences are seamlessly included into the guest's subsequent stays, thereby increasing the guest's level of pleasure (Rane, 2023). When combined with artificial intelligence and machine learning, blockchain technology can significantly improve customization (Upreti et al., 2024). Using artificial intelligence algorithms allows for implementing dynamic pricing models based on past data recorded on the blockchain. This ensures that guests receive the most competitive pricing possible. Internet of Things (IoT)-enabled smart rooms can communicate with the blockchain system to modify guests' temperature, lighting, and entertainment choices based on their previous preferences (Liu et al., 2021).

BLOCKCHAIN'S ROLE IN SUSTAINABLE TOURISM AND GREEN PRACTICES

Because clients are increasingly interested in eco-friendly solutions, sustainability is an essential priority in the hotel industry. Blockchain technology significantly ensures transparency in sustainable processes, such as ethical sourcing, waste management, and energy conservation (Tham & Sigala, 2020). To ensure that organizations not only claim but also verify their efforts to be environmentally responsible, blockchain technology has the potential to create immutable recordings of environmentally friendly actions taking place. The research conducted by Özgit & Adalıer (2022) sheds light on utilizing blockchain technology to monitor the carbon footprint of the hotel business. Using blockchain systems, hotels can record their energy consumption, waste management procedures, and carbon offsets, providing guests real-time access to this information. Consequently, this contributes to establishing a model for sustainable tourism that is transparent and accountable, allowing customers to make well-informed decisions regarding the impact that their stay has on the environment. In addition, blockchain technology makes it easier to monitor green certificates, which helps ensure that hotels comply with the necessary standards for environmentally friendly activities (Pranita et al., 2023).

BLOCKCHAIN AND INDUSTRY RECOVERY: FUTURE TRENDS AND PROSPECTS

As the hospitality industry begins to recover from the epidemic's effects, the future of blockchain appears to be bright, with additional developments on the horizon. Blockchain models that combine public and private blockchains are gaining popularity because they provide flexibility in scalability and regulatory compliance (Makridakis & Christodoulou, 2019). Hybrid blockchains combine both types of blockchains. This hybrid strategy is advantageous for the hospitality business, which must comply with various national and international rules and maintain a high level of transparency and security. The confluence of blockchain technology with artificial intelligence, the Internet of Things, and other developing technologies presents the sector with new opportunities (A. Verma et al., 2022). For instance, blockchain-based NFTs, also known as Non-Fungible Tokens, are now being investigated for use in hotel bookings. These NFTs would allow visitors to trade or sell their reservations on platforms driven by blockchain technology. This may create a new market for unused reservations and increase operational flexibility (Hussien et al., 2021). As blockchain technology advances, smart tourist ecosystems integrate more with technologies like 5G networks, driverless vehicles, and augmented reality (AR). Through the utilization of blockchain's transparent and tamper-proof system, the integration of these technologies will result in travel experiences that are highly tailored, efficient, and secure (Belchior et al., 2022).

FINDINGS FROM LITERATURE

The research on blockchain technology in the hospitality industry provides several significant discoveries that demonstrate the transformational potential of this technology. The capacity of blockchain technology to deliver transparency, data security, and decentralization has substantial advantages for the recovery of the hospitality industry following the epidemic. The reduction of fraudulent activity, the simplification of bookings, and the facilitation of contactless payments improve operational efficiency. In addition to enhancing consumer trust by ensuring tamper-proof booking records and health safety compliance, using smart contracts in blockchain technology has made it possible to conduct secure, automated transactions and service delivery (Onifade et al., 2024). Furthermore, the capability of blockchain to maintain self-sovereign identities assures that customer data is secure and under the control of the visitors, so addressing the growing concern over data privacy in the digital age. A further significant discovery is that blockchain technology has the potential to facilitate the customization of guest experiences and loyalty programs. By utilizing immutable guest profiles maintained on the blockchain, hotels can provide individualized services based on previous bookings, preferences, and feedback, increasing the level of pleasure experienced by guests.

Additionally, combining blockchain technology with cryptocurrencies and tokenized loyalty points has dramatically simplified the process of conducting financial transactions and increasing customer engagement. According to Vardhan et al. (2022), blockchain technology ensures these systems are secure, transparent, and efficient. It also helps build consumer loyalty by providing tamper-proof records of loyalty points and personalized offers.

The research shows hurdles to adopting blockchain technology in the hospitality industry, including high implementation costs, scalability issues, and regulatory ambiguity. However, despite its promising advantages, the literature also notes some challenges. While the initial investment in blockchain technology and infrastructure can be substantial, there are problems regarding the speed of transactions and the scalability of networks that need to be solved before blockchain can be broadly deployed in high-demand environments such as hotels and resorts (Nimkar & Makhijani, 2024). Additionally, the lack of worldwide legislative frameworks around blockchain presents difficulties in legal compliance, particularly concerning the protection of personal data and the transactions of cryptocurrencies (Kayani, 2025). It is necessary to surmount these obstacles so that blockchain technology can realize its full potential in changing the hospitality industry.

Figure 1. Conceptual Framework of Blockchain Technology Enhancing Hospitality Recovery and Safeguarding Data Privacy

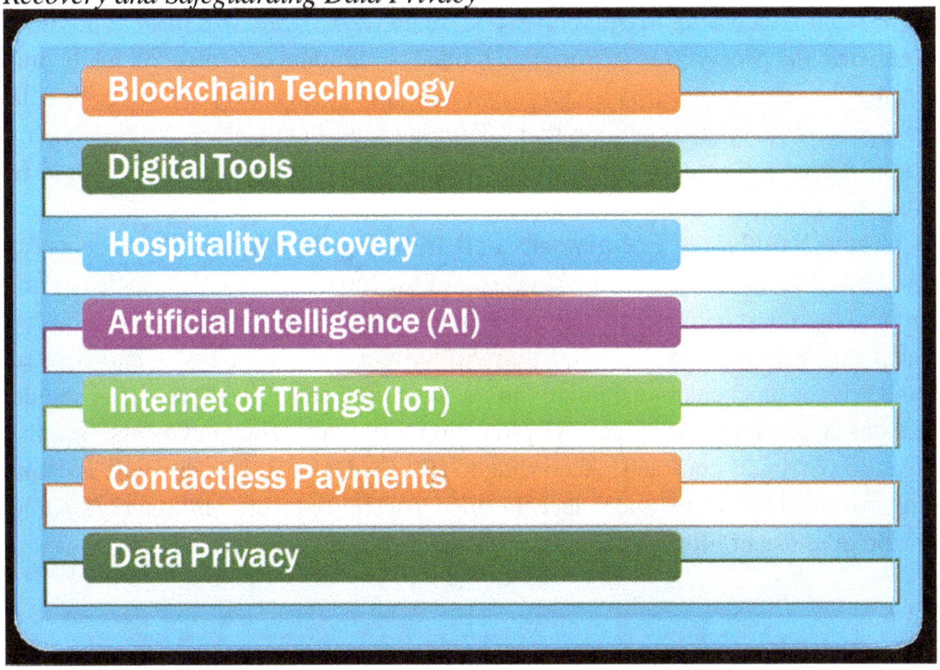

Source: Author Compilation

RECOMMENDATIONS

Numerous recommendations can be made based on the findings from the literature to integrate blockchain technology in the hospitality industry efficiently. These recommendations aim to ensure the successful adoption of blockchain technology and overcome potential hurdles.

Invest in Blockchain Education and Training: Companies in the hospitality industry should emphasize teaching their teams about the advantages and challenges of blockchain technology. This involves providing employees with training on how to use blockchain technologies for making reservations, making payments, and interacting with customers. According to (Panigrahi et al., 2021), establishing dedicated blockchain training programs would assist in minimizing the hurdles to entrance, such as a lack of technical understanding. It will empower staff members to arrive at educated decisions on the usage of blockchain technology.

Collaborate with Technology Providers to Explore Scalable Solutions: To address scalability concerns, hospitality organizations should collaborate with blockchain developers and technology providers to investigate hybrid blockchain solutions. These solutions incorporate the advantages of both public and private blockchains. According to Mukherjee and Singh (2023), this will make it possible to enhance the pace of transactions and reduce operational expenses, all while preserving the level of security and transparency that is necessary for efficient data management. It is also possible that adopting cloud-based blockchain platforms would reduce the price of infrastructure, making blockchain more accessible to small and medium-sized organizations.

Create Regulatory Frameworks and Industry Standards: The absence of standardized regulatory frameworks is one of the most significant obstacles to implementing blockchain technology in the hotel industry. Governments and industry leaders must collaborate to build transparent and internationally acknowledged standards for blockchain technology in the hotel industry. These standards should concentrate on topics such as data protection, cryptocurrency payments, and the execution of smart contracts. According to (Ray & Dash, 2022), this will assist in promoting customer trust and reduce the impact of legal concerns, ultimately leading to a broader use of blockchain solutions.

CONCLUSION

The conclusion is that blockchain technology presents excellent prospects for the hospitality industry to transform, notably in operational efficiency, data security, consumer trust, and recovery after a pandemic. Blockchain technology's decentralized and transparent nature makes improving fraud detection, simplifying bookings, and facilitating contactless transactions possible. These features are essential for the sector's recovery after the COVID-19 pandemic. Integrating blockchain technology with loyalty programs and cryptocurrency payments can also increase customer involvement and happiness. It is necessary to address scalability, high initial costs, and regulatory ambiguity to encourage the widespread adoption of blockchain technology in the hotel industry. The benefits of blockchain technology are readily apparent.

FUTURE STUDY

Future research should investigate hybrid blockchain models to overcome scalability and transaction speed issues. These models integrate the benefits of both public and private blockchains on a single platform. It is also possible for research to explore blockchain technology's influence on customers' behavior and pleasure, particularly concerning tailored services and loyalty programs. Furthermore, additional study is required to build unified regulatory frameworks that govern the use of blockchain technology in the hospitality industry. These frameworks should ensure compliance with data protection laws and financial regulations in various locations. Exploring the integration of blockchain technology with new technologies, such as artificial intelligence and the Internet of Things (IoT), could provide a complete understanding of how these technologies can work together to develop hospitality operations that are smarter and more efficient in the future.

REFERENCES

Acikgoz, F., Stylos, N., & Lythreatis, S. (2024). Identifying capabilities and constraints in utilizing blockchain technology in hospitality and tourism. *International Journal of Contemporary Hospitality Management*, *36*(10), 3493–3514. DOI: 10.1108/IJCHM-07-2023-1083

Agarwal, P., Malhotra, S. K., & Swami, S. (2024). The role of smart technologies in managing supply chain post pandemic: An exploratory scientific procedures and rationales for systematic literature review. *Journal of Science and Technology Policy Management*. DOI: 10.1108/JSTPM-07-2023-0106

Avi, Md. A. R., Nasrin, M., & Hassan, A. (2021). Application of Innovative Technologies in the Tourism and Hospitality Industry of Bangladesh: The Present Scenario. In A. Hassan (Ed.), *Technology Application in the Tourism and Hospitality Industry of Bangladesh* (pp. 81–95). Springer Singapore. DOI: 10.1007/978-981-16-2434-6_5

Balagolla, E. M. S. W., Fernando, W. P. C., Rathnayake, R. M. N. S., Wijesekera, M. J. M. R. P., Senarathne, A. N., & Abeywardhana, K. Y. (2021). Credit Card Fraud Prevention Using Blockchain. *2021 6th International Conference for Convergence in Technology (I2CT)*, 1–8. DOI: 10.1109/I2CT51068.2021.9418192

Bandara, E., Liang, X., Foytik, P., Shetty, S., Hall, C., Bowden, D., Ranasinghe, N., & De Zoysa, K. (2021). A blockchain empowered and privacy preserving digital contact tracing platform. *Information Processing & Management*, *58*(4), 102572. DOI: 10.1016/j.ipm.2021.102572 PMID: 33727760

Belchior, R., Vasconcelos, A., Guerreiro, S., & Correia, M. (2022). A Survey on Blockchain Interoperability: Past, Present, and Future Trends. *ACM Computing Surveys*, *54*(8), 1–41. DOI: 10.1145/3471140

Bissessar, D., Adams, C., & Stoianov, A. (2016). Privacy, Security and Convenience: Biometric Encryption for Smartphone-Based Electronic Travel Documents. In Abielmona, R., Falcon, R., Zincir-Heywood, N., & Abbass, H. A. (Eds.), *Recent Advances in Computational Intelligence in Defense and Security* (Vol. 621, pp. 339–366). Springer International Publishing., DOI: 10.1007/978-3-319-26450-9_13

Chauhan, A., Tripathi, S., Singh, S. V., Singh, K., & Talukdar, M. B. (2025). Eco-Friendly Practices of Ghost Kitchens Through Smart Technology. In Singh, K., Kumar, S., & Talukder, M. (Eds.), *Impact of AI and the Evolution of Future Ghost Kitchens* (pp. 231–246). IGI Global Scientific Publishing., DOI: 10.4018/979-8-3373-0432-8.ch011

Dewangan, S., & Kumar, S. (2025). Frontiers of Innovation: Unveiling the Future Opportunities in Fintech. In *Financial Landscape Transformation: Technological Disruptions* (pp. 153–165). Emerald Publishing Limited.

Elkhwesky, Z., & Elkhwesky, E. F. Y. (2022). A systematic and critical review of Internet of Things in contemporary hospitality: A roadmap and avenues for future research. *International Journal of Contemporary Hospitality Management, ahead-of-print*.

Filimonau, V., & Naumova, E. (2020). The blockchain technology and the scope of its application in hospitality operations. *International Journal of Hospitality Management, 87*, 102383. DOI: 10.1016/j.ijhm.2019.102383

Grima, S., Chaudhary, S., Sood, K., & Kumar, S. (2024). *Business Drivers in Promoting Digital Detoxification*.

Gurtu, A., & Johny, J. (2019). Potential of blockchain technology in supply chain management: A literature review. *International Journal of Physical Distribution & Logistics Management, 49*(9), 881–900. DOI: 10.1108/IJPDLM-11-2018-0371

Hamledari, H., & Fischer, M. (2021). Construction payment automation using blockchain-enabled smart contracts and robotic reality capture technologies. *Automation in Construction, 132*, 103926. DOI: 10.1016/j.autcon.2021.103926

Hassan, S. C., & Kumar, S. (2024). Artificial Intelligence as a Promising Technology: Possibilities and Challenges Across Different Areas of Human Life. *Exploring Ethical Dimensions of Environmental Sustainability and Use of AI*, 54–66.

Hole, Y., Hole, S., Leonardo Cavaliere, L. P., Nair, B., Hasyim, M., & Bapat, H. B. (2023). Blockchain Usages In Hospitality Management. *2023 3rd International Conference on Advance Computing and Innovative Technologies in Engineering (ICACITE)*, 2798–2801. DOI: 10.1109/ICACITE57410.2023.10183291

Huda, M. N., Talukder, M. B., & Kumar, S. (2024). Securing Healthcare AI: Applied Federal Learning. In Bhattacharya, P., Liu, H., Dutta, P. K., Rodrigues, J. J. P. C., & Sethi, G. (Eds.), *Revolutionizing Healthcare 5.0: The Power of Generative AI. Studies in Systems, Decision and Control* (Vol. 571). Springer., DOI: 10.1007/978-3-031-75771-6_17

Hussain, A., Akbar, W., Hussain, T., Bashir, A. K., Dabel, M. M. A., Ali, F., & Yang, B. (2024). Ensuring Zero Trust IoT Data Privacy: Differential Privacy in Blockchain using Federated Learning. *IEEE Transactions on Consumer Electronics*, •••, 1–1. DOI: 10.1109/TCE.2024.3444824

Hussien, H. M., Yasin, S. M., Udzir, N. I., Ninggal, M. I. H., & Salman, S. (2021). Blockchain technology in the healthcare industry: Trends and opportunities. *Journal of Industrial Information Integration*, *22*, 100217. DOI: 10.1016/j.jii.2021.100217

Jain, P., Singh, R., Mishra, R., & Rana, N. P. (2023). Emerging dimensions of blockchain application in tourism and hospitality sector: A systematic literature review. *Journal of Hospitality Marketing & Management*, *32*(4), 454–476. DOI: 10.1080/19368623.2023.2184440

Kamath, S. K., Pendekanti, S. K., Kanumuri, N. V., & Rao, D. (2024). Towards Sustainable Wellness: Leveraging Technology for Addiction Recovery Support. *2024 3rd International Conference on Artificial Intelligence For Internet of Things (AIIoT)*, 1–6. DOI: 10.1109/AIIoT58432.2024.10574651

Karim, R. A., Rabiul, M. K., Ishrat, M., Promsivapallop, P., & Kawser, S. (2023). Can Blockchain Payment Services Influence Customers' Loyalty Intention in the Hospitality Industry? A Mediation Assessment. *Administrative Sciences*, *13*(3), 85. DOI: 10.3390/admsci13030085

Kayani, U. N. (2025). Exploring prospects of blockchain and fintech: Using SLR approach. *Journal of Science and Technology Policy Management*, *16*(1), 5–41. DOI: 10.1108/JSTPM-01-2023-0005

Khanna, A., Sah, A., Choudhury, T., & Maheshwari, P. (2020). Blockchain Technology for Hospitality Industry. In Themistocleous, M., Papadaki, M., & Kamal, M. M. (Eds.), *Information Systems* (Vol. 402, pp. 99–112). Springer International Publishing., DOI: 10.1007/978-3-030-63396-7_7

Ktari, J., Frikha, T., Rekik, M., Gassara, O., Boujelben, M., & Amor, N. B. (2024). Decentralized Hotel Reservations: Blockchain Integration for Incentivized Data Sharing and Smart Contracts. *2024 IEEE 4th International Maghreb Meeting of the Conference on Sciences and Techniques of Automatic Control and Computer Engineering (MI-STA)*, 41–45. DOI: 10.1109/MI-STA61267.2024.10599713

Kumar, S., Talukder, M. B., & Kaiser, F. (2024). Artificial Intelligence in Business: Negative Social Impacts. In *Demystifying the Dark Side of AI in Business* (pp. 81–97). IGI Global.

Legris, P., Ingham, J., & Collerette, P. (2003). Why do people use information technology? A critical review of the technology acceptance model. *Information & Management*, *40*(3), 191–204. DOI: 10.1016/S0378-7206(01)00143-4

Lim, Y. H., Hashim, H., Poo, N., Poo, D. C. C., & Nguyen, H. D. (2019). Blockchain Technologies in E-commerce: Social Shopping and Loyalty Program Applications. In Meiselwitz, G. (Ed.), *Social Computing and Social Media. Communication and Social Communities* (Vol. 11579, pp. 403–416). Springer International Publishing., DOI: 10.1007/978-3-030-21905-5_31

Liu, A., Zhang, D., Wang, X., & Xu, X. (2021). Blockchain-based customization towards decentralized consensus on product requirement, quality, and price. *Manufacturing Letters*, *27*, 18–25. DOI: 10.1016/j.mfglet.2020.12.001

Makridakis, S., & Christodoulou, K. (2019). Blockchain: Current Challenges and Future Prospects/Applications. *Future Internet*, *11*(12), 258. DOI: 10.3390/fi11120258

Meng, D. N. K., & Bhutia, L. D. (2025). Leveraging Digital Technologies and Sustainable Practices for Post-Pandemic Tourism Recovery: A Focus on Malaysia. In Hassan, V. I. (Ed.), *Navigating Mass Tourism to Island Destinations* (pp. 151–178). IGI Global., DOI: 10.4018/979-8-3693-9107-5.ch006

Mittal, R., & Sinha, P. (2022). Framework for a resilient religious tourism supply chain for mitigating post-pandemic risk. *International Hospitality Review*, *36*(2), 322–339. DOI: 10.1108/IHR-09-2020-0053

Mohammad B.T. (2020a). An Appraisal of the Economic Outlook for the Tourism Industry, Specially Cox's Bazar in Bangladesh. *i-manager's Journal on Economics & Commerce,* 2(1), 23-35. DOI: 10.26634/jecom.2.1.17285

Mohammad, B. T. (2020b). The Future of Culinary Tourism: An Emerging Dimension for the Tourism Industry of Bangladesh. I-Manager's. *Journal of Management*, *15*(1), 27. DOI: 10.26634/jmgt.15.1.17181

Mohammad, B. T. (2021). An assessment of the roles of the social network in the development of the Tourism Industry in Bangladesh. *International Journal of Business, Law, and Education*, *2*(3), 85–93. DOI: 10.56442/ijble.v2i3.21

Mohammad, B.T. and Sanjeev, k. (2025), "Culinary Experiences and Food Tourism in Bangladesh", Tyagi, P.K., Nadda, V. and Singh, A.K. (Ed.) Meaningful Tourism (Building the Future of Tourism), Emerald Publishing Limited, Leeds, pp. 201-219. DOI: 10.1108/978-1-83797-837-320251028

Mohammad, B. T. (2025a). Maximizing Impact: The Role of Influencer Marketing in Contemporary Tourism Management. In Özsungur, F. (Ed.), *Navigating Organizational Behavior in the Digital Age with AI* (pp. 277–304). IGI Global Scientific Publishing., DOI: 10.4018/979-8-3693-8442-8.ch011

Mohammad, B. T. (2025b). Revolutionizing Hospitality: Leveraging Mobile Apps and Cutting-Edge Room Technologies in the Hotel Industry. In B. Varghese & S. H. (Eds.), *Advancing Smart Tourism Through Analytics* (pp. 315-332). IGI Global Scientific Publishing. DOI: 10.4018/979-8-3693-3715-8.ch017

Mohammad, B. T. (2025c). Climate change adaptation strategies for a tourism destination: A study of Kuakata beach. *Acta Scientiarum Polonorum. Administratio Locorum*, *24*(1), 165–179. DOI: 10.31648/aspal.10073

Morrone, D., Tarulli, A., Silvestri, R., & Santovito, S. (2024). Generation Z, tourism and hospitality: The legacy of COVID-19. *British Food Journal*, *126*(1), 205–222. DOI: 10.1108/BFJ-11-2022-0972

Motahhir, S., & Maleh, Y. (2022). *Security Engineering for Embedded and Cyber-Physical Systems* (1st ed.). CRC Press., DOI: 10.1201/9781003278207

Mukherjee, A. G., Wanjari, U. R., Chakraborty, R., Renu, K., Vellingiri, B., & George, A., CR, S. R., & Gopalakrishnan, A. V. (. (2021). A review on modern and smart technologies for efficient waste disposal and management. *Journal of Environmental Management*, *297*, 113347. DOI: 10.1016/j.jenvman.2021.113347 PMID: 34314963

Nam, K., Dutt, C. S., Chathoth, P., & Khan, M. S. (2021). Blockchain technology for smart city and smart tourism: Latest trends and challenges. *Asia Pacific Journal of Tourism Research*, *26*(4), 454–468. DOI: 10.1080/10941665.2019.1585376

Nimkar, S., & Makhijani, S. (2024). Blockchain and Cloud Computing in Healthcare: A Critical Analysis and Future Prospects. *2024 IEEE 3rd International Conference on Electrical Power and Energy Systems (ICEPES)*, 1–5. DOI: 10.1109/ICEPES60647.2024.10653489

Onder, I., & Acikgoz, F. (2023). *Blockchain for Tourism and Hospitality Industries* (1st ed.). Routledge., DOI: 10.4324/9781003351917

Önder, I., & Gunter, U. (2022). Blockchain: Is it the future for the tourism and hospitality industry? *Tourism Economics*, *28*(2), 291–299. DOI: 10.1177/1354816620961707

Onifade, M., Adebisi, J. A., & Zvarivadza, T. (2024). Recent advances in blockchain technology: Prospects, applications and constraints in the minerals industry. *International Journal of Mining, Reclamation and Environment*, *38*(7), 497–533. DOI: 10.1080/17480930.2024.2319453

Özgit, H., & Adalıer, A. (2022). Can Blockchain technology help small islands achieve sustainable tourism? A perspective on North Cyprus. *Worldwide Hospitality and Tourism Themes*, *14*(4), 374–383. DOI: 10.1108/WHATT-03-2022-0037

Pande, L., Pandey, U., & Sengupta, S. (2025). The Convergence of 5G, Contactless Technology and Blockchain in Tourism: Assessing Impacts, Adoption, and Future Trends. SSRN *Electronic Journal*. DOI: 10.2139/ssrn.5086775

Panigrahi, C. R., Pati, B., Rath, M., & Buyya, R. (2021). *Computational Modeling and Data Analysis in COVID-19 Research (C. Rani Panigrahi* (Pati, B., Rath, M., & Buyya, R., Eds.; 1st ed.). CRC Press., DOI: 10.1201/9781003137481

Patel, K. (2024). Revolutionizing Customer Experience: Integrating Blockchain with AR and VR in Retail. In B. Verma, A. Mittal, M. Raman, & B. Sindhav (Eds.), *Augmenting Retail Reality, Part B: Blockchain, AR, VR, and AI* (pp. 1–22). Emerald Publishing Limited. DOI: 10.1108/978-1-83608-708-320241003

Patel, Y., Chovatia, N., & Kaur, H. (2024). Securing Payment Transactions: A Comprehensive Review of Smart Cards and Contactless Payments with Cryptographic Methods. *2024 11th International Conference on Computing for Sustainable Global Development (INDIACom)*, 785–790. DOI: 10.23919/INDIACom61295.2024.10498568

Pranita, D., Sarjana, S., Musthofa, B. M., Kusumastuti, H., & Rasul, M. S. (2023). Blockchain Technology to Enhance Integrated Blue Economy: A Case Study in Strengthening Sustainable Tourism on Smart Islands. *Sustainability (Basel)*, *15*(6), 5342. DOI: 10.3390/su15065342

Queiroz, M. M., Telles, R., & Bonilla, S. H. (2019). Blockchain and supply chain management integration: A systematic review of the literature. *Supply Chain Management*, *25*(2), 241–254. DOI: 10.1108/SCM-03-2018-0143

Rafique, H., Almagrabi, A. O., Shamim, A., Anwar, F., & Bashir, A. K. (2020). Investigating the Acceptance of Mobile Library Applications with an Extended Technology Acceptance Model (TAM). *Computers & Education*, *145*, 103732. DOI: 10.1016/j.compedu.2019.103732

Rane, N. (2023). Enhancing customer loyalty through Artificial Intelligence (AI), Internet of Things (IoT), and Big Data technologies: Improving customer satisfaction, engagement, relationship, and experience. *Internet of Things (IoT), and Big Data Technologies: Improving Customer Satisfaction, Engagement, Relationship, and Experience (October 13, 2023).*

Rane, N., Choudhary, S., & Rane, J. (2023). Blockchain and Artificial Intelligence (AI) integration for revolutionizing security and transparency in finance. SSRN *Electronic Journal*. DOI: 10.2139/ssrn.4644253

Rashideh, W. (2020). Blockchain technology framework: Current and future perspectives for the tourism industry. *Tourism Management*, *80*, 104125. DOI: 10.1016/j.tourman.2020.104125

Ratna, S., Saide, S., Putri, A. M., Indrajit, R. E., & Muwardi, D. (2024). Digital transformation in tourism and hospitality industry: A literature review of blockchain, financial technology, and knowledge management. *EuroMed Journal of Business*, *19*(1), 84–112. DOI: 10.1108/EMJB-04-2023-0118

Ray, P. P., & Dash, D. (2022). Blockchain for IoT-based medical delivery drones. In *Blockchain Technology for Emerging Applications* (pp. 137–176). Elsevier., DOI: 10.1016/B978-0-323-90193-2.00002-8

Rodríguez Bolívar, M. P., Sepe, F., Nanu, L., & Roberto, F. (2025). Perceptions and challenges of blockchain adoption in tourism industry: A study on trust, privacy and security. *Journal of Hospitality and Tourism Technology*, *16*(3), 429–449. DOI: 10.1108/JHTT-03-2024-0193

Rongali, B., Mohapatra, S., & Nayak, S. K. (2023). A Secure Contactless Payment System with Bidirectional Blockchain and Blake Hash Function. *2023 IEEE 22nd International Conference on Trust, Security and Privacy in Computing and Communications (TrustCom)*, 318–325. DOI: 10.1109/TrustCom60117.2023.00061

Rouhani, S., & Deters, R. (2021). Data Trust Framework Using Blockchain Technology and Adaptive Transaction Validation. *IEEE Access : Practical Innovations, Open Solutions*, *9*, 90379–90391. DOI: 10.1109/ACCESS.2021.3091327

Saberi, S., Kouhizadeh, M., Sarkis, J., & Shen, L. (2019). Blockchain technology and its relationships to sustainable supply chain management. *International Journal of Production Research*, *57*(7), 2117–2135. DOI: 10.1080/00207543.2018.1533261

Sahoo, S., Kumar, S., Sivarajah, U., Lim, W. M., Westland, J. C., & Kumar, A. (2024). Blockchain for sustainable supply chain management: Trends and ways forward. *Electronic Commerce Research*, *24*(3), 1563–1618. DOI: 10.1007/s10660-022-09569-1

Santos, A. F., Marinho, J., & Bernardino, J. (2023). Blockchain-Based Loyalty Management System. *Future Internet*, *15*(5), 161. DOI: 10.3390/fi15050161

Saxena, M., Senthilkumar, N., & Girimurugan, B. P, L. A., Hasan, K. S., & Sanjay. (2024). Customer Relationship Management in the Digital Age by Implementing Blockchain for Enhanced Data Security and Customer Trust. *2024 2nd International Conference on Disruptive Technologies (ICDT)*, 56–59. DOI: 10.1109/ICDT61202.2024.10489537

Sharma, M., Sehrawat, R., Daim, T., & Shaygan, A. (2021). Technology assessment: Enabling Blockchain in hospitality and tourism sectors. *Technological Forecasting and Social Change, 169*, 120810. DOI: 10.1016/j.techfore.2021.120810

Singh, K., Kumar, S., & Talukder, M. B. (Eds.). (2025). *Impact of AI and the Evolution of Future Ghost Kitchens*. IGI Global., DOI: 10.4018/979-8-3373-0432-8

Srinivasan, S., Raja, R., Jehan, C., Murugan, S., Srinivasan, C., & Muthulekshmi, M. (2024). IoT-Enabled Facial Recognition for Smart Hospitality for Contactless Guest Services and Identity Verification. *2024 11th International Conference on Reliability, Infocom Technologies and Optimization (Trends and Future Directions) (ICRITO)*, 1–6. DOI: 10.1109/ICRITO61523.2024.10522363

Talukder, M. B., Hoque, M., & Kumar, S. (2024). Impact of Cybersecurity in the Aviation, Tourism, and Hospitality Industries. In *Corporate Cybersecurity in the Aviation, Tourism, and Hospitality Sector* (pp. 200–215). IGI Global.

Talukder, M. B., Hoque, M., & Kumar, S. (2025). Understanding the Blend of Work and Leisure in Hospitality: The Era of Bleisure. In *Smart Travel and Sustainable Innovations in Bleisure Tourism* (pp. 179–200). IGI Global.

Talukder, M. B., & Kumar, S. (2024). The Development of Human Capital in The Hospitality Business. In S. Taneja, P. Kumar, Reepu, B. Balusamy, K. Sood, & S. Grima (Eds.), *Contemporary Studies in Economic and Financial Analysis* (pp. 21–38). Emerald Publishing Limited. DOI: 10.1108/S1569-375920240000114002

Talukder, M. B., Kumar, S., & Tyagi, P. K. (Eds.). (2024). *Impact of AI and Tech-Driven Solutions in Hospitality and Tourism*. IGI Global., DOI: 10.4018/979-8-3693-6755-1

Talukder, M. B., Lina, F. Y., Kumar, S., & Khan, M. R. (2024). Data-Driven Personalization in the Sharing Economy. In Ordóñez De Pablos, P. (Ed.), (pp. 277–300). Advances in Finance, Accounting, and Economics. IGI Global., DOI: 10.4018/979-8-3693-5673-9.ch012

Tham, A., & Sigala, M. (2020). Road block(chain): Bit(coin)s for tourism sustainable development goals? *Journal of Hospitality and Tourism Technology, 11*(2), 203–222. DOI: 10.1108/JHTT-05-2019-0069

Upreti, K., Gangwar, D., Vats, P., Bhardwaj, R., Khatri, V., & Gautam, V. (2024). Artificial Neural Networks for Enhancing E-commerce: A Study on Improving Personalization, Recommendation, and Customer Experience. In Shaw, R. N., Siano, P., Makhilef, S., Ghosh, A., & Shimi, S. L. (Eds.), *Innovations in Electrical and Electronic Engineering* (Vol. 1115, pp. 141–153). Springer Nature Singapore., DOI: 10.1007/978-981-99-8661-3_11

Vanini, P., Rossi, S., Zvizdic, E., & Domenig, T. (2023). Online payment fraud: From anomaly detection to risk management. *Financial Innovation*, *9*(1), 66. DOI: 10.1186/s40854-023-00470-w

Vardhan Singh Rawat, H., Bisht, D., Kumar, S., & Dangi, S. (2022). Rise of Blockchain-Based Non-fungible Tokens (NFTs): Overview, Trends, and Future Prospects. In V. Skala, T. P. Singh, T. Choudhury, R. Tomar, & Md. Abul Bashar (Eds.), *Machine Intelligence and Data Science Applications* (Vol. 132, pp. 1–10). Springer Nature Singapore. DOI: 10.1007/978-981-19-2347-0_1

Verma, A., Bhattacharya, P., Madhani, N., Trivedi, C., Bhushan, B., Tanwar, S., Sharma, G., Bokoro, P. N., & Sharma, R. (2022). Blockchain for Industry 5.0: Vision, Opportunities, Key Enablers, and Future Directions. *IEEE Access : Practical Innovations, Open Solutions*, *10*, 69160–69199. DOI: 10.1109/ACCESS.2022.3186892

Vijayvergiya, R., Goto, T., & Sen, S. (2024). A Framework for Direct Benefit Transfer for Fertilizer Distribution and Payment Using Blockchain. In H. N. Saha, H. Ray, & P. G. Bradford (Eds.), *International Conference on Systems and Technologies for Smart Agriculture* (pp. 839–850). Springer Nature Singapore. DOI: 10.1007/978-981-97-5157-0_69

Waheed, S., & Kumar, S. (2024). Challenges and Future Directions for Promoting Sustainable Gastronomy Tourism. In *Promoting Sustainable Gastronomy Tourism and Community Development* (pp. 1–16). IGI Global. DOI: 10.4018/979-8-3693-1814-0.ch001

Wang, H., Ma, S., Dai, H.-N., Imran, M., & Wang, T. (2020). Blockchain-based data privacy management with Nudge theory in open banking. *Future Generation Computer Systems*, *110*, 812–823. DOI: 10.1016/j.future.2019.09.010

Wang, L., Luo, X., & Lee, F. (2019). Unveiling the interplay between blockchain and loyalty program participation: A qualitative approach based on Bubichain. *International Journal of Information Management*, *49*, 397–410. DOI: 10.1016/j.ijinfomgt.2019.08.001

Yadav, A. S., Charles, V., Pandey, D. K., Gupta, S., Gherman, T., & Kushwaha, D. S. (2023). Blockchain-based secure privacy-preserving vehicle accident and insurance registration. *Expert Systems with Applications*, *230*, 120651. DOI: 10.1016/j.eswa.2023.120651

Yeh, K.-H. (2018). A Secure Transaction Scheme With Certificateless Cryptographic Primitives for IoT-Based Mobile Payments. *IEEE Systems Journal*, *12*(2), 2027–2038. DOI: 10.1109/JSYST.2017.2668389

Chapter 11
Risks, Challenges, and Ethical Considerations in Tokenized Economic Systems

Virender Singh Thakur
https://orcid.org/0009-0003-8947-7517
Chandigarh University, India

Akanksha Kaushik
https://orcid.org/0009-0000-1688-8727
Chandigarh University, India

ABSTRACT

Tokenized economic systems, powered by blockchain and distributed ledger technologies, are reshaping ownership, finance, and governance through digital tokens representing assets, rights, or value. While offering transparency, efficiency, and new economic models, these systems introduce significant risks—technical vulnerabilities, market volatility, regulatory gaps, and governance flaws. Ethical concerns such as exclusion, manipulation, environmental harm, and lack of accountability are also prevalent. Through analysis of token types, systemic risks, and real-world failures (e.g., TerraUSD, The DAO, OpenSea), this chapter highlights both the promise and pitfalls of token economies. It proposes principles for responsible tokenization—including transparency, equity, sustainability, and hybrid governance—supported by interdisciplinary collaboration. The chapter aims to guide developers, regulators, and researchers in building resilient, ethical, and inclusive digital economies.

DOI: 10.4018/979-8-3373-3371-7.ch011

1. INTRODUCTION

The way money is handled and financial systems work, is being transformed like never before. Recently, the rise of tokenized economic systems has been made possible by blockchain and distributed ledger technologies (DLT). With these systems, digital tokens stand in for real-world assets and allow for exchange, decision-making and value trading, all done without a central authority. Because of this, the ecosystems are drastically changing ownership, investment and supervision methods, giving hope for future value systems based on transparency, decentralization and inclusion (Buterin, 2014; Tapscott & Tapscott, 2016).

What is attractive about tokenization is that it can give equal access to capital, cut out middlemen and improve how transactions happen. A token on a blockchain network allows you to own part of artwork, real estate or business shares, trade them and oversee their use. This method leads to cost savings as well as allows more countries to participate in markets they could not join before (OECD, 2020). Even so, there are a lot of big challenges tied to these benefits. Tokenized systems have also created different types of risks which include issues with technology, changing regulations and conflicts related to privacy, fairness and environmental impact (Zetzsche, Buckley, & Arner, 2020).

We can observe the need for attention to these issues by observing the collapse of TerraUSD (UST), the DAO hack and issues with NFTs on platforms such as OpenSea. Such major incidents have shown the weaknesses of current tokenization schemes and revealed reasons why centralized structures cannot be fully trusted (Goforth, 2021).

This chapter carefully looks at tokenized economic systems, including their main workings, the problems they may bring and the ethical issues that arise. Using perspectives from computer science, law, ethics and economics, we want to provide an in-depth look and practical tools to guide the development of responsible, equitable and sustainable token economies.

2. UNDERSTANDING TOKENIZATION

Tokenization happens when any properties of an asset such as ownership, are assigned to a digital token on a distributed ledger. They may be used to show ownership of assets, for example, money, land, inventions, stocks or roles in governance. Because of tokenized economies, ownership can now be programmed, records are permanent and transactions are automatic, so finance and exchange are no longer the same as before (Catalini & Gans, 2016).

2.1 Overview of the Types of Tokens

The token economy has many types of tokens and every token differs in its features, requirements under the law and how it is used.

Utility Tokens act as tickets that let you use an application or service in the blockchain. Some cryptocurrencies developed for these purposes are Golem (GNT) for computing and Filecoin (FIL) for storage (Narayanan et al., 2016).

Security Tokens are like share or bond offerings and must usually follow securities rules. These tokens are helpful during Security Token Offerings (STOs), as mentioned by Goforth (2021).

These tokens have real-world tie-ups with items like real estate, precious metals or different commodities (OECD, 2020).

An NFT is a special kind of asset that cannot be broken up, so we often see them used for digital art, gaming items or intellectual property (Tapscott & Tapscott, 2016).

Having a Governance Token means users can join in or influence governance in decentralized protocols (Binance Research, 2021).

All types of tokens affect regulatory compliance, the market's behavior and the way users use them in various ways.

The main features of tokenized systems are explained below.

There are a number of basic principles that define tokenized systems:

- In decentralization, everyone participating in the network is equal in managing and operating it instead of a single central figure (World Economic Forum, 2020).
- They allow programmers to automate functions like voting, dividing royalties and issuing new tokens (Buterin, 2014).
- Because the ledger on blockchain is public, anyone can look at the transactions, making the industry more trustworthy (Coin Center, 2022).
- Connected Access: Many token systems are built so that they can work together across different platforms and worlds (Allen et al., 2020).
- Tokens are given out as rewards to motivate people to take part in activities such as protocols or network checking (Catalini & Gans, 2016).

2.2 There are many benefits and opportunities involved.

Tokenization has several good sides:

- Making it easier for people to start investing (World Bank, 2022).
- Helping to make markets where trading tends to be low more liquid (OECD, 2020).

- Making the system less dependent on middlemen (Tapscott & Tapscott, 2016).
- Working to make sure that underserved communities can get access to financial services (Giudici, Milne, & Vinogradov, 2020).
- Helping to create innovative ways for people to make money online, like play-to-earn and decentralized finance schemes (Zetzsche, Buckley, & Arner, 2020).

3. RISK LANDSCAPE IN TOKENIZED ECONOMIES

There are many dangers associated with tokenized economies and they come from technological, financial, regulatory, organizational and general system risks. If these problems are not taken care of, it could endanger the acceptance, maintenance and survival of decentralized ecosystems. It is important for researchers, policymakers and developers to know and understand this landscape when building ethical and strong platforms.

3.1 Technological Risks

Smart Contract Vulnerabilities

Tokenized systems are built on smart contracts which do transactions and governance without needing intermediaries. Nonetheless such contracts are susceptible to coding problems, wrong assumptions and security problems. A significant instance is the "The DAO" hack in 2016 using a recursive call which caused about $60 million in Ether to be taken and led to Ethereum being divided into Ethereum and Ethereum Classic (Siegel, 2016; Zetzsche et al., 2020).

It is almost impossible to change a smart contract's function even when serious errors are discovered after deployment. This leads to a conflict between the expectation for transparency and the occasional need for someone to control the network (Buterin, 2014).

Security Weakness Exploits and Hacking

Because of weak cryptography, careless key handling and skipped security reviews, token platforms are breached often. Events like the 2022 Ronin Network hack, where over $625 million was stolen from Axie Infinity, clearly show that blockchain networks can be easily attacked if proper security measures are not taken (Chainalysis, 2022).

Risks are greater for custodial wallets, bridges and oracles. Although crypto networks are meant to be decentralized, relying on centralized components can cause the whole system to fail (Narayanan et al., 2016).

Networks Can Become Overloaded and are Not Scalable

Networks like Ethereum may slow down, transactions may fail and gas fees can surge when a lot of people use them at the same time for NFT drops or yield farming. Ethereum has experienced issues with being able to process transactions fast enough, so new Layer-2 protocols are being developed and the move to proof-of-stake consensus has been made (Wood, 2022). Issues like these badly affect user experience and weaken the system's ability to be trusted.

3.2 Financial and Economic Risks

There can be market changes due to manipulation and actors trying to benefit from trading.

These markets are very unstable, mainly because of speculation, similar decisions by many and the lack of sufficient liquidity in a lot of altcoins. Social media opinions, when famous people promote a product or when several traders make similar trades can all change prices greatly (Giudici et al., 2020). Because Bitcoin, Ethereum and smaller tokens frequently rise or fall in value, they are no longer reliable for saving money.

A lot of NFT markets are affected by practices like pump-and-dump and wash trading. Because token markets are unregulated, these practices can happen with few legal consequences (Goforth, 2021).

Concerns about liquidity and being unable to exit an investment work against bonds.

Buyers and sellers for smaller tokens are often rare which leads to problems when processing trades as prices can fluctuate a lot. Because protocol tokens are hard to liquidate, investors face high exit risk when the market is weak or if the protocol experiences technical issues. What happened to Bitconnect and many "rug pulls" in DeFi reveals that liquidity can disappear instantly (Zetzsche et al., 2020).

Speculative Bubbles

In both 2017 and 2021, the increase in popularity of ICOs and NFTs was mostly about hype and not about their actual worth. In these situations, investors who joined these projects sometimes ended up with tokens that were not useful (Tapscott & Tapscott, 2016). It is similar to other financial manias when promises are made that cannot be met and then things collapse rapidly.

3.3 Legal and Regulatory Risks

Regulatory Arbitrage and Ambiguity

Issuers of tokens usually set up shop in places with light regulation, taking advantage of the difference in laws (Allen et al., 2020). Because of regulatory arbitrage, it becomes more difficult to enforce laws and protect investors. Since standards are missing when categorizing if a token is a security, commodity or utility, countries have taken different approaches (Goforth, 2021).

Putting rules like the EU's MiCA Regulation in place aims to solve the ambiguity, but it is still far off for the entire world (European Union, 2023).

AML and KYC Compliance Gaps

Because they do not always apply KYC and AML rules such platforms are attractive to illegal activity. The U.S. Department of the Treasury says that DeFi protocols could be used for money laundering and other illegal activities (FinCEN, 2021). If businesses do not have on-chain compliance, regulators could place major restrictions or outlaw these activities entirely.

Unclear Legal Recourse

Where cases of fraud, hacking or failure in governance occur, users have few or no legal rights to protect them. For example, as DAOs are unrecognized legal entities in most areas, it makes contract enforcement and liability much harder (Zetzsche et al., 2020).

3.4 Governance and Organizational Risks

Centralization of Power in Decentralized Systems

While claiming to decentralize, most of these platforms are still influenced by a small group of developers or early investors who control the governance tokens. Because this governance is centralized, the system does not support democratic participation and could face issues like corruption, censorship or people making decisions for personal gain (Coin Center, 2022).

Governance Tokens Being Held by Few

If whales hold a big number of governance tokens, they can warp voting to benefit their own needs. Under this plutocratic model, minority voices become less important and the community may become less unified (according to Gans in 2019).

Different Protocol Versions and Splitting

When disagreements happen, those differences may cause a hard fork which splits the blockchain into rival networks. The disagreement between Ethereum and Ethereum Classic and later the Bitcoin Cash forks, demonstrate that community disputes can both harm cryptocurrency networks and cause users confusion (Buterin, 2014).

3.5 Operational and Infrastructure Risks

Custodial Failures

Many third-party wallets and centralized crypto exchanges hold the funds of their users. Any problems with managing or protecting these custodians can be disastrous. The cases of Mt. Gox and FTX going bust in 2022 underline the ongoing threat of trusting custodial businesses (Narayanan et al., 2016).

Errors from users and cases where mistakes cannot be fixed

Because transactions are permanent on the blockchain, anything done mistakenly cannot be corrected. When money is sent to the wrong place or the contract is not properly set up, those funds cannot be recovered which results in permanent losses (OECD, 2020).

Interoperability Failures

Using different blockchains and decentralized finance (DeFi) protocols can lead to failed transactions, assets that are locked up and challenging ways to get them back. These bridging technologies are not fully developed and are frequently targeted by people trying to steal funds (Chainalysis, 2022).

3.6 Systemic and Contagion Risks

Protocol Interdependence and Domino Failures

DeFi platforms are strongly connected. An incident in any one—because of a loophole, insolvency or incorrect setup—can start a chain of issues with liquidity, loans and farming. A clear example of this was the Terra ecosystem collapse in 2022 which strongly affected Anchor and Mirror Protocol (World Bank, 2022).

Stablecoin De-Pegging

Stablecoins which are meant to provide liquidity, can become unstable and lose their peg if the underlying systems are not reliable or have not been backed up properly. When TerraUSD (UST) collapsed, it made investors everywhere fearful and this resulted in the loss of over $40 billion in cryptocurrencies (Zetzsche et al., 2020).

Falling reputation and losing trust from others

Problems such as scandals, rug pulls or government actions against big projects make people doubt blockchain as well as the platforms involved. For instance, the FTX scandal led to people asking for greater regulation in crypto and this even reached unrelated projects in the European Union (2023).

Conclusion

There are many risks involved in tokenized economies and those risks keep changing over time. Whether caused by fraudulent trades or failures of the system, each risk points out the importance of better technical rules, governance procedures and clear laws. Since we are using more token-based technology, it is important to plan for and address issues in a way that helps both advancement and security.

4. ETHICAL DILEMMAS AND SOCIAL CHALLENGES

With financial and organizational models being reshaped by tokenized systems, serious ethical dilemmas are introduced. They are not limited to issues like faulty technology or rules—people are also concerned with who gets what, users' personal rights, environmental protection and how these are managed. To prevent token-based breakthroughs from making things worse, these concerns must be addressed (Zetzsche et al., 2020; Goforth, 2021).

4.1 Equity, Access, and Inclusion

Digital Exclusion and the Global Divide

Getting involved in tokenized economy means users must be digital literate, online most of the time and understand blockchain tools and these resources are not evenly available everywhere. Some rural or low-income people may not have the facilities or understanding needed to make use of digital currencies, making the digital divide an even bigger problem (OECD, 2020).

But making things difficult for non-technical users by using technical words, complex setup procedures and unstable interfaces is also a problem. Because of these problems, women, the elderly and uneducated individuals are less likely to join in with what is often seen as a democratizing innovation (as stated by the World Bank, 2022).

Having a lot of wealth and operating early on allows a company to succeed

Contrary to what decentralization implies, most of the wealth and influence in token economies remains with early investors, venture capitalists and the people who build the platforms. Whales get hold of a lot of crypto through airdrops, mining and access to pre-sale rounds before the public can pitch in (Allen et al., 2020).

Therefore, finance in Web3 can mirror a system where the rich have the biggest influence in making decisions (Coin Center, 2022).

4.2 Privacy and Surveillance Risks

Pseudonymity vs. Anonymity

It is common for blockchain networks not to show the real names of those who use them, but just their wallet addresses. Still, everything done through a crypto wallet is recorded in public ledgers, so it can be traced in the future. Should identity be linked to the information, it may lead to focused surveillance, unfair treatment or being barred from some things (Narayanan et al., 2016).

On one hand, this transparency leads to more accountability; on the other hand, people lose their financial privacy and some control over their accounts. For instance, people who try to use blockchain for economic deals could be traced by harmful groups or regimes (FinCEN, 2021).

Consent and who owns the data

As decentralized identification (tokenized ID) becomes more common, questions arise about who owns a user's data, how data is given access and whether people can choose to not participate. Data-driven smart contracts may make transfers or change access rules without having specific consent in place. Because of this, personal privacy is undermined and new opportunities for abuse are created (Goforth, 2021).

4.3 Manipulation, Addiction, and Behavioral Engineering

Gamification and Compulsive Engagement

Using gamification such as points, levels, rewards and streaks is common in token-based systems to capture users' attention. Although these mechanics help gain participation, they may use tactics from behavioral psychology. Users of Axie Infinity and other play-to-earn platforms sometimes reported becoming addicted, playing for long periods and spending lots of money, but they didn't raise much token revenue (Chainalysis, 2022).

Using psychological triggers in gamification might result in more young people or people with limited money becoming addicted which raises ethical issues about exploitation, according to Giudici et al. (2020).

Problems of incentives and Ponzi-style structures

High rewards in certain protocols (staking and liquidity mining) tend to attract people seeking fast returns, not those wanting to build value over the long term. Applying these mechanisms may cause interest rates to rise or fall unexpectedly. Because TerraUSD was using an unsustainable yield protocol called Anchor, luring users with promises of high returns, its tokenomics turned out to be vulnerable (Zetzsche et al., 2020).

They are much like Ponzi schemes, where money to pay early users comes from the contribution of new investors. Once markets turn against these investments, the systems quickly fail and leave those who got in last with major losses.

4.4 Governance, Accountability, and Transparency

DAO Governance and the Myth of Democracy

Many people see Decentralized Autonomous Organizations (DAOs) as models of democracy. Even so, having more tokens in the system allows the wealthy to have a bigger impact during governance, according to Gans (2019). It conflicts with the important idea of decentralized participation.

It is not always easy for people to access or understand how rules are made. Most proposals are written using technical jargon and the menus for voting are not easy for all users. This situation makes it hard for people to participate and it questions the fairness and equality of these processes (Binance Research, 2021).

No Systematic Legal or Ethical Oversight

In older organizations, ethics committees, the legal team or ombudspersons may deal with ethical breaches. There is less clarity in who is held accountable in a DAO. When issues occur such as treasury theft or a breach in the protocol, it remains uncertain who is responsible and how things can be settled (as Goforth describes in 2021).

Developers and founders of protocols usually have a significant effect, even though they claim to be neutral. Interventions in the system such as delaying smart contracts, adjusting how tokens are designed or going against community decisions, often make people doubt the project (Tapscott & Tapscott, 2016).

4.5 Environmental Sustainability

Energy Consumption

It takes a large amount of energy to operate proof-of-work (PoW) blockchains, including Bitcoin. Cambridge Bitcoin Electricity Consumption Index shows that Bitcoin mining uses as much power annually as countries like Argentina. This causes us to worry about the effect tokenized systems have on the environment (Narayanan et al., 2016).

Ethereum now uses a PoS method that uses much less energy, yet a lot of older blockchains and systems stick with PoW. It stresses that we need to switch to better consensus mechanisms for ethical reasons.

The issues associated with E-Waste and tiny cellphones are E-Waste and the problem of fewer minerals.

Because their profitability ends quickly, many companies toss out their mining equipment after using it. This increases electronic waste and reduces the availability of rare earth minerals, adding more stress on the environment as related to blockchain (OECD, 2020).

4.6 Moral Hazard and Exploitation of Hype

Unregulated Promotion and Influencer Risk

Anyone can issue tokens and offer new projects in a decentralized system, usually with little government regulation. Occasionally, social media influencers take money from project founders to generate hype about the launch which can be misleading to users. Usually, these promotions come without warnings or overpromise rewards which leads to people basing their investment decisions on wrong information (European Union, 2023).

Many pump-and-dump schemes happen when insiders hype and then sell their own tokens at a high price. The result for retail investors, on the other hand, is worthless assets and profits for promoters, showing an ethical problem in the way the market operates (Chainalysis, 2022).

Laws have a hard time catching up with new innovations since they are moving rapidly.

DeFi and NFT growth happens so fast that it usually prevents anyone from considering ethics. Projects are set up in just a few days which means there is little time for testing and reviewing impacts. The approach, passed down from Silicon Valley, where developers swiftly release their work without deep testing, goes against the potentially very high stakes of such economies (Allen et al., 2020).

Token projects may not realize the damage their behavioral choices cause until harm to society, the environment or users is already extensive.

Conclusion

Dealing with ethics in tokenized systems directly affects how the ecosystem acts, endures and is seen as legitimate. Developers, regulators and researchers are being challenged by inequality, monitoring, manipulation and harm to the environment to look at innovation from an ethical standpoint. We should control technology, so it serves both human worth, ensures social justice and results in sustainable growth long-term.

5. CASE STUDIES OF TOKENIZED SYSTEMS: LESSONS FROM PRACTICE

Experiences in the real economy have helped greatly improve theoretical ideas about tokenized systems. This section of case studies is meant to show how difficult decentralized technologies can be to manage, listing the successes as well as their failures. These cases support the risks, issues and ethical dilemmas mentioned earlier and also give helpful advice to developers, policy makers and researchers.

5.1 The DAO Hack (2016): Smart Contracts and Code Inflexibility

Background and Significance

The Decentralized Autonomous Organization (The DAO) went live on the Ethereum blockchain in April 2016 as a fund managed by its investors. In total, the campaign collected more than $150 million in Ether from 11,000 people which made it the biggest crowdfunding effort in history (Siegel, 2016).

Incident

Shortly after The DAO was launched, a hacker used a flaw called recursive call in the smart contract to take away one-third of the money. Because smart contracts can't change, the Ether taken by the attack could not be brought back without major intervention (Buterin, 2014).

Resolution and the Effect it Creates

The community behind Ethereum performed a hard fork which basically allowed them to edit the blockchain and bring back the compromised funds. The outcome of this choice was the development of two new blockchains, Ethereum (ETH) and Ethereum Classic (ETC). As a result of the fork, there was a lot of debating about how decentralized the network should be, what was ethically right and the boundaries of "code is law" (Zetzsche et al., 2020).

Key Lessons

- It is important to combine immutability with ways to fix issues.
- It is not optional to audit smart contracts and ensure they are formally verified.
- Governance actions should be built on legitimacy and the agreement of the wider community.

5.2 TerraUSD and the Collapse of Algorithmic Stablecoins (2022)

Background

TerraUSD (UST) is a kind of stablecoin that tried to keep a value equal to the dollar by doing bi-token transactions with LUNA. Nearly all DeFi platforms began using UST as it provided a stable means to engage in yield farming and adding liquidity especially because Anchor offered a 20% return (World Bank, 2022).

Incident

In May 2022, large numbers of people withdrawing from UST pools caused it to depart from being tied to the dollar. With everyone trying to sell UST for LUNA, the value of both tokens plunged as LUNA became severely over-valued. The fall in value removed around $40 billion from the sector and impacted millions of investors worldwide (2022, Chainalysis).

Key Lessons

Generally, those algorithmic pegs are not truly stable because they are not backed by anything.

High and unsustainable ways of farming make the system more at risk of failure.

Not revealing the information about reserves and how the project is governed causes users to lose trust.

5.3 Axie Infinity: Token Economies and Gamified Labor

Background

The blockchain game Axie Infinity by Sky Mavis popularized the idea of "playing to earn" money. By getting involved in the game, players could gather tokens such as Smooth Love Potion (SLP) and Axie Infinity Shards (AXS). Because of the COVID-19 pandemic, more people started using the platform, especially in developing countries such as the Philippines (Giudici et al., 2020).

Incident

As players increased, the game's financial resources could no longer support the player base. More SLP was being created than people wanted to buy, pushing down its prices. A lot of players, especially those who had advanced money to join, saw their earnings drop to virtually nothing. The Ronin bridge used for the game was hacked in March 2022, resulting in the loss of $625 million (Chainalysis, 2022).

Key Lessons

- Financialized video games can result in exploitative ways of getting players to work.
- Poorly designed tokens and token economics can threaten the entire system.
- Safeguarding infrastructure is very important on interconnected token platforms.

5.4 ConstitutionDAO: Collective Action and Legal Limitations

Background

On November 14, 2021, ConstitutionDAO tried to bid on the U.S. Constitution in a public auction. The goal was reached with $40 million in ETH collected from nearly 17,000 supporters. The original plan was to assign ownership by giving out governance tokens called $PEOPLE (Binance Research, 2021).

Incident

Because of high gas fees and not having a suitable legal structure, the DAO failed to return everyone's money after losing the auction. Some who provided funding had to spend more than they originally invested and a lot of people wondered why their $PEOPLE tokens were still important after the bid did not go through (Goforth, 2021).

Key Lessons

- It is important for DAOs to have well-formed policies for refunds, law and governance.
- Being discouraged by the fees involved and blockchain infrastructure may prevent some people from taking part.
- Hype-driven actions by groups should make use of achievable logistics.

5.5 OpenSea: Market Manipulation and Insider Trading

Background

OpenSea is the biggest NFT marketplace and was important in the rise of digital art and collectibles. It helped billions trade in NFTs and supported many artists and art lovers (OECD, 2020).

Incidents

It became known in 2021 that an employee at OpenSea had used insider information to purchase NFTs ahead of their placement on the homepage which is a clear example of front-running. When the company heard the allegations, it asked the employee to leave and made changes to their internal guidelines. The platform also came across continual problems caused by fake NFTs, infringement of IP and wash trading (European Union, 2023).

Key Lessons

- NFT markets can still suffer from traditional types of financial scams.
- Decentralized markets need platforms to be responsible and accountable.
- Legal guidance on who owns these cryptocurrencies and their security is instantaneously required.

Conclusion

They reveal two sides of what tokenized economies offer. Cases from the podcast highlight the importance of efficient oversight, as examples with innovative uses such as decentralized governance and algorithmic finance, might end in issues with ethics, finances or technology. Furthermore, these examples have shown that some aspects of regulation, monitoring and effect on society were missed by the authorities.

It is necessary for developers, regulators and communities to absorb these principles to encourage responsible development. Losing control in tech industries could mean users suffering, trust being broken and economic actions becoming unstable in the future.

6. TOWARD RESPONSIBLE TOKENIZATION

With more tokenized systems in the global digital economy, it becomes all the more important to regulate them properly. Because of the frequent risks and ethical problems, there is a need for systems that hold designers and regulators accountable, promote inclusion and enhance resilience. Responsible tokenization works to steer and shape innovation for outcomes that meet societal values and are good for the public in the long run (Allen et al., 2020; Zetzsche et al., 2020).

Guidelines, rules, regulatory approaches and technological tools are explained here for building responsible tokenized economies.

6.1 Principles for Ethical and Inclusive Token Design

1. **Transparency** For users to feel secure and take part, a company must be transparent. All projects have to clarify their token price model, introduce their team members, list the processes for community decisions and mention the dangers related to their project. This means code is open, it can be checked by the public and all documentation is clear (Buterin, 2014). Good transparency should apply to the way decisions are made. It is important for users to be able to check both past and current information on voting results, money movements and updates on the blockchain so they are well aware of how things are operating (OECD, 2020).
2. **Security by Design** Tokenized systems ought to be secure without configuration. It includes strict security tests on each smart contract, independent verification and looking over the system by outside security organizations. Bug bounty programs and modular architectures reduce the amount a system can be exploited and increase its strength (Narayanan et al., 2016). Steps for safety should be taken regarding wallets, bridges and user interfaces. Multi-signature signatures can be used instead of relying on one point of failure for important actions in the system (Chainalysis, 2022).
3. **Equity and Inclusion** Structural barriers to participation need to be dealt with directly in token economies. Interventions in design, for example: Using money distributors that help less popular users get involved. Changing the way people vote to lessen the influence of plutocrats, also known as quadratic voting. Onboarding for people living in regions with low income is subsidized. Promoting digital assets can offer equal access and give more authority to people in decision-making (Coin Center, 2022; Gans, 2019). It is also important that interfaces can be used in several languages and that educational resources are included during user journeys (World Bank, 2022).

4. **Sustainability** The design of systems has to take the environment into account. If proof-of-stake is used in consensus, smart contracts are built carefully and infrastructure is handled wisely, the ecological effect of blockchains can be reduced (Narayanan et al., 2016). High-traffic platforms should be offered the option of getting a lifecycle analysis and an energy audit. According to the OECD (Organisation for Economic Co-operation and Development), sustainability metrics may be shared with financial disclosures (OECD, 2020).
5. **User Autonomy and Privacy** Self-sovereign identity (SSI), along with zero-knowledge proofs (ZKPs) and selective disclosure protocols, helps users handle their own information. Consent systems need to be detailed, able to be withdrawn and confirmed by both parties (FinCEN, 2021). User transactions in a tokenized ID system ought to be separate from their personal ID unless users expressly agree to a link. By default, new blockchain protocols should keep privacy protection in mind, rather than seeing it as something optional (Goforth, 2021).

6.2 Ethical Governance Models for Tokenized Systems Hybrid Governance Structures

While these mechanisms offer visibility and automated processes, they are usually missing flexibility. Adding forums, working groups and advisory councils is a good way to increase how legitimate and thoroughly decisions are made (Binance Research, 2021).

A combination governance model supports:

- Responding to emergencies when protocol crises occur,
- More elaborate policy discussion than just occasional votes,
- Ways to appeal and deal with problems that arise from the outcomes (Zetzsche et al., 2020).
- Ethics Committees and Sub-DAOs work to set standards for the community.

It is important for token ecosystems to put ethics review systems in place. Ethics focused sub-DAOs or advisory groups can check new plans for risks to society, the environment or the system.

Besides experts in the field such bodies may also invite legal scholars, ethical specialists, economists and people from affected communities (Allen et al., 2020).

Getting Involved in the Local Community and Involving the Community

Users ought to be able to impact both how governance takes place and the rules by which it happens. Ways such as representing people by district, allowing public involvement in budgeting and involving citizens in deliberations can bring democracy to token economies (Coin Center, 2022).

Hosting workshops, collecting users' thoughts and organizing hackathons supports a culture of being open-minded and responsive.

6.3 Regulatory Engagement and Legal Harmonization

Proactive Regulatory Collaboration

Rather than avoiding accountability, token projects need to actively get involved with regulators to help design testing zones and sandboxes. Thanks to these managed settings, new ideas can be tried out as compliance systems are being tested (European Union, 2023).

Starting discussions early helps reduce legal issues and increases understanding between people working in technology and policymaking (Goforth, 2021).

Worldwide Guidelines for Categorizing Tokens

Standard bodies and regulators are advised to set up a common way of categorizing tokens (e.g., utility, security, governance, stablecoin). It would make it easier for both users and issuers to know their rights, who is liable and what needs to be disclosed (OECD, 2020).

Making rules on custody, KYC/AML compliance and investor protections the same across borders is important to stop regulatory arbitrage (FinCEN, 2021).

There are Mechanisms to Protect Consumers

Solutions such as these mentioned above, could be very effective for user protection in token websites.

It helps protect the business in case the internet or technology platform is down,

Dispute resolution policies that function automatically as well as those conducted by mediators.

Safer token sales and DAO voting require having several clearly outlined rules for refunds (Gans, 2019).

User contracts have to be understandable, available in several languages and enforceable in the relevant areas.

Changes in technology are needed together with improved governance and literacy for users to achieve as much risk reduction as possible (Narayanan et al., 2016).

6.5 Building Resilience through Education and Culture

Digital and Financial Literacy

Database platforms ought to contain educational pieces, for example:

- Handy instructions and tutorials displayed when needed,
- User experience levels determine the stages in their onboarding,
- Exercises that simulate main blockchain activities (such as voting and staking).

The cooperation between public and private sectors can help bring blockchain education into schools, universities and centers for the community (World Bank, 2022).

Always Be Careful and Do What is Right as an Entrepreneur

A builder shouldn't aim only at going quickly and raising market cap. Reflection and explicit attention to ethics should be a regular part of life in token ecosystems.

Particularly, founders and influencers are responsible in how they communicate about their products to others. Every project is expected to lay out and implement community codes of conduct (Coin Center, 2022).

Focusing Innovation on Benefiting the Public

Innovation in responsible tokenization should benefit others and not just earn profits; it should help by including, sustaining and developing communities.

Across organizations, things like promoting development of open-source software, educational efforts, green activities and helping communities can be rewarded by creating new incentives (Tapscott & Tapscott, 2016).

6.6 The Role of Interdisciplinary Collaboration

Problems associated with tokenized systems affect the technical, social, legal and environmental fields simultaneously. Solving these cannot be done by only one discipline. Moving forward into a responsible future, token economies require a long-term and systemic effort from:

- Those dealing with computer systems (systems architecture, safety),
- Experts who study the law (jurisdiction, liability, what is regulated).
- Theories of Ethicists and Philosophers (equity, power, autonomy).
- Economists (regarding incentives and the stability of markets).
- Environmental scientists (how we use energy and support sustainability).

Creating research groups, policy labs and ethics boards among universities allows them to share knowledge and look after collective interests (Allen et al., 2020).

To sum up the section

What matters most for the future of tokenized economic systems are the principles, structures and cultures behind them, more than only technological improvements. If we focus on being transparent, employ ethical design, practice inclusion and make things more sustainable, we will upgrade from just trying new things to making change that counts online.

Tokenization should not repeat the inequalities in current systems, but rather introduce a new way focused on the good of the public. Achieving that goal calls for planning, professionals from different fields and a group effort to help everyone benefit from the economy.

7. CONCLUSION AND FUTURE OUTLOOK

Tokens in the economy play a key role in digital transformation by proposing innovative ways to deal with value, control and management in the 21st century. Such changes, from programmable things to decentralized organizations, could make the economy less centralized, let more liquidity flow and allow people to be involved in new types of economic acts. Still, it is clear from the chapter that there are many risks that come with such potential: technological, financial, regulatory and ethical in nature.

7.1 Synthesis of Key Findings

It began by giving an overview of the basic technologies and varieties of tokens which include utility, governance and non-fungible assets. Beyond that, we outlined the risks faced by blockchain by identifying weaknesses in smart contracts, the unstable nature of crypto-assets and since regulations may change, all of which can reduce trust and stability (Narayanan et al., 2016; OECD, 2020).

The situations discussed—including issues involving wealth concentration, surveillance, environmental damage and changes in behavior—show that tokenized systems can also perpetuate or magnify the disadvantages found in traditional systems (Zetzsche et al., 2020; Goforth, 2021).

Examples used in the courses like The DAO, TerraUSD, Axie Infinity, ConstitutionDAO and OpenSea made it clear what went wrong and what consequences these failures had. Such events underline the importance of having guidelines in place that address ethics, equity, openness and anticipate new rules in the creation of token systems (Chainalysis, 2022; World Bank, 2022).

For this reason, we structured a multidimensional framework covering the security and transparency of design, allowing communities to shape decision-making, being involved in regulatory efforts and encouraging various experts to collaborate. They exist to guarantee that token economies are advanced, accessible, ongoing and able to cope with challenges.

7.2 The Road Ahead: Trends and Strategic Priorities

The future course of tokenized economies will be set by how successfully stakeholders deal with a series of challenges and possibilities. You are likely to see five major themes guide the new phase of evolution.

1. **Regulatory Maturation and Harmonization** Groups from both the national and international levels are stepping up actions to oversee digital assets. The EU's MiCA Regulation and the SEC's activities in the U.S. are helping to define exactly what are the rights and obligations of tokens (European Union, 2023; FinCEN, 2021). Moving ahead, successful token economies should make sure their procedures are in line with regulations, include features required by law and allow cross-border legal operations (Goforth, 2021).
2. **Institutional Adoption and Integration** Major financial players, technology companies and governments are looking into token-based innovations, ranging from central bank digital currencies (CBDCs) to security tokens and technologies for checking the movement of goods in supply chains. From these developments, it is clear that token economies will cooperate with, rather than replace, traditional infrastructure (OECD, 2020). So, attention should be given to interoperability, auditability and standardization during the design process to make tokens suitable for use by enterprises and governments.
3. **Ethical and Inclusive Innovation** Token systems in the future should focus on protecting people's dignity and what matters to the public. This includes: • Creating ways for everyone to be included and have similar rights, • Including environmental sustainability in the way core infrastructure works, • Helping give marginalized people more input in the political process (Allen et al., 2020; Coin Center, 2022). With no proper priorities, tokenization might lead to new digital colonization and algorithmic abuse.
4. **Decentralized Identity and Data Autonomy** As SSI systems and token technology progress, users will get to decide how much personal info they share in each platform. With all these changes, there is likely to be a shift in understanding digital citizenship, who owns data and reputation-related matters (FinCEN, 2021; Tapscott & Tapscott, 2016). Ensuring privacy and consent, so that no one

is spied on or abused, should be more important than allowing surveillance and deceit.

5. **Cultural Shifts and the Ethics of Design** People need to stop paying attention mainly to short-term speculation and hype and focus more on building lasting value and responsible stewardship. Anyone involved in web3 should value care, reflection and community more than making quick profits and acting alone (Gans, 2019; World Bank, 2022).

Just like the open-source community changed software, a commitment to ethics in tokenization can drive stable digital economies based on working together.

7.3 Final Reflections

Having tokenized economic systems appear means we now face major chances and important duties. Because digital tokens are now part of financial, social and political systems, we are called upon to consider basic questions:

- What decisions are made about who can use and receive the wealth?
- Which principles direct the way systems are designed or managed?
- What makes sure people are held accountable in decentralized societies?
- How does the way nations and regions govern themselves affect digital developments?

The chapter has tried to offer a guide to address these issues in a clear and ethical way. The purpose is to help innovation thrive, so our systems support justice, sustainability and happiness.

Tokenization can happen by accident and it is not always a positive thing. What the internet achieves will be determined by the ideas it contains, the rules that follow it and the people who use it.

REFERENCES

Allen, D. W., Berg, C., Markey-Towler, B., Novak, M., & Potts, J. (2020). Blockchain and the evolution of institutional technologies. *Research Policy*, *49*(1), 103865. DOI: 10.1016/j.respol.2019.103865

Binance Research. (2021). An Overview of Decentralized Governance. https://research.binance.com

Buterin, V. (2014). A Next-Generation Smart Contract and Decentralized Application Platform. Ethereum White Paper.

Chainalysis. (2022). Crypto Crime Report. https://www.chainalysis.com

Coin Center. (2022). Decentralization: Why It Matters. https://www.coincenter.org

European Union. (2023). Markets in Crypto-Assets (MiCA) Regulation. European Parliament.

FinCEN. (2021). *Advisory on Illicit Finance Risks of Decentralized Finance*. U.S. Department of the Treasury.

Gans, J. (2019). The Case for an ICO Contract. *Journal of Institutional and Theoretical Economics*, *175*(1), 34–51.

Giudici, G., Milne, A., & Vinogradov, D. (2020). Cryptocurrencies: Market analysis and perspectives. *Economia e Politica Industriale*, *47*(1), 1–18. DOI: 10.1007/s40812-019-00138-6

Goforth, C. (2021). Token Regulation and the Challenges of Classification. *Fordham Journal of Corporate & Financial Law*, *26*(2), 197–239.

Narayanan, A., Bonneau, J., Felten, E., Miller, A., & Goldfeder, S. (2016). *Bitcoin and Cryptocurrency Technologies*. Princeton University Press.

OECD. (2020). *The Tokenisation of Assets and Potential Implications for Financial Markets*. OECD Blockchain Policy Series.

Siegel, D. (2016). *Understanding the DAO Attack*. Coindesk.

Tapscott, D., & Tapscott, A. (2016). *Blockchain Revolution: How the Technology Behind Bitcoin is Changing Money, Business, and the World*. Penguin.

World Bank. (2022). Digital Economy for Development. https://www.worldbank.org

Zetzsche, D. A., Buckley, R. P., & Arner, D. W. (2020). Decentralized Finance (DeFi). *Journal of Financial Regulation*, *6*(2), 172–203. DOI: 10.1093/jfr/fjaa010

Chapter 12
Risks, Challenges, and Ethical Considerations in Tokenized Systems:
Supplementary Illustrative Indigenous Case Study

Shahinaz Hanem (Sherry) Rashad Sayed Abdellatif
https://orcid.org/0009-0005-1528-1567
University Canada West, Canada

Larry Earnhart
https://orcid.org/0009-0005-2377-1814
University Canada West, Canada

Jack E. Smith
University Canada West, Canada

Bismark Addai
https://orcid.org/0000-0003-0550-5983
University Canada West, Canada

ABSTRACT

Blockchain technology has disrupted traditional business models through tokenization. Tokenized systems offer opportunities while presenting risks and challenges for global investors. This chapter critically examines the risks, challenges, and ethical considerations in tokenized systems. It analyzes risks, such as financial, liquidity, market, operational, fraud, and cybersecurity risks. Further, it addresses constraints related to blockchain networks, adoption, scalability, sustainability, and governance,

DOI: 10.4018/979-8-3373-3371-7.ch012

including the integration of artificial intelligence (AI). The chapter also evaluates ethical concerns related to tokenization, such as algorithmic bias, data privacy, accountability, and sustainability. To address these critical issues, it proposes a conceptual framework and concludes with policy insights and an outlook to guide the ethical and responsible adoption of tokenized systems globally and within indigenized contexts. This discussion is further illustrated through an Indigenous-focused case study, framed by the lens of "two-eyed seeing", as presented in Annex Chapter 12.

1. INTRODUCTION

Blockchain technology reshaped the global economic and financial landscape and disrupted businesses through tokenization (Stability Board, 2024). As shown in Figure 1, tokenized systems provide several opportunities and challenges to global investors. Recently, there has been a wide acceptance of tokenized systems across both conventional and Islamic markets (Mousavi et al.,2025), in terms of fractionalization and partial ownership of high-value assets like real estate. The potential of blockchain technology to provide value in achieving various social impacts has been widely discussed. The benefits range from assisting vulnerable populations to global supply chains (Barclay, I., Cooper, M., Hackel, J., & Perrin, P., 2022).

While tokenized systems are potentially transformative for conventional and Islamic financial markets, there are numerous challenges and risks associated with their introduction and full utilization (Financial Stability Board, 2024). There are many barriers to adoption, including a lack of regulation, fast-paced changes in technology, and overall organizational resistance. In addition, technological vulnerability is demonstrated by cyberattacks and theft (Chainalysis 2025; La Morgia et al. 2023), while scalability issues currently restrict wide-scale application (Deval et al., 2024; Li et al., 2024). Proof of ownership of tokenized assets is a problem, especially where there is an existing system that is legally accepted. Questions of market manipulation and volatility of the assets prevent acceptance as well (Briola et al., 2023; Liu et al., 2023). There are other concerns, including governance, environmental sustainability, indigenization, and integration of artificial intelligence (Mulligan, et al., 2024; Upadhyay, 2020).

Figure 1. Opportunities, risks, challenges and ethical considerations frameworks for tokenized systems

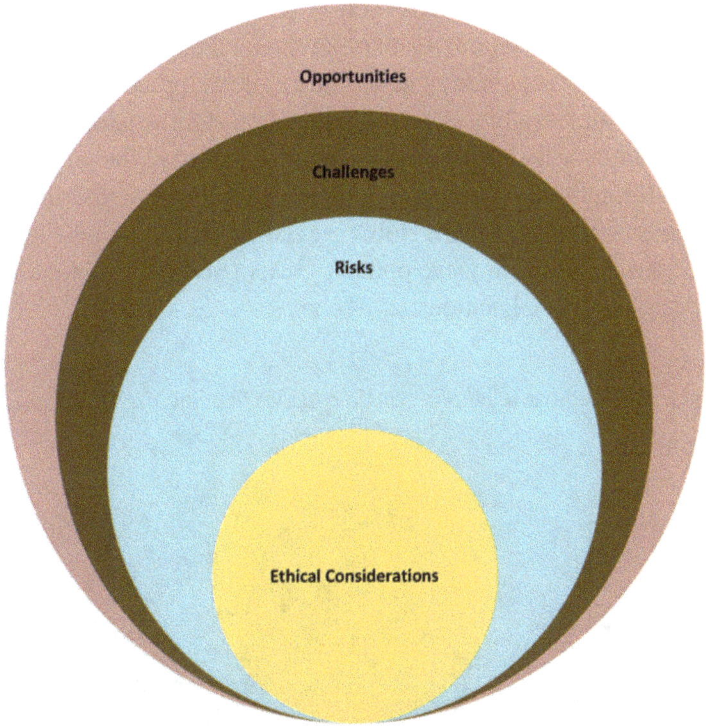

Chapter 12 aims to investigate the risks, challenges, and ethical concerns in tokenized systems as illustrated in the conceptual RCE framework for Tokenized Systems in Figure 2. At the beginning of this chapter, the key risks associated with tokenization are analysed, such as financial risks, liquidity risks, security risks, fraud, Environmental, Social, Governance (ESG) risks, as well as regulatory and compliance risks and other types of risks (Zhang et al., 2024; BIS, 2023). Those risks are analysed in terms of the complexity of enforcing anti-money laundering (AML) and Know Your Customer (KYC) regulations, and the lack of standardized legal frameworks across jurisdictions (Financial Stability Board, 2024).

Next, the chapter critically examines the challenges in implementing tokenized systems in terms of adoption barriers, technical complexities, and scalability issues related to blockchain networks and tokenized systems (Dehghani et al., 2022; Zhang, Tavalaei, and Parry, 2024).

Third, the chapter addresses the contemporary trends and ethical considerations regarding the integration of AI with blockchain in tokenized systems and the ethical concerns in terms of algorithmic bias and data privacy concerns (Abdellatif,

2025). This chapter also highlights the ethical implications of innovative financial structures, such as decentralized finance (DeFi) and tokenized crowdfunding. It also addresses ethical considerations such as sustainability and governance in an indigenized context (First Nations Technology Council, 2021; Mousavi et al., 2021).

Finally, this chapter concludes with a future outlook, practical insights, and policy recommendations from multilateral organizations for the adoption of tokenized systems. The chapter provides solutions to mitigate the risks, challenges, and ethical considerations through transparent technology design and implementation, risk mitigation strategies, compliance with global regulations, and responsible governance that promote the Sustainable Development Goals (SDG) and Economic, Social, Governance (ESG) (United Nations, 2024)

Figure 2. risks, challenges and ethical considerations frameworks for tokenized systems

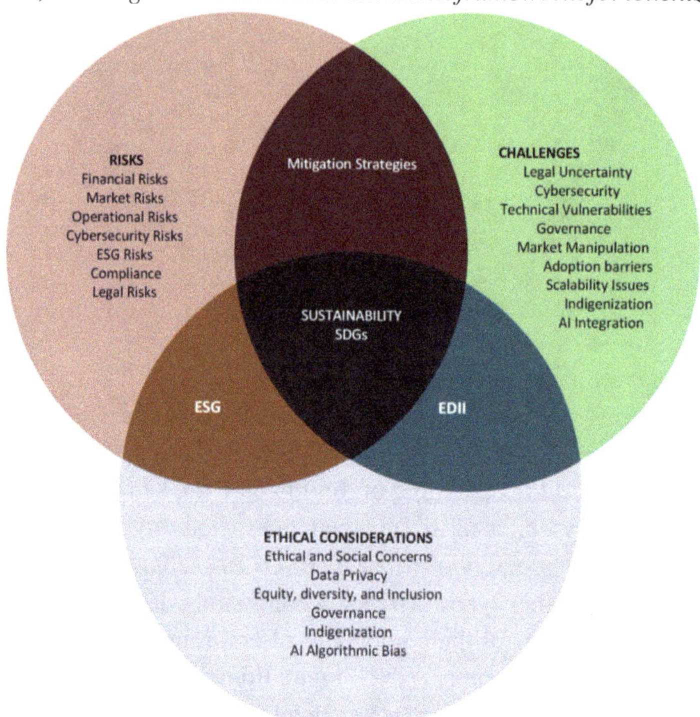

2. RISKS IN TOKENIZED SYSTEMS

Tokenization introduces a new set of risks, necessitating the development of new risk management tools and the re-evaluation of existing ones. Real and digital assets can be represented in a distributed ledger through tokenization. This unlocks tremendous potential for efficiency gains through a faster settlement, fractional ownership, and expanded market access. At the same time, distributed, borderless, and asset-class value transfer in tokenized systems has implications for an equally distributed and complex set of risks that cut across finance, technology, and regulation.

The risks of a tokenized system are likely to be more systemic in nature and magnified by the distributed and borderless nature of the underlying technology, as well as the speed and transparency of blockchain transactions, which can make shocks more immediately visible and amplify them across markets (Zhang et al., 2024; BIS, 2023). Regulators and market participants alike thus face the urgent need for a coherent risk framework that is not purely derived from a legacy "off-chain" mindset or the existing infrastructure, but instead adequately balances financial stability considerations and decentralized cross-border infrastructures and the risks that they present. This is especially true for tokenized finance, as decentralized finance (DeFi) challenges many existing risk-related assumptions about traditional asset ownership, investor protection, and systemic contagion channels.

2.1. Financial Risks

Endemic to tokenized systems endures financial risks, including valuation volatility, counterparty default, and collateral instability. Valuation of many tokens is imperfect, and liquidity, concentration, and basis risks are compounded by many market and protocol participants taking highly leveraged positions in the same underlying assets. A complete unwinding of trust and sudden, massive devaluation of TerraUSD (UST), a decentralized algorithmic stablecoin, occurred in May 2022, exposing crypto-asset markets to large and systemic financial risk (Briola et al., 2023; Liu et al., 2023). In this case, a highly leveraged DeFi lending market combined with automatic liquidation mechanisms effectively triggers large and rapid downdrafts in the price of associated assets. A further related risk arises from the fact that tokens generally trade across a combination of on- and off-chain markets. In the absence of a central clearinghouse or central bank of the last resort as a liquidity provider, shocks from one market can cascade more easily into another. Thus, the underlying combination of leverage, automation, and fragmentation represents a powerful source of innovation and a point of systemic fragility (Badev & Watsky, 2023; Carapella, F., Swem, N., & Gerszten, J., 2023).

2.2. Liquidity risks

Tokenization is often discussed as a significant liquidity enabler, especially for real assets. However, the market depth for several tokenized assets remains low and can suffer from sudden drawdowns in market-making capital during stressful periods. The price impact is significant due to volatility (Moncada, et al., 2024), especially for institutional adoption, which is further hindered by low turnover, order-book fragmentation, and the absence of two-sided markets (International Monetary Fund, 2025).

This is especially true for tokens that represent privately issued or otherwise niche assets, where the effective cost of unwinding a position is especially high. Additionally, liquidity provision in tokenized markets is typically dominated by a small set of Automated Market Makers (AMMs) or exchanges. Liquidity can also be withdrawn from these tokens if the provision is solely algorithmic, such as through AMM liquidity pools, and rapid changes in the token price can drain liquidity and lead to significantly wider spreads (Mills & Carapella, 2012). In extreme cases, an outright shortage of liquidity can even lead to so-called "token freezes," where an asset becomes effectively untradeable for extended periods. Unlike regulated financial securities with transparent price ranges, tokenization may result in price opacity with widening bid-ask spreads, which may lead to speculative bidding (Ebadi, R., 2025; OECD, 2025). Accordingly, liquidity risk mitigation requires standardized measures for linkages and clearing.

2.3. Security Risks

Tokenized systems also pose several security risks, as transaction finality is provided by the immutability of smart contracts, which, unfortunately, also makes any design or coding vulnerabilities persistent. The 2016 DAO Hack drained approximately \$50 million in Ether from a DAO via a recursive call vulnerability (Mehar et al., 2019; Morrison, 2020). More recently, a technical review found multiple additional security risks, such as re-entrancy attacks, oracle manipulation, and flash-loan exploits, which, in combination, are representative of the much broader phenomenon of composability in tokenized decentralized finance DeFi, which has been shown to significantly increase systemic risk (Werner et al., 2022). Security risks have been found to be positively correlated with risks related to governance. When the pace of innovation is faster than the capacity of security audits, attack surfaces increase; this creates gaps that can be exploited by malicious actors (i.e., automated bots). Therefore, security issues must be monitored, and governance structures need to be dynamic to evolve around the threat.

2.4. Fraud and Cybersecurity Risks

Fraud and cybersecurity risks represent significant concerns in tokenized systems because of the "pseudonymous" and borderless nature of blockchain transactions, which can facilitate new types of fraud, such as "rug pulls, insider trading, and coordinated pump-and-dump schemes". Cyberattacks against exchanges, custodians, and wallet providers also remain a major source of risk, especially when stolen assets frequently remain unrecovered because of fragmented law enforcement. The lack of standardized identity verification mechanisms also increases the risks of phishing, credential compromise, and unauthorized transfers. Social engineering attacks against users can also be effective in exploiting a general lack of familiarity with private key management, leading to a permanent loss of assets. Tokenization also increases the risk of fraud by creating entirely fictitious asset-backed tokens (Chainalysis 2025; La Morgia et al. 2023).

In addition, investors often need to rely on unchecked marketing claims due to a lack of standardization and uniform disclosure or auditing practices for tokenized projects, which can be misleading. Fraud is further facilitated by the opaque and often highly unregulated nature of OTC token trading in both institutional and retail markets. Fraud risks are especially acute in rapidly tokenized assets that have undergone limited vetting procedures. The jurisdictional fragmentation of enforcement multiplies the challenges of combating these risks. Thus, international cooperation needs to be strengthened, and investor education efforts need to be prioritized.

2.5. Environmental, Social, and Governance (ESG) Risks

There are environmental, social, and governance risks associated with tokenization. Environmentally, Proof of work systems raise concerns due to high energy and carbon costs (Stoll et al., 2019; de Vries, 2022). Socially, digital access inequality can happen due to financial or technological exclusion precludes certain users or actors from accessing these ecosystems. Governance risks can materialize when tokens become concentrated in the hands of early adopters, thereby distorting outcomes in on-chain voting mechanisms and centralizing decision-making power.

From an ESG perspective, a lack of standardization and uniform reporting practices for tokenized projects presents a major challenge for responsible investors, who would like to incorporate ESG criteria, especially environmental and governance criteria, into their investment decisions. Tokenized projects that fail to meet these standards run a risk of exclusion from important institutional portfolios. The reputational damage and negative financial externalities associated with a project that is perceived as environmentally damaging, socially exclusive, or otherwise unresponsive to governance concerns are nontrivial.

2.6. Regulatory and Compliance Risks

Enforcing anti-money laundering (AML) and Know Your Customer (KYC) regulations in tokenized markets is not easy to implement due to different laws across countries, cross-border data issues, and the ease of decentralized trading. All of these factors encourage regulatory avoidance and hinder safe institutional growth (Zhang et al., 2024; FATF, 2021; IOSCO, 2023).

Projects may even structure tokens to bypass current securities laws, while taking advantage of the lack of clear legal precedents regarding smart contract disputes and creating additional uncertainty for investors. This is a further disincentive for participation by institutional market players, which also retards wider adoption. The lack of regulatory and compliance frameworks is perceived as a significant disincentive for financial institutions to join. The perception of risk to financial institutions is another hurdle that needs to be overcome. However, excessive regulation can suffocate innovation; therefore, finding the balance between innovation and financial integrity is also important (IOSCO, 2023).

2.7. Market Risks

The three principal drivers of tokenized market risk are the high volatility of many tokens, the underdeveloped hedging infrastructure, and the swift transmission of shocks across fragmented ecosystems. The prices of many tokens are highly sensitive to changes in macroeconomic news and regulatory announcements. Owing to the lack of fundamental drivers, token prices can be disproportionately affected by speculative sentiment (International Monetary Fund, 2025).

Risk management tools such as futures, options, and other derivatives are still in their early stages of development in tokenized asset markets, unlike traditional asset markets, which can leave traders exposed to wild swings in prices. Fragmented liquidity across exchanges and L1/L2 blockchains can result in distorted price discovery and regulatory arbitrage opportunities, which may lead to instability and give rise to risk-based supervision by global regulators (IOSCO, 2023). The correlation between crypto markets and traditional equity markets is growing, and the shock has the potential for cross-domain contagion (Financial Stability Board, 2022). As the Federal Reserve disclosed, there is a possibility that tokenized market volatility will spread to the traditional reference-asset market, especially when the assets in question have no traditional cash flows, thereby creating systemic risk (Federal Reserve, 2024). The development of tokenized markets has led to multilayered volatility.

2.8. Other Risks

Beyond the main risks covered in this section, there are several more legal uncertainties around, for example, a lack of clarity in on-chain asset transfer recognition, the systemic implications of dependency on external oracles that introduce third-party data integrity risks, and susceptibility to market manipulation in thin order books (Eskandari et al., 2021). Custodial and interoperability risks, as well as potential contagion through cross-market linkages, are important, but do not seem to capture the full complexity of the systemic vulnerabilities present in tokenized ecosystems (Law Commission of England and Wales, 2023). Relying only on native blockchain tokens for transaction fees can lead to significant friction if network congestion coincides with the high fee volatility. Consequently, these remaining risks play a role in shaping the resilience of these markets in the long run. In addition to the key risks described in this section, tokenized markets are also exposed to the risk of technological obsolescence because rapid technological development could render certain standards or blockchains infeasible, extend the resolution of disputes, and lessen investors' trust. As adoption expands, the role of risk-based supervision becomes more vital (IOSCO, 2023).

3. CHALLENGES IN TOKENIZED SYSTEMS

Blockchain has the potential to revolutionize the global financial system, yet there are several impediments. In this section, the potential challenges of tokenized systems are addressed in the current research on blockchain and summarized under technical complexities and vulnerabilities, governance, compliance and regulatory, sustainability and AI legal, security and privacy, and other aspects.

3.1. Regulatory and Legal Uncertainty

Most jurisdictions do not yet recognize blockchain tokens as legally binding ownership records. The appearance of such a token may not necessarily be proof that an asset is owned by the token holder. For this to occur, it is necessary for the token to be integrated into the existing system and to be recognized by all parties as an enforceable property right instead of an economic interest. For example, Sweden's Lantmäteriet (land-mapping registry) conducted a pilot of blockchain property transfer in 2016, but this was not supported by legislative action and was discontinued (Haaramo, 2017).

In contrast, in the U.S., UCC Article 12 on Controllable Electronic Records (2022) created a Federal legal framework for digital ownership. The individual states, however, have not followed suit and maintain their own registries in many areas. The Republic of Georgia was among One of the first countries to integrate blockchain technology into a national land registry was the Republic of Georgia. In 2016, the government united with the Bitfury Group and the National Agency of Public Registry to link property transactions to the Bitcoin blockchain. By doing that, they created tamper-resistant digital records that served as cryptographic proofs of ownership (The Bitfury Group & National Agency of Public Registry, 2016). The later expansions of this initiative demonstrated how token-like digital hashes could secure millions of property titles, which leads to the improvement of transparency and increase trust in land governance (Exonum, n.d.; Santiso, 2022). More recent analyses highlight how this model continues to serve as a reference point for using blockchain in public registries and land rights management (BlockApps, 2024).

Cross-border transactions, particularly, may provide entry points for fraud and other risk factors. For example, in Anti Money-Laundering (AML) and Know-Your-Client (KYC) rules for investors, due to differences in the way different countries enforce these regulations currently, criminals may take advantage of the free flow of tokens across borders to exploit the weakest link in the system to launder money (Zhang et al., 2024). To address this concern, MiCA introduced a new European Union regulation EU 2023/1114) to adopt a legal framework for crypto assets, to verify transactions across EU countries (Regulation (EU) 2023/1114 (MiCA)) (European Parliament & Council of the European Union, 2023; Hogan 2023). In another study (Zhang, Y., Gong, B., & Zhou, P., 2024) summarized the regulatory and legislative frameworks of currency/asset tokenization in seven major economies (the US, EU, UK, Switzerland, Australia, Japan, and South Korea). The study concluded that policymakers in these countries should follow a "gradual, eclectic, and collaborative" approach to tokenization. In a different context, tokenized systems in Islamic countries may face additional challenges in the application of Islamic finance as an issuer requires a Shariah Advisor to examine the blockchain algorithm programming and ensure its alignment with the underlying Shariah contract (Kunhibava et al., 2021).

3.2. Cybersecurity and Technical Vulnerabilities

There are numerous ways in which technical risks in tokenized systems may be exploited, including smart contract exploits, cyberattacks, and operational flaws. There have been recurring vulnerabilities found in Ethereum smart contracts, which included re-entrancy and access-control failures (Atzei et al., 2017). In 2016, Ethereum created a crowdfunding smart contract called DAO or Decentralized Autonomous Organization, which allowed investors to pool their ETH bitcoins and determine projects to fund. Through this, they raised 12 million ETH worth $150M. However, the contract code contained a re-entry bug, a flaw that was exploited to drain one-third of the Ether into a separate account. Due to a 28-day holding period the Ethereum community responded by splitting the account into two separate parts. In one, the code was modified to reverse the hack and restore the funds. Many Ethereum holders followed this chain and received some reimbursement. In the other chain, the code was not changed due to the concept that the code is considered law and must be accepted as-is. (Mehar et al., 2017).

In practice, much of the vulnerability in tokenized systems stems from the same problems that everyday internet users face. Private keys are necessary to control access to the various chains, and these are subject to the same types of attacks, such as phishing, SIM-swaps, and poor security, such as storing keys on vulnerable servers.

Hackers exploited poor key management at Mt. Gox, a bitcoin exchange located in Shibuya, Tokyo, Japan, to steal 950,000 Bitcoin worth $9B over many years (Carlisle, Y. 2019; Chainalysis, 2019). In 2016, attackers accessed private keys through flawed integration from the Bitfinex currency exchange in Hong Kong, stealing 120,000 BTC (worth $72 million at the time). U.S. federal Law Enforcement obtained a search warrant for a cloud storage server thought to have received the stolen Bitcoin and were able to obtain a spreadsheet of wallet addresses and passwords linked to the hack after various attempts at money laundering were traced back to the account (Chainalysis, 2023). More recently, in 2025, macOS users have been targeted with malware disguised as the legitimate "Ledger Live" app by presenting a fake error message that tricks users into entering their seed phrase, which is a 12 or 24-word recovery key. The seed phrase is then sent to cybercriminals, in turn giving them full access to the victim's crypto assets. Measures to mitigate this risk include encrypting the seed phrase and using the "splitting" technique to store the crypto wallet seed phrase (Bukhari et al., 2024)

Arbitrage bots are used for predatory front-running in decentralized markets (DEXes), which exploit market inefficiencies like high-frequency trading done in traditional financial markets. They generate Maximal Extractable Value (MEV) by observing user transactions and placing their own orders in front by paying higher fees. Other risks are fee-based forking attacks and time-bandit attacks, which can lead to significant financial losses and threaten the integrity of smart contracts (Daian et al., 2019). These are examples of flaws that can be exploited, which would erode trust and slow adoption. It is crucial to use preventive security systems for exchanges in a way that includes safeguards such as time-delayed withdrawals or vaults, which can be activated after a breach, to protect user assets and controls such as formal verification, audits, runtime monitoring, and strong custody arrangements.

3.3. Market Volatility and Manipulation

Tokenization involves constructing digital representations (crypto tokens) for non-crypto assets (reference assets), which establish interconnections between the digital asset ecosystem and the traditional financial system. Thus, tokenized assets could spread volatility from crypto asset markets to the markets for the crypto token's reference assets (Mills & Carapella, 2012).

"Wash trading" occurs when market actors artificially inflate trading volume by trading with themselves, creating misleading measures of activity and demand (Cong, Li, et al., 2021). Valuing real assets in tokenized form poses complexity. Without standardized appraisal protocols and solid comparables, tokenization of art or land creates price opacity, fueling speculative bidding and widening bid-ask spreads (Ebadi, R., 2025; OECD, 2025). Unlike financial securities with transparent benchmarks, these assets have difficulty being valued consistently, leading to failures of price discovery.

These behaviors hinder the integrity of token markets because when speculative and manipulative practices predominate, the confidence in decentralized platforms gets shaken, as a result, tokenization becomes less viable for institutional investors and stable infrastructure (European Securities and Markets Authority, 2025).

To adjust for this, there should be an increase in regulatory oversight and transparent exchange infrastructure, plus stablecoins and asset-backed tokens, which provide more reliable valuation anchors.

3.4. Adoption Barriers

Although tokenization and blockchain hold immense potential, their adoption remains slow due to many factors, including unclear regulations, perceived risks, and cultural resistance (Dehghani et al., 2022; Zhang, Tavalaei, and Parry, 2024).

Regulatory conservatism and fragmentation also function as a barrier to adoption. Without a harmonized framework, institutions remain especially hesitant to expand tokenization across borders. OECD (2025). As an example, the Financial Action Task Force's (*Financial Action Task Force [FATF], 2021)* Inconsistent enforcement of Anti Money Laundering and Countering the Financing of Terrorism (AML/CFT) standards undermines confidence, particularly for institutions that operate in multiple jurisdictions.

There is also a lack of skilled personnel and infrastructure. Several businesses lack in-house expertise to assess and implement blockchain-based systems (Deval et al., 2024). This is especially visible in industries with legacy IT systems, where integration with distributed ledger technologies requires costly modernization, which discourages businesses from investing. When applied to Indigenization, adoption barriers in tokenized markets are even more critical.

3.5. Environmental Sustainability Challenges

Bitcoin mining alone is estimated to consume more electricity annually than entire mid-sized nations (de Vries, 2023). Thus, the environmental impact of blockchain infrastructure creates strong challenges to the concept of sustainable tokenization. In addition to the adverse climate impact, it also risks damaging the reputation of tokenization projects in general. Although there is progress on this issue, it does come with risk (Task Force on Climate-related Financial Disclosures, 2021).

Major networks such as Bitcoin continue to rely on an energy-intensive proof-of-work (PoW) process, while the Ethereum network's cut its energy consumption by 99.95% (European Union Blockchain Observatory and Forum [EUBOF], 2023).

3.6. Scalability Issues

Scalability remains a challenge as tokenized systems become more integrated into the mainstream. Without sufficient throughput, these systems tend to recreate more complex legacy bottlenecks platforms risk undergoing the same bottlenecks of legacy infrastructures, but with added technical complexity.

In tokenized systems, scalability is determined by the balance between throughput, decentralization, and security (Deval et al., 2024). Increasing throughput often requires compromising decentralization (such as concentrating validation in fewer nodes) or reducing security guarantees. Where the tokenized system is involved with real assets such as tokenized bonds, cross-border settlements, and supply-chain efforts, there is a demand for high throughput and low latency, but these requirements directly conflict with the architectural limits of public blockchains.

To deal with throughput constraints, developers have pursued Layer 2 solutions such as rollups and sidechains, which offload transactions from the main chain and later settle them in an aggregated form. Although this significantly improves performance, it poses new risks around interoperability, cross-chain consensus, and bridge security (McGuire, 2023). Similarly, sharding, which means partitioning the blockchain into smaller subsets of nodes that process transactions in parallel, improves scalability but complicates network coordination and consensus, raising concerns about cross-shard attacks or validator collusion (Li et al., 2024).

Without making settlement systems scalable, tokenization risks will replicate inefficiencies from traditional finance, leading to delays and aggravated costs. Tokenized systems promise fast settlement, but if networks cannot support high transaction volumes securely, they may not be able to compete in the real world with common centralized infrastructures such as SWIFT or central securities depositories (CSDs). Without robust throughput, tokenized settlement frameworks will struggle to meet systemic requirements for resilience and finality (The Bank for International Settlements 2023).

Institutional players are particularly sensitive to congestion risks. Events such as the Ethereum "gas fee spikes" of 2021 demonstrated how surges in demand through NFT minting and DeFi activity can make transaction costs soar unpredictably and settlement times become unstable (Werner et al., 2022). For tokenization of real-world assets (RWAs), where investors expect reliable settlement like traditional markets, this volatility undermines trust and slows adoption.

For example, during the NFT boom of 202, demand on Ethereum surged, which severely outpaced its capacity of 15–30 transactions per second, which in turn caused extreme congestion and fee spikes—averaging up to $196 per transaction in May (Bitinfocharts, n.d.; Liu et al., 2022). These spikes made Ethereum prohibitively expensive for casual users and eroded trust in its utility for mass applications.

Ethereum's gas system operates on a supply-and-demand model, and base fees adjust dynamically with congestion. To get around this, users can tip validators to prioritize transactions. During network surges, this model amplifies costs and unpredictability through dynamic pricing (Investopedia, 2018; Thirdweb, 2024). To increase throughput, a Layer-2 scaling solution was overlaid on top of the main blockchain. This second layer processes transactions offline, which are then settled into the Layer 1 main blockchain later. The Layer-2 networks can process thousands of transactions per second, thus dramatically increasing throughput and reducing cost to pennies per transaction. However, this comes at a cost of higher risk due to greater complexity, greater opportunity for fraud and theft, along with an increased probability of interoperability problems (Ethereum.org, 2025a, 2025b).

3.7. AI Integration Challenges

Scalability challenges, as mentioned earlier, embody a structural bottleneck where tokenized markets can't attain institutional trust without robust settlement systems. While layer 2 rollups, sharding, and hybrid architectures are promising, each introduces governance and security trade-offs. Unless these constraints are addressed, tokenized infrastructures risk replicating legacy inefficiencies in more complex technical environments, thereby undermining the very efficiency gains that make tokenization attractive (Financial Stability Board, 2024).

Scalability of tokenized systems through the Integration of AI into tokenization holds the promise of efficiency but introduces complex governance challenges, such as algorithmic bias, data privacy, and other related challenges (Abdellatif, 2025), leading to more complexity in performing audits or contesting outcomes (Alvarez et al., 2024). Within DeFi, AI systems are commonly used to optimize trading, which often leads to governance risks (Aramonte, Huang, and Schrimpf, 2021) and sustainability challenges in DeFi (Sorensen, 2023).

3.8. Governance Challenges

Governance challenges in tokenized systems are very common, as it is heavily controlled by a few large token holders or DAOs, which dominate decision-making. User participation in governance is low (Eisermann et al., 2025; Esposito et al., 2025; Fritsch, 2024). Examples of Governance issues from several DeFi industries cited include, but are not limited to, the following:

Aava uses token-based voting to set risk parameters, liquidity incentives, and protocol upgrades (Cornelli et al., 2024). Aave has been innovative in bringing in cross-chain risk management, but governance is a concern (Esposito et al., 2025).

Uniswap is governed through UNI token holders, who can submit and vote on public proposals. Governance is also a concern with a few token holders or DAOs (Eisermann et al., 2025; Fritsch, 2024).

MakerDAO issues DAI, a decentralized stablecoin pegged to the U.S. dollar. Governance is conducted through MKR token holders (Feng, Z., 2024; Sun, X., 2024).

YearnFinance (YFI) moves user funds between DeFi protocols to optimize yields. Its token holders govern strategy approvals, treasury management, and development direction. Its founder, Andre Cronje, renounced his YFI allocation, forcing governance to be entirely community-driven (Stevens, R. 2020).

In short, governance challenges in tokenized systems require attention as smart contracts may lead to market speculation (Dotan et al., 2023; Messias et al., 2023) and manipulation (Daian et al., 2019; Manzano Kharman & Smyth, 2024) due to thin liquidity (European Securities and Markets Authority, 2025), and fiduciary risk across borders (OECD, 2025).

4. ETHICAL CONSIDERATIONS IN TOKENIZED SYSTEMS

4.1. Governance

Governance capture can happen through insiders or developers, which end up replicating centralized financial structures under the guise of decentralization (Alvarez et al., 2024). A “Plutocracy” can occur due to token accumulation by individuals or corporations (Whales). Since tokens by their very nature are technologically complex, this can result in a Technocratic governance system of core developers and specialized teams (Feichtinger et al., 2023; Eisermann et al., 2025). The decentralized nature of blockchain through the tokenization of transactions removes the need for a centralized process to document and track transactions and accounts. However, governance of these systems can present a challenge; the decision-making process for a particular asset is often concentrated among founding developers, which undermines claims of broad-based democratic participation. For example, the Bybit hack of 2025 (Berkowitz, 2025) and the 2016 DAO hack showed the difficulty of collective governance when, as noted above, the Ethereum community faced the dilemma of either upholding blockchain immutability or intervening to reverse losses, which ultimately ended up with the contentious Ethereum–Ethereum Classic split (Mehar et al., 2017). This has been called the 'Decentralisation Illusion' (Aramonte, Huang, and Schrimpf, 2021). These DAO failures further illustrate unresolved governance issues, particularly in crisis management.

Risks of collusion and censorship persist in blockchains, which raises ethical concerns in terms of equity due to the underdevelopment of accountability mechanisms and dispute resolution frameworks. Issues such as having emergency overrides, risk of collusion, and censorship are essential for accountability. In addition, formal dispute resolution methods and transparency requirements are key areas of concern (De Filippi, P., & Loveluck, B., 2016; Hassan, S., & De Filippi, P., 2021). In a nutshell, regulatory divergence and legal uncertainty remain a key concern (Aramonte et al., 2021; Laatikainen, 2021; Lacity, 2018).

While tokenized systems using defi remove banks and other traditional finance intermediaries from defi transactions, a persistent governance paradox persists. Power imbalances now manifest themselves in a different form through token-weighted voting, developer dominance, technocratic dominance, and reliance on external oracles. Since voter turnout is persistently low, sophisticated delegates and funds dominate governance outcomes (Dotan et al., 2023; Messias et al., 2023). Since tokenized products are technologically complex, design and codebase ownership, core developers, and specialized teams can control governance (Feichtinger et al., 2023; Eisermann et al., 2025).

Hidden failure modes due to Oracles, bridges, and upgrade keys function as governance chokepoints, concentrating power regardless of the level of decentralization of the product. Liquidity mining and governance token incentives attract market speculators who may be at odds with appropriate governance. Oracles and bridges should be mandated to have fail-safe and circuit-breaker procedures to be ready for market crashes and governed by transparent, well-considered rules (Barbereau et al., 2022; Manzano Kharman & Smyth, 2024).

4.2. AI Ethical Use in Tokenized Systems

The integration of AI into tokenized systems is interconnected with broader debates about fairness and governance in digital contexts (Cath, 2018). This section builds on the theoretical foundations of the AI-Ethics CSR Governance Framework to address the ethical concerns of the use of AI in the financial services sector, such as data privacy, algorithmic bias, and inequity, and provides a more balanced approach to this ethical dilemma. The framework also presents policy recommendations for the adoption of AI, aligning AI-ethics and Corporate Social Responsibility (CSR) goals, while addressing the needs of the various stakeholders and bringing about sustainability (Abdellatif, 2025).

In contrast, Paramasivan et al. (2022) in their study explored how Artificial Intelligence (AI) in combination with the tokenization methods suggested can help mitigate risks, such as data leakage and fraudulent activities. Abdellatif (2025) also emphasized the role of AI in safeguarding against fraud and Anti-money laundering activities if used ethically and responsibly.

4.3. Sustainability

Ethical concerns in tokenized systems arise when considering tokenization in the context of Sustainable Development Goals (SDGs) & Environmental, Social, and Governance (ESG). For example, in carbon markets, where carbon offsets or credits are fractionalized and traded, there is a risk of double-counting where the same offset is claimed by multiple parties (Environmental Defense Fund, 2019; Gold Standard, n.d.; Cambridge Engage, 2025). Other concerns include "Additionality", where credits are rendered without real emissions reductions, and the issue of "Permanence," in which offsets are not long-term reductions (Sorensen, 2023). Platforms such as KlimaDAO, which tokenize voluntary carbon credits, may not be able to ensure auditability, creating uncertainty around whether these markets deliver genuine decarbonization benefits or simply financial speculation (Ballesteros-Rodríguez et al., 2024). Tokenization without robust oversight raises sustainability concerns (Kumar, 2025) and risks regarding systemic risks (Financial Stability Board, 2024) and "green bubble" (OECD, 2025).

Tokenization also introduces ethical concerns when applied to Islamic finance and Indigenous economic systems. Accordingly, ethical considerations are crucial to ensure the integrity of Islamic Shariah and Indigenous governance traditions and to promote the equitable adoption of blockchain technology (First Nations Technology Council, 2021; Mousavi et al., 2021).

5. CONCLUSION

In this chapter, the risks, challenges, and ethical considerations in tokenized systems were critically examined. While tokenization promises efficiency, transparency, and new avenues for participation of users, it also introduces vulnerabilities that must be managed to encourage broader adoption of tokenized assets and avoid incorporating the failures of traditional finance while adding new risks specific to blockchain-based assets. In this chapter, Section 1 discussed the risks in tokenized systems. In this section, we explained that financial risks in terms of financial stability in tokenized systems matter in a similar way to those in traditional finance. Liquidity risk is a concern for all financial instruments, whether DeFi or TradFi. Since pricing is frequently opaque in tokenized environments, valuation volatility, counterparty defaults, and collateral instability are magnified. Market depth for many tokens is thin, turnover is low, and order books are fragmented. Automated Market Makers dominate liquidity but can themselves amplify shocks. This makes markets prone to sudden drawdowns and rapid contagion. Second, the section discusses security, fraud, and cybersecurity risks. Security risks stem largely from the immutability of smart contracts. Once it is deployed, flawed code cannot be revised due to governance rules, and without extensive coordination, leaving vulnerabilities unchangeable. This, in turn, creates opportunities for rug pulls, insider trading, and pump-and-dump schemes. The complexity of decentralized finance introduces further attack vectors such as "reentrancy, flash-loan exploits, and oracle manipulation", while fraudulent creation of asset-backed tokens and inadequate vetting processes have added to the problem. Third, the risks section addressed the Environmental, Social, and Governance (ESG) risks, including how tokenized systems, especially with the integration of AI, raise not only environmental concerns but also social and governance risks, creating more barriers to participation in tokenized ecosystems, undermining democratic participation, and creating centralized power structures. Next, the section discussed regulatory and compliance risks and how decentralized trading platforms create opportunities for regulatory arbitrage. Traditional finance operates under strict anti-money laundering and know-your-customer requirements, while decentralized finance has little or no governance structure to provide compliance. Some tokens are deliberately structured to avoid securities law, thus creating disincentives for institutional uptake and prompting inevitable government scrutiny. The lack of harmonized frameworks is still a major obstacle to institutional trust, even as regulatory initiatives such as the European Union's MiCA framework begin to provide clearer standards for tokenized assets. Fifth, the section discusses market risks due to the volatility of tokenized assets, underdeveloped hedging tools, and fragmented market infrastructure. Token prices are sensitive to news and regulatory announcements. In thinly traded markets, price manipulation and sharp market corrections are common. Tokenized representations of real assets, such as land or art, face valuation difficulties due to the absence of approved appraisal methods. Sixth, this section discusses other risks, such as uncertainty over on-chain asset transfer recognition remains unresolved. Tokens representing real assets are useful only if all parties accept them as binding proofs of ownership. In addition, rapid technological change creates obsolescence risks, while dependence on external oracles introduces third-party data integrity problems, and thin order books also expose markets to manipulation.

This chapter discussed in section 2 the challenges in tokenized systems. First, technical vulnerabilities such as smart contract exploits, operational flaws, and poor private key management continue to create significant exposures. Market volatility and manipulation are seen to be major concerns. For example, "Pump-and-dump schemes, wash trading, and fabricated asset backing" are frequent in TradFi markets with low liquidity. Institutions face adoption barriers linked to regulatory uncertainty, lack of technological standards, and limited expertise. Smaller firms lack the capacity to transition to tokenized infrastructures.

Second, the section discussed security, fraud, and cybersecurity risks. There are ongoing threats arising from smart contract vulnerabilities, exchange hacks, governance manipulation, and fraud risks due to inadequate verification and due diligence in Know Your Client (KYC) and Anti-money laundering (AML). Proactive monitoring and adaptive safeguards, which include formal KYC verification, runtime audits, custody protections, time-delayed withdrawals, and investor education, are crucial to instill investor trust, consumer protection, and the integrity of the financial system globally. Third, the section analyzed regulatory and compliance challenges. The absence of legal recognition and enforceability of tokenized ownership rights across several jurisdictions deters institutional adoption. Adoption of models such as the European Union's MiCA regulation illustrates how cross-border interoperability and regional regulatory frameworks can build trust for tokenization across regions. In this regard, market risk and manipulation in terms of systematic hazards can occur when volatility in tokenized assets spills over into reference markets, leading to speculative behavior and weakening the financial stability of markets globally. Regulations thus play a major role along with derivatives markets in ensuring market stability, providing hedging opportunities, and mitigating these mechanisms, asset-backed tokens and stablecoins can serve as valuation anchors along with derivatives markets that provide hedging opportunities. Policymakers should follow a gradual and collaborative approach to tokenization. Fifth, the section examines the technical scalability and infrastructure in tokenized systems. Scalability remains a structural barrier to institutional trust. Available solutions, such as "rollups, sharding, and hybrid architectures", offer promise to mitigate this issue but require governance and security trade-offs. Reliance on oracles and cross-chain bridges creates single points of failure, necessitating diversification and the inclusion of circuit-breakers governed by transparent rules. Without such safeguards, tokenized infrastructures risk the same vulnerabilities found in traditional systems. Sixth, the section discussed governance as a major challenge. Poorly designed governance framework structures allow whale dominance, delegate capture, and low voter engagement, and are major obstacles to trust. Governance power often consolidates among founding developers, large token holders, or venture capital firms, preventing representative participation in governance of the asset. Smart contract vulnerabilities add to the risks, as do flash loan and oracle exploits, which may lead to speculative trading and undermine the governance aspects of the token. Seventh, the section discussed adoption barriers and AI integration. Regulatory uncertainty, fragmented standards, and limited organizational expertise are hindrances to institutional adoption. The use of AI enhances efficiency while risking the incorporation of algorithmic bias, opacity, and manipulation that undermine legitimacy due to "black box" issues.

Finally, the chapter in section 3 concludes with ethical considerations in tokenized systems. Tokenized systems face questions of transparency, fairness, equity, and accountability. First, the section discussed how weak governance structures are a critical ethical consideration for earning user trust in tokenized systems. Reforms should include delegated voting with revocation, quorum thresholds, and time-lock mechanisms. Protocol stewardship should be separated from treasury and risk management, supported by independent councils with clear responsibilities. It highlights the importance of good governance through creating transparency, accountability, fairness, and equity to meet the needs and interests of all stakeholders. This section discusses the role of hybrid governance models that integrate "blend token-based voting" with independent audits and disclosures within tokenized systems to ensure transparency, mitigate concentration of power, and maintain accountability to the owners.

Next, the integration of artificial intelligence introduces additional risks. One of those risks is that AI enabled oracles can exhibit biased risk since AI algorithms can operate as opaque "black boxes.". To mitigate these risks, AI policy guidelines should ensure data governance, explainability, human oversight, and independent audits. Next, the section raised ethical concerns regarding the integration of AI in tokenized systems, which can unintentionally undermine transparency and accountability, centralize control, embed algorithmic bias, weaken user trust, create inequity, and reduce social sustainability. In addition, environmental sustainability is a growing issue due to tokenized asset creation, and AI use is also a key challenge. In carbon credit markets, there are integrity issues, such as double-counting and non-permanent offsets. Without proper auditability, Carbon markets can end up being speculation tools instead of becoming a tool to decarbonize.

In conclusion, tokenization is a transformative innovation, but its success depends on dealing with all the present weaknesses, such as financial, technical, governance, and ethical vulnerabilities. It will be necessary to employ transparent design, sustainable practices, and regulatory interoperability. As a result, tokenized systems would become trusted building blocks of future financial markets. Tokenization offers opportunities but also poses several risks and challenges. Its success depends on addressing financial instability, liquidity shortages, security vulnerabilities, and fraud. Scalability and AI integration present technical and ethical challenges that also require careful management.

As a final outlook, tokenization has the potential to revolutionize financial systems and expand opportunities if regulators, institutions, and other stakeholders globally collaborate to provide clear regulatory frameworks, technical cybersecurity safeguards, and robust governance processes. To ensure ethical alignment across countries, institutions are recommended to adopt ESG principles. Further, strengthening governance, regulatory, and compliance systems is essential to ensure their legitimacy and create shared value. Importantly, tokenization must also respect diverse governance traditions, including Indigenous systems, to ensure financial inclusion and equitable adoption - as discussed in the book chapter case study.

REFERENCES

Abdellatif, S. H. R. (2025). The Intersection of AI Ethics and Corporate Social Responsibility: A Case of AI-Driven RegTech in the Banking Industry. Available at *SSRN* 5261863.

Abdellatif, S. H. R. The Intersection of AI Ethics and Corporate Social Responsibility: A Case of AI-Driven RegTech in the Banking Industry (February 28, 2025). Available at *SSRN*: https://ssrn.com/abstract=5261863 or DOI: 10.2139/ssrn.5261863

Alvarez, J. M., Colmenarejo, A. B., Elobaid, A., Fabbrizzi, S., Fahimi, M., Ferrara, A., Ghodsi, S., Mougan, C., Papageorgiou, I., Reyero, P., Russo, M., Scott, K. M., State, L., Zhao, X., & Ruggieri, S. (2024). Policy advice and best practices on bias and fairness in AI. *Ethics and Information Technology*, *26*(2), 97. DOI: 10.1007/s10676-024-09746-w

Aramonte, S., Huang, W., & Schrimpf, A. (2021, December). DeFi risks and the decentralisation illusion. BIS Quarterly Review, 21–36. https://www.bis.org/publ/qtrpdf/r_qt2112b.htm

Atzei, N., Bartoletti, M., & Cimoli, T. (2017). A survey of attacks on Ethereum smart contracts (SoK). In Maffei, M., & Ryan, M. (Eds.), *Principles of Security and Trust* (pp. 164–186). Springer., DOI: 10.1007/978-3-662-54455-6_8

Badev, A., & Watsky, C. (2023). Interconnected DeFi: Ripple effects from the terra collapse. DOI: 10.17016/feds.2023.044

Ballesteros-Rodríguez, A., De-Lucio, J., & Sicilia, M.-Á. (2024). Tokenized carbon credits in voluntary carbon markets: The case of KlimaDAO. *Frontiers in Blockchain*, *7*, 1474540. DOI: 10.3389/fbloc.2024.1474540

Bank for International Settlements. (2023). *Blueprint for the future monetary system: Improving the old, enabling the new.* BIS Annual Economic Report 2023. https://www.bis.org/publ/arpdf/ar2023e3.htm

Bank for International Settlements. (2023). Blueprint for the future monetary system: improving the old, enabling the new. https://www.bis.org/publ/arpdf/ar2023e3.htm

Barbereau, T., Sedlmeir, J., Smethurst, R., Fridgen, G., & Rieger, A. (2022). Tokenization and regulatory compliance for art and collectibles markets: From regulators' demands for transparency to investors' demands for privacy. In *Blockchains and the Token Economy* (pp. 213–236). Springer., DOI: 10.1007/978-3-030-95108-5_8

Barclay, I., Cooper, M., Hackel, J., & Perrin, P. (2022). Tokenizing behavior change: A pathway for the Sustainable Development Goals. *Frontiers in Blockchain, 4*, 730101. DOI: 10.3389/fbloc.2021.730101

Bartlett, C., Marshall, M., & Marshall, A. (2012). Two-Eyed Seeing and other lessons learned with-in a co-learning journey of bringing together Indigenous and mainstream knowledges and ways of knowing. *Journal of Environmental Studies and Sciences, 2*(4), 331–340. 10.1007/s13412-012-0086-8

Berkowitz, J. (2025, March 14). *The Bybit hack of 2025 - potential implications.* Paul Hastings. https://www.paulhastings.com/insights/crypto-policy-tracker/the-bybit-hack-of-2025-potential-implications

Bitinfocharts. (n.d.). *Ethereum avg. transaction fee—historical chart.* Retrieved August 29, 2025, from https://bitinfocharts.com/comparison/ethereum-transactionfees.html

BlockApps. (2024). *Securing land rights and property records with blockchain.* BlockApps. https://blockapps.net/blog/securing-land-rights-and-property-records-with-blockchain/

Blockchain, U. B. C. (2021). *Decolonizing blockchain: Indigenous pathways to digital sovereignty.* University of British Columbia.

Briola, A., Vidal-Tomás, D., Wang, Y., & Aste, T. (2023). Anatomy of a Stablecoin's failure: The Terra-Luna case. *Finance Research Letters, 51*, 103358. DOI: 10.1016/j.frl.2022.103358

Bukhari, S. T., Janjua, M. U., & Qadir, J. (2024). Secure Storage of Crypto Wallet Seed Phrase Using ECC and Splitting Technique. *IEEE Open Journal of the Computer Society, 5*, 278–289. DOI: 10.1109/OJCS.2024.3398794

Carapella, F., Swem, N., & Gerszten, J. (2023). Tokenization: Overview and Financial Stability implications. Finance and Economics Discussion Series, issue. DOI: 10.17016/feds.2023.060r1

Carlisle, Y. (2019). Mt. Gox: Lessons from the biggest Bitcoin hack. *Journal of Financial Crime, 26*(3), 764–773. DOI: 10.1108/JFC-06-2018-0060

Cath, C. (2018). Governing artificial intelligence: Ethical, legal and technical opportunities and challenges. *Philosophical Transactions. Series A, Mathematical, Physical, and Engineering Sciences, 376*(2133), 20180080. DOI: 10.1098/rsta.2018.0080 PMID: 30322996

Chainalysis. (2019). *Crypto Crime Report.* (includes forensic study of Mt. Gox and private key vulnerabilities). https://go.chainalysis.com/2019-Crypto-Crime-Report.html

Chainalysis. (2025). The 2025 Crypto Crime Report. https://go.chainalysis.com/2025-Crypto-Crime-Report.html

Cong, L. W., Li, X., Tang, K., & Yang, Y. (2021). *Crypto Wash Trading.* arXiv. /arXiv.2108.10984DOI: 10.48550

Cornelli, G., Gambacorta, L., Garratt, R., & Reghezza, A. (2024, May). *Why DeFi lending? Evidence from Aave V2* (BIS Working Papers No. 1183). Bank for International Settlements. https://www.bis.org/publ/work1183.htm

Cramer, A.J. (2025, August 28). Indigenous data sovereignty in IT blockchain systems: Seminar Lecture. University Canada West (UCW).

Daian, P., Goldfeder, S., Kell, T., Li, Y., Zhao, X., Bentov, I., Breidenbach, L., & Juels, A. (2019). Flash Boys 2.0: Frontrunning, transaction reordering, and consensus instability in decentralized exchanges. arXiv. /arXiv.1904.05234DOI: 10.48550

De Filippi, P., & Loveluck, B. (2016). The invisible politics of Bitcoin: Governance crisis of a decentralized infrastructure. *Internet Policy Review*, *5*(3). Advance online publication. DOI: 10.14763/2016.3.427

De Vries, A. (2023). Revisiting Bitcoin's carbon footprint. *Joule*, *7*(3), 615–619. DOI: 10.1016/j.joule.2023.02.002

De Vries, A., Gallersdörfer, U., Klaaßen, L., & Stoll, C. (2022). Revisiting Bitcoin's carbon footprint. *Joule*, *6*(3), 498–502. DOI: 10.1016/j.joule.2022.02.005

Dehghani, M., Chen, Y., Wang, Y., & Kietzmann, J. (2022). High interest, low adoption: A mixed-method investigation into organisational blockchain adoption. *Journal of Business Research*, *149*, 393–411. DOI: 10.1016/j.jbusres.2022.05.015

Deval, V., Dwivedi, V. K., Dixit, A., Norta, A., Shah, S. A., Sharma, R., & Draheim, D. (2024). Mobile smart contracts: Exploring scalability challenges and consensus mechanisms. *IEEE Access : Practical Innovations, Open Solutions*, *12*, 34265–34288. DOI: 10.1109/ACCESS.2024.3371901

Doebeli, G., & Giang, A. (nd). Trans Mountain Pipeline Expansion Project, Open Case Studies: Trans Mountain Pipeline Expansion Project, retrieved (July 3, 2024) from https://wiki.ubc.ca/Documentation:Open_Case_Studies/IRES/Trans_Mountain_Pipeline_Expansion_Project

Dotan, M., Yaish, A., Yin, H.-C., Tsytkin, E., & Zohar, A. (2023). *The vulnerable nature of decentralized governance in DeFi. arXiv.* /arXiv.2308.04267DOI: 10.1145/3605768.3623539

Ebadi, R. (2025, May 21). Real Estate Tokenization: From Theory to Practice. *SSRN.* DOI: 10.2139/ssrn.5366013

Eisermann, T., Campajola, C., Tessone, C. J., & Teixeira, A. S. (2025, January 23). *Concentration in governance control across decentralized finance protocols.* arXiv. /arXiv.2501.13377DOI: 10.48550

Engage, C. (2025). *Scientific credibility for high-integrity voluntary carbon markets.* https://www.cambridge.org/engage/coe/article-details/679385946dde43c9082f7009

Environmental Defense Fund. (2019). *Addressing leakage, additionality, and permanence so that credits deliver real climate benefits.* https://www.edf.org/sites/default/files/Environmental_Integrity_TFS_3.4.19.pdf. Environmental Defense

Eskandari, S., Salehi, M., Gu, W. C., & Clark, J. (2021, September). Sok: Oracles from the ground truth to market manipulation. In *Proceedings of the 3rd ACM Conference on Advances in Financial Technologies* (pp. 127-141). DOI: 10.1145/3479722.3480994

Esposito, C., Ficco, M., & Moscato, V. (2025). Governance challenges in decentralized autonomous organizations: A systematic analysis. *Frontiers in Blockchain, 7,* 1538227. Advance online publication. DOI: 10.3389/fbloc.2025.1538227

Ethereum.org. (2025a, February 17). *Scaling.* https://ethereum.org/en/developers/docs/scaling/ ethereum.org

Ethereum.org. (n.d.). *Optimistic rollups.* Retrieved August 29, 2025, from https://ethereum.org/en/developers/docs/scaling/optimistic-rollups/

European Parliament & Council of the European Union. (2023, May 31). Regulation (EU) 2023/1114 of the European Parliament and of the Council of 31 May 2023 on markets in crypto-assets, and amending Regulations (EU) No 1093/2010 and (EU) No 1095/2010 and Directives 2013/36/EU and (EU) 2019/1937 (MiCA). *Official Journal of the European Union, L, 150,* 40–205. https://eur-lex.europa.eu/eli/reg/2023/1114/oj

European Securities and Markets Authority. (2025, July 1). *Maximal Extractable Value: Implications for crypto markets* (ESMA TRV Risk Analysis). European Securities and Markets Authority. DOI: 10.2856/328752

European Union Blockchain Observatory and Forum. (2023). Ethereum Merge: Trend report. https://blockchain-observatory.ec.europa.eu/document/download/3f78c885-d14e-47cb-b183-f22ef529a258_en

Exonum. (n.d.). *Improving the security of a government land registry: Georgia.* Exonum. https://exonum.com/story-georgia

Federal Reserve Bank of New York. (2024). The Financial Stability Implications of Digital Assets. Economic Policy Review (Vol. 30, Issue 2, pp. 1–2). https://www.newyorkfed.org/medialibrary/media/research/epr/2024/EPR_2024_digital-assets_azar.pdf

Feichtinger, R., Fritsch, R., Vonlanthen, Y., & Wattenhofer, R. (2023, February 23). *The hidden shortcomings of (D)AOs—An empirical study of on-chain governance.* arXiv. /arXiv.2302.12125DOI: 10.48550

Feng, Z. (2024). DAI's transparent and decentralized governance ensures stability through MKR token-holder voting. *Frontiers in Blockchain*. DOI: 10.3389/fbloc.2024.1392812

Financial Action Task Force. (2021). *Updated guidance for a risk-based approach to virtual assets and virtual asset service providers.* FATF. https://www.fatf-gafi.org/en/publications/Fatfrecommendations/Updated-Guidance-VA-VASPs.html

Financial Action Task Force. (2021). *Updated guidance for a risk-based approach to virtual assets and virtual asset service providers.* FATF. https://www.fatf-gafi.org/en/publications/Fatfrecommendations/Guidance-rba-virtual-assets-2021.html

Financial Stability Board. (2024, October 22). The financial stability implications of tokenisation. https://www.fsb.org/2024/10/the-financial-stability-implications-of-tokenisation

First Nation Bank of Canada. (2025, August 31) https://www.fnbc.ca

First Nations Technology Council. (2021). Indigenous Digital Equity Strategy. Retrieved from https://technologycouncil.ca August 1, 2025

First Nations Technology Council. (2021). *Indigenous digital sovereignty: A framework for reconciliation.* First Nations Technology Council. https://technologycouncil.ca

Gibson, G., & O'Faircheallaigh, C. (2015). *IBA Community Toolkit: Negotiation and Implementation of Impact and Benefit Agreements*. Walter and Duncan Gordon Foundation.

Haaramo, E. (2017, July 5). Sweden trials blockchain for land registry management. ComputerWeekly. https://www.computerweekly.com/news/450421958/Sweden-trials-blockchain-for-land-registry-management

Hassan, S., & De Filippi, P. (2021). Decentralized Autonomous Organizations and Governance by Code. *Internet Policy Review, 10*(2). Advance online publication. DOI: 10.14763/2021.2.1556

International Monetary Fund. (1980, January 1). *World economic outlook.* International Monetary Fund. https://openlibrary.org/works/OL1336051W

International Monetary Fund. (2025). *Tokenization: A framework and key considerations.* (Fintech Notes No. 2025/001). International Monetary Fund. DOI: 10.5089/9798400298905.063

International Organization of Securities Commissions. (2023). *Policy recommendations for crypto and digital asset markets.* IOSCO. https://www.iosco.org/library/pubdocs/pdf/IOSCOPD747.pdf

Investopedia. (2018). *What is gas (Ethereum)?* Investopedia. https://www.investopedia.com/terms/g/gas-ethereum.asp

Jeffrey, T., Kurtz, D. L. M., & Jones, C. A. (2021). Two-Eyed Seeing: Current Approaches, and Discussion of Medical Applications. *BC Medical Journal, 68*(8).

Kumar, B., Kumar, A., Sassanelli, C., & Kumar, L. (2025). Exploring the role of finance in driving circular economy and sustainable business practices. *Journal of Cleaner Production, 486*, 144480. DOI: 10.1016/j.jclepro.2024.144480

Kunhibava, S., Mustapha, Z., Muneeza, A., Sa'ad, A. A., & Karim, M. E. (2021). *ukūk on blockchain: a legal, regulatory and Sharī'ah review.* ISRA International Journal of Islamic Finance., DOI: 10.1108/IJIF-06-2020-0120

La Morgia, M., Mei, A., Sassi, F., & Stefa, J. (2023). The doge of wall street: Analysis and detection of pump and dump cryptocurrency manipulations. *ACM Transactions on Internet Technology, 23*(1), 1–28. DOI: 10.1145/3561300

Laatikainen, G., Li, M., & Abrahamsson, P. (2021). Blockchain Governance: A Dynamic View. In Wang, X., Martini, A., Nguyen-Duc, A., & Stray, V. (Eds.), *Software Business. ICSOB 2021. Lecture Notes in Business Information Processing* (Vol. 434). Springer., DOI: 10.1007/978-3-030-91983-2_6

Lacity, M. (2018). Addressing key challenges to making enterprise blockchain applications a reality. *MIS Quarterly Executive, 17*(3), 3. https://aisel.aisnet.org/misqe/vol17/iss3/3/

Law Commission of England and Wales. (2023). Digital assets: Final report (Law Com No. 256). The Stationery Office. https://lawcom.gov.uk/project/digital-assets/

Li, M., Luo, X., Xue, K., Xue, Y., Sun, W., & Li, J. (2024). A secure and efficient blockchain sharding scheme via hybrid consensus and dynamic management. *IEEE Transactions on Information Forensics and Security, 19*, 5911–5924. DOI: 10.1109/TIFS.2024.3406145

Liu, J., Makarov, I., & Schoar, A. (2023). *Anatomy of a run: The terra luna crash (No. w31160)*. National Bureau of Economic Research., DOI: 10.3386/w31160

Liu, Y., Lu, Y., Nayak, K., Zhang, F., Zhang, L., & Zhao, Y. (2022). *Empirical analysis of EIP-1559: Transaction fees, waiting time, and consensus security*. arXiv. https://arxiv.org/abs/2201.05574 DOI: 10.1145/3548606.3559341

Manzano Kharman, A., & Smyth, B. (2024, June 12). *Perils of current DAO governance* [Preprint]. *arXiv*. /arXiv.2406.08605DOI: 10.48550

McGuire. (2023, May 29). *Explore cross-chain interoperability in Layer 2*. Blockphere. https://blockphere.com/explore-cross-chain-interoperability-in-layer-2/

Meadows, J., Annandale, M., & Ota, L. (2019). Indigenous Peoples' participation in sustainability standards for extractives. *Land Use Policy, 88*, 104118.

Mehar, M. I., Shier, C. L., Giambattista, A., Gong, E., Fletcher, G., Sanayhie, R., Kim, H. M., & Laskowski, M. (2019). Understanding a revolutionary and flawed grand experiment in blockchain: The DAO attack. [JCIT]. *Journal of Cases on Information Technology, 21*(1), 19–32. DOI: 10.4018/JCIT.2019010102

Messias, J., Benevenuto, F., Wachs, J., & De Cristofaro, E. (2023). *Evidence of centralization in decentralized finance*. In *Proceedings of the Web Conference 2023 (WWW '23)* (pp. 1192–1202). ACM. DOI: 10.1145/3543507.3583235

Mills, D. C., & Carapella, F. (2012, March 9). *Information-insensitive securities: The benefits of central counterparty clearing* (Bank of Canada Working Paper No. 2012-20). Bank of Canada. https://www.bankofcanada.ca/wp-content/uploads/2012/07/Carapella-Francesca-paper.pdf

Moncada, R., Ferro, E., Fiaschetti, M., & Medda, F. (2024). Blockchain Tokens, Price Volatility, and Active User Base: An Empirical Analysis Based on Tokenomics. *International Journal of Financial Studies., 12*(4), 107. DOI: 10.3390/ijfs12040107

Morrison, R., Mazey, N. C., & Wingreen, S. C. (2020). The DAO controversy: The case for a new species of corporate governance? *Frontiers in Blockchain, 3*, 25. DOI: 10.3389/fbloc.2020.00025

Mousavi, S. H., Tohidinia, A., & Mousavi, S. M. (2025). Transforming Islamic finance: The impact of blockchain and Smart Sukuk [November.]. *Access Journal, Access Press Publishing House*, *6*(1), 184–201. DOI: 10.46656/access.2025.6.1(10)

Mulligan, C., Morsfield, S., & Cheikosman, E. (2024). Blockchain for sustainability: A systematic literature review for policy impact. *Telecommunications Policy*, *48*(2), 102676. DOI: 10.1016/j.telpol.2023.102676

O'Faircheallaigh, C. (2020). Impact and Benefit Agreements as Monitoring Instruments in the Minerals and Energy Industries. *The Extractive Industries and Society*, *7*(4), 1338–1346.

OECD. (2025). Tokenisation of assets and distributed ledger technologies in financial markets: Potential impediments and policy implications. *OECD Business and Finance Policy Papers*, (75). Advance online publication. DOI: 10.1787/bf84ff64-en

One Canadian Economy Act (Bill C-5). (2025).. . *Statutes of Canada*, *c*, 2.

Ostrowski, W. (2020). Transparency and Global Resources: Exploring Linkages and Boundaries. *The Extractive Industries and Society*, *7*(4), 1472–1479.

Paramasivan, A. (2022). AI and tokenization: Safeguarding sensitive card data in the digital economy. *International Journal on Science and Technology*, *13*(2), 1–19. DOI: 10.5281/zenodo.14551590

Santiso, C. (2022). *A blockchain-based land-titling project in the Republic of Georgia: Rebuilding public trust and lessons for future pilot projects.* ResearchGate. https://www.researchgate.net/publication/330069648_A_Blockchain-Based_Land_Titling_Project_in_the_Republic_of_Georgia_Rebuilding_Public_Trust_and_Lessons_for_Future_Pilot_Projects

Sayed, Y. J., Shishegaran, A., Smith, J., & Saeedi, M. (2025). Sustainability Reporting & Transparency. In Taherdoost, H., Saeedi, M., & Shishegaran, A. (Eds.), *Applications of Blockchain Technology and Computational Intelligence in Environmental Sustainability* (1st ed.). CRC Press., 10.1201/9781003609865

Sorensen, D. (2023). Tokenized carbon credits. *Ledger*, *8*, 76–91. DOI: 10.5195/ledger.2023.294

Sosa, I., & Keenan, K. (2001). Impact Benefit Agreements Between Aboriginal Communities and Mining Companies: Their Use in Canada. Report: Canadian Environmental Law Association, Environmental Mining Council of British Columbia, and Cooper Accion: Accion Solidaria para el Desarrollo.

Standard, G. (n.d.). *Our new double-counting guidelines*. https://www.goldstandard.org/publications/our-new-double-counting-guidelines. Gold Standard

Stevens, R. (2020, August 7). *YFI's Andre Cronje is tired, broke and close to quitting DeFi*. Decrypt. Retrieved August 29, 2025, from https://decrypt.co/37995/exclusive-yfi-andre-cronje-broke-quitting-defi

Stoll, C., Klaaßen, L., & Gallersdörfer, U. (2019). The carbon footprint of bitcoin. *Joule*, *3*(7), 1647–1661. DOI: 10.1016/j.joule.2019.05.012

Sun, X., Stasinakis, C., & Sermpinis, G. (2024). Decentralization illusion in decentralized finance: Evidence from tokenized voting in MakerDAO polls. *Journal Name* (preprint basis). /arXiv.2203.16612DOI: 10.48550

Task Force on Climate-related Financial Disclosures. (2021, July). *Metrics, targets, and transition plans guidance* [PDF]. https://assets.bbhub.io/company/sites/60/2021/07/2021-Metrics_Targets_Guidance-1.pdf

The Bitfury Group, & National Agency of Public Registry. (2016, February 7). *The Bitfury Group and Government of Republic of Georgia expand historic blockchain land-titling project* [Press release]. Bitfury. https://bitfury.com/content/downloads/the_bitfury_group_republic_of_georgia_expand_blockchain_pilot_2_7_16.pdf

Thirdweb. (2024, April 29). *What is EIP-1559? Ethereum gas fees and how they work*. Third web Blog. https://blog.thirdweb.com/eip-1559-ethereum-gas-fees

Trans Mountain Corporation. (2023). Trans Mountain: 2023 Environmental, Social & Governance Report. Retrieved (August 2025) from https://docs.transmountain.com/ESG-Reports/TransMountain_2023-ESG-Report.pdf

Uniform Law Commission. (2022). Uniform Commercial Code 2022 Amendments: Controllable electronic records (Article 12). ULC. https://www.uniformlaws.org

United Nations. (2008). "United Nations Declaration on the Rights of Indigenous Peoples".

United Nations Conference on Trade and Development. (2024, April 9). Financing for sustainable development report 2024: Financing for development at a crossroads. UNCTAD. Retrieved from https://unctad.org/publication/financing-sustainable-development-report-2024

Upadhyay, N. (2020). Demystifying blockchain: A critical analysis of challenges, applications and opportunities. *International Journal of Information Management*, *54*, 102120. DOI: 10.1016/j.ijinfomgt.2020.102120

Werner, S., Perez, D., Gudgeon, L., Klages-Mundt, A., Harz, D., & Knottenbelt, W. (2022, September). Sok: Decentralized finance (defi). In *Proceedings of the 4th ACM Conference on Advances in Financial Technologies* (pp. 30-46). DOI: 10.1145/3558535.3559780

Zhang, Y., Gong, B., & Zhou, P. (2024). Centralized use of decentralized technology: Tokenization of currencies and assets. *Structural Change and Economic Dynamics, 71*, 15–25. DOI: 10.1016/j.strueco.2024.06.006

Zhang, Y., Tavalaei, M., Parry, G., & Zhou, P. (2024): Evolution or involution? A systematic literature review of organisations' blockchain adoption factors, Cardiff Economics Working Papers, No. E2024/19, Cardiff University, Cardiff Business School, Cardiff

APPENDIX: SUPPLEMENTARY ILLUSTRATIVE INDIGENOUS CASE STUDY

Shahinaz Hanem (Sherry) Rashad Sayed Abdellatif, University Canada West, Canada & Jack E. Smith, University Canada West, Canada

The Trans Mountain Expansion Project Case Study

Chapter 12 discusses the risks, challenges, and ethical considerations in tokenized systems. This chapter presents an opportunity for illustration by reference to the Indigenous experience through an indigenous case study. Unpacking the case of the Trans Mountain Expansion Project (TMX) is informative to our discussion in three regards; it necessarily compels contextual discussion in the form of a brief history of Indigenous/settlor relationships in Canada provides a baseline opportunity to showcase the potential of technological advances like blockchain technology and its associated risks, challenges and ethical considerations from the perspective of Indigenous worldview and Two-eyed seeing approach (Bartlett, C., Marshall, M., & Marshall, A., 2012; Jeffrey, T., Kurtz, D.L.M., & Jones, C.A.,2021).

TMX is an extractive industry project where there has been a small-scale measure of Indigenous participation in the form of Indigenous Local Knowledge (ILK) acquired through negotiations leading to several signed Mutual Benefit Agreements (MBA) between First Nations and TMX (Doebali and Giang, n.d.). The project, which is now fully operational, twinned an existing 1150-kilometer-long, 50+ year old pipeline that ran from Edmonton, Alberta, to an export port in Burnaby, British Columbia, Canada. The intent of the original owners, Kinder Morgan, in 2012 was to increase the transportation capacity of crude, refined, and semi-refined oil by approximately 300% (from 300k to 890k barrels per day) (Doebali and Giang, n.d. Remarkably, the original pipeline built in 1951, unconstrained by environmental assessment regulation, was constructed in two years. Conversely, Kinder Morgan first introduced the TMX twinning pipeline project in 2012, but TMX did not obtain National Energy Board (NEB) certification until 2019, one year after Canada acquired Kinder Morgan's interest in the pipeline and project in 2018. TMX was officially operational in May 2024, 12 years after it was originally proposed (Doebali and Giang, n.d.) Much of the 10-year difference can be attributed to changes in Canadian environmental laws that reflected growing public concerns with the societal and environmental degradation impacts, and economic sustainability of large-scale resource extraction projects (Sayed, Y.J. et.al., 2025).

Complicating the approval process were Canadian common law developments supporting expanded recognition of Aboriginal rights and title within their traditional territories, creating a legal duty to consult with Indigenous Peoples and to avoid unjust abrogation of Indigenous rights and title interests. (Sayed, Y.J. et.al., 2025) Federal and provincial environmental assessment agencies fulfill the 'duty to consult' obligations. In the case of TMX, the NEB fulfilled this role as a function of its interprovincial legal mandate (Doebali and Giang, n.d). NEB provided some funding for stakeholder engagement but relied on TMX as the proponent to negotiate with stakeholders, including Indigenous stakeholders, over the 'accommodation' aspect of the project. Notably, Indigenous rights are protected UNDRIP through a 'free, prior, and informed consent' (FPIC) (Doebali and Giang, n.d.; United Nations, 2008).

The TMX pipeline crosses the traditional territories of 133 Indigenous communities, including Metis and First Nation territories. Only forty-three (43) Nations signed MBAs and were often under protest, indicating little support and considerable opposition to the project. (Doebali and Giang, n.d.). Canada's ongoing support for large-scale projects like TMX is evident in the recent passage of Bill C-5, One Canadian Economy Act (Statutes of Canada, 2025, c.2), which includes the Building Canada Act (S.C. 2025, c.2, s.4), created to expedite the review of large-scale infrastructure projects considered to be in the national interest despite stakeholder resistance and opposition. This points to the ongoing colonization object of Indigenous-settlor relations, which in its essence pits the individualist nature of capitalism against the collective nature of Indigenous societies, and 'man's domination over all others' (Ostrowski, 2020). Additionally, the secretive nature of the extractive industry before the 21st century, which invoked perceptions of corruption and collusion in colonial and neo-colonial contexts, continues to fuel feelings of distrust to this day (Sayed, Y.J. et.al., 2025; Ostrowski, 2020). The history of extractive industry players and Indigenous Peoples' relations is characterized by self-interest on the part of industry, accompanied by considerable negative impacts on the environment and on the social and cultural fabric of the communities and the territories within which they operate (Sosa and Keenan, 2001), as well as disregard to ILK (Meadows, J., Anandale, M., & Ota, L., 2019) Compounding this is the minimal participation afforded to Indigenous representatives in the revision of environmental assessment processes and extractive industry self-regulation standards, and the weak governmental enforcement of contractual MBA monitoring requirements. Finally, distrust of extractive industry players is exacerbated by a lack of transparency in monitoring and reporting that meets minimal government, industry, and often societal standards. TMX, for its part, engaged with its Indigenous stakeholders through the environmental assessment process (Doebali and Giang, n.d.). Indigenous stakeholders, not surprisingly, therefore protested and litigated the TMX project from the beginning, providing opposition that continues today. Furthermore, this will continue to plague large-scale resource extraction projects and other projects that infringe upon or abrogate Indigenous rights and title in Canada.

Companies such as TMX and others in the extractive industries are compelled to apply for and receive environmental assessment certificates, along with other licenses and permits, before commencing construction of the project (Gibson and O'Faircheallaigh, 2015; O'Faircheallaigh, C. (2020)). The application process for major projects requires considerable technical research and detail in support of a project's viability. The TMX proposal was interprovincial in nature; thus, federal and provincial governments granted TMX's request to harmonize or combine the processes in the interest of efficiency and cost, allowing one of the government agencies to take the lead (Gibson and O'Faircheallaigh, 2015; O'Faircheallaigh, C., 2020). In the instance of the TMX project, the National Energy Board (NEB) took the lead on behalf of Canada. (Doebali and Giang, n.d.). The TMX applications were reviewed by NEB, which then sent invitations out to potentially affected or impacted stakeholders, including the 133 Indigenous community stakeholders. Consultation and accommodations discussions often ensue, leading to formal MBAs or IBAs with stakeholders that usually include restitution for project impacts, and sometimes accommodation in the form of financial compensation. MBAs often identify a proponent's motivation to obtain a societal license to operate from impacted stakeholders such as communities along the proposed TMX route (Gibson and O'Faircheallaigh, 2015; O'Faircheallaigh, C., 2020), who often have their own views of indigenous knowledge and sustainability (Meadows, J., Anandale, M., & Ota, L., 2019). Consequently, TMX began negotiations with affected Indigenous nations to discuss accommodation details (Doebali and Giang, n.d.).

Finally, Indigenous stakeholders find themselves in a weak negotiation situation from the start when requested to respond to sophisticated applications (Sayed, Y.J. et.al., 2025). Since most First Nations lack the financial resources and technical and administrative expertise to respond effectively to technically rigorous proposals such as the TMX pipeline proposal, governments, usually in support of the proposed project, and proponents, as part of the cost of doing business, will provide capacity funding for the review and response (O'Faircheillaigh, 2020). And so, it was with the TMX project, when Canada became the owner of the mega project (Doebali and Giang, n.d.). Canada, in its capacity as the new owner of the pipeline project, as well as holding jurisdiction over the lead EA agency with authority to grant EA certification, found itself in a conflict-of-interest situation that is an aspect of the ongoing protest and litigation brought forward by non-supportive Indigenous stakeholders.

Analysis of the TMX case exposes that Indigenous engagement is key to equitable participation in large-scale development projects, and where the application of tokenization systems would enhance active Indigenous input and participation, provided caution is taken to address the risks, ethical challenges, and ethical considerations discussed in Chapter 12. The TMX pipeline expansion project, now fully operational as the Trans Mountain Corporation (TMC), postulated that adopting blockchain technology could enhance stakeholder, and particularly Indigenous stakeholder, participation in the context of sustainability (ESG) reporting due to its inherent attributes of immutability, decentralization, and especially transparency (Sayed, Y.J. et.al., 2025). Notably, these attributes are highly sought after by stakeholders seeking assurance, accuracy, and confidence in sustainability reporting, especially with stakeholder participation in relevant ESG standards selection. Thus, TMX sustainability reporting could become transparent and work to re-establish multi-party trust that was historically lost and restore stakeholder confidence in TMC's efforts at gaining an expanded social license to operate (Sayed, Y.J. et.al., 2025).

Throughout Chapter 12, in addressing the risks, challenges, and ethical considerations of adopting tokenized systems, consideration was given to mitigation strategies and solutions that could minimize ethical concerns and suggested that, through inclusive and transparent technology design and implementation, and other measures, the challenges presented could be mitigated. Arguably, the potential for the application of blockchain can be expanded to facilitate those occasions where Indigenous stakeholders are indeed 'holding the pen.' This is provided that blockchain ledgers are transparent and co-designed to incorporate the indigenous ways of learning consultations, and through a 'free, prior, and informed consent' (FPIC) from the onset. The goal is to allow for indigenous sovereignty and governance to prevail (Cramer, 2025) while ensuring the responsible and ethical use of technology to fulfil corporate social responsibility and ensure fairness and equity aligned with the United Nations Sustainable Development Goals (Abdellatif, 2025). Additionally, to reap the benefits of blockchain technology, especially with the integration of Artificial intelligence technology, it is crucial to consider the ''two-eyed seeing" approach (Bartlett, C., Marshall, M., & Marshall, A., 2012; Jeffrey, T., Kurtz, D.L.M., & Jones, C.A., 2021), smart contracts should address the risks, challenges, and ethical considerations of adopting tokenized systems, consideration was given to mitigation strategies and solutions that could minimize ethical concerns, such as algorithmic bias and data privacy (Abdellatif, 2025), and suggested that through inclusive and transparent technology design and implementation, and other measures, the challenges presented could be mitigated. The key effort in adopting tokenized systems in the Indigenous context is bringing together Western and Indigenous perspectives using a ''two-eyed seeing" approach as highlighted earlier. To this end, Indigenous stakeholders could exert their considerable influence to suggest and even demand that parties also adopt an approach that respects the worldview of each party.

To address the application of tokenized systems, the question then moves to consideration of how to locate the technology to avoid any misperception about unfair control and access. With the goal of maintaining a measure of equity in business relations, stakeholders could consider, again utilizing a two-eyed seeing approach, a neutral third-party agency to provide stewardship and manage the tokenized system.

The third-party steward of the technology would, of necessity, appeal to the confidence of Indigenous and non-Indigenous stakeholders alike. The appeal to Indigenous stakeholders of using an Indigenous banking institution, such as the First Nation Bank of Canada (FNBC) would be its commitment to uphold Indigenous values. FNBC or its subsidiary, FNB Trust, could conceivably be situated to develop the tokenization architecture to position itself as a contender for the role of steward and manager of the tokenization system. (FNBC, 2025) This is a potential growth area for other Indigenous owned financial institutions as well. Assuming that to be the case, then acceptable institutions or agencies could leverage tokenized systems like blockchain technology to achieve transparency, immutability, and decentralization that respond to the concerns raised earlier. What could this achieve on the ground?

Turning back to the situation of Indigenous stakeholders in the TMC case scenario, and to other players in the extraction industry, third-party stewards could assist in developing an appropriate Indigenous framework, preparing the way for the adoption of tokenized systems using smart contracts to enforce consent and governance. Assuming this can be achieved in relation to business dealings in the resource extraction industry, where much of the Indigenous-Settlor economic and commercial activity is situated, then presumably the adoption of a two-eyed seeing approach and the utilization of a third-party tokenization system stewards like the FNBC could potentially be achieved - a topic that begs further research and study.

Compilation of References

Abdellatif, S. H. R. (2025). The Intersection of AI Ethics and Corporate Social Responsibility: A Case of AI-Driven RegTech in the Banking Industry. Available at *SSRN* 5261863.

Abdellatif, S. H. R. The Intersection of AI Ethics and Corporate Social Responsibility: A Case of AI-Driven RegTech in the Banking Industry (February 28, 2025). Available at *SSRN*: https://ssrn.com/abstract=5261863 or DOI: 10.2139/ssrn.5261863

Abubakari, M. S. (2025a). Digital Competence for Enhancing Financial Inclusion in FinTech Adoption: Addressing the Digital Divide. In Masri, M., Sait, M. A., & Anshari, M. (Eds.), *Promoting Inclusivity and Accessibility With FinTech* (pp. 65–102). IGI Global Scientific Publishing., DOI: 10.4018/979-8-3373-1112-8.ch003

Abubakari, M. S. (2025b). Digital Technologies Adoption in Islamic Education for Fostering Lifelong Learning Culture: Pilot Survey Preliminary Insights. In Anshari, M., Almunawar, M. N., & Ordóñez de Pablos, P. (Eds.), *Multi-Industry Digitalization and Technological Governance in the AI Era* (pp. 103–126). IGI Global., DOI: 10.4018/979-8-3373-1681-9.ch005

Abubakari, M. S., & Kalinaki, K. (2024). Digital Competence in Islamic Education for Lifelong Learning: Preliminary Analysis Using DigComp 2.1 Framework. In Hawamdeh, M. M. K., & Abdelhafid, F. (Eds.), *Embracing Technological Advancements for Lifelong Learning* (pp. 1–31). IGI Global., DOI: 10.4018/979-8-3693-1410-4.ch001

Abubakari, M. S., Zakaria, G. A. N., & Musa, J. (2025). Validating the DigComp framework among university students across different educational systems. *Discover Education*, *4*(1), 200. DOI: 10.1007/s44217-025-00652-x

Acar, A., Aksu, H., Uluagac, A. S., & Conti, M. (2018). A survey on homomorphic encryption schemes: Theory and implementation. *ACM Computing Surveys*, *51*(4), 79. Advance online publication. DOI: 10.1145/3214303

Accenture, Chainlink, & RWA.xyz. (2025, forthcoming). *Liquidity without borders: Why cross-chain interoperability matters.*

Acikgoz, F., Stylos, N., & Lythreatis, S. (2024). Identifying capabilities and constraints in utilizing blockchain technology in hospitality and tourism. *International Journal of Contemporary Hospitality Management, 36*(10), 3493–3514. DOI: 10.1108/IJCHM-07-2023-1083

ADDX. (2023). Digital securities exchange platform. https://addx.co/

Adel, N. (2024). The impact of digital literacy and technology adoption on financial inclusion in Africa, Asia, and Latin America. *Heliyon, 10*(24), e40951. DOI: 10.1016/j.heliyon.2024.e40951 PMID: 39720071

Adler, J., Berryhill, R., Veneris, A., Poulos, Z., Veira, N., & Kastania, A. (2018). Astraea: A decentralized blockchain oracle. *2018 IEEE International Conference on Internet of Things.*

Agarwal, P., Malhotra, S. K., & Swami, S. (2024). The role of smart technologies in managing supply chain post pandemic: An exploratory scientific procedures and rationales for systematic literature review. *Journal of Science and Technology Policy Management.* DOI: 10.1108/JSTPM-07-2023-0106

Agbo, C. C., Mahmoud, Q. H., & Eklund, J. M. (2019). Blockchain technology in healthcare: A systematic review. *Health Care, 7*(2), 56. Advance online publication. DOI: 10.3390/healthcare7020056 PMID: 30987333

Aggarwal, S., & Kumar, N. (2021). A Consortium Blockchain-Based Energy Trading for Demand Response Management in Vehicle-to-Grid. *IEEE Transactions on Vehicular Technology, 70*(9), 9480–9494. DOI: 10.1109/TVT.2021.3100681

Alam, M. A., Sohel, A., Hossain, A., Eshra, S. A., & Mahmud, S. (2023). Medical imaging for early cancer diagnosis and epidemiology using artificial intelligence: Strengthening national healthcare frameworks in the USA. *American Journal of Scholarly Research and Innovation, 2*(1), 24–49. DOI: 10.63125/matthh09

Aldasoro, I., Aramonte, S., Huang, W., & Zoss, M. (2024). Stablecoins: A safe haven or a source of instability? Bank for International Settlements. https://www.bis.org

Aldasoro, I., Cornelli, G., Frost, J., Koo W. P., & Shreeti, V. (2025). *Tokenisation of government bonds*, mimeo

Allen, D. W., Berg, C., Markey-Towler, B., Novak, M., & Potts, J. (2020). Blockchain and the evolution of institutional technologies. *Research Policy, 49*(1), 103865. DOI: 10.1016/j.respol.2019.103865

Allen, F. (1990). The market for information and the origin of financial intermediation. *Journal of Financial Intermediation, 1*(1), 3–30. DOI: 10.1016/1042-9573(90)90006-2

Allen, F., & Santomero, A. (1998). The theory of financial intermediation. *Journal of Banking & Finance, 21*(11–12), 1461–1485. DOI: 10.1016/S0378-4266(97)00032-0

Allen, J. G. (2018). Wrapped and stacked: "Smart contracts" and the interaction of natural and formal language. *European Review of Contract Law, 14*(4), 307–343. DOI: 10.1515/ercl-2018-1023

Alnafrah, I., & Mouselli, S. (2021). Revitalizing blockchain technology potentials for smooth academic records management and verification in low-income countries. *International Journal of Educational Development, 85*, 102460. DOI: 10.1016/j.ijedudev.2021.102460

Alvarez, J. M., Colmenarejo, A. B., Elobaid, A., Fabbrizzi, S., Fahimi, M., Ferrara, A., Ghodsi, S., Mougan, C., Papageorgiou, I., Reyero, P., Russo, M., Scott, K. M., State, L., Zhao, X., & Ruggieri, S. (2024). Policy advice and best practices on bias and fairness in AI. *Ethics and Information Technology, 26*(2), 97. DOI: 10.1007/s10676-024-09746-w

AMF. (2023). Position-recommendation DOC-2023-04: Guide to the regulatory framework applicable to initial coin offerings (ICOs). Autorité des marchés financiers.

AMF. FMA, & CONSOB (2025). European crypto-asset markets' framework: proposals from the French, the Austrian, and the Italian financial markets authorities. Available at https://www.amf-france.org/sites/institutionnel/files/private/2025-09/final_amf-fma_conso b_mica-2-position-paper_clean-consob_logo.pdf

Ammous, S. (2021). *The fiat standard: The debt slavery alternative to human civilization*. Saifedean.com Publishing.

Andrae, S. (2022). The role of BigTech in emerging markets. In Nguyen, D. K. (Ed.), *Handbook of Banking and Finance in Emerging Markets* (pp. 433–463). Edward Elgar., DOI: 10.4337/9781800880900.00032

Andrae, S. (2026a). Money as a cultural artifact: An economic anthropology analysis of its social and environmental impacts. In Christiansen, B., & Branch, J. D. (Eds.), *Examining modern economic anthropology* (pp. 31–72). IGI Global Publishing., DOI: 10.4018/979-8-3373-1260-6.ch002

Andrae, S. (2026b). U.S. strategy to dominate the Dollar with stablecoins: Geopolitical and economic implications. In Akhtar, S., Khan, M., Almaqtari, F. A G., Selvam, V., & Bahl, S. (Eds.), *Policy implications on international financial economics and banking* (pp. 195–236). IGI Global Publishing., DOI: 10.4018/979-8-3373-3725-8.ch007

Andreoni, J. (1988). Why free ride? Strategies and learning in public goods experiments. *Journal of Public Economics*, *37*(3), 291–304. DOI: 10.1016/0047-2727(88)90043-6

Annunziata, F. (2020). Speak, if you can: What are you? An alternative approach to the qualification of tokens and initial coin offerings. *European Company and Financial Law Review*, *17*(2), 129–154. DOI: 10.1515/ecfr-2020-0007

Antonopoulos, A. M., & Wood, G. (2018). *Mastering Ethereum: Building smart contracts and DApps*. O'Reilly Media.

Aramonte, S., Huang, W., & Schrimpf, A. (2021, December). DeFi risks and the decentralisation illusion. BIS Quarterly Review, 21–36. https://www.bis.org/publ/qtrpdf/r_qt2112b.htm

Aramonte, S., Huang, W., & Schrimpf, A. (2022). DeFi risks and the decentralisation illusion. Bank for International Settlements. https://www.bis.org/publ/qtrpdf/r_qt2112b.htm

Arner, D. W., Auer, R., & Frost, J. (2020). Stablecoins: Risks, potential and regulation. Bank for International Settlements. https://www.bis.org/publ/bisbull21.pdf

Arner, D. W., Barberis, J., & Buckley, R. P. (2017). *FinTech and RegTech in a nutshell, and the future in a sandbox*. CFA Institute Research Foundation. DOI: 10.2139/ssrn.3088303

Arner, D. W., Barberis, J., & Buckley, R. P. (2017). FinTech, RegTech, and the reconceptualization of financial regulation. *Northwestern Journal of International Law & Business*, *37*(3), 371–413.

Arrow, K. J. (1962). Economic welfare and the allocation of resources for invention. In *The rate and direction of inventive activity* (pp. 609–626). Princeton University Press. DOI: 10.1515/9781400879762-024

Art, A. (2023). Programmable art platform. https://async.art/

Artory. (2023). Blockchain registry for art and collectibles. https://artory.com/

Asgaonkar, A., & Krishnamachari, B. (2018). Token curated registries: A game theoretic approach. arXiv. https://arxiv.org/abs/1809.01756

Association for Financial Markets in Europe (AFME) (2024). *Use of DLT and tokenisation in financial markets.*

Ast, F., & Dimov, D. (2021). The crowdjury, a crowdsourced justice system for the collaboration era. In *Legal Tech and the New Sharing Economy* (pp. 45–67). Springer.

Atzei, N., Bartoletti, M., & Cimoli, T. (2017). A survey of attacks on Ethereum smart contracts (SoK). In Maffei, M., & Ryan, M. (Eds.), *Principles of Security and Trust* (pp. 164–186). Springer., DOI: 10.1007/978-3-662-54455-6_8

Atzori, M. (2017). Blockchain technology and decentralized governance: Is the state still necessary? *Journal of Governance and Regulation*, *6*(1), 45–62. DOI: 10.22495/jgr_v6_i1_p5

Audius. (2023). Decentralized music streaming protocol. https://audius.co/

Auer, R. (2019). Embedded supervision: How to build regulation into blockchain finance. BIS Working Papers No. 811.

Auer, R., Cornelli, G., & Frost, J. (2023). CBDC development and cross-country experiences. Bank for International Settlements. https://www.bis.org/publ/bppdf/bispap136.pdf

Auer, R., Haslhofer, B., Kitzler, S., Saggese, P., & Friedhelm, V. (2023). *The technology of decentralized finance (DeFi).* Bank for International Settlements (BIS), Monetary and Economic Department, Working Papers, No. 1066

Ava Labs & Mastercard (2024). Asset tokenization: A comprehensive report and why you should start caring about the technology

Avi, Md. A. R., Nasrin, M., & Hassan, A. (2021). Application of Innovative Technologies in the Tourism and Hospitality Industry of Bangladesh: The Present Scenario. In A. Hassan (Ed.), *Technology Application in the Tourism and Hospitality Industry of Bangladesh* (pp. 81–95). Springer Singapore. DOI: 10.1007/978-981-16-2434-6_5

Azoulay, P., Zivin, J. S. G., & Manso, G. (2011). Incentives and creativity: Evidence from the academic life sciences. *The RAND Journal of Economics*, *42*(3), 527–554. DOI: 10.1111/j.1756-2171.2011.00140.x

Bacon, J., Bazinas, G., Goldenfein, J., Grigera-Naón, J. J., & Rauchs, M. (2021). *Blockchain and digital assets: International legal and regulatory challenges.* Sweet & Maxwell.

Badev, A., & Watsky, C. (2023). Interconnected DeFi: Ripple effects from the terra collapse. DOI: 10.17016/feds.2023.044

Baker, M. (2016). 1,500 scientists lift the lid on reproducibility. *Nature*, *533*(7604), 452–454. DOI: 10.1038/533452a PMID: 27225100

Balagolla, E. M. S. W., Fernando, W. P. C., Rathnayake, R. M. N. S., Wijesekera, M. J. M. R. P., Senarathne, A. N., & Abeywardhana, K. Y. (2021). Credit Card Fraud Prevention Using Blockchain. *2021 6th International Conference for Convergence in Technology (I2CT)*, 1–8. DOI: 10.1109/I2CT51068.2021.9418192

Baldwin, R., Cave, M., & Lodge, M. (2012). *Understanding regulation: Theory, strategy, and practice*. Oxford University Press.

Ballesteros-Rodríguez, A., De-Lucio, J., & Sicilia, M.-Á. (2024). Tokenized carbon credits in voluntary carbon markets: The case of KlimaDAO. *Frontiers in Blockchain*, *7*, 1474540. DOI: 10.3389/fbloc.2024.1474540

Bamakan, S. M., Nezhadsistani, N., Bodaghi, O., & Qu, Q. (2022). Patents and intellectual property assets as non-fungible tokens: Key technologies and challenges. *Scientific Reports*, *12*(1), 1–13. DOI: 10.1038/s41598-022-05920-6 PMID: 35140251

Banda, P., & Schwienbacher, A. (2023). Blockchain-based corporate governance. *Journal of Corporate Finance*, *78*, 102338.

Bandara, E., Liang, X., Foytik, P., Shetty, S., Hall, C., Bowden, D., Ranasinghe, N., & De Zoysa, K. (2021). A blockchain empowered and privacy preserving digital contact tracing platform. *Information Processing & Management*, *58*(4), 102572. DOI: 10.1016/j.ipm.2021.102572 PMID: 33727760

Banerjee, A., Sevillano, J., Higginson, M., Rigo, D., & Spanz, G. (2024). From ripples to waves: The transformational power of tokenizing assets. McKinsey Company. https://www.mckinsey.com/industries/financial-services/our-insights/from-ripples-to-waves-the-transformational-power-of-tokenizing-assets

Bank for International Settlements (BIS). (2021). CBDCs: Financial stability implications. https://www.bis.org/publ/bppdf/bispap114.pdf

Bank for International Settlements (BIS). (2023). *Blueprint for the future monetary system: Improving the old, enabling the new*. BIS Annual Economic Report 2023. https://www.bis.org

Bank for International Settlements (BIS). (2023a). A blueprint for the future monetary system: Improving the old, enabling the new. BIS Annual Economic Report, Chapter III. https://www.bis.org/publ/arpdf/ar2023e3.pdf

Bank for International Settlements (BIS). (2023b). Project mBridge: Connecting economies through CBDC. BIS Innovation Hub. https://www.bis.org/about/bisih/topics/cbdc/mcbdc_bridge.htm

Bank for International Settlements. (2021). CBDCs: An opportunity for the monetary system. https://www.bis.org/publ/othp42.pdf

Bank for International Settlements. (2022). *The future monetary system: A BIS perspective.* https://www.bis.org/publ/arpdf/ar2022e3.htm

Bank for International Settlements. (2023). *Blueprint for the future monetary system: Improving the old, enabling the new.* BIS Annual Economic Report 2023. https://www.bis.org/publ/arpdf/ar2023e3.htm

Bank for International Settlements. (2023). Blueprint for the future monetary system: improving the old, enabling the new. https://www.bis.org/publ/arpdf/ar2023e3.htm

Barbereau, T., Sedlmeir, J., Smethurst, R., Fridgen, G., & Rieger, A. (2022). Tokenization and regulatory compliance for art and collectibles markets: From regulators' demands for transparency to investors' demands for privacy. In *Blockchains and the Token Economy* (pp. 213–236). Springer., DOI: 10.1007/978-3-030-95108-5_8

Barclay, I., Cooper, M., Hackel, J., & Perrin, P. (2022). Tokenizing behavior change: A pathway for the Sustainable Development Goals. *Frontiers in Blockchain, 4*, 730101. DOI: 10.3389/fbloc.2021.730101

Barnett, J., & Treleaven, P. (2018). Algorithmic dispute resolution—The automation of professional dispute resolution using AI and blockchain technologies. *The Computer Journal, 61*(3), 399–409. DOI: 10.1093/comjnl/bxx103

Bartlett, C., Marshall, M., & Marshall, A. (2012). Two-Eyed Seeing and other lessons learned with-in a co-learning journey of bringing together Indigenous and mainstream knowledges and ways of knowing. *Journal of Environmental Studies and Sciences, 2*(4), 331–340. 10.1007/s13412-012-0086-8

Belchior, R., Vasconcelos, A., Guerreiro, S., & Correia, M. (2022). A Survey on Blockchain Interoperability: Past, Present, and Future Trends. *ACM Computing Surveys, 54*(8), 1–41. DOI: 10.1145/3471140

Belen-Saglam, R., Altuncu, E., Lu, Y., & Li, S. (2023). A systematic literature review of the tension between the GDPR and public blockchain systems. *Blockchain: Research and Applications, 4*(2), 100129. DOI: 10.1016/j.bcra.2023.100129

Belleflamme, P., Lambert, T., & Schwienbacher, A. (2014). Crowdfunding: Tapping the right crowd. *Journal of Business Venturing*, *29*(5), 585–609. DOI: 10.1016/j.jbusvent.2013.07.003

Benedetti, H., & Kostovetsky, L. (2021). Digital tulips? Returns to investors in initial coin offerings. *Journal of Corporate Finance*, *66*, 101786. DOI: 10.1016/j.jcorpfin.2020.101786

Benet, J. (2014). IPFS - Content Addressed, Versioned, P2P File System. ArXiv. https://arxiv.org/abs/1407.3561

Benkler, Y. (2002). Coase's Penguin, or, Linux and the nature of the firm. *The Yale Law Journal*, *112*(3), 369–446. DOI: 10.2307/1562247

Benkler, Y. (2006). *The wealth of networks: How social production transforms markets and freedom*. Yale University Press.

Bennett, K. (2025). The ReFi movement in Web3: Implications for the global commons. *Frontiers in Blockchain, 8*, Article 1564073. https://www.frontiersin.org/articles/10.3389/fbloc.2025.1564073/full

Ben-Sasson, E.. (2014). *Zerocash: Decentralized anonymous payments from Bitcoin*. IEEE S&P.

Berkowitz, J. (2025, March 14). *The Bybit hack of 2025 - potential implications*. Paul Hastings. https://www.paulhastings.com/insights/crypto-policy-tracker/the-bybit-hack-of-2025-potential-implications

Berne Convention for the Protection of Literary and Artistic Works. Sept. 9, 1886, as revised at Paris on July 24, 1971, and amended on September 28, 1979, S. Treaty Doc. No. 99-27 (1986).

Bhuiyan, S. M. Y., Mostafa, T., Schoen, M. P., & Mahamud, R. (2024). Assessment of machine learning approaches for the predictive modeling of plasma-assisted ignition kernel growth. *ASME 2024 International Mechanical Engineering Congress and Exposition*. DOI: 10.1115/IMECE2024-145906

Bin, A. F., Kumar, R. P., & Majharul, I. M. (2023). AI-Powered predictive failure analysis in pressure vessels using real-time sensor fusion: Enhancing industrial safety and infrastructure reliability. *American Journal of Scholarly Research and Innovation*, 2(2), 102–134. DOI: 10.63125/wk278c34

Binance Research. (2021). An Overview of Decentralized Governance. https://research.binance.com

Binns, R. (2018). Fairness in machine learning: Lessons from political philosophy. In Friedler, S. A., & Wilson, C. (Eds.), *Proceedings of the 1st Conference on Fairness, Accountability and Transparency* (pp. 149–159). PMLR.

Bischof, E., Botezatu, A., Jakimov, S., Suharenko, I., Ostrovski, A., Verbitsky, A., Yanovich, Y., Zhavoronkov, A., & Zmudze, G. (2022). Longevity foundation: Perspective on decentralized autonomous organizations for special-purpose financing. *IEEE Access : Practical Innovations, Open Solutions, 10*, 33048–33058. DOI: 10.1109/ACCESS.2022.3161392

Bissessar, D., Adams, C., & Stoianov, A. (2016). Privacy, Security and Convenience: Biometric Encryption for Smartphone-Based Electronic Travel Documents. In Abielmona, R., Falcon, R., Zincir-Heywood, N., & Abbass, H. A. (Eds.), *Recent Advances in Computational Intelligence in Defense and Security* (Vol. 621, pp. 339–366). Springer International Publishing., DOI: 10.1007/978-3-319-26450-9_13

Bitinfocharts. (n.d.). *Ethereum avg. transaction fee—historical chart.* Retrieved August 29, 2025, from https://bitinfocharts.com/comparison/ethereum-transactionfees.html

BlackRock. (2024). *Introducing the BlackRock BUIDL Fund: The next evolution of digital assets.* https://www.blackrock.com

Blandin, A., Cloots, A. S., Hussain, H., Rauchs, M., Saleuddin, R., Allen, J. G., & Cloud, K. (2019). *Global cryptoasset regulatory landscape study.* Cambridge Centre for Alternative Finance. DOI: 10.2139/ssrn.3379219

BlockApps. (2024). *Securing land rights and property records with blockchain.* BlockApps. https://blockapps.net/blog/securing-land-rights-and-property-records-with-blockchain/

Blockcerts. (2018). *FAQ - Blockcerts: The Open Standard for Blockchain Credentials.* Blockcerts.Org. https://www.blockcerts.org/guide/faq.html

Blockchain, U. B. C. (2021). *Decolonizing blockchain: Indigenous pathways to digital sovereignty.* University of British Columbia.

Boston Consulting Group (BCG). (2023). *Revolution in asset markets: The trillion-dollar potential of tokenization.*

Bourdieu, P. (1975). The specificity of the scientific field and the social conditions of the progress of reason. *Social Sciences Information. Information Sur les Sciences Sociales, 14*(6), 19–47. DOI: 10.1177/053901847501400602

Bourdieu, P. (2004). *Science of science and reflexivity.* University of Chicago Press.

Boyle, J. (2003). The second enclosure movement and the construction of the public domain. *Law and Contemporary Problems*, *66*(1/2), 33–74.

Braithwithe, C. (2025, June 25). What is private credit tokenization and how does it work? *Onchain*. Retrieved from https://onchain.org/magazine/what-is-private-credit-tokenization-and-how-does-it-work/

Breidenbach, S., Glatz, F., Schrey, J., & Schmid, A. (2021). *Rechtshandbuch Smart Contracts*. C.H. Beck.

Brennan, S. (2025, February 28). BioAgents: Accelerating decentralized science with AI agents. Bio Protocol. https://www.bio.xyz/blog-posts/bioagents-pioneering-decentralized-science-with-ai-agents

Bridge Liechtenstein, I. P. (2023). Intellectual property tokenization platform. https://ipbridge.li/

Briola, A., Vidal-Tomás, D., Wang, Y., & Aste, T. (2023). Anatomy of a Stablecoin's failure: The Terra-Luna case. *Finance Research Letters*, *51*, 103358. DOI: 10.1016/j.frl.2022.103358

Brody, P., Halamka, J., & Singh, H. (2021). *Decentralized data marketplaces: The future of digital information sharing*. IEEE Computer Society Press.

Brownsword, R. (2019). *Law, technology and society: Reimagining the regulatory environment*. Routledge. DOI: 10.4324/9781351128186

Brownsword, R., Scotford, E., & Yeung, K. (Eds.). (2017). *The Oxford handbook of law, regulation and technology*. Oxford University Press.

Budish, E. B. (2018). The economic limits of Bitcoin and the blockchain (Chicago Booth Research Paper No. 18-07). SSRN. DOI: 10.2139/ssrn.3197300

Bukhari, S. T., Janjua, M. U., & Qadir, J. (2024). Secure Storage of Crypto Wallet Seed Phrase Using ECC and Splitting Technique. *IEEE Open Journal of the Computer Society*, *5*, 278–289. DOI: 10.1109/OJCS.2024.3398794

Bünz, B., Bootle, J., Boneh, D., Poelstra, A., Wuille, P., & Maxwell, G. (2018). Bulletproofs: Short proofs for confidential transactions and more. *2018 IEEE Symposium on Security and Privacy (SP)*, 315-334. DOI: 10.1109/SP.2018.00020

Burst, I. Q. (2023). Blockchain and AI in healthcare: Securing precision medicine through intelligent automation. *HealthTech Journal*, *14*(1), 32–47.

Busch, C., Mak, V., Twigg-Flesner, C., & Schulze, R. (2021). The EU digital services act and the EU digital markets act: A primer. *EuCML*, *10*(6), 256–261.

Buterin, V. (2014). A Next-Generation Smart Contract and Decentralized Application Platform. Ethereum White Paper.

Buterin, V. (2021). *Retroactive public goods funding*. Medium. https://medium.com/ethereum-optimism/retroactive-public-goods-funding-33c9b7d00f0c

Buterin, V. (2021, August 16). *Moving beyond coin voting governance* [Blog post]. https://vitalik.eth.limo/general/2021/08/16/voting3.html

Buterin, V., Hitzig, Z., & Weyl, E. G. (2018). Liberal radicalism: A flexible design for philanthropic matching funds [Working paper]. *SSRN*. DOI: 10.2139/ssrn.3243656

Buterin, V., Hitzig, Z., & Weyl, E. G. (2019). A flexible design for funding public goods. *Management Science*, *65*(11), 5171–5187. DOI: 10.1287/mnsc.2019.3337

Calliess, G. P., & Zumbansen, P. (2010). *Rough consensus and running code: A theory of transnational private law*. Hart Publishing.

Canadian Securities Administrators. (2023). CSA Staff Notice 21-332: Crypto Asset Trading Platforms: Term and Conditions of Trading. Retrieved from https://www.securities-administrators.ca/news/csa-publishes-updated-approach-to-crypto-asset-trading-platforms/

Cannarsa, M. (2019). Interpretation of contracts and smart contracts: Smart interpretation or interpretation of smart contracts? *European Review of Private Law*, *27*(4), 773–785.

Capetillo, A., Camacho, D., & Alanis, M. (2022). Blockchained education: Challenging the long-standing model of academic institutions. [IJIDeM]. *International Journal on Interactive Design and Manufacturing*, *16*(2), 791–802. DOI: 10.1007/s12008-022-00886-1 PMID: 40477579

Capitol Records, LLC v. ReDigi Inc., 934 F.Supp.2d 640 (S.D.N.Y. 2013).

Capponi, A., Iyengar, G., & Sethuraman, J. (2023). Decentralized finance: Protocols, risks, and governance. Foundations and Trends® in Privacy and Security, 5(3), 144-188. DOI: 10.1561/3300000036

Carapella, F., Chuan, G., Gerszten, J., Hunter, C., & Swem, N. (2023). *Tokenization: Overview and financial stability implications* (Finance and Economics Discussion Series No. 2023-060). Board of Governors of the Federal Reserve System. DOI: 10.17016/feds.2023.060

Carapella, F., Swem, N., & Gerszten, J. (2023). Tokenization: Overview and Financial Stability implications. Finance and Economics Discussion Series, issue. DOI: 10.17016/feds.2023.060r1

Cardoso, S., Mamede, H. S., & Santos, V. (2020a). Reference model for academic results certification in student mobility scenarios : Position paper. *2020 15th Iberian Conference on Information Systems and Technologies (CISTI)*, 1–4. DOI: 10.23919/CISTI49556.2020.9141134

Cardoso, S., Mamede, H., & Santos, V. (2020b). Reference Model for Academic Results Certification in Student Mobility Scenarios. *Journal of Information Systems Engineering & Management*, *5*(4), em0125. Advance online publication. DOI: 10.29333/jisem/8491

Carlisle, Y. (2019). Mt. Gox: Lessons from the biggest Bitcoin hack. *Journal of Financial Crime*, *26*(3), 764–773. DOI: 10.1108/JFC-06-2018-0060

Carstens, A. (2020). Shaping the Future of Payments. BIS Quarterly Review, March 2020, Available at *SSRN*: https://ssrn.com/abstract=3561177

Casey, A. J., & Niblett, A. (2019). Framework for the new personalization of law. *The University of Chicago Law Review. University of Chicago. Law School*, *86*(2), 333–358.

Casino, F., Dasaklis, T. K., & Patsakis, C. (2019). A systematic literature review of blockchain-based applications: Current status, classification and open issues. *Telematics and Informatics*, *36*, 55–81. DOI: 10.1016/j.tele.2018.11.006

Catalini, C., & Gans, J. S. (2016). *Some simple economics of the blockchain* (MIT Sloan Research Paper No. 5191-16). DOI: 10.3386/w22952

Catalini, C., & Gans, J. S. (2016). Some simple economics of the blockchain (Working Paper No. 22952). National Bureau of Economic Research.

Catalini, C., & Gans, J. S. (2020). Some simple economics of the blockchain. *Communications of the ACM*, *63*(7), 80–90. DOI: 10.1145/3359552

Cath, C. (2018). Governing artificial intelligence: Ethical, legal and technical opportunities and challenges. *Philosophical Transactions. Series A, Mathematical, Physical, and Engineering Sciences*, *376*(2133), 20180080. DOI: 10.1098/rsta.2018.0080 PMID: 30322996

Centrifuge. (2022). *Protocol overview and Tinlake documentation.* https://docs.centrifuge.io

Chainalysis. (2019). *Crypto Crime Report.* (includes forensic study of Mt. Gox and private key vulnerabilities). https://go.chainalysis.com/2019-Crypto-Crime-Report.html

Chainalysis. (2022). Crypto Crime Report. https://www.chainalysis.com

Chainalysis. (2025). The 2025 Crypto Crime Report. https://go.chainalysis.com/2025-Crypto-Crime-Report.html

Chang, Y., Iakovou, E., & Shi, W. (2019). Blockchain in global supply chains and cross border trade: A critical synthesis of the state-of-the-art, challenges and opportunities. *International Journal of Production Research*, *58*(7), 2082–2099. DOI: 10.1080/00207543.2019.1651946

Chauhan, A., Tripathi, S., Singh, S. V., Singh, K., & Talukdar, M. B. (2025). Eco-Friendly Practices of Ghost Kitchens Through Smart Technology. In Singh, K., Kumar, S., & Talukder, M. (Eds.), *Impact of AI and the Evolution of Future Ghost Kitchens* (pp. 231–246). IGI Global Scientific Publishing., DOI: 10.4018/979-8-3373-0432-8.ch011

Chen, X., He, S., Sun, L., Zheng, Y., & Wu, C. Q. (2024). A Survey of Consortium Blockchain and Its Applications. *Cryptography*, *8*(2), 12. DOI: 10.3390/cryptography8020012

Chen, Y., & Bellavitis, C. (2020). Blockchain disruption and decentralized finance: The rise of decentralized business models. *Journal of Business Venturing Insights*, *13*, e00151. DOI: 10.1016/j.jbvi.2019.e00151

Chiu, J., & Monnet, C. (2024). Public and private money creation for distributed ledgers: Stablecoins, tokenized deposits, or central bank digital currencies? Bank of Canada. https://www.bankofcanada.ca/wp-content/uploads/2024/10/swp2024-35.pdf

Chiu, J., Koeppl, T., Yu, H., & Zhang, S. (2023). Understanding DEFI through the lens of a Production-Network model. Bank of Canada. DOI: 10.34989/swp-2023-42

Chuing, S. S., & Kutty, F. M. (2025). The Effectiveness of Implementing a Token Economy System in Reducing Disruptive Behavior among Preschool Students. *International Journal of Academic Research in Progressive Education and Development*, *14*(1), 1812–1828. DOI: 10.6007/IJARPED/v14-i1/24769

Ciccio, C. D. (2024). *Blockchain and Distributed Ledger Technologies*. Cambridge University Press., DOI: 10.1017/9781009411783.003

Clark, B. (2018). Blockchain and IP law: A match made in crypto heaven? WIPO Magazine, February 2018.

Coase, R. H. (1960). The problem of social cost. *The Journal of Law & Economics*, *3*, 1–44. DOI: 10.1086/466560

Cohney, S., Hoffman, D., Sklaroff, J., & Wishnick, D. (2019). Coin-operated capitalism. *Columbia Law Review*, *119*(3), 591–676.

Coin Center. (2022). Decentralization: Why It Matters. https://www.coincenter.org

Commodity Futures Trading Commission (CFTC). (2024, November 21). *CFTC's Global Markets Advisory Committee advances recommendation on tokenized non-cash collateral* [Press release]. https://www.cftc.gov/PressRoom/PressReleases/9009-24

Commodity Futures Trading Commission (CFTC). Digital assets primer (2020). https://www.cftc.gov/LabCFTC/primers

Commons Stack. (2019). *Deep dive: Augmented bonding curves* [Medium article by A. Titcomb]. https://medium.com/commonsstack/deep-dive-augmented-bonding-curves-b5ca4fad4436

Commons Stack. (2021a). *The augmented bonding curve, part 1: A Web3 way to fund public goods.* https://medium.com/commonsstack/the-augmented-bonding-curve-part-1-a-web3-way-to-fund-public-goods-7c9d1a871ae2

Commons Stack. (2021b). *Augmented Bonding Curve whitepaper.* https://www.commonsstack.org/augmented-bonding-curve

Cong, L. W., Li, X., Tang, K., & Yang, Y. (2021). *Crypto Wash Trading.* arXiv. / arXiv.2108.10984DOI: 10.48550

Cong, L. W., & He, Z. (2019). Blockchain disruption and smart contracts. *Review of Financial Studies, 32*(5), 1754–1797. DOI: 10.1093/rfs/hhz007

Cong, L. W., Li, Y., & Wang, N. (2021). Tokenomics: Dynamic adoption and valuation. *Review of Financial Studies, 34*(3), 1105–1155. DOI: 10.1093/rfs/hhaa089

Cornelli, G., Gambacorta, L., Garratt, R., & Reghezza, A. (2024). Decoding DeFi lending: Motivations, risks, and investor behaviours. CEPR. https://cepr.org/voxeu/columns/decoding-defi-lending-motivations-risks-and-investor-behaviours

Cornelli, G., Gambacorta, L., Garratt, R., & Reghezza, A. (2024, May). *Why DeFi lending? Evidence from Aave V2* (BIS Working Papers No. 1183). Bank for International Settlements. https://www.bis.org/publ/work1183.htm

Cornes, R., & Sandler, T. (1996). *The theory of externalities, public goods, and club goods* (2nd ed.). Cambridge University Press. DOI: 10.1017/CBO9781139174312

Cramer, A.J. (2025, August 28). Indigenous data sovereignty in IT blockchain systems: Seminar Lecture. University Canada West (UCW).

Croman, K., Decker, C., Eyal, I., Gencer, A. E., Juels, A., Kosba, A., Miller, A., Saxena, P., Shi, E., Sirer, E. G., Song, D., & Wattenhofer, R. (2016). On scaling decentralized blockchains. In Clark, J., Meiklejohn, S., Ryan, P., Wallach, D., Brenner, M., & Rohloff, K. (Eds.), *Financial cryptography and data security: FC 2016 international workshops* (pp. 106–125). Springer., DOI: 10.1007/978-3-662-53357-4_8

Crosby, M., Nachiappan, Pattanayak, P., Verma, S., & Kalyanaraman, V. (2016). Blockchain technology: Beyond bitcoin. *Applied Innovation Review*, *2*, 6–19.

Crypto Valley Association. (2023). CV VC Top 50 Report. https://cryptovalley.swiss

Cutts, T. (2019). Smart contracts and consumers. *West Virginia Law Review*, *122*(2), 389–447.

Daniels, J. (2025). *Introducing FIL ProPGF: A new era in community-led public goods funding for the Filecoin ecosystem*. Filecoin. https://filecoin.io/blog/posts/introducing-fil-propgf-a-new-era-in-community-led-public-goods-funding-for-the-filecoin-ecosystem

Darlin, M., Palaiokrassas, G., & Tassiulas, L. (2022, September). Debt-financed collateral and stability risks in the defi ecosystem. In 2022 4th Conference on Blockchain Research & Applications for Innovative Networks and Services (BRAINS) (pp. 5-12). IEEE. DOI: 10.1109/BRAINS55737.2022.9909090

Dasgupta, A., Islam, M., Nahid, M., Omar, F., Rahmatullah, R. (2024). Engineering management perspectives on safety culture in chemical and petrochemical plants: A systematic review. *Academic Journal On Science, Technology, Engineering & Mathematics Education, 1*(1), 10.69593.

David, P. A. (2004). Understanding the emergence of 'open science' institutions: Functionalist economics in historical context. *Industrial and Corporate Change*, *13*(4), 571–589. DOI: 10.1093/icc/dth023

Davis, F. D. (1989). Perceived usefulness, perceived ease of use, and user acceptance of information technology. *Management Information Systems Quarterly, 13*(3), 319–340. DOI: 10.2307/249008

de Alwis, A., Shrestha, A., & Sarker, T. (2025). Exploring Governance for accreditation in the education sector using blockchain technology: A systematic literature review. *Discover Education*, *4*(1), 57. DOI: 10.1007/s44217-025-00449-y

De Filippi, P. (2016). The interplay between decentralization and privacy: The case of blockchain technologies. Journal of Peer Production, 7.

De Filippi, P., & Wright, A. (2019). Decentralized blockchain technology and the rise of lex cryptographia. SSRN Electronic Journal.

De Filippi, P., & Hassan, S. (2016). Blockchain technology as a regulatory technology: From code is law to law is code. *First Monday, 21*(12). Advance online publication. DOI: 10.5210/fm.v21i12.7113

De Filippi, P., & Loveluck, B. (2016). The invisible politics of Bitcoin: Governance crisis of a decentralized infrastructure. *Internet Policy Review, 5*(4). Advance online publication. https://ssrn.com/abstract=2852691. DOI: 10.14763/2016.3.427

De Filippi, P., Mannan, M., & Reijers, W. (2021). The alegality of blockchain technology. *Policy and Society, 41*(3), 358–372. DOI: 10.1093/polsoc/puac006

De Filippi, P., & Wright, A. (2018). *Blockchain and the law: The rule of code.* Harvard University Press.

De Vries, A. (2023). Revisiting Bitcoin's carbon footprint. *Joule, 7*(3), 615–619. DOI: 10.1016/j.joule.2023.02.002

DeFi Pulse. (2021). Centrifuge and Tinlake overview: Real-world assets on DeFi. https://defipulse.com/blog/centrifuge-real-world-assets/

DeFi Rate. (2024). *Compare crypto lending rates.* Available at https://defirate.com/lend/

DeFiLlama. (n.d.) Total value locked (DeFi) all chains. *DeFiLlama.* Retrieved from https://defill ama.com/ chains

DeFrancesco, L., & Klevecz, A. (2022). Decentralized investor communities gain traction in biotech. *Nature Biotechnology, 40*(9), 1310–1315. DOI: 10.1038/s41587-022-01459-z PMID: 36042297

Dehghani, M., Chen, Y., Wang, Y., & Kietzmann, J. (2022). High interest, low adoption: A mixed-method investigation into organisational blockchain adoption. *Journal of Business Research, 149*, 393–411. DOI: 10.1016/j.jbusres.2022.05.015

Delgado-von-Eitzen, C., Anido-Rifón, L., & Fernández-Iglesias, M. J. (2024). NFTs for the Issuance and Validation of Academic Information That Complies with the GDPR. *Applied Sciences (Basel, Switzerland), 14*(2), 706. DOI: 10.3390/app14020706

Dell'Erba, M. (2020). Initial coin offerings: The response of regulatory authorities. *NYU Journal of Law & Business, 16*(3), 543–608.

Deval, V., Dwivedi, V. K., Dixit, A., Norta, A., Shah, S. A., Sharma, R., & Draheim, D. (2024). Mobile smart contracts: Exploring scalability challenges and consensus mechanisms. *IEEE Access : Practical Innovations, Open Solutions, 12*, 34265–34288. DOI: 10.1109/ACCESS.2024.3371901

Dewangan, S., & Kumar, S. (2025). Frontiers of Innovation: Unveiling the Future Opportunities in Fintech. In *Financial Landscape Transformation: Technological Disruptions* (pp. 153–165). Emerald Publishing Limited.

Diamond, D. W. (1984). Financial intermediation and delegated monitoring. *The Review of Economic Studies, 51*(3), 393–414. DOI: 10.2307/2297430

Dickinson, A. (2019). Cryptocurrencies and the conflict of laws. In Fox, D., & Green, S. (Eds.), *Cryptocurrencies in public and private law* (pp. 253–289). Oxford University Press. DOI: 10.1093/law/9780198826385.003.0005

Digibrixx. (2021). *Infrastructure tokenization platform documentation*. https://www.digibrixx.eu/docs

Digital Dubai & Dubai Future Foundation. (2025). Dubai State of AI Report. Government of Dubai. https://www.digitaldubai.ae/knowledge-hub/publications/dubai-state-of-ai-report-2025

Digital Dubai. (2024). *AI integration in public services*. Digital Dubai Office.

Digital Signatures Act, RT I 2000, 26, 150 (Estonia).

Dinh, T. T. A., Liu, R., Zhang, M., Chen, G., Ooi, B. C., & Wang, J. (2018). Untangling Blockchain: A Data Processing View of Blockchain Systems. *IEEE Transactions on Knowledge and Data Engineering, 30*(7), 1366–1385. DOI: 10.1109/TKDE.2017.2781227

Dinwoodie, G. B. (2009). Developing a private international intellectual property law: The demise of territoriality. *William and Mary Law Review, 51*(2), 711–800.

Directive 2001/29/EC of the European Parliament and of the Council of 22 May 2001 on the harmonisation of certain aspects of copyright and related rights in the information society, OJ L 167, 22.6.2001.

Directive 2001/84/EC of the European Parliament and of the Council of 27 September 2001 on the resale right for the benefit of the author of an original work of art, OJ L 272, 13.10.2001.

Directive 2014/65/EU of the European Parliament and of the Council of 15 May 2014 on markets in financial instruments, OJ L 173, 12.6.2014.

DMCC. (2025). *Blockchain and AI for government efficiency*. Dubai Multi Commodities Centre.

Do, B.-L., Nguyen, V.-T., Dinh, H.-N., Dao, T.-C., & Nguyen, B. (2022). Blockchain for Education: Verification and Management of Lifelong Learning Data. *Computer Systems Science and Engineering*, *43*(2), 591–604. DOI: 10.32604/csse.2022.023508

Doebeli, G., & Giang, A. (nd). Trans Mountain Pipeline Expansion Project, Open Case Studies: Trans Mountain Pipeline Expansion Project, retrieved (July 3, 2024) from https://wiki.ubc.ca/Documentation:Open_Case_Studies/IRES/Trans_Mountain_Pipeline_Expansion_Project

Doshi-Velez, F., & Kim, B. (2017). Towards a rigorous science of interpretable machine learning. arXiv. https://arxiv.org/abs/1702.08608

Dotan, M., Yaish, A., Yin, H.-C., Tsytkin, E., & Zohar, A. (2023). *The vulnerable nature of decentralized governance in DeFi. arXiv.* /arXiv.2308.04267DOI: 10.1145/3605768.3623539

Douceur, J. R. (2002). The Sybil attack. In Druschel, P., Kaashoek, F., & Rowstron, A. (Eds.), *Peer-to-Peer Systems (IPTPS 2002)* (pp. 251–260). Springer., DOI: 10.1007/3-540-45748-8_24

Durovic, M., & Janssen, A. (2019). The formation of blockchain-based smart contracts in the light of contract law. *European Review of Private Law*, *27*(4), 753–771.

Easley, D., O'Hara, M., & Basu, S. (2019). From mining to markets: The evolution of bitcoin transaction fees. *Journal of Financial Economics*, *134*(1), 91–109. DOI: 10.1016/j.jfineco.2019.03.004

Ebadi, R. (2025, May 21). Real Estate Tokenization: From Theory to Practice. *SSRN*. DOI: 10.2139/ssrn.5366013

Efroni, Z., & Geiger, C. (2018). Limitations in the digital single market: Has the court of justice developed a crystal clear vision? IIC - International Review of Intellectual Property and Competition Law, 49(8), 881-885.

Eichhorn, K. (2019). *The end of forgetting: Growing up with social media*. Harvard University Press. DOI: 10.4159/9780674239333

Elkhwesky, Z., & Elkhwesky, E. F. Y. (2022). A systematic and critical review of Internet of Things in contemporary hospitality: A roadmap and avenues for future research. *International Journal of Contemporary Hospitality Management, ahead-of-print*.

Else, H. (2024). 'Getting paid to review is justice': Journal pays peer reviewers in cryptocurrency. *Nature*. Advance online publication. DOI: 10.1038/d41586-024-04027-4 PMID: 39663443

Engage, C. (2025). *Scientific credibility for high-integrity voluntary carbon markets*. https://www.cambridge.org/engage/coe/article-details/679385946dde43c9082f7009

Environmental Defense Fund. (2019). *Addressing leakage, additionality, and permanence so that credits deliver real climate benefits*. https://www.edf.org/sites/default/files/Environmental_Integrity_TFS_3.4.19.pdf. Environmental Defense

Eskandari, S., Salehi, M., Gu, W. C., & Clark, J. (2021, September). Sok: Oracles from the ground truth to market manipulation. In *Proceedings of the 3rd ACM Conference on Advances in Financial Technologies* (pp. 127-141). DOI: 10.1145/3479722.3480994

ESMA. (2019). Advice on Initial Coin Offerings and Crypto-Assets. ESMA50-157-1391.

Esposito, C., Ficco, M., & Moscato, V. (2025). Governance challenges in decentralized autonomous organizations: A systematic analysis. *Frontiers in Blockchain*, *7*, 1538227. Advance online publication. DOI: 10.3389/fbloc.2025.1538227

Ethereum.org. (2025a, February 17). *Scaling*. https://ethereum.org/en/developers/docs/scaling/ ethereum.org

Ethereum.org. (n.d.). *Optimistic rollups*. Retrieved August 29, 2025, from https://ethereum.org/en/developers/docs/scaling/optimistic-rollups/

European Central Bank (ECB). (2023). Progress on the investigation phase of a Digital Euro. ECB Reports. https://www.ecb.europa.eu/paym/digital_euro/investigation/progress/html/index.en.html

European Commission. (2020). *Proposal for a Regulation of the European Parliament and of the Council on Markets in Crypto-assets and amending Directive (EU) 2019/1937*. Retrieved from https://eur-lex.europa.eu/legal-content/EN/TXT/?uri=CELEX%3A52020PC0593

European Commission. (2020). Proposal for a Regulation on Markets in Crypto-assets. COM(2020) 593 final.

European Commission. (2020). White paper on artificial intelligence: A European approach to excellence and trust. Publications Office of the European Union.

European Convention on Human Rights, November 4, 1950, E.T.S. 5, 213 U.N.T.S. 221.

European Parliament & Council of the European Union. (2023, May 31). Regulation (EU) 2023/1114 of the European Parliament and of the Council of 31 May 2023 on markets in crypto-assets, and amending Regulations (EU) No 1093/2010 and (EU) No 1095/2010 and Directives 2013/36/EU and (EU) 2019/1937 (MiCA). *Official Journal of the European Union, L, 150*, 40–205. https://eur-lex.europa.eu/eli/reg/2023/1114/oj

European Securities and Markets Authority. (2022). *ESMA report on trends, risks and vulnerabilities*. https://www.esma.europa.eu/sites/default/files/library/esma50-165-2238_trv_1_2022.pdf

European Securities and Markets Authority. (2025, July 1). *Maximal Extractable Value: Implications for crypto markets* (ESMA TRV Risk Analysis). European Securities and Markets Authority. DOI: 10.2856/328752

European Securities and Markets Authority. (n.d.). Markets in Crypto-Assets Regulation (MiCA). https://www.esma.europa.eu/esmas-activities/digital-finance-and-innovation/markets-crypto-assets-regulation-mica

European Union (2023). Regulation (EU) 2023/1114 on markets in crypto-assets (MiCA). Official Journal of the EU. https://eur-lex.europa.eu/eli/reg/2023/1114/oj

European Union Blockchain Observatory and Forum. (2023). Ethereum Merge: Trend report. https://blockchain-observatory.ec.europa.eu/document/download/3f78c885-d14e-47cb-b183-f22ef529a258_en

European Union. (2023). Markets in Crypto-Assets (MiCA) Regulation. European Parliament.

Evans, D. (2024). Permissioned DeFi goes live with Aave Arc + Fireblocks. Fireblocks. https://www.fireblocks.com/blog/permissioned-defi-goes-live-with-aave-arc-fireblocks/#:~:text=We're%20excited%20to%20announce,active%20whitelister%20for%20the%20protocol

Exonum. (n.d.). *Improving the security of a government land registry: Georgia.* Exonum. https://exonum.com/story-georgia

Eyal, I., & Sirer, E. G. (2014). Majority is not enough: Bitcoin mining is vulnerable. *Communications of the ACM*, *61*(7), 95–102. DOI: 10.1145/3212998

Fairfield, J. (2021). Tokenized: The law of non-fungible tokens and unique digital property. *Industrial Law Journal*, *97*(4), 1261–1331.

Fantaccini, S., Grassi, L., & Rampoldi, A. (2024). The potential of DAOs for funding and collaborative development in the life sciences. *Nature Biotechnology*, *42*(4), 555–562. DOI: 10.1038/s41587-024-02189-0 PMID: 38565972

FATF. (2021). *Updated guidance for a risk-based approach to virtual assets and virtual asset service providers*. Financial Action Task Force.

Federal Act on the Adaptation of Federal Law to Developments in Distributed Ledger Technology (DLT Act), AS 2021 33 (Switzerland).

Federal Reserve Bank of New York. (2024). The Financial Stability Implications of Digital Assets. Economic Policy Review (Vol. 30, Issue 2, pp. 1–2). https://www.newyorkfed.org/medialibrary/media/research/epr/2024/EPR_2024_digital-assets_azar.pdf

Feng, Z. (2024). DAI's transparent and decentralized governance ensures stability through MKR token-holder voting. *Frontiers in Blockchain*. DOI: 10.3389/fbloc.2024.1392812

Fernandes, F., & Werner, C. (2023). Towards a Blockchain-based Software Engineering Education. *Proceedings of the 1st Colloquium on Blockchain and Decentralized Web*, 25–30. DOI: 10.5753/cblockchain.2023.230488

Ferrari, V. (2020). The regulation of crypto-assets in the EU – Investment and payment tokens under the radar. *Maastricht Journal of European and Comparative Law*, *27*(3), 325–342. DOI: 10.1177/1023263X20911538

Fetch.AI. (2023). *Technical whitepaper: Building autonomous economic systems with agents and smart contracts. Fetch*. AI Foundation.

Filimonau, V., & Naumova, E. (2020). The blockchain technology and the scope of its application in hospitality operations. *International Journal of Hospitality Management*, *87*, 102383. DOI: 10.1016/j.ijhm.2019.102383

Finance, U. K. (2024, November). *Digital gilt roadmap 2024*. https://www.ukfinance.org.uk/system/files/2024-11/UK%20Finance%20Digital%20Gilt%20roadmap%202024.pdf

Financial Action Task Force. (2021). *Updated guidance for a risk-based approach to virtual assets and virtual asset service providers*. FATF. https://www.fatf-gafi.org/en/publications/Fatfrecommendations/Guidance-rba-virtual-assets-2021.html

Financial Action Task Force. (2021). *Updated guidance for a risk-based approach to virtual assets and virtual asset service providers*. FATF. https://www.fatf-gafi.org/en/publications/Fatfrecommendations/Updated-Guidance-VA-VASPs.html

Financial Action Task Force. (2021). *Updated guidance for a risk-based approach to virtual assets and virtual asset service providers.* https://www.fatf-gafi.org/content/dam/fatf-gafi/guidance/Updated-Guidance-VA-VASP.pdf

Financial Stability Board (FSB). (2022). Assessment of risks to financial stability from crypto-assets. https://www.fsb.org/2022/02/assessment-of-risks-to-financial-stability-from-crypto-assets

Financial Stability Board (FSB). (2024). The financial stability implications of tokenisation. October 22, 2024. https://www.fsb.org/uploads/P221024-2.pdf

Financial Stability Board (FSB). (2024). *The financial stability implications of tokenization.* Financial Stability Board.

Financial Stability Board. (2024, October 22). The financial stability implications of tokenisation. https://www.fsb.org/2024/10/the-financial-stability-implications-of-tokenisation

Financial Times. (2025). UAE experiments with AI-driven legislative drafting. Financial Times Middle East Edition.

FinCEN. (2021). *Advisory on Illicit Finance Risks of Decentralized Finance.* U.S. Department of the Treasury.

Finck, M. (2018). *Smart contracts as a form of private ordering: An empirical study* (Max Planck Institute for Innovation and Competition Research Paper No. 18-10). https://doi.org/DOI: 10.2139/ssrn.3266668

Finck, M. (2019). *Blockchain and the General Data Protection Regulation: Can distributed ledgers be squared with European data protection law?* European Parliamentary Research Service.

FINMA. (2018). *Guidelines for enquiries regarding the regulatory framework for initial coin offerings (ICOs).* Swiss Financial Market Supervisory Authority.

First Nation Bank of Canada. (2025, August 31) https://www.fnbc.ca

First Nations Technology Council. (2021). Indigenous Digital Equity Strategy. Retrieved from https://technologycouncil.ca August 1, 2025

First Nations Technology Council. (2021). *Indigenous digital sovereignty: A framework for reconciliation.* First Nations Technology Council. https://technologycouncil.ca

Floridi, L., Cowls, J., Beltrametti, M., Chatila, R., Chazerand, P., Dignum, V., Luetge, C., Madelin, R., Pagallo, U., Rossi, F., Schafer, B., Valcke, P., & Vayena, E. (2018). AI4People—An ethical framework for a good AI society: Opportunities, risks, principles, and recommendations. *Minds and Machines*, *28*(4), 689–707. DOI: 10.1007/s11023-018-9482-5 PMID: 30930541

Foucault, M. (2014). On the government of the living (A. Davidson, Ed.). Palgrave.

Franceschet, M., Colavizza, G., Smith, T., Finucane, B., Ostachowski, M. L., Scalet, S., Perkins, J., Morgan, J., & Hernández, S. (2021). Crypto art: A decentralized view. *Leonardo*, *54*(4), 402–405. DOI: 10.1162/leon_a_02003

Franklin Templeton. (2022). *Franklin OnChain U.S. Government Money Fund launched on Stellar.* https://www.franklintempleton.com

Freitas, L., & Maldonado, W. (2024). Quadratic funding with incomplete information. *Social Choice and Welfare*, *64*(1), 43–67.

Freni, P., Ferro, E., & Moncada, R. (2022). Tokenomics and blockchain tokens: A design-oriented morphological framework. *Blockchain: Research and Applications*, *3*(1), 100069. DOI: 10.1016/j.bcra.2022.100069

Friday, S. (2023, June 18). VitaDAO letter: Zuzalu & shaping the future of autophagy research. VitaDAO.

Frischmann, B. M., Madison, M. J., & Strandburg, K. J. (2014). *Governing knowledge commons*. Oxford University Press. DOI: 10.1093/acprof:oso/9780199972036.001.0001

Gans, J. (2019). The Case for an ICO Contract. *Journal of Institutional and Theoretical Economics*, *175*(1), 34–51.

Garcia-Costa, D., Squazzoni, F., Mehmani, B., & Grimaldo, F. (2022). Measuring the developmental function of peer review: A multi-dimensional, cross-disciplinary analysis of peer review reports from 740 academic journals. *PeerJ*, *10*, e13539. DOI: 10.7717/peerj.13539 PMID: 35694383

Garcia-Font, V. (2020). Blockchain: Opportunities and Challenges in the Educational Context. In Baneres, D., Rodríguez, M., & Guerrero-Roldán, A. (Eds.), *Engineering Data-Driven Adaptive Trust-based e-Assessment Systems* (Vol. 34, pp. 133–157). Springer., DOI: 10.1007/978-3-030-29326-0_7

Gatteschi, V., Lamberti, F., Demartini, C., Pranteda, C., & Santamaría, V. (2018). Blockchain and smart contracts for insurance: Is the technology mature enough? *Future Internet*, *10*(2), 20. DOI: 10.3390/fi10020020

Geiger, C., Frosio, G., & Bulayenko, O. (2018). The exception for text and data mining (TDM) in the proposed directive on copyright in the digital single market. Centre for International Intellectual Property Studies Research Paper No. 2018-02.

Gensler, G. (2023). You may have seen this before - Remarks before the Piper Sandler Global Exchange and FinTech Conference. U.S. Securities and Exchange Commission. https://www.sec.gov/newsroom/speeches-statements/gensler-remarks-piper-sandler-060823

Gibson, G., & O'Faircheallaigh, C. (2015). *IBA Community Toolkit: Negotiation and Implementation of Impact and Benefit Agreements*. Walter and Duncan Gordon Foundation.

Gitcoin. (2023). *Gitcoin impact report – Funding stats 2019–2023.*

Gitcoin. (2023, April 18). *WTF is retro funding* [Blog post by S. Smith].

Gitcoin. (2025a). *GG23 results & recap*. Gitcoin Blog.

Giudici, G., Milne, A., & Vinogradov, D. (2020). Cryptocurrencies: Market analysis and perspectives. *Economia e Politica Industriale*, *47*(1), 1–18. DOI: 10.1007/s40812-019-00138-6

Giveth. (2021, May 10). *Deep dive: Augmented bonding curves*. Giveth Blog. https://blog.giveth.io/deep-dive-augmented-bonding-curves-3f1f7c1fa751/

Goforth, C. (2021). Token Regulation and the Challenges of Classification. *Fordham Journal of Corporate & Financial Law*, *26*(2), 197–239.

Goforth, C. R. (2021). Regulation of crypto: Who is the securities and exchange commission protecting? *American Business Law Journal*, *58*(3), 643–705. DOI: 10.1111/ablj.12192

Gogel, D., Baker-Taylor, T., Cloots, A. S., Forster, B., Gustave, J. L., Schär, F., & Sokolin, L. (2021). DeFi Beyond the Hype: The Emerging World of Decentralized Finance. Wharton Blockchain and Digital Asset Project, in collaboration with the World Economic Forum. https://wifpr.wharton.upenn.edu/wp-content/uploads/2021/05/DeFi-Beyond-the-Hype.pdf

Government of the Hong Kong Special Administrative Region (HKSAR). (2025, February 26). *The 2025–26 budget: Speech by the financial secretary*, the Hon Paul MP Chan. https://www.budget.gov.hk/2025/eng/pdf/e_budget_speech_2025-26.pdf

Graeber, D. (2014). *Debt: The First 5,000 Years*. Melville House.

Grech, A., Balaji, V., & Miao, F. (2022). *Education and Blockchain*. Commonwealth of Learning (COL). DOI: 10.56059/11599/4131

Grech, A., Camilleri, A. F., & Inamorato dos Santos, A. (2017). *Blockchain in Education*. Publications Office of the European Union., DOI: 10.2760/60649

Grima, S., Chaudhary, S., Sood, K., & Kumar, S. (2024). *Business Drivers in Promoting Digital Detoxification*.

Grobys, K., Kolari, J. W., & Niang, J. (2022). Man versus machine: On artificial intelligence and hedge funds performance. *Applied Economics*, *54*(40), 4632–4646. DOI: 10.1080/00036846.2022.2032585

Group of Central Banks. (2020). Central bank digital currencies: Foundational principles and core features. https://www.bis.org/publ/othp33.pdf

Guillaume, F. (2019). Blockchain: La réponse de la CNUDCI et d'UNIDROIT. *Revue de Droit Commercial Belge*, *6*, 513–532.

Gulf News. (2025). *AI transforms public services in Dubai*. Gulf News Tech.

Gurrea-Martínez, A., & Remolina, N. (2020). Global challenges and regulatory strategies to fintech. *SSRN*, *35*(3), 421–465. DOI: 10.2139/ssrn.3576506

Gurtu, A., & Johny, J. (2019). Potential of blockchain technology in supply chain management: A literature review. *International Journal of Physical Distribution & Logistics Management*, *49*(9), 881–900. DOI: 10.1108/IJPDLM-11-2018-0371

Gutiérrez, A., Tran, T. T., & Wainwright, S. (2023). Governance of the ReFi ecosystem and the integrity of voluntary carbon markets as a common resource. *The International Journal of the Commons*, *17*(1), 1–24. DOI: 10.5334/ijc.1410

Haaramo, E. (2017, July 5). Sweden trials blockchain for land registry management. ComputerWeekly. https://www.computerweekly.com/news/450421958/Sweden-trials-blockchain-for-land-registry-management

Hacker, P., Lianos, I., Dimitropoulos, G., & Eich, S. (Eds.). (2019). *Regulating blockchain: Techno-social and legal challenges*. Oxford University Press. DOI: 10.1093/oso/9780198842187.001.0001

Hagendorff, T. (2020). The ethics of AI ethics: An evaluation of guidelines. *Minds and Machines*, *30*(1), 99–120. DOI: 10.1007/s11023-020-09517-8

Hagiu, A., & Yoffie, D. B. (2013). The new patent intermediaries: Platforms, defensive aggregators, and super-aggregators. *The Journal of Economic Perspectives*, *27*(1), 45–66. DOI: 10.1257/jep.27.1.45

Hall, B. H., & Lerner, J. (2010). The financing of R&D and innovation. In Hall, B. H., & Rosenberg, N. (Eds.), *Handbook of the economics of innovation* (Vol. 1, pp. 609–639). North-Holland. DOI: 10.1016/S0169-7218(10)01014-2

Hamledari, H., & Fischer, M. (2021). Construction payment automation using blockchain-enabled smart contracts and robotic reality capture technologies. *Automation in Construction*, *132*, 103926. DOI: 10.1016/j.autcon.2021.103926

Hanson, R. (2000). Shall we vote on values, but bet on beliefs? Department of Economics, George Mason University. https://mason.gmu.edu/~rhanson/futarchy2000.pdf

Hardin, G. (1968). The tragedy of the commons. *Science*, *162*(3859), 1243–1248. DOI: 10.1126/science.162.3859.1243

Harvey, C., Ramachandran, A., & Santoro, J. (2021). *DeFi and the future of finance*. Wiley.

Hassan, S. C., & Kumar, S. (2024). Artificial Intelligence as a Promising Technology: Possibilities and Challenges Across Different Areas of Human Life. *Exploring Ethical Dimensions of Environmental Sustainability and Use of AI*, 54–66.

Hassan, S., & De Filippi, P. (2021). Decentralized Autonomous Organizations and Governance by Code. *Internet Policy Review*, *10*(2). Advance online publication. DOI: 10.14763/2021.2.1556

Heines, R., Dick, C., Pohle, C., & Jung, R. (2021). The tokenization of everything: Towards a framework for understanding the potentials of tokenized assets. In PACIS 2021 Proceedings (Paper 40). Pacific Asia Conference on Information Systems. https://aisel.aisnet.org/pacis2021/40

Heines, R., Dick, C., Pohle, C., & Jung, R. (2021). *The tokenization of everything: Towards a framework for understanding the potentials of tokenized assets*. Proceedings of the Pacific Asia Conference on Information Systems (PACIS). https://aisel.aisnet.org/pacis2021/86

Heizelman, I., Bittner, N., Alvarez Vazquez, E., Ewert, D., & Striker, R. (2024). Empowering Engineering Students: Blockchain Learning Tokens for Assessing ABET Student Outcomes and Enhancing Quality Control in Innovation-Based Education. *2024 ASEE Annual Conference & Exposition Proceedings*. DOI: 10.18260/1-2--47245

Heller, M. A., & Eisenberg, R. S. (1998). Can patents deter innovation? The anticommons in biomedical research. *Science*, *280*(5364), 698–701. DOI: 10.1126/science.280.5364.698 PMID: 9563938

Hellmann, T. (2007). The role of patents for bridging the science to market gap. In Academic science and entrepreneurship: Dual engines of growth (pp. [insert page range if known]). National Bureau of Economic Research. DOI: 10.1016/j.jebo.2006.05.013

Helms, K. (2025, June 27). XRP legal saga concludes as Ripple withdraws appeal, SEC expected to follow. *Bitcoin*. Retrieved from https://news.bitcoin.com/xrp-legal-saga-concludes-as-ripple-withdraws-appeal-sec-expected-to-follow/

Henderson, M. T., & Raskin, M. (2019). A regulatory classification of digital assets: Toward an operational Howey test for cryptocurrencies, ICOs, and other digital assets. *Columbia Business Law Review, 2019*(2), 443–493.

Henriquez, R., Cohen, I., Bittan, N., & Tulbassiyev, K. (2019). Blockchain and business model innovation: Designing a P2P mortgage lending system. SSRN *Electronic Journal*. DOI: 10.2139/ssrn.3371850

Hentov, E., & Gorshkov, V. (2024). *Asset tokenization in capital markets: A primer*. State Street Global Advisors (SSGA) White Paper. https://www.ssga.com

Hess, C., & Ostrom, E. (Eds.). (2007). *Understanding knowledge as a commons*. MIT Press.

Hirshleifer, J. (1971). The private and social value of information and the reward to inventive activity. *The American Economic Review, 61*(4), 561–574.

Hockett, R. C. (2022). *The citizens' ledger digitizing our money, democratizing our finance*. Springer., DOI: 10.1007/978-3-030-99566-9

Hockett, R. C., & Omarova, S. (2017). The finance franchise. *Cornell Law Review, 102*, 1143–1218. https://scholarship.law.cornell.edu/clr/vol102/iss5/2

Hole, Y., Hole, S., Leonardo Cavaliere, L. P., Nair, B., Hasyim, M., & Bapat, H. B. (2023). Blockchain Usages In Hospitality Management. *2023 3rd International Conference on Advance Computing and Innovative Technologies in Engineering (ICACITE)*, 2798–2801. DOI: 10.1109/ICACITE57410.2023.10183291

Hong Kong Monetary Authority. (2023, February 16). *HKSAR Government announces successful offering of the world's first tokenised government green bond*. https://www.hkma.gov.hk/eng/news-and-media/press-releases/2023/02/20230216-3/

HSBC. (2023). *HSBC Orion platform completes EIB digital bond issuance*. https://www.hsbc.com

HSBC. (2023). *HSBC Orion platform pilot on digital gold*. https://www.hsbc.com/news-and-insight/2023/hsbc-launches-digital-gold-token

Huda, M. N., Talukder, M. B., & Kumar, S. (2024). Securing Healthcare AI: Applied Federal Learning. In Bhattacharya, P., Liu, H., Dutta, P. K., Rodrigues, J. J. P. C., & Sethi, G. (Eds.), *Revolutionizing Healthcare 5.0: The Power of Generative AI. Studies in Systems, Decision and Control* (Vol. 571). Springer., DOI: 10.1007/978-3-031-75771-6_17

Hussain, A., Akbar, W., Hussain, T., Bashir, A. K., Dabel, M. M. A., Ali, F., & Yang, B. (2024). Ensuring Zero Trust IoT Data Privacy: Differential Privacy in Blockchain using Federated Learning. *IEEE Transactions on Consumer Electronics*, **•••**, 1–1. DOI: 10.1109/TCE.2024.3444824

Hussien, H. M., Yasin, S. M., Udzir, N. I., Ninggal, M. I. H., & Salman, S. (2021). Blockchain technology in the healthcare industry: Trends and opportunities. *Journal of Industrial Information Integration*, *22*, 100217. DOI: 10.1016/j.jii.2021.100217

Hyperledger Foundation. (2023). *AI-integrated compliance monitoring in distributed networks*. Hyperledger Technical Reports.

Images, G. (2023). Stock photo licensing platform. https://www.gettyimages.com/

ImmuneBytes. (2024). Crypto hacks directory. *ImmuneBytes*. Retrieved from https://immunebyte s.com/blog/category/web3-security/crypto-hacks-directory/

Information Services Department. HKSAR Government. (2023, February 16). *World's first tokenised government green bond issued*. https://www.info.gov.hk/gia/general/202302/16/P2023021600466.htm

InsurAce Protocol. (2023). Decentralized insurance protocol. https://www.insurace.io/

International Monetary Fund. (1980, January 1). *World economic outlook*. International Monetary Fund. https://openlibrary.org/works/OL1336051W

International Monetary Fund. (2021). *The rise of digital money*. https://www.imf.org/en/Publications/fintech-notes/Issues/2019/07/12/The-Rise-of-Digital-Money-47097

International Monetary Fund. (2025). *Tokenization: A framework and key considerations*. (Fintech Notes No. 2025/001). International Monetary Fund. DOI: 10.5089/9798400298905.063

International Organization of Securities Commissions (IOSCO). (2023, December). Final report with policy recommendations for decentralized finance (DeFi) (FR/14/2023). https://www.iosco.org/library/pubdocs/pdf/IOSCOPD753.pdf

International Organization of Securities Commissions. (2023). *Policy recommendations for crypto and digital asset markets*. IOSCO. https://www.iosco.org/library/pubdocs/pdf/IOSCOPD747.pdf

International Securities Services Association (ISSA). (2023, July). *DLT in the real world survey 2023 – key findings.* https://issanet.org/content/uploads/2023/07/DLT-in-the-Real-World-2023_Survey-Key-Findings.pdf

International Shoe Co. v. Washington, 326 U.S. 310 (1945).

Internet Archive. (2025, August 1). *Do you accept cryptocurrency?* Internet Archive Help Center. https://help.archive.org/help/do-you-accept-cryptocurrency/

Investopedia. (2018). *What is gas (Ethereum)?* Investopedia. https://www.investopedia.com/terms/g/gas-ethereum.asp

Ioannidis, J. P. A. (2005). Why most published research findings are false. *PLoS Medicine*, *2*(8), e124. DOI: 10.1371/journal.pmed.0020124 PMID: 16060722

IOSCO. (2022). Decentralized Finance Report. International Organization of Securities Commissions. https://www.iosco.org/library/pubdocs/pdf/IOSCOPD699.pdf

IOSCO. (2023). *Policy recommendations for crypto and digital asset markets.* International Organization of Securities Commissions.

IPwe. (2023). Global patent marketplace. https://ipwe.com/

ISO/IEC. (2023). *ISO/IEC 38505-1: Information governance—Governance of data—Part 1: Application of ISO/IEC 38500 to the governance of data.* International Organization for Standardization.

Ivanov, D. (2022). The industry 5.0 framework: Viability-based integration of the resilience, sustainability, and human-centricity perspectives. *International Journal of Production Research*, *61*(5), 1683–1695. DOI: 10.1080/00207543.2022.2118892

Jacobs, L. (2021). Financial regulation of crypto-assets under MiFID II/MiFIR and MiCA. *European Company and Financial Law Review*, *18*(6), 844–878.

Jain, P., Singh, R., Mishra, R., & Rana, N. P. (2023). Emerging dimensions of blockchain application in tourism and hospitality sector: A systematic literature review. *Journal of Hospitality Marketing & Management*, *32*(4), 454–476. DOI: 10.1080/19368623.2023.2184440

Jeffrey, T., Kurtz, D. L. M., & Jones, C. A. (2021). Two-Eyed Seeing: Current Approaches, and Discussion of Medical Applications. *BC Medical Journal*, *68*(8).

Jha, S. (2025). The Complete Guide for Types of Blockchain. In *Simplilearn*. Simplilearn. https://www.simplilearn.com/tutorials/blockchain-tutorial/types-of-blockchain

Jin, C., Wang, J., & Li, Y. (2023). Blockchain and AI integration: Opportunities, challenges and future directions. *Journal of Network and Computer Applications*, *214*, 103513. Advance online publication. DOI: 10.1016/j.jnca.2023.103513

Jirgensons, M., & Kapenieks, J. (2018). Blockchain and the Future of Digital Learning Credential Assessment and Management. *Journal of Teacher Education for Sustainability*, *20*(1), 145–156. DOI: 10.2478/jtes-2018-0009

Johnson, K. (2020). *Downtown Stimulus Program Review.* Medium.https://medium .com/@katiebrenjohnson/downtown-stimulus-program-review-e89f67e29f4f

Kaal, W. A. (2020). Blockchain innovation in wealth and asset management: The RealT case. *Journal of Financial Transformation*, *52*(2), 34–45.

Kamath, S. K., Pendekanti, S. K., Kanumuri, N. V., & Rao, D. (2024). Towards Sustainable Wellness: Leveraging Technology for Addiction Recovery Support. *2024 3rd International Conference on Artificial Intelligence For Internet of Things (AIIoT)*, 1–6. DOI: 10.1109/AIIoT58432.2024.10574651

Kamiyama, S., Sheehan, J., & Martinez, C. (2006). Valuation and exploitation of intellectual property. OECD Science, Technology and Industry Working Papers 2006/05.

Karim, R. A., Rabiul, M. K., Ishrat, M., Promsivapallop, P., & Kawser, S. (2023). Can Blockchain Payment Services Influence Customers' Loyalty Intention in the Hospitality Industry? A Mediation Assessment. *Administrative Sciences*, *13*(3), 85. DOI: 10.3390/admsci13030085

Kassen, M. (2022). Blockchain and e-government innovation: Automation of public information processes. *Information Systems*, 103, 101862. https://doi.org/. 101862DOI: 10.1016/j.is.2021

Katzenbach, C., & Ulbricht, L. (2019). Algorithmic governance. *Internet Policy Review*, *8*(4). Advance online publication. DOI: 10.14763/2019.4.1424

Kaul, I., Grunberg, I., & Stern, M. A. (Eds.). (1999). *Global public goods: International cooperation in the 21st century*. Oxford University Press., DOI: 10.1093/0195130529.001.0001

Kaur, G. (2024, December 11). What are tokenized debt instruments? A beginner's guide. *Cointelegraph*. Retrieved from https://cointelegraph.com/learn/articles/what -are-tokenized -debt-instruments

Kavazi, D., Smirnov, V., Shilina, S., Li, M., Contreras, R., Gajera, H., & Lavrenov, D. (2021). You are [not] a bot. arXiv preprint arXiv:2111.13189. https://arxiv.org/abs/2111.13189

Kayani, U. N. (2025). Exploring prospects of blockchain and fintech: Using SLR approach. *Journal of Science and Technology Policy Management*, *16*(1), 5–41. DOI: 10.1108/JSTPM-01-2023-0005

Kelsen, H. (1967). *Pure theory of law*. University of California Press. DOI: 10.1525/9780520312296

Kenyon, C., Berrahoui, M., & Macrina, A. (2022). Transparency principle for carbon emissions drives sustainable finance. *arXiv Preprint*. https://arxiv.org/abs/2202.07689

Kerr, W. R., & Nanda, R. (2015). Financing innovation. *Annual Review of Financial Economics*, *7*(1), 445–462. DOI: 10.1146/annurev-financial-111914-041825

Khanna, A., Sah, A., Choudhury, T., & Maheshwari, P. (2020). Blockchain Technology for Hospitality Industry. In Themistocleous, M., Papadaki, M., & Kamal, M. M. (Eds.), *Information Systems* (Vol. 402, pp. 99–112). Springer International Publishing., DOI: 10.1007/978-3-030-63396-7_7

Kiviat, T. I. (2015). Beyond Bitcoin: Issues in regulating blockchain transactions. *Duke Law Journal*, *65*(3), 569–608.

Klima, D. A. O. (2024). *The Klima Protocol Dashboard (Part 1)*. https://www.klimadao.finance/resources/the-klima-protocol-dashboard-pt1

Koepsell, D. (2022). NFTs, IP rights, and policy. *Frontiers in Blockchain*, *5*, 1077343.

Konashevych, O. (2019). Constraints and benefits of the blockchain use for real estate and property rights. Journal of Property. *Planning and Environmental Law*, *12*(2), 109–127.

Konashevych, O. (2020). General concept of real estate tokenization on blockchain. *European Property Law Journal*, *9*(1), 21–66. DOI: 10.1515/eplj-2020-0003

Kowsar, M. M., & Mintoo, A. A. (2025). Blockchain in banking: A review of distributed ledger applications in loan processing, credit history, and compliance. *American Journal of Scholarly Research and Innovation*, *4*(1), 101–138. DOI: 10.63125/gp61va54

Kramer, X. (2021). Swiss DLT Act enters into force. *Computer Law Review International*, *22*(2), 51–53.

Kroll, J. A., Davey, I. C., & Felten, E. W. (2013). The economics of Bitcoin mining, or Bitcoin in the presence of adversaries. In Proceedings of WEIS 2013. https://w .econinfosec.org/archive/weis2013/papers/KrollDaveyFeltenWEIS2013.pdf

Ktari, J., Frikha, T., Rekik, M., Gassara, O., Boujelben, M., & Amor, N. B. (2024). Decentralized Hotel Reservations: Blockchain Integration for Incentivized Data Sharing and Smart Contracts. *2024 IEEE 4th International Maghreb Meeting of the Conference on Sciences and Techniques of Automatic Control and Computer Engineering (MI-STA)*, 41–45. DOI: 10.1109/MI-STA61267.2024.10599713

Kumar, S., Talukder, M. B., & Kaiser, F. (2024). Artificial Intelligence in Business: Negative Social Impacts. In *Demystifying the Dark Side of AI in Business* (pp. 81–97). IGI Global.

Kumar, B., Kumar, A., Sassanelli, C., & Kumar, L. (2025). Exploring the role of finance in driving circular economy and sustainable business practices. *Journal of Cleaner Production, 486*, 144480. DOI: 10.1016/j.jclepro.2024.144480

Kunhibava, S., Mustapha, Z., Muneeza, A., Sa'ad, A. A., & Karim, M. E. (2021). *ukūk on blockchain: a legal, regulatory and Sharī'ah review*. ISRA International Journal of Islamic Finance., DOI: 10.1108/IJIF-06-2020-0120

La Morgia, M., Mei, A., Sassi, F., & Stefa, J. (2023). The doge of wall street: Analysis and detection of pump and dump cryptocurrency manipulations. *ACM Transactions on Internet Technology, 23*(1), 1–28. DOI: 10.1145/3561300

La Salla, F. (2024, January 16). *Why standards and controls are essential to the future offinancial assets.* World Economic Forum. https://www.weforum.org/stories/ 2024/01/digital-financia l-markets-developing-standards-controlsdavos24/

Laatikainen, G., Li, M., & Abrahamsson, P. (2021). Blockchain Governance: A Dynamic View. In Wang, X., Martini, A., Nguyen-Duc, A., & Stray, V. (Eds.), *Software Business. ICSOB 2021. Lecture Notes in Business Information Processing* (Vol. 434). Springer., DOI: 10.1007/978-3-030-91983-2_6

Lacity, M. (2018). Addressing key challenges to making enterprise blockchain applications a reality. *MIS Quarterly Executive, 17*(3), 3. https://aisel.aisnet.org/ misqe/vol17/iss3/3/

Laeven, L. (2011). Banking crises: A review. *Annual Review of Financial Economics, 3*(1), 17–40. DOI: 10.1146/annurev-financial-102710-144816

Lalley, S., & Weyl, E. G. (2017). Quadratic voting: How mechanism design can radicalize democracy. *American Economic Association Papers and Proceedings, 1*(1). https://ssrn.com/abstract=2003531

Lam, T. Y., & Dongol, B. (2022). A blockchain-enabled e-learning platform. *Interactive Learning Environments, 30*(7), 1229–1251. DOI: 10.1080/10494820.2020.1716022

Latour, B., & Woolgar, S. (1986). *Laboratory life: The construction of scientific facts* (2nd ed.). Princeton University Press.

Lavayssière, X. (2025). Legal structures of tokenised assets. *European Journal of Risk Regulation*, •••, 1–13. DOI: 10.1017/err.2024.88

Law Commission of England and Wales. (2023). Digital assets: Final report (Law Com No. 256). The Stationery Office. https://lawcom.gov.uk/project/digital-assets/

Ledger Insights. (2024, November 26). EIB issues second €100m digital bond in a week using wCBDC. *Ledgerinsights*. https://www.ledgerinsights.com/eib-issues-second-e100m-digital -bond-in-a-week-using-wcbdc/

Ledger Insights. (2024, October 28). *Hong Kong partners with Brazil and Thailand for tokenization, to offer digital bond grants*. https://www.ledgerinsights.com/hong-kong-partners-central-banks-of-brazil-thailand-for-tokenization-to-offer-digital-bond-grants

Lee, C. J., Sugimoto, C. R., Zhang, G., & Cronin, B. (2013). Bias in peer review. *Journal of the American Society for Information Science and Technology, 64*(1), 2–17. DOI: 10.1002/asi.22784

Legris, P., Ingham, J., & Collerette, P. (2003). Why do people use information technology? A critical review of the technology acceptance model. *Information & Management, 40*(3), 191–204. DOI: 10.1016/S0378-7206(01)00143-4

Lehmann, M. (2019). Who owns Bitcoin? Private law facing the blockchain. *SSRN, 21*(1), 93–136. DOI: 10.2139/ssrn.3402678

Lekhi, P. (2024). Central Bank Digital Currencies: Concept, Benefit, Impact, and Challenges. In *Exploring Central Bank Digital Currencies: Concepts, Frameworks, Models, and Challenges* (pp. 13-20). IGI Global Scientific Publishing.

Lekhi, P. (2024). Megatrends and Innovations Shaping the Future of Finance. *Innovation, Sustainability, and Technological Megatrends in the Face of Uncertainties: Core Developments and Solutions*, 41.

Lekhi, P., & Kaur, G. (Eds.). (2023). *Concepts, Technologies, Challenges, and the Future of Web 3*. IGI Global. DOI: 10.4018/978-1-6684-9919-1

Leland, H. E., & Pyle, D. H. (1977). Informational asymmetries, financial structure and financial intermediation. *The Journal of Finance, 32*(2), 371–387. DOI: 10.2307/2326770

Lessig, L. (2001). *The future of ideas: The fate of the commons in a connected world*. Random House.

Lessig, L. (2006). *Code: Version 2.0*. Basic Books.

Lev, B. (2001). *Intangibles: Management, measurement, and reporting*. Brookings Institution Press.

Lim, C., Saw, T. J., & Sargeant, C. (2019). Smart contracts: Bridging the gap between expectation and reality. Oxford Law Faculty Research Paper.

Li, M., Luo, X., Xue, K., Xue, Y., Sun, W., & Li, J. (2024). A secure and efficient blockchain sharding scheme via hybrid consensus and dynamic management. *IEEE Transactions on Information Forensics and Security*, *19*, 5911–5924. DOI: 10.1109/TIFS.2024.3406145

Li, M.-Y., Jiang, Z.-H., & Wang, L. (2024). Grain storage security in context of government digital governance: A tripartite evolutionary game analysis of speculative behavior. *Kybernetes*. Advance online publication. DOI: 10.1108/K-12-2023-2670

Lim, Y. H., Hashim, H., Poo, N., Poo, D. C. C., & Nguyen, H. D. (2019). Blockchain Technologies in E-commerce: Social Shopping and Loyalty Program Applications. In Meiselwitz, G. (Ed.), *Social Computing and Social Media. Communication and Social Communities* (Vol. 11579, pp. 403–416). Springer International Publishing., DOI: 10.1007/978-3-030-21905-5_31

Liu, A., Zhang, D., Wang, X., & Xu, X. (2021). Blockchain-based customization towards decentralized consensus on product requirement, quality, and price. *Manufacturing Letters*, *27*, 18–25. DOI: 10.1016/j.mfglet.2020.12.001

Liu, J., Makarov, I., & Schoar, A. (2023). *Anatomy of a run: The terra luna crash (No. w31160)*. National Bureau of Economic Research., DOI: 10.3386/w31160

Liu, Y., Lu, Y., Nayak, K., Zhang, F., Zhang, L., & Zhao, Y. (2022). *Empirical analysis of EIP-1559: Transaction fees, waiting time, and consensus security*. arXiv. https://arxiv.org/abs/2201.05574 DOI: 10.1145/3548606.3559341

Longchamp, Y., Gupta, A., & Goel, K. (2021). *Tokenomics*. SEBA Bank AG.

Low, K. F. K., & Teo, E. (2017). Bitcoins and other cryptocurrencies as property? *Law, Innovation and Technology*, *9*(2), 235–268. DOI: 10.1080/17579961.2017.1377915

Maas, T. (2019). Initial coin offerings: When are tokens securities in the EU and US? SSRN Electronic Journal. DOI: 10.2139/ssrn.3337514

Madison, M. J., Frischmann, B. M., & Strandburg, K. J. (2010). Constructing commons in the cultural environment. *Cornell Law Review, 95*(4), 657–709.

Makarov, I., & Schär, F. (2022). *Permissionless blockchains and the future of financial intermediation*. National Bureau of Economic Research., DOI: 10.3386/w30006

MakerDAO Governance Forum. (2022–2024). *Real-world asset proposals and research*. https://forum.makerdao.com/c/rwa/16

Makridakis, S., & Christodoulou, K. (2019). Blockchain: Current Challenges and Future Prospects/Applications. *Future Internet, 11*(12), 258. DOI: 10.3390/fi11120258

Mandin, J. (2025, March 21). *Risk free uncollateralized lending in decentred markets*. https://www.bankofcanada.ca/wp-content/uploads/2025/03/sdp2025-6.pdf

Mangano, R. (2018). Blockchain securities, insolvency law and the sandbox approach. *European Business Organization Law Review, 19*(4), 715–735. DOI: 10.1007/s40804-018-0123-5

Mann, M. (2019). Technological architecture as law: Affordances and the dynamics of digital regulation. *Regulation & Governance, 14*(3), 466–481.

Marois, T. (2023). *Public Banks: Decarbonisation, Definancialisation and Democratisation*. Cambridge University Press. DOI: 10.4324/9781003344292

Marwell, G., & Ames, R. E. (1979). Experiments on the provision of public goods. I. Resources, interest, group size, and the free-rider problem. *American Journal of Sociology, 84*(6), 1335–1360. DOI: 10.1086/226937

MAS (Monetary Authority of Singapore). (2023). *Project Guardian expands cross-border tokenized asset pilots*. https://www.mas.gov.sg

MAS. (2016). *FinTech regulatory sandbox guidelines*. Monetary Authority of Singapore.

McGreal, R. (2023). Blockchain and Micro-Credentials in Education. *International Journal of E-Learning & Distance Education, 38*(1), 1–17. DOI: 10.55667/ijede.2022.v38.i1.1250

McGuire. (2023, May 29). *Explore cross-chain interoperability in Layer 2*. Blockphere. https://blockphere.com/explore-cross-chain-interoperability-in-layer-2/

McKinsey & Company. (2024, July). What is tokenization? https://www.mckinsey.com/featured-insights/mckinsey-explainers/what-is-tokenization

Meadows, J., Annandale, M., & Ota, L. (2019). Indigenous Peoples' participation in sustainability standards for extractives. *Land Use Policy, 88*, 104118.

Mehar, M. I., Shier, C. L., Giambattista, A., Gong, E., Fletcher, G., Sanayhie, R., Kim, H. M., & Laskowski, M. (2019). Understanding a revolutionary and flawed grand experiment in blockchain: The DAO attack. [JCIT]. *Journal of Cases on Information Technology*, *21*(1), 19–32. DOI: 10.4018/JCIT.2019010102

Mendoza-Chan, J., & Pee, L. G. (2024). Digital skilling of working adults: A systematic review. *Computers & Education*, *218*(March 2023), 105076. DOI: 10.1016/j.compedu.2024.105076

Meng, D. N. K., & Bhutia, L. D. (2025). Leveraging Digital Technologies and Sustainable Practices for Post-Pandemic Tourism Recovery: A Focus on Malaysia. In Hassan, V. I. (Ed.), *Navigating Mass Tourism to Island Destinations* (pp. 151–178). IGI Global., DOI: 10.4018/979-8-3693-9107-5.ch006

Merton, R. K. (1973). *The sociology of science: Theoretical and empirical investigations*. University of Chicago Press.

Messari. (2022). State of Centrifuge Q2 2022. https://messari.io/report/state-of-centrifuge-q2-2022

Messari. (2023). *Goldfinch Q3 Report: Decentralized credit growth*. https://messari.io

Messari. (2024). *State of OP Mainnet Q3 2024*.

Messias, J., Benevenuto, F., Wachs, J., & De Cristofaro, E. (2023). *Evidence of centralization in decentralized finance*. In *Proceedings of the Web Conference 2023 (WWW '23)* (pp. 1192–1202). ACM. DOI: 10.1145/3543507.3583235

Mezei, P. (2020). Revisiting the concept of exhaustion in the online environment. *GRUR International*, *69*(11), 1107–1120.

Michels, J. D. (2018). Blockchain in securities markets: Toward a new ecosystem. *Journal of Securities Operations & Custody*, *10*(4), 310–321.

Mik, E. (2017). Smart contracts: Terminology, technical limitations and real world complexity. *Law, Innovation and Technology*, *9*(2), 269–300. DOI: 10.1080/17579961.2017.1378468

Mikroyannidis, A., Third, A., & Domingue, J. (2025). Blockchain-based decentralised micro-accreditation for lifelong learning. *Interactive Learning Environments*, *33*(3), 2201–2215. DOI: 10.1080/10494820.2024.2401485

Miles, M. B., & Huberman, A. M. (1994). *Qualitative data analysis: An expanded sourcebook* (2nd ed.). Sage Publications.

Mills, D. C., & Carapella, F. (2012, March 9). *Information-insensitive securities: The benefits of central counterparty clearing* (Bank of Canada Working Paper No. 2012-20). Bank of Canada. https://www.bankofcanada.ca/wp-content/uploads/2012/07/Carapella-Francesca-paper.pdf

Minsky, H. (1992). The financial instability hypothesis. The Jerome Levy Economics Institute Working Paper No. 74. https://www.levyinstitute.org/pubs/wp74.pdf

Mirowski, P. (2011). *Science-mart: Privatizing American science*. Harvard University Press. DOI: 10.4159/harvard.9780674061132

Mirowski, P., & Sent, E.-M. (2007). The Commercialization of Science, and the Response of STS. In *Edward Hackett, Olga Amsterdamska, Michael Lynch & Judy Wajcman, The Handbook of Science and Technology Studies* (pp. 635–689). MIT Press.

Mittal, R., & Sinha, P. (2022). Framework for a resilient religious tourism supply chain for mitigating post-pandemic risk. *International Hospitality Review, 36*(2), 322–339. DOI: 10.1108/IHR-09-2020-0053

Mohammad B.T. (2020a). An Appraisal of the Economic Outlook for the Tourism Industry, Specially Cox's Bazar in Bangladesh. *i-manager's Journal on Economics & Commerce,* 2(1), 23-35. DOI: 10.26634/jecom.2.1.17285

Mohammad, B. T. (2025b). Revolutionizing Hospitality: Leveraging Mobile Apps and Cutting-Edge Room Technologies in the Hotel Industry. In B. Varghese & S. H. (Eds.), *Advancing Smart Tourism Through Analytics* (pp. 315-332). IGI Global Scientific Publishing. DOI: 10.4018/979-8-3693-3715-8.ch017

Mohammad, B.T. and Sanjeev, k. (2025), "Culinary Experiences and Food Tourism in Bangladesh", Tyagi, P.K., Nadda, V. and Singh, A.K. (Ed.) Meaningful Tourism (Building the Future of Tourism), Emerald Publishing Limited, Leeds, pp. 201-219. DOI: 10.1108/978-1-83797-837-320251028

Mohammad, B. T. (2020b). The Future of Culinary Tourism: An Emerging Dimension for the Tourism Industry of Bangladesh. I-Manager's. *Journal of Management, 15*(1), 27. DOI: 10.26634/jmgt.15.1.17181

Mohammad, B. T. (2021). An assessment of the roles of the social network in the development of the Tourism Industry in Bangladesh. *International Journal of Business, Law, and Education*, 2(3), 85–93. DOI: 10.56442/ijble.v2i3.21

Mohammad, B. T. (2025a). Maximizing Impact: The Role of Influencer Marketing in Contemporary Tourism Management. In Özsungur, F. (Ed.), *Navigating Organizational Behavior in the Digital Age with AI* (pp. 277–304). IGI Global Scientific Publishing., DOI: 10.4018/979-8-3693-8442-8.ch011

Mohammad, B. T. (2025c). Climate change adaptation strategies for a tourism destination: A study of Kuakata beach. *Acta Scientiarum Polonorum. Administratio Locorum, 24*(1), 165–179. DOI: 10.31648/aspal.10073

Moncada, R., Ferro, E., Fiaschetti, M., & Medda, F. (2024). Blockchain Tokens, Price Volatility, and Active User Base: An Empirical Analysis Based on Tokenomics. *International Journal of Financial Studies., 12*(4), 107. DOI: 10.3390/ijfs12040107

Monetary Authority of Singapore. (2023). MAS partners financial industry to expand asset tokenisation initiatives. https://www.mas.gov.sg/news/media-releases/2023/mas-partners-financial-industry-to-expand-asset-tokenisation-initiatives

Mora, C., Rollins, R. L., Taladay, K., Kantar, M. B., Chock, M. K., Shimada, M., & Franklin, E. C. (2018). Bitcoin emissions alone could push global warming above 2°C. *Nature Climate Change, 8*(11), 931–933. DOI: 10.1038/s41558-018-0321-8

Mori, T. (2016). Financial technology: Blockchain and securities settlement. *Journal of Securities Operations & Custody, 8*(3), 208. DOI: 10.69554/YEJN7450

Morrison, R., Mazey, N. C., & Wingreen, S. C. (2020). The DAO controversy: The case for a new species of corporate governance? *Frontiers in Blockchain, 3*, 25. DOI: 10.3389/fbloc.2020.00025

Morrone, D., Tarulli, A., Silvestri, R., & Santovito, S. (2024). Generation Z, tourism and hospitality: The legacy of COVID-19. *British Food Journal, 126*(1), 205–222. DOI: 10.1108/BFJ-11-2022-0972

Möslein, F. (2019). Conflicts of laws and codes: Defining the boundaries of digital jurisdictions. In Hacker, P., Lianos, I., Dimitropoulos, G., & Eich, S. (Eds.), *Regulating blockchain* (pp. 264–282). Oxford University Press. DOI: 10.1093/oso/9780198842187.003.0016

Motahhir, S., & Maleh, Y. (2022). *Security Engineering for Embedded and Cyber-Physical Systems* (1st ed.). CRC Press., DOI: 10.1201/9781003278207

Mousavi, S. H., Tohidinia, A., & Mousavi, S. M. (2025). Transforming Islamic finance: The impact of blockchain and Smart Sukuk [November.]. *Access Journal, Access Press Publishing House, 6*(1), 184–201. DOI: 10.46656/access.2025.6.1(10)

Mukherjee, A. G., Wanjari, U. R., Chakraborty, R., Renu, K., Vellingiri, B., & George, A., CR, S. R., & Gopalakrishnan, A. V. (. (2021). A review on modern and smart technologies for efficient waste disposal and management. *Journal of Environmental Management, 297*, 113347. DOI: 10.1016/j.jenvman.2021.113347 PMID: 34314963

Mulligan, C., Morsfield, S., & Cheikosman, E. (2024). Blockchain for sustainability: A systematic literature review for policy impact. *Telecommunications Policy, 48*(2), 102676. DOI: 10.1016/j.telpol.2023.102676

Munir, K. A. (2015). A loss of power in institutional theory. *Journal of Management Inquiry, 24*(1), 90–92. DOI: 10.1177/1056492614545302

Murray, A. (2019). *The regulation of cyberspace: Control in the online environment*. Routledge.

Nägele, T., & Xander, P. (2020). Liechtenstein's innovative Blockchain Act. *Trusts & Trustees, 26*(10), 876–888.

Nakamoto, S. (2008). Bitcoin: A peer-to-peer electronic cash system. https://bitcoin .org/bitcoin.pdf

Nam, K., Dutt, C. S., Chathoth, P., & Khan, M. S. (2021). Blockchain technology for smart city and smart tourism: Latest trends and challenges. *Asia Pacific Journal of Tourism Research, 26*(4), 454–468. DOI: 10.1080/10941665.2019.1585376

Narayanan, A., Bonneau, J., Felten, E., Miller, A., & Goldfeder, S. (2016). *Bitcoin and Cryptocurrency Technologies*. Princeton University Press.

Nelson, R. R. (1959). The simple economics of basic scientific research. *Journal of Political Economy, 67*(3), 297–306. DOI: 10.1086/258177

New York Convention on the Recognition and Enforcement of Foreign Arbitral Awards, June 10, 1958, 21 U.S.T. 2517, 330 U.N.T.S. 38.

Nguyen, D.-H., Nguyen-Duc, D.-N., Huynh-Tuong, N., & Pham, H.-A. (2018). CVSS: A Blockchainized Certificate Verifying Support System. *Proceedings of the Ninth International Symposium on Information and Communication Technology - SoICT 2018*, 436–442. DOI: 10.1145/3287921.3287968

Nielsen, M. (2012). *Reinventing discovery: The new era of networked science*. Princeton University Press.

Nikolaidi, M., & Stockhammer, E. (2017). Minsky models: A structured survey. *Journal of Economic Surveys, 31*(5), 1304–1331. DOI: 10.1111/joes.12222

Nimkar, S., & Makhijani, S. (2024). Blockchain and Cloud Computing in Healthcare: A Critical Analysis and Future Prospects. *2024 IEEE 3rd International Conference on Electrical Power and Energy Systems (ICEPES)*, 1–5. DOI: 10.1109/ICEPES60647.2024.10653489

Nordic Institute for Interoperability Solutions. (2021). X-Road: Data exchange layer technology. https://niis.org/x-road

Nosek, B. A.. (2015). Estimating the reproducibility of psychological science. *Science*, *349*(6251), aac4716. Advance online publication. DOI: 10.1126/science.aac4716 PMID: 26315443

Nzaro, E. K., Ondimu, K., & Mwakondo, F. (2022). A Blockchain-Based Conceptual Model for Curbing Institutional Academic Certificate Fraud. *International Journal of Computer Applications Technology and Research*, *11*(07), 255–263. DOI: 10.7753/IJCATR1107.1002

O'Dair, M., & Owen, R. (2019). Monetizing music in the blockchain age. *Journal of Revenue and Pricing Management*, *18*(4), 330–337.

O'Faircheallaigh, C. (2020). Impact and Benefit Agreements as Monitoring Instruments in the Minerals and Energy Industries. *The Extractive Industries and Society*, *7*(4), 1338–1346.

Odinet, C. K., & Tosato, A. (2025). Regulating stablecoins: Comparing MiCAR and the GENIUS Act. DOI: 10.2139/ssrn.5383158

OECD. (2020). *The Tokenisation of Assets and Potential Implications for Financial Markets*. OECD Blockchain Policy Series.

OECD. (2021). *Micro-credential innovations in higher education : Who, What and Why* (Vol. 39). OECD Publishing., DOI: 10.1787/f14ef041-

OECD. (2022). Institutionalisation of crypto-assets and DeFi–TradFi interconnectedness. OECD. https://www.oecd.org/en/publications/institutionalisation-of-crypto-assets-and-defi-tradfi-interconnectedness_5d9dddbe-en.html

OECD. (2023). *The tokenisation of assets and potential implications for financial markets*. OECD Publishing.

OECD. (2025). Tokenisation of assets and distributed ledger technologies in financial markets: Potential impediments and policy implications. *OECD Business and Finance Policy Papers*, (75). Advance online publication. DOI: 10.1787/bf84ff64-en

Official Monetary and Financial Institutions Forum (OMFIF). (2025). *Global public investor 2025*. London.

Ohlhaver, P., Weyl, E. G., & Buterin, V. (2022). Decentralized society: Finding Web3's soul. *SSRN*. DOI: 10.2139/ssrn.4105763

Olson, M. (1965). *The logic of collective action: Public goods and the theory of groups*. Harvard University Press. DOI: 10.4159/9780674041660

Omarova, S. (2021). The People's Ledger: How to democratize money and finance the economy. *Vanderbilt Law Review*, *74*(5), 1231–1314. https://scholarship.law.vanderbilt.edu/vlr/vol74/iss5/3

Onder, I., & Acikgoz, F. (2023). *Blockchain for Tourism and Hospitality Industries* (1st ed.). Routledge., DOI: 10.4324/9781003351917

Önder, I., & Gunter, U. (2022). Blockchain: Is it the future for the tourism and hospitality industry? *Tourism Economics*, *28*(2), 291–299. DOI: 10.1177/1354816620961707

Ondo Finance. (2023). *OUSG and USDY product documentation*. https://ondo.finance/whitepaper

One Canadian Economy Act (Bill C-5). (2025).. . *Statutes of Canada*, *c*, 2.

Onifade, M., Adebisi, J. A., & Zvarivadza, T. (2024). Recent advances in blockchain technology: Prospects, applications and constraints in the minerals industry. *International Journal of Mining, Reclamation and Environment*, *38*(7), 497–533. DOI: 10.1080/17480930.2024.2319453

Optimism Collective. (2023). *Optimism case study – Retroactive public goods funding results*.

Optimism Collective. (2024). *Retro funding 5: OP Stack – Round details*. Governance Forum.

Optimism Collective. (n.d.). *How retro funding works*. Optimism Docs. https://community.optimism.io/citizens-house/how-retro-funding-works

Optimism. (2021, July 20). Retroactive public goods funding. Optimism PBC Blog. https://medium.com/ethereum-optimism/retroactive-public-goods-funding-33c9b7d00f0c

Orchard, J., & Voloder, E. (2025, October 6). European regulators jostle for control of MiCA. *OMFIF*. Retrieved from https://www.omfif.org/2025/10/european-regulators-jostle-for-contro l-of-mica/?mc_cid=d482b2a27d&mc_eid=1fd274c085

Organisation for Economic Co-operation and Development (OECD). (2021). *Understanding the tokenisation of assets in financial markets*. OECD Blockchain Policy Series. https://www.oecd.org

Ortolani, P. (2016). Self-enforcing online dispute resolution: Lessons from Bitcoin. *Oxford Journal of Legal Studies, 36*(3), 595–629. DOI: 10.1093/ojls/gqv036

Ortolani, P. (2019). The impact of blockchain technologies and smart contracts on dispute resolution: Arbitration and court litigation at the crossroads. *Uniform Law Review, 24*(2), 430–448. DOI: 10.1093/ulr/unz017

Ostrom, E. (1990). *Governing the commons: The evolution of institutions for collective action*. Cambridge University Press. DOI: 10.1017/CBO9780511807763

Ostrom, E. (2010). Polycentric systems for coping with collective action and global environmental change. *Global Environmental Change, 20*(4), 550–557. DOI: 10.1016/j.gloenvcha.2010.07.004

Ostrowski, W. (2020). Transparency and Global Resources: Exploring Linkages and Boundaries. *The Extractive Industries and Society, 7*(4), 1472–1479.

Ouellette, L. L. (2012). How many patents does it take to make a drug? *Nature Biotechnology, 30*(6), 556–560.

Özgit, H., & Adalıer, A. (2022). Can Blockchain technology help small islands achieve sustainable tourism? A perspective on North Cyprus. *Worldwide Hospitality and Tourism Themes, 14*(4), 374–383. DOI: 10.1108/WHATT-03-2022-0037

Ozili, P. K. (2023). Institutional theory of financial inclusion. (Munich Personal RePEc Archive Paper No. 115770). Retrieved from https://mpra.ub.uni-muenchen.de/115770/

Pactual, B. T. G. (2019). *ReitBZ whitepaper*. https://www.reitbz.io/whitepaper.pdf

Pande, L., Pandey, U., & Sengupta, S. (2025). The Convergence of 5G, Contactless Technology and Blockchain in Tourism: Assessing Impacts, Adoption, and Future Trends. SSRN *Electronic Journal*. DOI: 10.2139/ssrn.5086775

Panigrahi, C. R., Pati, B., Rath, M., & Buyya, R. (2021). *Computational Modeling and Data Analysis in COVID-19 Research (C. Rani Panigrahi* (Pati, B., Rath, M., & Buyya, R., Eds.; 1st ed.). CRC Press., DOI: 10.1201/9781003137481

Paramasivan, A. (2022). AI and tokenization: Safeguarding sensitive card data in the digital economy. *International Journal on Science and Technology, 13*(2), 1–19. DOI: 10.5281/zenodo.14551590

Paris Convention for the Protection of Industrial Property, March 20, 1883, as revised at Stockholm on July 14, 1967, 21 U.S.T. 1583, 828 U.N.T.S. 305.

Park, J. (2021). Promises and challenges of Blockchain in education. *Smart Learning Environments, 8*(1), 33. DOI: 10.1186/s40561-021-00179-2 PMID: 40477765

Partha, D., & David, P. A. (1994). Toward a new economics of science. *Research Policy, 23*(5), 487–521. DOI: 10.1016/0048-7333(94)01002-1

Pasquini, R. A. (2020). *Quadratic funding and matching funds requirements*. SSRN Working Paper (Revised August 2022).

Pasquini, R. A. (2022). *Optimal allocation of limited funds in quadratic funding. arXiv Preprint.*

Patel, K. (2024). Revolutionizing Customer Experience: Integrating Blockchain with AR and VR in Retail. In B. Verma, A. Mittal, M. Raman, & B. Sindhav (Eds.), *Augmenting Retail Reality, Part B: Blockchain, AR, VR, and AI* (pp. 1–22). Emerald Publishing Limited. DOI: 10.1108/978-1-83608-708-320241003

Patel, Y., Chovatia, N., & Kaur, H. (2024). Securing Payment Transactions: A Comprehensive Review of Smart Cards and Contactless Payments with Cryptographic Methods. *2024 11th International Conference on Computing for Sustainable Global Development (INDIACom)*, 785–790. DOI: 10.23919/INDIACom61295.2024.10498568

Payment Services Act. 2019, No. 2 of 2019 (Singapore).

People's Bank of China. (2021). Progress of Research & Development of e-CNY in China. PBoC Report. https://www.pbc.gov.cn/en/3688110/3688172/4157443/4293696/2021071614584691871.pdf

Peters, B. G. (2022). Institutional theory. In *Handbook on Theories of Governance*. Edward Elgar Publishing. DOI: 10.4337/9781800371972.00039

Peukert, A. (2021). Fictitious commodities: A theory of intellectual property inspired by Karl Polanyi's "Great Transformation". Fordham Intellectual Property. *Media & Entertainment Law Journal, 29*(4), 1151–1210.

Pinna, A., & Ruttenberg, W. (2016). *Distributed ledger technologies in securities post-trading* (ECB Occasional Paper No. 172). European Central Bank. https://www.ecb.europa.eu/pub/pdf/scpops/ecbop172.en.pdf

Pistor, K. (2019). *The Code of Capital: How the Law Creates Wealth and Inequality*. Princeton University Press.

Polanyi, M. (1962). The republic of science: Its political and economic theory. *Minerva, 1*(1), 54–73. DOI: 10.1007/BF01101453

Posner, E. A., & Weyl, E. G. (2018). *Radical markets: Uprooting capitalism and democracy for a just society*. Princeton University Press.

Pranita, D., Sarjana, S., Musthofa, B. M., Kusumastuti, H., & Rasul, M. S. (2023). Blockchain Technology to Enhance Integrated Blue Economy: A Case Study in Strengthening Sustainable Tourism on Smart Islands. *Sustainability (Basel)*, *15*(6), 5342. DOI: 10.3390/su15065342

Protocol, M. (2023). Intellectual property NFTs for biotech. https://molecule.to/

Protocol, O. (2023). Data tokenization protocol. https://oceanprotocol.com/

Pulmano, C. E., Estuar, M. R. J. E., De Leon, M. M., Tan, H. C. L., Co, N. A. S., & Tamayo, L. P. V. (2023). Towards the Development of a Blockchain-based Decentralized Digital Credential System using Hyperledger Fabric for Participatory Governance. *Procedia Computer Science*, *219*, 99–106. DOI: 10.1016/j.procs.2023.01.269

Qin, K., Zhou, L., Gamito, P., Jovanovic, P., & Gervais, A. (2021, November). An empirical study of defi liquidations: Incentives, risks, and instabilities. In *Proceedings of the 21st ACM internet measurement conference* (pp. 336-350). DOI: 10.1145/3487552.3487811

Queiroz, M. M., Telles, R., & Bonilla, S. H. (2019). Blockchain and supply chain management integration: A systematic review of the literature. *Supply Chain Management*, *25*(2), 241–254. DOI: 10.1108/SCM-03-2018-0143

Quintais, J. P. (2017). *Copyright in the age of online access: Alternative compensation systems in EU law*. Kluwer Law International.

Rafique, H., Almagrabi, A. O., Shamim, A., Anwar, F., & Bashir, A. K. (2020). Investigating the Acceptance of Mobile Library Applications with an Extended Technology Acceptance Model (TAM). *Computers & Education*, *145*, 103732. DOI: 10.1016/j.compedu.2019.103732

Rane, N. (2023). Enhancing customer loyalty through Artificial Intelligence (AI), Internet of Things (IoT), and Big Data technologies: Improving customer satisfaction, engagement, relationship, and experience. *Internet of Things (IoT), and Big Data Technologies: Improving Customer Satisfaction, Engagement, Relationship, and Experience (October 13, 2023).*

Rane, N., Choudhary, S., & Rane, J. (2023). Blockchain and Artificial Intelligence (AI) integration for revolutionizing security and transparency in finance. SSRN *Electronic Journal*. DOI: 10.2139/ssrn.4644253

Rashideh, W. (2020). Blockchain technology framework: Current and future perspectives for the tourism industry. *Tourism Management*, *80*, 104125. DOI: 10.1016/j.tourman.2020.104125

Ratna, S., Saide, S., Putri, A. M., Indrajit, R. E., & Muwardi, D. (2024). Digital transformation in tourism and hospitality industry: A literature review of blockchain, financial technology, and knowledge management. *EuroMed Journal of Business*, *19*(1), 84–112. DOI: 10.1108/EMJB-04-2023-0118

Ray, P. P., & Dash, D. (2022). Blockchain for IoT-based medical delivery drones. In *Blockchain Technology for Emerging Applications* (pp. 137–176). Elsevier., DOI: 10.1016/B978-0-323-90193-2.00002-8

Redman, J. (2025, June 19). Blockchain lending boom: Tokenized private credit nears $14 billion. *Bitcoin.* Retrieved from https://news.bitcoin.com/blockchain-lending-boom-tokenized-priv ate-credit-nears-14-billion/

Reed, C. (2018). How should we regulate algorithms? *Philosophical Transactions of the Royal Society A*, *376*(2128), 20170360. DOI: 10.1098/rsta.2017.0360

Regen Network Registry. (2024). *Indigenous-led biocultural jaguar corridor credits.* https://registry.regen.network

Regen Network. (2021). *Regen Network whitepaper v1.3.* https://regen.network

Regen Network. (2023, May). *Digital carbon market case study. Frontiers in Blockchain.* https://frontiersin.org

Regulation (EU) 2017/1129 of the European Parliament and of the Council of 14 June 2017 on the prospectus to be published when securities are offered to the public or admitted to trading on a regulated market, OJ L 168, 30.6.2017.

Regulation (EU) 2023/1114 of the European Parliament and of the Council of 31 May 2023 on markets in crypto-assets (MiCA), OJ L 150, 9.6.2023.

Regulation (EU) No 1215/2012 of the European Parliament and of the Council of 12 December 2012 on jurisdiction and the recognition and enforcement of judgments in civil and commercial matters (recast), OJ L 351, 20.12.2012.

Reidenberg, J. R. (1998). Lex informatica: The formulation of information policy rules through technology. *Texas Law Review*, *76*(3), 553–593.

Reyes, C. L. (2019). If Rockefeller were a coder. *The George Washington Law Review*, *87*(2), 373–429.

Roam Network. (2025). *Building a credential-based wireless network.* Messari. https://messari.io

Robinson, R. (2020). The new digital wild west: Regulating the explosion of initial coin offerings. *Tennessee Law Review, 85*(4), 897–960.

Rodrigues, U. R. (2019). Law and the blockchain. *Iowa Law Review, 104*(2), 679–729.

Rodríguez Bolívar, M. P., Sepe, F., Nanu, L., & Roberto, F. (2025). Perceptions and challenges of blockchain adoption in tourism industry: A study on trust, privacy and security. *Journal of Hospitality and Tourism Technology, 16*(3), 429–449. DOI: 10.1108/JHTT-03-2024-0193

Rogers, E. M. (2003). *Diffusion of innovations* (5th ed.). Free Press.

Rohr, J., & Wright, A. (2019). Blockchain-based token sales, initial coin offerings, and the democratization of public capital markets. *The Hastings Law Journal, 70*(2), 463–524.

Rongali, B., Mohapatra, S., & Nayak, S. K. (2023). A Secure Contactless Payment System with Bidirectional Blockchain and Blake Hash Function. *2023 IEEE 22nd International Conference on Trust, Security and Privacy in Computing and Communications (TrustCom)*, 318–325. DOI: 10.1109/TrustCom60117.2023.00061

Roughgarden, T. (2020). Transaction fee mechanism design. *ACM SIGecom Exchanges, 19*(1), 52–55. DOI: 10.1145/3476436.3476445

Rouhani, S., & Deters, R. (2021). Data Trust Framework Using Blockchain Technology and Adaptive Transaction Validation. *IEEE Access : Practical Innovations, Open Solutions, 9*, 90379–90391. DOI: 10.1109/ACCESS.2021.3091327

Royal. (2023). Music NFT marketplace. https://royal.io/

Rozas, D., Tenorio-Fornés, A., Díaz-Molina, S., & Hassan, S. (2021). When Ostrom meets blockchain: Exploring the potentials of blockchain for commons governance. *Environmental Innovation and Societal Transitions, 69*, 100678.

Russell, S. J., & Norvig, P. (2021). *Artificial intelligence: A modern approach* (4th ed.). Pearson.

S&P Global. (2024). *Tokenized Private Credit: A New Digital Frontier for Real World Assets.* Retrieved from https://www.spglobal.com/en/research-insights/special-reports/tokenized-private-credit

Saberi, S., Kouhizadeh, M., Sarkis, J., & Shen, L. (2019). Blockchain technology and its relationships to sustainable supply chain management. *International Journal of Production Research, 57*(7), 2117–2135. DOI: 10.1080/00207543.2018.1533261

Saengchote, K. (2023). Decentralized lending and its users: Insights from Compound. *Journal of Banking & Finance, 151*, 106839. DOI: 10.1016/j.jbankfin.2023.106839

Sahoo, S., Kumar, S., Sivarajah, U., Lim, W. M., Westland, J. C., & Kumar, A. (2024). Blockchain for sustainable supply chain management: Trends and ways forward. *Electronic Commerce Research, 24*(3), 1563–1618. DOI: 10.1007/s10660-022-09569-1

Samuelson, P. A. (1954). The pure theory of public expenditure. *The Review of Economics and Statistics, 36*(4), 387–389. DOI: 10.2307/1925895

Santana, C., & Albareda, L. (2022). Blockchain and the emergence of Decentralized Autonomous Organizations (DAOs): An integrative model and research agenda. *Technological Forecasting and Social Change, 182*, 121806. DOI: 10.1016/j.techfore.2022.121806

Santiso, C. (2022). *A blockchain-based land-titling project in the Republic of Georgia: Rebuilding public trust and lessons for future pilot projects.* ResearchGate. https://www.researchgate.net/publication/330069648_A_Blockchain-Based_Land_Titling_Project_in_the_Republic_of_Georgia_Rebuilding_Public_Trust_and_Lessons_for_Future_Pilot_Projects

Santos, A. F., Marinho, J., & Bernardino, J. (2023). Blockchain-Based Loyalty Management System. *Future Internet, 15*(5), 161. DOI: 10.3390/fi15050161

Saraji, S., & Borowczak, M. (2021). A blockchain-based carbon credit ecosystem. *arXiv Preprint.* https://arxiv.org/abs/2107.00185

Sarewitz, D. (2016). The pressure to publish pushes down quality. *Nature, 533*(7602), 147. DOI: 10.1038/533147a PMID: 27172010

Savelyev, A. (2017). Contract law 2.0: 'Smart' contracts as the beginning of the end of classic contract law. *Information & Communications Technology Law, 26*(2), 116–134. DOI: 10.1080/13600834.2017.1301036

Savelyev, A. (2018). Copyright in the blockchain era: Promises and challenges. *Computer Law & Security Review, 34*(3), 550–561. DOI: 10.1016/j.clsr.2017.11.008

Saxena, M., Senthilkumar, N., & Girimurugan, B. P, L. A., Hasan, K. S., & Sanjay. (2024). Customer Relationship Management in the Digital Age by Implementing Blockchain for Enhanced Data Security and Customer Trust. *2024 2nd International Conference on Disruptive Technologies (ICDT)*, 56–59. DOI: 10.1109/ICDT61202.2024.10489537

Sayed, Y. J., Shishegaran, A., Smith, J., & Saeedi, M. (2025). Sustainability Reporting & Transparency. In Taherdoost, H., Saeedi, M., & Shishegaran, A. (Eds.), *Applications of Blockchain Technology and Computational Intelligence in Environmental Sustainability* (1st ed.). CRC Press., 10.1201/9781003609865

Schär, F. (2021). Decentralized finance: On blockchain- and smart contract-based financial markets. *Review - Federal Reserve Bank of St. Louis*, *103*(2), 153–174.

Schär, F. (2021). Decentralized finance: On Blockchain- and Smart Contract-based financial markets. *Review - Federal Reserve Bank of St. Louis*, *103*(2), 153–174. DOI: 10.20955/r.103.153-74

Schmitz, A. J., & Rule, C. (2019). Online dispute resolution for smart contracts. *Journal of Dispute Resolution*, *2019*(1), 103–126.

Schrepel, T. (2021). Smart contracts and the digital single market through the lens of a "Law + Technology" approach. European Commission. SEC v. Kik Interactive Inc., No. 19-cv-5244 (S.D.N.Y. 2020). SEC v. Ripple Labs, Inc., No. 20-cv-10832 (S.D.N.Y. July 13, 2023). SEC v. W.J. Howey Co., 328 U.S. 293 (1946).

Scott, W. R. (2001). *Institutions and organizations* (2nd ed.). Sage Publications.

Scott, W. R. (2005). Institutional theory: Contributing to a theoretical research program. *Great Minds in Management: The Process of Theory Development*, *37*(2), 460–484. DOI: 10.1093/oso/9780199276813.003.0022

Securities Act of 1933, 15 U.S.C. §§ 77a–77aa.

Securities and Exchange Commission. (2020). *Framework for "investment contract" analysis of digital assets*. https://www.sec.gov/corpfin/framework-investment-contract-analysis-digital-assets

Securitize. (2023). Digital asset securities platform. https://securitize.io/

Senftleben, M. (2019). User-generated content: Towards a new use privilege in EU copyright law. In Aplin, T. (Ed.), *Research handbook on intellectual property and digital technologies* (pp. 136–162). Edward Elgar Publishing.

Sharma, M., Sehrawat, R., Daim, T., & Shaygan, A. (2021). Technology assessment: Enabling Blockchain in hospitality and tourism sectors. *Technological Forecasting and Social Change, 169*, 120810. DOI: 10.1016/j.techfore.2021.120810

Shilina, S. (2023). Decentralized science (DeSci): Web3-mediated future of science. URL: https://medium. com/paradigm-research/decentralized-science-desci-web3-mediated-future-of-science-2547f9a88c40

Shilina, S. (2025). Worlds that verify themselves: DeScAI as a recursive epistemic ecology. *SSRN*. DOI: 10.2139/ssrn.5272669

Siegel, D. (2016). *Understanding the DAO Attack.* Coindesk.

Siemens, A. G. (2023). *Siemens issues first digital bond on blockchain under eWpG.* https://press.siemens.com

Silaghi, D. L., & Popescu, D. E. (2025). A Systematic Review of Blockchain-Based Initiatives in Comparison to Best Practices Used in Higher Education Institutions. *Computers, 14*(4), 141. DOI: 10.3390/computers14040141

Smart Dubai Office & Dubai Future Foundation. (2023). *Dubai Blockchain Strategy progress and implementation.* Government of Dubai.

Smith, R. (2006). Peer review: A flawed process at the heart of science and journals. *Journal of the Royal Society of Medicine, 99*(4), 178–182. DOI: 10.1177/014107680609900414 PMID: 16574968

So, H.-J., Lee, C., Lee, G.-Y., & Kim, M. J. (2024). *Artificial intelligence, blockchain and extended reality in lifelong learning*. UNESCO Institute for Lifelong Learning.

Solulab (2025). *Top DeFi Lending Platforms in 2025.* Available at https://www .solulab.com/top-defi-lending-platforms/

Sorensen, D. (2023). Tokenized carbon credits. *Ledger, 8*, 76–91. DOI: 10.5195/ ledger.2023.294

Sosa, I., & Keenan, K. (2001). Impact Benefit Agreements Between Aboriginal Communities and Mining Companies: Their Use in Canada. Report: Canadian Environmental Law Association, Environmental Mining Council of British Columbia, and Cooper Accion: Accion Solidaria para el Desarrollo.

Srinivasan, S., Raja, R., Jehan, C., Murugan, S., Srinivasan, C., & Muthulekshmi, M. (2024). IoT-Enabled Facial Recognition for Smart Hospitality for Contactless Guest Services and Identity Verification. *2024 11th International Conference on Reliability, Infocom Technologies and Optimization (Trends and Future Directions) (ICRITO)*, 1–6. DOI: 10.1109/ICRITO61523.2024.10522363

Standard, G. (n.d.). *Our new double-counting guidelines*. https://www.goldstandard.org/publications/our-new-double-counting-guidelines. Gold Standard

Statista. Retrieved June 13, 2025, from https://www.statista.com/statistics/1272181/defi-tvl-in-multiple-blockchains/

Steiu, M.-F. (2020). Blockchain in education: Opportunities, applications, and challenges. *First Monday*, *25*(9). Advance online publication. DOI: 10.5210/fm.v25i9.10654

Stephan, P. (1996). The economics of science. *Journal of Economic Literature*, *34*(3), 1199–1235.

Stephan, P. (2012). *How economics shapes science*. Harvard University Press. DOI: 10.4159/harvard.9780674062757

Stevens, R. (2020, August 7). *YFI's Andre Cronje is tired, broke and close to quitting DeFi*. Decrypt. Retrieved August 29, 2025, from https://decrypt.co/37995/exclusive-yfi-andre-cronje-broke-quitting-defi

Stokel-Walker, C. (2023, January 18). ChatGPT listed as author on research papers: Many scientists disapprove. Nature. https://www.nature.com/articles/d41586-023-00107-z

Stokes, D. E. (1997). *Pasteur's quadrant: Basic science and technological innovation*. Brookings Institution Press.

Stoll, C., Klaaßen, L., & Gallersdörfer, U. (2019). The carbon footprint of bitcoin. *Joule*, *3*(7), 1647–1661. DOI: 10.1016/j.joule.2019.05.012

Suddaby, R. (2010). Challenges for institutional theory. *Journal of Management Inquiry*, *19*(1), 14–20. DOI: 10.1177/1056492609347564

Sun, H., Wang, X., & Wang, X. (2018). Application of Blockchain Technology in Online Education. [IJET]. *International Journal of Emerging Technologies in Learning*, *13*(10), 252–259. DOI: 10.3991/ijet.v13i10.9455

Sunyaev, A., Kannengießer, N., Beck, R., Treiblmaier, H., Lacity, M., Kranz, J., Fridgen, G., Spankowski, U., & Luckow, A. (2021). Token Economy. *Business & Information Systems Engineering*, *63*(4), 457–478. DOI: 10.1007/s12599-021-00684-1

Swan, M. (2015). *Blockchain: Blueprint for a new economy*. O'Reilly Media.

Swift. (n.d.). Unlocking the potential of digital asset securities. Retrieved April 14, 2025, from https://www.swift.com/campaign/unlocking-potential-digital-asset-securities

Swiss Code of Obligations, SR 220 (as amended by the DLT Act).

Sygnum Bank. (2022). *Sygnum tokenizes own shares and distributes first tokenized dividend.* https://www.sygnum.com

Szabo, N. (1997). Formalizing and securing relationships on public networks. *First Monday*, *2*(9). Advance online publication. DOI: 10.5210/fm.v2i9.548

Tahlil, T., Gomasta, S. S., & Ali, A. B. M. S. (2022). AlgoCert: Adopt Non-transferable NFT for the Issuance and Verification of Educational Certificates using Algorand Blockchain. *2022 IEEE Asia-Pacific Conference on Computer Science and Data Engineering (CSDE)*, 1–8. DOI: 10.1109/CSDE56538.2022.10089274

Talukder, M. B., & Kumar, S. (2024). The Development of Human Capital in The Hospitality Business. In S. Taneja, P. Kumar, Reepu, B. Balusamy, K. Sood, & S. Grima (Eds.), *Contemporary Studies in Economic and Financial Analysis* (pp. 21–38). Emerald Publishing Limited. DOI: 10.1108/S1569-375920240000114002

Talukder, M. B., Hoque, M., & Kumar, S. (2024). Impact of Cybersecurity in the Aviation, Tourism, and Hospitality Industries. In *Corporate Cybersecurity in the Aviation, Tourism, and Hospitality Sector* (pp. 200–215). IGI Global.

Talukder, M. B., Hoque, M., & Kumar, S. (2025). Understanding the Blend of Work and Leisure in Hospitality: The Era of Bleisure. In *Smart Travel and Sustainable Innovations in Bleisure Tourism* (pp. 179–200). IGI Global.

Talukder, M. B., Kumar, S., & Tyagi, P. K. (Eds.). (2024). *Impact of AI and Tech-Driven Solutions in Hospitality and Tourism.* IGI Global., DOI: 10.4018/979-8-3693-6755-1

Talukder, M. B., Lina, F. Y., Kumar, S., & Khan, M. R. (2024). Data-Driven Personalization in the Sharing Economy. In Ordóñez De Pablos, P. (Ed.), (pp. 277–300). Advances in Finance, Accounting, and Economics. IGI Global., DOI: 10.4018/979-8-3693-5673-9.ch012

Tan, E., & Du Seuil, D. (2025). European Digital Infrastructure Consortium (EDIC): A New Governance Framework for the European Blockchain Services Infrastructure (EBSI). In *Public Governance and Emerging Technologies* (pp. 83–101). Springer Nature Switzerland. DOI: 10.1007/978-3-031-84748-6_5

Tan, E., Lerouge, E., Du Caju, J., & Du Seuil, D. (2023). Verification of Education Credentials on European Blockchain Services Infrastructure (EBSI): Action Research in a Cross-Border Use Case between Belgium and Italy. *Big Data and Cognitive Computing*, *7*(2), 79. DOI: 10.3390/bdcc7020079

Tanveer, U., Ishaq, S., & Hoang, T. G. (2025). Tokenized assets in a decentralized economy: Balancing efficiency, value, and risks. *International Journal of Production Economics*, *282*, 109554. DOI: 10.1016/j.ijpe.2025.109554

Tapscott, D., & Tapscott, A. (2016). *Blockchain Revolution: How the Technology Behind Bitcoin is Changing Money, Business, and the World.* Penguin.

Tariq, A., Binte Haq, H., & Ali, S. T. (2023). Cerberus: A Blockchain-Based Accreditation and Degree Verification System. *IEEE Transactions on Computational Social Systems*, *10*(4), 1503–1514. DOI: 10.1109/TCSS.2022.3188453

Task Force on Climate-related Financial Disclosures. (2021, July). *Metrics, targets, and transition plans guidance* [PDF]. https://assets.bbhub.io/company/sites/60/2021/07/2021-Metrics_Targets_Guidance-1.pdf

Taurus Group. (2021). *SCCF-Taurus trade finance tokenization report.* https://www.taurusgroup.ch/reports/sccf

Tennant, J. P.. (2017). A multi-disciplinary perspective on emergent and future innovations in peer review. *F1000 Research*, *6*, 1151. DOI: 10.12688/f1000research.12037.3 PMID: 29188015

Tepelidis, A., Mitsopoulou, E. E., Patenidis, A. T., Votis, K., & Tzovaras, D. (2024). A Multi-blockchain System for Verifiable Academic Credentials. In *Open Science in Engineering (REV 2023)* (Vol. 763, pp. 917–926). Springer., DOI: 10.1007/978-3-031-42467-0_86

Terzi, S., Ioannis, S., Votis, K., & Tsiatsos, T. (2022). A Life-Long Learning Education Passport Powered by Blockchain Technology and Verifiable Digital Credentials: The BlockAdemiC Project. In *Software Engineering and Formal Methods. SEFM 2021 Collocated Workshops* (pp. 249–263). Springer Publishing Company. DOI: 10.1007/978-3-031-12429-7_18

Thaler, J. (2013). Time-optimal interactive proofs for circuit evaluation. CRYPTO 2013.

Tham, A., & Sigala, M. (2020). Road block(chain): Bit(coin)s for tourism sustainable development goals? *Journal of Hospitality and Tourism Technology*, *11*(2), 203–222. DOI: 10.1108/JHTT-05-2019-0069

The Bank for International Settlements. (2025). *The next-generation monetary and financial system* (Annual Report, Chapter III). https://www.bis.org/publ/arpdf/ar2025e3

The Bitfury Group, & National Agency of Public Registry. (2016, February 7). *The Bitfury Group and Government of Republic of Georgia expand historic blockchain land-titling project* [Press release]. Bitfury. https://bitfury.com/content/downloads/the_bitfury_group_republic_of_georgia_expand_blockchain_pilot_2_7_16.pdf

Thirdweb. (2024, April 29). *What is EIP-1559? Ethereum gas fees and how they work.* Third web Blog. https://blog.thirdweb.com/eip-1559-ethereum-gas-fees

Tiits, M., & Kaska, K. (2018). *Estonian digital government architecture and the role of emerging technologies.* Estonian Information System Authority.

Token and Trusted Technology Service Provider Act (TVTG). LGBl. 2019 No. 301 (Liechtenstein).

Token Engineering Academy. (2025). *TE Fundamentals course overview.* https://te-academy.netlify.app

Token Engineering Commons. (2022). [Medium article by S. Voshmgir]. https://sherminvoshmgir.medium.com/token-engineering-commons-69398048209a

Token Engineering Commons. (2023). *Tunable quadratic funding: Incorporating expertise into QF* [Medium article by G. Rosenblatt]. https://medium.com/token-engineering-commons/expertise-and-quadratic-funding-bd4f0c5c3e23

Tokengate. (2023). DLT securities platform. https://tokengate.io/

Tokeny. (2022). *ERC-3643 and ERC-1400 token standards overview.* https://www.tokeny.com/erc-3643-overview

Torbey, C. (2020). Reconciling music streaming and blockchain: Transparency and smart contracts. *Hastings Communications and Entertainment Law Journal, 42*(2), 145–178.

Trans Mountain Corporation. (2023). Trans Mountain: 2023 Environmental, Social & Governance Report. Retrieved (August 2025) from https://docs.transmountain.com/ESG-Reports/TransMountain_2023-ESG-Report.pdf

Trimble, M. (2012). The future of cybertravel: Legal implications of the evasion of geolocation. Fordham Intellectual Property. *Media & Entertainment Law Journal, 22*(3), 567–657.

Turkanovic, M., Holbl, M., Kosic, K., Hericko, M., & Kamisalic, A. (2018). EduCTX: A Blockchain-Based Higher Education Credit Platform. *IEEE Access : Practical Innovations, Open Solutions, 6*, 5112–5127. DOI: 10.1109/ACCESS.2018.2789929

U.S. Securities and Exchange Commission (SEC). Ongoing enforcement releases on crypto assets. https://www.sec.gov/about/divisions-offices/division-enforcement/cyber-crypto-assets-emerging-technology/enforcement-actions#crypto

U.S. Securities and Exchange Commission. (2024, January 10). *Order approving the application for the ProShares Bitcoin Strategy ETF.* Retrieved from https://www.sec.gov/news/press-release/2024-6

UNCITRAL Model Law on Electronic Commerce. G.A. Res. 51/162, U.N. Doc. A/RES/51/162 (Dec. 16, 1996).

Uniform Law Commission. (2022). Uniform Commercial Code 2022 Amendments: Controllable electronic records (Article 12). ULC. https://www.uniformlaws.org

United Nations Conference on Trade and Development. (2024, April 9). Financing for sustainable development report 2024: Financing for development at a crossroads. UNCTAD. Retrieved from https://unctad.org/publication/financing-sustainable-development-report-2024

United Nations. (2008). "United Nations Declaration on the Rights of Indigenous Peoples".

Upadhyay, N. (2020). Demystifying blockchain: A critical analysis of challenges, applications and opportunities. *International Journal of Information Management, 54*, 102120. DOI: 10.1016/j.ijinfomgt.2020.102120

Upreti, K., Gangwar, D., Vats, P., Bhardwaj, R., Khatri, V., & Gautam, V. (2024). Artificial Neural Networks for Enhancing E-commerce: A Study on Improving Personalization, Recommendation, and Customer Experience. In Shaw, R. N., Siano, P., Makhilef, S., Ghosh, A., & Shimi, S. L. (Eds.), *Innovations in Electrical and Electronic Engineering* (Vol. 1115, pp. 141–153). Springer Nature Singapore., DOI: 10.1007/978-981-99-8661-3_11

UsedSoft GmbH v. Oracle International Corp., Case C-128/11, ECLI:EU:C:2012:407.

Ustawa z dnia 4 lutego 1994 r. o prawie autorskim i prawach pokrewnych, Dz.U. 1994 nr 24 poz. 83 (Poland).

Van Hoecke, M. (2002). *Law as communication.* Hart Publishing.

Vanini, P., Rossi, S., Zvizdic, E., & Domenig, T. (2023). Online payment fraud: From anomaly detection to risk management. *Financial Innovation, 9*(1), 66. DOI: 10.1186/s40854-023-00470-w

Vardhan Singh Rawat, H., Bisht, D., Kumar, S., & Dangi, S. (2022). Rise of Blockchain-Based Non-fungible Tokens (NFTs): Overview, Trends, and Future Prospects. In V. Skala, T. P. Singh, T. Choudhury, R. Tomar, & Md. Abul Bashar (Eds.), *Machine Intelligence and Data Science Applications* (Vol. 132, pp. 1–10). Springer Nature Singapore. DOI: 10.1007/978-981-19-2347-0_1

Vaultie. (2023). Trademark tokenization platform. https://vaultie.io/

Verma, A., Bhattacharya, P., Madhani, N., Trivedi, C., Bhushan, B., Tanwar, S., Sharma, G., Bokoro, P. N., & Sharma, R. (2022). Blockchain for Industry 5.0: Vision, Opportunities, Key Enablers, and Future Directions. *IEEE Access : Practical Innovations, Open Solutions, 10*, 69160–69199. DOI: 10.1109/ACCESS.2022.3186892

Vijayvergiya, R., Goto, T., & Sen, S. (2024). A Framework for Direct Benefit Transfer for Fertilizer Distribution and Payment Using Blockchain. In H. N. Saha, H. Ray, & P. G. Bradford (Eds.), *International Conference on Systems and Technologies for Smart Agriculture* (pp. 839–850). Springer Nature Singapore. DOI: 10.1007/978-981-97-5157-0_69

VitaDAO. (2023). Decentralized biotech research collective. https://vitadao.com/

Waheed, S., & Kumar, S. (2024). Challenges and Future Directions for Promoting Sustainable Gastronomy Tourism. In *Promoting Sustainable Gastronomy Tourism and Community Development* (pp. 1–16). IGI Global. DOI: 10.4018/979-8-3693-1814-0.ch001

Wamba, S. F., & Queiroz, M. M. (2020). Blockchain in the operations and supply chain management: Benefits, challenges and future research opportunities. *International Journal of Information Management*, 52, 102064. https://doi.org/. ijinfomgt.2019.102064DOI: 10.1016/j

Wang, L., Yu, J., Bennett, A., Gao, B., & Joseph, R. (2025). Evaluating voting design vulnerabilities for retroactive funding. *arXiv Preprint, arXiv:2505.16068.* https://arxiv.org/abs/2505.16068

Wang, D., Wu, S., Lin, Z., Wu, L., Yuan, X., Zhou, Y., Wang, H., & Ren, K. (2021). Towards a first step to understand flash loan and its applications in DeFi ecosystem, *Proceedings from Ninth International Workshop on Security in Blockchain and Cloud Computing* (pp. 22-28). DOI: 10.1145/3457977.3460301

Wang, H., Ma, S., Dai, H.-N., Imran, M., & Wang, T. (2020). Blockchain-based data privacy management with Nudge theory in open banking. *Future Generation Computer Systems, 110*, 812–823. DOI: 10.1016/j.future.2019.09.010

Wang, L., Luo, X., & Lee, F. (2019). Unveiling the interplay between blockchain and loyalty program participation: A qualitative approach based on Bubichain. *International Journal of Information Management*, *49*, 397–410. DOI: 10.1016/j.ijinfomgt.2019.08.001

Wang, X., Younas, M., Jiang, Y., Imran, M., & Almusharraf, N. (2025). Transforming Education Through Blockchain: A Systematic Review of Applications, Projects, and Challenges. *IEEE Access : Practical Innovations, Open Solutions*, *13*, 13264–13284. DOI: 10.1109/ACCESS.2024.3519350

Weber, M. (1919). *Politik als Beruf*. Duncker & Humblot.

Websima, D. M. C. C. (2025). *AI and blockchain in Dubai government services: Case studies and insights*. Websima DMCC.

Weidener, L., & Boltz, L. (2025). Challenges of DAOs in decentralized science: A qualitative analysis of expert interviews. *SSRN*. DOI: 10.3389/fbloc.2025.1641294

Weidener, L., & Spreckelsen, C. (2024). Decentralized science (DeSci): Definition, shared values, and guiding principles. *Frontiers in Blockchain*, *7*, 1375763. DOI: 10.3389/fbloc.2024.1375763

Weiss, J., & Salman, Z. (2022). How Blockchain Can Encourage Learning. In *Stanford GSE Office of Innovation and Technology*. Stanford GSE Office of Innovation and Technology. https://medium.com/@stanfordgseit/blockchain-enthusiasts-eye-challenges-in-education-3064058fdfb2

Weiss, K. (2022). Gitcoin grants – Quadratic funding for the world. Gitcoin. https://gitcoin.co

Werbach, K. (2018). *The blockchain and the new architecture of trust*. MIT Press. DOI: 10.7551/mitpress/11449.001.0001

Werner, S., Perez, D., Gudgeon, L., Klages-Mundt, A., Harz, D., & Knottenbelt, W. (2022, September). Sok: Decentralized finance (defi). In *Proceedings of the 4th ACM Conference on Advances in Financial Technologies* (pp. 30-46). DOI: 10.1145/3558535.3559780

Wiki Contributors. (2025). X-Road. In Wikipedia. Retrieved December 23, 2025, from https://en.wikipedia.org/wiki/X-Road

Wilkinson, M. D., Dumontier, M., Aalbersberg, I. J. J., Appleton, G., Axton, M., Baak, A., Blomberg, N., Boiten, J.-W., da Silva Santos, L. B., Bourne, P. E., Bouwman, J., Brookes, A. J., Clark, T., Crosas, M., Dillo, I., Dumon, O., Edmunds, S., Evelo, C. T., Finkers, R., & Mons, B. (2016). The FAIR guiding principles for scientific data management and stewardship. *Scientific Data*, *3*(1), 160018. DOI: 10.1038/sdata.2016.18 PMID: 26978244

Williams, S., Diordiiev, V., Berman, L., Raybould, I., & Uemlianin, I. (n.d.). Arweave: A protocol for economically sustainable information permanence (DRAFT-1). Arweave. Retrieved from https://www.arweave.org/yellow-paper.pdf

Willmott, H. (2015). Why institutional theory cannot be critical. *Journal of Management Inquiry*, *24*(1), 105–111. DOI: 10.1177/1056492614545306

WIPO. (2022). WIPO Blockchain Whitepaper: Blockchain technologies and IP ecosystems: A WIPO white paper. World Intellectual Property Organization.

Wolfers, J., & Zitzewitz, E. (2004). Prediction markets. *The Journal of Economic Perspectives*, *18*(2), 107–126. DOI: 10.1257/0895330041371321

World Bank Group. (2020). *Blockchain Technology for Youth Empowerment and Value Exchange: Final Project and Evaluation Report* (Vol. 1). World Bank Group. https://documents.worldbank.org/curated/en/948241602654046284

World Bank. (2020). *Digital financial services for development*. https://www.worldbank.org/en/topic/financialinclusion/publication/digital-financial-services

World Bank. (2020). Trade finance gaps, growth, and jobs survey. https://www.worldbank.org/en/topic/trade/publication/trade-finance-gaps-growth-and-jobs-survey

World Bank. (2022). Digital Economy for Development. https://www.worldbank.org

World Economic Forum (WEF). (2025). *Asset tokenization in financial markets: The next generation of value exchange*. Cologny, Switzerland

World Economic Forum. (2020). The tokenization of products and services. https://www.weforum.org/reports/the-tokenization-of-products-and-services

World Economic Forum. (2020). *Tokenization of assets and the future of finance*. https://www.weforum.org/reports/tokenization-of-assets-and-potential-implications-for-financial-markets

World Economic Forum. (2022). Tokenization of real estate and the future of property investment. https://www.weforum.org/reports/tokenization-in-real-estate-2022/

Wright, A., & De Filippi, P. (2015). Decentralized blockchain technology and the rise of lex cryptographia. SSRN Electronic Journal. DOI: 10.2139/ssrn.2580664

Wright, A. (2021). The rise of decentralized autonomous organizations: Opportunities and challenges. *Stanford Journal of Blockchain Law & Policy*, *4*(2), 152–203.

Wyman, O., De Lima, L., Ekberg, J., Ho, M., & Hung, T. (n.d.). It's Time to Explore Institutional DeFi. Oliver Wyman Forum. https://www.oliverwymanforum.com/future-of-money/2022/Nov/institutional-defi.html

Wyoming Digital Assets Act, W.S. § 34-29-101 (2019).

Yadav, A. S., Charles, V., Pandey, D. K., Gupta, S., Gherman, T., & Kushwaha, D. S. (2023). Blockchain-based secure privacy-preserving vehicle accident and insurance registration. *Expert Systems with Applications*, *230*, 120651. DOI: 10.1016/j.eswa.2023.120651

Yeh, K.-H. (2018). A Secure Transaction Scheme With Certificateless Cryptographic Primitives for IoT-Based Mobile Payments. *IEEE Systems Journal*, *12*(2), 2027–2038. DOI: 10.1109/JSYST.2017.2668389

Yeoh, P. (2017). Regulatory issues in blockchain technology. *Journal of Financial Regulation and Compliance*, *25*(2), 196–208. DOI: 10.1108/JFRC-08-2016-0068

Yeung, K. (2019). Regulation by blockchain: The emerging battle for supremacy between the code of law and code as law. *The Modern Law Review*, *82*(2), 207–239. DOI: 10.1111/1468-2230.12399

Yin, R. K. (2018). *Case study research and applications: Design and methods* (6th ed.). Sage Publications.

Zachariadis, M., Hileman, G., & Scott, S. V. (2019). Governance and control in distributed ledgers: Understanding the challenges facing blockchain technology in financial services. *Information and Organization*, *29*(2), 105–117. DOI: 10.1016/j.infoandorg.2019.03.001

Zargham, M., Shorish, J., & Paruch, K. (2020). *From curved bonding to configuration spaces*. BlockScience. https://blog.block.science/from-curved-bonding-to-configuration-spaces/

Zeiß, C., Schaschek, M., Straub, L., Tomitza, C., & Winkelmann, A. (2024). Re-intermediation of the crypto asset ecosystem by banks: An empirical study on acceptance drivers among the populace. *Electronic Markets*, *34*(1), 37. DOI: 10.1007/s12525-024-00720-4

Zeroual, N., Lamia, M., & Hafidi, M. (2024). Blockchain-Based Payment System for Registration Fees in higher education: A Case Study of Algeria. *CEUR Workshop Proceedings: 7th International Conference on Informatics and Applied Mathematics, 3922*, 124–138.

Zetzsche, D. A., Buckley, R. P., & Arner, D. W. (2020). Decentralized finance (DeFi). *Journal of Financial Regulation*, *6*(2), 172–203. DOI: 10.1093/jfr/fjaa010

Zetzsche, D. A., Buckley, R. P., Arner, D. W., & Barberis, J. N. (2020). The future of data-driven finance and RegTech. *European Business Organization Law Review*, *21*(3), 353–394.

Zetzsche, D. A., Buckley, R. P., Arner, D. W., & Föhr, L. (2021). The ICO gold rush: It's a scam, it's a bubble, it's a super challenge for regulators. *Harvard International Law Journal*, *60*(2), 267–315.

Zhang, Y., Tavalaei, M., Parry, G., & Zhou, P. (2024): Evolution or involution? A systematic literature review of organisations' blockchain adoption factors, Cardiff Economics Working Papers, No. E2024/19, Cardiff University, Cardiff Business School, Cardiff

Zhang, Y., Gong, B., & Zhou, P. (2024). Centralized use of decentralized technology: Tokenization of currencies and assets. *Structural Change and Economic Dynamics*, *71*, 15–25. DOI: 10.1016/j.strueco.2024.06.006

Zhao, L. (2021). How blockchain is changing real estate: A case study of RealT. Forbes Technology Council. https://www.forbes.com/sites/forbestechcouncil/2021/06/21/how-blockchain-is-changing-real-estate

Ziman, J. (2000). *Real science: What it is, and what it means*. Cambridge University Press. DOI: 10.1017/CBO9780511541391

About the Contributors

Guneet Kaur holds a Professional Doctorate in Data Science and is a multidisciplinary expert in fintech, blockchain, and digital finance education. With over a decade of experience bridging academia and industry, she specializes in crypto strategy, decentralized finance (DeFi) ecosystems, and data-driven financial innovation. She is currently Senior Editor at CCN.com and a Science Fellow at Exponential Science, where she contributes thought leadership and research at the intersection of emerging technologies, data science, and global financial systems. Previously, she served as Head of Learn at Cointelegraph for four years, leading editorial strategy and content development for the Learn section, with a focus on educational resources covering cryptocurrency, blockchain technology, and Web3 ecosystems. Dr. Kaur is also a fintech educator and assessor for executive education programs at 2U, specializing in blockchain, digital payments, and the transformation of global finance. In recognition of her contributions to the Web3 and AI ecosystem, she was named to Unstoppable Women of Web3's "Most Inspiring Women of Web3 and AI" 2025 list. An active academic contributor, Dr. Kaur serves as a peer reviewer for leading journals, including Springer's Financial Innovation, IGI Global's E-Business Research, and the International Journal of Big Data Intelligence and Applications. She has authored multiple research papers and book chapters spanning fintech, blockchain, crypto and decentralized technologies, and data science. She is a sought-after speaker and has presented at conferences and events worldwide. Her research interests encompass digital finance, blockchain, cryptocurrencies, Central Bank Digital Currencies (CBDCs), monetary policy innovation, and financial technologies.

Lorena Nessi, Ph.D., specializes in digital technology, cryptocurrency and blockchain. With a background in international relations and digital communication, she examines how emerging technologies reshape financial systems, regulation and geopolitical dynamics. She covers crypto markets, stablecoin policy, decentralized finance, artificial intelligence, and regulatory developments. She serves as Researcher and Op-Ed Editor at CCN.com, where she leads opinion strategy, commissions expert commentary, and produces in-depth analysis on digital finance, blockchain innovation, and global policy. Her work emphasizes evidence-based reporting and regulatory clarity. Dr. Nessi is also a lecturer at Fairleigh Dickinson University, teaching social media and digital culture. Her research focuses on platform governance, digital ecosystems, technological disruption, and the societal impact of decentralized systems.

Pooja Lekhi is the Chair of the Department of Quantitative Studies and a Finance Professor at University Canada West. With over a decade of experience in teaching and research, she specializes in making complex financial and technical concepts accessible through innovative teaching and assessment methodologies. Dr. Lekhi's research interests encompass asset quality management in financial institutions, cryptocurrencies, cybersecurity, financial technologies (FinTech), blockchain, and other emerging trends in the financial sector. Her work has been published in Fintech Magazine, Blockchain Tribune, and Money and Finance Magazine, and her insights have been featured in Express.co.uk, Currency.com, The New York Times Post, News Nation USA, World ABC News, and Forbes Alert. Beyond research and publishing, Dr. Lekhi has authored numerous book chapters and peer-reviewed journal articles. She has also played a key role in academic publishing by editing books for leading publishers, further establishing her expertise in finance and financial technologies.

***

Shahinaz Hanem (Sherry) Abdellatif brings over 25 years of diverse experience across academia and industry in Canada and international markets. She has an extensive background in senior advisory, financial planning, and policymaking, with a proven track record at leading financial institutions, earning multiple awards as a top advisor across Canada. She is an Associate Professor (Continuing Faculty) in the Department of Quantitative Studies at University Canada West, where she teaches corporate finance, fintech, financial planning, and investments. In addition, she serves as Vice-Chair of the Research and Scholarly Activities Committee and actively contributes to curriculum development, innovation, and training committees. Dr. Abdellatif's teaching philosophy is grounded in a student-centered approach, where she excels as both a mentor and subject matter expert. She holds a Doctorate in Business Administration and a master's in Business Administration from Heriot-Watt University. Her interdisciplinary research focuses on Sustainability, Fintech, AI, Blockchain, Decentralized Finance, Ethics, and Policymaking

Lawal Olamilekan Abdulwahab is a dedicated scholar and educator, pursuing a PhD in Economics at Universiti Brunei Darussalam, an AACSB-accredited institution, under a fully funded scholarship. With a Master's degree in Health Economics and a Bachelor's degree in Economics Education from Taraba State University, Nigeria, his expertise spans natural resources, health, development, and macroeconomics. He has over six years of university-level teaching and research experience across Africa and Asia, having lectured at Accord University (Somalia), Unity University (Somaliland), and Peacock College of Education (Nigeria). At Universiti Brunei Darussalam, he tutors undergraduate students in the School of Business and Economics, while actively supervising postgraduate and undergraduate theses that have led to impactful publications and conference presentations. Lawal's research and academic contributions have been showcased at multiple international conferences in Nigeria, Indonesia, Portugal, Türkiye, India, and the United Arab Emirates. He is skilled in advanced data analysis using Stata, SPSS, EViews, and MS Excel, and impressively integrates AI-powered tools into research and education. His work reflects a commitment to bridging economic theory with policy-relevant solutions that enhance governance, healthcare financing, and sustainable development. He maintains an active academic presence through Google Scholar, Scopus, and ORCID and continues to contribute to global knowledge exchange through publications, mentorship, and collaborative research.

Mussa S Abubakari, PhD, is an enthusiastic educational technology researcher and associate researcher with the Dig Connectivity Research Laboratory (DCRLab) in Kampala, Uganda, since 2024. He's an instructor in the Department of Physics and Mathematics at Kondoa Islamic Secondary School, Tanzania. He has a PhD in Educational Technology from Sultan Hassanal Bolkiah Institute of Education, Universiti Brunei Darussalam, and graduated in 2025. Dr. Mussa obtained a Master of Education degree in Electronics and Informatics Engineering at Yogyakarta State University, Indonesia, in July 2021. He obtained his BSc. in Telecommunications Engineering at the University of Dodoma in June 2016. His academic and research interests include educational technology, technology-enhanced learning, technology acceptance, open and distance learning, generative AI, and digital competence, among others. He has over 15 journal articles published in internationally reputable journals, several book chapters, and papers presented at international conferences.

Bismark Addai is an Assistant Professor at the University Canada West. He holds a Ph.D. in Economics with a specialization in Finance from Zhongnan University of Economics and Law. He is a Consulting Review Editor for Editage and previously a Guest Editor for the *Journal of Economic Policy Reform*. He was also a Research Integrity Consultant for Wiley Publishing. Before joining University

Canada West, he served in other research and teaching capacities, including his role as a Postdoctoral research fellow at Changsha University of Science and Technology. He also has industry experience as a financial consultant. He is widely published in many reputable journals, including *Journal of Multinational Financial Management, Economic Change and Restructuring, Journal of Applied Economics, Energy, Marine Policy, Resources Policy, Technology in Society, Journal of Industry, Competition & Trade, Aquaculture Economics & Management, and Environmental Science and Pollution Research.*

Silvio Andrae has been an independent researcher, senior consultant, project manager, and business partner in the financial sector since 1995. His specialization is inclusive finance, and he has over 25 years of experience advising financial institutions in Latin America, Africa, and Asia. It includes implementing credit technologies based on statistical methods and machine learning. Notably, he is a dedicated senior lecturer and trainer at various universities and teaching institutions, where he shares his expertise with the next generation of professionals, inspiring them to make a difference in the field.

Larry Earnhart has a Ph.D. in Chemistry from Georgia Institute of Technology and an MBA from Pepperdine University. For much of my career he has worked as an operations manager in the chemical production industry in the US. He moved to Canada and since then has been an entrepreneur and became an instructor at University Canada West for the MBA program teaching Finance and Operations Management since 2010. He was the Chair of the Dept. of Quantitative Studies from 2022-2025.

Samyukta Gurudanti is a dedicated professional currently pursuing her MBA Tech program at SVKM's NMIMS Mukesh Patel School of Technology Management and Engineering, Mumbai, with a specialization in Data Science for her B.Tech and Finance for her MBA. With a strong interdisciplinary background combining quantitative analytics and financial insight, she brings a unique perspective to solving complex problems at the intersection of business and technology. Samyukta has a deep interest in research and analytics, which is reflected in her hands-on projects, academic work, and industry-focused explorations.

Adjei Gyamfi Gyimah is a development finance expert who currently works in the Sustainable Finance Department with the Eastern and Southern African Trade and Development Bank. His research spans regional banking dynamics, agricultural value chain finance, rural development, financial inclusion, digital finance, clean energy economics, climate finance and waste management.

Firoj Kabir is a researcher, Lecturer of the Department of "Tourism and Hospitality Management" at the Daffodil International University, Dhaka, Bangladesh, with a solid academic background in BBA and MBA majoring in Tourism and Hospitality Management from the University of Dhaka. His passion lies in exploring the intersection of travel and culture. His diverse areas of interest include archaeological tourism, sustainable tourism, and the unique characteristics of Generation Z travelers. Through extensive research and insightful writing, he sheds light on the intricate connections between historical sites, responsible tourism, and the evolving preferences of the next generation of travelers. His work not only enriches the field of tourism but also inspires readers to engage with the world around them in meaningful and responsible ways.

Yashodhan K. Karulkar is the Assistant Professor and Area Chair (Marketing) at NMIMS University's Mukesh Patel School since September 2016. With nearly 20 years of leadership experience in top Indian and multinational firms, he now drives curriculum delivery and pedagogy innovation in NMIMS University. He has published numerous research papers, case studies, and book chapters in reputed Scopus and ABDC-indexed journals.

Przemysław Kępczyński, is a graduate of the Łódź University of Technology, specializing in software engineering, where he researched stock price forecasting using artificial neural networks. Furthering his academic pursuits, he completed postgraduate studies at the Warsaw School of Economics, where he wrote his thesis on the valuation of capital companies using exotic options. Kępczyński began his professional journey in investment finance, playing a key role in the formation of the trading department at XTB. He later contributed to the establishment of the Alior Trader and efx platforms at Alior Bank. In 2013, he pivoted to the rapidly evolving blockchain industry, collaborating with investors on projects related to cryptocurrency exchanges and token issuance. A significant aspect of Kępczyński's research concentrates on the intricate interplay between game theory and consensus mechanisms in decentralized protocols and organizations, particularly DAOs (Decentralized Autonomous Organizations). Through this, he explores how game-theoretical models can be leveraged to ensure honesty, fairness, and efficiency in decentralized systems, ensuring that participants act in the best interests of the network. Such studies are pivotal in understanding the sustainability and security of emerging decentralized structures, as they operate based on mutual trust and collaboration among anonymous entities. Besides this, Kępczyński is the esteemed author of a publication that delves into the application of game theory in mediation, published by the Institute of Justice. His current academic venture involves comprehensive research for his doctoral thesis, focusing on the legal implications and status of smart contracts in Polish private law.

Musfiqur Rahoman Khan is an accomplished author and Teaching Assistant at the Department of Tourism and Hospitality Management at Daffodil Institute of IT (DIIT), Dhaka, Bangladesh. He holds a Bachelor's degree in Business Administration (BBA), majoring in Tourism and Hospitality Management, from the same institute. With a strong academic background and a passion for exploring the intersection of travel and culture, Musfiq's diverse areas of interest include Adventure tourism, Cultural tourism, and Wildlife tourism. Through his teaching and writing, he strives to inspire others to discover the richness and diversity of the world through travel.

Sanjeev Kumar is a Professor in Lovely Professional University Punjab India. He received Undergraduate in Hotel Management from Osmania University, Postgraduate in Tourism Management from Madurai Kamaraj University. He completed Doctor of Philosophy in Hospitality Management in 2019 from Amity University Jaipur India. His research areas lies in food Service Industry, his research focuses on Alcoholic beverages, Event management and Sustainable Management Practices, Metaverse, AI Machine Learning and Artificial Intelligence. He published more than 60 research papers, articles and chapters in Scopus Indexed, UGC Approved and peer reviewed Journals and books. Dr. Sanjeev Kumar participated and acted as resource person in various National and International conferences, seminars, session chair, research workshops and industry talks and his work has been widely cited. Dr. Sanjeev also edited more than 12 books with various International Publishers such as IGI Global, Cambridge Scholars, Emerald, CABI, Bentham Science, Taylor & Francis. Dr Sanjeev is an active researcher and has published numerous research articles in prestigious national and international journals and books.

Peilin Li is a finance professional and passionate educator with over ten years of experience in the finance, banking, and mortgage sectors. Currently he is an Associate Professor at University Canada West, Peilin specializes in teaching financial management, bringing practical, real-world applications into the classroom. With a PhD in Physical & Theoretical Chemistry from the University of Oxford and an MSc from Imperial College London, Peilin seamlessly combines analytical skills in a microscopic view with a deep understanding of finance.

Vinod Krishna Makkimane is an Professor at Department of Management Studies, Dayananda Sagar College of Engineering with over 34 years of experience in corporate, entrepreneurship, and academia. His expertise spans personal finance, fintech, cybersecurity, and marketing. He holds a PhD in Management and has co-founded ventures in education, consulting, and financial services.

Aneta Napieralska is an independent expert in financial law and blockchain technology regulation. An advocate and graduate of Jagiellonian University, she has specialized in emerging technologies since 2017, beginning her career with investment projects in real estate tokenization and ICO token issuance. In her practice, she combines legal expertise with deep understanding of blockchain technologies and digital assets. Her collaboration with Swiss legal firms has provided extensive experience in international investment projects, AML procedures, and cryptocurrency-related legal challenges. She specializes in investment agreements in the blockchain sector, tokenization of financial instruments, and intellectual property rights in new technologies and AI. As a distinguished author and researcher, she has published extensively on cutting-edge fintech topics, including smart contracts in financial security, legal frameworks for decentralized autonomous organizations, and Central Bank Digital Currencies. Her research addresses critical issues in DeFi regulation, participant liability in blockchain governance, and the legal implications of Web 3 technologies. Her approach combines traditional legal expertise with innovative solutions for the rapidly evolving fintech landscape, making her a sought-after speaker at industry conferences and a trusted advisor for blockchain investment projects.

Kamal Nain Sharma is an accomplished academic and researcher with over 21 years of teaching experience in computer science and IT. He holds a Ph.D. in Computer Science from IKGPTU, specializing in medical image processing for breast cancer detection. Currently serving as an Assistant Professor at Lovely Professional University, he has previously held key positions such as Associate Dean (Research) and Head of IT at LKCTC, Jalandhar. Dr. Sharma's research interests include medical image processing, software engineering, and network security, with numerous publications in Scopus/UGC Care journals and international conferences. He is also a co-author of the book Blockchain Technology and its Applications and holds a patent on an IoT and AI-based physiotherapy apparatus. Beyond research, he has contributed as a resource person for guest lectures, coordinated academic and administrative initiatives, and actively engaged in professional bodies such as ISTE and CSI.

Maria Shilina is Senior Researcher at the Paradigm Research Institute, where she advances work at the intersection of International Law, FinTech, and Sustainability. Maria is also the co-founder of Episteme, an AI-powered decentralized prediction-market platform for forecasting scientific breakthroughs, where she leads research, partnerships and market design. Beyond her work there, she also serves as a Senior Specialist at the Skolkovo Institute of Science and Technology (Skoltech), contributing her expertise to innovation-focused projects that bridge academic research and real-world deployment.

Sasha Shilina is Managing Partner and Chief Research Officer at the Paradigm Research Institute, where she explores the frontiers of decentralized technologies, tokenized economies, and the philosophy of distributed systems. A Ph.D. graduate of Lomonosov Moscow State University and a founding member of Humanode, she has been active in the blockchain field since 2018. Her work integrates academic theory and experimental practice, with publications on trust, governance, decentralized science (DeSci), and artificial intelligence (AI). She is currently developing *Episteme*, a decentralized AI-driven prediction market for scientific discovery. Sasha Shilina's writing moves between technical precision and philosophical inquiry, framing tokenized infrastructures not only as economic engines but as cultural architectures of the future.

Jack Smith, J.D., M.B.A., is a Plains Cree Indigenous person with an extensive consultation background in Indigenous business and economic development, special projects, and treaty and intergovernmental negotiations. He has taught in the Marketing, Strategy, and Entrepreneurship (MSE) department at UCW since 2021.

Mohammad Badruddoza Talukder is an Associate Professor, College of Tourism and Hospitality Management, IUBAT - International University of Business Agriculture and Technology, Dhaka, Bangladesh. He holds PhD in Hotel Management from Lovely Professional University, India. He has been teaching various courses in the Department of Tourism and Hospitality at various universities in Bangladesh since 2008. His research areas include tourism management, hotel management, hospitality management, food & beverage management, and accommodation management, where he has published research papers in well-known journals in Bangladesh and abroad. Mr. Talukder is one of the executive members of the Tourism Educators Association of Bangladesh. He has led training and consulting for a wide range of hospitality organizations in Bangladesh. He just became an honorary facilitator at the Bangladesh Tourism Board's Bangabandhu international tourism and hospitality training institution.

Honnur Thazuddin is an MBA graduate specializing in Finance and Analytics from Visvesvaraya Technological University (VTU), Dayananda Sagar College of Engineering, Bengaluru. His/her research interests include financial markets, business analytics, and data-driven decision-making.

Index

A

B

C

D

E

F

G

H

I

M

O

P

Q

R

S

T

www.ingramcontent.com/pod-product-compliance
Lightning Source LLC
LaVergne TN
LVHW062334300926
849161LV00007B/1690